**Channel Islands,
Cherbourg Peninsula
& North Brittany**

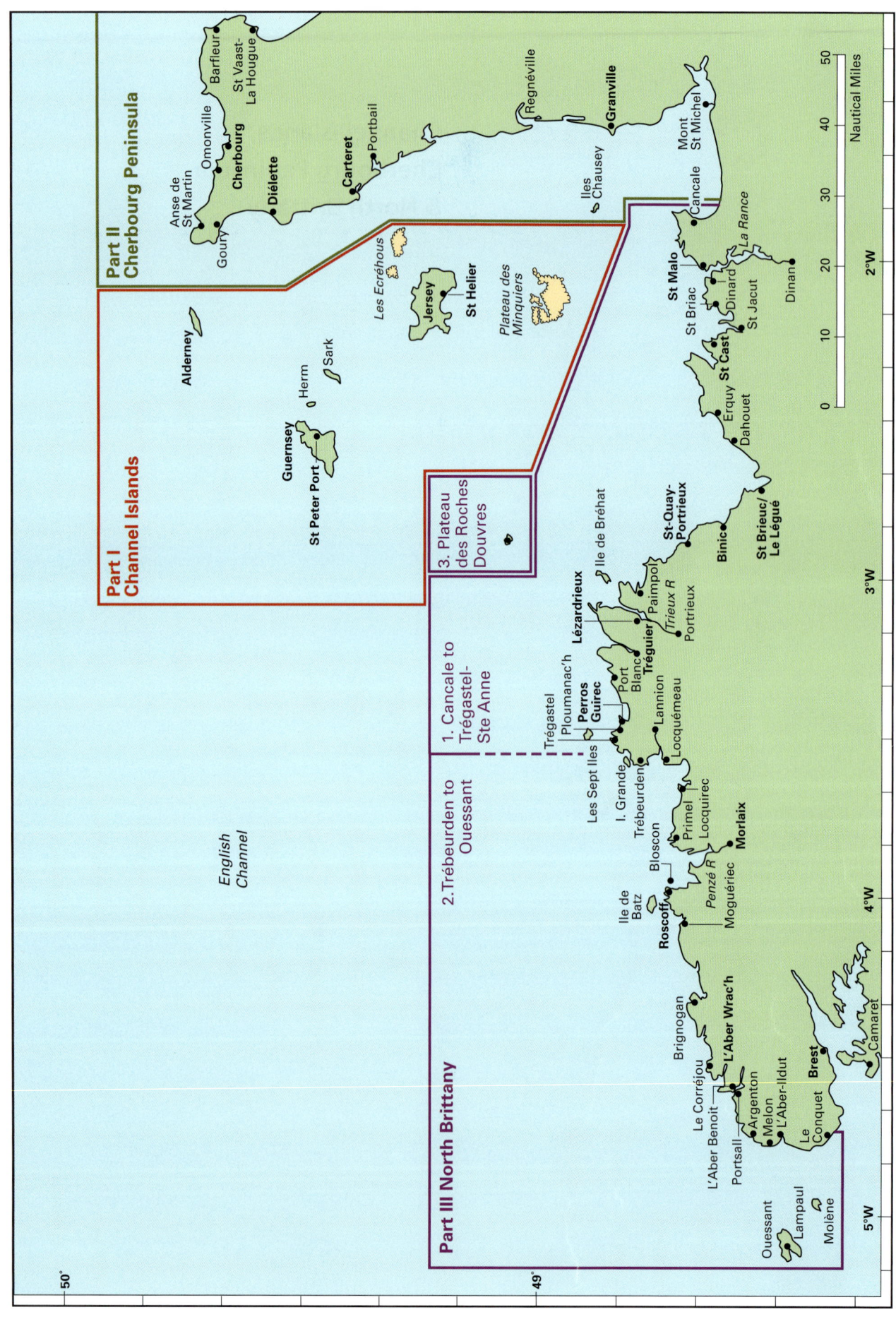

Channel Islands, Cherbourg Peninsula & North Brittany

St Vaast-La Hougue to Ouessant

 RCC PILOTAGE FOUNDATION

Peter Carnegie

Imray Laurie Norie & Wilson

Published by
Imray Laurie Norie & Wilson Ltd
Wych House The Broadway St Ives
Cambridgeshire PE27 5BT England
☎ +44 (0)1480 462114
www.imray.com
2018

© Text: Royal Cruising Club Pilotage Foundation 2018
© Plans: Imray Laurie Norie & Wilson Ltd 2018
© Photographs: Peter Carnegie 2018 or as acknowledged in the captions

All rights reserved. No part of this publication may be reproduced, transmitted or used in any form by any means – graphic, electronic or mechanical, including photocopying, recording, taping or information storage and retrieval systems or otherwise – without the prior permission of the Publishers.

First combined edition 2015
Revised first edition 2018

ISBN 978 184623 943 4

British Library Cataloguing in Publication Data.
A catalogue record for this title is available from the British Library.

This product has been derived in part from material obtained from the UK Hydrographic Office with the permission of the UK Hydrographic Office, Her Majesty's Stationery Office and SHOM (Service hydrographique et océanographique de la marine).

© British Crown Copyright, 2018. All rights reserved.

Licence number GB AA - 005 - Imrays

© SHOM Licence No 44/2013

THIS PRODUCT IS NOT TO BE USED FOR NAVIGATION

NOTICE
The UK Hydrographic Office (UKHO), its licensors and SHOM make no warranties or representations, express or implied, with respect to this product. The UKHO, its licensors and SHOM have not verified the information within this product or quality assured it.

The last input of technical data was March 2018

Printed in Croatia by Zrinski

CAUTION
Whilst the RCC Pilotage Foundation, the author and the publishers have used reasonable endeavours to ensure the accuracy of the content of this book, it contains selected information and thus is not definitive. It does not contain all known information on the subject in hand and should not be relied on alone for navigational use: it should only be used in conjunction with official hydrographical data. This is particularly relevant to the plans, which should not be used for navigation. The RCC Pilotage Foundation, the authors and the publishers believe that the information which they have included is a useful aid to prudent navigation, but the safety of a vessel depends ultimately on the judgment of the skipper, who should assess all information, published or unpublished. The information provided in this pilot book may be out of date and may be changed or updated without notice. The RCC Pilotage Foundation cannot accept any liability for any error, omission or failure to update such information. To the extent permitted by law, the RCC Pilotage Foundation, the author and the publishers do not accept liability for any loss and/or damage howsoever caused that may arise from reliance on information contained in these pages.

Positions and Waypoints
All positions and waypoints are to datum WGS 84. They are included to help in locating places, features and transits. Do not rely on them alone for safe navigation.

Bearings and Lights
Any bearings are given as °T and from seaward. The characteristics of lights may be changed during the lifetime of this book. They should be checked against the latest edition of the UK Admiralty *List of Lights*.

Updates and supplements
Any mid-season updates or annual supplements are published as free downloads available from www.imray.com. Printed copies are also available on request from the publishers.

Find out more
For a wealth of further information, including passage planning guides and cruising logs for this area visit the RCC Pilotage Foundation website at www.rccpf.org.uk

Feedback
The RCC Pilotage Foundation is a voluntary, charitable organisation. We welcome all feedback for updates and new information. If you notice any errors or omissions, please let us know at www.rccpf.org.uk

Contents

Foreword *vii*
Preface *viii*
Acknowledgements *viii*

Introduction

Part I. The Channel Islands

Introduction *5*

Alderney *23*

Guernsey *43*

Herm *71*

Sark *87*

Jersey *103*

Les Ecréhous and Plateau des Minquiers *131*

Part II. The Cherbourg Peninsula

Introduction *143*

1 St Vaast-La Hougue to Goury *145*

2 Diélette to Granville *170*

3 Iles Chausey *187*

Part III. North Brittany

Introduction *197*

1 Cancale to Trégastel-Ste Anne *201*

2 Trébeurden to Ouessant *283*

3 Plateau des Roches Douvres *359*

Appendix *364*
Index *380*

# RCC PILOTAGE FOUNDATION

The RCC Pilotage Foundation was formed as an independent charity in 1976 supported by a gift and permanent endowment made to the Royal Cruising Club by Dr Fred Ellis. The Foundation's charitable objective is 'to advance the education of the public in the science and practice of navigation'.

The Foundation is privileged to have been given the copyrights to books written by a number of distinguished authors and yachtsmen. These are kept as up to date as possible. New publications are also produced by the Foundation to cover a range of cruising areas. This is only made possible through the dedicated work of our authors and editors, all of whom are experienced sailors, who depend on a valuable supply of information from generous-minded yachtsmen and women from around the world.

Most of the management of the Foundation is done on a voluntary basis. In line with its charitable status, the Foundation distributes no profits. Any surpluses are used to finance new publications and to subsidise publications which cover some of the more remote areas of the world.

The Foundation works in close collaboration with three publishers – Imray Laurie Norie & Wilson, Bloomsbury (Adlard Coles Nautical) and On Board Publications. The Foundation also itself publishes guides and pilots, including web downloads, for areas where limited demand does not justify large print runs. Several books have been translated into French, Spanish, Italian and German and some books are now available as digital versions.

For further details about the RCC Pilotage Foundation and its publications visit **www.rccpf.org.uk**

PUBLICATIONS OF THE RCC PILOTAGE FOUNDATION

Imray
Arctic and Northern Waters
Atlantic France
Atlantic Islands
Atlantic Spain & Portugal
Black Sea
Cape Horn and Antarctic Waters
Channel Islands, Cherbourg Peninsula and North Brittany
Chile
Corsica and North Sardinia
Islas Baleares
Isles of Scilly
Mediterranean Spain
North Africa
Norway
South Biscay
The Baltic Sea and Approaches

Adlard Coles Nautical
Atlantic Crossing Guide
Pacific Crossing Guide

On Board Publications
South Atlantic Circuit
Havens and Anchorages for the South American Coast

RCC Pilotage Foundation
Supplement to Falkland Island Shores
Guide to West Africa
Argentina

RCCPF website www.rccpf.org.uk
Supplements
Support files for books
Passage Planning Guides
ePilots - from the Arctic to the Antarctic Peninsula

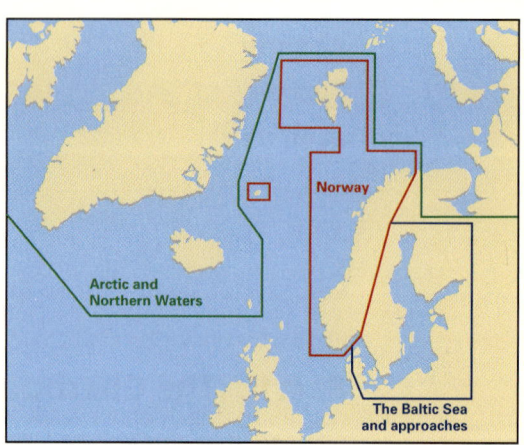

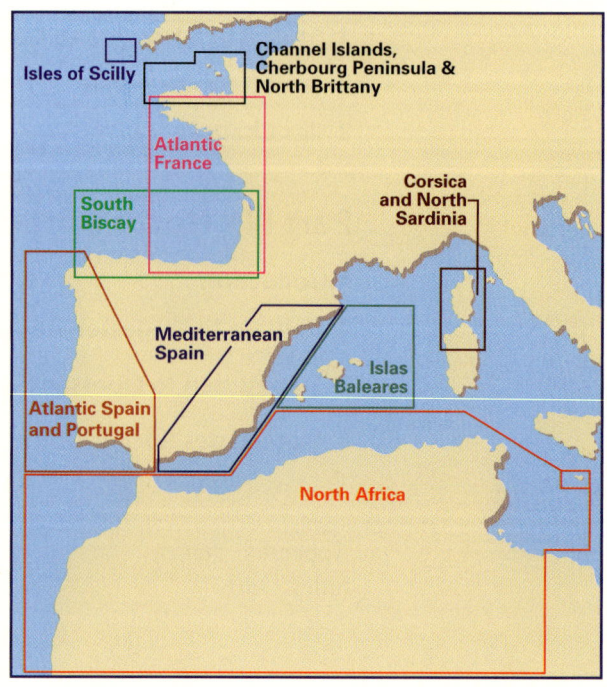

Trinity House   PATRON OF THE RCC PILOTAGE FOUNDATION

The RCC Pilotage Foundation is privileged to have Trinity House as its Patron. Trinity House, established in 1514 under King Henry VIII, is a charity dedicated to safeguarding shipping and seafarers by providing education, support and welfare to the seafaring community as well as by delivering and monitoring reliable aids to navigation for the benefit and safety of all mariners. Proud of its long history and traditions in navigation and pilotage, Trinity House is nevertheless at the forefront of technological developments and works closely with other organisations around the world to improve aids to navigation and to optimise global navigation satellite systems and e-navigation. The ongoing safety of navigation and education of mariners are common goals of Trinity House and of the RCC Pilotage Foundation.
To find out more go to www.trinityhouse.co.uk

FOREWORD

It is nearly 130 years since Claud Worth sailed his 33ft cutter, *Foam*, from Itchen Ferry across to Guernsey, on to Lézardrieux, Les Roches Douvres and back to the Petite Rade at Cherbourg before returning across The Channel. It was really just a quick dash for a few enjoyable days of adventure, recorded in the third chapter of Worth's *Yacht Cruising*. Similarly brief cross-Channel cruises to the Channel Islands and neighbouring French coasts continue to be enjoyed by a wide variety of sailing and motor boats today. For those with more time, this is an extensive and rewarding cruising ground. The landscape varies appreciably between the sandy and low-lying shores of the Cherbourg Peninsula, the rivers of North Brittany leading inland to sylvan tranquillity, and the multitude of rocks and islands off the coast.

Careful passage planning is essential to enjoying the region to the full. The whole area is subject to strong tidal streams and areas of very high tidal ranges, with associated tidal races off headlands and in constricted channels. The Atlantic swell can cause many an anchorage to become untenable. Fog is a common occurence, particularly in the west of the region. However, modern weather and sea state forecasts, GPS and chart plotters, radar, AIS and all the other electronic navigational aids are a considerable comfort in navigating these waters. And, even in 1888, Worth reported that: 'the coast is so admirably marked and lighted that the pilotage is very much easier than a study of the chart might lead one to suppose'.

Peter Carnegie advises us all to think of the rocks as our 'friends', providing vital signposts in the safe pilotage of the area. Peter's first-hand knowledge of these 'friends', and his clear descriptions and annotated plans of routes and approaches through and around them, provides an essential guide for both visitors and locals.

The RCC Pilotage Foundation is extremely grateful to Peter Carnegie for all the meticulous research, both on the water and from the air, which has gone into this book. Peter has done a wonderful job of updating his own work on the Channel Islands and then extending the coverage to include pilotage information for the neighbouring coasts of North Brittany and the Cherbourg Peninsula. John Lawson's previous work on RCC Pilotage Foundation *North Brittany* served as a useful basis for this integrated material and the RCC Pilotage Foundation remains grateful to all the contributors over the years who have freely provided information and photographs for the benefit of other sailors. Peter Carnegie's wife, Julia, daughter Fiona and son James have supported Peter's work in a multitude of ways, and they also deserve our sincere thanks.

Finally, huge thanks to the team at Imray who have brought this revised first edition to publication. It is always a privilege to work with them and to benefit from their expertise.

Jane Russell
Editor in Chief
RCC Pilotage Foundation
March 2018

PREFACE

Following the success of *The Channel Islands* I was given the task of putting together an updated and extended version that would take in the neighbouring French coastline of Normandy and Brittany.

The Cherbourg Peninsula, Le Cotentin, has close historical and cultural links with the islands which at their nearest point are a mere eight miles away. In addition to covering its main ports and harbours, St Vaast - La Hougue, Cherbourg and Granville, I have included several minor ones which may be considered off limits for anything larger than the small shallow-draught boats that use them. They are nevertheless interesting places.

The major part of this book is taken up with the classic cruising area of North Brittany. There are over sixty harbours and anchorages between Cancale east of St Malo and the far west if you include the islands of Ouessant and Molène.

This section concludes with a chapter devoted to Plateau des Roches Douvres. This hitherto unpublished information is the result of research from the air and by sea including a visit to the Subdivision des Phares et Balises at Lézardrieux that is responsible for maintenance of the lighthouse.

Over the decades since my early ventures in the area covered by this book, much has changed. The number of marinas has sprouted from a handful to some 20 in 2017 and the uniform system of buoyage with many new marks, most of which are well maintained, together with updated charts has made the area safer and more user friendly.

With dependence on GPS as a means of navigation more or less universal, the aim in writing this book has been to steer a middle course between waypoint navigation and traditional methods. Situational awareness through visual observation continues to be a vital element of pilotage and good seamanship.

My hope is that it will assist those that take up the challenge of discovering new harbours and anchorages to achieve their objective safety.

Peter Carnegie
March 2018

Acknowledgements

The author is grateful for the assistance of yachtsmen and professional seafarers in the preparation of this book. The following require special mention and thanks:

Channel Islands
Stephen Arthur
Nick Bailhache, RCC
John Elliott
Bill Harris
Richard Klein
Jane Russel, RCCl
Steve Shaw
Ian Tardivel, Grève de Lecq Boatowners
Mark Tucker

Cherbourg Peninsula
Richard and Juliet Gillam
Aurélie Leroy, Maison de Normandie, Jersey
Lionel Mesnil
Luc Pingeon

North Brittany
Hervé Allain
Paul Bryans, RCC
David Endacott
Robin and Zillah Faulkner, RCC
Chris Gladish
John Marc Hercelin
Bobby Lawes, RCC
John Nugent
Subdivision des Phares et Balises – Port de Lézardrieux
Bob Wright Jersey Aero Club

General
William Bourne, RCC
Julia Carnegie
Fiona Scott
John Searson, Jersey Meteorological Department
Société Jersiaise
Tom Vallois

Photography
All photography is by the author and James Carnegie unless stated otherwise.
Détail de la Tapisserie de Bayeux. Avec autorisation spéciale de la Ville de Bayeux.

The author has sailed most of the marks described in this pilot with *Caprice*, a 42' sloop with 65hp auxiliary and 1·6m draught

Introduction

The Channel Islands area, with its unique blend of French and English culture, has always held a fascination for yachtsmen. As a cruising ground, the islands themselves and the neighbouring coasts of Normandy and Brittany offer a great diversity of harbours and anchorages, more than can be explored in a lifetime. A climate milder than in the UK and spread over a longer season, together with a lack of air and sea pollution, adds to the appeal of this extensive cruising ground.

Passage planning

Strong tides and changeable weather are common to all areas covered in this book. Although such topics are focussed on the Channel Islands in the first section, they are equally applicable to the Cherbourg Peninsula and North Brittany. When planning a passage anywhere in the area, readers are therefore recommended to study the introductory chapters of the Channel Islands.

A suitable boat

Any well-found yacht capable of making a safe Channel crossing and properly equipped for coastal cruising will meet the demands of these waters. Special consideration must be given to the auxiliary, which should be reliable and sufficiently powerful to make headway into a foul tide of up to 5 knots or more. With a lee shore never far away the ability to beat out into a fresh breeze with a short sea is essential. Keel type and draught will dictate cruise plans. A draught of more than 2m (6ft) will rule out some of the best anchorages in the area and limit options particularly at neap tides, when there may be insufficient water. It is worth knowing before a visit if the yacht can be dried out on its keel if necessary. Multihulls, bilge keelers and yachts fitted with beaching legs come into their own as the majority of harbours and anchorages dry: Herm, Creux (Sark), St Aubin and Gorey (Jersey) and Les Minquiers and Les Ecréhous, to mention a few in the Channel Islands. On the Cherbourg Peninsula there is no alternative to taking the ground at Barfleur and in the sandy inlets on the west coast. North Brittany offers myriads of similar drying anchorages.

Ground tackle should be comprehensive, chain marked and a reliable electric/manual windlass fitted. Visitors unprepared for a large tidal range may find they are short of chain when anchored over high water – particularly in Sark anchorages where depths can be in excess of 17m (55ft) at spring tides.

Navigational equipment

The yacht should be equipped with VHF radio, GPS and a depth sounder but note that GPS should not be relied upon for pilotage among rocks. With the prevalence of advection and frontal fog in the autumn and winter, and radiation fog in anticyclonic conditions at any time, radar is a useful navigational aid. It can mean less time and tide lost while waiting for visibility to improve, and at sea provides a means of detecting navigational marks and traffic, particularly high-speed inter-island ferries.

Technical information

Nautical miles, cables and metres, bearings

As the metric system is rapidly replacing imperial measures and since vertical heights and soundings are already shown in metres on charts, the practice in this edition will be to give short distances that the navigator is expected to estimate by eye in metres (m).

For these estimated distances, the navigator who normally estimates in cables and yards can, to within 10%, take 200m as 1 cable (in fact 218·7yds) and 30m as 30yds (in fact 32·8yds).

However, since it is normal practice to use the latitude scale on a Mercator chart to measure nautical miles and tenths and although the traditional cable is very close to a tenth of a nautical mile, when referring to a chart and especially when the required track may be plotted on the chart, distances will be given in nautical miles (M) and decimals (e.g. 3·8M, 0·3M).

All bearings are expressed in degrees True. Times are expressed in UTC unless otherwise stated.

Marks

Note that positions are given in the text to the nearest tenth of a minute of latitude and longitude. A large-scale chart should be consulted for a more precise position.

Striking marks and clearing lines

These traditional but effective measures may be used to clear or pinpoint the position of a submerged rock or obstruction. All that is needed is a handbearing compass and an identified mark which will usually be on the shore.

A position line from the mark and crossing the hazard gives the critical bearing at the point where one is likely to strike the hazard. A mark used in this way is known as a striking mark.

The bearing of a mark can also be used to provide safe clearance of a hazard. This position line is known as a clearing line.

Such critical bearings may also be derived from the transit of two marks.

Introduction

Illustration of transit marks
In many instances of marks described, the front mark obscures the back mark. For the sake of clarity, such marks have been photographed offset (opened). If this slight deviation is permissable, no mention is made in the text. (See *Transits* on page 10.)

Positions
The latitude and longitude coordinates given under the name of a port or harbour and in some cases an anchorage are not waypoints. They are for the purpose of indicating their general position.

Waypoints
A numbered waypoint is shown in a safe-water position. In most cases this is on an approach line to a port, harbour or anchorage to indicate where pilotage may take over from GPS navigation.
See *Appendix*. *Waypoint list* page 376.

Safety note Waypoints and tracks between them should be plotted and checked on an up-to-date chart before being used for navigation.

Waypoints on plans These are shown on the relevant plan and listed with number and coordinates in an information box. A blue symbol indicates that the position is off the plan.

Tides
All tidal information is based on standard port St Helier, unless stated otherwise.

Depths
Depths or drying heights given in metres (m) for passages and channels are based on Chart Datum – the level below which sea level seldom falls.

Charts
There are three main publishers of charts covering the area of this pilot:

British Admiralty (BA) www.admiralty.gov.uk

Service Hydrographique et Oceanographique de La Marine (SHOM) www.shom.fr

Imray Laurie Norie & Wilson (Imray) www.imray.com

Additionally, all charts for particular ports, harbours and anchorages are detailed in individual chapters.

A directory of BA and Imray charts is available at www.imray.com. SHOM charts (www.shom.fr) are detailed and supplied by www.riviera-charts.com

The traditional firing of a cannon from the ramparts of Castle Cornet in St Peter Port signals midday

St Servan

Herm harbour

The regions covered in this book are noted for gastronomy, shellfish in particular

2 CHANNEL ISLANDS, CHERBOURG PENINSULA & NORTH BRITTANY

Introduction

Dried out on the sands, Portbail

GPS and chart datum

As of May 2004 editions of all British Admiralty and SHOM charts covering the area of this book are on WGS 84 datum and positions are based on this datum.

Caution should be exercised if using pre-metric or old French or private charts which do not show any correction. There may be significant discrepancies between the latitude and longitude on the chart and that shown by GPS set to any datum.

Electronic charts

Electronic or digital charts may be used in chart plotters and increasingly iPads and other tablets. In all cases, care needs to be taken to ensure that software and hardware are compatible. New apps and options are appearing all the time, but at the time of writing, the main providers and chart numbers for the Channel Islands and North Brittany area are:

Imray Download the free Imray Navigator app for iPad and iPhone. ID20 English Channel includes a full range of Imray charts for the area, and FR3 North France, derived from SHOM charts, also covers the entire area.

Navionics Gold charts XL9 46XG (Europe West) provides coverage of the whole area. Small Gold charts 555 (Lorient-Paimpol), 556 (Ile de Batz-Carentan), and 557 (Jersey-Le Tréport) are suitable for chart plotters only and provide coverage of parts of the area at a cheaper price. The Gold charts are also purchasable through the iNavX app for iPad.

Garmin Blue Chart EU001R (English Channel) and EU4575 (Bretagne) provide full coverage of the area, EU008R (Bay of Biscay) and EU4565 (English Channel Central-East) partial coverage of west and eastern half respectively.

AIS (Automatic Identification System)

AIS enables monitoring of other nearby AIS equipped vessels that may pose a collision risk. Increasingly lights, buoys and other navigation aids are fitted with AIS transmitters. This VHF system transmits and receives data on a vessel's position, course, speed, identity and status – under power or sail, constrained by draught, restricted, not under command.

1 The Channel Islands

4 CHANNEL ISLANDS, CHERBOURG PENINSULA & NORTH BRITTANY

I. The Channel Islands

History

The coastal forts and defences of the islands, many of which serve as pilotage marks, are evidence of centuries of struggle between England and France and in more recent times the German occupation from 1940–45.

How the islands came to be included in the British Isles but not in the United Kingdom, or the European Union, is the result of a quirk of history. Originally part of the Duchy of Normandy, they were annexed to England at the time of the Norman Conquest in 1066, thus becoming one of the oldest possessions of the Crown. Following the loss of the Duchy to France in the reign of King John (one of William the Conqueror's successors), Channel Islanders had to decide where their allegiance lay. In 1204 they chose to remain loyal to the English crown. They were rewarded by an exemption from all taxes made by Parliament and given the freedom to govern themselves. Such privileges have been confirmed by successive sovereigns – there is still no VAT in the Channel Islands but Jersey has introduced GST (Goods and Services Tax). This is currently 5% (2018).

Getting there

Getting to the islands will, for many, mean a Channel crossing. In suitable conditions this can be a straightforward 8–10 hour sail from the UK south coast with en route staging posts such as Cherbourg, St Vaast-La Hougue, Diélette and Carteret. Braye Harbour, Alderney is a popular port of entry where visitors first experience the friendly atmosphere of the islands and meet with a minimum of formalities. Further south the marinas at Beaucette and St Peter Port, Guernsey and at St Helier in Jersey provide a secure base for those wishing to enjoy attractions ashore and day cruising to nearby anchorages and beaches.

From St Peter Port it is a short sail to Herm and Sark and for the experienced there are the spectacular LW anchorages in the protected sites of Les Écréhous and Les Minquiers off Jersey. Vessels able to take the ground can retreat to drying harbours such as Herm, Creux (Sark) or St Aubin and Gorey in Jersey. On the Normandy coast Portbail is a popular haven for bilge keelers.

Pilotage around the Channel Islands

With its rock-strewn waters and some of the most powerful tides in the world, the Channel Islands area offers something of a challenge. Seasoned locals will refer to their home waters as 'a cruising ground but not a playground' and talk of currents twice a boat's speed, overfalls, fog-banks that roll in without warning and tricky pilotage. While it is true that safe sailing here calls for a degree of alertness and unremitting care, the basic requirement is a good working knowledge of sound coastal navigation. There are three golden rules for survival: know the weather; know the tides; know where you are.

Today, first time visitors to the islands enjoy a head start unknown to earlier generations of cruising yachtsmen. Over the past twenty years the system of buoyage and marks has been greatly extended, the area has been comprehensively charted by both British and French authorities, and yachting guides and pilots abound. Dedicated visitors' moorings will be found in most islands as well as a choice of marinas in St Peter Port, St Helier and the adjacent French coast. With weather bulletins regularly beamed to all corners of the area and navigation revolutionised through GPS, there are fewer excuses for getting caught out or lost.

Finding your destination is one thing; getting safely in is another. Pilotage is that element of a passage concerned with the conduct of a vessel into and out of a harbour or anchorage, and is often a test of the navigator's skill. The yacht will be in relatively shallow waters and in close proximity to rocks and other hazards. Visibility may be reduced and inshore streams unpredictable. At such times the rocks are your 'friends', providing vital signposts. Since time immemorial they have played a key role in Channel Islands pilotage. (See *Appendix. Channel Island rock names*, page 374.)

This pilot is intended as a resource and backup for those with limited local knowledge. It belongs in the cockpit along with other tools of the pilot's trade: binoculars and a handbearing compass. It is *no substitute for up-to-date charts of suitable scale* which should be thoroughly consulted when passage planning, together with the tidal atlas and tables.

Weather

Despite the Channel Islands being tucked away in the most southerly corner of the British Isles they are still subject to the 'mishmash' of English weather. Atlantic depressions are borne in on the prevailing westerly flow, punctuated by ridges or longer-lasting highs. Air is funnelled from all points of the compass, providing a wide range of conditions to keep yachtsmen on their toes.

The islands can claim to enjoy more sunshine on average than elsewhere in the British Isles. Spring comes earlier, summer hangs on longer and winters are mild. One only has to compare BBC shipping forecasts for Portland sea area with local bulletins to appreciate the difference.

1 The Channel Islands

Depressions tracking across northern sea areas may bring dismal conditions to the English Channel while those in the islands will often be moderated, offering pleasant sailing. Within the area itself there are subtle variations due to the surrounding French mainland. The Cherbourg peninsula provides shelter from easterly winds but with less effect around Alderney and Guernsey. There will often be a regime of fresh northeasterlies accompanied by a fine spell early in the season. In such situations, however, the peninsula can be responsible for a localised low that develops to windward of the islands, causing a narrowing of the isobars and resulting in a stiff afternoon breeze (Force 7), strongest in the southern isles. Elsewhere there may be little more than Force 5. See Figs 1a and 1b.

The Brittany peninsula to the S gives shelter from winds from that direction, the degree of which is shown in Figs 2 and 3.

S and SE winds are the least frequent, often associated with thundery conditions or a warm front moving in from the W.

The islands are fully exposed to winds from the W and NW, the prevailing direction (see diagram right).

Gales

Gales, which are mostly westerly, can occur at any time of the year but are most frequent between October and January with the lowest incidence between June and August. As a general rule the N part of the area, from Guernsey to latitude 50°N, picks up stronger winds than the S. With comprehensive local forecasting services and a sensitive 'weather nose', it should always be possible to anticipate likely changes and tailor plans accordingly.

If a gale threatens, good shelter with plenty of interest ashore to sustain a weather-bound crew is seldom more than a 4–6 hours' sail away.

St Helier and St Malo are excellent bolt-holes but Alderney (Braye) should be avoided in northeasterlies when it is totally exposed. St Peter Port can be entered in almost all weathers but can be uncomfortable in easterlies. Beaucette Marina should not be approached in strong easterlies.

St Helier's marinas are well sheltered but an approach to the port in a southerly gale could be hazardous.

Gorey (Jersey) is particularly exposed around HW in gales from between SSE and SSW, when taking the ground can be a painful experience.

Sea state

From Alderney southwards the effects of the surrounding coast, other islands and above all strongly tidal waters, will be felt. The longer seas of the English Channel give way to short seas with frequent local changes in shape and direction – the effect of varying depth, shoals, reefs, headlands, gaps and above all the state and run of the tide. (See figs 4, 5 and 6 opposite.)

Throughout the area there are several notorious patches where wind against tide conditions can throw up short steep seas. Passage through such areas can range from a barely noticeable sea state to a highly dangerous situation for small craft. Transit through the **Alderney Race** or the neighbouring **Swinge** should be carefully timed to coincide with fair weather and slack tide or avoided altogether in bad weather. There are notorious patches around The Race

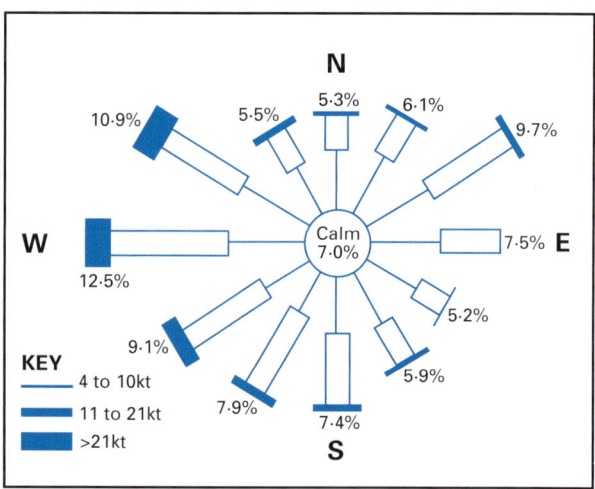

Average wind direction and strength based on observations at Jersey Airport Met Office over the period 1971-2000   *Courtesy of Jersey Meteorological Department*

Rocks and further S over Milieu and Banc de la Schôle. Other areas to be wary of are:

Guernsey Big Russel W of Brecqhou, Little Russel between Platte Fougère lighthouse and Roustel beacon tower
Sark East coast
Jersey Grosnez Point, Point Corbière and Noirmont Point
Cherbourg Peninsula Le Raz Blanchard and eastern approaches, Pointe de Barfleur.

Swell and fetch

Swell is usually developed by deep Atlantic lows. As it enters the strongly tidal waters of the Channel it will become more pronounced, particularly over spring tides.

At such periods many anchorages become untenable around HW. Sark anchorages are notorious in this respect.

Wave height is monitored by wave rider buoys and features in Channel Island weather forecasts and reports. The longer the fetch the higher the waves, so winds from a westerly direction will produce higher waves and longer swell in contrast to easterlies and southerlies where the fetch is short. See Fig 1.

Visibility

Fog and poor visibility is traditionally a major hazard in Channel Island waters, although GPS and radar have taken some of the sting out of it.

Fog is mostly of the advection type, being associated with mild moist air tracking over the cooler seas of spring and early summer. It will usually disperse with a shift in wind direction or the passage of a front. In the summer months, predominantly June and July, radiation fog associated with clear nights in anticyclonic weather tends to generate in the low-lying areas of the Cherbourg peninsula and Brittany. This will often waft towards the islands causing fog that will not lift until late morning when the surface has warmed up.

Fog can also develop suddenly in summer when a very warm southeasterly at the onset of a thundery spell gives way to a cooler westerly flow towards the end of the day. Fog in the islands is rare from mid-August to October.

Introduction

CHARACTER OF THE WINDS

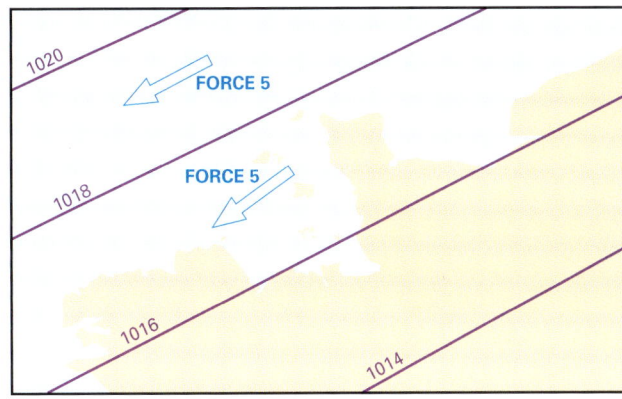

Fig 1a Typical isobaric situation and winds with a northeasterly in the early morning

Fig 1b Typical isobaric situation and winds in the afternoon after heating over France

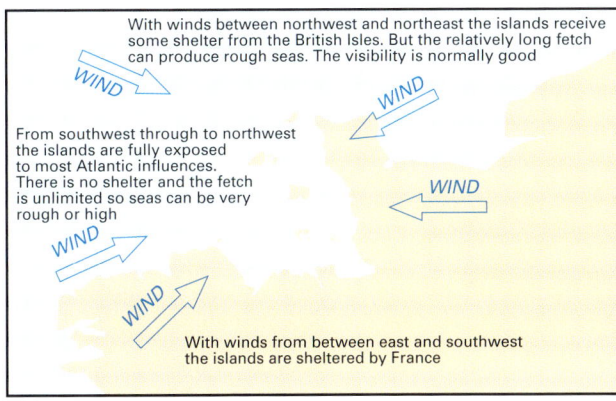

Fig 2 Position of the Channel Islands and the main wind/sea effects

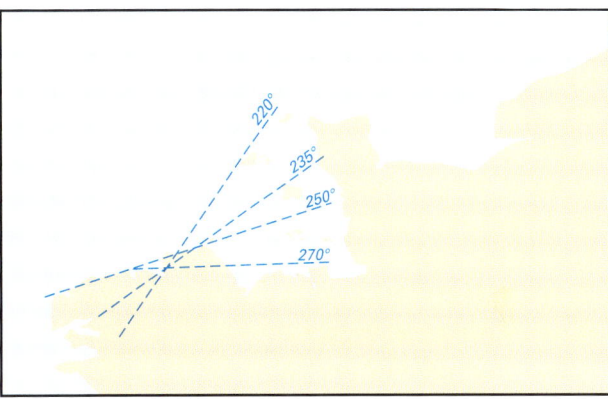

Fig 3 Lines to the south of which there is substantial shelter from Brittany from given wind directions

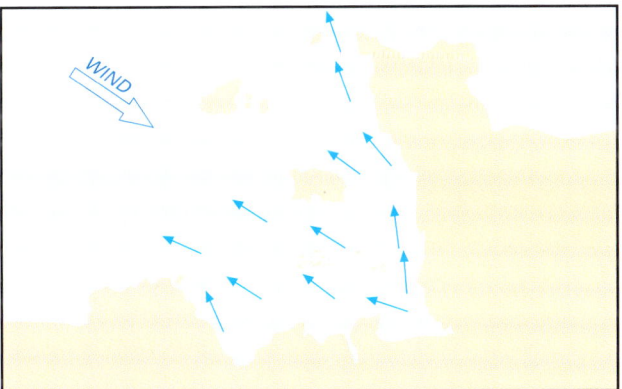

Fig 4 Areas where strong northwest-flowing tides can produce very rough seas in northwesterly wind situations

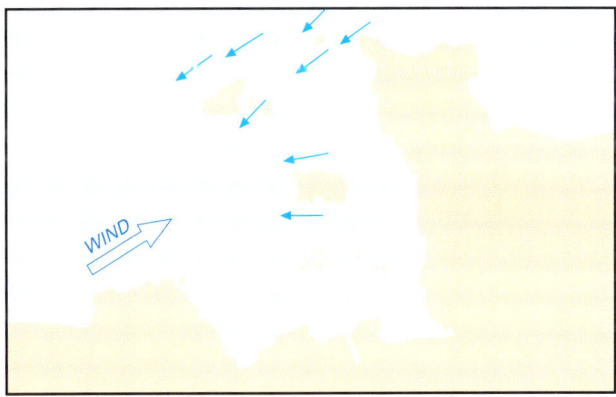

Fig 5 Areas where strong-flowing tides produce very rough seas in southwesterly wind situations

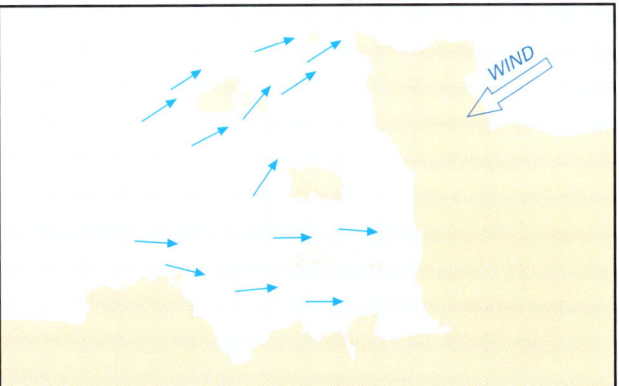

Fig 6 Areas where strong-flowing tides can produce very rough seas in northeasterly wind situations

CHANNEL ISLANDS, CHERBOURG PENINSULA & NORTH BRITTANY

1 The Channel Islands

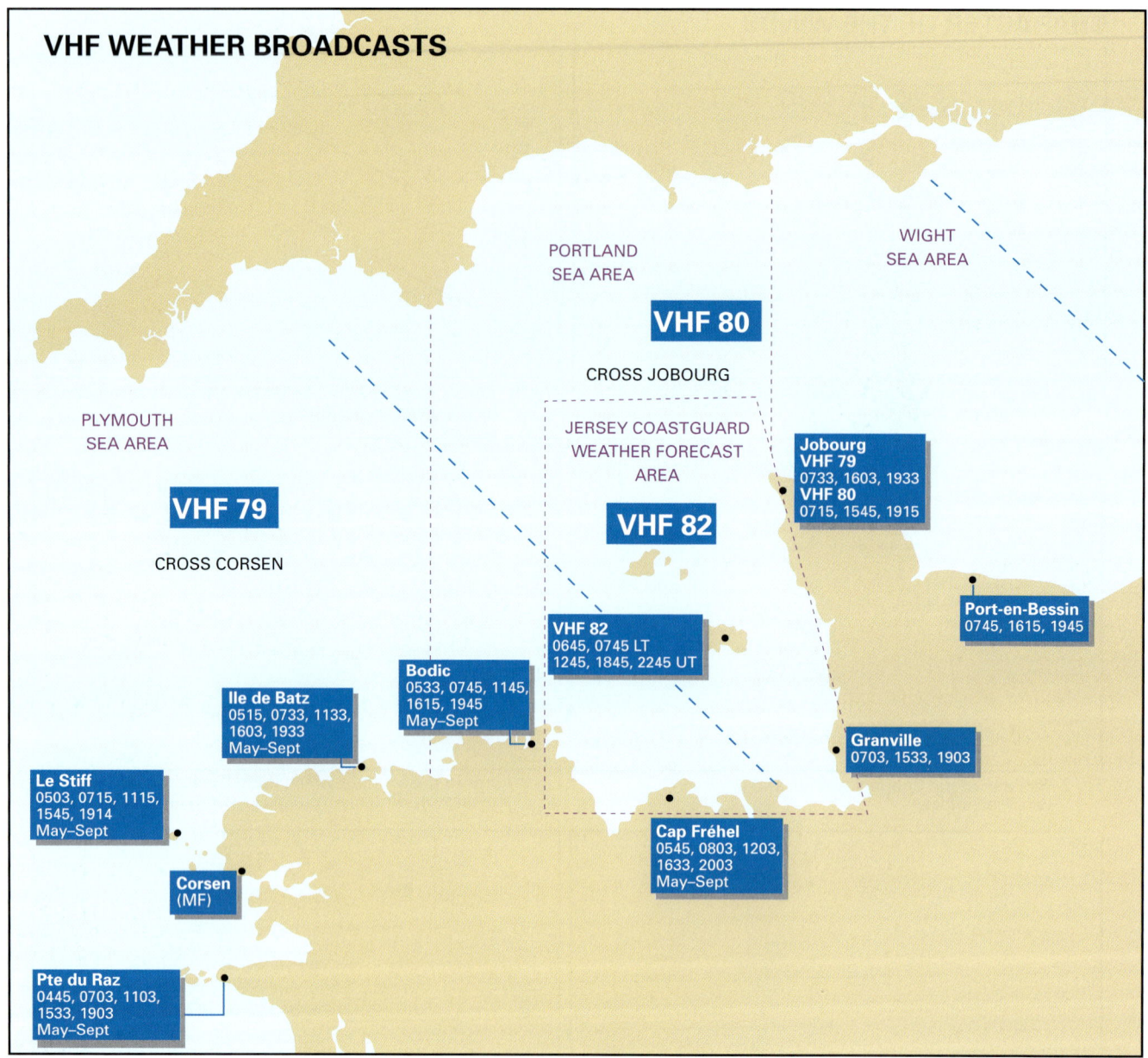

Sources of weather information

VHF

CHANNEL ISLANDS

JERSEY COASTGUARD (check website for details)
Channel Islands Shipping Forecast
Ch 25, 82 at 0645, 0745, 0845 (LT), 1245, 1845, 2245 (UT) for area bounded by 50°N, French Coast from Cap de la Hague to Île de Bréhat and 3°W
Gale and strong wind warnings
On receipt and at 0307, 0907, 1507, 2107 (UT).
Internet services www.portofjersey.je

ST HELIER PIERHEADS INFORMATION SERVICE
Ch 18. An automatic broadcast of wind direction and strength at St Helier pierheads. Updated every 2 minutes. Range is about 5 miles.

FRANCE

CROSS JOBOURG
Ch 80 at Jobourg 0715, 1545, 1915 (LT). Granville 0703, 1533, 1903 (LT). For area Cap d'Antifer to Mont St Michel
Gale and strong wind warnings
In French and English on receipt and at H+20 and H+50 (LT)
Warnings for coastal areas on receipt and at H+03.

CROSS CORSEN
Ch 79 0815, 2015 (LT). For area Mont St Michel to Pte de Penmarc'h

FRENCH SÉMAPHORES (COASTAL SIGNAL STATIONS)
Weather forecasts broadcast including gale warnings at regular intervals or on demand - VHF Ch 16 and 10. Most maintain a 24h lookout. Main stations are (E–W);

St Vaast-La Hougue (Pte de Saire)
Gatteville (Pte de Barfleur)
Cherbourg
Cap de la Hague
Carteret
Granville (Pte du Roc)
St Cast
St Quay, Portrieux
Bréhat
Ploumanach
Batz
Brignogan
Stiff (Ouessant)
St Mathieu

Introduction

JERSEY MET SERVICES
Internet services www.gov.je/weather
Services are continually being updated, so check the website for any updates. At the time of going to press, the Channel Islands Shipping Forecast, coastal reports, live wind at St Helier Harbour, local weather radar and satellite pictures were all available on this site. Wind is now measured by Jersey Met on Les Maisons (Les Minquiers) and on Grand Rousse (Les Ecrehous) as well as on the Jersey data buoy (WMO 62027). These are also available online. The Channel Islands Shipping Forecast is also available by telephone and fax.
Recorded ✆ 0900 669 00 22 (60p per min)
Fax 0960 100 466 (£1 per min)
Personal Consultation Service ✆ 0905 807 77 77

BBC RADIO 4 SHIPPING FORECAST (Sea Area Portland)
LW 198kHz. MW 756kHz. FM Channel Islands: 94·8mHz
Times (LT) 0048 LW, MW, FM
 0520 LW, MW, FM
 1201 LW only
 1754 LW, FM (Sat/Sun)

LOCAL RADIO
BBC Radio Jersey
1026kHz, 88·8Mhz
Shipping forecast for local waters Mon–Fri 0635, 1800 LT. Sat/Sun 0735 LT. Sat/Sun at H+00 (0700–1300 after the news) and 0725 LT

BBC Radio Guernsey
93·2Mhz, 1116kHz
Weather bulletins for the waters around Guernsey, Herm & Sark.
Mon–Fri 0630, 0730, 0830 LT. Sat/Sun 0730, 0830 LT

INTERNET WEATHER WEBSITES
www.metoffice.gov.uk
www.rnli.org.uk/weather.asp
www.metbrief.com
www.portofjersey.je/weather
www.magicseaweed.com
www.windguru.cz/int/
www.windfinder.com/forecast/guernsey

Planning and navigation
Understanding the tides

The Channel Islands area and its tides are synonymous and the lives of local mariners are governed by them. They should therefore be the first consideration when planning a passage, which whenever possible should be timed to take advantage of favourable streams.

The basic essentials for working the tides are the current *Almanac* for its tide tables and other information, and the *Tidal Stream Atlas*. The Atlas is worth more than any number of words on the subject and should be studied carefully. There are several covering the areas of this book:

The Channel Islands
British Admiralty *Tidal Stream Atlas for The Channel Islands and adjacent coasts of France* (NP 264)
SHOM *Courants de Marée dans Le Golfe Normand-Breton de Cherbourg a Paimpol* (SHOM 562-UJA).

East coast of Cherbourg peninsula
SHOM *Baie de Seine* (SHOM 561-UJA)

North Brittany
British Admiralty *The English Channel* (NP 250)
SHOM *Côte Nord de Bretagne* (SHOM 563-UJA)

West Brittany
SHOM *Côte ouest de Bretagne* (SHOM 560-UJA)

Tidal differences based on standard port St Helier

	Times (approx)		Times (approx)
Lézardrieux	–0033		
Ile de Bréhat	–0025	Chausey	–0014
Paimpol	–0022	Carteret	+0010
St Quay/Portrieux	–0022	Diélette	+0020
Erquy/Dahouët	–0020	St Peter Port (Guernsey)	+0005
St Malo	–0020	Braye (Alderney)	+0045
Granville	–0015	Cherbourg	+0135

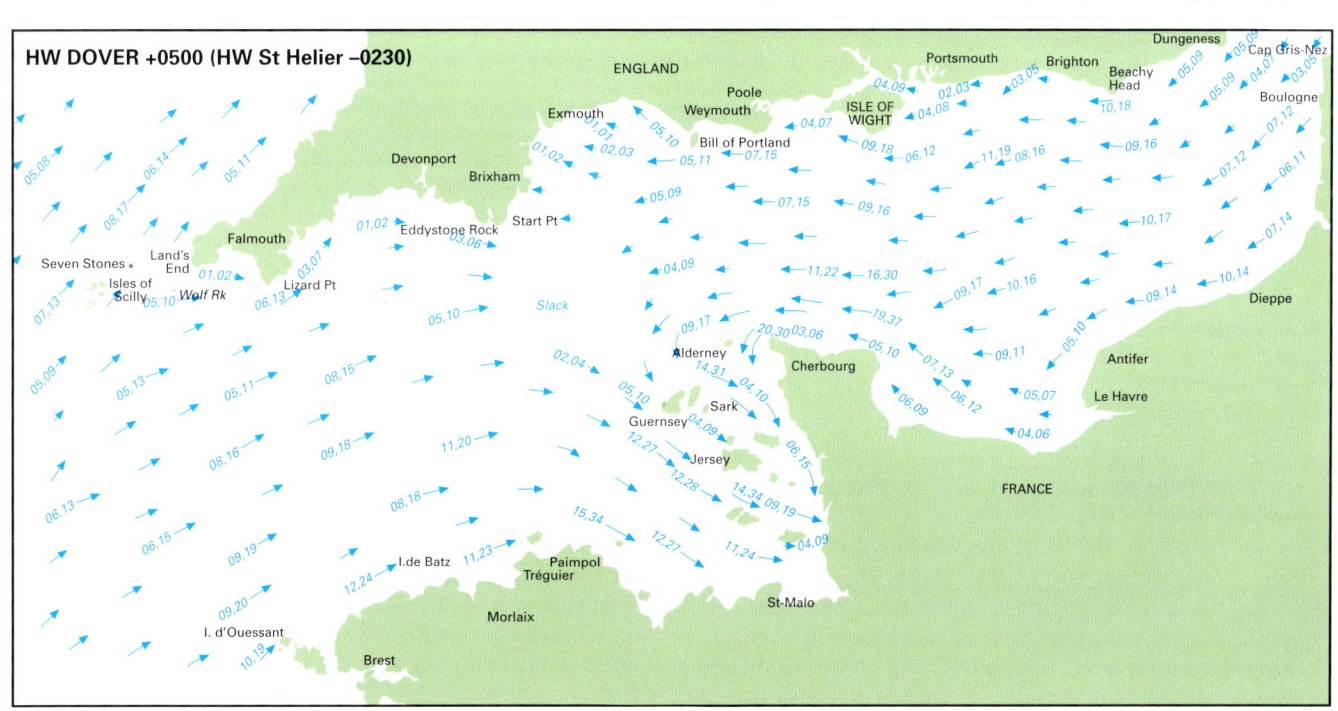

CHANNEL ISLANDS, CHERBOURG PENINSULA & NORTH BRITTANY

1 The Channel Islands

See *Appendix* for large-scale tidal stream diagrams for individual Channel Islands. They indicate many of the complex inshore eddies that do not feature on small-scale diagrams.

An understanding of how the area happens to have one of the world's largest tidal ranges starts with the concept of a tidal wave surging up and down the English Channel every 12 hours. In general, ports to the W will experience HW earlier and ports to the E will be later, so when it is HW at St Helier it will be about 30 minutes after HW at Paimpol and about 1½ hours before HW at Cherbourg. There are, of course, exceptions to this within the area due to the flow around the islands.

A look at the plan on page 9 for HW Dover +0500 (the equivalent of HW at St Helier –0230) clearly shows the Channel Islands at the confluence of 2 waves of tide. The outgoing wave in the E Channel is turning sharply S through the Alderney Race to bear down on the islands. At the same time the incoming wave is racing in from the W becoming accelerated along the Brittany coast. Both waves converge on the Baie de Mont St Michel SE of Jersey, where the tide is said to run at the speed of a galloping horse and HW rises to a height of nearly 15m (50ft) at spring tides. The outgoing tide is equally savage with the sea retreating up to seven miles offshore. At nearby St Malo this energy is harnessed to generate electricity. Within this relentless swirl will be found eddies, rotary currents, acceleration zones and bay effects. It can never be said to be boring!

Tidal hints

Imray's Tides Planner app provides quick and easy reference to tidal data, streams and coefficients.

- Calculate the best time to leave by working back from the deadline for arriving at your destination. This may be influenced by limitations such as a marina sill, tidal conditions or depth in a channel
- Decide the minimum boat speed that needs to be made good and consider using engine if falling behind.
- Mark each page of the *Tidal Atlas* with clock times so you can easily find the set and strength of the stream at any time or place. In the Channel Islands to avoid confusion use St Helier as your standard port rather than Dover. East of Cherbourg it may be useful to use Cherbourg and in N Brittany St Malo and Brest
- Add at least 10% to published rates if navigating over spring tides and beware of unstable inshore eddies which may not be shown. The first turn of the tide will tend to be felt close inshore, where rates are also likely to be stronger
- Try to keep up-tide of the rhumbline and guard against being set onto dangers
- In areas where reference marks are sparse it is easy to become unaware of drift. A useful clue can be provided by GPS cross track error
- Arrange your passage so as to be in strong tidal areas (off headlands, in narrow channels) when the stream is going your way and to be in weak tidal areas when the tide is against you
- The Rule of Twelfths for estimating the height of tide works better in the north of the area where the rise and fall total more or less six hours each. In the south, the rise is quicker than the fall, so apply with caution

- Bear in mind that in this area HW at springs occurs morning and evening with LW at noon. At neaps HW occurs at noon and midnight. Spring tides are, therefore, the best time for planning lunchtime stops in sheltered pools left by the retreating tide.

Transits

Identifying marks and being able to hold accurately in transit, paticularly in a cross set, is essential for survival in these waters. Electronics can let you down.

Tidal coefficients

The French use a simplified method of expressing the range of the tide as a 'coefficient'. This shows without the need for calculation whether it is neaps, springs or in between. Typical values are:

20 = A very small neap tide (mort-eau)
45 = Mean neaps
70 = An average tide
95 = Mean springs
120 = A very big spring tide (vive-eau)

The coefficient for the day may also be used to decide the correction(s) to apply when calculating time and height differences between Standard and Secondary ports.

Vive eau (spring) corrections should be applied when a coefficient is over 70 and morte eau (neap) corrections when it is less than 70.

Formalities and regulations

Jersey, along with Le Plateau des Minquiers and Les Ecréhous reefs, makes up the Bailiwick of Jersey, while the Bailiwick of Guernsey includes Alderney, Herm and Sark, the latter being more or less self-governing and a law unto itself. Both Bailiwicks have separate parliaments known as 'The States' and their own customs and immigration services.

Passports are required for entry into the Channel Islands. On arrival in France you may also be required to show proof of competence in the form of the International Certificate of Competence (ICC) which should be endorsed for 'inland waters' if entry into French canals is planned. Ship's Papers should include Certificate of Registration, Certificate of Insurance, proof of VAT status and, if the yacht is chartered, a copy of the charter contract.

Q flag

This formality is no longer enforced, although some harbour authorities favour use of the Q flag as a means of identifying new arrivals in the Channel Islands. All vessels are required to complete a customs and immigration form at the port of entry. The French Courtesy Flag (Tricolour) should be flown when in French territorial waters.

Introduction

Official ports of entry
Alderney Braye
Guernsey, Herm and **Sark** St Peter Port, St Sampson (for commercial vessels only) and Beaucette Marina
Jersey St Helier and Gorey
France Normally it is only necessary to report at Bureau du Port or Marina office but be prepared for a visit by Les Douaniers anywhere or anytime.

Prevention of rabies
The Channel Islands is a rabies-free area and all the islands have legislation that prohibits the landing of animals without a licence. An exception is made if the vessel is arriving from within the Bailiwicks of Guernsey or Jersey, the United Kingdom, the Republic of Ireland or the Isle of Man. A vessel arriving from outside these territories and with an animal on board should first obtain inward clearance from port control and will be directed to an isolated berth. The animal must be securely confined and will not be permitted to land. There are severe penalties for breaking the law.

Marinas and moorings

Marinas
Guernsey Victoria Marina, QE2 Marina, Beaucette Marina, St Sampsons (locals only)
Jersey St Helier Marina, Elizabeth Marina, La Collette Yacht Basin
Cherbourg peninsula St Vaast-La Hougue, Cherbourg, Diélette, Carteret, Granville.

Visitors' moorings
Alderney Braye Harbour
Guernsey St Peter Port
Herm N and W of harbour (drying)
Sark La Grève de la Ville, Havre Gosselin
Jersey Gorey (drying)

Yacht clubs
Yacht clubs in the islands welcome visitors:
Alderney Alderney Sailing Club, Braye
  ☎ 01481 822758/822959/725500
Guernsey Royal Channel Islands Yacht Club, St Peter Port ☎ 01481 723154
  Guernsey Yacht Club, St Peter Port
  ☎ 01481 725342
Jersey Royal Channel Islands Yacht Club, St Aubin,
  ☎ (01534) 741023/745783
  St Helier Yacht Club, St Helier
  ☎ (01534) 732229/721307

Search and rescue
Marine Search and Rescue is coordinated by the Coastguard Stations at Jersey (St Helier), Guernsey (St Peter Port) and Alderney (Braye). Communications are undertaken by Jersey and Guernsey with both stations maintaining a 24 hour/7 day watch on Ch 16 and DSC calls on Ch 70. Alderney Coastguard (not 24 hr) coordinates its own operations with the backup of Guernsey Coastguard. There are three RNLI offshore lifeboats and several inshore lifeboats based in the islands.

Channel Islands Air Search aircraft on service over Les Roches Douvres *CIAS*

Channel Islands Air Search
The Channel Islands Air Search charity was founded in 1980 and is funded by voluntary donations. Its main benefactor, the Lions Clubs of Guernsey and Jersey, enabled the acquisition of the PBN 2B Islander *Lions Pride*. This dedicated search and rescue aircraft, based in Guernsey, is equipped with a heat seeking infrared camera, search radar, night-vision sight, air droppable life-raft (11 man), smoke markers, night strobe markers, marine VHF, VHF/EPIRB homer, loudhailer and searchlight.
  CIAS receive some forty callouts a year by Channel Island, French and occasionally UK Rescue Centres. www.ci-airsearch.com

French search and rescue
FRENCH SAR is coordinated by CROSS centres (Centre Régionaux Opèrationneis de Surveillance et de Sauvetage) with 24hr watch on VHF ch 16 and DSC.
  The French lifeboat service is operated by SNSM (Société National de Sauvetage en Mer).

A local hazard
The fouling of propellers and rudders on fishing pots, traps and nets is the most common cause of calls to rescue services in the Channel Islands. Although local regulations ban the laying of fishing gear in main channels, it is safer to assume that such obstacles may be found anywhere. Maintain a sharp lookout for markers and always aim to pass downtide of them. It is recommended that a rope cutter be fitted to the propeller shaft and a snorkel, mask and diver's knife kept aboard.

High speed ferries
High speed ferries ply between the Islands and the UK south coast (Poole and Weymouth) and adjacent French coast (Granville and St Malo). The larger catamarans proceed at speeds of around 37 knots and a good lookout should be maintained.

Telecommunications

Dialling French numbers
If using a UK or Channel Island phone it is necessary to prefix the number with the country code 0033 and delete the 0 from the NW France area code 02. Calls to a French mobile number must be preceeded by 06.

1 The Channel Islands

Mobile phone service

The whole area is well served by Channel Islands and French networks, and apart from mid-Channel there are very few areas where it will not be possible to receive a signal of sufficient strength to make and receive calls.

Mobile phone subscribers to UK and French networks will usually find that their provider has roaming agreements with local networks, but some are limited and it is worth checking before visiting the area. Unless you manually select a new network the handset will automatically connect to the strongest signal. This means that sailing around Jersey, for instance, you could be using a French network off the E coast and a Guernsey network around the NW corner and a Jersey network elsewhere.

Medical emergencies

112 pan-European emergency number may be called from any phone including a mobile. In France this service is known as SAMU (Service d'Aide Medicale Urgent). An English speaking operator is available on request.

Internet services - WiFi

Guernsey WiFi is enabled in Victoria Marina and elsewhere in the port. A password issued to visitors on arrival is required to access the system. Internet facilities are available at Guernsey Information Centre, St Peter Port library and the Harbour Office.

Jersey Jersey Marinas supply complimentary WiFi throughout the port. Follow onscreen directions to register for free access. Internet access is available at the Marina Office, Post Office and public library

France WiFi is available in all major ports and marinas but may require an external antenna where the signal is weak. A code to gain access is issued on receipt of payment of dues.

NetABord offers high-speed WiFi at a wide range of marinas in the English Channel and North Brittany. Users can buy one, two or 24 hours of WiFi access from www.netabord.fr. Payment is via credit/debit card or PayPal. Technical support ☏ +33 2 97 56 57 97.

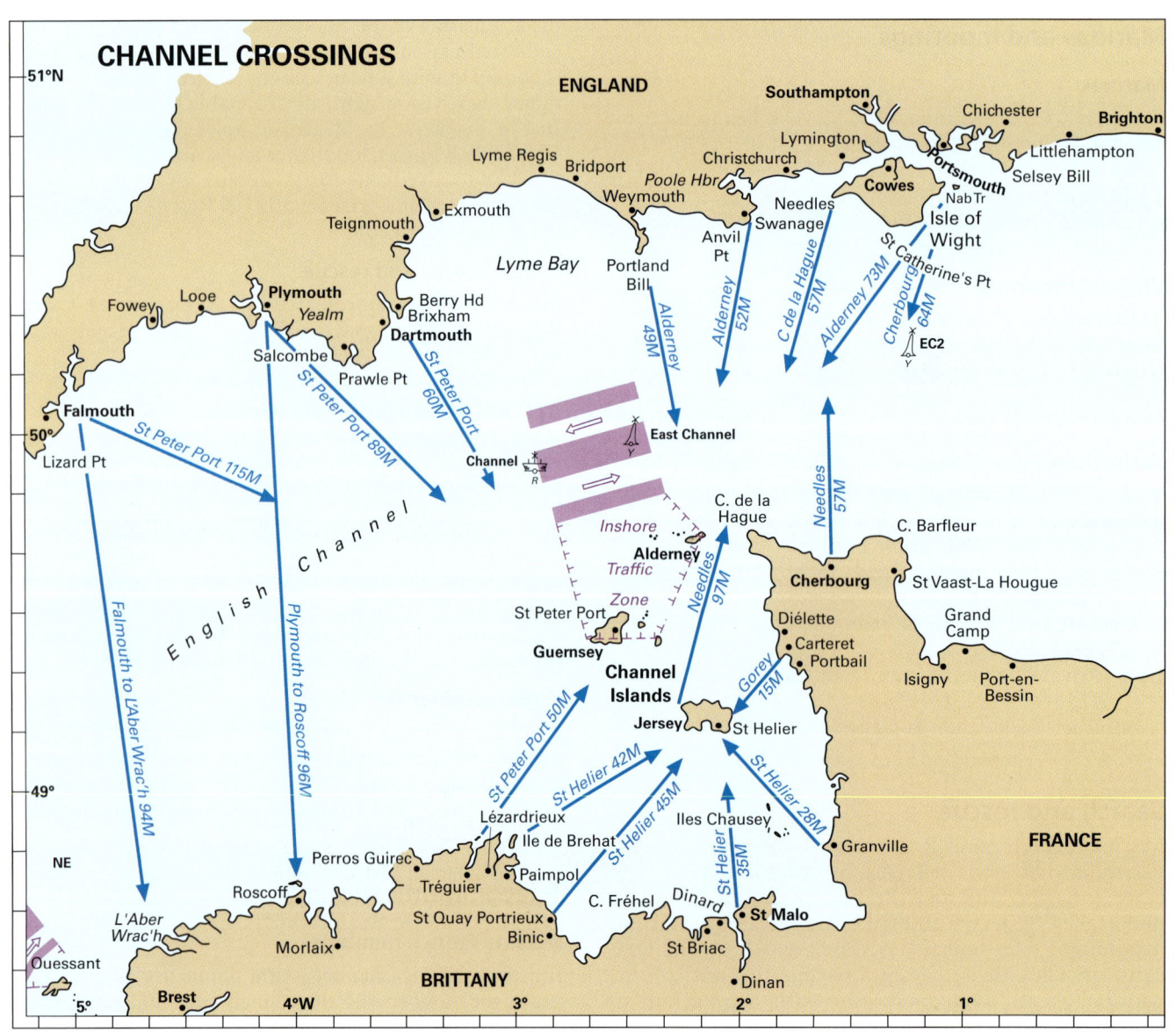

12 CHANNEL ISLANDS, CHERBOURG PENINSULA & NORTH BRITTANY

Introduction

Getting to the islands

The Channel crossing

For the majority of yachtsmen, a visit to the Channel Islands will involve a Channel crossing. This should be achieved within a day but can nevertheless be a challenging hurdle, calling for thorough preparation. (See *Formalities and regulations*, page 10.)

Weather

As with any passage, finding a window of settled weather is the first consideration. Follow the trend during the run-up period to your departure and obtain the latest forecast before casting off. Once underway, monitor weather bulletins broadcast by UK coastguards, Cross Jobourg (French coastguards) and Jersey Coastguard. Should conditions call for a change of plan, such as a return or diversion. There are fewer alternatives in the Channel Islands than on the South Coast and many a yachtsman has been glad of the shelter provided by the Cherbourg peninsula or the port itself with its ease of access. Barfleur and St Vaast-La Hougue on the east side are good bolt-holes in westerly weather. (See *II. The Cherbourg Peninsula*.)

Fog anywhere in the Channel can be unnerving – more so if you are without radar or AIS (see page 3). If this is forecast to affect your route it is better to stay put.

Tidal strategy

For most passages to the islands there is a deadline for arrival at a given point. When this is due to tidal considerations it is known as a 'tidal gate' and will dictate departure time. For instance, on a crossing from the Needles to Jersey via the Alderney Race, the tidal gate is the entry to the Alderney Race at HW Dover (HW St Helier +0500). With an average speed of 6 knots and a distance of 60 miles, departure from the Needles Fairway buoy will need to be 10 hours earlier (2 hours after the previous HW Dover).

With the ebb and flow running E–W in the Channel, the majority of crossings will be across the stream, setting the yacht east and west of track. Since most crossings to the islands can take less than 12 hours under sail, you will not receive equal amounts of ebb and flood. In practice, adjustment will be required to compensate for this imbalance and also the stronger streams on the French side (see diagram below).

Collision avoidance

Every day some 500 ships pass through the English Channel, making it one of the world's busiest shipping routes. With crossing traffic in conflict with the prevailing flow up and down the Channel there is a serious risk of near misses and collisions. When these do occur, small craft come off worst.

A Traffic Separation Scheme (TSS) operates north of the Casquets, which has the effect of concentrating shipping into a small area. Cross-Channel routes followed by yachts will tend to avoid crossing a TSS, where special rules apply, but will pass close to entry and exit points where shipping will be more spread out and movements less predictable. In such areas the normal Regulations for Preventing Collisions at Sea apply and should be followed.

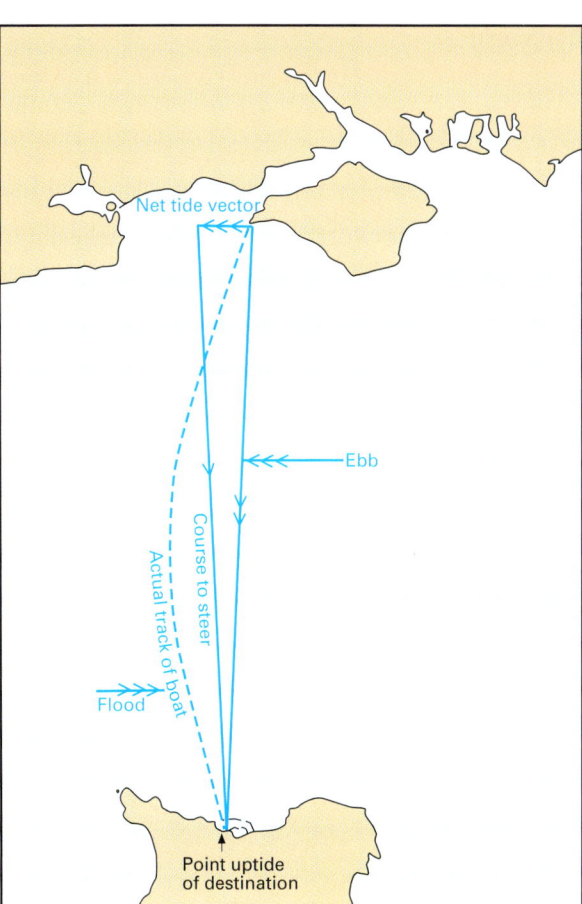

A tidal vector is drawn to calculate the degree of compensation required to offset an imbalance between east and west-going stream. On this cross-Channel passage the sum total of west-going stream exceeded that of the east-going stream, the difference being represented by the length of the net tide vector arrow

A sharp lookout must be maintained at all times and frequent bearings taken of conflicting vessels, some of which may be little short of 1,300ft long and steaming at 20 knots in good visibility. It may be safer to assume that they are not going to alter course for a sailing vessel.

See *AIS (Automatic Identification System)*, page 3.

Crossing from the Solent area between Portsmouth and Poole

Departure points Nab Tower, St Catherine's Point, Needles Fairway buoy, Anvil Point

Crossings to Alderney and its Race, or perhaps to Cherbourg, are among the shortest. It is 52M from Anvil Point to The Race.

To Alderney (Braye)

The Alderney landfall from a northeasterly direction when the island is seen end-on can make it elusive. Since it is low-lying compared with the high land of the adjacent Cherbourg peninsula, it is also slower to lift above the horizon.

The approach to Braye Harbour should be carefully controlled to avoid being swept west into The Swinge with its dangerous overfalls or east into The Race. Arrival should coincide with slack water, which is about half tide up or down off Braye (HW St Helier –0215 or +0215).

1 The Channel Islands

To Cherbourg

Cherbourg, with its easy landfall and entrance at any time by day or night, makes a good stop over en route to the islands but, in the prevailing westerlies, the 15M haul onwards to The Race can be hard going. See *Alderney Race, Cherbourg to Braye*; also *Cherbourg Part II*.

To Guernsey (St Peter Port) and Jersey (St Helier)

If the stream is fair, the logical route is to continue through The Race. This presents no hazard in fair weather when patches of overfalls may be barely noticeable; but if in doubt, avoid The Race Rocks SE of Alderney, the 16m bank off Cap de la Hague, Milieu 4M SSE of Alderney and Banc de la Schôle with only 2.4m at chart datum.

Aim to arrive at a waypoint midway between Cap de la Hague and Quénard Point (⊕1) just before HW Dover (HW St Helier +0500) when the stream is slack. Get it right and it can be a fast passage on the tidal escalator to St Peter Port or all the way to St Helier.

If outbound from Poole for St Peter Port, conditions may favour routeing W of the Casquets. This is described below in *Crossings from the West Country*. Guernsey will usually be approached from the N following a landfall NE of Platte Fougère Lighthouse. An alternative in poor visibility is to route via the Big Russel where there is more sea room and the possibility of diversions via Sark or Herm. Approach to St Peter Port will then be from the Lower Heads S cardinal buoy S of Jethou.

The most direct route to St Helier is via Banc Desormes W cardinal buoy off the NW Corner (⊕28), round Point Corbière and on to the S coast. If routeing via the E coast, approach between the Paternosters and Les Dirouilles. Directions for the NE Corner to St Helier are described under *Approaches to Gorey. From the west (St Helier)* and *From the north*.

Crossing from the west country between Weymouth and Plymouth

Departure Points Portland Bill, Berry Head, River Dart entrance, Prawle Pt, Plymouth Sound.

To Guernsey (St Peter Port)

At just 70 miles from the River Dart, Guernsey is the nearest and most popular arrival point in the Islands. Prevailing westerlies and a more favourable slant on the tidal streams can make for a good passage.

If bound for St Peter Port, routeing via Les Hanois Lighthouse at the SW corner and St Martin's Point on the SE corner can be quicker than the N approach, providing the tides are worked intelligently. Care must be taken not to be set onto the W coast of Guernsey, a notorious lee shore. Keep at least 3M off. By contrast, the S coast is well marked and straightforward. Stay just outside the 50m contour and you will be about 1M off all the way along.

The inbound track from Weymouth will pass close to E Channel light buoy at the E end of the Casquets Traffic Separation Scheme. This may involve crossing the lanes, in which case a diversion E to keep clear should be made if it is not possible to comply with the Rules.

The passage close E of the Casquets is the wide Ortac Channel. Overfalls and eddies can be expected anywhere in this area, but providing passage through the channel is made in fair weather and at slack water, HW Dover–0100 (HW St Helier+0400), it presents no hazard. Keep a distance off the lighthouse of at least 1M – more if the tidal stream is setting you onto it. With an average speed of 6 knots, departure from Weymouth will have to be some 8 hours earlier (5 hours before the previous HW Dover) in order to meet this tidal gate. This will also ensure a fair stream for the remaining 13M of the passage to Little Russel. Slower boats should consider departing earlier or routeing via an intermediate port if practicable.

To Alderney (Braye)

As with other crossings from the West Country, the prospect of navigating across or around the Casquets Traffic Separation Scheme will need to be considered.

Approaching the island from the NW it is important to guard against being set towards the Casquets and Burhou with its outlying reefs to the N. All will be left safely to the SW if Fort Albert (E of the harbour) is kept open E of the breakwater head on 115°. An alternative clearing line is Quénard Point lighthouse on a bearing of no less than 120°. At night stay in the W sector of Château L'Etoc light (Iso.WR.4s) until the leading lights (both Q) are aligned.

To avoid ending the passage in a tidal battle, aim to arrive well before HW Dover (HW St Helier +0500) when the main English Channel stream turns to run W with a vengeance.

To northwest Brittany

Crossings to Brittany from harbours between Salcombe and Plymouth range from 90 to 100M, representing a passage time of about 24 hours for the average yacht. Compared to the coastal route to west Brittany - which is often thwarted by head winds and unhelpful tides, these N–S crossings offer the chance of a good off the wind sail and the taste of an ocean passage.

When passage planning there are several factors which should be considered. Wait for a 48 hour window of settled conditions. If N'lies are forecasted assess the risk of closing a lee shore. Poor visibility with fog is prevalent in west Brittany and could prejudice a safe landfall. Atlantic swell will often be experienced in the Western approaches - no hazard in itself but it can put more demands on the crew.

Although there are no TSS zones to be crossed, expect concentrations of commercial traffic around the zones off Casquets, Lands End and Ouessant.

Overall the tidal effect on any crossing is likely to be marginal over 20 hours. However, tides run strongly along the N Brittany coast - particularly to the west. Be sure to

Ortac with Alderney in the distance

Introduction

err up tide on arrival. Also the tidal range will be greater than the English west country which may affect suitable arrival times at some harbours - especially those with half tide gates.

The choice of a landfall anywhere on this rocky coastline needs careful planning. Between Ile de Bréhat and L'Aber Wrac'h there are the conspicuously tall lighthouses of Les Héaux, Ile de Batz and Ile Vierge which provide good initial marks from which to set up an approach. Pilotage into a safe haven is preferable in daylight and good visibility.

Should problems force a diversion to a more easterly destination, there are several bolt holes between the Channel Islands and Tréguier. Be prepared for a longer passage and carry sufficient information on alternative harbours. There is always the option of turning back.

Crossing from the south

North Brittany and lower Normandy

Departure Points Tréguier, Lézardrieux, Île de Bréhat, St Quay Portrieux, St Malo, Granville

To Guernsey (St Peter Port)

At around 50M these passages are among the longest to the islands from the French coast. As they do not quite fit into one tide some compromise is required. Assuming you want to make the best use of the flood tide when the streams are generally setting ENE, it will be necessary to get underway on the last of the ebb, or earlier if you want to avoid a foul tide in the final approach to St Peter Port.

The initial W-going stream can set like a mill race at spring tides on this corner of the Brittany coast and care should be taken to avoid being set towards Les Roches Douvres and Plateau de Barnouic – an area to be avoided. (See *Part III, Plateau des Roches Douvres*.)

A landfall off the S coast of Guernsey, with its steep cliffs, is among the easiest and the channel up to St Peter Port from St Martin's Point is broad and comparatively clear of dangers.

To Jersey (St Helier)

Inbound from the more southwesterly departure points gives a better slant on the streams. By working the tides it should be possible to make the Passage Rock buoy in St Helier W Passage at HW just before the ebb.

A passage from St Malo will route either E or W about the Plateau des Minquiers depending on wind and tide.

Westabout the Minquiers (40M)

Leave St Malo by the main channel (La Petite Porte) at half ebb (HW St Helier+0300). The turning points are SW Minquiers W cardinal buoy and NW Minquiers W cardinal buoy which will be reached at about LW. The rest of the passage to the Passage Rock N cardinal buoy in the St Helier Western Passage will be made on the first hours of the flood, arriving at about HW St Helier–0300.

Eastabout the Minquiers (36M)

Leave St Malo at HW St Helier–0300 (about 2½ hours before local HW) by La Grande Conchée Channel. Set a course for NE Minquiers E cardinal buoy, at which point alter course for the Demie de Pas light tower. Entry to St Helier will initially be by the South Passage then the Red and Green Passage. A slightly earlier departure from St Malo means that you may make it over St Helier marina sills, which close at half ebb.

Any approach to the island from the SE, particularly from Granville and Iles Chausey, will route close S of the dangers that extend some 8 miles out from the SE corner. On a spring ebb care should be taken to avoid being set N.

The Demie de Pas light tower tends to be inconspicuous, in which case initial approach can be made with the Power Station Chimney (95m) (conspic) on a bearing of 350° (see *Jersey, Electric Passage* page 112).

Coq passage

This route E of Les Minquiers saves a few miles. It is frequently used by high speed ferries when there is 7m or more rise above Chart Datum. Stay on the 2°W meridian and you will pass, N–S, 0·4M E of N Minquiers buoy, 0·8M E of Le Coq bn and 200m E of SE Minquiers buoy. See page 140. (Chart BA 3656)

Returning from the islands

It is easier to leave the Channel Islands for the UK South Coast than to arrive.

Before casting off, one of the main considerations, along with the weather and routeing across or round the Traffic Separation Scheme, will be the powerful streams on the south side of the Channel. Getting a good send-off is all a matter of timing.

Departure from St Peter Port, Guernsey should be timed to ensure a favourable tide for whichever route is chosen. A departure at HW St Helier–0230 or as

Recif Le Coq beacon (Coq passage) looking W

Maîtresse Ile — Le Coq bn

CHANNEL ISLANDS, CHERBOURG PENINSULA & NORTH BRITTANY

1 The Channel Islands

soon as the marina sill can be cleared will take the first of the N-going stream out of Little Russel and then carry nearly 7 hours fair to the NE. This will mean passing through The Race at its greatest rate and an alternative plan should be made if strong winds from the N or NE are likely. In the Ortac Channel NW of Alderney beware of a strong set to the E towards reefs N of Ortac.

Departure for the N from St Helier is more complicated. A N-going eddy starts at La Corbière at about HW St Helier–0200 (HW Dover+0530), but to catch it one must stem the tide from St Helier. There are then a good six hours of favourable tide to get up to and through the Alderney Race over 30 miles away – plenty of time at a reasonable speed – but unlike a departure time from St Peter Port there may not be time to carry the tide all the way to Cherbourg. Conditions may favour routeing E-about Jersey, leaving St Helier at HW–0300. At the NE corner, the N-going stream starts just before HW.

At Braye one is best poised for a Channel crossing, just 56M to the Needles, but keep a sharp lookout for shipping leaving the E-going lane of the Casquets Traffic Separation Scheme. The time of departure should be calculated to catch a fair stream through the Needles Channel if bound for the Solent or up to the Nab Tower if bound for Portsmouth.

Some inter-island passages

These passages cover some of the well-trodden tracks around the Channel Islands.

Charts
The charts listed are those editions on which the whole passage may be plotted. Additional large-scale charts will be required to cover departure and approach.

Distance
(M) is in nautical miles by the shortest navigable route.

Time
(h) is based on an average speed of 6 knots through the water. Since most passages will be made on a fair tidal stream, speeds made good will be higher, possibly into double figures at spring tides. Most inter-island passages fall within 30 miles so are achievable on one tidal cycle i.e. 6 hours.

Tides
Passages should be made wherever possible using all of the fair stream. If a part must be taken during a foul stream, dodge out of the worst if possible and use the engine to maintain progress. Punching a strong adverse stream can be a negative experience.

Best time to leave
For most passages there will be a 'gate' to be met and such deadlines dictate the time of departure.

Dangers en route
These include areas of overfalls, banks, shoals and drying rocks, which call for particular vigilance if not a diversion. Navigation and pilotage at LW when many potential dangers are visible is more straightforward than when they are covered.

Tracks and waypoints
Tracks shown on the sketch plans represent typical inter island passages rather than text book routes to be followed. Selected waypoints are those that may be useful for the passage. Navigators should plot any waypoint they intend to use to check that it serves their intended route.

Between Alderney and Guernsey

BRAYE TO ST PETER PORT VIA THE SWINGE
Charts
BA 2669, BA Leisure Folio SC 5604 (sheet 3)
Imray C33A, Imray 2500 Chart Atlas (sheet 4)
SHOM 6966
Distance 24M
Time 4h

Tides
The main consideration is safe passage through The Swinge where slack water is around HW St Helier +0300. Arrival in the Little Russel should also be before the N-going stream starts at HW St Helier –0300 but with a fair stream there should be time in hand to achieve both objectives.

Refer to the Admiralty *Tidal Stream Atlas: The Channel Islands and adjacent coasts of France*. See also tidal diagrams on pages 364–373 in the Appendix to this book.

Best time to leave
This is local HW+0230 (HW St Helier+0300).

Dangers en route
Submerged end of Braye harbour breakwater – do not turn W until well clear. (See *Alderney. Clearing the submerged breakwater*). The Swinge can throw up dangerous overfalls in wind against tide conditions, when it is prudent to consider the alternate route via The Race. Pierre au Vraic (drying 1·2m) lurks 2 miles WSW of Les Etacs (Garden Rocks).

For clearing marks see *Alderney. Approaches to Braye from the S and SW via The Swinge*.

By night
It is inadvisable to use The Swinge due to lack of suitable lights.

The top of Little Russel from the southeast. The flood stream is setting hard to the south

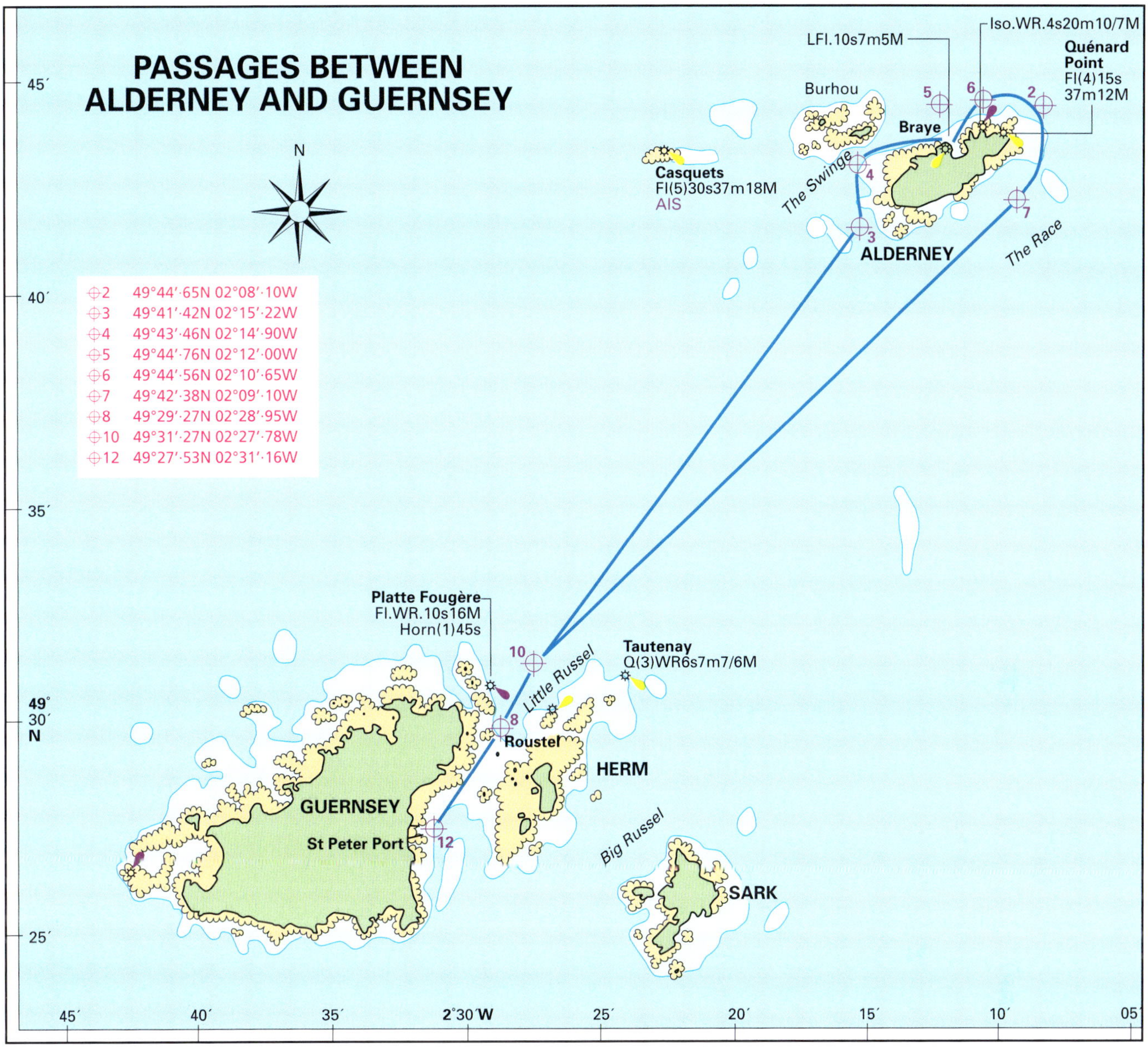

Introduction

I. THE CHANNEL ISLANDS

PASSAGES BETWEEN ALDERNEY AND GUERNSEY

⊕ 2	49°44'·65N 02°08'·10W
⊕ 3	49°41'·42N 02°15'·22W
⊕ 4	49°43'·46N 02°14'·90W
⊕ 5	49°44'·76N 02°12'·00W
⊕ 6	49°44'·56N 02°10'·65W
⊕ 7	49°42'·38N 02°09'·10W
⊕ 8	49°29'·27N 02°28'·95W
⊕ 10	49°31'·27N 02°27'·78W
⊕ 12	49°27'·53N 02°31'·16W

Passage waypoints

⊕ 5, 4, 3, 10, 8, 12
For detailed pilotage information see *Alderney* and *Guernsey*.

BRAYE TO ST PETER PORT VIA THE RACE

Charts
  BA 2669, BA Leisure Folio SC 5604 (sheet 3)
  Imray C33A, Imray 2500 Chart Atlas (sheet 4)
  SHOM 6966
Distance 25M
Time 4h

Tides

This roundabout route to St Peter Port may be necessary if conditions in The Swinge are unsuitable. Between Braye and Quénard Point at the E end of the island there are only 2 hours of E-going stream (from HW St Helier –0200 to HW St Helier). The Race does not start running to the SW until HW St Helier+0430 so

Looking NNE over The Garden Rocks (Les Etacs) off Alderney's west end. It is just after HW springs and the stream is setting N at 6–8 knots

CHANNEL ISLANDS, CHERBOURG PENINSULA & NORTH BRITTANY

1 The Channel Islands

a foul stream round the NE corner of the island must be punched for 2M before getting into the SW-going Race.

Best time to leave
Leave Braye at HW St Helier+0400 and make good speed while the current is comparatively weak.

Dangers en route
Drying rocks extending 0·3M off the N coast. Potentially heavy overfalls along the Brinchetais (Brimtides) Ledge particularly around Blanchard Rock 0·8M E of Quénard Point. Keep 0·5M off the N coast and 1·0M off Quénard Point before altering course SW for Guernsey.

By night
Depart on leading lights (A9 ⊕6) and turn E when Casquets light Fl(5)30s bears 262°(A1 ⊕2). If not visible, an alternative is to turn E when Quénard Point light Fl(4)15s bears 140°. Clear Quénard Point by at least 1·0M and hold Platte Fougère light Fl.WR.10s N of Little Russel on a bearing of 230° while keeping in W sector of Tautenay light Q(3)6s.

Align Roustel (Q) and Brehon Tower Iso.4s on 198° (G3 ⊕10). This will intercept the leading lights (on 220°) for St Peter Port leaving Roustel to port.

Passage waypoints
⊕ 6, 2, 7, 10, 8, 12

For detailed pilotage information see *Alderney* and *Guernsey* below.

ST PETER PORT TO BRAYE VIA THE SWINGE

Charts
BA 2669, BA Leisure Folio SC 5604 (sheet 3)
Imray C33A, Imray 2500 Chart Atlas (sheet 4)
SHOM 6966

Distance 24M
Time 4h

Tides
In order to carry a favourable stream through to Braye, The Swinge must be taken before HW St Helier+0300 when the stream turns to run W. (See *The Swinge* tidal strategy on page 27.)

Best time to leave
Bearing in mind your deadline for slack water in The Swinge, it would be prudent to get under way by just before HW St Helier−0230. At this time the N-going stream in the Little Russel is established.

Dangers en route
See *Alderney. The Swinge; Approaches to Alderney from SW via The Swinge Channel*; and also *Braye to St Peter Port via The Swinge*.

By night
It is inadvisable to use The Swinge due to lack of lights.

Passage waypoints
⊕ 12, 8, 10, 3, 4, 5

For detailed pilotage information see *Alderney* and *Guernsey* below.

ST PETER PORT TO BRAYE VIA THE RACE

Charts
BA 2669, BA Leisure Folio SC 5604 (sheet 3)
Imray C33A, Imray 2500 Chart Atlas (sheet 4)
SHOM 6966

Distance 25M
Time 4h

Tides
The 6½ hour slot between HW St Helier−0230 and HW St Helier+0320 is the right time for this passage. The deadline for catching the last of the E-going stream up through The Race is HW St Helier+0400. After this there will be a brief period of slack before the SW-going stream takes over.

Best time to leave
Leave St Peter Port at HW St Helier−0200 when the N-going stream off Guernsey's E coast is established.

Dangers en route
See *Alderney. Alderney Race* (below) and also *Braye to St Peter Port via The Race* (above).

By night
Directions are as for Braye to St Peter Port via The Race, but in reverse order. When abeam Platte Fougère light take up a course to a suitably positioned waypoint S of the area of overfalls within the 30m contour S of Alderney. Keep outside until Quénard Point light, which will have been obscured for most of the passage, bears 310° or less, when course may be altered towards N to pass round Quénard Point, and onto transit A1.

Passage waypoints
⊕ 12, 8, 10, 7, 26

For detailed pilotage information see *Alderney* and *Guernsey*.

Victoria Marina, St Peter Port *Jane Russell*

18 CHANNEL ISLANDS, CHERBOURG PENINSULA & NORTH BRITTANY

Introduction

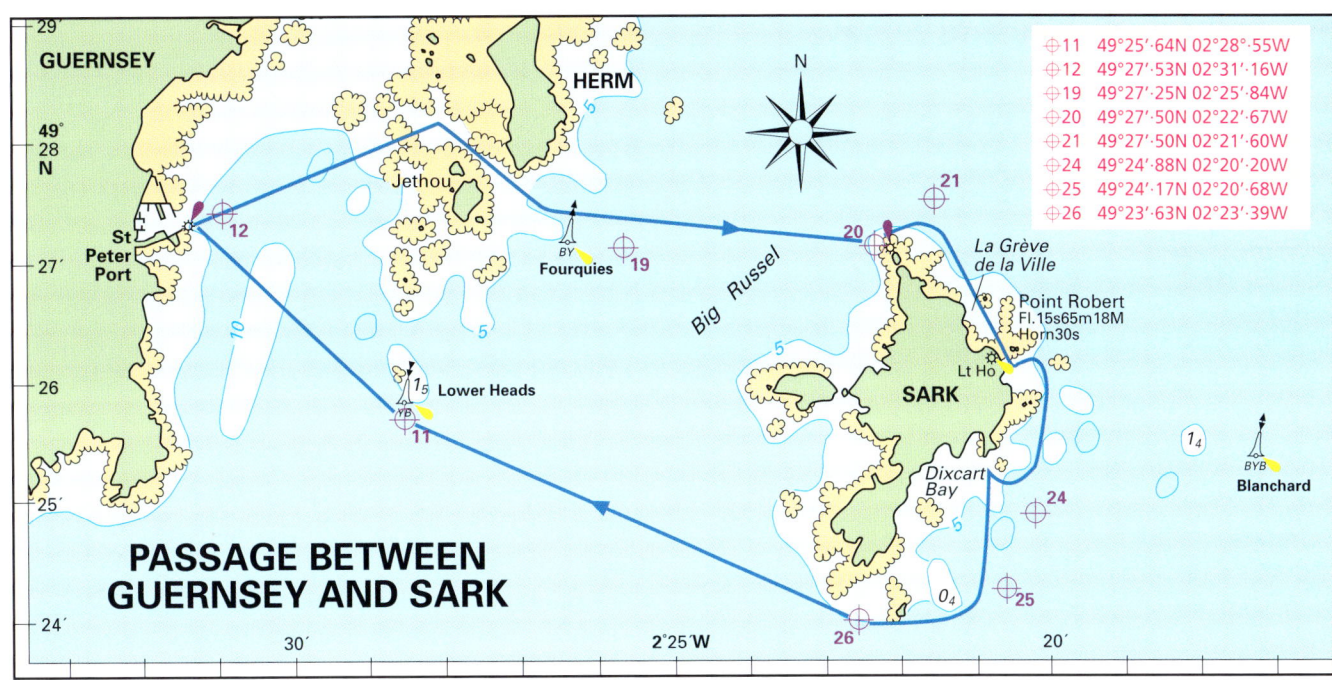

Between Guernsey and Sark

ST PETER PORT TO LA GRÈVE DE LA VILLE ANCHORAGE VIA HERM, ROUTEING BY ALLIGANDE PASSAGE, PERCÉE PASSAGE AND BEC DU NEZ

Charts BA 808, Imray 2500 Chart Pack (sheet 5), SHOM 6904
Distance 7·5M
Time 1–2h

Tides

The best time to cross the Big Russel is over the half tide period when streams here and all round Sark are comparatively weak. At this time there will also be a least depth of about 4m in the Alligande Passage.

Best time to leave

HW St Helier–0300

Dangers en route

Most of this passage involves pilotage among rocks so visibility of at least 3·5M is required to sight marks. The marks in the Alligande and Percée Passages must be held accurately until Meulettes (drying 1·7m) are cleared (see plan page 72). On the E side of Sark the inshore channel between Bec du Nez and Pécheresse (drying 8·9m) has a least width of 200m (see *Sark. East Coast. Approaches from the N*, page 91).

By night

Pilotage round Sark is not possible after dark.

Passage waypoints

⊕ 12, 19, 20, 21
For detailed pilotage information see *Guernsey* and *Sark*.

DIXCART BAY ANCHORAGE TO ST PETER PORT SOUTHABOUT

Charts BA 808, Imray 2500 Chart Atlas (sheet 5), SHOM 6904
Distance 9M
Time 2h

Tides

The decision whether to go N or S of Sark will depend on wind and tide. If leaving for St Peter Port at about half tide on a rising tide (HW St Helier–0300) and just before HW, it is better to go S of Sark. Initially the stream will be unhelpful but once L'Etac has been rounded and the course altered for the Lower Heads buoy, there will be a NE-going stream till about HW St Helier+0230.

Best time to leave

HW St Helier–0300.

Note An alternative return N of Sark will make use of the S-going eddy in Banquette Bay (W coast) which runs from just before HW St Helier to HW St Helier+0300, while the stream in the Big Russel is running NE. It may be practical to take the Percée Passage and Alligande Passage, or with caution one of the passages S of Jethou.

Best time to leave

HW+0200

Dangers en route

When rounding the S of Sark take care not to be swept towards Balmée which may be covered, Les Vingt Clos and dangers S of Sercul.

By night

If bad weather is forecast, leave before nightfall, as pilotage round the island is not possible after dark.

Passage waypoints

⊕ 24, 25, 26, 11, 12
For detailed pilotage information see *Sark* and *Guernsey*.

1 The Channel Islands

Between Guernsey and Jersey

ST PETER PORT TO ST HELIER

Charts
 BA 2669, BA Leisure Folio SC 5604 (sheet 4)
 Imray C33A, Imray 2500 Chart Atlas (sheet 8)
 SHOM 6966
Distance 26M
Time 4h

Tides

Fair from HW St Helier+0420 at the earliest to just before HW St Helier. The best hours are from HW St Helier–0500 to HW St Helier–0030. For much of the passage the stream is square on the port beam, so expect to be set S of track. This is not a bad thing as you will want to pass clear of Point Corbière.

Dangers en route

To clear reefs off Point Corbière, known as the Jailers, keep a distance of at least 1 mile off the lighthouse. In wind against tide conditions, more particularly around HW springs, overfalls can extend up to 2M off the Point.

By night

Soon after passing Lower Heads S cardinal buoy it should be possible to identify Grosnez Point light Fl(2) and Corbière Point light Iso.10s on Jersey. Keep in the W sector of both. Use ⊕37 to clear dangers W of Point Corbière and approach St Helier by the Northwest Passage (J2) or Western Passage (J6) ⊕36.

Passage waypoints

⊕ 12, 11, 37

For detailed pilotage information see *Guernsey* and *Jersey*.

ST HELIER TO ST PETER PORT

Charts
 BA 2669, BA Leisure Folio SC 5604 (sheet 4)
 Imray C33A, Imray 2500 Chart Atlas (sheet 8)
 SHOM 6966
Distance 27M
Time 4h

Tides

Fair from HW St Helier–0100 to HW St Helier+0320.

Inshore streams turn to the N on the W coast of Jersey at HW St Helier–0300 but only turn fair to the W along the S coast of the island at HW–0100. The later the

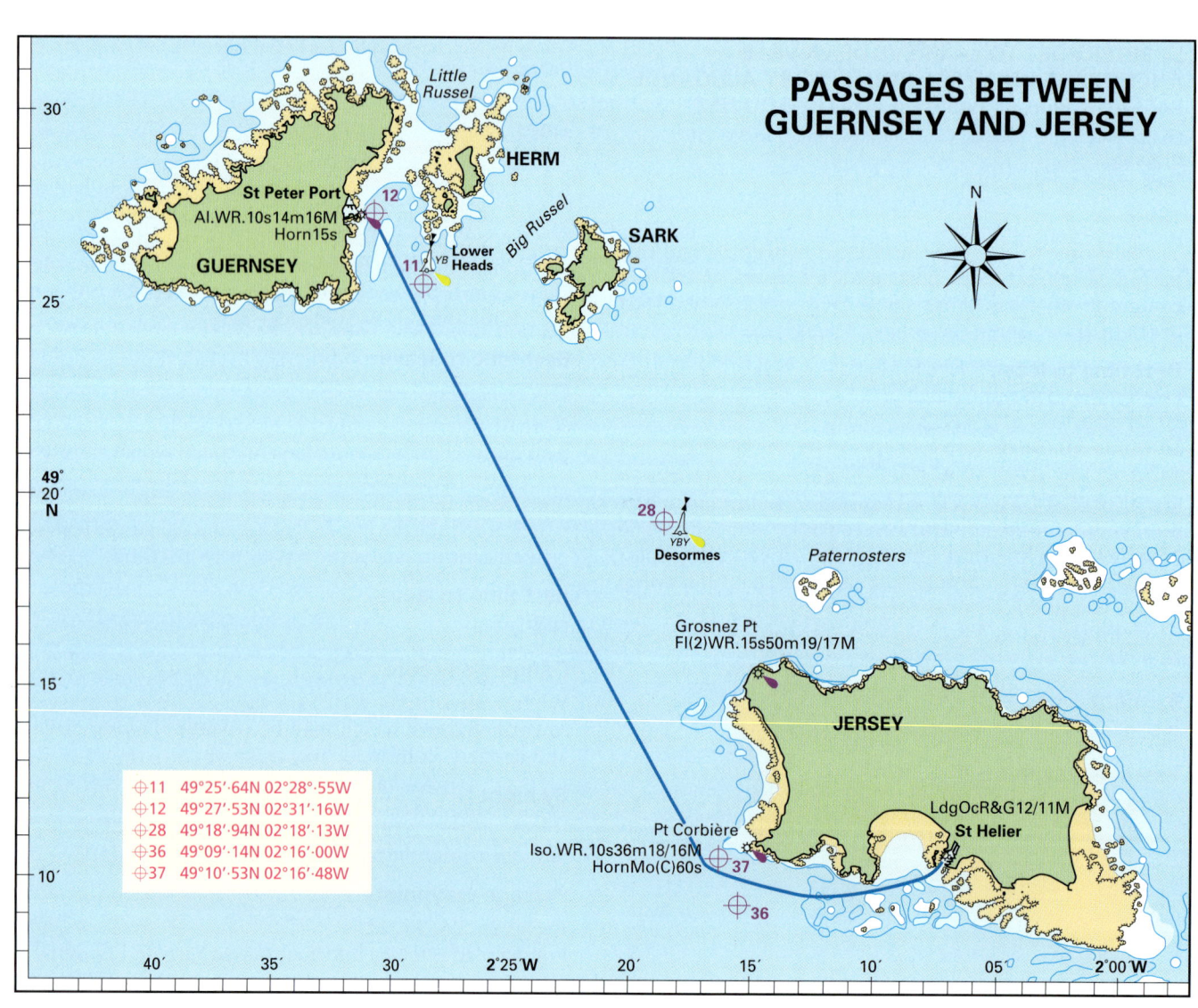

Introduction

Castle Cornet lighthouse, St Peter Port

departure after HW the greater the likelihood of overfalls off La Corbière. A compromise is to leave at HW St Helier–0100 which should carry a fair stream between the islands and, if good speed is maintained, the last of the N-going up the Little Russel.

Best time to leave
HW St Helier –0100

Dangers en route
Lobster pot markers off Point Corbière and into St Ouen's Bay.

By night
Leave on Red and Green Passage (J11) then take up W Passage (J6). Pass midway between Noirmont Point light Fl(4)12s and Les Fours N cardinal buoy. Take up a westerly heading into the W sector of La Corbière light Iso. Keep at least 1·0M off as you round Point Corbière. ⊕37 is aligned with the turning point which is the FR on the shore on with La Corbière light. Set course for Lower Heads S cardinal buoy (⊕11) and then directly to Castle Cornet breakwater light Al.WR.

Passage waypoints
⊕ 37, 11, 12

For detailed pilotage information see *Guernsey* and *Jersey*.

Between Sark and Jersey

DIXCART BAY ANCHORAGE TO GOREY
Charts
  BA 2669, BA Leisure Folio SC 5604 (sheet 4)
  Imray C33A, Imray 2500 Chart Atlas (sheet 8)
  SHOM 6966
Distance 20M
Time 3h

Tides
The most favourable period is from HW St Helier–0500 to HW St Helier, a total of 5 hours. The strongest stream is close inshore off the NE corner of Jersey, up to 6 knots at springs, a tidal 'gate' to be met before the turn of the tide at just before HW.

Best time to leave
HW St Helier–0500.

Dangers en-route
With the stream on the port beam for most of the passage, take care not to be set S onto the Paternosters Reef.

By night
Departure should be made before darkness. The route from Banc Desormes W cardinal buoy ⊕28 along the N coast of Jersey to Gorey is not easy by night, due to the Paternosters reef and few lights.

Approach in the W sector of Sorel Point light LFl.7.5s and keep no less than 1·0M off the coast until established on Gorey leading lights.

Conditions may favour a more direct route N of the Paternosters with ⊕29 as shown.

Passage waypoints
⊕ 25, 29, 30, 31, 32

For detailed pilotage information see *Sark* and *Jersey*.

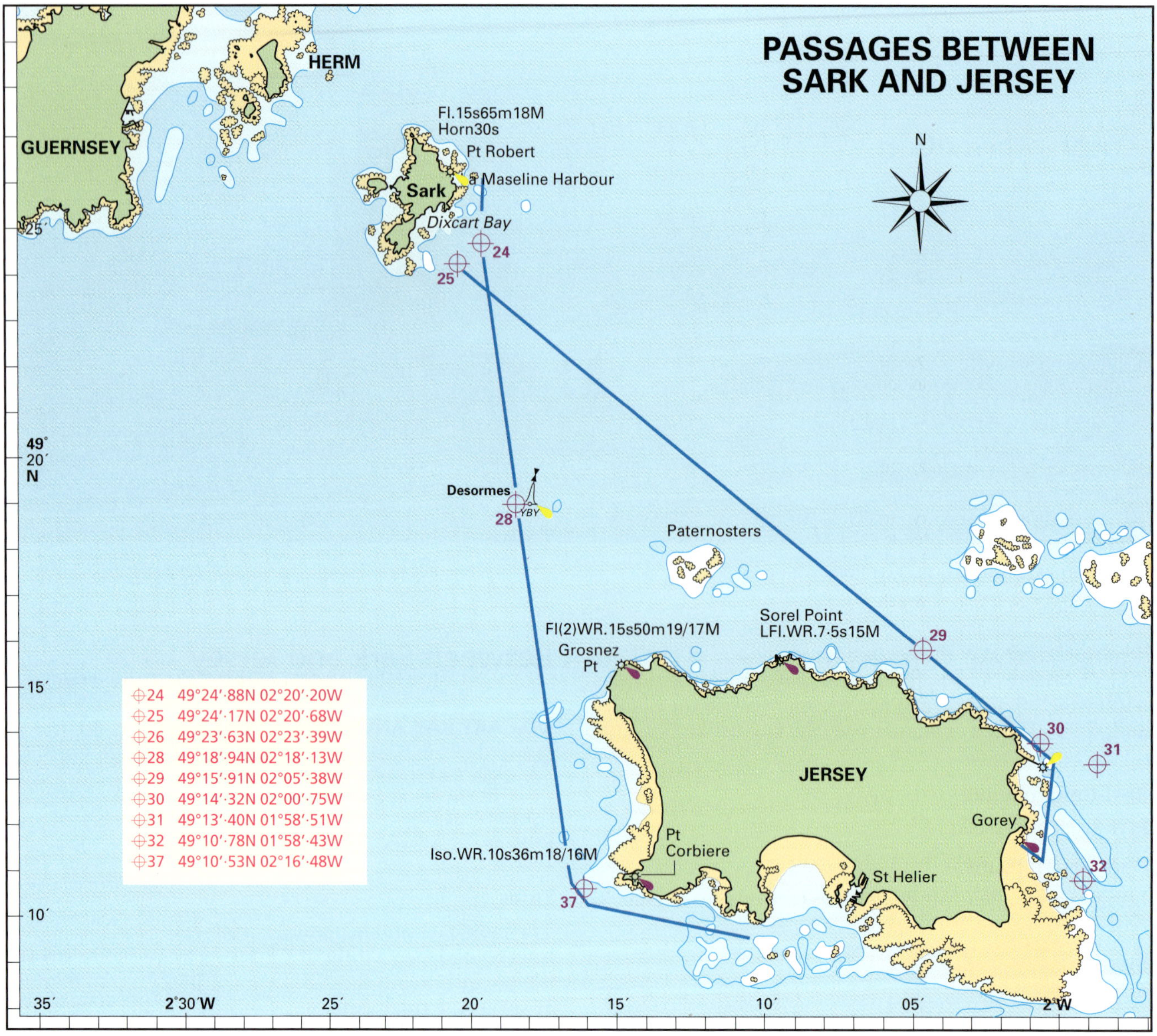

1 The Channel Islands

PASSAGES BETWEEN SARK AND JERSEY

Waypoint	Position
⊕24	49°24'·88N 02°20'·20W
⊕25	49°24'·17N 02°20'·68W
⊕26	49°23'·63N 02°23'·39W
⊕28	49°18'·94N 02°18'·13W
⊕29	49°15'·91N 02°05'·38W
⊕30	49°14'·32N 02°00'·75W
⊕31	49°13'·40N 01°58'·51W
⊕32	49°10'·78N 01°58'·43W
⊕37	49°10'·53N 02°16'·48W

ST HELIER TO LA MASELINE HARBOUR

Charts
BA 2669, BA Leisure Folio SC 5604 (sheet 4)
Imray C33A, Imray 2500 Chart Atlas (sheet 8)
SHOM 6966
Distance 21M
Time 3h

Tides
The most favourable period is from just before HW St Helier to St Helier HW+0320, after which the first of the flood tide sweeps in from the Alderney Race with increasing strength. Either keep the speed up or leave earlier.

Best time to leave
HW St Helier–0100

Dangers en route
See *St Helier to St Peter Port*.

By night
Approach to La Maseline Harbour is not possible after dark.

Passage waypoints
⊕ 37, 28, 24
For detailed pilotage information see *Jersey* and *Sark*.

La Maseline
Sark Tourism

22 CHANNEL ISLANDS, CHERBOURG PENINSULA & NORTH BRITTANY

Alderney

Local information

☏ STD code: 01481

TRAVEL
Air
  Direct flights from Southampton and inter-Island
  Aurigny Air Services ☏ 822886
  Blue Islands ☏ 824567
Sea
  Connections with Diélette and St Peter Port
  Manche Iles Express ☏ 822881
  www.vedettesducotentin.com
Charter boats
  Lady Maris ☏ 823666
  Voyager ☏ 823532
  www.bumblebee.gg ☏ 720200

PORTS OF ENTRY
The official ports of entry into the Bailiwick of Guernsey are Braye in Alderney and Beaucette Marina, St Sampson (for commercial vessels only) and St Peter Port in Guernsey. At St Peter Port, all visiting yachts must clear in at the main harbour irrespective of which marina they moor in.

CHARTS
British Admiralty
  60 Alderney and the Casquets (1:25 000)
  2845 Alderney Harbour (1:6 000)
  3653 Guernsey to Alderney and Adjacent Coast of France (1:50 000)
  SC 5604 The Channel Islands Leisure Folio:
    7 Alderney (1:25 000)
    8 Alderney Harbour (1:6 000)
    11c The Casquets (1:25 000)
Imray
  C33A Channel Islands*
    *includes plan: Alderney Harbour (1:9000)
  2500 The Channel Islands and adjacent coast of France Chart Atlas:
    3 Alderney & Burhou (1:25 000)
    3a Alderney Harbour (1:12 500)
SHOM
  6934 Alderney (Aurigny) et Les Casquets (1:25 000)
  7158 Du Cap de Carteret au Cap de la Hague - Raz Blanchard (1:48 000)

RADIO
Alderney Radio
  Harbourmaster's office ☏ 822620 www.alderney.net
  Hours of operation October–April Mon–Fri 0800–1700. May 0800–1800. June–September 0800–2000. 7 days a week. Outside these hours call Jersey Coastguard, Guernsey Coastguard VHF 16, 20 or Crossma (French coastguard) who can activate Alderney Coastguard within minutes in an emergency.
  VHF Call *Alderney Coastguard* on VHF Ch 16, 20, 74 and 67. The harbour launch, operated by the harbour officials, also listens on Ch 74, call *Harbour Launch*

NAVIGATIONAL AIDS
Radiobeacon (Aeronautical NDB)
Ident: ALD Position: 49°42'·6N 02°11'·9W. Freq 383kHz. Range 50M
Radar, VTS and RDF service available on request

USEFUL CONTACTS
  Harbourmaster, Customs, Coastguard, Lifeboat ☏ 822333
  Alderney Tourist Information Centre ☏ 822811
  Alderney Sailing Club ☏ 822758/822959
  Doctor: Eagle Medical Practice ☏ 822494

SUPPLIES AND SERVICES
Chandlers Mainbrayce in Little Crabby Harbour provide water, diesel (duty free), bottled gas, spares and mechanical assistance. A tide gauge at the entrance indicates depth of water alongside. Access to yachts is approximately 2 hours either side of local HW. Mainbrayce is open 0830–1800 7 days a week in the summer. ☏ 822772 Mobile 07781 415420
Email mainbrayce.alderney@virgin.net VHF Ch 80.
Water taxi Call Mainbrayce Taxi on VHF Ch 37 (M) or the chandlery on Ch 80. Hours of operation are the same as the chandlery but can extend well into the evening during the season.
  www.vedettesducotentin.com - 8 and 12 seater
  www.bumblebee.gg - ex Gsy Mark Gaudin
  2 *vedettes* between Alderney and Diélette
Boat charters, round-island trips Voyager ☏ 823666, Lady Maris 2 ☏ 823532 or ask at Harbour Office
Alderney Sailing Club next to the harbourmaster's office welcomes visiting yachtsmen.
Restaurants, bars and shopping Good selection in harbour area. The First and Last Restaurant ☏ 823162
Alderney Duty Free Consortium on the harbour quay (☏ 823414 Mobile 07781 112309). Goods will be delivered to your boat. Le Riches Supermarket, Braye Street; is one of several duty free outlets in the island. Goods will be delivered to your boat on departure – but don't forget to supply your buoy number.
Car and bike hire
  Braye Hire, Braye Street ☏ 823352
  Top Gear ☏ 822000.
  Braye Hire Cars ☏ 823881
  Cycle and Surf bike hire ☏ 822286
Alderney Fuel Services
  (Total Garage) ☏ 823352
Taxis
  A.B.C Taxis ☏ 823760, Island Taxis ☏ 823823, J S Taxis ☏ 07781 100830
Alderney Society Museum
  High Street
Alderney Cinema
  Victoria Street

St Anne, with an adequate selection of shops, pubs and restaurants, is a twenty-minute walk up from the harbour
Alderney Tourism

1 The Channel Islands

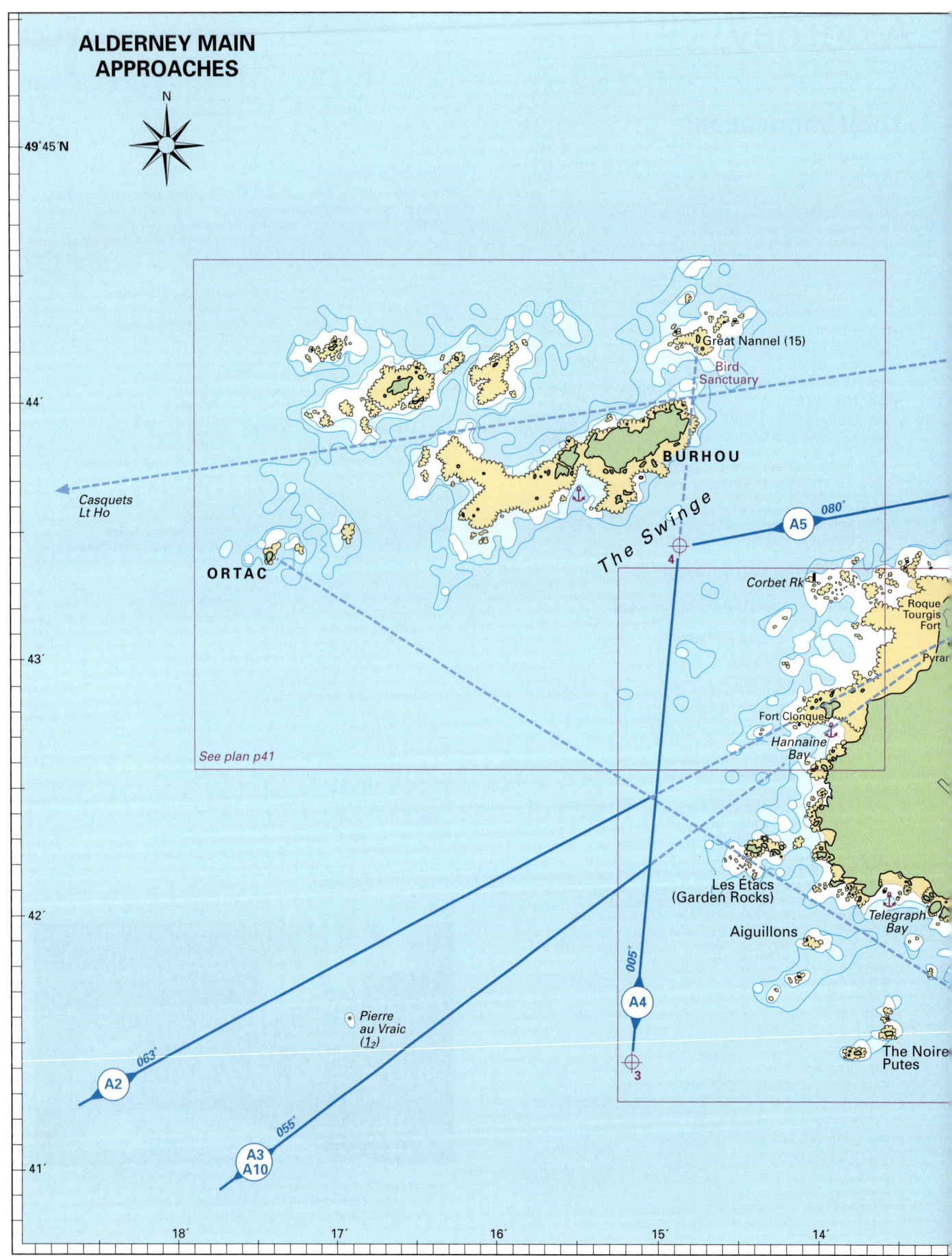

24 CHANNEL ISLANDS, CHERBOURG PENINSULA & NORTH BRITTANY

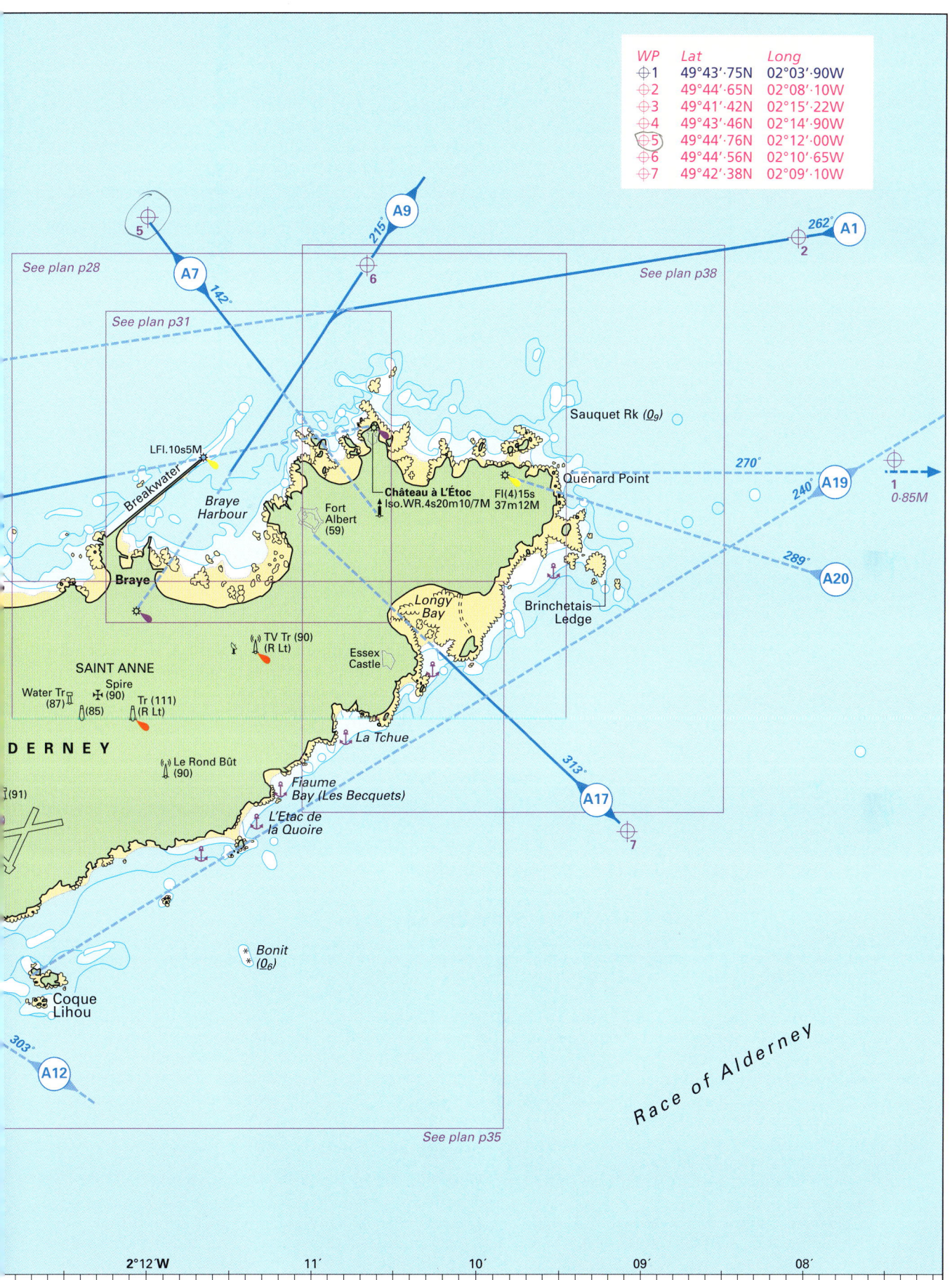

Alderney

I. THE CHANNEL ISLANDS

1 The Channel Islands

Tidal information

Braye 49°43'·60N 2°11'·70W

MHWS	MHWN	MLWN	MLWS	MTL
6·3m	4·7m	2·6m	0·8m	3·6m

HW Braye in relation to other ports

Dover	–0400
St Helier, Jersey	+45
Cherbourg	–50
Carteret	+36
Diélette	+25
St Peter Port, Guernsey	+40

Tidal streams
The Admiralty *Tidal Stream Atlas* for the Channel Islands and adjacent coasts of France (NP 264) includes large-scale plans of Alderney and the Casquets. Additional information on inshore directions and rates may also be found in the tidal section of the *Appendix*.

Inshore eddies
Like a boulder in the rapids, Alderney lies in the main NE–SW English Channel stream and the associated stream that scurries up and down the Normandy coast. Directions and rates are modified round the coast, particularly in the tide shadow at either end. There are numerous and complex eddies which may be used to advantage. Some will not be indicated in the *Tidal Atlas* and in the absence of local knowledge, the navigator should be on the lookout for changes in set and act accordingly.

Main eddies around Alderney

Northeast corner Here the NE stream turns to follow the coast W towards The Swinge from just after HW St Helier to HW St Helier–0220 attaining over 3 knots.

South Coast Along the S coast from off Houmet Herbé Fort on the NE corner to Coupé Rock on the SW corner, there is a narrow eddy close inshore. The stream sets E and NE for 9 hours out of 12, only running W from about HW St Helier+0300 to HW St Helier+0530.

TIDAL RACES AND OVERFALLS
Caution
Where the streams are accelerated through gaps, tidal races occur. Passing over shoals, ledges or uneven seabed, overfalls will form in all but calm weather. The main tidal races off Alderney are The Alderney Race to the east and The Swinge to the northwest. See below.

For many, the first glimpse of this small northern outrider of the Channel Islands will be seen towards the end of a crossing from the UK south coast. The trail of shipping lies behind and as the island comes into view, concentration is very much focusexd on tidal streams that are amongst the fiercest in Europe. The area between the Casquets and Alderney Race has something of a reputation as a ship's graveyard and should be approached with respect and caution.

Once safely moored in Braye Harbour, visitors will discover a peaceful, unpretentious island with a friendly and relaxed atmosphere. Although only 8M from the Normandy coast, the feel is more English than French – the legacy of 160 years of occupancy by English garrison troops and a total evacuation during the last war.

To the Romans, Alderney was Vecta Riduna and its natives Ridunians. They established a station at Longis (Longy) Bay, which became the island's first port until it silted up in the Middle Ages.

The era of privateering brought wealth to the island and led to the building of the Old Jetty at Braye in 1736.

The Great Admiralty Breakwater was constructed in response to the threat from France in the 19th century. Like St Catherine Bay in Jersey, it was intended to enclose a large harbour to shelter the British Fleet. The plan was abandoned but the breakwater was completed to a length of 5,000 feet in 1864. By 1900, Atlantic rollers had undermined most of it and the outer 600m (2,000ft) was abandoned. Maintenance and reinforcement of the remaining 900m (3,000ft) has been a constant and expensive battle against the elements ever since. The cost is covered by the States of Guernsey as the Bailiwick's contribution to Britain's defence of the islands.

Alderney is famous for its seabirds, especially the gannet. About 5,000 pairs nest on the Channel Islands' two gannetries, Ortac and Les Etacs (Garden Rocks) both W of Alderney.

Ashore

With over forty miles of walks and paths the best way to discover Alderney is on foot or by bike.

The Alderney Visitor Information Centre (① 823737) and Alderney Wildlife Trust (① 822935) both in Victoria Street, St Anne, provides advice and leaflets on recommended walks and bird watching tours.

www.visitalderney.com *Email* tourism@alderney.gov.gg

www.alderneywildlife.org *Email* info@alderneywildlife.org

There are several historical sites worth visiting including the Victorian forts and more recent German fortifications and bunkers.

The less energetic can hire a car or electric bicycle, or use the seasonal bus service that calls at the harbour. Alderney has the only working railway in the Channel Islands. This runs at weekends in summer between Braye harbour station and the northeast coast. From the station at Mannez you can take a short walk to visit Quénard Point lighthouse.

Beaches

The most accessible from the harbour are Braye Bay and further east Saye (pronounced 'soy'), Arch and Corblets. On the south coast Longy Bay is reputed to be the best in the island.

Alderney Race

This 8 mile gap between Cap de La Hague on the Normandy coast and the E end of Alderney is the commonly used gateway to and from the Channel Islands. With spring rates in the order of 10–12 knots and dangerous overfalls, yachtsmen justifiably approach The Race with some trepidation. Even in the lightest conditions skippers would be wise to re-check stowage, hatches and harnesses well before reaching The Race. The secret lies in timing and avoiding areas of overfalls.

OVERFALLS

West side When overfalls are active and at night, the Brinchetais (pronounced Brimtides) Ledge should be given a clearance of at least 1M. The area around Race Rock (5·5m) and Inner Race Rock (5·5m) and Blanchard Rock (3·7m) SE of Quénard Point should be treated with caution and avoided in wind against tide conditions.

Alderney

Alderney from the east

Middle There is a clear fairway 2·5M wide undisturbed by rocks and shoals between Race Rocks and the 16m bank with heavy overfalls which lie 4M WSW from Cap de la Hague; this passage should be used whenever possible.

East side To the E of the 16m bank referred to above is another 17m bank which does not break so heavily but should be avoided in wind over tide conditions. Between the 17m bank and La Foraine beacon off Cap de la Hague is a 1·5M passage which, although situated in the fiercest streams, may be used if rounding the Cap to or from Cherbourg in suitable conditions (see BA Chart 60).

South of Alderney While clear of the fierce streams of The Race there are three banks where overfalls may occur. From N to S these are:

South Banks (11m) 1M SSE of Alderney
Milieu (14m) 4M SSE of Alderney
Banc de la Schôle (2·4m) 8M S of Alderney. This bank is constantly shifting and depths may be less than charted. There is now a wreck 1M N of the bank with 3·2m over it and marked by a N cardinal buoy.

Tidal strategy

Southbound Aim to be at least 2M NW of Cap de la Hague at HW Dover–0040 (HW St Helier+0410). ⊕1 (see plan on pages 24–5) is a recommended safe-water waypoint 3·8M due E of Quénard Point lighthouse. This will ensure that your passage through The Race is made at dead slack, following which the stream will turn in your favour. The initial push in a SW direction will gradually swing to a southerly direction and strengthen. You could carry a fair stream all the way to St Helier.

Northbound Departing from St Helier or St Peter Port, there is always the risk of running out of fair stream just short of The Race. The deadline is about HW St Helier+0430 or earlier if proceeding to Cherbourg. It may be better to leave early and maintain the best possible speed.

Cherbourg to Braye The main concern is to avoid rough conditions off Cap de la Hague and make a smooth passage across the top of The Race without getting sucked into it. The answer is to cross at about HW St Helier+0400. Keep a good 2M off the Cap and aim to stay N (uptide) of the rhumbline.

The Swinge

This channel lies between the NW of Alderney and the islets between the Nannels and Ortac to the N. It is the quickest passage between Alderney and Guernsey.

OVERFALLS

Caution

BA chart 60 warns, 'Dangerous overfalls form in the main Swinge Channel. Their position varying with the tidal stream.' They cover a smaller area than those in the Race but are less easy to avoid. Seas can be short and steep when wind and tide are opposed. As with the Race, timing is of the essence and in general the channel should be taken near slack water at neap tides. The calmest area is often on the S side near Corbet (pronounced Kerby) Rock (0·5m) (see *Approaches to Alderney from the S and SW* on page 29).

Tidal strategy

The published advice in Alderney is straightforward. Slack in The Swinge is 0230 after both local HW and local LW. If heading SW pass through at 0230 after local HW (HW St Helier +0315). If heading NE pass through at 0230 after local LW (HW St Helier - 0235). The latter period gives a short interval when the stream is slackest but not truly slack.

For tidal diagrams of overfalls in *Alderney Race* and *The Swinge* see Appendix.

Ortac, one of the largest colonies of gannets in Europe

1 The Channel Islands

Approaches to Alderney

All directions given here are focused on Braye Harbour. Approaches are straightforward providing key marks are identified and the yacht's position confirmed as early as possible. Compensation can then be made for any cross-set which can be powerful. Strategically it is best to arrive at slack water, but if late and being carried SW down the Race, it may be necessary to give up the fight, particularly at spring tides, and change plans.

The final stage of an approach to Braye from any direction, apart from NE, involves clearing the hazardous remains of the submerged breakwater. For directions see *Entry to Braye Harbour: clearing the submerged breakwater*, page 30.

FROM THE EAST OR NORTHEAST
(See plan page 24)

A1 Until the breakwater and leading marks are identified it is necessary to keep 0·5M offshore. The transit for this, which is aligned with ⊕2, is as shown on the photo.

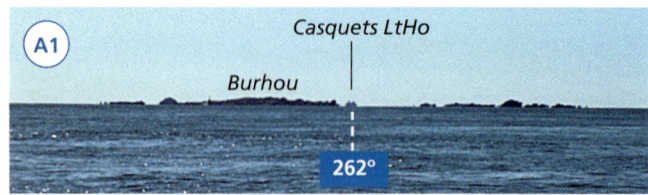

A1 *262° (⊕2) Casquets LtHo open to N of Burhou will clear the Grois Rocks (drying 5·5m) to N of the island*

By night
Keep Casquets (Fl(5)30s37m18M) bearing no more than 260° until leading lights are aligned.

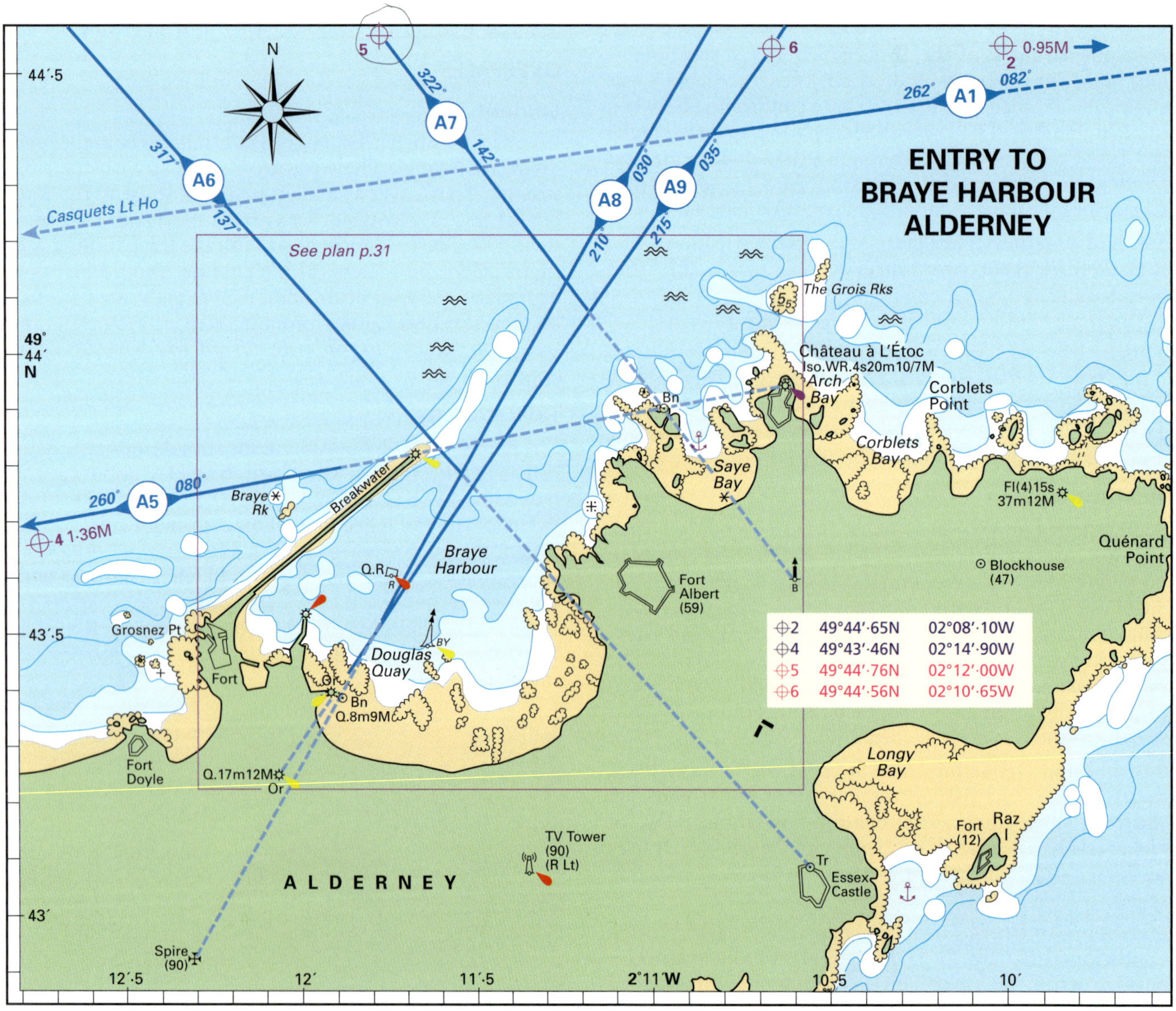

ENTRY TO BRAYE HARBOUR ALDERNEY

⊕2	49°44'·65N	02°08'·10W
⊕4	49°43'·46N	02°14'·90W
⊕5	49°44'·76N	02°12'·00W
⊕6	49°44'·56N	02°10'·65W

28 CHANNEL ISLANDS, CHERBOURG PENINSULA & NORTH BRITTANY

Alderney

Features on the northeast coast of Alderney

FROM THE NORTHWEST

(See plan page 28)

The aim is to avoid being set SW towards Casquets and Burhou with its surrounding reefs.

Approach with Quénard Point lighthouse Fl(4)15s37m12M bearing no less than 120°. This is a powerful light that flashes by day and night.

A useful transit is:

115° Fort Albert (E of the harbour) kept open E of the breakwater head

There are marks to clear the outer end of the submerged breakwater by day. See *Clearing the submerged breakwater* below.

When the harbour opens up, turn onto Transit A8 or A9 ⊕6 to enter as described under *Braye Harbour. Entry Marks.*

By night

Stay in the W sector of Château a L'Etoc light (Iso.WR.4s20m10/7M) until leading lights are aligned on A9 ⊕6. (See *Braye Harbour. Entry.*)

FROM THE SOUTH AND SOUTHWEST VIA THE SWINGE

(Plan page 24)

Caution

The SW approach to The Swinge would be straightforward were it not for the inconveniently positioned Pierre au Vraic (49°41'·60N 02°16'·92W) (drying 1·2m) 2M WSW of Les Etacs (Garden Rocks) which continues to be a hazard to shipping. The key to clearance is the use of transits using Fort Clonque (20m) on the island's W end.

Clearing North of Pierre au Vraic

A2 063° A white pyramid S of Roque Tourgis Fort to the N of Fort Clonque

CHANNEL ISLANDS, CHERBOURG PENINSULA & NORTH BRITTANY

1 The Channel Islands

Clearing South of Pierre au Vraic

A3 055°. The same pyramid to S of Fort Clonque

Note This transit is also used for approach to Hannaine Bay (**A10**) (see *Round the island westabout*).

Entry to The Swinge is made on a northerly course using transit:

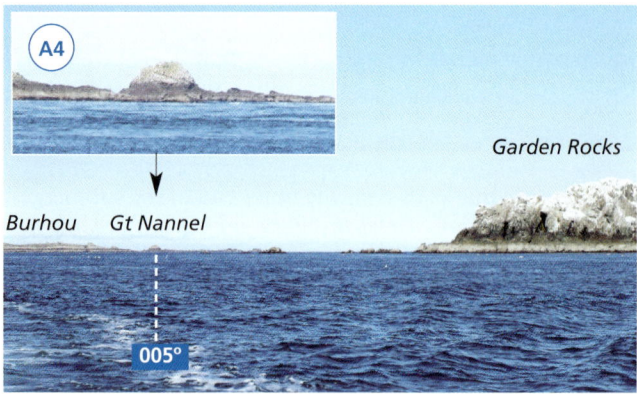

A4 005° ⊕3 Great Nannel open E of Burhou Island

This will leave Les Etacs (Garden Rocks) with their colony of gannets about 0·5M to the E and lead well into The Swinge. There are offlying reefs on this corner and all the way up to Braye Harbour breakwater. Corbet Rock (0·5m) (its beacon was destroyed in 1993) lying 0·5M from the shore, is the main consideration in The Swinge. It reduces its width to 0·5M between Burhou and Corbet.

Continue N until:

A5 080° N side of Château à L'Etoc in line with N end of breakwater. Follow this transit up to the breakwater head giving due clearance to Braye Rock and The Follets (dry 4·3m)

VIA ALDERNEY RACE

(See page 26-27 and plans pages, 25, 38)

Yachts from Jersey and ports on its adjacent coasts will usually approach Braye via the Race. This offers more sea room and fewer navigational obstacles but, as with the Swinge, it is a question of weather and timing the tide.

The passage northbound through the Race is covered under Alderney Race above. The pilotage round the E end of the island and into Braye is covered under *Round the island westabout: Longy Bay to Braye*, page 40.

Entry to Braye Harbour: clearing the submerged breakwater (by day only)

(See plan page 28)

Pieces of the old wall lying on their side on top of the original foundation are a hazard for vessels approaching the harbour from between SW and N. The least charted depth is 1·2m but there is a crossing over a relatively flat area with a minimum of 2·3m 50m off the breakwater head (BA chart 2845). The harbour may be entered over this 2·3m section of the submerged breakwater with caution not less than 3 hours either side of local LW (LW St Helier–0430) when there is no ground swell. The transit is as shown below.

A6 137° Turret (known as 'Pepper Pot') on Essex Castle, over gap in slope below Fort Albert. A bush has recently grown beside the turret, as shown on the inset

Outside this period, in less than ideal conditions or if in any doubt, it is safer to pass well N of the submerged breakwater using Transit **A7** ⊕5:

Alderney

Braye Harbour
49°43'·83N 02°11'·45W (0·15M E of breakwater head)

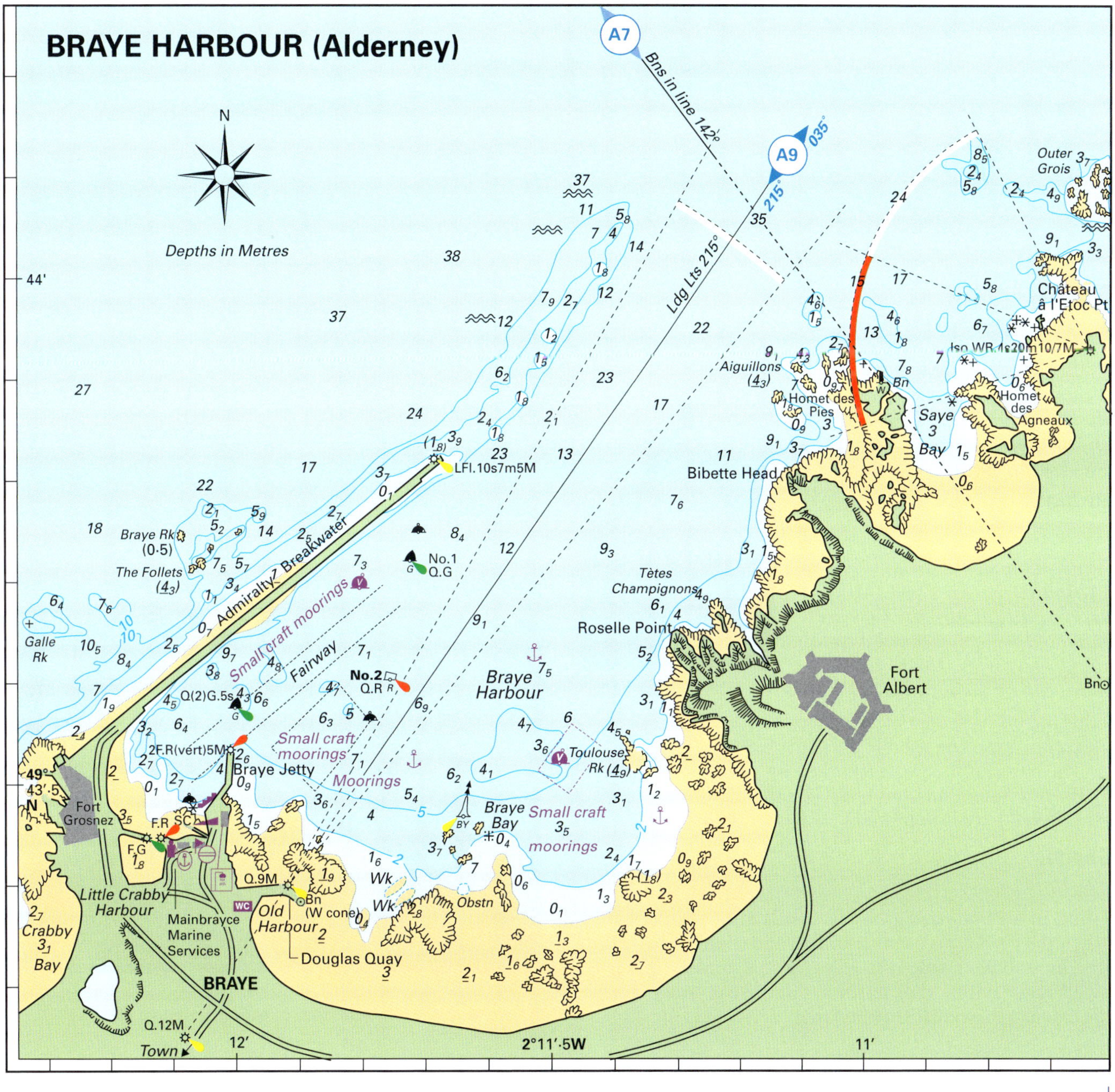

A7 142° ⊕5 *The beacon on the foreshore (the 'Ball') in line with beacon with triangle 0·25M E of Fort Albert*

Note *Both these marks are inconspicuous, particularly when viewed into the sun*

I. THE CHANNEL ISLANDS

CHANNEL ISLANDS, CHERBOURG PENINSULA & NORTH BRITTANY

1 The Channel Islands

Entry marks
(See plan page 28)

A8 *210° White pyramid on Douglas Quay in transit with St Anne's church spire*

This should be held accurately as the line passes within 200m of the submerged remains off the breakwater head.

By night

A9 *215° ⊕6*

The leading lights (front Q.8m9M, rear Q·17m12M) serve as day marks and they are mounted on conspicuous dayglo orange triangles. The forward mark can be inconspicuous.

Rear leading light/mark

Entering on these marks gives about 200m more clearance from the submerged breakwater.

The harbour fairway is marked by 3 buoys, Q.G and Q.R at its outer end, and Q(2)G.5s towards its inner end. Braye Jetty is marked by 2F.R(vert) lights.

Shelter

Caution

Good in all but strong N–NE winds and ground swell, when the harbour is totally exposed and should be avoided in winds above Force 5. In gales from W and SW a heavy swell can enter the harbour and seas may break spectacularly over the breakwater.

Moorings

There are 70 yellow visitors' buoys and it is possible to raft up on these in calm weather. With the exception of the first five rows in from the entrance which are intended for use by larger vessels, all moorings are suitable for vessels up to 40ft. If all visitors' moorings are taken it may be possible to use one of the moorings to S of fairway between jetty and No.2 (Q.R).

Some moorings are located SW of Toulouse Rock on the E side of the bay, which may offer some shelter from northeasterlies, if not the swell which tends to bend its way round the island and find its way in. Here there is a minimum depth of between 3·5m and 5·5m at Chart

Braye moorings are still tenable in NE winds as long as there is no accompanying swell from that direction: here in a ENE F5-6
Jane Russell

32 CHANNEL ISLANDS, CHERBOURG PENINSULA & NORTH BRITTANY

Alderney

Braye

Little Crabby Harbour

Datum. It is not permitted to dry out in Braye or Saye bays unless in an emergency and with authorisation from the harbourmaster.

Little Crabby inner harbour is reserved for local craft but may be entered for fuel and water. See *Harbour Facilities* below.

Anchoring

The anchorage in the middle of Braye Bay has good holding in sand, but there are areas of rock and weed. Towards the entrance of the harbour, the bottom is generally more rocky. Due to the tidal range at springs (up to 6·9m) a good scope should be put out. It is not permitted to anchor in the fairway or close to Braye Jetty.

Entry formalities

Vessels entering from outside the Bailiwick of Guernsey must complete a customs form at the harbourmaster's office. Channel Islands Regulations concerning the prevention of rabies apply. There is a 4-knot speed limit in the harbour.

The harbourmaster's office is located at the SW end of the harbour and fulfils the function of customs, coastguard, Alderney Radio Station and lifeboat. Excellent weather forecasts are available. Hours are as for Alderney Radio (see *Radio Facilities* page 23).

Harbour facilities

Dinghy pontoon, slipway, showers, toilets, launderette, telephones, chandlers and rubbish skip are all located near the harbourmaster's office.

Harbour launch, taxi service Ch 74. (see supplies and services, Water taxi page 23).

Alderney Sailing Club next to the harbourmaster's office welcomes visiting yachtsmen. It offers WiFi and weather information. Bar and occasional restaurant.

CHANNEL ISLANDS, CHERBOURG PENINSULA & NORTH BRITTANY

1 The Channel Islands

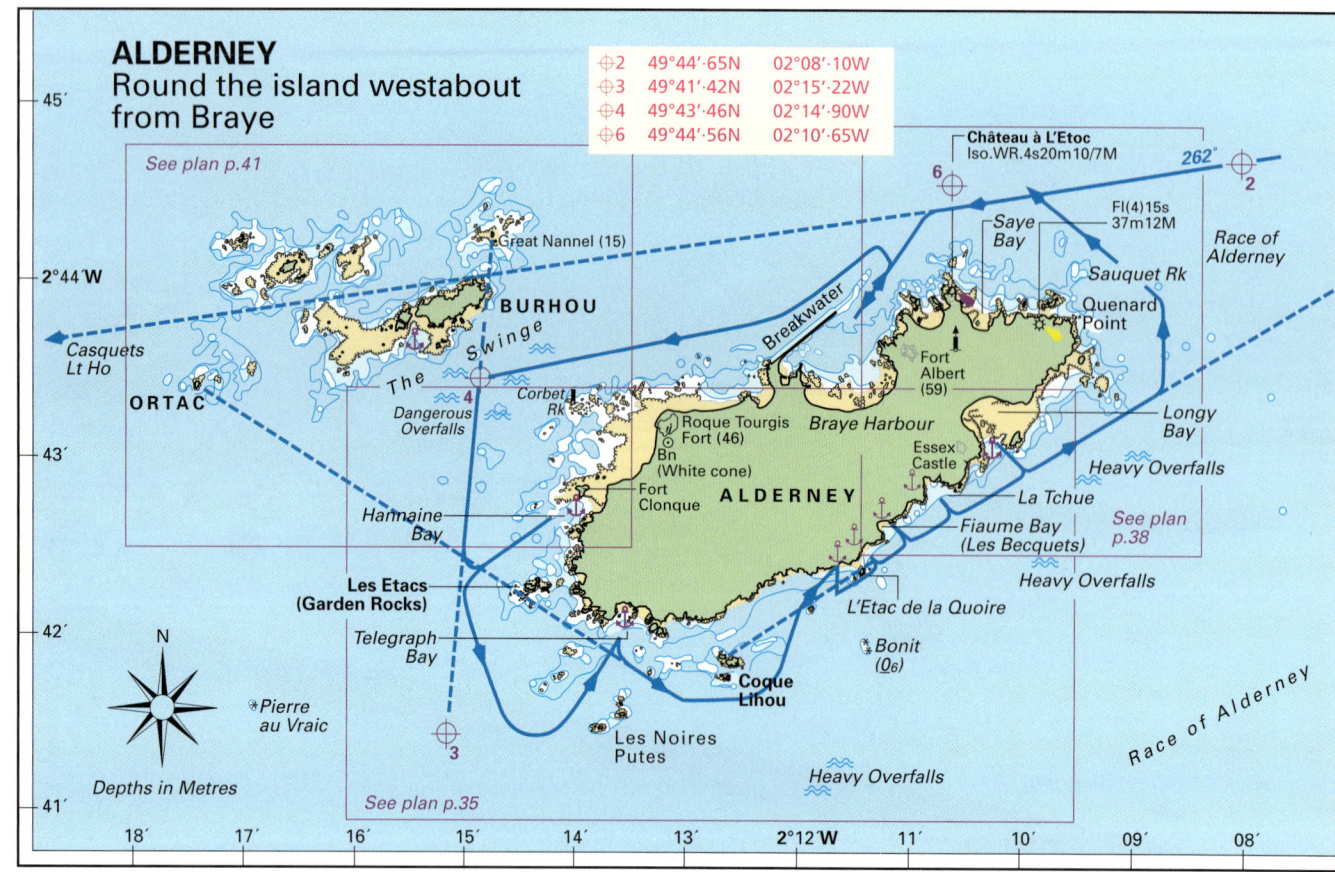

Alderney from the west

Round the Island westabout from Braye (by day only)

There is a 9-hour tidal envelope in which to make a circumnavigation to include a few anchorages. Choose settled weather and avoid large spring tides. These directions assume an average boat speed of 6 knots.

A visit to Burhou Island is not included in this trip but described separately at the end of this section.

Caution

Overnighting in any of the anchorages described is not recommended. A departure after dark could be hazardous.

CHART
BA 60 Alderney and the Casquets
DISTANCE
Approximately 11M (Outside Garden Rocks)
TIDAL STRATEGY
The aim is to carry a fair tide as much as possible and catch The Swinge and the Race near slack water. The period around local LW (HW St Helier+0515) is the time to visit S coast anchorages. Return to Braye just before local HW (HW St Helier+0045).

Leaving at local HW+0415 (HW St Helier+0330) will give a fairly slack W-going stream through The Swinge. From HW St Helier+0430 and over the LW period up to HW St Helier–0400, the S coast is in the grip of a SW-going stream. This gives way to a NE-going stream for the best part of 6 hours. The Race is best taken around HW St Helier–0230 when there is slack water N of the island.

Alderney

Braye to Longy Bay
(See plan pages 24–25 and 28)

Using reciprocal transits, depart from Braye on the leading marks (A8 or A9 ⊕6) then A7 ⊕5 to clear the submerged breakwater or A6 subject to depth. When clear, take up A5 ⊕4 to enter The Swinge. Continue until Great Nannel (15m) bears 005° then come S onto Transit A4 ⊕3. Avoid cutting the corner.

Hannaine Bay
49°42'·73N 02°14'·02W
(See plan above)

A10 This anchorage S of Fort Clonque provides excellent protection in NE–E winds and can be useful to yachts approaching from the SW that need to wait for a fair tide up through The Swinge. Entry from Transit A4 is not easy, particularly if there is a strong current across the 200m wide entrance between rocks. Marks must therefore be held accurately. These are shown below.

Hannaine Bay

A10 *055° White pyramid beacon S of Roque Tourgis Fort open to S of Fort Clonque and midway between Fort Clonque and white gable*

Note This is the same transit as A3, the southerly clearing line for Pierre au Vraic (drying 1·2m) (see plan page 24 and *Approaches to Braye from the S and SW*). Anchor in 3m (sand) 100m or more S of Fort Clonque. Depart using same marks to rejoin A4.

CHANNEL ISLANDS, CHERBOURG PENINSULA & NORTH BRITTANY

1 The Channel Islands

Caution
The coast between Les Etacs (Garden Rocks) and Noire Roque is peppered with rocks. Short cuts close inshore are not advised without local knowledge aboard. (See plan page 35.)

Alderney west end looking northwest

Leave Garden Rocks 0·3M to port and steer 160° to leave Orbouée (0·5m) and Coupé (7m) NE of it 0·3M to port.

Alderney west end looking northeast

Telegraph Bay
49°42'·04N 02°13'·55W
(See plan page 35)

Approach between Coupé (7m) and Les Noires Putes (19m, 12m and 6m) with clearing line A11. The tower is on the skyline, so will not be visible close in. Holding is good but the bay is encumbered with rocks, so consult the chart carefully.

A11 *035° The Old Telegraph tower (85m) on a bearing of 035°*

Depart on 215° and hold until:

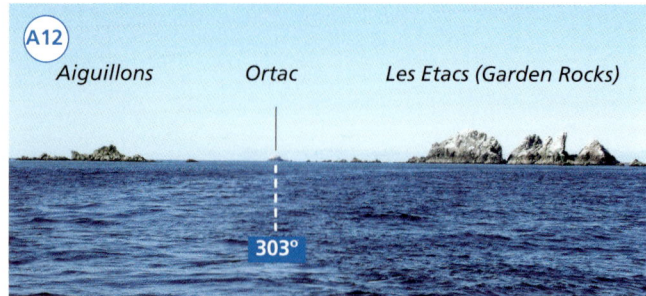

A12 *303° Ortac is open S of the Les Etacs (Garden Rocks) and midway between them and Aiguillons (5m)*

If Ortac is not visible keep the S edge of the Garden Rocks on 310°. Steer out on 130° with attention to tidal stream, leaving Joyeux (dries 5·4m) to port and the Noires Putes to starboard. When the tallest of the Noires Putes (19m) is abeam identify:

A13 *050° La Rocque Pendante (48m) is just touching the left (E) edge of L'Étac de la Quoiré*

Then turn E. Leave Coque Lihou (14m) 200m to port and steer in to pass either side of Noire Roque (4m) but well inside the isolated rock Bonit (dries 0·6m) (see *Clearing Bonit* below).

Note Noire Rocque should be given a wide berth to the NW and N, particularly at low water, as reefs run off the main rock.

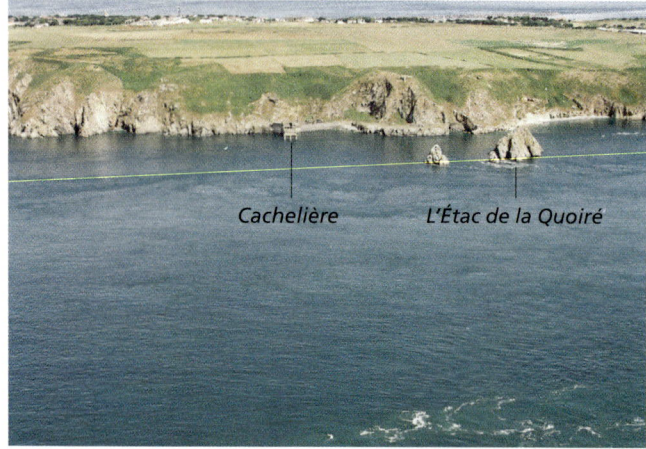

Tidal disturbance marks the position of Bonit 0·5M SSE of the ruined pier at Cachelière

Alderney

Clearing Bonit (Boneay)
(See plan page 35)

The marks for clearing this danger are:

To the west **A14** *007° White pyramid open left (W) of L'Etac de la Quoiré*

To the east **A15** *350° White pyramid open right (E) of L'Etac de la Quoiré*

To the south **A16** *270° All the Noires Putes are open S of Coque Lihou Rocks*

To allow safe clearance of Bonit, make good 090° after leaving Coque Lihou 200m to port and hold this until transit A15 is obtained.

Les Becquets (Vaulto)
49°42'·65N 02°11'·13W

(See plan page 35)

When entering this obscure bay (locally known as Vaulto) from the SW, beware of drying rock (dries 4·3m) off the S point. When the whole of the old pier at Cachalière is visible between L'Etac and the cliff, it is clear to enter with the centre of the bay on a bearing of 307°.

La Tchué
(See plan page 38)

49°42'·87N 02°10'·71W

This bay affords the next more attractive anchorage. Approach with the middle of the bay on 330°. The spectacular Rocque Pendante (48m) may be seen hanging out of the cliff to the E. The bottom is generally sand and the holding good.

Longy Bay
49°43'·12N 02°10'·21W

(See plan page 38)

This is the island's most popular anchorage and has a fine beach. It provides a good bolt-hole when Braye is suffering from northeasterlies or while waiting for the tide up through the Race. it can be exposed at HW.

Approach on

A17 *313° ⊕7. The W wall of Fort Albert in line with the Nunnery (the E end of Château de Longy)*

This transit will leave Queslingue (10m) 250m to port and a drying rock (dries 0·5m) in the middle of the bay 80m to port.

1 The Channel Islands

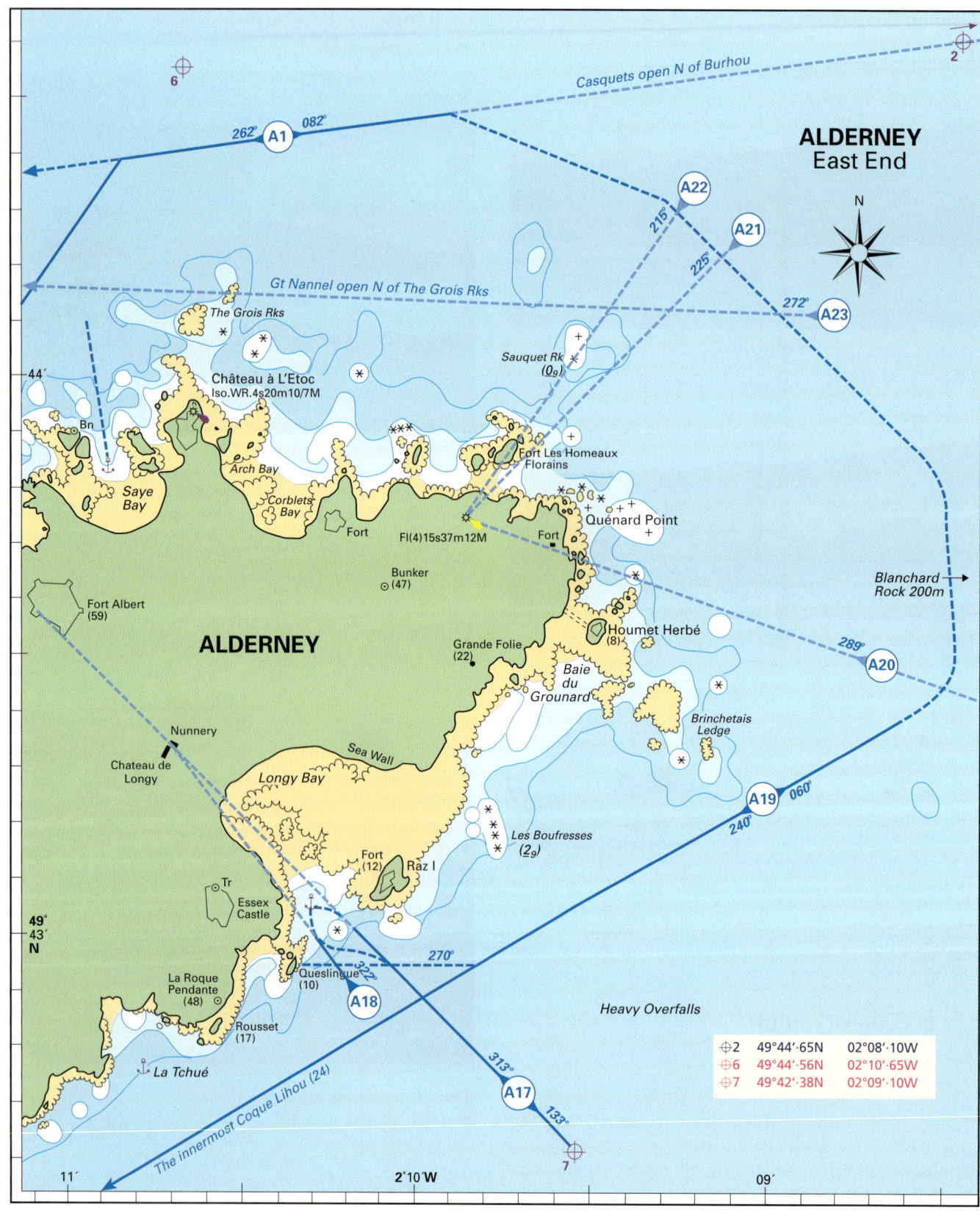

Alderney

I. THE CHANNEL ISLANDS

Anchorage

The preferred anchorage, offering more room and better holding, is to the NW of this drying rock, therefore when Queslingue bears W (as shown on plan page 38), come to port, west of your approach line, and transfer to:

Sound in carefully, the bottom is sand with rocky patches. Anchor when:

A18 322° The Nunnery is just open of the W side of the bay

La Rocque Pendante is open of the end of the wall on 235°

Historical

The Nunnery has the best preserved small Roman fort in Britain. Much of the site is open to visitors.

CHANNEL ISLANDS, CHERBOURG PENINSULA & NORTH BRITTANY

1 The Channel Islands

Longy Bay to Braye

(See plans pages 34 and 38)

Leaving Longy Bay steer SE until Brinchetais Ledge can be cleared. The clearing marks are as shown below.

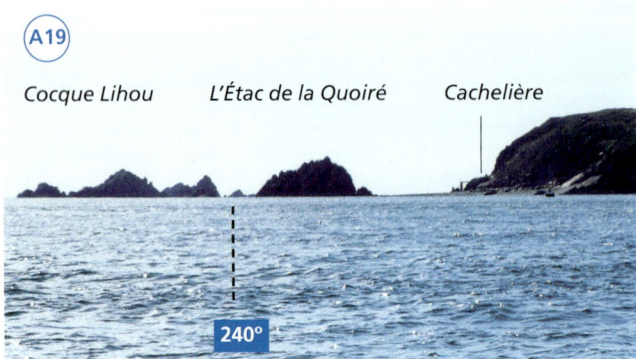

A19 240° *The innermost Coque Lihou open E of L'Etac de la Quoiré*

Steer NE until the turning point:

A20 289° *Quénard Point LtHo is over a small yellow house with black roof and a chimney at each end*

Then steer N taking care to avoid the overfalls round Blanchard Rock (3·7m).

Clearing Sauquet rock (dries 0·9m)
49°44'·02N 02°09'·56W

The final hazard is the much-hit Sauquet Rock and its reef. **E clearance is:**

A21 225° *Quénard Point LtHo open to S of the bunker and Fort Homeaux Florains*

Striking marks

A22 215° *Quénard Point LtHo in line with Fort Homeaux Florains*

With these marks on, locals use the horizontal WBW stripes to estimate distance off. If all the stripes are visible you are outside Sauquet. If none of the black stripe is visible you are passing inside it. **N clearance is:**

A23 272° *Gt Nannel open N of all the Grois Rocks (dry 5·5m)*

Come round to the NW and leaving Sauquet Rock to port regain Transit A1, then A9 ⊕6 for entry to Braye Harbour.

Saye Bay
49°43'·85N 02°10'·87W
(See plan page 38)

Just 0·5M short of the breakwater, this cove offers one final diversion in settled weather. There is a safe sandy beach for bathing and good holding. Enter between the high heads on either side and anchor with reference to the chart. *Note* Saye is pronounced 'soy'. Ashore is a campsite with facilities.

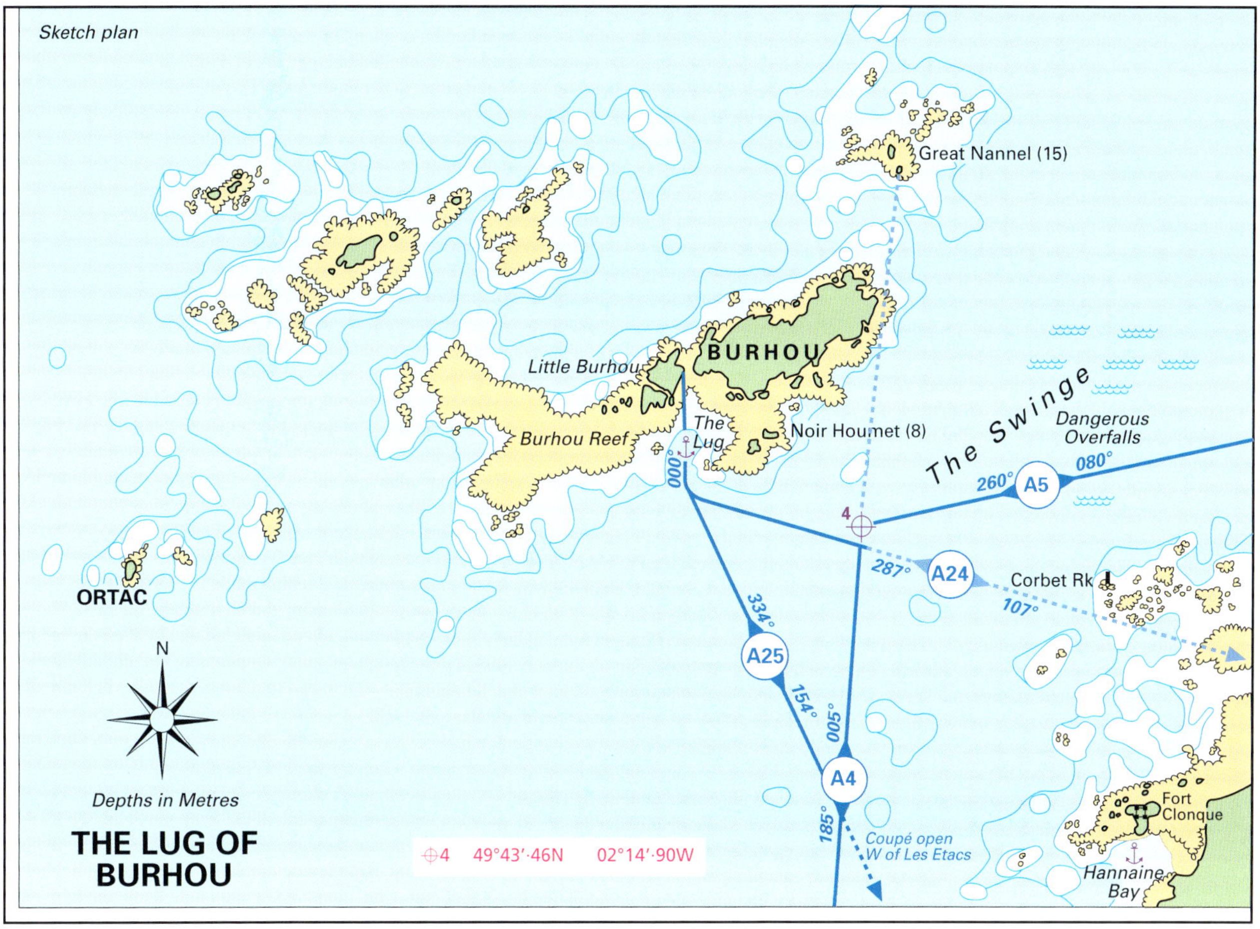

Alderney

Burhou from the east

Burhou Island
49°43'·64N 02°15'·49W

This island 2M WNW of Braye has the distinction of being home to the largest colony of puffins in the Channel Islands. For this reason landing is prohibited in their breeding season (15 March–21 July).

In settled weather and preferably at LW neaps when the reefs afford some protection, there is an anchorage known as The Lug (La Logue in local patois), between Burhou Island and Burhou Reef. As with Hannaine Bay this is a useful LW anchorage in which to await slack water if a yacht fails to make Braye before the tide turns. It can be dangerous approaching at HW springs when the NE-going flood stream courses through the anchorage.

There is a refuge hut on the island, maintained by the States of Alderney.

Caution

The Lug should only be used towards LW and on the ebb. It should be left before the easterly flood stream sets in or if there is any likelihood of the anchorage becoming exposed to the weather. Approaching from the S or E, allowance must be made for a westerly set which can be strong.

CHANNEL ISLANDS, CHERBOURG PENINSULA & NORTH BRITTANY

1 The Channel Islands

The Lug viewed from WNW at low water springs

Approach from Braye

(See plan page 41)

Hold stern Transit A5 080° ⊕4 down The Swinge until Gt Nannel bears N then transfer to stern transit:

A24 *107° St Anne's church spire on the right (S) edge of Rocque Tourgis fort (white pyramid). This line will clear the rocky shoreline E of the anchorage by 100m*

Approach from SW

(See plan page 24)

Make initial approach on A4 005° ⊕4 then transfer to stern transit A25 (154°) for entry.

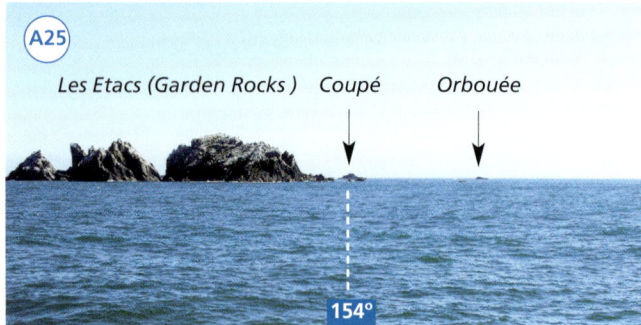

A25 *154° Coupé Rock open to the W of Les Etacs (Garden Rocks)*

Avoid any overfalls in The Swinge and keep a check on any cross set.

Anchorage

When the broad anchorage opens up, enter from the S. The anchorage is deep, gradually shelving around the edge. The bottom is sand with rocky patches and the holding is good. The scenery is starkly beautiful.

Entering the Lug from the south

CHANNEL ISLANDS, CHERBOURG PENINSULA & NORTH BRITTANY

Guernsey

Local information

STD code: 01481

TRAVEL INFORMATION
The island is well served by air and ferry routes. Regular flights operate from Southampton, Exeter, Gatwick and elsewhere. Condor high-speed ferries cross the Channel from Weymouth or Poole in less than three hours and the terminal is a short walk away from the marinas. They also operate the St-Malo route via Jersey. Inter-island ferries regularly ply the short distance between St Peter Port, Herm and Sark.

Air
Direct flights from Gatwick, Southampton, Stansted and many regional airports
Flybe (British European) ☎ 0871 7000123
Inter-Island and several UK airports. Dinard (France):
Aurigny Air Services ☎ 882888
Blue Islands ☎ 727567 / 08456 202122

Sea
Jersey, St Malo, Weymouth, Poole:
Condor Ferries ☎ 0845 3452000
Jersey, Alderney Diélette, Granville, Sark:
Manche Iles Express ☎ 01534 766566

PORTS OF ENTRY
The official Ports of Entry into the Bailiwick of Guernsey are Braye in Alderney and Beaucette Marina, St Sampson (for commercial vessels only) and St Peter Port in Guernsey. At St Peter Port, all visiting yachts must clear in at the main harbour irrespective of which marina they moor in.

CHARTS
British Admiralty
807 Guernsey and Herm (1:25 000)*
808 East Guernsey, Herm and Sark (1:25 000)*
  *both include plan: Beaucette Marina (1:15 000)
3140 Saint Peter Port (1:6000)
3654 Guernsey, Herm and Sark (1:50 000)
SC 5604 The Channel Islands Leisure Folio:
  9 Guernsey, Herm and Sark (1:50 000)
  10 Approaches to Saint Peter Port (1:25 000)
  11a Saint Peter Port (1:6 000)
  11b Beaucette Marina (1:15 000)

Imray
C33A Channel Islands*
  *includes plans: Beaucette Marina (1:15 000), St Sampson Harbour (1:20 000), St Peter Port (1:10 000), Little Russel (1:50 000)
2500 The Channel Islands and adjacent coast of France
Chart Atlas:
  5 Guernsey, Herm & Sark (1:60 000)
  6 East Guernsey & Herm (1:25 000)
  7a St Peter Port & Havelet Bay (1:6 000)
  7b Beaucette Marina (1:15 000)
  7d Guernsey – South Coast Anchorages (1:25 000)

SHOM
6903 Guernsey et Herm (1:25 000)*
6904 Guernsey Est, Herm et Sark (1:25 000)*
  *both include plan: Beaucette Marina (1:15 000)
7159 De Guernsey, Herm et Sark à Alderney - Bancs des Casquets (1:48 000)

RADIO
Guernsey Coastguard VHF CH 12
  ☎ 720672, ☎ 710277 for shore to ship calls
  Email guernsey.harbour@gov.gg
  MMSI: 00 232 00 64
  Hours of operation 24
  VHF Ch16, 20 (direct calling), 62 (link calls), 70 (DSC)
  Traffic Lists Vessels are initially called on Ch 16. Lists are broadcast on Ch 20 after navigation warnings at 0133, 0533, 0933, 1333, 1733, 2133 UT
  VHF Direction-finding Bearings can be provided on Ch 16 or 67. Note the aerial position for D/F purposes is 49°26'·27N 02°35'·77W (Guernsey Airport)
  Port Control Ch 12 This channel should be monitored entering/exiting St Peter Port but is not to be used for berthing information and general enquiries
Water taxi Summer months only 0700–2200. Ch 18
Victoria Marina Ch 80 (no 24h watch)

NAVIGATIONAL AIDS
Racons (radar beacons):
Platte Fougère LtHo 49°30'·88N 02°97'·05W (P)

USEFUL CONTACTS
Harbourmaster's office ☎ 720229
Duty dockmaster ☎ 712422
Customs ☎ 741400
Victoria Marina office (dockmaster) ☎ 725987
Visitor Information Centre ☎ 723552
Guernsey Yacht Club ☎ 722838 Bar ☎ 725342
Guernsey Sailing Trust ☎ 710877
Royal Channel Islands Yacht Club ☎ 723154/725500
White Rock Signal Station ☎ 720672
St Sampson (Dockmaster) ☎ 720229
Beaucette Marina Office ☎ 245000
Victoria Marina WiFi Hotspot is free for visiting yachts. Contact Marina staff for log-in details.

SUPPLIES AND SERVICES
St Peter Port
  Chandlery, fuel, bottled gas Boatworks+ ☎ 726071
  Engine servicing and repairs Herm Seaway Marine
    ☎ 726829
  Sailmaker Katy Barrett ☎ 246741
St Sampson
  Marine and General Boatyard ☎ 243048
  Fuel ☎ 200800
  Chandleries Quayside ☎ 245881
    Seaquest Marine ☎ 721773
  Sailmaker Warren Hall ☎ 444280 Mobile 07781 444 280
  Marine Electronic Equipment ☎ 728837
  Lifecraft servicing AB Marine ☎ 722378

1 The Channel Islands

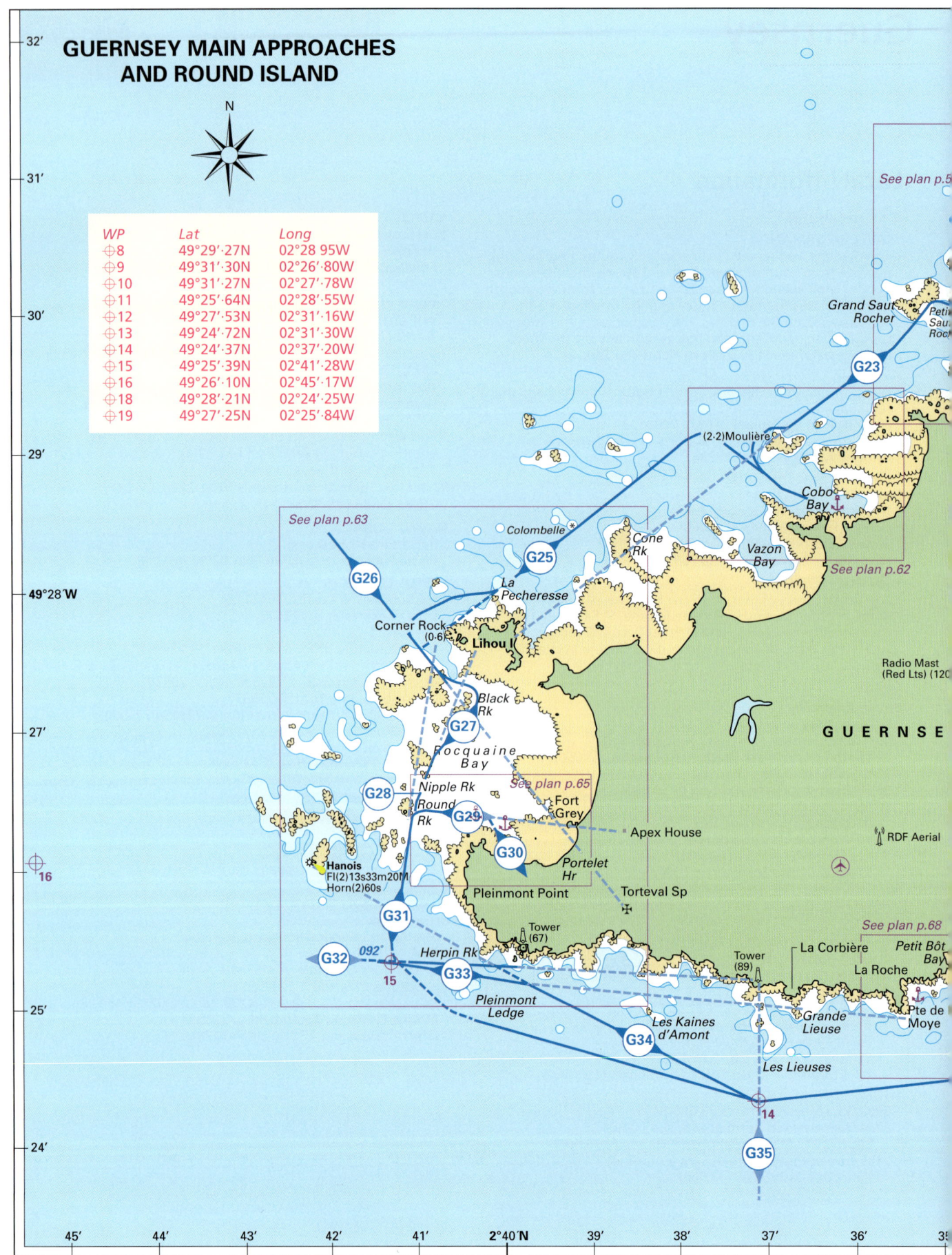

GUERNSEY MAIN APPROACHES AND ROUND ISLAND

WP	Lat	Long
8	49°29'·27N	02°28·95W
9	49°31'·30N	02°26'·80W
10	49°31'·27N	02°27'·78W
11	49°25'·64N	02°28'·55W
12	49°27'·53N	02°31'·16W
13	49°24'·72N	02°31'·30W
14	49°24'·37N	02°37'·20W
15	49°25'·39N	02°41'·28W
16	49°26'·10N	02°45'·17W
18	49°28'·21N	02°24'·25W
19	49°27'·25N	02°25'·84W

44 CHANNEL ISLANDS, CHERBOURG PENINSULA & NORTH BRITTANY

1 The Channel Islands

Introduction

Guernsey is the second largest of the Channel Islands and 'big sister' to the group of dependent isles that make up the Bailiwick – Alderney, Sark, Herm and Jethou. Despite sharing common roots, Guernsey has managed to retain the more leisurely pace of life that is threatened by commercialism elsewhere.

One of the island's greatest assets is St Peter Port harbour and the sheltered waters of the roadstead outside, which together provide the safest haven in the Channel Islands, accessible at any state of tide and in almost any weather. This has been exploited throughout the centuries, establishing Guernsey as a vital staging post on lucrative trading routes. Evidence of this goes back to Roman times, thanks to the discovery in 1984 of the remains of a flat-bottomed Gallo-Roman vessel in the harbour entrance. Its cargo of tiles and pottery confirms that it is the oldest wreck to be discovered in the British Isles.

The harbour is dominated by Castle Cornet which was an important stronghold up to Napoleonic times. Apart from being captured by the French on three occasions, it was a Royalist stronghold during the Civil War – the last in the British Isles to be overcome. It is now a museum.

Today it is yacht crews that throng the waterfront and in high season the harbour can brim with pleasure craft of all flags. Somehow the friendly marina staff can always find room for one more. For the cruising fraternity, St Peter Port is a popular stopover en route to N Brittany, while day sailors find that the excellent facilities and close proximity of Sark and Herm make it an ideal holiday base.

Ashore

There is a comprehensive selection of shops, restaurants and bars close to St Peter Port Marinas. Pier 17 Restaurant and Bar on Albert Quay (☎ 720823) specialising in local seafood is recommended. Castle Cornet Fortress has a fascinating Maritime Museum.

Before venturing out of town, the Visitor Information Centre on the Esplanade can advise on the numerous environmental and historical sites in the island. Rent a car or take the bus to visit to the west coast and Lihou Island with its bird sanctuary.

Beau Sejour Leisure Centre on the outskirts of St Peter Port is a sports centre with a gym and 25m pool.

Approaches to St Peter Port

FROM THE NORTH

Via Little Russel

The gateway to this well-worn route lies between Platte Fougère lighthouse off the island's NE corner and Tautenay beacon tower a mile N of Herm.

The key to a successful approach is positive and early identification of the main marks.

Make the initial approach with Platte Fougère LtHo on a bearing of 220° until other marks have been identified. A suitable arrival waypoint would be ⊕9 or ⊕10 both about 1M ENE of the lighthouse. Off Roustel beacon tower the channel narrows to little more than 1M wide before opening out to the broad roads off St Peter Port.

Tidal information

(Tidal levels referred to chart datum)
St Peter Port 49°27 N 2°31 W

MHWS	MHWN	MLWN	MLWS	MTL
9·3m	7·0m	3·6m	1·5m	5·3m

St Peter Port is a standard port with its own predictions. The mean difference on St Helier is +0005 to 0010.

Guernsey is positioned in the main tidal flow as much as Alderney, with the N-going stream running from about local HW–0300 to +0300, and the S-going from local LW–0300 to +0300.

Streams are generally not as strong as around Alderney but the island's triangular shape and the close proximity of its neighbours create complexities and locally accelerated rates up to 6kn. Overfalls, severe at spring tides, can be expected in wind against tide conditions. Areas to be wary of are:

Little Russel
Beware of cross set navigating the channels at the northern end off Beaucette and Roustel beacon tower. Overfalls around Roustel are notorious and on the flood with fresh northeasterlies can be vicious

SW of Brehon Tower smaller overfalls may occur on the ebb in southwesterlies

Off St Martin's Point
The stream is strongest just after HW and LW and should be given a good clearance when wind is against tide

Big Russel
Numerous overfalls can be expected on a line between Brecqou and the Lower Heads S of Jethou, especially in wind against tide conditions.

There are several options for approach which may be used in conjunction with each other. Selection will depend on the range of visibility.

Good visibility

By day only

G1 208° ⊕9 St Martin's Point open of Brehon Tower

This transit if held will pass close E of Roustel beacon tower. While there may be reasons for taking this route note it is more usual to pass W of this beacon (⊕8) to intercept the leading marks (G2). Note rock (dries 0·6m) close NE of the beacon and Cavale (dries 1·2m) 0·3M E of it.

Moderate visibility

G2A 223° ⊕8 Belvedere House in line with Castle Cornet white mark

Guernsey

This is the main approach line through Little Russel to St Peter Port. Belvedere House is the most northerly and prominent of a group of white houses SW of Castle Cornet. Note that Belvedere light is NW of the House.

By night
Align rear light (Belvedere Oc.10s61m14M) and front light (Castle Breakwater Al.WR.10s14m16M) on 220°. This transit is easier to see by night than by day, but as it passes over Boue Agenor (2·1m) which is guarded by the red sector of Platte beacon (Fl.WR.3s) it is necessary for deep draught vessels to borrow 100m to port when abreast of Brehon tower.

Poor visibility
This option requires visibility of at least 2M. If the weather is, or seems likely to become foggy, it is better to approach St Peter Port by Big Russel.

G3 198° ⊕10 *Roustel beacon tower in line with Brehon tower*

Leave Roustel and Brehon to port and then transfer to the main approach line (see *Moderate visibility* (by day) above).

By night
Align Roustel (Q.8m7M) with Brehon (Iso.4s19m9M).

Via Big Russel
(See plans pages 45, 75 and 76)

When beating down to St Peter Port by day from the NE against a southwester, Big Russel provides a channel seldom less than 2·5M wide between Herm and Sark which is largely free of traffic.

Apart from overfalls in the S there are only two offlying dangers: Noire Pute (2m) is marked by a lit beacon (Fl(2)WR.15s) and Fourquies (dry 2·3m) marked by a lit N cardinal buoy (Q). The buoy should be given a good clearance as it tends to drift around in this area of powerful streams. Once round the Lower Heads S cardinal buoy (⊕11) you can head up to St Peter Port (see *St Peter Port from the East* below).

FROM THE NORTHWEST
(See plans pages 45 and 56)

The marks to clear NE of the Brayes reefs are as shown on BA chart 807:

149° SW extremity of Little Sark on the (low) NE point of Herm

This will leave Platte Fougère lighthouse 0·3M to the W. Proceed as for *Approach from the north via Little Russel*, above.

Doyle Passage (by day only)
(See plan page 56)

This approach from the NW provides a useful cut inside Platte Fougère to join Beaucette Marina channel and Little Russel approaches to St Peter Port. It calls for fair weather

Looking SSW over Doyle Passage into Little Russel

1 The Channel Islands

and good visibility. The streams are strong on this corner and this passage should only be attempted on the flood when the stream is setting E. HW–0300 is a good time.

There is one mark which should be held accurately:

G16 *146° Corbette d'Amont beacon tower midway between Herm and Jethou*

For view and details for entry to this passage from the S see *Round the island northabout from St Peter Port. St Peter Port north to Fort Doyle*, below.

FROM THE EAST
(See plans pages 45, 75 and 76)

Getting around Sark, Herm and Jethou and into Little Russel offers interesting pilotage. From N of Sark one option is to cross Big Russel into Percée Passage between Herm and Jethou and then, subject to enough water, to join Alligande Passage across to St Peter Port (see *Herm, Passages N of Jethou*).

From S of Sark, route via Lower Heads S cardinal buoy (⊕11) and then make good a NNW track to St Peter Port pier heads with initial transit to clear W of Lower Heads:

G39 *312° ⊕11 White Rock LtHo open S of Castle cornet breakwater LtHo*

By day and in good visibility a more direct route is possible via the Musé Passage (see *Herm. Passages S of Jethou*). When 0·25M off Castle Cornet LtHo come to starboard to open pierheads as shown in G6 below.

By night
Sark waters are not an option and the Percée Passage and Alligande Passage should not be used without local knowledge (see *St Peter Port from the South* below).

FROM THE SOUTH
(See plans pages 45 and 69)

Via Little Russel

Enter Little Russel anywhere between Lower Heads S cardinal buoy (⊕11) and a point 800m E of St Martin's Point. The only dangers are those on Guernsey's E coast between St Peter Port and St Martin's Point (See *Round the Island. St Martin's Point to St Peter Port*).

Good visibility

G4 *004° ⊕13 Vale Mill over the middle shed of a group of three (green) at St Sampson*

Poor visibility

G5 *350° White Rock LtHo open to the E of Castle Cornet clears dangers off the coast as far as Oyster beacon (O)*

200m NE of Oyster lies Ferico (0·9m). To clear both steer out into Little Russel after passing Moulinet beacon (M) until the pier heads are open:

Guernsey

G6 298° St Peter Port pier heads open will clear Ferico

By night
Approaching off St Martin's Point you will be clear of all dangers off the S coast, providing Hanois (Fl(2)13s33m20M) is visible. The red sector of St Martin's Pt (Fl(3)WR.10s15m14M) guards the rocks off the point but note this does not include Longue Pierre (LP) beacon (unlit) and its reef, which extends 400m NE of the point. Aim to keep at least 0·75M off the point and steer E until Castle Breakwater (Al.WR.10s16M) is on a safe bearing of between 312° and 345°. This will put White Rock (Oc.G.5s) open W of Castle Breakwater (Al.WR.10s) and open E of Castle Cornet. The E side of the approach is marked by The Lower Heads S cardinal lit buoy. Approaching the breakwater, come E until White Rock light is just open E of Castle Breakwater light in order to open up the entrance.

See also *Round the island northabout from St Peter Port. St Martin's Point to St Peter Port*, below.

St Peter Port visitors' pontoons and ferry beyond, looking NE from the harbour office *Jane Russell*

St Peter Port

St Peter Port
49°27'·44N 02°31'·60W White Rock port control

Entry

Port Control Signal Station

Entry signals
These are displayed from Port Control Signal Station on White Rock Pier.

Red: Large vessels are under way. Entry and exit of other vessels prohibited except small boats of 15m or less under power, which may proceed keeping well clear.
See *Local information. Radio Facilities*, page 43.

Speed limit
4kn in the inner harbour to 6kn in the outer harbour.

Entry is midway between the pier heads:

G7 265° Green church spire over Victoria Marina Lt Tower

By night
265° Lights in line
Front (on light tower) Oc.R.5s.10m14mM,
Rear (on building behind) Iso.R.2s22m3M

This transit will give a good indication of the cross set outside the entrance. Contrary to the usual convention yachts entering must keep to the port and S side where the yacht approach channel is marked by a green conical buoy (Q.G) and three red can buoys (Fl.R). When the last port-hand buoy is reached and just past the fuel jetty, turn hard to starboard towards the waiting and visitors' pontoons.

CHANNEL ISLANDS, CHERBOURG PENINSULA & NORTH BRITTANY

1 The Channel Islands

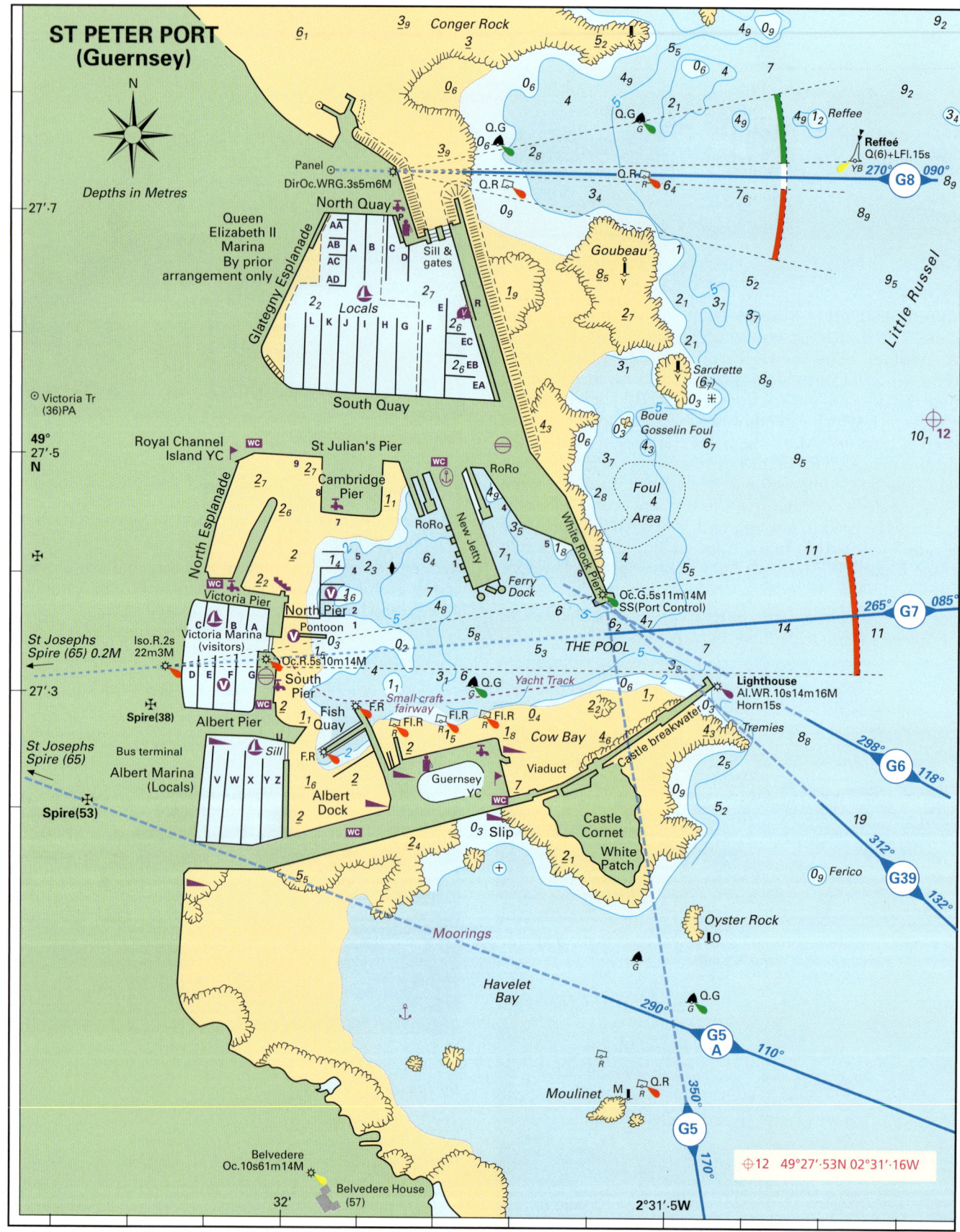

50 CHANNEL ISLANDS, CHERBOURG PENINSULA & NORTH BRITTANY

Guernsey

Entry formalities
Visiting yachts will be met by the marina dory to issue mooring instructions and deliver a customs and immigration form. This should be completed and deposited in one of the yellow customs boxes ashore or returned to the customs official afloat.

Q Flag It is appreciated if yachts entering from outside the Bailiwick of Guernsey display a Q flag as this assists harbour authorities in identifying new arrivals.

Harbour facilities
St Peter Port is a yachtsman's mecca where all amenities can be found just a short walk or row from Victoria Marina and the outer harbour (The Pool). The marina itself has a shower and launderette block. On Castle Emplacement on the south side of the harbour there are chandleries, marine engineers, electricians and a boatyard. Guernsey Yacht Club at Castle Emplacement and the Royal Channel Islands Yacht Club above the Crown Pub on the waterfront welcome visiting yachtsmen (see *Local information* on page 43). There is a wide selection of shops, restaurants, hotels and bars found in the town. The ferry terminals are located on the N side of the harbour near the entrance. Buses and taxis at the waterfront serve the airport.

Fuel (diesel, petrol, (LRP, ULMS))
The fuelling pontoon on Castle Emplacement is operated by Boatworks+. It is accessible about 3–4 hours either side of local HW. There is also a fuelling berth in the QE2 Marina where LPG is available (see *Local information. Supplies and Services*).

Drying out
There are pads in Victoria Marina and QE2 Marina where yachts can dry out alongside. The careening hard N of Victoria Marina is suitable for bilge keelers and yachts with beaching legs.

Anchoring
Permitted in Havelet bay well clear of private moorings. For entry see page 70, *Havelet Bay*.

Looking E over Victoria marina and the drying entrance sill with holding pontoon beyond *Jane Russell*

Marinas

VICTORIA MARINA AND THE POOL
(Plan page 50)

Approach and entry
Visitors have the choice of crossing a half tide sill (dries 4·2m) into Victoria Marina on the W side of the harbour, or mooring to a visitors' pontoon in the outer harbour (The Pool). The decision will depend on the state of the tide, availability of space in the marina and intended length of stay.

Yachts waiting to enter the marina will be directed to the waiting pontoon, or if the marina is full, to The Pool. Getting ashore will involve the tender or there is a water taxi (see *Local Information. Radio Facilities* at the beginning of the chapter). Albert Marina in the SW corner of the harbour is for local residents. During the season, all five pontoons in The Pool, excluding the waiting pontoon outside Victoria Marina, are connected to the shore by a walkway. There are no power points on the walk ashore pontoons in the Pool (2016).

Signals
R/G traffic lights above the marina sill control entry and exit.

Water Available on all marina pontoons and two pontoons in The Pool.
Electricity Available on marina pontoons only.
Depth Victoria Marina is dredged to 2m at CD but depths are less on the westerly pontoons. The bottom is soft mud.
Shelter Excellent in all but easterlies when surge can enter the harbour. In strong to gale force conditions this will penetrate into the marina at HW and life in The Pool can become untenable. Apart from stout fenders and lines, the

Victoria Marina
Depth over sill in metres (sill dries 4·2m)
Given in hourly and half hourly intervals either side of HW

Height of HW at St Peter Port	HW	+/–1hr	+/–2hr	+/–2½hr	HALF TIDE +/–3hr	+/–3½hr	+/–4hr	+/–5hr	+/–6hr
6·00	1·65	1·50	1·20	0·96	0·75	0·52	0·30	0·00	0·00
6·20	1·85	1·67	1·30	1·03	0·75	0·47	0·20	0·00	0·00
6·40	2·05	1·84	1·40	1·08	0·75	0·42	0·10	0·00	0·00
6·60	2·25	2·00	1·50	1·13	0·75	0·37	0·00	0·00	0·00
6·80	2·45	2·17	1·60	1·18	0·75	0·32	0·00	0·00	0·00
7·00	2·65	2·34	1·70	1·23	0·75	0·27	0·00	0·00	0·00
7·20	2·85	2·50	1·80	1·26	0·75	0·22	0·00	0·00	0·00
7·40	3·05	2·67	1·90	1·33	0·75	0·17	0·00	0·00	0·00
7·60	3·25	2·84	2·00	1·38	0·75	0·12	0·00	0·00	0·00
7·80	3·45	3·00	2·10	1·43	0·75	0·07	0·00	0·00	0·00
8·00	3·65	3·17	2·20	1·48	0·75	0·02	0·00	0·00	0·00
8·20	3·85	3·34	2·30	1·53	0·75	0·00	0·00	0·00	0·00
8·40	4·05	3·50	2·40	1·58	0·75	0·00	0·00	0·00	0·00
8·60	4·25	3·67	2·50	1·63	0·75	0·00	0·00	0·00	0·00
8·80	4·45	3·84	2·60	1·68	0·75	0·00	0·00	0·00	0·00
9·00	4·65	4·00	2·70	1·73	0·75	0·00	0·00	0·00	0·00
9·20	4·85	4·17	2·80	1·78	0·75	0·00	0·00	0·00	0·00
9·40	5·05	4·34	2·90	1·83	0·75	0·00	0·00	0·00	0·00
9·60	5·25	4·50	3·00	1·88	0·75	0·00	0·00	0·00	0·00
9·80	5·45	4·67	3·10	1·93	0·75	0·00	0·00	0·00	0·00
10·00	5·65	4·84	3·20	1·98	0·75	0·00	0·00	0·00	0·00

All the above figures are in metres. The depths are only approximate and can be affected by winds and changes in barometric pressure.
At all times check actual depth on the gauge at the marina.
Instructions:
1. Look up predicted height and time of HW at St Peter Port for the day.
2. Select the line corresponding to the predicted height of HW.

1 The Channel Islands

only option may be to apply for a berth in the QE2 Marina or relocate to the W coast of Herm. The Marina Office is manned 0600–2200 throughout the year.

QUEEN ELIZABETH II MARINA (QE2)
(Plan page 50)

This is reserved for local residents although an application can be made for a berth on the E arm for vessels drawing over 2m or requiring an extended stay. The marina has its own entrance 0·4M N of the main harbour entrance and a half tide sill drying 4·5m. Gates ensure total shelter. These are lowered about 3 hours either side of HW depending on whether it is spring or neap tides.

Approach and entry

Approach on 270°, passing close S of Reffée S cardinal light buoy

G8 270° Leading marks in line

Marina leading marks are two rather inconspicuous panels above a white patch on the loose rocks of the breakwater N of the entrance. The front panel is yellow with a RWG directional light and the rear panel is a red square attached to a lamp post. Proceed along the buoyed channel and, when 40m from the breakwater, turn hard to port round the inner port-hand buoy to enter the marina. The centre section in the entrance should be left to port on entry and departure.

At night use a directional light Oc.WRG.3s.

Signals

Green: Entry permitted. There is at least 2m over the sill
Red: No entry

Electronic depth gauge at entrance indicates the actual depth above the gate in either closed or open position.

Beaucette Marina looking W

BEAUCETTE MARINA
49°30'·14N 02°30'·10W Entrance (Plan page 53)

This unusual marina perched on the NE corner of Guernsey was created by blasting out an 8m wide passage linking an empty granite quarry to the open sea, thereby flooding it. Pond level is retained by a sill. It is privately owned and of the 115 berths, 30 are allocated to visitors. Its isolation will appeal to those seeking the quiet life. Facilities are comprehensive and include a restaurant.

Approaches to Beaucette

All approaches are from Little Russel.

Caution

Entry not advised in strong onshore winds or heavy swell. Channel markers are liable to be changed.

From the north

Approach Little Russel as for St Peter Port (see above). Identify Petite Canupe S cardinal beacon 0·65M S of Platte Fougère lighthouse. On passing the beacon turn due W and into the buoyed channel that leads to the marina entrance. There is also a good approach from the NW through the Doyle Passage. This is described under *Approaches to St Peter Port from NW*, page 47.

Drying hard in QE2 *Jane Russell*

Beaucette Marina office from the visitors' berth

52 CHANNEL ISLANDS, CHERBOURG PENINSULA & NORTH BRITTANY

Guernsey

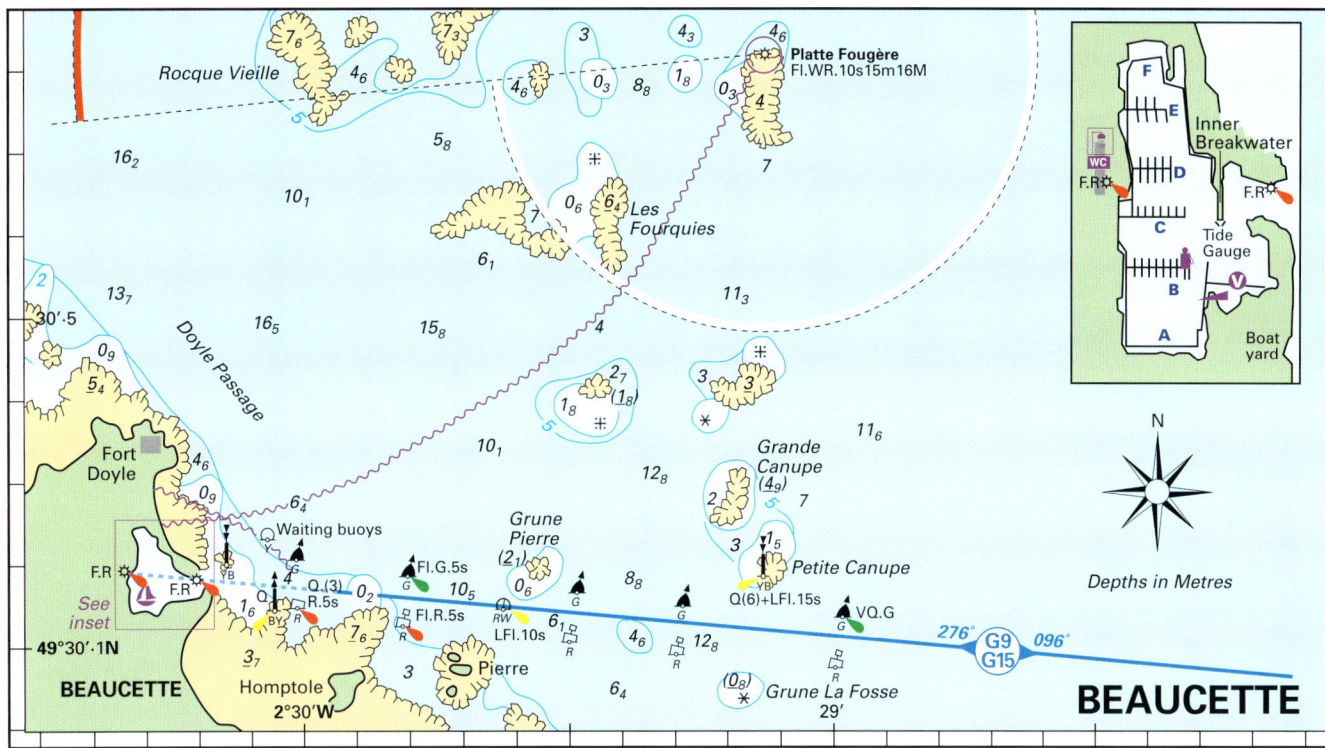

From the south

Proceed N up Little Russel as for St Peter Port (see above) to pass between Platte beacon tower and Roustel beacon tower. Once past, head towards Petite Canupe S cardinal beacon and proceed as described above.

Access

The sill dries at 2·4m giving access about three hours either side of local HW. Six yellow visitors' buoys are located just to the N of the buoyed approach channel for vessels waiting to enter. These are seasonal (Apr–Oct). Vessels should call the marina for berthing instructions (see *Local information. Radio Facilities* on page 43) before entering the Beaucette channel.

Depth

16m at CD.

Entry and berthing

Entry marks are:

G9/G15 276° Front: Situated N of entrance; red arrow on white background Rear: Situated on marina building with windsock: white arrow on red background

The rocks either side of the narrow entrance are painted white. Inside, a concrete wall provides a wave breaker.

There are depth boards situated either side of N head and inside. These indicate depth over the sill.

On entering turn to port and proceed to visitors' berths. Priority is given to vessels departing.

Channel Island Yacht Marina (Beaucette)
Depth over sill in metres (sill dries 2·37m)
Given in hourly and half hourly intervals either side of HW

Height of HW at St Peter Port	HW	+/–1hr	+/–2hr	+/– 2½hr	HALF TIDE +/–3hr	+/– 3½hr	+/–4hr	+/–5hr	+/–6hr LW
6·00	3·63	3·51	3·28	3·11	2·93	2·76	2·58	2·35	2·23
6·20	3·83	3·68	3·38	3·16	2·93	2·71	2·48	2·18	2·03
6·40	4·03	3·85	3·48	3·21	2·93	2·66	2·38	2·01	1·83
6·60	4·23	4·01	3·58	3·26	2·93	2·61	2·28	1·85	1·63
6·80	4·43	4·18	3·68	3·31	2·93	2·56	2·18	1·68	1·43
7·00	4·63	4·35	3·78	3·36	2·93	2·51	2·08	1·51	1·23
7·20	4·83	4·51	3·88	3·41	2·93	2·46	1·98	1·35	1·03
7·40	5·03	4·68	3·98	3·46	2·93	2·41	1·88	1·18	0·83
7·60	5·23	4·85	4·08	3·51	2·93	2·36	1·78	1·01	0·63
7·80	5·43	5·01	4·18	3·56	2·93	2·31	1·68	0·85	0·43
8·00	5·63	5·18	4·28	3·61	2·93	2·26	1·58	0·68	0·23
8·20	5·83	5·35	4·38	3·66	2·93	2·21	1·48	0·51	0·03
8·40	6·03	5·51	4·48	3·71	2·93	2·16	1·38	0·35	0·00
8·60	6·23	5·68	4·58	3·76	2·93	2·11	1·28	0·18	0·00
8·80	6·43	5·85	4·68	3·81	2·93	2·06	1·18	0·01	0·00
9·00	6·63	6·01	4·78	3·86	2·93	2·01	1·08	0·00	0·00
9·20	6·83	6·18	4·88	3·91	2·93	1·96	0·98	0·00	0·00
9·40	7·03	6·35	4·98	3·96	2·93	1·91	0·88	0·00	0·00
9·60	7·23	6·51	5·08	4·01	2·93	1·86	0·78	0·00	0·00
9·80	7·43	6·68	5·18	4·06	2·93	1·81	0·68	0·00	0·00
10·00	7·63	6·85	5·28	4·11	2·93	1·76	0·58	0·00	0·00

All the above figures are in metres. The depths are only approximate and can be affected by winds and changes in barometric pressure.
At all times check actual depth on the gauge at the marina.
Instructions:
1. Look up predicted height and time of HW at St Peter Port for the day.
2. Select the line corresponding to the predicted height of HW.

1 The Channel Islands

By night
This is possible in settled weather and good visibility using Tautenay light (Q(3)WR.6s7/6M), Petite Canupe beacon (Q(6)+LFl.15s) and the 2F.R lights on the leading marks. The channel buoys are lit (see plan).

Formalities
As a port of entry into the Bailiwick of Guernsey, visitors must complete a customs and immigration form. These can be obtained from the port office.

Supplies and services
16-ton travel-hoist
Customs clearance
Water and electricity on pontoons
Fuel (diesel)
Gas
Launderette
Restaurant ☎ 247066
Toilets and showers
Shop: Dolphin stores is a 5-minute walk away, as is the bus service to St Sampson's and St Peter Port.
Marina office ☎ 245000
Mobile 07781 102302
Email info@beaucettemarina.com
www.beaucettemarina.com

Radio facilities
VHF 80 (0700–2200). Call *Beaucette Marina*.

St Sampson
49°28'·97N 02°30'·66W Pier head

The growth of St Sampson is attributable to the quarrying industry of the 19th century when granite was exported worldwide from its solid wharves and piers. Today this drying harbour 1·5M N of St Peter Port is mainly concerned with commercial traffic carrying bulk cargoes. It is seldom used by yachts but an ambitious engineering project to provide marina berthing for up to 350 shallow-draught local craft was completed in 2005. 'Space

St Sampson Marina

St Sampson Marina looking SE

Guernsey

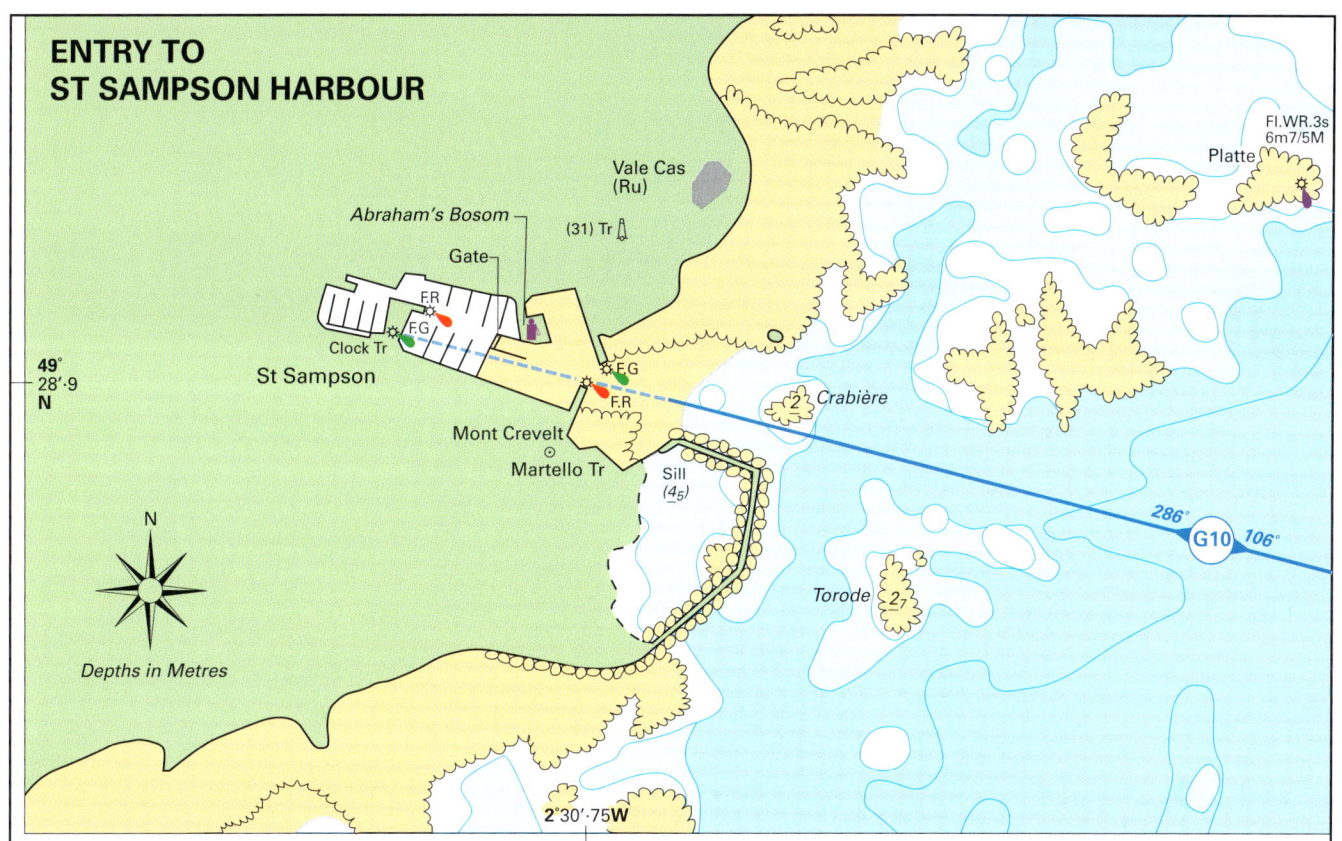

permitting and subject to prior arrangement' there may also be some provision for visitors but at the time of going to press entry for visitors was for commercial services only and there were no special facilities.

Entry

G10 286° *The clock tower in line with white band on southern breakwater head*

Entry signals
R on S pier: large vessels under way and have priority. Keep clear.

By night
The marks are lit, front F.R, rear F.G.

Marina signals
Traffic lights on SW corner of Abraham's Bosom (visible from land).
Green – entry over sill permitted
Red – no entry.

Supplies and services
Marine and General Boatyard is the main commercial shipyard in the Channel Islands. It offers a comprehensive range of services to larger vessels including a 75-ton travel-hoist.
Dockmaster (St Peter Port) ✆ 720229
Marine and General Boatyard ✆ 243048
Chandlery: Quayside ✆ 245881.

Fuel
Obtainable at commercial rates by prior arrangement with fuelling companies. The fuelling pontoon is alongside Abraham's Bosom and dries. ✆ 200800.

Radio facilities
VHF 12 (24 hours)

CHANNEL ISLANDS, CHERBOURG PENINSULA & NORTH BRITTANY

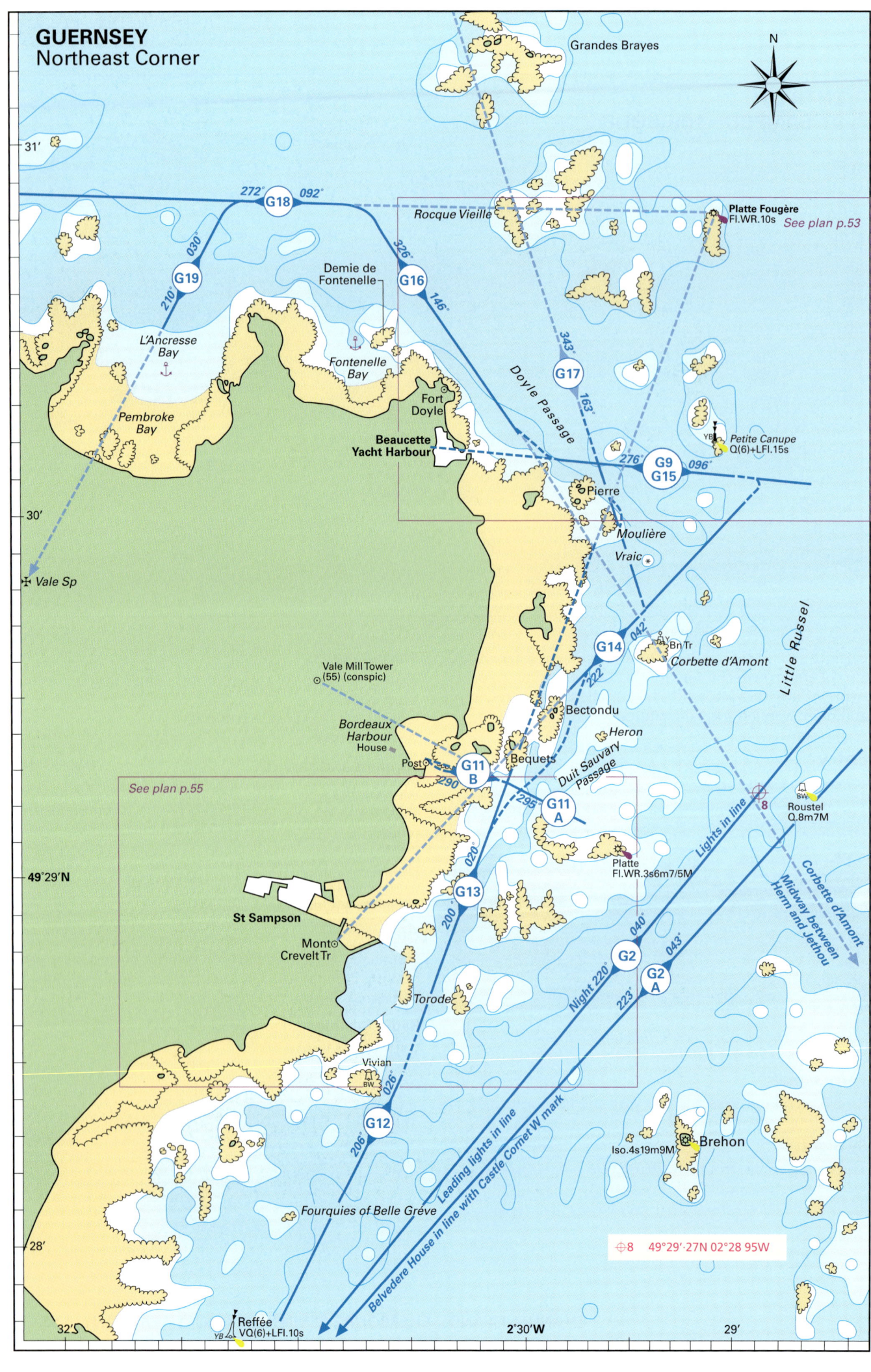

Guernsey

Bordeaux
49°29'·28N 02°30'·30W Pier head

Bordeaux at HW

This shallow drying harbour is 0·5M N of St Sampson and may be of interest to a small yacht able to take the ground. It is exposed to the E.

Approach

G11A *295° Vale Mill in line with the flat-topped Jumelle rock*

Entry

G11B *290° A white post on the end of a short pier, which covers at HW, in line with the gable of a house (partially obscured by trees)*

The rock Jumelle has a long flat spur extending some 12m. Hold the transit until 30m from Jumelle then turn to port and round the spur to enter the harbour.

Facilities
None except a bus stop.

Round the island northabout from St Peter Port (by day only)
(See plan pages 44-5)
CHART
  BA 807 Guernsey and Herm

Caution
Most of the pilotage in this section should appeal to those looking for a challenge. It passes inside reefs that extend up to 2 miles off the coast and is generally tortuous, particularly in Rocquaine Bay where there are reputed to be 130 rocks. A circumnavigation should only be attempted with local knowledge aboard and in quiet weather with at least 5 miles' visibility. When conditions fall below this minimum the N and W coast between Platte Fougère and Hanois lighthouses should be given substantial clearance.

At the N end of the island are three bays offering secluded pit stops and on the SW corner is Portelet Harbour. With little of interest to the yachtsman in between it follows that a visit to Portelet and its anchorages is more logically achieved south about from St Peter Port, following directions below in reverse (see *Portelet Harbour southabout from St Peter Port* on page 67).

All anchorages described (with the exception of those on the S and E coast) are not recommended for use at night as it could be treacherous to leave if the weather changed.

Tidal strategy
As much of the circumnavigation as possible should be made over the LW period and preferably at springs when rocks are visible. With a distance of around 23 miles, target time for a sailing vessel should be about 6 hours, aiming to make the SW corner at LW. Leaving St Peter Port just after half ebb, it is possible to dodge the S-going stream out in Little Russel by keeping close to the shore. At the NE corner, the W-going stream will give a good ride down into Rocquaine Bay, but beware of accelerated streams close inshore. From LW up to HW the stream sets conveniently E along the S coast and N up the E coast until HW+0300.

Note Tidal information is based on St Peter Port (St Helier +0005).

St Peter Port north to Fort Doyle 3·5M (3·0m)
(See plan page 56)

Departing St Peter Port take up stern transit G12:

G12 *206° White patch on S edge of Castle Cornet open E of Castle Cornet LtHo by its width (shown here open half width)*

I. THE CHANNEL ISLANDS

1 The Channel Islands

This transit leads into the Duit Sauvary Passage clearing E of Fourquies of Belle Grève (dries 1·5m) and Vivian BW beacon tower. When NE of this beacon tower and abeam St Sampson's reclamation site take up:

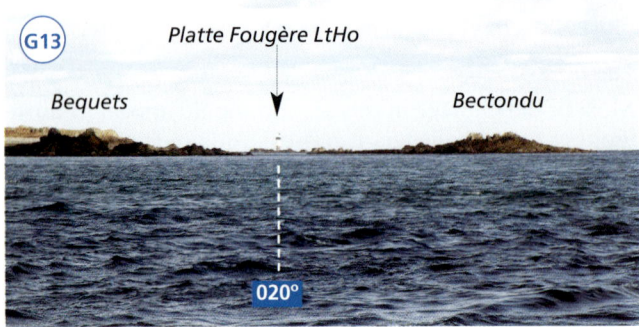

G13 020° Platte Fougère LtHo midway between Bequets and Bectondu (4·4m)

Run up to Bectondu and make a close turn to starboard to pass midway between it and Heron (dries 2·4m). Stop the turn when stern Transit G12 is regained or, if this is no longer visible, when the next transit is seen astern.

G14 222° Mont Crevelt Tower (S of St Sampson's Harbour entrance) above the N head of Bectondu. Steer out to pass N of Corbette d'Amont beacon tower

When abeam Corbette d'Amont bn tower there is a choice of two entries into Doyle Passage.

Either steer out into Little Russel on stern transit G14 until Petit Canupe S cardinal beacon bears NW then take up Beaucette Marina leading marks:

G9/G15 276° Front: red arrow on white background on the N head. Rear: windsock pole on marina building above white arrow on red background

Note that this leading line crosses a shallow patch (0·2m) 400m short of the entrance (see plan p.53).

Continue towards the marina entrance until looking SE identify stern transit:

G16 146° Corbette d'Amont beacon tower midway between Herm and Jethou. This leads into Doyle Passage

Or from a position 200m NW of Corbette d'Amont beacon tower look NW to identify sugar-loaf-shaped Rocque Vieille (dries 7·6m) and beyond the whitewashed Grandes Brayes (2m). Take up:

G17 343° Grandes Brayes open to the E of Rocque Vieille. This will clear W of Vraic (dries 0·6m) but a close turn to starboard should be made to clear the E edges of Moulière (dries 4·8m) and Pierre

Return to Transit G16 as described above to enter Doyle Channel.

The turning point onto a W heading is stern transit:

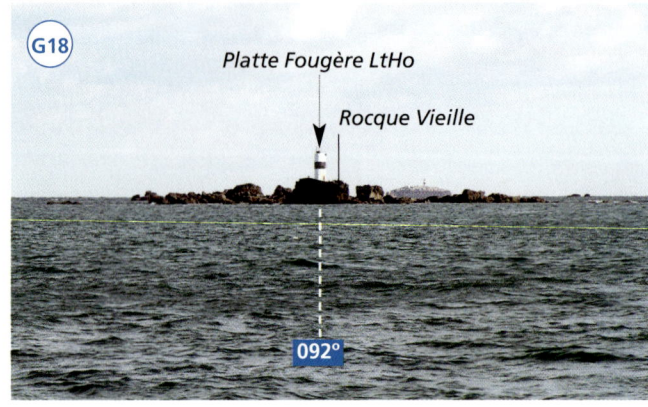

G18 092° Platte Fougère LtHo in line with Rocque Vieille

Guernsey

Fort Doyle west to Grand Havre 3·0M (1·4m)

(See plans page 56 and below)

Transit G18 must be held accurately for almost 2 miles. Now is the time to identify a few marks. Ahead is Rousse de Mer (dries 6·8m) and off the starboard bow is Silleuse (dries 6·4m) and Roque au Nord (ht 0·5m). On the land look for Vale church spire to the SW and Victoria Tower to the SSW, both of which will be needed later.

S of Silleuse the line passes through the narrowest gap in the channel – barely 200m wide.

There is plenty of depth, at least 11m at datum, but it may be necessary to 'borrow' S to clear an isolated rock (dries 1·2m) to the N. When 0·25M short of Rousse de Mer alter course to WSW and pass 200m S of it and onto Transit G22 as described below.

If early on the tide, branch off the transit G18 and discover several peaceful anchorages on this stretch of coast. All offer good shelter at LW in offshore breezes.

FONTENELLE BAY

49°30'·43N 02°30'·70W

(See plan page 56)

Less sheltered than its neighbouring bays to the W and vulnerable to swell.

There are no formal marks and entry should be made with reference to the chart. Beware of Demie de Fontenelle (dries 4·6m) a half tide rock on the E side.

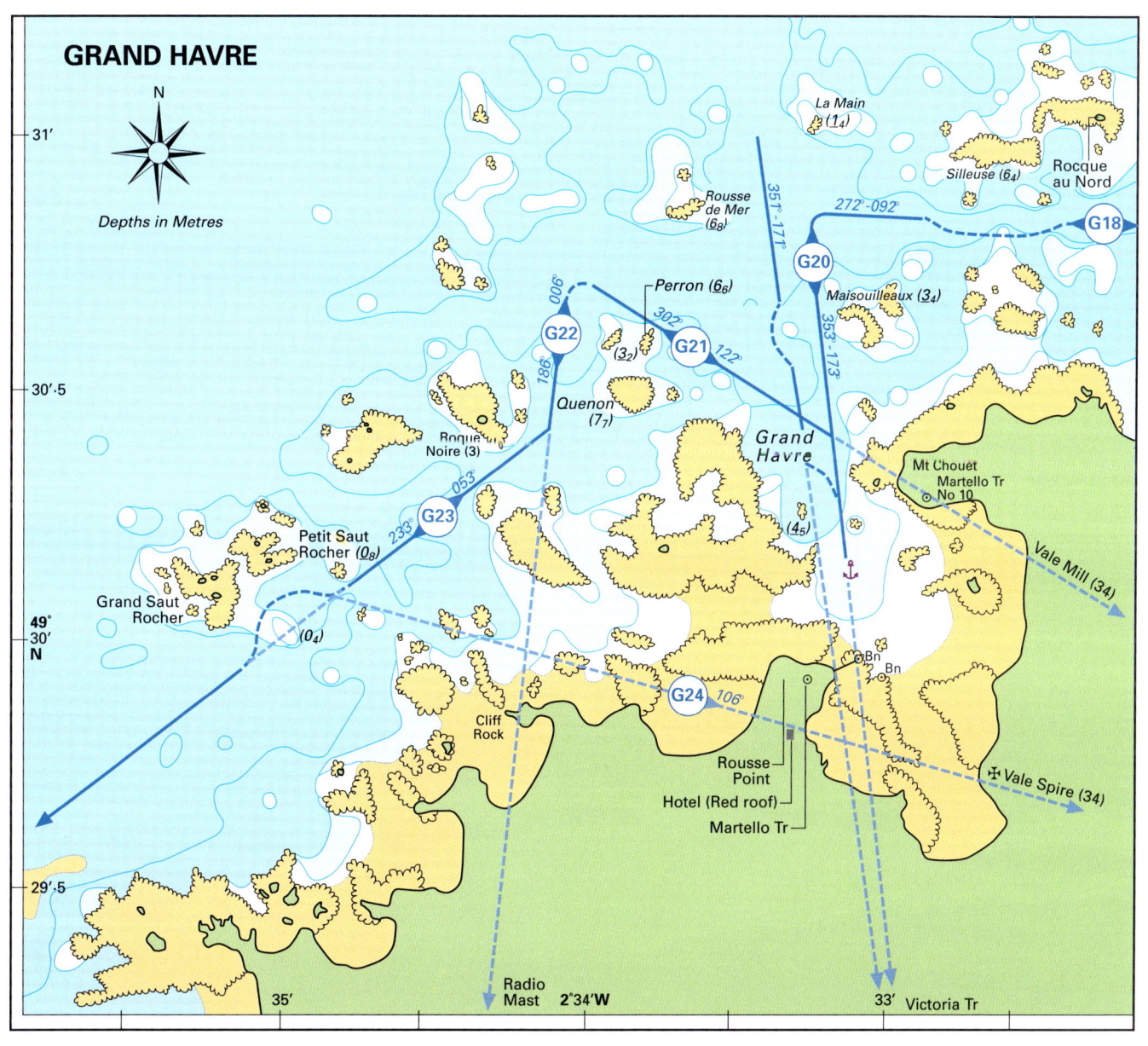

1 The Channel Islands

L'ANCRESSE BAY (PEMBROKE BAY)
49°30'·55N 02°31'·45W
(See plan page 56)

L'Ancresse Bay looking south

Entry
When the bay has opened up find:

G19 *210° Martello Tower No. 7 in the S of the bay in line with Vale Church spire (34m)*

Anchorage
There is good holding in sand in the middle of the bay. (see air view above). Take care to avoid drying rocks (2·8m and 0·5m - see chart BA 807).

Grand Havre
49°30'·18N 02°33'·01W
(See plan page 59)

Entry

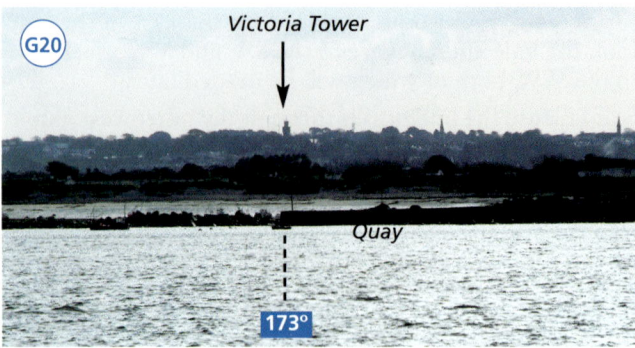

G20 *173° From G18 identify:*

Beacon (B) on the end of the quay off Rousse Point is in transit with Victoria Tower. Make sure the correct spire is identified!

Approaching from further N use transit shown on BA chart 807/808 (Victoria Tower in line with Rousse Point 171°) (see plan). This will clear between La Main (dries 1·4m) and Rousse de Mer (dries 6·8m) but crosses a shoal patch of 1·4m 200m W of Maisouilleaux when it will be necessary to borrow a bit to the W. To clear the drying rock (dries 4·5m) further S transfer to G20 on entry to give it a clearance of 175m.

Anchorage
Anchor with reference to the chart. Beware of several drying rocks in the bay. There is a stone slipway on the 130m long quay.

Facilities
Bars, grocery shops and a hotel. Regular buses to town.

Grand Havre looking south

Guernsey

Grand Havre south to Pleinmont Point
9·0M (2·1m)
(See plans pages 59, 62, 63)

Departure from Grand Havre

Proceeding W depart on stern transit:

G21 *122° Vale Mill tower closed behind Martello Tower No. 10 on Mt Chouet (shown open for clarity)*

Close the transit to give Perron (dries 6·6m) a respectable distance then make a close turn to pass 300m N of the rock and its westerly neighbour (dries 3·2m).

Next look SSW to identify the radio mast in the middle of the island. This is the rear mark for:

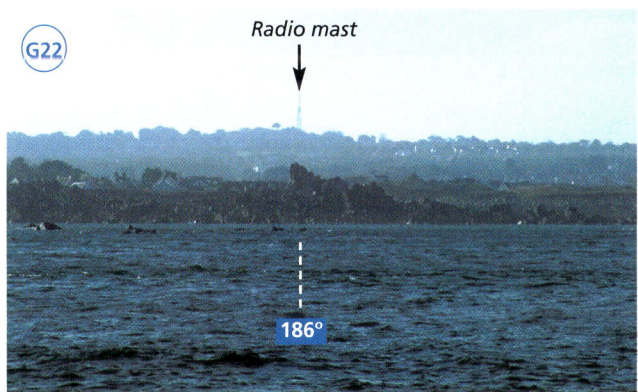

G22 *186° radio mast in line with Cliff Rock*

This short transit line will clear between Roque Noire (3m) with its drying neighbours and Quenon (dries 7·7m). Looking SW identify Lihou Island and Moulière (2·2m) with its reef. Take up transit:

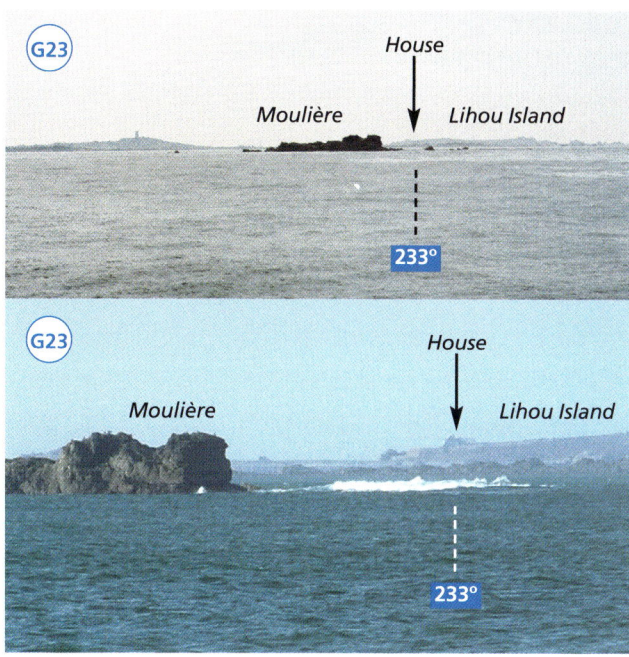

G23 *233° House on Lihou is on the W side of Moulière (2·2m) (here shown too far open)*

A minor detour from this transit is required to clear a rocky shoal (0·4m) S of the extensive Grand Saut Rocher (6m) and Petit Saut Rocher (2m) reefs. For the turning point look ESE for the prominent red roof on an hotel on Rousse Point.

G24 *106° The N end of the red roof is in line with Vale church spire*

Commence a turn to starboard and head for Grand Saut Rocher (6m). When 200m off the rock alter course to port to regain transit G23.

You have cleared the dangers when Hanois lighthouse, if visible, is open to the E of Moulière. (See plan page 62).

Break off transit G23 to pass N of Moulière.

Continuing SW, a brief alteration onto a WNW heading is now required to find the next transit (G25) as described below. This will clear dangers lurking to the S. If time permits, take a break in Cobo Bay to plan the next stage.

1 The Channel Islands

COBO BAY
49°28'·66N 02°36'·33W

There are no formal marks for this fair weather anchorage and it is a question of feeling your way in with reference to the chart. When entering or leaving the bay note Boue Vazon (dries 3m) 0·5M SW of Moulière.

Anchorage
SW of local moorings there is good holding in sand.
  Returning to seaward, identify:

Cobo Bay

G25 233° La Pécheresse (dries 7·9m) to the SW aligned with Corner Rock (0·8m) at the most westerly end of Lihou

Holding this transit accurately is vitally important for clearing between dangers ahead. It will clear between Colombelle (dries 1·5m) and the reef extending W of La Conchée (4m).

Leave Pécheresse close to port to shape a course to pass midway between Corner Rock (0·6m) and Grand Etacré (dries 6·7m). Now is the time to decide whether to continue on to the S coast outside Rocquaine Bay or alter course S into Rocquaine Bay.

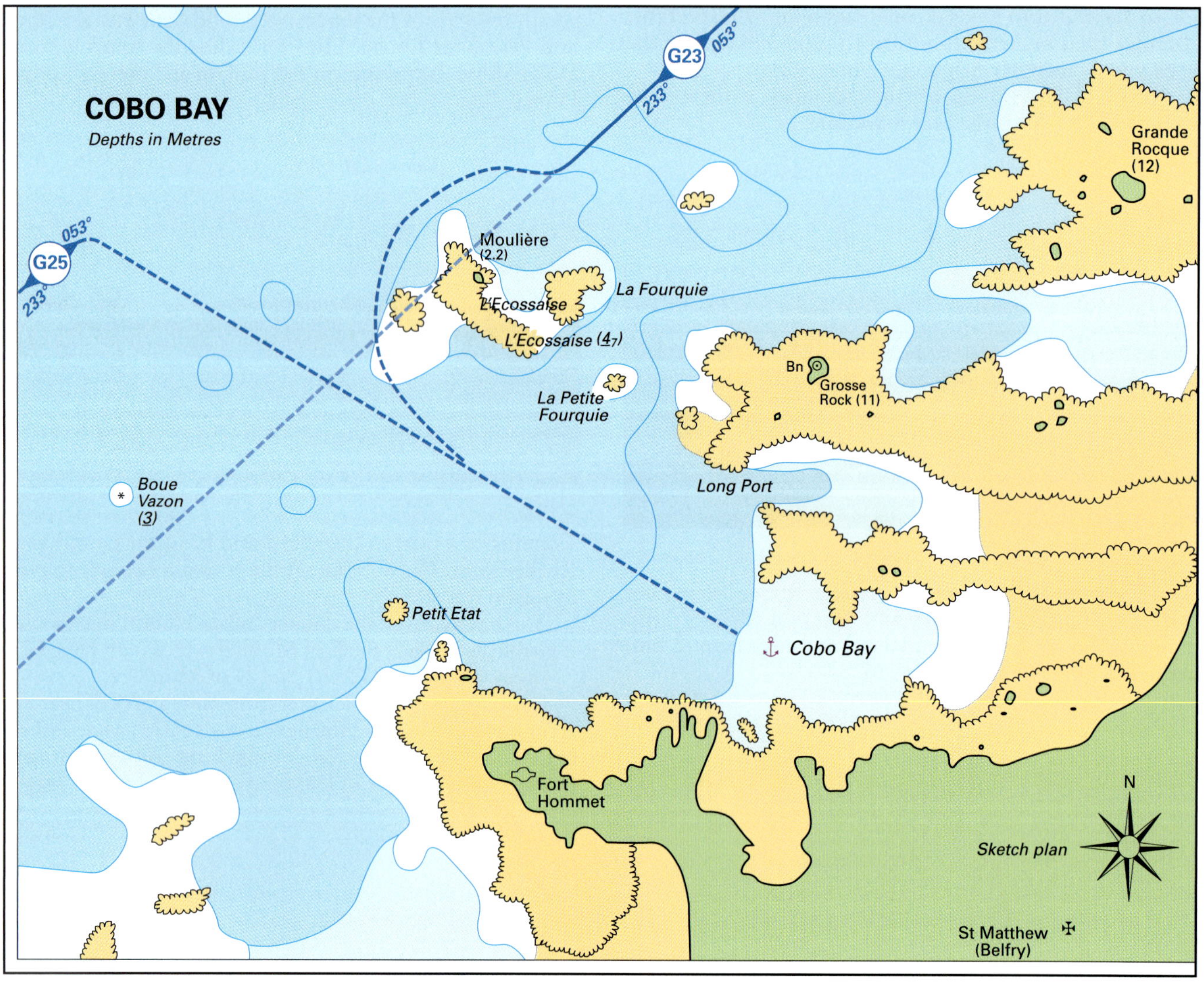

Guernsey

CHANNEL ISLANDS, CHERBOURG PENINSULA & NORTH BRITTANY

1 The Channel Islands

Looking SE into Roquaine Bay

ROCQUAINE BAY (see plan page 63)

Entry from N

From a position 400m WNW of Corner Rock (0·6m) identify the white Fort Grey tower (locally known as the 'Cup and Saucer') to the SE and take up:

G26 141° *Torteval church aligned with the N side of Fort Grey tower*

Line G26 will leave La Fourquie (dries 6·1m) close to port. When just short of Perron (dries 3·5m) open out the transit and commence a turn to port leaving both Perron and Black Rock (dries 8·2m) to the S of it close to starboard (see view above). Turn to starboard onto a heading of 215° with transit:

G27 215° *Round Rock (6m) is just open to the S of Nipple Rock (dries 8·5m)*

The next transit indicated on BA chart 807 is difficult to identify. Hold G27 until looking astern:

G28 023° *Saddle Rock on Lihou Is is aligned with Black Rock*

This transit is held until a good 200m E of Round Rock (6m) at which point you can either continue SSW out of the bay using stern transit G31 (described below) or relax at anchor off Portelet Harbour.

Rocquaine Bay from Fort Grey looking WSW towards Les Hanois lighthouse *Jane Russell*

64 CHANNEL ISLANDS, CHERBOURG PENINSULA & NORTH BRITTANY

Guernsey

PORTELET HARBOUR AND ANCHORAGES
49°26'·15N 02°39'·84W

This minuscule drying harbour has two quays which cover at HW. When there is no swell, bilge keelers can take the ground on firm sand below Trinity Cottages (see aerial views).

Approach
(See plans page 63 and below)

Branch off line G28 when

G29 *095° Apex House is aligned with the N side of Fort Grey tower*

This clears S of a rock awash at datum and, further in, N of La Tour (dries 7·9m).

Note The rear mark can be partially obscured by trees.

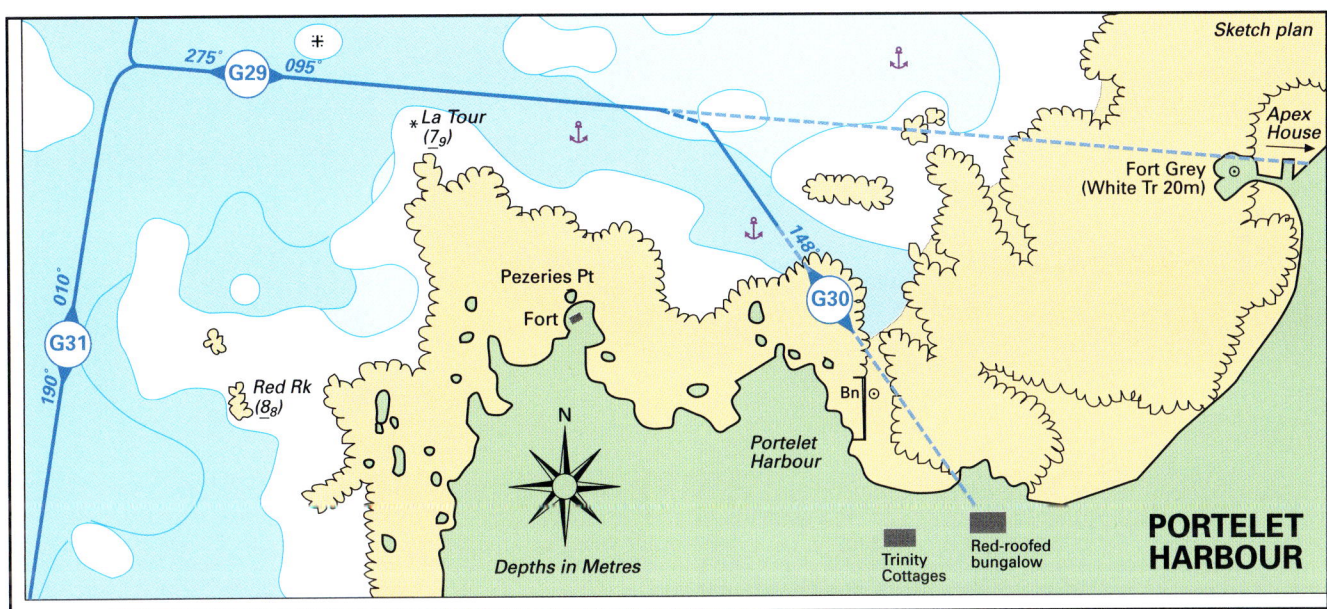

Portelet harbour from the north

CHANNEL ISLANDS, CHERBOURG PENINSULA & NORTH BRITTANY

1 The Channel Islands

A further useful transit for locating a suitable anchoring position N of the harbour is:

G30 *Red-roofed bungalow in line with Portelet Pier beacon 148°*

Note This transit is preferred to that shown on BA 807.

Anchorages

N of Pezeries Point as shown on BA 807 and plan page 65.

Portelet harbour from the WSW. The yacht is anchored NE of Pezeries Point and just S of approach line G29

E of Pezeries Point below the 2m contour NW of small boat moorings.

Facilities

Ashore there is a grocery shop and several restaurants: oysters and mussels are a local speciality.

Clearing S out of Rocquaine Bay on Transit G31

Departure

Continuing round the island, leave by the arrival transit (see plan page 65):

When a good 200m short of Round Rock, note Hanois lighthouse touching its S edge. At this point take up the final stern transit that leads out onto the S coast:

G31 *010° ⊕15 The westernmost rock off Lihou Is over the eastern edge of Nipple Rock*

Note At 0·5M S of Round Rock the line passes a rock (1·5m) close to port. Depending on the height of tide it may be necessary to open the transit to give a wider berth. As these marks are difficult to identify use Hayes Rock

66 CHANNEL ISLANDS, CHERBOURG PENINSULA & NORTH BRITTANY

Guernsey

(1m) 0·45M SSW of the break-off point from G29. If you are on the right track you will pass 200m E of this rock. 0·25M on you are clear of all dangers.

Portelet Harbour southabout from St Peter Port
(See plans pages 44-5, 63, 65, 69)

For a more straightforward passage to Portelet Harbour, go southabout from St Peter Port. Leave at HW St Helier +0230, just before the marina sill closes. There will be a S-going stream to St Martin's Point where it will be slack and on the S coast a W-going stream until LW which is the right time to be in Rocquaine Bay.

All dangers along the S coast will be cleared if you stay just outside the 50m contour – about 1M off.

Pleinmont Point east to St Martin's Point 7·6M (2·0m)
(See plans pages 44-5, 63, 69)

This stretch of Guernsey's coastline is generally steep-to and presents a somewhat confusing succession of similar shaped headlands. There are hazards extending up to 0·5M off, the main ones being Pleinmont Ledge, Les Kaines d'Amont, Les Lieuses, Baleine Rock and the Grunes de Jerbourg.

Locals have their marks for passing inside all but the Grunes. These directions take a moderate route S of most of these dangers, providing short detours into several attractive fair weather anchorages between Pte de la Moye and Jerbourg Point.

The inshore turning point off line G31 and onto the S coast is achieved with:

G32 092° ⊕15 The conspicuous lookout tower (89m) near La Corbière Point (not to be confused with Pleinmont Tower) bears 092°

At the same time and subject to good visibility identify the marks for transit:

G33 095° L'Etac (65m) S of Sark open of Pte de La Moye and midway between the Pte and Grande Lieuses 095° (no view)

Routeing inside Pleinmont Ledge

This line clears midway between Pleinmont Ledge and Herpin Rock (1·5m). Confirmation can be obtained by taking stern bearings of Hanois LtHo. When on 298° hold transit:

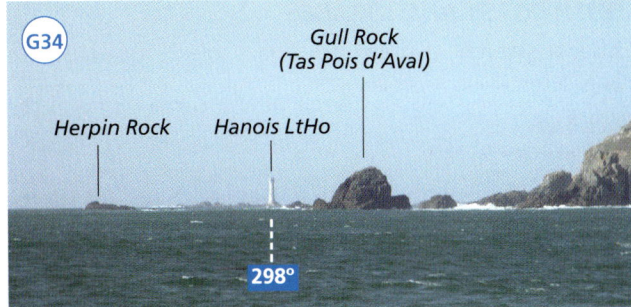

G34 298° Hanois LtHo is seen midway between Gull Rock (14m) and Herpin Rock (1·5m). This clears Les Kaines d'Amont and Les Lieuses

Les Kaines d'Amont are off the stripey headland Les Tielles

Routeing outside Pleinmont Ledge

An alternative is to pass outside (S) of Pleinmont Ledge then route ESE to the turning point S of Corbière lookout tower. This is:

G35 (⊕14) 000° Corbière lookout tower bearing N (no view)

At this point steer towards Jerbourg Pt but note there are dangers extending up to 0·25M off Pointe de la Moye, Icart Point and Jerbourg Point. The turning point SSE of Jerbourg Point is a fix derived from 2 bearings. These are:

G36 305° The Martello tower above Saints Bay is well open south of Les Tas de Pois d'Amont. (This should not be used as an entry line into Moulin Huet Bay.)

and:

G38 026° Brehon Tower is open E of Longue Pierre beacon

1 The Channel Islands

SOUTH COAST ANCHORAGES

The last stretch of the south coast passes some of the island's finest anchorages.

Icart Bay
49°25'·18N 02°34'·70W

Petit Bôt (pronounced 'Bo') **Bay** and its southerly neighbour **Le Portelet** are snug anchorages in offshore winds. Petit Bôt is identified by its Martello Tower (15m). To clear Fourquie de la Moye (dries 3·1m) approach with:

G37 353° the tower open of the point

Anchor in 3m E of transit.

Le Gouffre
49°25'·10N 02°35'·30W

This small cove N of Pointe de la Moye offers some shelter in quiet weather. Anchor clear of rocks and moorings.

Le Jaonnet and La Bette

Le Jaonnet and **La Bette** bays in the NE of Icart Bay provide secluded anchorage, but note the drying rocks between them. Approach with reference to the chart.

Moulin Huet Bay
49°25'·41N 02°32'·55W

The main obstruction in this superb bay to the E of Icart Point is the drying rock Mouilière (dries 8·5m) at its centre, which is usually visible. The holding is generally good in fine sand and there are several options depending on wind direction.

Approach and anchor with reference to the chart.

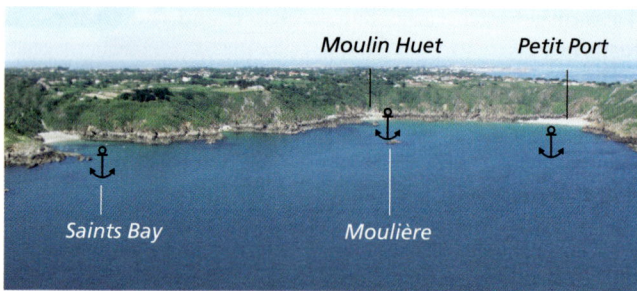

Moulin Huet Bay

Saints Bay
49°35'·23N 02°33'·20W

This small cove offers good holding in sand but beware of a drying rock close in and keep clear of local moorings. A path above the beach leads inland. The beacon marks the entry of old telephone cables. These have now been replaced by a fibre optic cable.

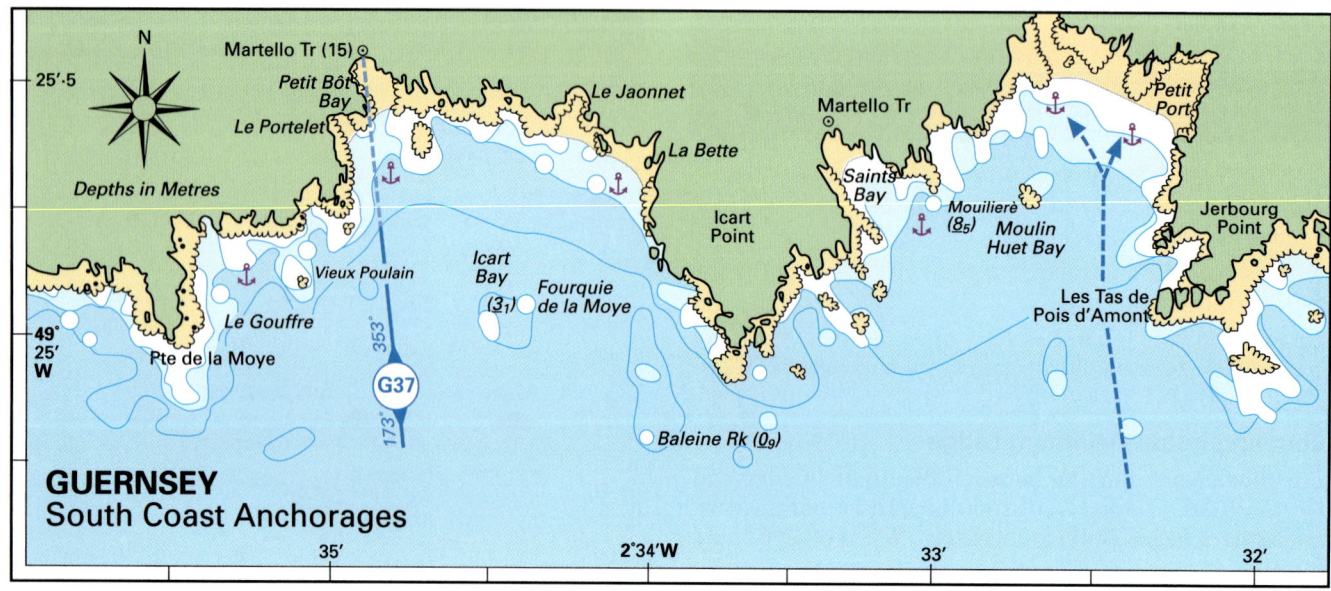

GUERNSEY South Coast Anchorages

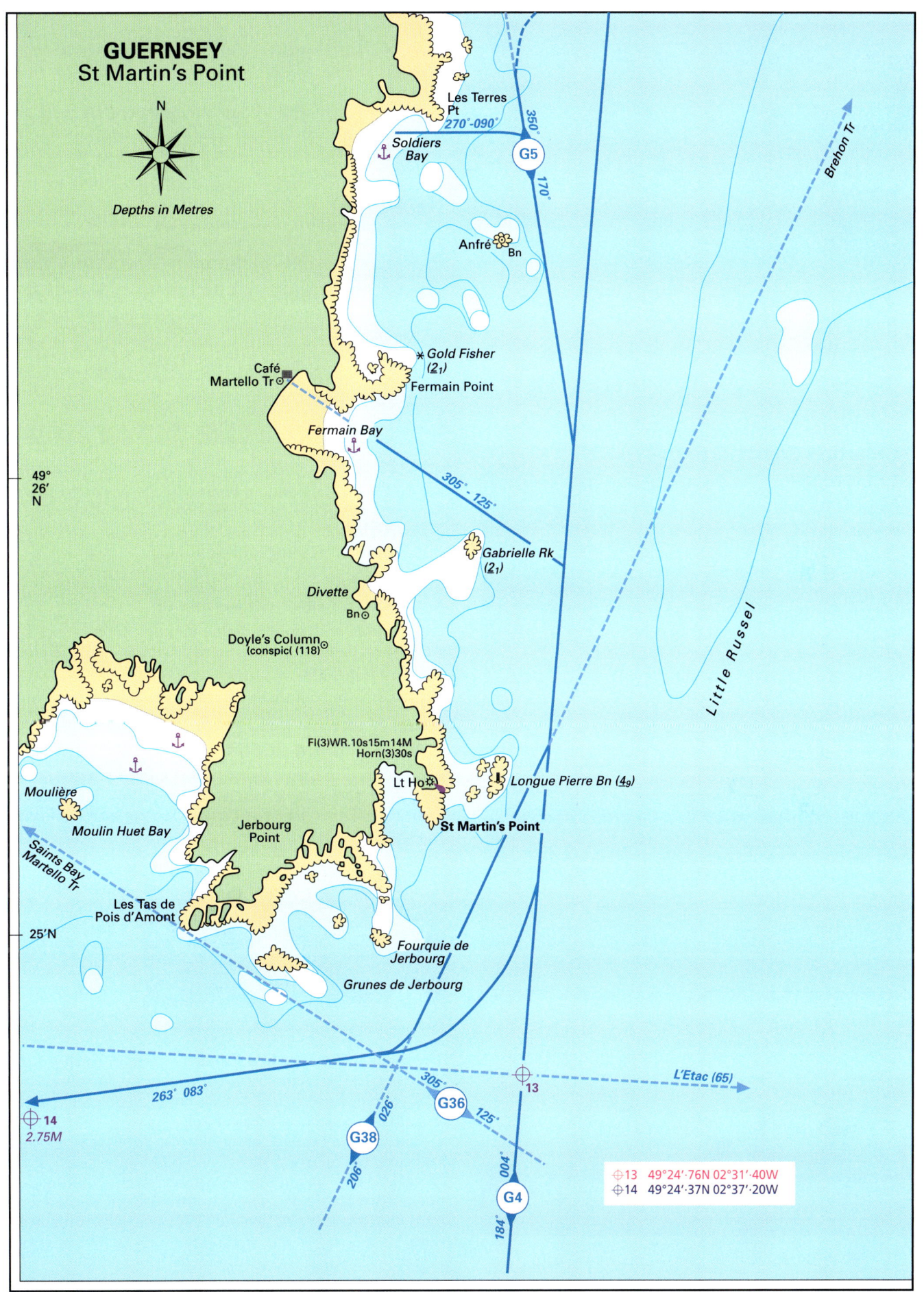

1 The Channel Islands

Saints Bay

Off Petit Port

In winds between N and E, the best anchorage will be found NE of Moulière.

Facilities There are cafés ashore at Petit Bôt, Moulin Huet and Saints Bays.

St Martin's Point north to St Peter Port
2M (2·0m)

(See plans pages 45, 50, 69)

If possible arrange to make this last short leg between HW St Helier −0300 and +0100, when the stream is running N up to St Peter Port. Alternatively it is possible to dodge a S-going stream in Little Russel by routeing inside Gabrielle Rock (dries 2·1m) and Anfré (dries 3·3m) with its beacon. Directions below are for the offshore route outside all dangers. From turning point SSE of Jerbourg Pt or WP13 take up:

St Martin's Point Lighthouse

G4 004° ⊕13 *Vale Mill over the middle shed of a group of three (green) at St Sampsons*

G5 350° *White Rock light open to the E of Castle Cornet*

When Moulinet beacon (M) is abeam, steer out into Little Russel to clear Oyster beacon (0m) and Ferico (0·9m) and open the pier heads (see *Approaches to St Peter Port from S* above).

Between St Martin's Point and St Peter Port there are three possible anchorages offering perfect shelter in westerlies. They can be untenable in winds between S and E.

FERMAIN BAY
49°26'·12N 02°31'·79W   (See plan page 69)

An attractive bay with a popular beach. Approach with the café open S of Fermain Point with the Martello Tower bearing 305°. This line will clear N of Gabrielle Rk (dries 2·1m) and S of Fermain Point. Anchor as close to the shore as tide allows. Holding is good in sand.

SOLDIERS BAY
49°27'·06N 02°31'·68W   (See plan page 69)

A small inlet with good holding in sand. Reference to BA 807 shows dangers in the S so approach from the E close to Les Terres Point.

Facilities None, but there are steps to a cliff path.

HAVELET BAY
49°27'·06N 02°31'·68W   (See plan page 50)

A wide bay S of Castle Cornet that can be crowded at the height of the season when St Peter Port Harbour is saturated. Enter between Oyster beacon and Moulinet beacon with transit:

G5A 290° *St Joseph's church spire (green) in line with Salem church spire*

The channel is buoyed in the summer months. Anchor with reference to the chart avoiding local craft moorings and rocky patches at either side of the bay. The holding is good in sand but beware of areas of kelp.

Landing can be made at the slip just W of Castle Cornet and close to Guernsey Yacht Club building.

Note Havelet Bay tends to attract swell, making for uncomfortable nights. This is mostly tide-generated and particularly noticeable around HW, especially over spring tides.

Herm

Local information

STD code: 01481

TRAVEL INFORMATION
Sea only
In the season there is an hourly ferry service between St Peter Port and the island. The Sark ferry calls into Herm several times a week to pick up visitors for Sark
Travel Trident ☎ 721379
Herm Seaway Express ☎ 721379
www.traveltrident.com

PORTS OF ENTRY
The official Ports of Entry into the Bailiwick of Guernsey are Braye in Alderney and Beaucette Marina, St Sampson (for commercial vessels only) and St Peter Port in Guernsey. At St Peter Port, all visiting yachts must clear in at the main harbour irrespective of which marina they moor in.

CHARTS
British Admiralty
807 Guernsey and Herm (1:25 000)
808 East Guernsey, Herm and Sark (1:25 000)
3654 Guernsey, Herm and Sark (1:50 000)
SC 5604 The Channel Islands Leisure Folio:
9 Guernsey, Herm and Sark (1:50 000)
10 Approaches to Saint Peter Port (1:25 000)
12 Sark and The Big Russel (1:25 000)

Imray
C33A Channel Islands*
*includes plans: Herm Harbour & Rosière Anchorage (1:30 000), Little Russel (1:50 000)
2500 The Channel Islands and adjacent coast of France Chart Atlas:
5 Guernsey, Herm & Sark (1:60 000)
6 East Guernsey & Herm (1:25 000)

SHOM
6903 Guernsey et Herm (1:25 000)
6904 Guernsey Est, Herm et Sark (1:25 000)
7159 De Guernsey, Herm et Sark à Alderney - Bancs des Casquets (1:48 000)

RADIO
Guernsey Coastguard VHF Ch 20

NAVIGATIONAL AIDS
None

USEFUL CONTACTS
Herm Office ☎ 750000
www.herm.com

SUPPLIES AND SERVICES
Within the harbour area you will find: fresh water tap, toilets, showers, gift shops, rubbish collection point. Basic provisions are obtainable from The Mermaid Tavern shop.
Restaurants
The Boaters Restaurant (The Mermaid Tavern) ☎ 750050
The White House Hotel and Ship Restaurant ☎ 710075
The Boaters Restaurant ☎ 750050

Herm (right) and Jethou (left) from the south. Goubinière is in the foreground

I The Channel Islands

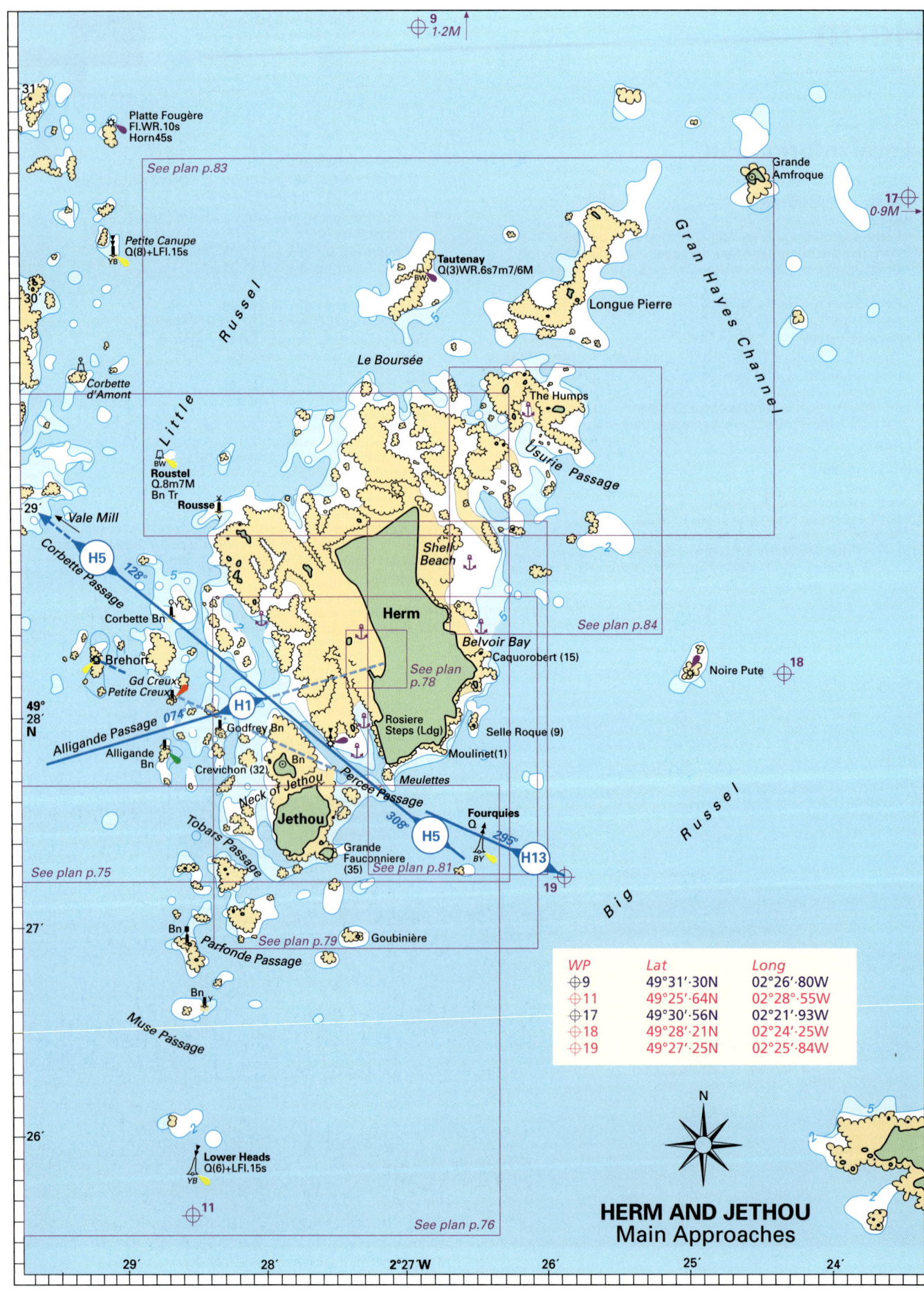

Herm

Tidal information

Tidal Levels referred to chart datum, as for St Peter Port. A look at the tidal plans in the *Appendix* indicates that the streams around Herm roughly conform to the pattern in the Russels. This is:

N-going from HW–0300 to HW+0300 and S-going from HW+0300 to HW–0300 with slack water around half tide. Close inshore there are subtle variations particularly among the reefs west of Herm and in the Percée Passage S of the island, where currents may exceed 5 knots.

When following the E–W channels the navigator should be particularly vigilant. Here a devious cross set can be experienced and if transits are not held accurately the yacht may quickly be swept towards dangers. *Always allow for tidal set.*

Shell beach, Herm *Visit Guernsey*

Introduction

A visit to Guernsey would be incomplete without making the three-mile hop across from St Peter Port to enjoy the tranquil charm of Herm. In 1949 the island was purchased in a dilapidated state by Guernsey from the Crown and has since been leased to the Wood family. Thanks to their vision and a strong commitment to conservation, it has been tastefully restored and is well maintained by a permanent community of about 40 people. In the centre of the island is the Manor House with its 12th-century Chapel of St Tugual. Clustered round the harbour are the highly rated White House Hotel and Restaurant, The Mermaid Tavern, self-catering cottages, a campsite and several small boutiques.

Visiting yachtsmen, along with ferry-loads of visitors are welcomed but regulated so the peaceful atmosphere is not threatened. Permission is required to remain on the island overnight and this is available without charge from the administrative office at the harbour.

Jethou and its neighbouring islets Crevichon and Grand Fauconnière are private and landing is prohibited.

Herm's minuscule drying harbour and its low-water anchorage to the south offer good shelter with the option of drying out or remaining afloat at all states of tide. There are several idyllic anchorages on the east coast.

Ashore

A walk round the island will take about two hours. Beaches are clean and safe, the best being Belvoir Bay and Shell Beach on the east coast.

The island's sole pub The Mermaid Tavern, sells basic provisions and meals at The Boaters Restaurant.

The White House Hotel (☎ 722159) has two restaurants, The Ship Restaurant which is open to the public and The Conservatory for hotel residents only.

Pilotage

Over a dozen passages cut through the extensive reef that stretches from Grande Amfroque in the NE through Herm and Jethou to the Lower Heads S cardinal buoy. Even given good visibility, sufficient water and large-scale chart BA 808, plying these channels is a challenge to the navigator. With a profusion of marks at close range, pilotage here becomes a precise art calling for a degree of concentration.

In contrast to the deep waters to the south, the north of Herm is an almost impenetrable area of drying sand and reefs. With strong and diverse streams and transits that are difficult to identify without local knowledge, the channels in this area are seldom used by visitors. They should not be attempted until the more straightforward channels in the south have been mastered.

Approaches to Herm

From St Peter Port

When approaching Herm from St Peter Port it is vital to locate key marks well before entering the reefs. Beacons can be difficult to identify against the backdrop of the island. Generally one is in safe water up to the point where Brehon Tower is bearing N. Whether to approach N or S of Jethou will depend on the state of the tide and the navigator's local knowledge.

Northabout (see pages 74–5), the direct Alligande Passage with a succession of beacons and a single transit is the most used channel, but caution is needed below half tide as there are some shallow patches. The LW option is Creux Passage which calls for confident pilotage.

Both these channels converge on a point in the Percée Passage from where you can, with sufficient water, enter the harbour on the leading beacons or proceed down the passage to Rosière Steps deep water landing and anchorage S of the harbour.

Percée Passage, which is a continuation of Corbette Passage (2·2m) provides a deep water NW–SE cut between Herm and Jethou.

Southabout (see pages 76–78), the Sark Ferries regularly ply the Tobars Passage S of Jethou at LW. This has greater depth and easily identified marks but there is little room for error. If uncertain take the easiest, if rather circuitous, option of going S for the Musé Passage or the Lower Heads S cardinal buoy. Approach to Rosière Steps is described under *Rosière Steps Landing* below.

All passages E of Herm are described from W to E.

By night

(See *Herm Harbour. By night.*)

Visitors are not encouraged to approach Herm at night. Locals use Alligande Passage (described below) and enter the harbour on the leading lights.

CHANNEL ISLANDS, CHERBOURG PENINSULA & NORTH BRITTANY

1 The Channel Islands

PASSAGES NORTH OF JETHOU
(See plans pages 75 and 79)

Alligande Passage (0·5m) (W to E)

Used by the Herm ferries, and the only passage that may be taken at night with caution and then only in summer. There are shallow patches so particular caution is required below half tide, when it may be necessary to choose an alternative passage. The key to entry is Alligande beacon (green with an A topmark and lit 49°87'·85N 02°27'·78W) this should be left 200m to starboard. Identify Vermerette beacon (yellow with a V topmark and lit) and take up:

H1 074° Vermerette beacon in line with white patch on end of quay

When 400m short of Vermerette beacon turn to port onto Transit H17 (see *Herm Harbour entrance* below) or to starboard to enter Percée Passage (H5).

Creux Passage (3·0m) (W to E)
(Plan pages 75, 79)

This is the low-water passage from St Peter Port to Herm; there are four doglegs and marks can be difficult to hold with any cross-set.

H2 095° Rosière Cottage (above Rosière Steps on Herm) open to the S of Petit Creux (C) beacon

When 100m from Petit Creux beacon, come to port and make a turn round it, leaving it 60m to starboard, then take up stern transit H3:

H3 257° Victoria Tower in line with Petit Creux beacon will clear N of Etacré (dries 0·9m) and its boue (dries 0·3m) and S of the Boue Lionnais (dries 0·7m)

This transit should be held for 400m then to clear the Boue, alter to 102° using stern transit:

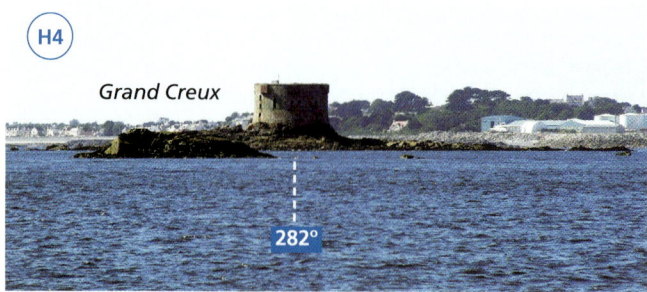

H4 282° Brehon Tower to the N of the highest part of Grand Creux

This course will intercept the Corbette Passage as described under *Approaches to Herm. From the northwest*, below

Percée Passage (Passe Percée) (3·4m) (N to S)
(Plan pages 75, 79)

This NW–SE passage (pronounced 'Per-she') offers a straightforward approach to Herm from either direction.
 As a continuation of the Corbette Passage it shares the same transit:

H5/H14 308° Vale Mill open as much as its elevation SW of Corbette de La Mare beacon

The mill must be kept open by about as much as the elevation of the mill in order to clear Percée Rock W cardinal beacon, also known as Gate Rock, and the sandbank (0·3m) S of Mouette. The above transit will also clear Meulettes (dries 1·7m), a reef off the S end of Herm, and Tinker (dries 2·5m) NE of Jethou.

74 CHANNEL ISLANDS, CHERBOURG PENINSULA & NORTH BRITTANY

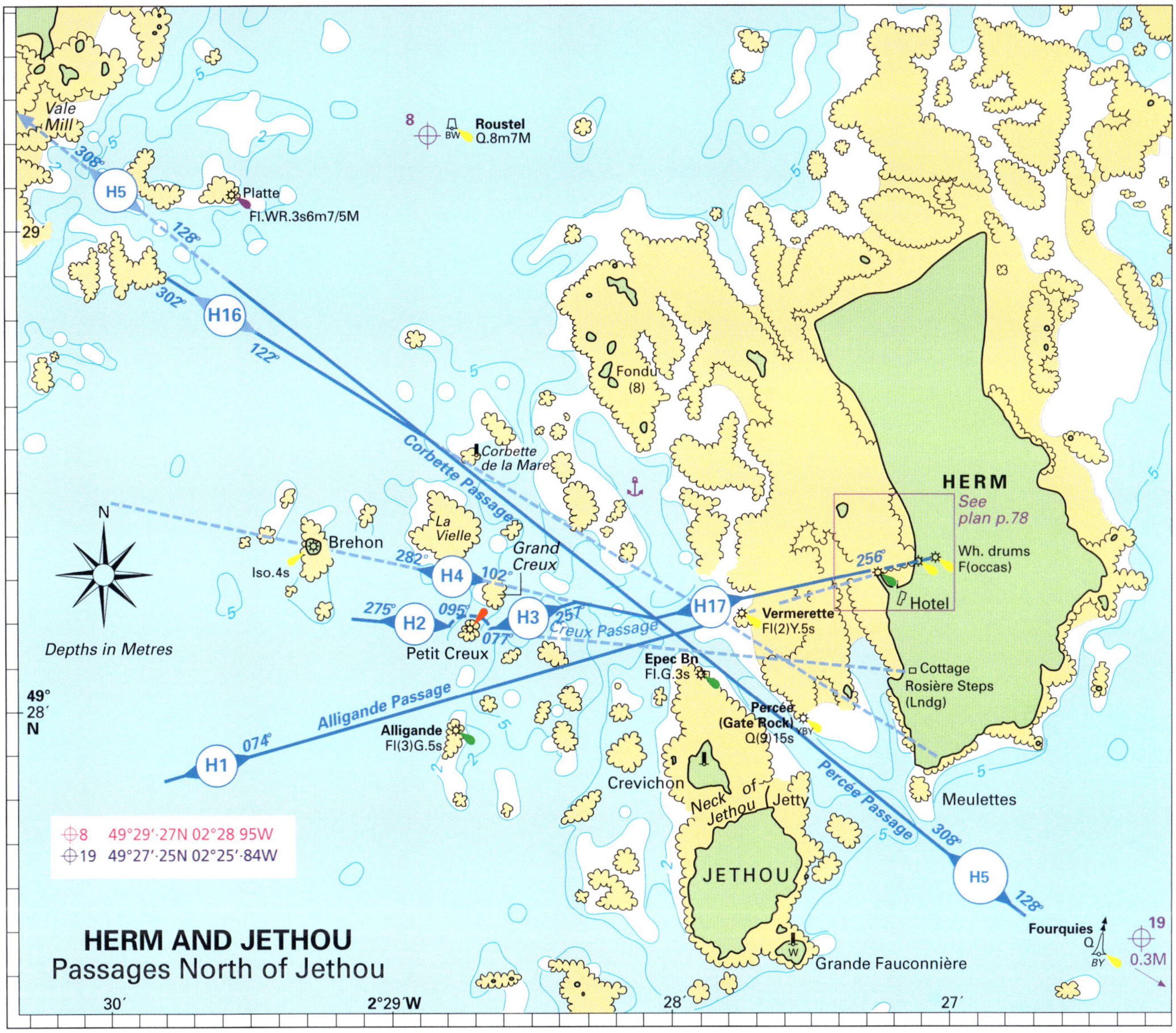

Herm

HERM AND JETHOU
Passages North of Jethou

⊕ 8 49°29'·27N 02°28·95W
⊕ 19 49°27'·25N 02°25'·84W

I. THE CHANNEL ISLANDS

CHANNEL ISLANDS, CHERBOURG PENINSULA & NORTH BRITTANY

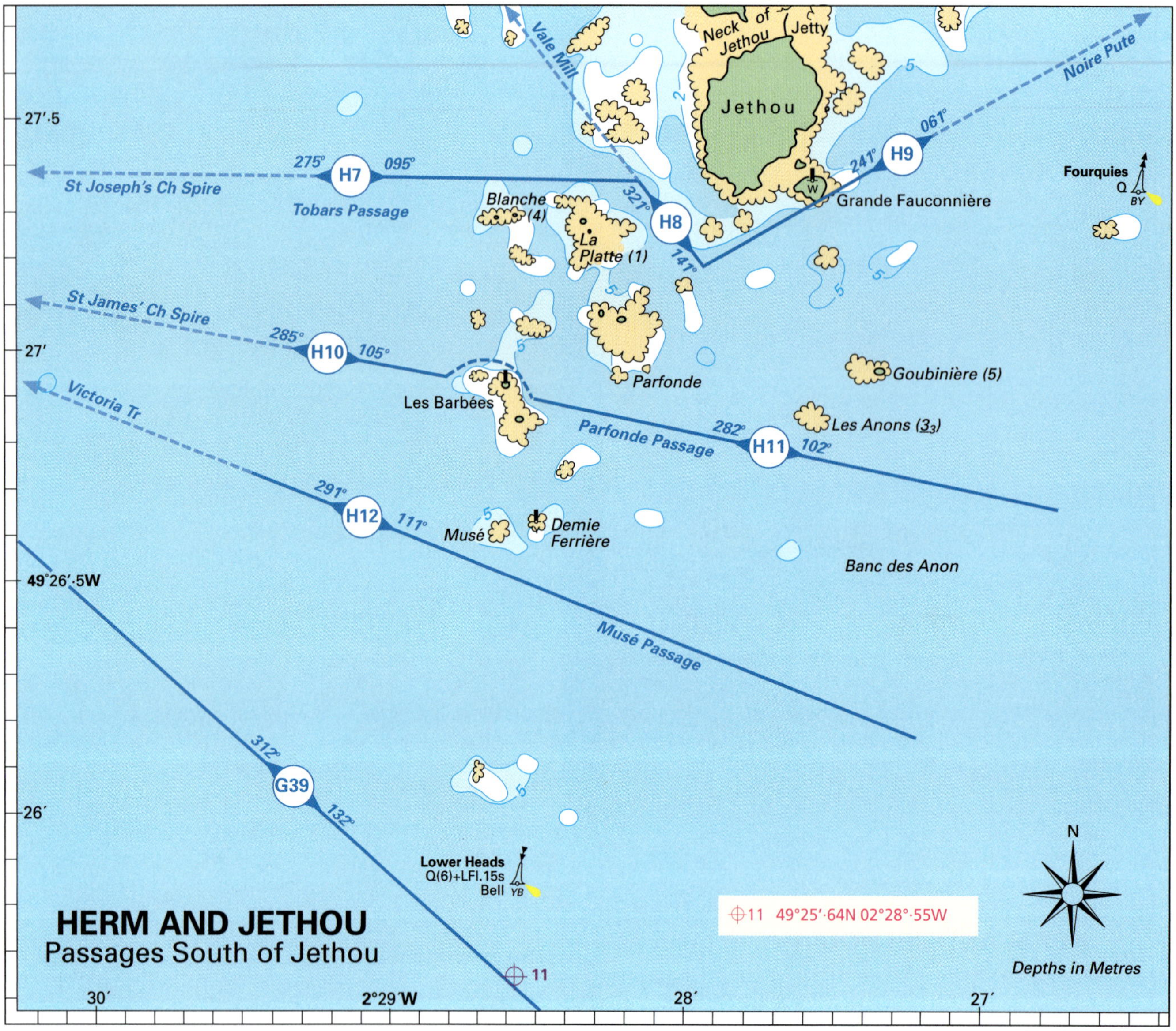

1 The Channel Islands

PASSAGES SOUTH OF JETHOU

Tobars Passage (5·0m) (W to E)

This is a more demanding passage and therefore best attempted once local knowledge has been gained. There are three doglegs and three sets of transits.

In very good visibility note that the Bec du Nez of Sark is just obscured behind the slope. When 400m short of Jethou turn to starboard and looking over the port quarter identify:

1. H7 095° Grande Fauconnière white beacon (pepper pot) touching the S slope of Jethou

2. H8 321° Vale Mill by the left (W) side of Brehon Tower

Herm

If poor visibility obscures Vale Mill, an alternative is Alligande beacon in the middle of the transit. Hold until:

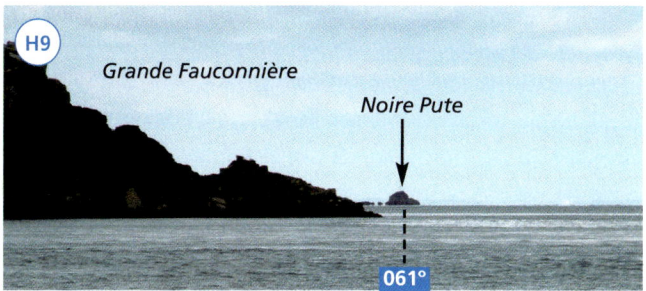

3. H9 061° *Noire Pute open of the southern slope of Grande Fauconnière*

Hold this transit leaving Grande Fauconnière 100m to Port.

Parfonde Passage (2·8m) (W to E)

H10 285° *St James' Church spire open left (S) of Castle Cornet breakwater LtHo*

After leaving Les Barbées beacon (red can topmark) 100m to starboard (note that a head 100m WNW of the bn dries 1·2m); alter to starboard to avoid Parfonde and ensure the tidal stream does not set you onto Les Anons (dries 3·3m).

Take stern transit:

H11 282° *Victoria Tower just to the N of Les Barbées beacon. Hold for 1M to clear between Les Anons and the Banc des Anons*

Musé Passage (12m) (W to E)

Take stern transit:

H12 291° *Victoria Tower over the N edge of Castle Cornet. This leaves Musé Rock 200m to the N and the beacon (M) 300m to the N*

PERCÉE PASSAGE (PASSE PERCÉE) (3·4m) (S TO N)

(See plans pages 75 and 79)

The approach to Herm from the SE and into this passage is the simplest. The key mark is Fourquies N cardinal buoy close N of the rock (dries 2·3m) that it guards. As its position can be unreliable make initial approach into the channel using:

H13 ⊕19 295° *Brehon Tower well open to the N of Crevichon*

This line will also clear Meulettes (dries 1·7m) off the S tip of Herm but on closing the 300m wide gap between Herm and Jethou the distant marks to the NW should be identified:

H5 308° *Vale Mill open twice its own width SW of Corbette de la Mare beacon*

Since the forward mark may be difficult to see from the S an alternative is to come E a bit to find:

308° *Vale Mill with Percée (Gate Rock) W cardinal lit bn seen to the E and Epec bn (with E topmark and lit) seen to the W*

CHANNEL ISLANDS, CHERBOURG PENINSULA & NORTH BRITTANY

1 The Channel Islands

See also *Passages North of Jethou. Percée Passage*.

Note Clearing marks for avoiding Meulettes (dries 1·7m) S of Herm and Tinker (dries 2·5m) NW of Jethou are described under *Rosière Steps Landing. Approaches from the S*, below.

From the northwest
(See plan page 75)

Corbette Passage (2·2m) N to S
The direct route from Beaucette Marina or St Sampson to Sark (see plans pages 72 and 75), as it leads into the Percée Passage and out to the S of Herm.
First locate Corbette de la Mare beacon at a distance of no less than 600m. Identify transit:

H16 *122° Sauzebourge Point on Herm in line with Corbette de La Mare Rock*

Pass close W of Corbette de la Mare Rock which is steep-to on its SW side then take up stern transit **H5** as for Percée Passage, described above.

Herm Harbour
49°28'·20N 02°27'·28W Pier head

Space in the inner drying harbour is extremely limited and available only to small bilge keelers and yachts with beaching legs which should moor fore and aft. It is possible to dry out alongside the pier but ferry movements take precedence.

Rosière Steps is the ferry terminal when there is insufficient water in the harbour.

Bilge keelers and multihulls will be in their element on the sandy beach east of the harbour where visitors' moorings are available on a first come first served basis. There is no charge but contributions to Flying Christine Sea Ambulance are accepted. This area can be very congested at weekends in the summer months and it is not possible to reserve a patch in advance.

Entrance
Depending on draught, there will usually be sufficient water to enter the harbour between HW St Helier–0300 and +0300. Main approaches converge on Vermerette beacon (V) 250m short of Herm pier. When the rock on which it stands (dries at 4·3m) is awash there is about 1·0m depth at the pier and its steps.

From a position 80m N of Vermerette beacon locate two white drums above the beach just N of pier end and align with **H17** *078°* (see view H1 page 74, plan and air view below).

By night
Lights available are the drums which are lit (F) throughout the summer, Vermerette beacon (Fl(2)Y.5s) and Alligande beacon (Fl(3)G.5s) (see plan page 75).

Local boats return to St Peter Port in the evening on the stern transit as above then round Vermerette beacon and into the Alligande Passage keeping one of the lit drums either side of Vermerette light.

Speed limit
6kn off beaches and in harbour area.

Herm harbour near HW

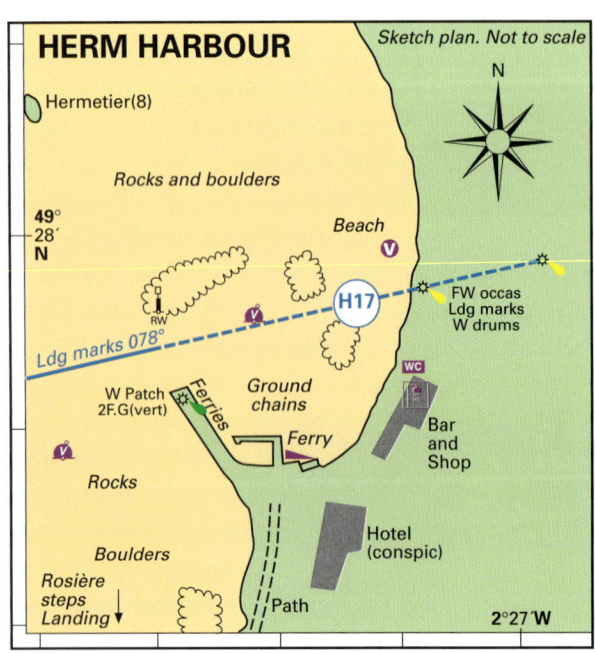

Herm

APPROACHES TO HERM HARBOUR AND ROSIÈRE STEPS

1 The Channel Islands

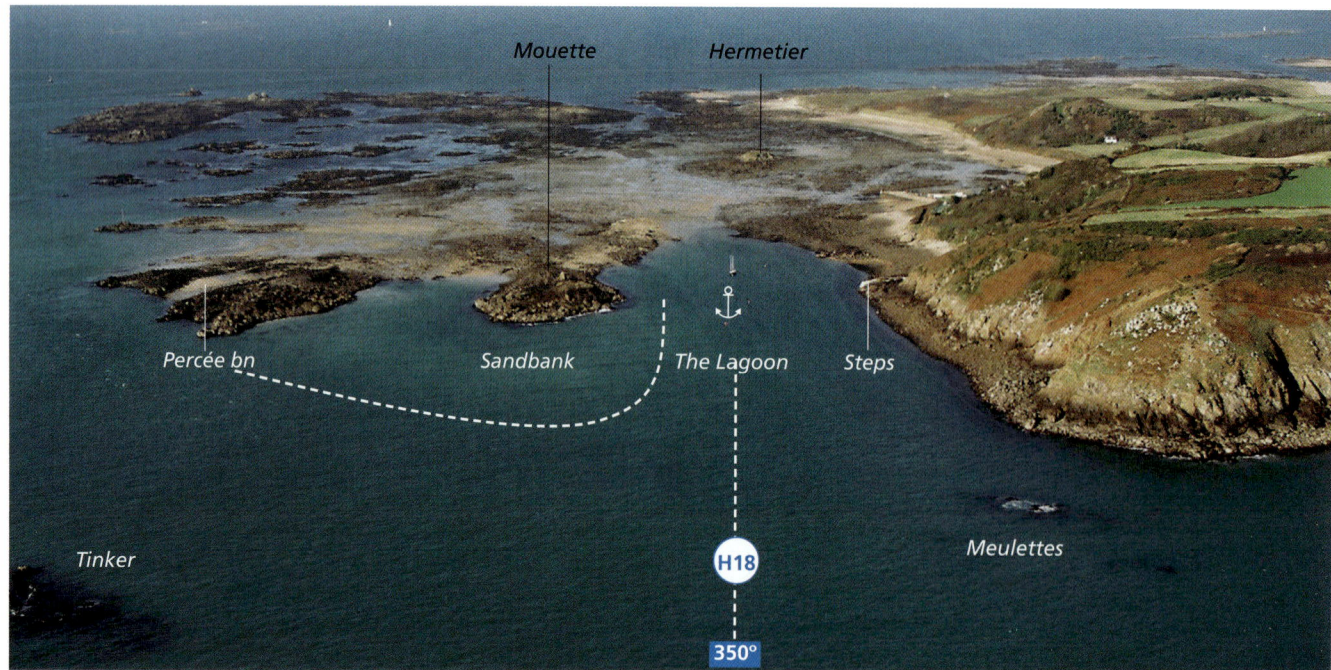

Rosière from the S at LW

Rosière Steps landing

49°27'·98N 02°27'·20W

APPROACHES

From the south

Approach is from SSE as follows:

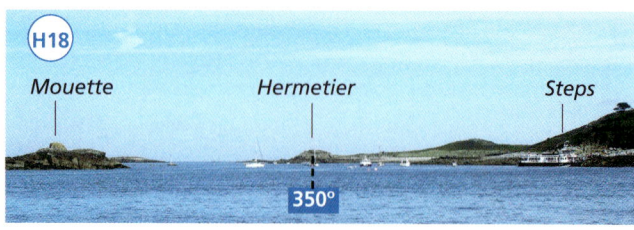

H18 350° Hermetier (Rat Island) should be well open to W of Rosière Steps (midway between the steps and Mouette (5m) to clear between Meulettes (dries 1·7m) and Tinker (dries 2·5m), see air view above.

An alternative transit for clearing E of Tinker is:

H15 327° Vermerette beacon open to the right (E) of Percée (Gate Rock) beacon

Rosière Steps Landing south of the harbour near HW

From the north

If approaching from the N in the Percée Passage avoid taking a short cut into the anchorage ('The Lagoon') by crossing the sandbank (0·3m) S of Mouette. Turn when the N point of Sark is just open of the S point of Herm.

'The Lagoon'

This is a snug anchorage in all but southerlies. Holding is good in sand and shingle if well clear of the rock and weed on the shoreline. Depths at CD are between 0·9m and 3·0m. At springs the whole area to the N dries and there is no flow in the remaining pool of water. At around HW a strong current sweeps S through the anchorage, making the short row to the landing demanding or even dangerous.

Mooring at the landing steps which are used by the ferries is not permitted, but here tenders may be manhandled ashore. A short track leads to the harbour.

80 CHANNEL ISLANDS, CHERBOURG PENINSULA & NORTH BRITTANY

Herm

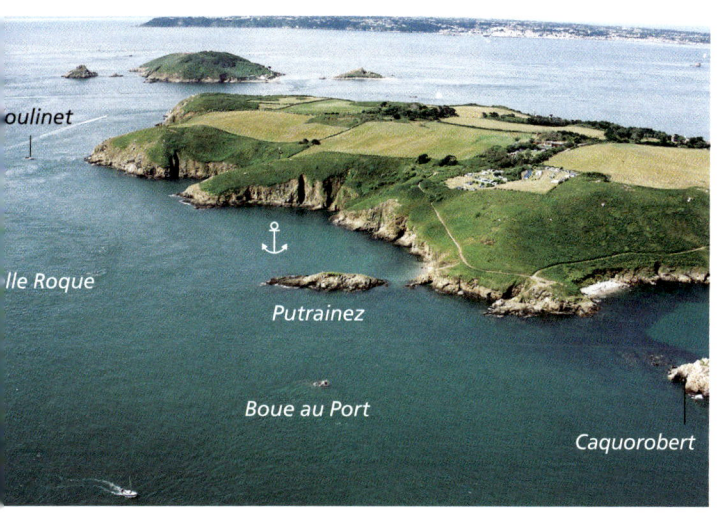

Herm east coast (HW springs)

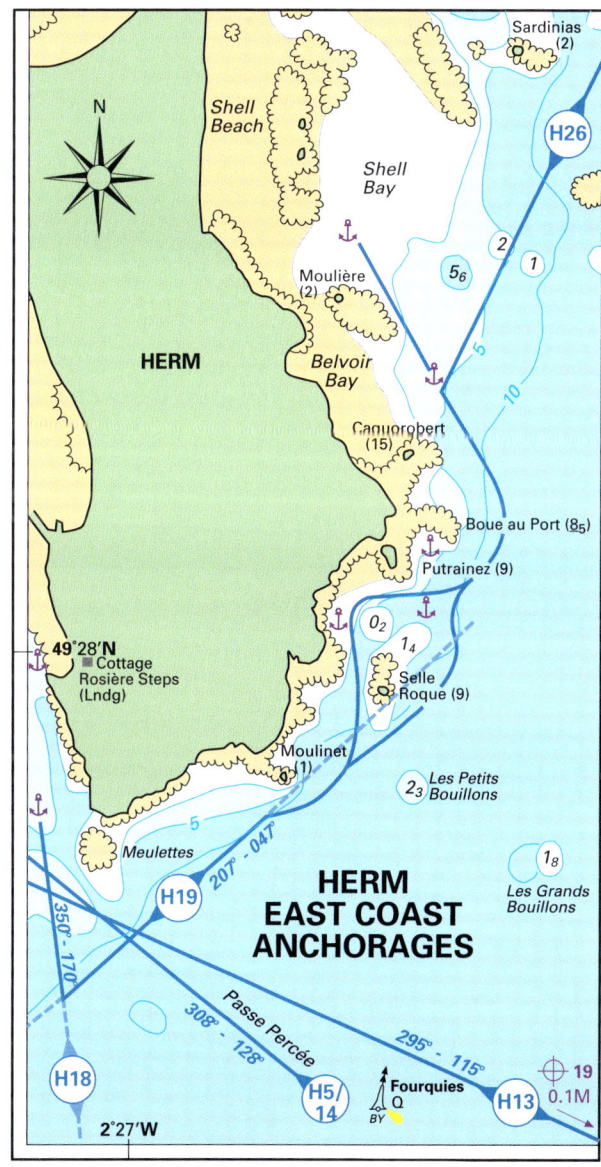

Herm east coast

APPROACHES

From the east

Approaching from the east is straightforward. The solitary rock Noire Pute (2m) situated one mile ESE of Belvoir Bay is a useful mark, but note it extends 300m N of its small beacon, so it is better to pass S of it. Guard against being set towards reefs to the NE if approaching with a N-going stream.

From the Percée Passage

Hold Transit H5 or H13 carefully and avoid wandering E of the line to risk a conflict with Meulettes. The turning point on to the E coast is reached when the conspicuous *Selle Roque (9m) is bearing 047° and open to the right (E) of Moulinet (1m)*. This is Breastmark H19 (047°):

There is the option of passing inside, with caution, or outside Selle Rocque (9m). 400M N is Putrainez (9m) with Putrainez Bay in between.

ANCHORAGES

Putrainez Bay 49°28'·05N 02°26'·39W

This is a pleasant alternative anchorage to Belvoir further N, particularly at LW.

Belvoir Bay 49°28'·40N 02°26'·34W

This bay lies between Caquorobert (Robert's helmet) (15m) in the S and Moulière (2m) in the N. This is a sheltered anchorage in W to SW winds and the holding is very good in sand. Taking the ground should be avoided as it shelves steeply and is subject to swell. The beach and small café are popular.

Shell Beach 49°28'·60N 02°26'·50W

Made of myriads of rare and exotic shells, this is entered close N of Moulière avoiding drying rocks further to the N. Watch the depth sounder carefully and anchor between Moulière and a group of rocks that dry 6·3m to the NW.

1 The Channel Islands

The north of Herm, an area of high rocks, sandbanks and rushing streams

North of Herm

Caution

Like many other Channel Island passages those N of Herm call for local knowledge, good visibility and should be taken between 2 hours either side of LW springs, when the majority of dangers are visible and currents comparatively weak. Much of the pilotage here is of the eyeball variety and should be taken at slow speed (see *Pilotage* page 73).

FROM LITTLE RUSSEL TO BIG RUSSEL BY LE BOURSEE (HAYES PASSAGE) (10m)

Le Boursée (10m) (W to E)

Best taken W to E and in visibility of at least three miles. Proceeding up Little Russel, make for a position 0·4M SW of Tautenay beacon tower (a truncated pyramid with BW vertical stripes). As a lead into the channel identify Corbette d'Amont yellow conical beacon and align this with Vale Mill (conspic) as a stern transit:

H20 264° *Vale Mill over Corbette d'Amont beacon*

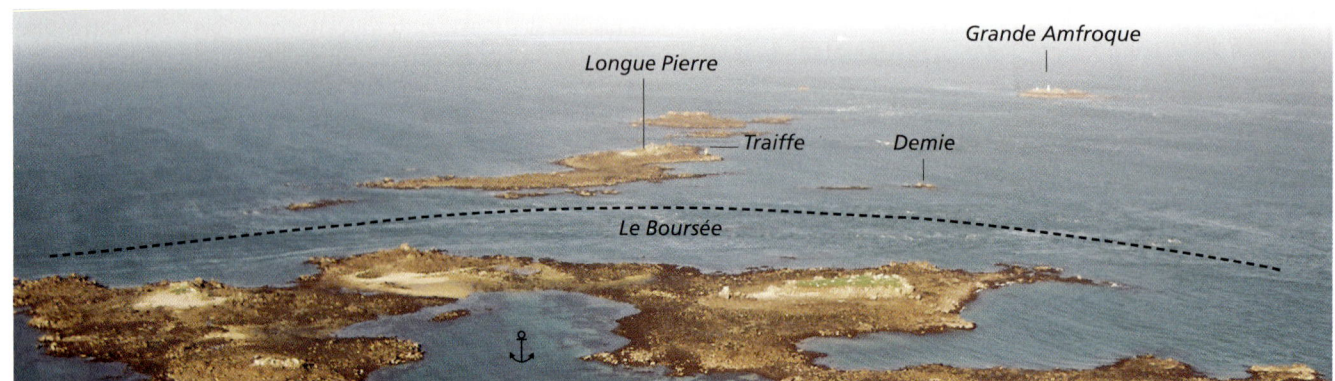

82 CHANNEL ISLANDS, CHERBOURG PENINSULA & NORTH BRITTANY

Herm

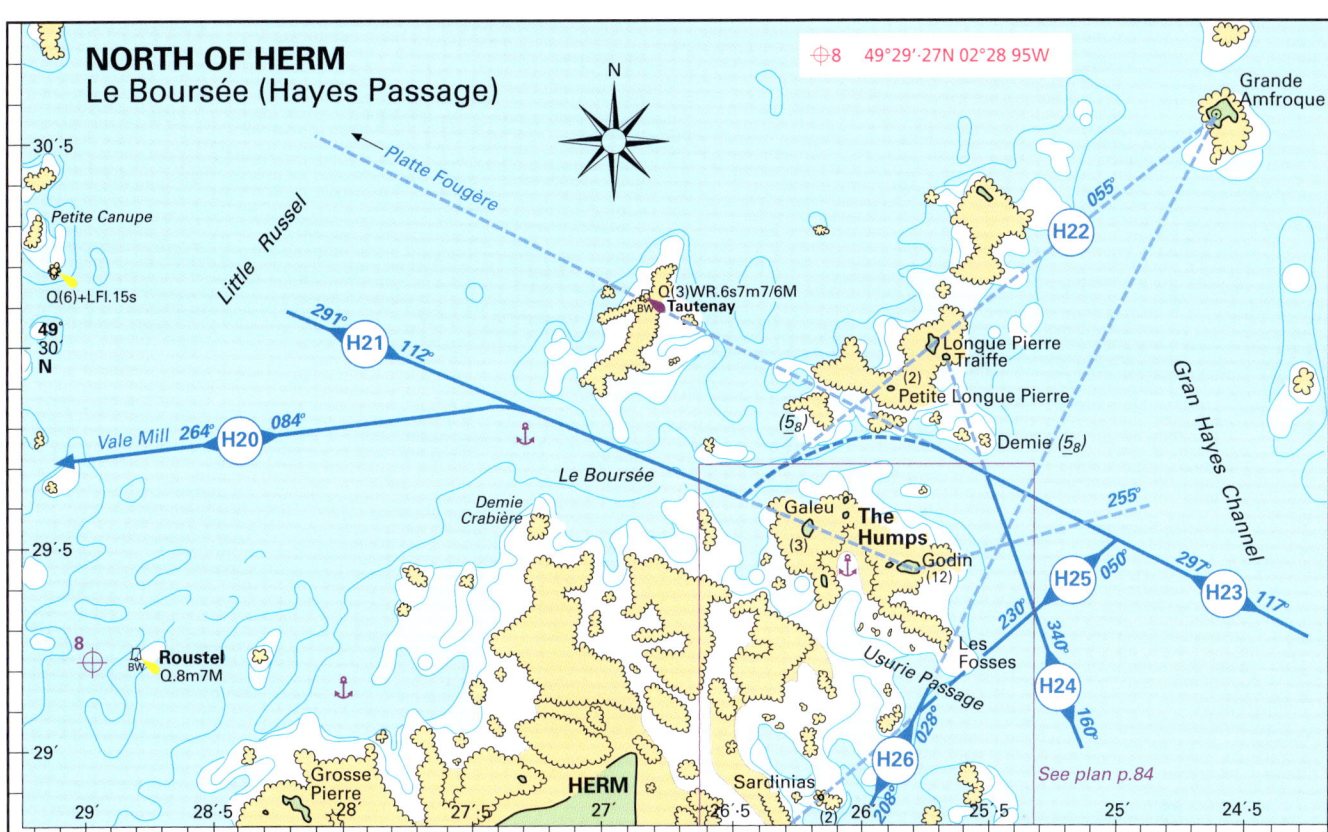

Next identify Godin (12m) and the smaller Galeu (3m) on the Humps. The transit is:

H21 112° *The highest point of Godin just to the N of the highest point of Galeu*

When 600m short of Galeu Island it is time to make the avoiding turn onto a NE heading with the next transit:

H22 055° *Gde Amfroque b/w beacon open to the N of Longue Pierre*

When 300m short of the 5·8m drying rock extending SW of Petite Longue Pierre (2m) commence a shallow turn onto an easterly heading into the middle of the 200m wide channel. Skirt the fringe of rocks to the N, keeping 100m off.

Continue the turn until:

H23 297° *Platte Fougère light tower (if visible) is just open S of Tautenay Bn Tower*

Steer to hold this transit on 297° into Big Russel until Godin bears 255°.

CHANNEL ISLANDS, CHERBOURG PENINSULA & NORTH BRITTANY

1 The Channel Islands

If proceeding S into The Humps anchorage, the following directions may be used to clear Les Fosses:

From a position 100m S of Demie (dries 5·8m) take up stern transit:

H24 340° *The left (W) edge of Demie in line with the column-like rock Traiffe*

Hold until:

H25 230° *Sardinias (2m) bears 230° and in transit with two isolated trees on the Herm skyline (see plan page 83)*

Hold until:

H26 028° *Gde Amfroque BW tower over the exposed end of Les Fosses*

Proceed as for The Humps anchorage as described:

USURIE PASSAGE AND THE HUMPS ANCHORAGE (S TO N)
49°29'·43N 02°26'·05W
(See plans page 83 and below)

The Humps anchorage

The Humps LW anchorage must rate as one of the most difficult to access in the Channel Islands and calls for local knowledge. Boat owners are requested not to land on The Humps between 1 January and 15 July to protect the important breeding sea bird colonies on these islets. The same applies to Brehon Tower.

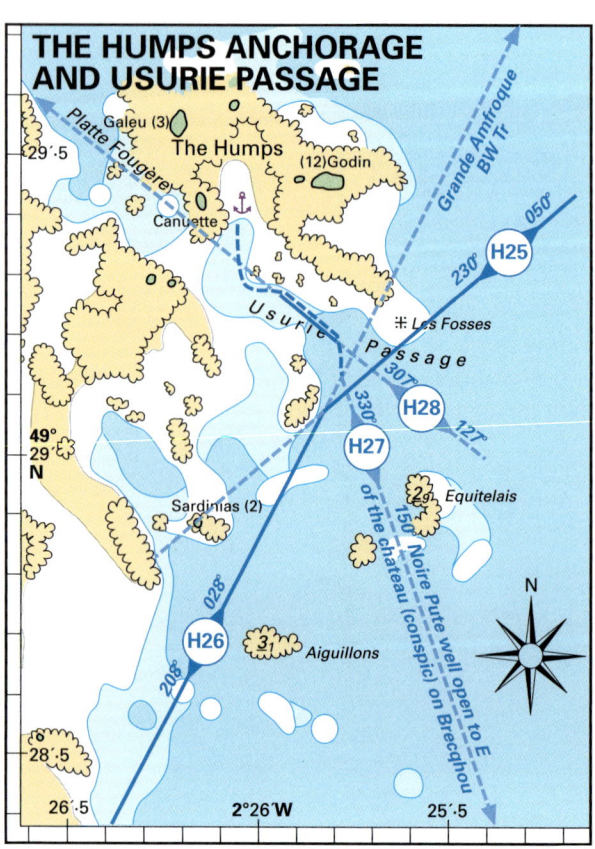

84 CHANNEL ISLANDS, CHERBOURG PENINSULA & NORTH BRITTANY

Herm

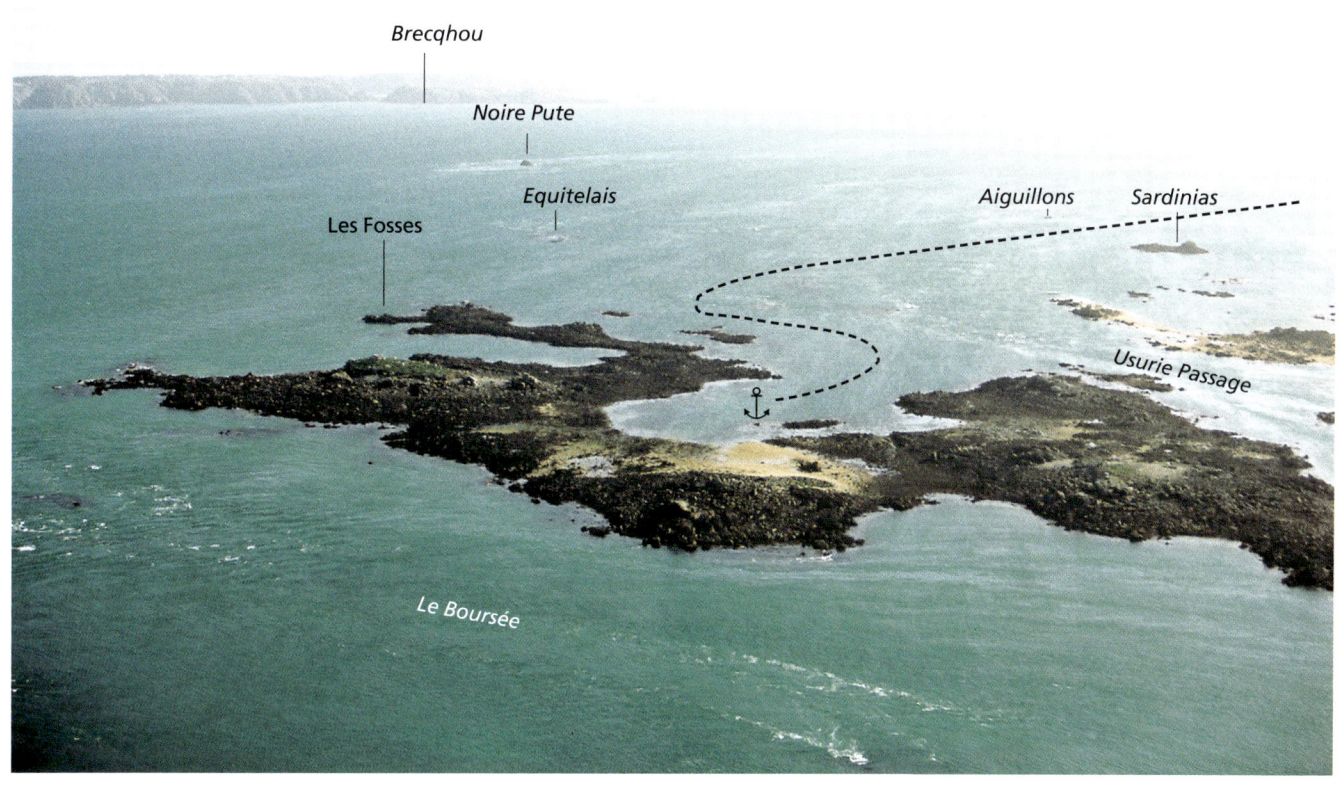

The approach to the Humps anchorage viewed from the NW above and the SE below

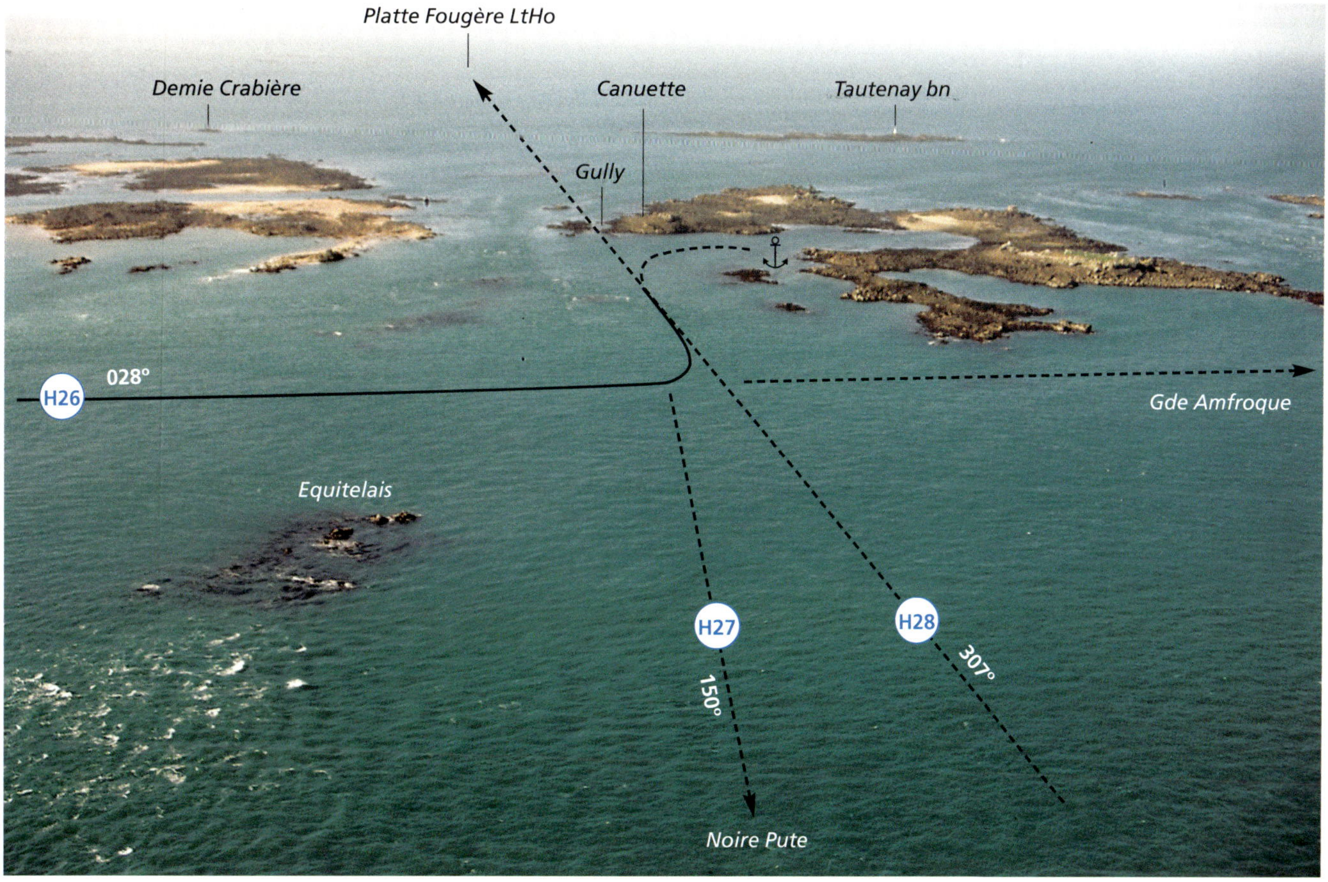

CHANNEL ISLANDS, CHERBOURG PENINSULA & NORTH BRITTANY

1 The Channel Islands

Approach from Belvoir Bay

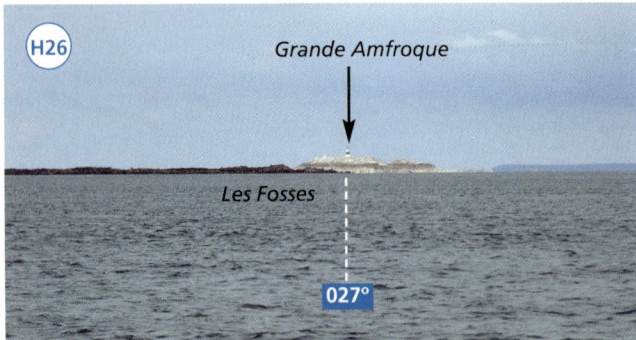

H26 *028° Grande Amfroque BW Tower over the exposed end of Les Fosses*

This is an important transit to be held carefully. It provides safe passage between Sardinias (2m) to the W and Aiguillons (dry 3·1m) and Equitelais (dries 2·9m) to the E. Next be ready for:

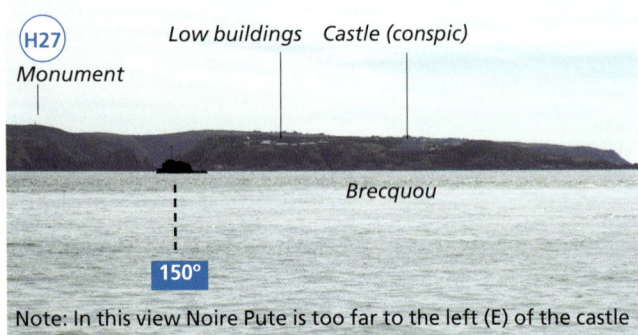

Note: In this view Noire Pute is too far to the left (E) of the castle

H27 *Identify Noire Pute (2m) to the SE on a stern bearing of 150° and well open to the E of the castle (conspic) on Brecqhou,*

Alter course to NW and ahead identify Canuette (12m). Keeping a good lookout over the bow make a small westerly diversion onto:

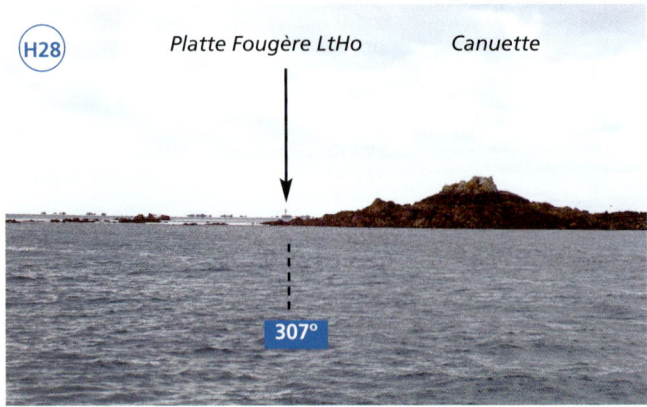

H28 *307° Platte Fougère LtHo in the gully S of Canuette*

Turn N to enter the anchorage. The bottom is sand with some weed and the holding good.

Depth in the anchorage

This is charted as 0·6m at CD. The author found 3·5m at LW when the predicted height at St Helier was 3m.

Looking N into the Humps anchorage at LWS

86 CHANNEL ISLANDS, CHERBOURG PENINSULA & NORTH BRITTANY

Sark

Local information

STD code: 01481

TRAVEL INFORMATION
Isle of Sark Shipping Company operates a regular ferry service between St Peter Port and the island. Guernsey office ℡ 724059. The French carrier *Manche Iles Express* (seasonal) links Sark with the other islands and French ports. ℡ 701316 and 01534 880756.

PORTS OF ENTRY
The official Ports of Entry into the Bailiwick of Guernsey are Braye in Alderney and Beaucette Marina, St Sampson (for commercial vessels only) and St Peter Port in Guernsey. At St Peter Port, all visiting yachts must clear in at the main harbour irrespective of which marina they moor in.

CHARTS
British Admiralty
  808 East Guernsey, Herm and Sark (1:25 000)
  3654 Guernsey, Herm and Sark (1:50 000)

  SC 5604 The Channel Islands Leisure Folio:
    9 Guernsey, Herm and Sark (1:50 000)
    12 Sark and The Big Russel (1:25 000)

Imray
  C33A Channel Islands*
    *includes plans: Creux Harbour Approaches (1:25 000), Bays of Sark (1:25 000)
  2500 The Channel Islands and adjacent coast of France Chart Pack:
    5 Guernsey, Herm & Sark (1:60 000)
    7c Sark Anchorages (1:25 000)

SHOM
  6904 Guernsey Est, Herm et Sark (1:25 000)
  7159 De Guernsey, Herm et Sark à Alderney - Bancs des Casquets (1:48 000)

RADIO FACILITIES
Sark Moorings VHF Ch 10
Guernsey Coastguard (west coast) VHF Ch 20
Jersey Coastguard (east coast) VHF Ch 82

NAVIGATIONAL AIDS
None

USEFUL CONTACTS
Duty harbourmaster ℡ 07781 135611, harbourmaster@gov.gg
Sark Mooring Sites: Andy Learman Mobile 07781 106065
Sark Vistor Centre ℡ 832345 www.sark.info
Doctor: Sark Medical Centre ℡ 832045

SUPPLIES AND SERVICES
Water from tap (Creux) within harbour area.
Showers at the N end of the tunnel.
Petrol and diesel (cans) via harbourmaster.
Bar, restaurant, provisions, bank walk or tractor up the hill to the village.
Bike hire Sark Cycle Hire ℡ 07781 454375
Hotels Stocks Hotel ℡ 832001
  La Sablonnerie Hotel ℡ 832061

Sark from the south

1 The Channel Islands

SARK Main Approaches
Depths in Metres

WP	Lat	Long
18	49°28'·21N	02°24'·25W
20	49°27'·50N	02°22'·67W
21	49°27'·50N	02°21'·60W
22	49°26'·95N	02°19'·34W
23	49°25'·35N	02°16'·65W
24	49°24'·88N	02°20'·20W
25	49°24'·17N	02°20'·68W
26	49°23'·63N	02°23'·39W
27	49°25'·25N	02°24'·40W

La Coupée *Jane Russell*

Sark

Introduction

Sark, the peaceful Channel Island, is a unique place where you can step back in time to an age before cars – there are none. For generations it has managed to retain its independence from the outside world and despite the annual deluge of visitors there is little to disturb the population of some five hundred, other than farm sounds and the call of sea birds. Sark has been declared the world's first 'dark sky island' in recognition of the exceptional blackness of its night sky.

The island's early history is sketchy. To the Romans it was Sargia. Under the Normans it was held sacred by its monks but was soon abandoned to hermits due to the Black Death and frequent raids by pirates. Sark's modern history starts in 1565 with the arrival of Helier de Carteret, Seigneur of St Ouen in Jersey. He was granted the island by Queen Elizabeth I on condition that it was continually inhabited and capable of defence. This he managed with the aid of 40 families, 35 from Jersey and the remainder from Guernsey. The feudal government they established remains largely intact to this day, the present Seigneur enjoying some of the rights and privileges of his predecessors. Sark is part of the Bailiwick of Guernsey but has its own parliament known as the Chief Pleas.

Rising to 116m (380ft), Sark is hard to miss. A rather sinister aspect from seaward belies the charm of the countryside on top of the plateau. As a place for the crew to stretch their legs it is unsurpassed. Secure the tender at one of the many landing places, scale up a narrow cliff path and walk or cycle the tracks in some of the cleanest air in the realm. For the less energetic, the island may be explored by horse and carriage and there is a tractor-drawn trailer that hauls visitors up the hill from La Maseline Harbour. The village offers basic shopping, two banks, a post office and a good scattering of hotels, restaurants and pubs. The lack of public lighting makes cliff paths hazardous after dark without a torch.

Little Sark to the S is joined to the main island by a spectacular causeway known as La Coupée.

Brecqhou Island

This island off the W coast is separated by the narrow Gouliot Passage. It is privately owned and landing is strictly prohibited. In recent years a conspicuous fort style residence has been built on the NW corner. As of 2011, Sark residents can apply to make an escorted visit to Brecqhou. Further details are available from Sark Island Hotel Reservations (✆ 832832).

Harbours and anchorages

The bays and coves beneath Sark's cliffs offer sheltered anchorage in offshore winds. Visitors' moorings have been laid in Havre Gosselin (W coast) and Grève de la Ville (E coast). There is no charge for use of moorings but donations will be accepted at Sark Visitor Centre.

The drying harbour of Creux on the E coast was built by the early settlers. It claims to be the smallest in the world and is certainly one of the wonders of Sark. It can only be used by small, shallow-draught boats (and service boats) and with caution.

The adjoining harbour of La Maseline is used by ferries and small cargo vessels. It is unsuitable for yachts.

TIDAL INFORMATION
Tidal levels referred to chart datum
La Maseline Jetty 49°26'·00N 02°20'·60W

MHWS	MLWS	MHWN	MLWN
8·9m	1·1m	6·6m	3·4m

High water at Sark is approximately 10 minutes after St Helier.

Positioned in the middle of the fast-moving stream that ebbs and flows through the Alderney Race just 20 miles to the NE, Sark's streams are vigorous, running approximately SW on the last of the ebb and first of the flood and NE on the last of the flood and first of the ebb. Slack water is around half tide. The shape of the island induces counter streams and reversals round the island which are too complex to show on the Tidal Stream Atlas in the appendix. For example, in the Gouliot, between Sark and Brecqhou, it may touch 7 knots on the top of a big spring tide. Outside Creux and Maseline harbours, the Goulet on the ebb reaches 6 knots.

Inbound to the E coast harbours from Guernsey, the decision whether to go N or S depends on the tide. The fastest streams run approximately NE around high water and SW around low. Thus it follows that from the Bec du Nez to the Grand Moie it is slack at high water and from Sercul to Grande Grève it is slack at low water. Therefore head N coming from the Big Russel at high water but S near low water. When leaving from Sark harbours towards St Peter Port, between half tide up to just before high water, go S. When clear of Sercul, bear away for the Lower Heads buoy. At most other times go N but if it is high water or soon after, circle the Bec du Nez and keep close to the Banquette Bay shore. Keep 200m off the N of Brecqhou, leave Moie Batard 100m to port, then head W across the Big Russel. Naturally, wind direction must be considered in any inshore pilotage around Sark. The high cliffs form a welcome lee but also cause downdrafts and accelerated gusts (see *Appendix. Tidal diagrams* page 370).

Approach and pilotage

There is nothing difficult in arriving within a mile or two of Sark but relevant coastal features should be identified before closing the coast. Initially key rocks tend to be illusive against the backdrop of cliffs with which they merge. Sark waters are not navigable after dark.

Pilotage round the island can be an awesome experience for newcomers. Many channels lie within 0·3M of the shore and rocks are passed close enough to disturb the cormorants. However, inshore waters are generally deep and life will be easier if arrival coincides with half tide, when streams are more or less slack all round the island and many charted dangers are safely covered.

Ashore

The only way to see the island is on foot, with a bike or by horse and cart. Not all bays have footpaths ashore and apart from the harbours, the easiest landings for the village are at Dixcart Bay and Grande Grève.

Sark Information Centre in The Avenue provides an excellent official map of footpaths and landmarks. It is worth visiting La Coupée, the causeway between Sark and Little Sark, and the formal gardens of La Seigneurie. This is the official residence of the Seigneur of Sark.

There are several restaurants ashore specialising in sea food. Dixcart Bay Hotel (✆ 832015) and Aval du Creux Hotel and Restaurant (✆ 852036) and La Sablonnerie Hotel, Little Sark (✆ 832061) are recommended.

If taking an evening meal ashore, be prepared to return to the yacht in total darkness – there is no street lighting!

1 The Channel Islands

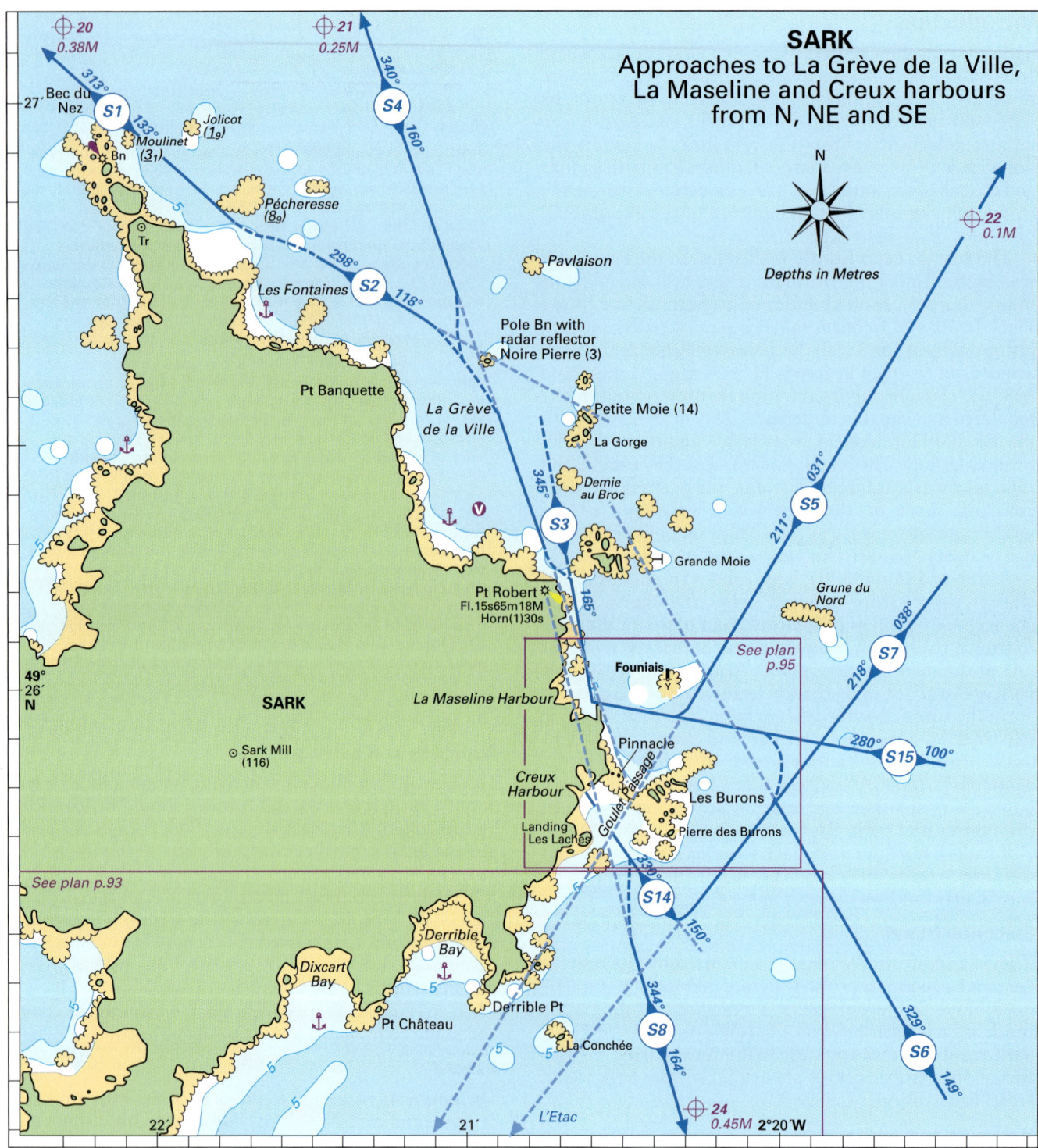

SARK Approaches to La Grève de la Ville, La Maseline and Creux harbours from N, NE and SE

⊕20 49°27'·50N 02°22'·67W
⊕21 49°27'·50N 02°21'·60W
⊕22 49°26'·95N 02°19'·34W
⊕24 49°24'·88N 02°20'·20W

Sark

East coast
(Creux Harbour, La Maseline Harbour, the anchorages)

Approaches

FROM THE NORTH
(See plan page 90)

Inside Pécheresse (dries 8·9m)

The run in from the N on initial transit S1 (⊕20) commences NNW of Bec du Nez. This point is steep-to and overfalls can be expected to the NW of it with wind against tide. The channel N of La Maseline Harbour is narrow (100m wide in one place) and should not be attempted at LW Springs. Coming from Guernsey or the Big Russel the passage is best taken at HW when the stream will be slack between Bec du Nez and the Grande Moie.

S1 133° (⊕20) 133° W side of Grande Moie in line with Banquette Point clears Pécheresse (dries 8·9m)

With Pécheresse abeam, identify the black above-water rock Noire Pierre (3m) and alter to port for:

S2 118° N face of Noire Pierre in line with N face of Petite Moie

When 200m off Noire Pierre (pole bn with radar reflector) steer for the gap between Point Robert (with the lighthouse) and Grande Moie.

The dangers in the narrow gap under the LtHo are cleared by S3:

S3 165° Pinnacle Rock of the Goulet just open of the end of La Maseline Jetty. Inner side of jetty visible.

If too open you will be over a patch of Grande Moie drying 1·6m.

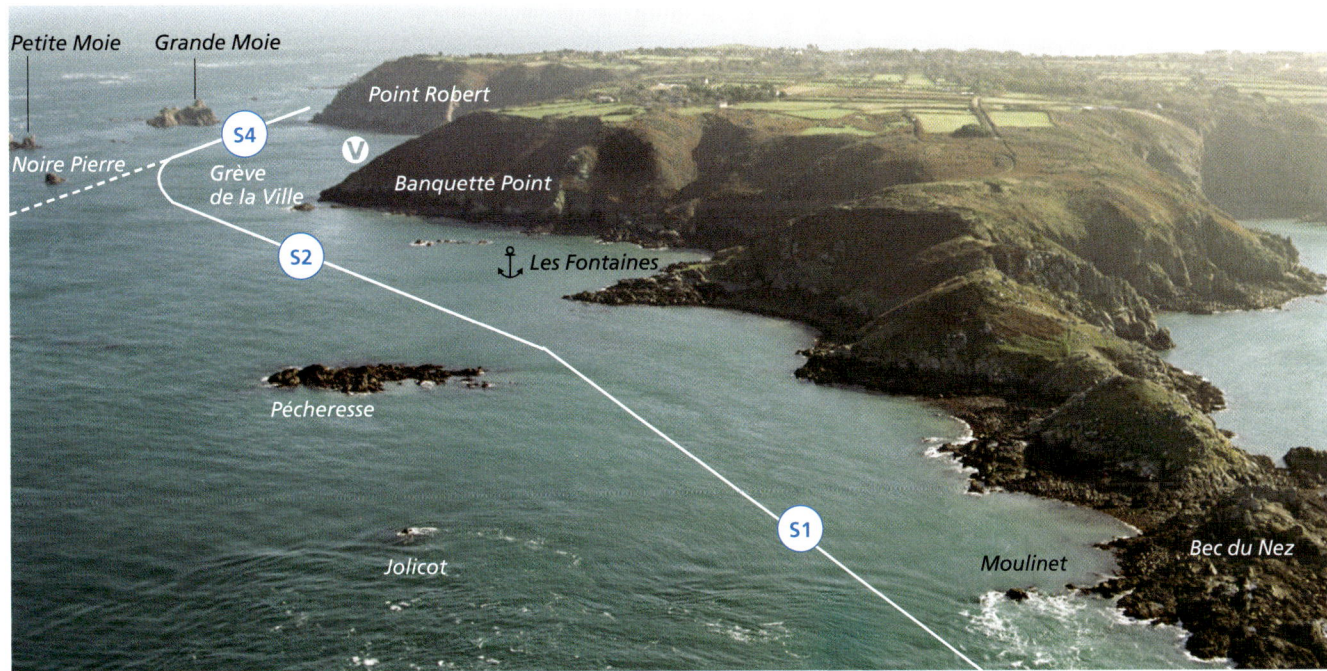

Sark's northeast coast looking south at LWS

CHANNEL ISLANDS, CHERBOURG PENINSULA & NORTH BRITTANY   91

Outside Pécheresse (dries 8·9m)

This easier approach, particularly if under sail, avoids overfalls off Bec du Nez and passes E of Pécheresse leaving Bec du Nez 0·5M to starboard. When St Martin's Pt (Guernsey) is open to the right (N) of Bec du Nez find:

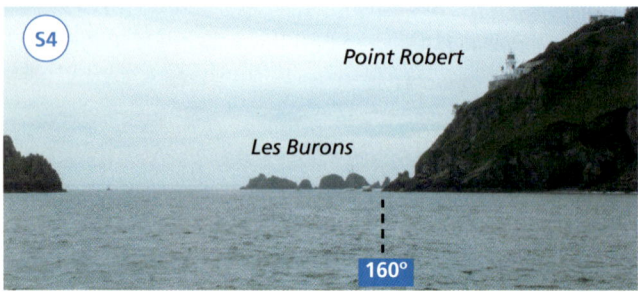

S4 160° (⊕21) All Les Burons are open of Point Robert

Hold this transit but leave Noire Pierre to port. Continue as for *Inside Pécheresse* as above.

FROM THE NORTHEAST

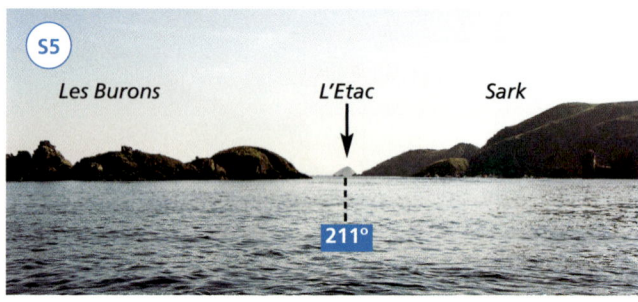

S5 211° (⊕22) L'Etac between Les Burons and Sark

This approach from the NE can be used for either La Maseline or Creux Harbour, passing N of Grune du Nord (dries 3·7m).

In the harbour approaches identify Founiais beacon (dries 6·7m) 300m ENE of the pierhead. This can be passed 100m either side (see Transit S15). (For La Maseline entry and information see *La Maseline Harbour. Entry* page 96.)

Goulet Passage (1·2m)
(See plans pages 90 and 95)

If intending to proceed S to Creux Harbour it is necessary to route outside Les Burons. It is prohibited to pass S through the drying Goulet Passage between Creux Harbour and Les Burons so, after passing Point Robert and Grande Moie or on leaving La Maseline take up stern transit:

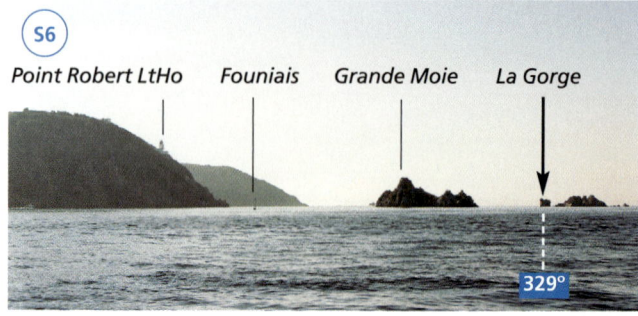

S6 329° La Gorge with its 'head' looking west open E of la Grande Moie by a distance equal to the distance between the two peaks of la Grande Moie

This transit will clear between Les Burons and the shallows with overfalls to the east. When Les Burons bear due W identify La Conchée (3m) and take up:

S7 218° L'Etac well open to the left (E) of La Conchée

This transit will clear drying rocks off Burons. It can be maintained if proceeding to Creux Harbour or to Baleine Bay anchorages.

FROM THE SOUTHEAST

There are several options if approaching from this direction, typically from Jersey. ⊕24 and ⊕25 are recommended safe-water positions. See plan page 88.

From N to S these are:
1. Transit S6 – described above – skirts S of the troubled waters W of Blanchard cardinal buoy and onto the approach to La Maseline (S 15).
2. Transit S8 ⊕24 Outer approach to Creux Harbour:

S8 344° ⊕24 Pt Robert LtHo in line with Creux Harbour tunnel

The lighthouse will dip below the headland when less than about 1 mile off. (For Creux Harbour entry and information see under *The Harbours. Creux Harbour*, below.
3. Transit S9 (⊕25) into Baleine Bay aimed at Dixcart Bay.

Sark

S9 340° ⊕25 *White house above Dixcart Bay over the westward slope of Point Chateau*

Note The transit shown on BA chart 808 is unreliable as Sark Mill is no longer conspicuous.

For entry to either of the harbours break off this transit before turning into Dixcart and head NE to join S8, S14 or S15. La Conchée (3m) may be passed either side. See plan page 90.

FROM THE SOUTH

An approach towards the south of the island is best made at low water when marks are visible and from St Helier HW–0500, the stream will run NE for nearly nine hours from Sercul Rock (5m) off Little Sark to Creux Harbour.

BA chart 808 shows the shallows and disturbed water SE of Little Sark and care should be taken not to be swept into Les Vingt Clos (dries 1·9m) or Balmée (dries 6·7m), when the stream is running.

Outside (E of) L'Etac (See plan page 88)

The easiest option is to approach well outside all dangers. Pass 0·5M S of L'Etac then steer 060° to reach Transit S9 340° for Dixcart Bay, or S8 344° Outer approach to Creux Harbour or S6 329° for La Maseline.

Inside (W of) L'Etac (See plans pages 88, 90 and below)

There are two passages, both of which require positive identification of key marks and precise pilotage.

1. **Outside Pierre du Cours S10 (⊕26)**
   Starting from a position 0·75M off the S point of Little

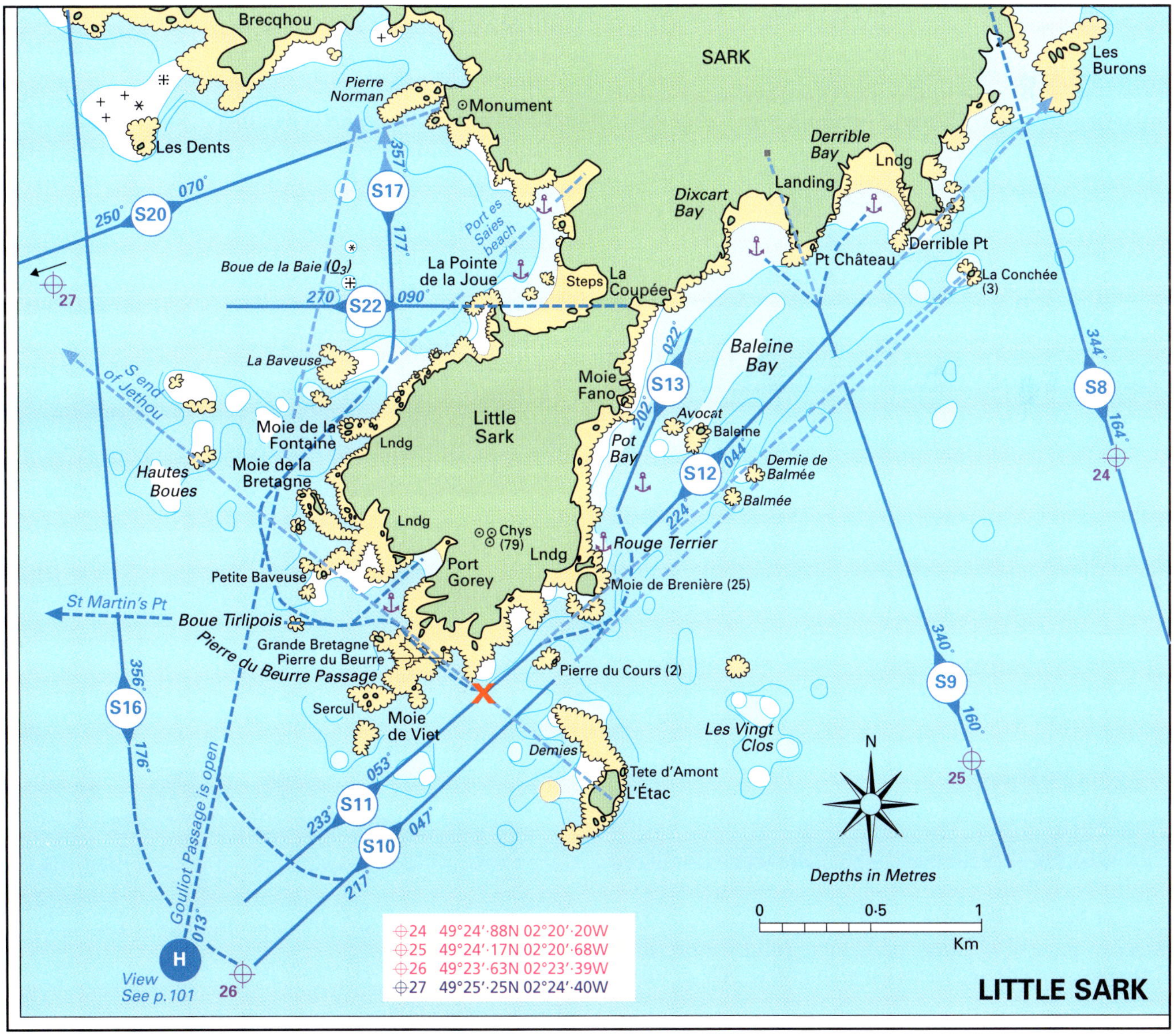

I. THE CHANNEL ISLANDS

⊕24	49°24'·88N 02°20'·20W
⊕25	49°24'·17N 02°20'·68W
⊕26	49°23'·63N 02°23'·39W
⊕27	49°25'·25N 02°24'·40W

LITTLE SARK

CHANNEL ISLANDS, CHERBOURG PENINSULA & NORTH BRITTANY

1 The Channel Islands

Looking NE over L'Etac at the south end of Sark

Sark bearing 030° make a positive identification of Pierre du Cours (2m) and La Conchée (3m) 2M beyond and SE of Derrible Point. Then take up S10.

S10 *047° ⊕26 La Conchée well open to the E of Pierre du Cours and Balmée (dries 6·7m) (if above water)*

When 200m from Pierre du Cours leave it close (50m) to port in order to keep well clear of the Demies that extend NW from l'Etac. Steer out to leave Balmée to port or take the inshore passages described under *Passages across Baleine Bay* below.

2. Inside Pierre du Cours S11

S11 *053° La Conchée and Balmée (if above water) on the edge of Moie de Brenière (25m)*

Steer to pass W of Pierre du Cours (2m) by more than 150m to avoid drying rocks extending W to NW of Pierre du Cours. When the rock bears S, steer E to avoid rocks S of Moie de Brenière. When Balmée is seen open E of La Conchée, come round to the N, leaving Moie de Brenière 200m to port.

PASSAGES ACROSS BALEINE BAY

Passage N to Dixcart Bay may be made inside Balmée (dries 6·7m) and Demie de Balmée (dries 3·4m) with transit:

S12 *044° Les Burons chimney in the 'V' of Derrible Pt (see air view below)*

Note that a shelf extends W of Balmée and there are drying heads 100m to the S of Baleine.

Passage N inside Baleine (6m) and Avocat (dries 3·7m) may be made using stern transit:

S13 *202° Daylight just showing through the hole in Moie de Brenière*

Beware of Avocat which may be covered and rocks drying 5m extending 100m E from Moie Fano.

Sark

The harbours

Creux Harbour

Location 49°25'·80N 02°20'·60W Pierhead

The harbour dries out completely and is prone to surge. It is therefore suitable for small shallow draught boats and only in fair weather. Surge enters the harbour in SE'lies. Access is HW St Helier ± approximately 2 hours. Anchoring outside the harbour, Les Laches, is prohibited.

Entry

On closing the harbour on Transit S8 as described above under *East coast. From the SE* transfer to entry transit S14.

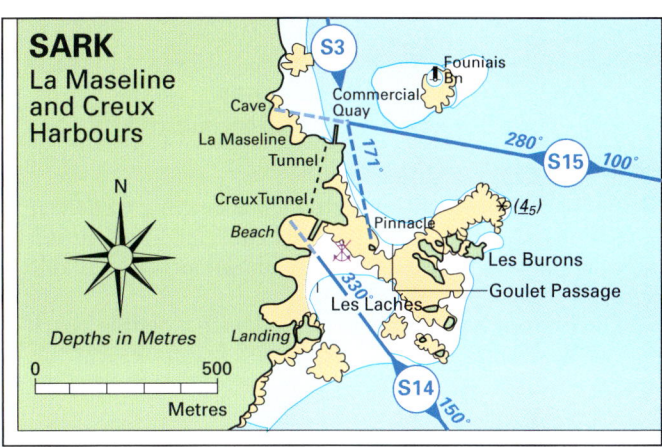

S14 *330° The beach at the back of the harbour fills the entrance*

Note This will only just clear drying rocks S of Les Burons so it may be necessary to borrow a bit to port.

Creux Harbour

La Maseline and Creux Harbour at LWS

CHANNEL ISLANDS, CHERBOURG PENINSULA & NORTH BRITTANY

1 The Channel Islands

Depths

At half tide there is 4m at the pierheads and 3m at the embarkation steps just inside the entrance on the N side. Entry can be made about 2 hours either side of HW.

Mooring

Dry bow to E wall and stern to anchor keeping well clear of embarkation steps at S end of the pier at all times. Drying out alongside may be possible subject to available space.

The bottom is generally firm sand with a pebble beach on the W side opposite the entrance.

La Maseline Harbour
49°25'·97N 02°20'·57W Jetty head

This deep-water commercial harbour is connected to Creux Harbour by a tunnel cut through the cliff.

Entry

Preferred entry is from NE, which provides a clear view of any activity in the harbour. If entering from E, beware of cross-set. Either way, give Founiais (dries 6·7m) with its beacon a clearance of 100m. Beware of drying rocks that extend NE from Les Burons (see plan page 95). A useful transit for an easterly entry or departure is shown below.

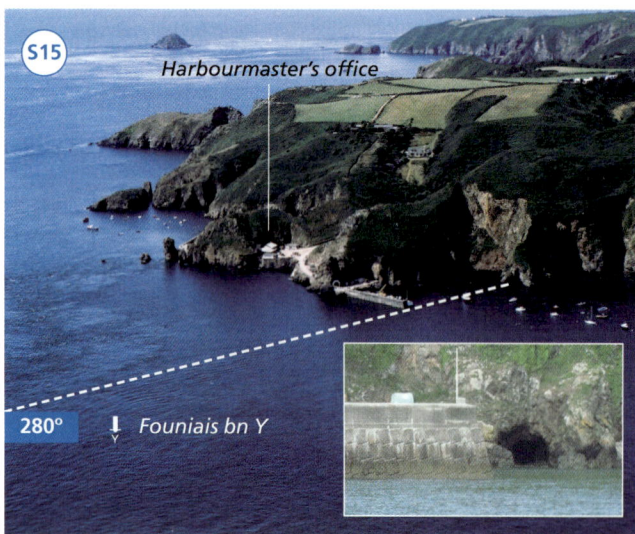

S15 280° *Cave just open of the pierhead*

Depth

Least depth is 4m.

Mooring

The quay is reserved for commercial vessels but coming alongside briefly is possible when it is clear. The harbourmaster may grant permission to lie alongside overnight but the vessel should not be left unattended and should be ready to move at any time.

Anchoring NW of the jetty is possible with harbourmaster's approval, but keep well clear of ferry movements. It can be uncomfortable in all but light winds from between NW and SE. Northwesterlies produce a swell.

Notes: East coast anchorages (N–S)

(See plans pages 88 and 90)

Caution

With a wind shift or a turn in the tide a tranquil anchorage can become exposed and anchors may drag. It is inadvisable to leave an anchored yacht unattended or out of effective control anywhere off Sark.

LES FONTAINES 49°26'·78N 02°21'·62W

Sand and shingle with fair holding. Anchor well clear of reefs with La Gorge of La Petite Moie on the edge of Banquette Point.

GREVE DE LA VILLE 49°26'·57N 02°21'·05W

Good shelter in southwesterlies. Anchor close in to stone steps in 4–7m. Visitors' moorings available. Good access to village by cliff path.

DERRIBLE BAY
49°25'·41N 02°21'·07W

Good holding in firm sand anywhere in the bay but swell can penetrate, making it uncomfortable. Used by ferries. Good access to shore by zig-zag path.

DIXCART BAY
49°25'·33N 02°21'·48W

Dixcart Bay looking S *Jane Russell*

(For approach and entry see *East coast approaches. From the SE.*) Good holding in firm sand. Popular with French and Jersey yachts due to good access to hotels, restaurants and shops. Swell can penetrate in southwesterlies.

POT BAY AND ROUGE TERRIER (LITTLE SARK)
49°24'·78N 02°21'·87W

Protected fair weather anchorages under high cliffs with a landing and cliff path to the top where there is an excellent hotel/restaurant La Sablonnerie ☎ 01481 832061. Mooring reserved for customers. Holding is good in sand.

Sark

West coast anchorages
(See notes page 101)

Approaches from the west

N of Brecqhou (Banquette Bay)
An approach to Sark between Bec du Nez and Gouliot Passage presents no major navigational obstacles. There are two small bays, Saignie Bay in the N and Port à la Jument in the S. See *Notes: W coast anchorages (N–S)* page 101.

South of Brecqhou (La Grande Grève)
Sark's most frequented anchorages within easy reach of St Peter Port are located in La Grande Grève. These are described in (N–S) order below and under *Notes: W coast anchorages (N–S)*.

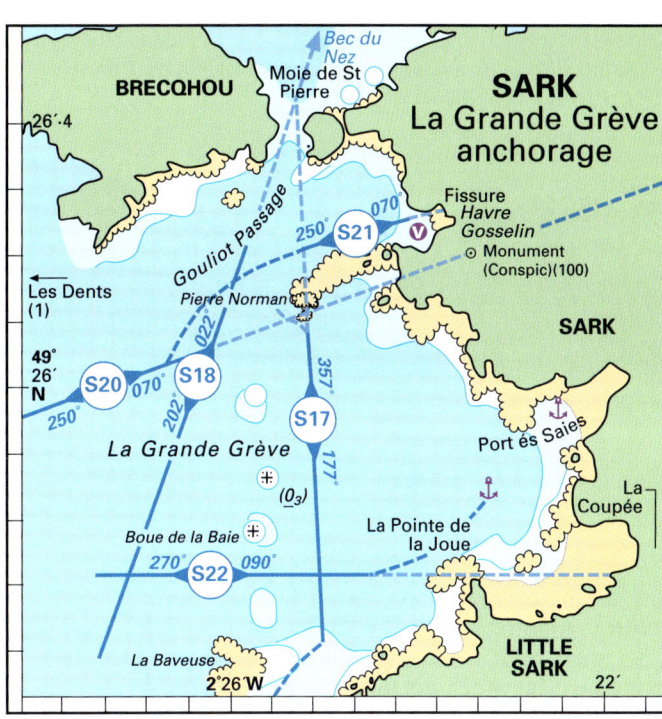

GOULIOT PASSAGE (3·6m)
Between Banquette Bay and La Grande Grève is the Gouliot.

Shooting through this narrow passage between Sark and Brecqhou has long provided Channel Island yachtsmen with a bit of excitement. On spring tides the stream courses through the gap at 5–7 knots, but it should be taken at half tide when the stream is slack. Stemming it head on can prove slow, if not impossible. Consult the *Appendix. Tidal diagrams*.

The passage is clean on both sides with a least depth of 3·6m. It is important to observe the transits as described below in order to keep clear of isolated drying rocks and shoal areas lurking at either end of the passage.

Passage north
(See plan above and page 88)

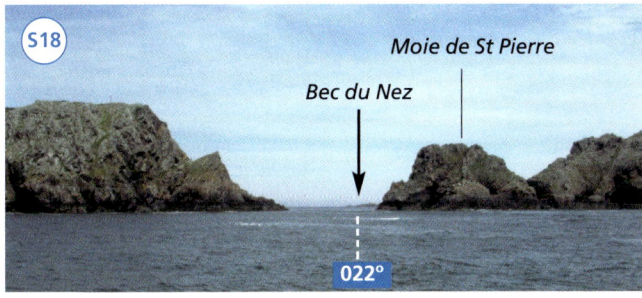

S18 022° *Bec du Nez just seen through Gouliot Passage*

This will clear dangers all the way to Bec du Nez. If proceeding to Herm do not turn W until well past Boue de Grune Gouliot (0·8m) NE of Brecqhou.

Passage south
(See plan page 88)

S19 186° *Moie de la Bretagne open of Moie de St Pierre*

TO HAVRE GOSSELIN S20 ⊕27 S21
49°25'·77N 02°22'·68W

Approach from the SW using recommended ⊕27. In the absence of any boats in the cove, it is easily located by reference to the conspicuous Pilcher Monument (100m) on the skyline to the S. To clear Les Dents (1m) S of Brecqhou the distant approach is made on transit S20:

S20 070° ⊕27 *Pilcher Monument in line with Sark Mill*

Note Sark Mill is no longer conspicuous.

CHANNEL ISLANDS, CHERBOURG PENINSULA & NORTH BRITTANY

1 The Channel Islands

Closer in, a further danger to be avoided is Pierre Norman (drying 8·8m) on the outer SW corner of Havre Gosselin. The transit available to clear this is:

S21 *070° Gosselin Fissure over to the left of Pierre Norman*

With Gouliot Passage opened up as above (S18) come to port to round Pierre Norman by 200m. This transit above will also clear the drying rock (2·6m) S of Brecqhou on the W side of Gouliot Passage.

TO PORT ES SAIES
(View 1 page 101)
49°25'·35N 02°22'·43W

Approach is straightforward with the bay opened up but adequate clearance should be given to isolated dangers in the bay as described above (see also *Approaches from the S. Inside La Baveuse*, below).

TO LA GRANDE GREVE S22 090°
(E of La Coupée)
49°25'·38N 02°22'·59W

This approach passes between La Baveuse (drying 7·6m) and Boue de la Baie awash at LW, to the N of the line. The marks for this transit are shown at top of right-hand column:

S22 *090° S edge of of La Coupée in line with Pointe de la Joue*

When 400m from Pointe de la Joue turn to port and come to anchor NE of the point. Landing can be made on the beach and there are steps to the top of the cliff. Not for the fainthearted!

Approaches from the south
(See plan page 88)

W of Les Hautes Boues

This is the easiest route passing outside all dangers. From a position 1·2M SW of L'Etac identify La Givaude (12m) to NNW off the westernmost tip of Brecqhou then take up the transit shown below.

S16 *356° Grande Amfroque (17m) open W of La Givaude clears all dangers to W of Sark*

Pierre du Beurre Passage

98 CHANNEL ISLANDS, CHERBOURG PENINSULA & NORTH BRITTANY

Sark

Break off this line for La Grande Grève or Havre Gosselin anchorages as required (see *West coast anchorages. Approaches from W*).

Inside La Baveuse
(See plans pages 93, 97 and below)

The passage S of Sercul (5m) and then inside La Baveuse (dries 7·6m) is difficult. Start from a position 0·8M SW of Sercul ⊕26 at LW when the stream is slack and marks are visible. Identify Transit S10 (page 94) and make a slow turn to NW. When the peak of Moie de St Pierre (at the Gouliot) bears 013° and is open its width to W of Moie de la Bretagne, steer on this transit with care, leaving Boue Tirlipois (drying 1·1m) 200m to starboard (see View H under *Pierre du Beurre Passage* below).

When Petite Baveuse (6m), which extends westward at LW, is 250m abeam, steer to leave Moie de la Bretagne (17m) at least 100m to starboard. Then come round to starboard, steering to leave Moie de la Fontaine (17m) at least 100m to starboard.

At this point proceed NE towards Port Es Saies to pass between La Baveuse and the shoreline. Entry to La Grande Grève anchorage is described above under *Approaches from the West*. If proceeding N across the bay to Havre Gosselin anchorage (see under *Sark Anchorages* below) beware of an isolated danger in the bay, Boue de la Baie (awash at CD), and its neighbour (dries 0·3m). Use the transit line S17 as follows to clear E of this (and see plans pages 93 and 97 and below).

S17 *357° Pierre Norman (dries 8·8m) in line with the middle of Gouliot Passage*

PIERRE DU BEURRE (BURRE) PASSAGE (APPROX. 3·6m) (E–W)
(See plan below and air view page 98)

Caution
Little Sark is no place to be at HW due to powerful streams, swell and a lack of reference points. This inshore passage that elbows its way through the rocks around the bottom of Little Sark is best attempted at LW Springs in quiet weather, good visibility and with sound knowledge of the area or a local expert aboard. There is about 4m in the passage at CD. At one point the passage is only 20m wide. Pilotage is by rock recognition rather than transits. Marks must be positively identified.

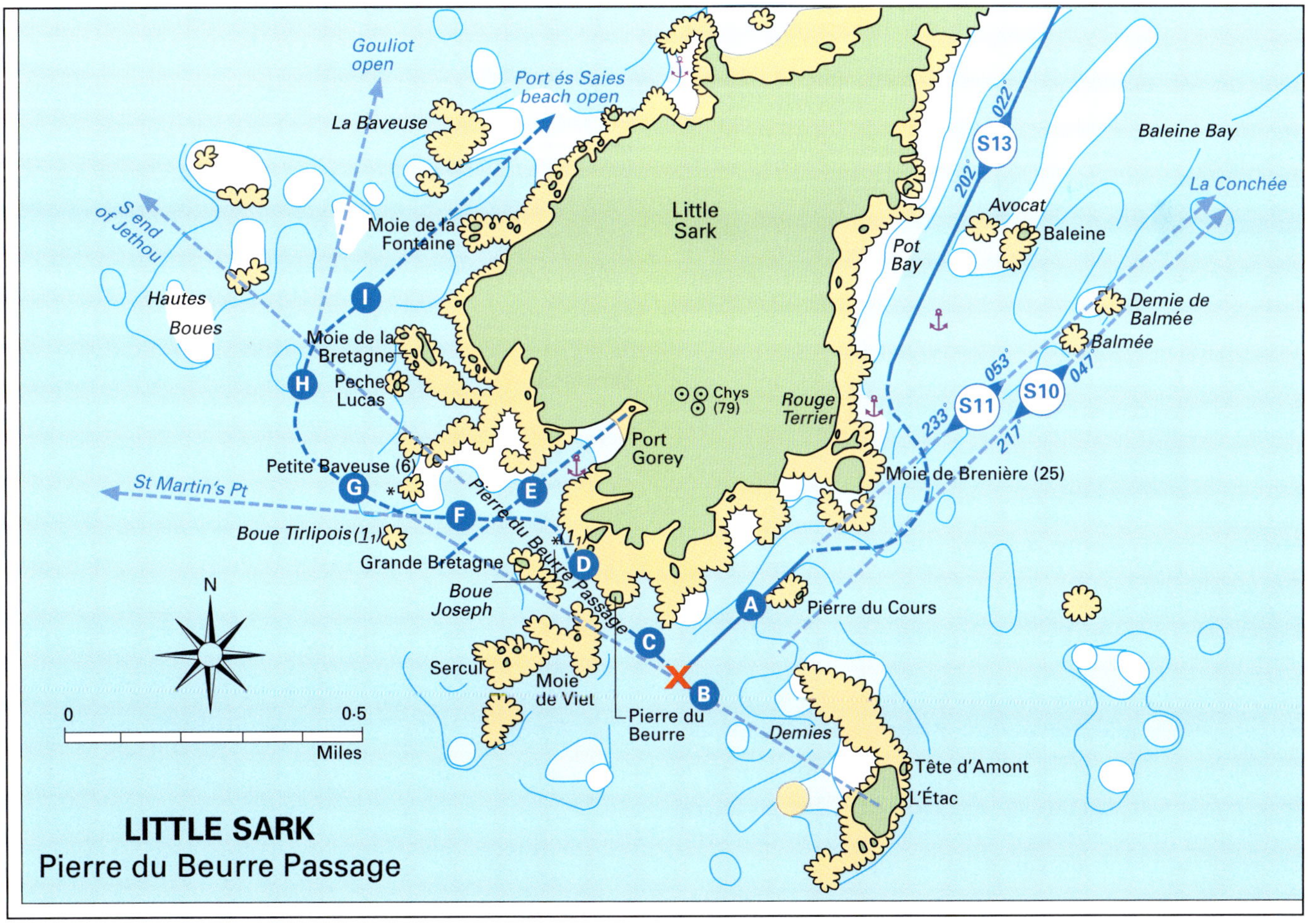

LITTLE SARK
Pierre du Beurre Passage

1 The Channel Islands

When the author made this passage from east to west, timed over LW with a predicted height of 2·5m at St Helier a minimum depth of 3·6m was found.

Starting from Dixcart Bay, a position 200m E of Moie de Brenière was reached by the inshore route across Baleine Bay (S13). This is described under *Approaches to the East Coast. From the South.* Alter heading towards Pierre du Cours and hold until the beach SW of Moie de Brenière comes into view, then take up:

S11 *053° La Conchee and Balmée on the East edge of Moie de Brenière*

In view A above and on the plan, Balmée is almost closed behind the E edge of Moie de Brenière and La Conchée is not visible. This is favoured by Sark pilot instructor Dick Adams as it gives more clearance of the drying extension on the W edge of Pierre du Cours.

Hold until 180m SW of Pierre du Cours which is the turning point into the passage (marked with a red X on the plan). Identify key marks as shown in View B.

Enter with View C on a NW heading:

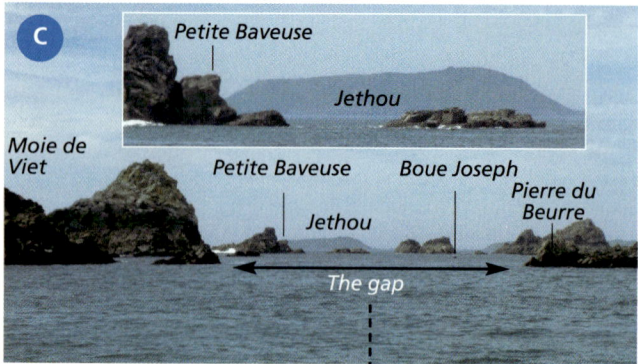

S end of Jethou is in the 'bottom step' of Petite Baveuse

This transit will lead through a narrow gap between Pierre du Beurre (dries approximately half tide) on the Sark shoreline and Moie de Viet (10m) to the S.

With Pierre du Beurre abeam identify the small isolated Boue Joseph (dries approximately 1·2m) lying midway between Grande Bretagne (18m) and the Sark shoreline.

Pierre du Beurre

Before Grande Bretagne comes abeam make a small alteration to starboard to within 20m of the shore in order to leave Boue Joseph 20m to port (View D). Then return to a northwesterly heading with C until:

The beach at Port Gorey is open

Now alter course to port towards the southern point of Guernsey:

The southern point of Guernsey

100 CHANNEL ISLANDS, CHERBOURG PENINSULA & NORTH BRITTANY

Hold this heading until, looking astern, Mark G is identified:

The chimney of Moie de Viet (10m) is on the peak of L'Etac

Turn to starboard onto a NW heading to hold these marks for clearing between Boue Tirlipois (dries 1·1m) to the S and Petite Baveuse (6m) to the north (see air view on following page).

Next look N for View H:

The Gouliot Passage is open

Turn onto a NNE heading to leave Les Hautes Boues to port and Moie de la Bretagne (17m) with Piquillon and Peche Lucas SW of it 100m to starboard.

When Moie de la Bretagne is on the quarter identify and head towards Port es Saies beach to the NE (View I):

The beach at Port es Saies is open

Moie de la Fontaine should be left 100m to starboard. Pass midway between La Baveuse (dries 7·6m and 0·2m) and the shoreline.

With Pointe de la Joue abeam either take up the leading marks S22 090° for entry to Grande Grève anchorage (see *Approaches from the S. Inside La Baveuse*) or proceed N using Transit S17 357° to clear E of dangers in the bay (see *Approaches from the W. To La Grande Grève*).

Sark Mill

Notes: West coast anchorages (N–S)

(See plans pages 88, 97, 99)

SAIGNIE BAY
49°26'·53N 02°22'·10W

Sand and shingle with fair holding. Anchor in 3–5m. Exposed to NW.

PORT À LA JUMENT
49°26'·17N 02°22'·42W

Sand and shingle with fair holding in 3m. Exposed to NW but potentially sheltered from SW'lies by Brecqhou. Path up to hotel at top.

HAVRE GOSSELIN
49°25'·77N 02°22'·68W

Popular small deep-water cove exposed to W and SW. Can be swelly particularly at springs when it is not recommended for overnight stay. Landing is in SE corner with 299 steps and steep zigzag path the top. The reward is an outstanding view. Most of the anchorage is now taken up by visitors' moorings. For entry see *West Coast anchorages* above.

PORT ES SAIES
49°25·44N' 02°22·22W

A sandy anchorage with good holding but exposed to W. A steep cliff path.

LA GRANDE GREVE
49°25'·38N 02°22'·59W

A snug anchorage in easterly winds under La Coupée. The bottom is fine sand and shingle and there are steep railed steps from the beach up to La Coupée. An alternative is Port es Saies in the N corner of the bay with good holding in sand. For entry see *West coast anchorages. Approaches from the west* above.

PORT GOREY
49°24'·54N 02°22'·80W

A narrow cove prone to HW swell and strictly a fine weather LW anchorage. Holding is good in sand at the entrance but there are boulders further in. The crumbling remains of a 19th-century silver mine are conspicuous on the skyline above the small beach. Landing is possible on S side with path to the top and a hotel, La Sablonnerie ☎ 01481 832061. Mooring reserved for customers.

1 The Channel Islands

Port Gorey

Approach
Starting from position 0·5M WSW of Sercul, approach with the beach open on a bearing of 050° and with the conspicuous mine chimney on the starboard bow. This will leave Grande Bretagne (18m) 100m to starboard (see *Pierre Du Beurre Passage, View E*).

Departure
Make good a course of 230°. If proceeding into the Big Russel, hold to pass between Grande Bretagne (18m) to the SE and Boue Tirlipois (dries 1·1m) to the NW. You are clear of all dangers when L'Etac bears E and Grande Amfroque is open W of La Givaude on 356° (see S16 on page 98 and air view above). If proceeding N, follow directions under *West Coast anchorages. Approaches from the S above.*

Jersey

Local information

① STD code: 01534

TRAVEL INFORMATION
There are regular flights to many UK and continental airports and ferry links with Portsmouth, Poole and Weymouth in the UK and Carteret, Granville and St Malo on the French coast.

Air
British Airways ① 711711
Flybe ① 498284
Aurigny Air Services ① 744735
Blue Islands ① 08456 202122

Sea
Condor Ferries ① 0845 1242004
Manche Iles Express ① 766566

PORTS OF ENTRY
Official Ports of Entry into the Bailiwick of Jersey are St Helier and Gorey

CHARTS
British Admiralty
   1136 Jersey – North Coast (1:25 000)
   1137 Approaches to Saint Helier (1:25 000)
   1138 Jersey – East Coast (1:25 000)
   3278 Saint Helier (1:6 000)
   3655 Jersey and Adjacent Coast of France (1:50 000)

   SC 5604 The Channel Islands Leisure Folio:
      13 Jersey (1:50 000)
      14 Approaches to Saint Helier (1:25 000)
      15a Saint Helier (1:6 000)
      15b Pierres de Lecq or Paternosters (1:25 000)
      16 East Coast of Jersey (1:25 000)

Imray
   C33A Channel Islands*
      includes plan: Gorey (1:20 000)
   C33B Channel Islands and North Coast of France*
      includes plans: St Helier Approaches (1:30 000), St Helier Harbour (1:12 500)
   2500 The Channel Islands and adjacent coast of France Chart Atlas:
      9 Jersey & Les Écrehous (1:75 000)
      10 Approaches to St Helier (1:30 000)
      10a St Helier Harbour (1:15 000)
      11 East Coast of Jersey (1:25 000)

SHOM
   6937 Jersey - Côte Nord (1:25 000)
   6938 Abords de Saint Hélier (1:25 000)
   6939 Jersey - Côte Est (1:25 000)
   7157 De la Pointe d'Agon au Cap de Carteret - Passage de la Déroute (1:48 400)
   7160 De Jersey à Guernsey (1:48 300)
   7161 Des îles Chausey à Jersey - Plateau des Minquiers (1:48 500)

RADIO
Jersey
Jersey Coastguard and VTS VHF Ch 82
① 447705
MMSI 002320060
Hrs of watch: 24
VHF Ch 16, 82, 25, 67 (small craft distress and safety working)
DSC Ch 70

Weather bulletins 0645, 0745, 0845 (LT), 1245, 1845, 2245 UTC
Strong wind and gale warnings: On receipt and at 0307, 0907, 1507, 2107 UTC
(See *Introduction. Sources of weather information* page 8)

Navigation warnings On receipt and at 0433, 0833, 1633, 2033
Link calls: Ch 25 only
VHF Direction Finding Vessel transmits and receives bearing from Station on Ch 16 or 82
Note The aerial position for D/F purposes is 49°10'·85N 02°14'·30W Lookout tower Point La Corbière

St Helier Pierhead Control Ch 14 Hours of watch: 24.
Range: approx 5 miles

St Helier Pierheads Information Service Transmits wind speed and direction at St Helier Pierhead Control every 2 minutes Ch 18

NAVIGATIONAL AIDS
Racons (Radar beacons):
Demie de Pas light tower 49°09'·00N 02°06'·15W (T) 10M

USEFUL CONTACTS
Emergency ① 112 or 999
Jersey Coastguard and Sea Rescue ① 447705
St Helier Marina, Elizabeth Marina and La Collette Yacht Basin
   ① 447708
St Helier VTS ① 447722
Jersey Harbours ① 447788 www.jersey-harbours.com
   Email jerseyharbours@jersey-harbours.com
Boat hoist office ① 447773
Jersey Tourism ① 859000
Customs and Immigration ① 448000

YACHT CLUBS
St Helier Yacht Club, South Pier St Helier ① 732229/721307
Royal Channel Islands Yacht Club, St Aubin ① 741023/747783
St Catherine's Sailing Club www.scsc.org.je

SUPPLIES AND SERVICES
For general supplies see under separate marinas.

Chandlery, bottled gas, charts, sail repairs
South Pier Marine ① 711000
IS Marine ① 850090
Jackson's Yacht Services ① 743819

Duty free supplies Boatfayre, Albert Quay ① 888852 / 07797 859592 boatfayrelimited@hotmail.fr

Car and bike hire Zebra ① 736556

Marine electronics
South Pier Marine ① 711008
Aquamarine Electronics ① 07797 722359

Fuel
Victoria Pier Fuel Berth ① 07700 347313
Marine 24/7 Fuel ① 525247
Elizabeth Marina, PC Boat Sales ① 737537/07797723090
Gorey Marine Fuel Supplies ① 07797 742384

Corporate Events
Jersey Sailing ① 747738

I The Channel Islands

JERSEY AND LES ECREHOUS
Main Approaches

TIDAL INFORMATION
Tidal levels referred to chart datum
St Helier 49°11 N 2°07 W

MHWS	MHWN	MLWN	MLWS	MTL
11·0	8·1	4·1	1·4	6·1

St Helier is a standard port for the Channel Islands and it is more accurate if all tidal calculations are based on St Helier rather than Dover when cruising in this area. HW St Helier is approximately HW Dover −0500. With spring tide means of 11·0m and 1·4m Jersey can claim the greatest tidal range of the islands. Equinoctial spring tides can be awesome, when height predictions modified by strong winds or extremes of barometric pressure may cause flooding and the exposure of vast areas of seabed.

Areas noted for rough seas and overfalls in strong wind against tide conditions are Grosnez point (with the Rigdon Bank) off the NW corner and Point La Corbière and Noirmont Point off the SW corner.

The *Tidal Atlas* shows the flood setting eastward and the ebb westward along the south coast. On the N coast the flood is generally SE and the ebb NW. The E coast presents something of an anomaly which is indicated on the large-scale tidal diagrams in the *Appendix* but not in the *Tidal Atlas*. The flood sets generally S offshore while inshore it is northerly for half the period. There is a similar contra-flow towards the latter part of the ebb. Inshore eddies also occur on the SW corner.

Jersey

WP	Lat	Long
28	49°18'·94N	02°18'·13W
29	49°15'·91N	02°05'·38W
30	49°14'·32N	02°00'·75W
31	49°13'·40N	01°58'·51W
32	49°10'·80N	01°59'·10W
33	49°07'·70N	01°57'·14W
34	49°07'·34N	02°01'·13W
35	49°08'·00N	02°06'·50W
36	49°09'·14N	02°16'·00W
37	49°10'·53N	02°16'·48W

I. THE CHANNEL ISLANDS

CHANNEL ISLANDS, CHERBOURG PENINSULA & NORTH BRITTANY

1 The Channel Islands

St Helier

Introduction

The Bailiwick of Jersey, which includes Les Ecréhous and Les Minquiers reefs, is the southernmost territory of the British Isles, and being the closest to France it is not surprising that the Normans left their strongest influence here. Their laws and system of government form the backbone of Jersey law and the Norman French they spoke still survives. The exploits of Jersey's seafarers between the 16th and 19th centuries are legendary and well documented in the Maritime Museum at St Helier Marina. The island's principal port of St Helier embraces several interesting historical sites. Elizabeth Castle that shelters the entrance was the official residence of the Governor until the 18th century, one of its most distinguished residents being Sir Walter Raleigh, whose term began in 1600. Part of the castle's breakwater is Hermitage Rock, reputed to be the home of St Helier, hermit, missionary and patron saint.

Today Jersey is the most commercial of the Channel Islands and has all the amenities to satisfy a cosmopolitan population. Despite a large influx of visitors during the season, there remain many areas of natural beauty and tranquillity in and around the island where it is possible to get away from it all. In recent years the States of Jersey has done much to improve facilities for visiting yachtsmen. Land reclamation has created three marinas, making St Helier a practical port of call or a longer-term base. Bilge keelers and multihulls can enjoy the option of small drying harbours such as Gorey and St Aubin which have a character all their own. In suitable conditions of wind and tide, the island's coastline offers a number of good anchorages.

Ashore

First time visitors will find all the information they need at Jersey Tourism Centre in Liberation Square off St Helier Marina. It is a short walk north across Royal Square to find the shopping precincts and a wide range of cafés and restaurants.

Sites of interest around the harbour are the Maritime Museum adjoining the Marina and Elizabeth Castle, which is reached at low tide by a causeway. The developing Waterfront Centre has an Aqua Centre with multiplex cinema, fast food outlets and a nightspot.

There is a comprehensive bus service, the terminus is off Liberation Square and several car rental depots nearby. It is worth taking the half hour coastal route along to Gorey for a visit to Mont Orgueil Castle. Alternatively, go west via St Aubin to St Ouen's Bay with its 5-mile beach – a popular venue with surfers.

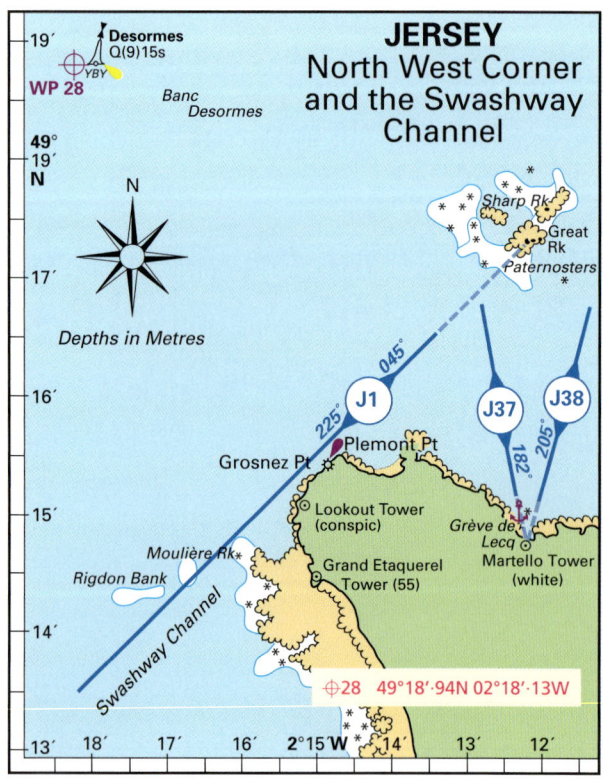

Jersey

Approaches to St Helier

From the north and west
(See also plans on pages 104–5 and 110–111)

Grosnez Point to Point La Corbière and into St Helier NW Passage and Western Passage

Grosnez Point at Jersey's NW corner and Point Corbière at its SW are vital reference points when making a landfall from the north or west.

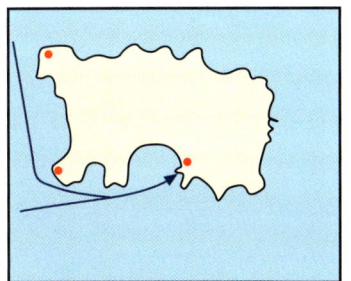

The approach channels in from the west run within a mile of the south coast and marks should be positively identified from a safe water position.

The sea off Grosnez Point can be rough in wind against tide conditions when the Rigdon Bank should be given a good clearance. In quiet weather the Swashway Channel may be used by day only.

The stern transit is:

J1 *045° Great Rock of the Paternosters open of Grosnez Point*

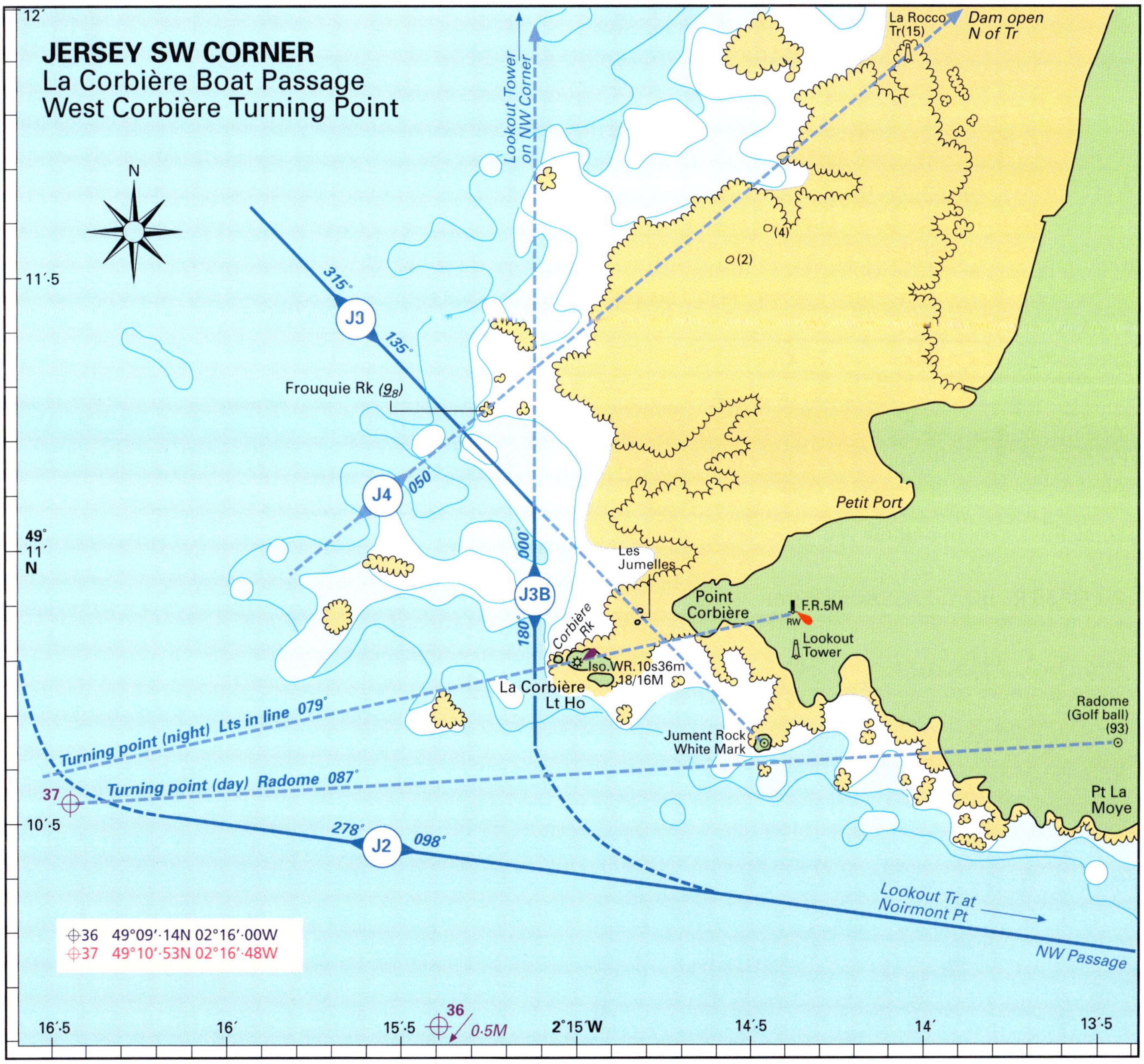

I. THE CHANNEL ISLANDS

CHANNEL ISLANDS, CHERBOURG PENINSULA & NORTH BRITTANY

1 The Channel Islands

This will pass between Rigdon Bank (minimum depth 3·1m) and Moulière (or Mouillière) Rock (dries 0·6m) leaving it 200m to port. It should be held until La Corbière lighthouse bears SSE when course may be altered towards Pt Corbière.

Round the point at a distance of 1 mile off the light to clear outlying dangers. This is achieved by keeping the top of the lighthouse level with the skyline.

With the lighthouse abeam run S until you identify Noirmont Pt light tower. When this comes onto an easterly bearing commence a turn onto:

J2 098° ⊕37 *The lookout tower on Noirmont Point open S of Le Fret Point*

West Corbière turning point

The Radome (93m) (known as The Golf Ball) on Point la Moye, makes a useful mark for a turning point by day. When it is open SE of the white-painted Jument Rock on 087° you are clear to commence a turn (see plan page 107).

By night

Approach in the white sector of Grosnez Point light Fl(2)WR.15s and then into the W sector of La Corbière light (Iso.WR.10s). Leave the LtHo at least 1M to port – in clear conditions a back bearing on Point Robert light (Fl.15s) on Sark can be useful. When the F.R (on the shore) and La Corbière light come in line (079°) identify Noirmont Tower light (Fl(4)12s) and when this bears 100° commence a turn to join the NW passage (see plan page 110).

LA CORBIÈRE BOAT PASSAGE (1·2m)

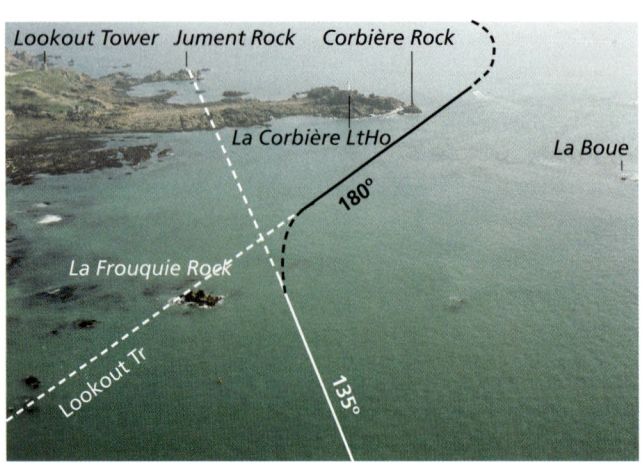

By day only

This short cut inside reefs to the W of Point Corbière provides a spectacular view of its lighthouse. The passage now prohibited to commercial traffic, has claimed several casualties over the years, not least the French ferry *St Malo* in 1995, which struck La Frouquie Rock (dries 9·8m). The passage carries a least depth of 1·2m at chart datum and should not be attempted in anything other than quiet weather with no W swell. If in doubt stay out.

Approach from the north

J3 135° *White patch on Jument Rock between the two heads of Les Jumelles (dry about 9m and 8m)*

When 200m SE of La Frouquie rock, if visible, steer just to the W of the LtHo until, looking astern, find:

J3B 000°. *The Lookout tower on the NW tip of the island bears due N, with La Frouquie if visible well open of the headland*

Take up a heading of 180°.

Note When Frouquie Rock is covered there is a striking mark to pinpoint its position:

J4 050° *La Rocco Tower bearing 050° with the dam open its width to the N*

When 400m off La Corbière Rock, which is steep-to, steer round it at a distance of 100m off. When the lighthouse bears 030° steer out on 130° to pick up mark J2 as described above and enter the NW passage.

Jersey

NORTHWEST PASSAGE (8·5m)

(See plan page 110)

Continue E on line J2 *098°* keeping the lookout tower well open S of Le Fret Point in order to clear Les Kaines (dry 8·5m). When St Brelade's Bay opens up take up stern transit for this passage:

J5 *290° La Corbière LtHo open S of La Jument white painted rock will clear Les Kaines (dry 8·5m)*

This should be held until abeam Noirmont Point when course should be altered into the Western Passage (see below and plan page 110).

By night

Hold Noirmont light Fl(4)12s on a steady bearing of no more than 095° to enter the red sector of La Corbière light astern. Identify Passage Rock N cardinal buoy (VQ), Les Fours N cardinal buoy (Q) and Ruaudière buoy (Fl.G.3s) beyond. As La Corbière light turns from red to white, steer to pass midway between Noirmont Point light and Les Fours (leaving Passage Rock buoy 0·5M to starboard) until the leading lights for the Western Passage come in line as described below.

WESTERN PASSAGE (4·0m)

J6 *082° ⊕36 Grève d'Azette lighthouse in line with Dog's Nest beacon*

This passes over Passage Rock, but if you borrow to the N to leave the Passage Rock N cardinal buoy to starboard the whole channel then carries 6m.

By night

The same transit is used, Dog's Nest beacon (Fl.Y3s3M), Mont Ubé light (Oc.R.5s46m12M) and Grève d'Azette LtHo (Oc.5s23m14M) in line.

From the south

(See also plan pages 110–111)

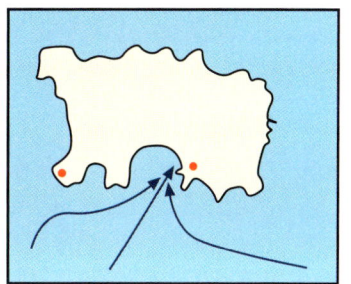

Caution

Reefs extend W from Demie de Pas light tower to Passage Rock N cardinal buoy off St Brelade's Bay.

Picking your way between them using some of the passages described below may be demanding as marks must be positively identified from safe water which can be up to 4 miles off. Transits may also be difficult to hold accurately with the stream setting E or W.

It may be safer to make for a poisition W of Passage Rock N cardinal buoy to approach by Western Passage, or a position S of Demie de Pas light tower to approach by South Passage.

DANGER ROCK PASSAGE (5·8m)

J7 *044° Fort Regent signal mast just open S of breakwater end*

The signal mast is hard to identify at a distance but the conspicuous white-painted pierhead control tower makes a good alternative.

This passage leaves Danger Rock (1·2m) 400m to starboard and two rocks (depth 0·3m and 0·9m) with Grunes aux Dardes (dry 1·8m) 200m to port so the line must be held exactly.

By night

The passage is unlit. Use the Red and Green Passage (see *Entry to St Helier Harbour* below) if there is sufficient water over the Fairway Rock (1·2m).

SOUTH PASSAGE (8m)

Once identified with binoculars the marks are conspicuous. With Demie de Pas light tower abeam to starboard, Les Têtards Rocks (one awash at LW and another depth 1·8m) lie 300m to port. Identify Hinguette buoy (R) which will be left 100m to port in this passage.

CHANNEL ISLANDS, CHERBOURG PENINSULA & NORTH BRITTANY

I The Channel Islands

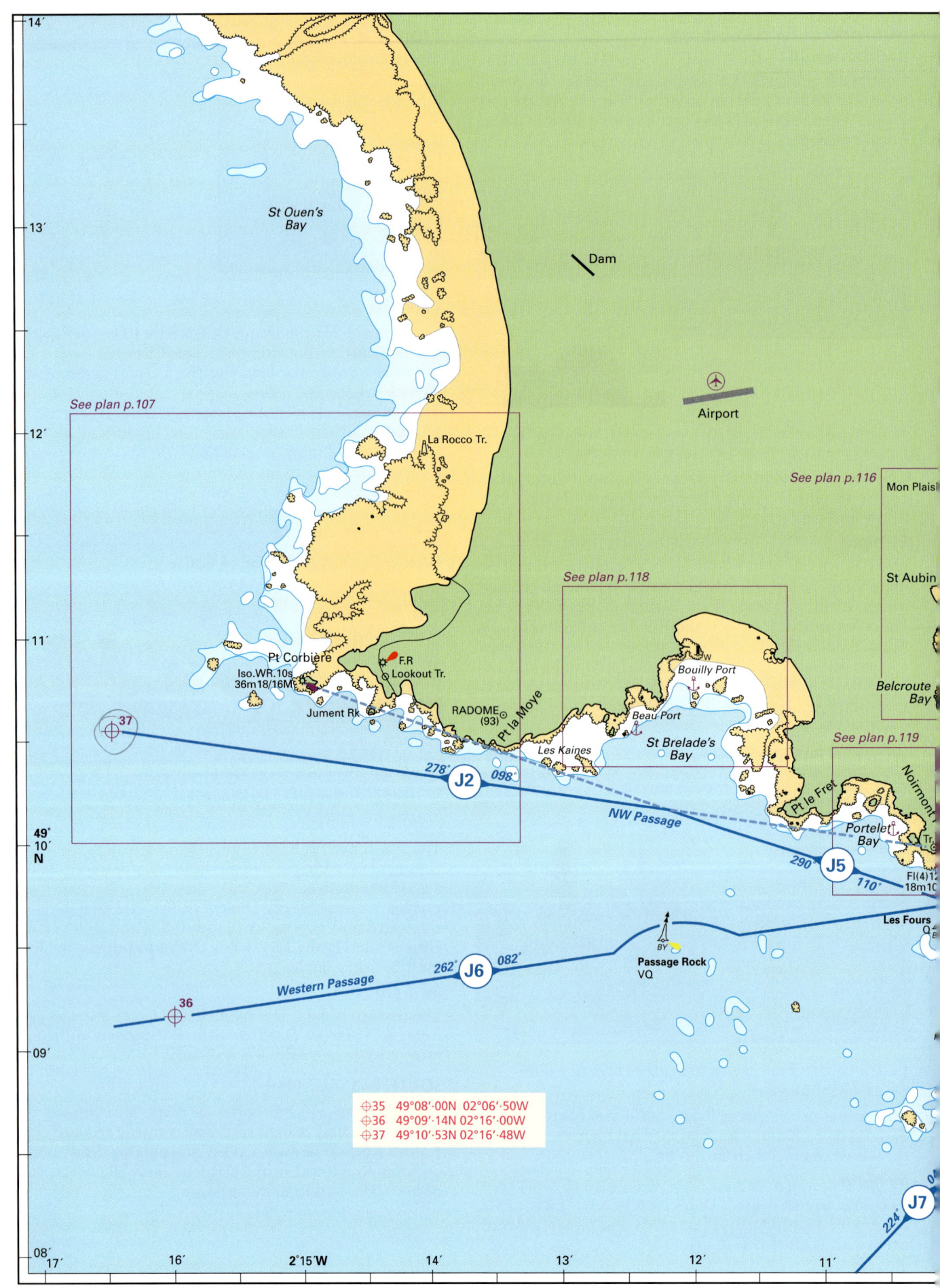

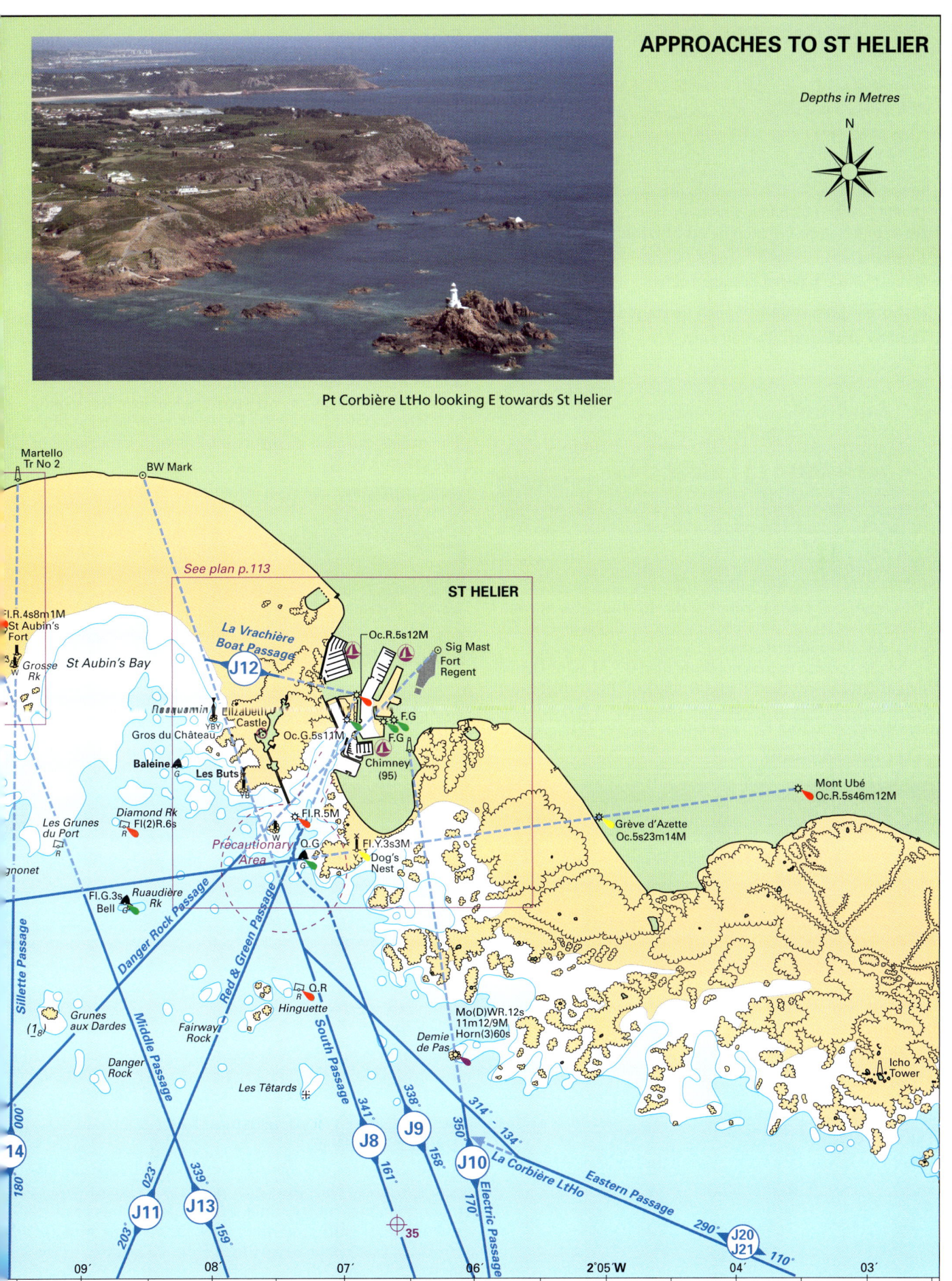

Pt Corbière LtHo looking E towards St Helier

1 The Channel Islands

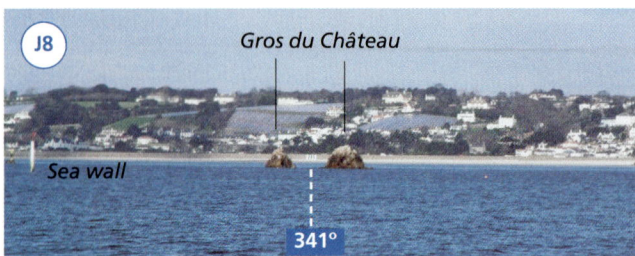

J8 341° ⊕35 *The black and white vertical stripes on the sea wall between the twin heads of Gros du Château*

By night
Unlit. Use the Eastern Passage below.

Inshore alternative to South Passage (2·5m)
Used by small craft. By day only.

J9 338° *Elizabeth Castle breakwater end on (BW stripes) in line with Platte Rock beacon (R)*

This unofficial passage runs parallel to South Passage but 400m closer inshore. It is useful when South Passage marks are difficult to identify.

Shape a course to pass not more than 0·5 M W of Demie de Pas light tower then align the marks. This transit must be left 200m short of E Rock buoy (G) when course should be altered W to join Red and Green Passage J11.

'ELECTRIC PASSAGE'

J10 350° *Demie de Pas light tower in line with power station chimney*

This unofficial passage may be used when approaching from the SE but must be left, steering 314°, to join the South Passage when 500m from Demie de Pas light tower, Hinguette buoy (R) will be left to port.

By night
This transit may be used by night if the chimney is floodlit.

From the east

EASTERN PASSAGE (7m)
There are no leading marks for this wide passage which joins the Red and Green Passage 0·5M S of Platte beacon.

By night
Keeping in the white sector of Demie de Pas light (Mo(D)WR.12s), steer to leave it 300m to starboard and the Hinguette port buoy (Qk.Fl.R) 400m to port until the Red and Green Passage lights (front Oc.G, rear Oc.R.5s) are in transit on 023°.

Entry to St Helier Harbour

RED AND GREEN PASSAGE (SHOAL PATCH 1·2m)
This passage covers the final entry to St Helier Harbour and its marinas via Small Road.

It is unsuitable as an entry passage S of East Rock buoy as it passes over Fairway Rock (1·2m) (see plan page 111). The marks can also be difficult to identify at a range of more than 1 mile.

J11 023°. *Two thin metal dayglo red columns, the rear on land and the front on a white painted caisson E side of the RoRo berth*

By night
Front mark (Oc.G.5s11M) and rear mark (Oc.R.5s12M) in transit. Despite their intensity the marks can be difficult to identify against the mass of background lighting.

LA VRACHIERE LOCAL BOAT PASSAGE (DRIES 5·3m) (W–E)
To reduce the volume of traffic in the Small Roads at peak periods, Jersey Harbours encourage local boat owners, rather than first-time visitors, to make use of this passage when there is sufficient water over the crossing point of Elizabeth Castle causeway (dries 5·3m). The table below shows depths over the causeway relative to the digital depth

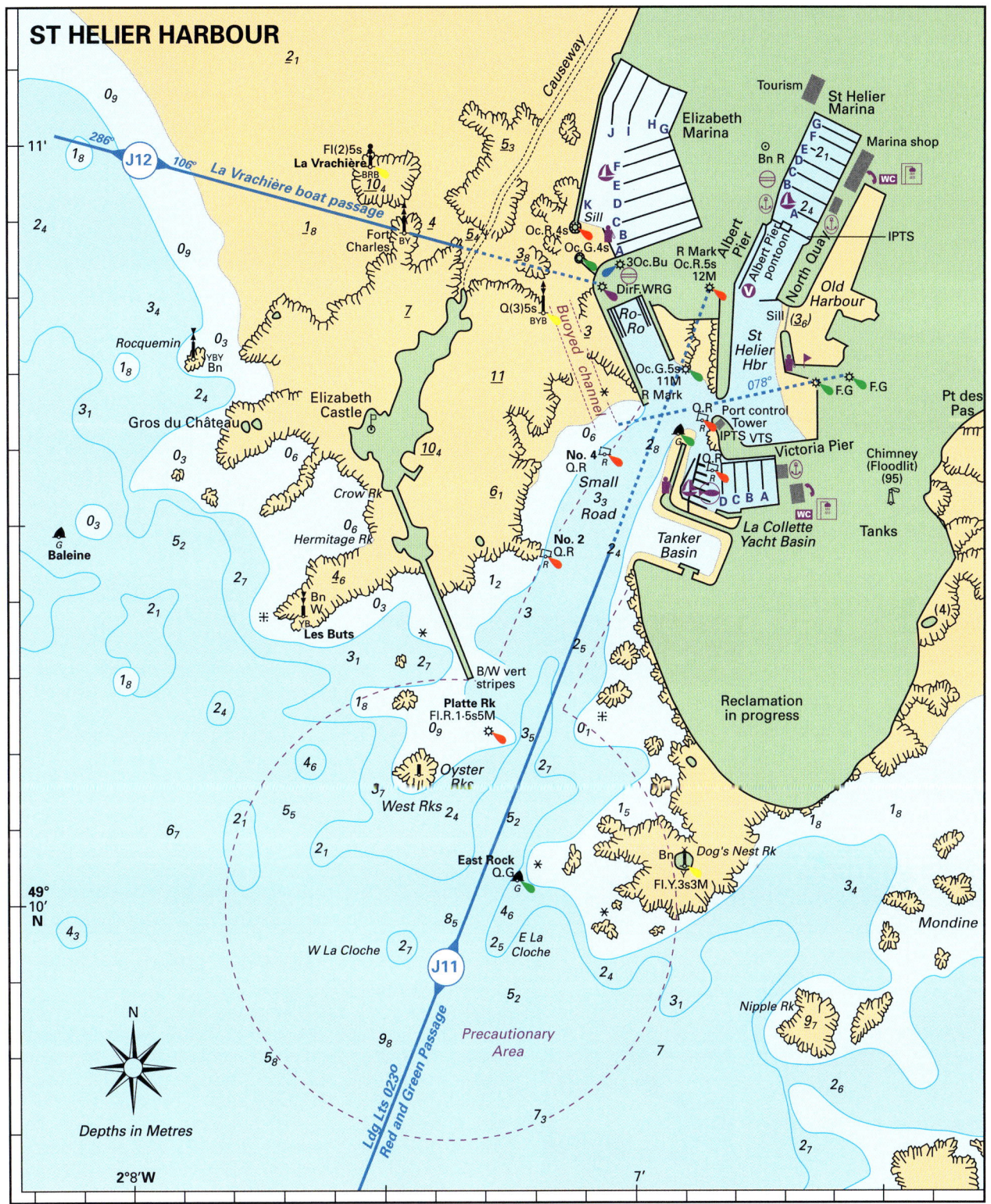

1 The Channel Islands

display at Elizabeth Marina entrance. At opening and closing time, approximately half tide, there is about 0·5m over the causeway crossing point.

Indicated depth over sill (m)	Depth over causeway crossing point
2·1m	0·5m
2·6m	1·0m
3·1m	1·5m
3·6m	2·0m
4·1m	2·5m
4·6m	3·0m

J12 106° The dayglo red marks positioned S of Elizabeth Marina entrance should be held in transit until 100m N of Fort Charles E cardinal Q(3)5s, when course may be altered for the marina entrance or St Helier Harbour pierheads

The passage passes 100m S of La Vrachière beacon (Fl(2)5s), shown here at HW.

By night
Keep in the W sector of Dir.WRG.4m1M positioned on the nearer day mark. When 3 lights (3Oc.Bu.8s4m1M) in the Elizabeth Marina entrance are in transit on 076° you may, subject to traffic signals, enter the marina or break off S to follow the lit buoyed channel into the Small Road.

St Helier Harbour
49°10'·57N 02°06'·87W Pier head control tower

TRAFFIC CONTROL SIGNALS
IALA signal lights are now exhibited on Elizabeth Harbour W wall in addition to VTS Port Control Tower.

F.R	Stop, vessels shall not proceed
Fl.R	Serious emergency. Stop and await instructions
F.G	Vessels may proceed. One-way traffic
F.G, F.G, FW	Vessels may proceed. Two-way traffic.

Fuel pontoon

VHF
St Helier VTS work on VHF Ch 14 and approaching vessels are advised to keep a listening watch for shipping movements. Range is about 5 miles. If berthing information is required, port control is in contact with marina staff. There is no marina channel.

Speed limit
A speed limit of 5 knots applies in the Small Road.

Entry formalities
If arriving from outside the Bailiwick of Jersey a customs and immigration declaration form must be completed on arrival. These may be obtained and delivered at marina office.

Marinas
ST HELIER MARINA
Located in the upper harbour in the town centre, this is the most sheltered of the three marinas.

St Helier Marina sill

Entry Approximately 3 hours either side of HW over a sill (dries 3·5m), with hinged gate which operates when tide level is 2·2m.
Entry signals Lights are displayed above the entrance and have the same meaning as Pierhead Control signals (see *Traffic Control Signals* above). A depth display and board indicates depth over the sill.
Retained depth 2·3m minimum. Deep draught yachts are advised not to manoeuvre within the marina when the gate is closed as there are shoal depths in places.
Waiting areas La Collette Yacht Basin or Albert Pier pontoon SW of the entrance (under development 2014).
Shore facilities In addition to a comprehensive facilities block there is a marina shop that keeps long hours during the season and a DIY laundry.
Fuel A fuel berth has been established on the La Collette Yacht Basin side of Victoria Pier, below Pierhead Control Tower. It dries out and is normally accessible three hours either side of HW. There is a tide gauge at the pontoon. Open April-September 0800-1830 seven days a week.
℡ 07700 347313
The fuel berth at South Pier has relocated to a pontoon off the end of the North Quay, adjacent to the Albert Pier pontoon. Open Monday-Saturday 0900-1700, Sunday 1200-1800. Diesel only.
Marina Fuel 24/7 ℡ 525247 self service. (Accepts debit/credit cards)
Hours of opening (tide permitting) Mon–Fri 0830–1700; Sat 0900–1700; Sundays and holidays 0900–1700 (see harbour plan).
Drying out A scrubbing pad is situated in the NE corner with water and electricity on hand. It is totally dry for approximately 5 hours. Pre-booking with the marina office is necessary. ℡ 01534 447708

Jersey

St Helier Marina

La Collette yacht basin. It is an exceptionally low spring tide and the channel is almost dry

Elizabeth Marina

LA COLLETTE YACHT BASIN

Well placed for chandlers, marine engineers and sailmaker, but some distance from the town. St Helier Yacht Club on nearby South Pier welcomes visiting yachtsmen. Bar with food facility.

Entry All states of tide, although the narrow buoyed channel has a least depth of 1·8m at MLWS when a close eye should be kept on the sounder – the bottom is soft mud.

Entry signals Port Control Tower.

Facilities Pontoons C and D are used as holding points while waiting for the tide and are often congested. Water and electricity are available on C but water only on D pontoon.

Drying blocks situated in SE corner are dry for approximately 6 hours from half ebb. Fishermen have priority so check with marina staff.

Fuel See *St Helier Marina* above.

Haul-out 16-ton slipway hoist and 65-ton docking hoist.

Maximum stay ashore is 3 months.

Shore facility block including showers.

ELIZABETH MARINA

Situated W of Albert Pier with 590 berths. A limited number of berths are available to visitors staying for a minimum of 1 month. Pre-booking is necessary.

Entry Over a sill (dries 3·5m) with hinged gate which operates approximately 3 hours either side of HW. A depth display and board indicate depth over the sill after tide level has reached 2·2m and the gate has been lowered. The entrance is narrow and the current can attain 4 knots at spring tides. The rate is displayed on a digital gauge.

Traffic signals One-way traffic is controlled by traffic lights at the entrance. A relay light positioned on W breakwater

CHANNEL ISLANDS, CHERBOURG PENINSULA & NORTH BRITTANY 115

1 The Channel Islands

is visible when approaching from the Small Road. A warning alarm sounds (0730–2300) when the gate is rising and the traffic lights go to red. They change every 10 minutes.
Waiting buoys 5 yellow buoys positioned either side of the approach channel are available to yachts waiting to enter. Most of the area dries at MLWS.
Retained depth 5·6m.
Shore facilities The facilities block consists of a large foyer, toilets and showers.
Fuel Complete Boat Care ☎ 07797 732 299.
Pump-out facilities (free) Available adjacent to the fuel berth. Enquire at the marina office.
Drying out There is a scrubbing pad close to the entrance. Arrangements should be made with the marina office.
☎ Marina office 01534 447708
Ashore Radisson Waterfront Hotel and Restaurant, Supermarket.

St Aubin Harbour and south coast anchorages
49°11'·21N 02°10'·04W N Pierhead

Historical note
From earliest times and until the development of St Helier as a deep-water harbour in the 19th century, St Aubin served as the island's port. This western corner of the bay enjoys almost total natural shelter from winds and swell, and extensive firm sands meant ships could take the ground and discharge their cargoes into carts. The addition of piers and fortifications in the 17th and 18th centuries gave further protection and created the town. The Old Court House Inn overlooking the S arm dates from this era. Its restaurant and bars are a popular venue.

Approach
(See plan on pages 110–111 and caution page 109)

From the south

MIDDLE PASSAGE (6·0m)
S of western passage intersection

First identify on BA chart 1137 several features on the W side of St Aubin Bay:

Pignonet S cardinal pole beacon
Les Grunes du Port port-hand buoy
St Aubin Fort with Platte Rock pole beacon and Grosse Rock pole beacon (G) close SE of the fort
Mon Plaisir House. Martello tower No.2

With good visibility and positive identification of marks (J13) Middle Passage may be used for entering the W side of St Aubin Bay.

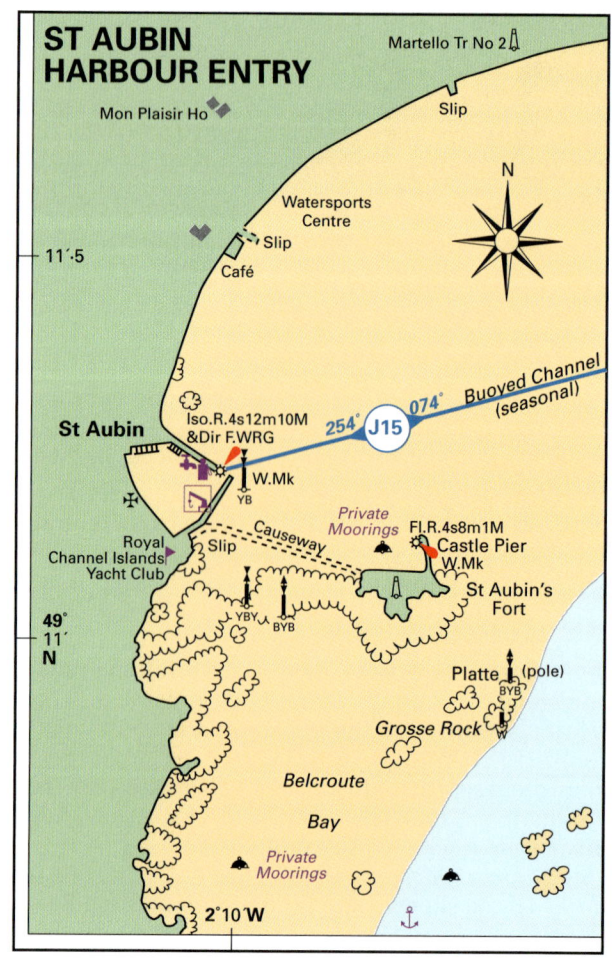

116 CHANNEL ISLANDS, CHERBOURG PENINSULA & NORTH BRITTANY

J13 339° Mon Plaisir House in line with St Aubin Fort

The line clears E of both Danger Rock (1·2m) and Frouquie of the Grunes aux Dardes (dry 0·9m) by 500m and W of Ruaudière Rock (dries 1·2m) by 400m. If extended N of its junction with Western Passage it will clear close E of Les Grunes du Port port-hand buoy. When abeam alter course N into the bay. Hold until N of the Fort and the harbour entrance has opened up.

SILLETTE PASSAGE (6·1m S OF WESTERN PASSAGE INTERSECTION)

This passage provides a transit that may be adapted to clear close W of Les Grunes du Port (dries 2·1m) when approaching from the S. Once past, borrow E to avoid Les Junées (0·9m)

J14 000° Martello Tr no. 2 on the E side of Grosse Rock

From the southeast

Use the South Passage. When East Rock buoy (G) is abeam alter course for St Aubin Fort to pass N of it and into the entry channel.

Caution

A strong cross-set may be experienced using N–S channels S of St Aubin Bay.

From St Helier Harbour

Subject to sufficient rise of tide use La Vrachière local boat passage (see *Entry to St Helier Harbour*) or depart via Red and Green Passage and proceed as from southeast.

Entry to St Aubin Harbour

J15 254° N pierhead light on a white mast

Enter by the channel which is buoyed during the season. There is a depth board at the entrance.

By night

St Aubin N pierhead light Iso.R.4s12m10M and DirF.WRG. Enter in the W sector of the directional light. St Aubin Fort Pier light Fl.R.4s8m1M. White Mast.

Shelter

Total from prevailing W to SW winds with some fetch entering the harbour in strong northeasterlies.

Access

The harbour and approaches dry out and entry is only possible approximately 2 hours either side of HW. At neaps the tide barely fills the harbour and there is only 1·5m at the entrance at the top of a 7·6m tide.

Mooring

There are no visitors' moorings but there is limited space alongside the N arm and the S arm up to the hand crane.

Nearby anchorages

In settled weather and with light offshore winds, bilge keelers can dry out between the harbour entrance and the mole at St Aubin Fort. Deep keel yachts have the option of remaining afloat at all states of tide in Belcroute Bay (see plan) or, with caution and in calm conditions, to dry out alongside the N end of the W side of St Aubin Fort mole. Here the yacht should not be left unattended.

Harbour facilities

Fuel Diesel only by arrangement with local boatyards 6 days a week.
Water From tap on N arm.
Crane A 4½-ton crane jointly operated by boatyards in the area is situated on the S arm.
Drying out There is a pad and two drying out grids. Book in advance through the St Helier harbour office or in case of emergency check availability with local boatyards.
Boatyards and chandlers Jackson's Yacht Service on the Bulwarks.
Yacht club The Royal Channel Islands Yacht Club overlooking the S arm welcomes visiting yachtsmen to their clubhouse. Showers, bar and restaurant available.
St Aubin village Telephone box on W side of parish hall, post office, supermarket and a variety of shops close by. Bus and taxi services into St Helier. Some of the best restaurants on the island.
St Helier harbour office ☎ 447788
Emergency out of hours ☎ 733908
Jackson's Yacht Services ☎ 743819
Gallichan Marine ☎ 746387
Royal Channel Islands Yacht Club ☎ 741023

1 The Channel Islands

South coast anchorages
(See plan pages 110–111)

ST BRELADE'S BAY
49°10'·64N 02°11'·84W

A wide bay sheltered between W through N to E but exposed to southwesterly swell. Most of the middle and E part is inaccessible, being strewn with rocks. There are two attractive anchorages on the W side and there is one entry transit into the bay. Do not close the bay until it has fully opened up and the marks have been identified:

J16 006° The E end of St Brelade's Bay Hotel (marked Hotel on BA chart 1137) above white patch on end of jetty

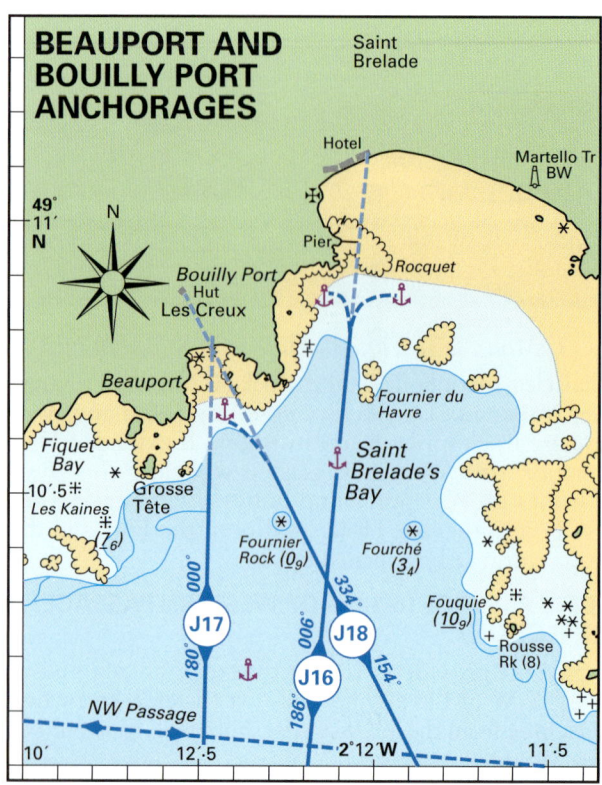

BEAUPORT
49°10'·62N 02°12'·40W

On entering St Brelade's Bay a small cove distinguished by its sandy beach and conspicuous pinnacle rock will open up. Beauport anchorage is considered by many to be the most beautiful anchorage on the island. There are two approaches passing either side of Fournier Rock (dries 0·9m):

Beauport and Bouilly Port

118 CHANNEL ISLANDS, CHERBOURG PENINSULA & NORTH BRITTANY

Jersey

W of Fournier Rock (3m)

J17 000° The middle of Beauport beach bearing N will give 200m clearance (no view)

E of Fournier Rock (3m)

J18 331° Pinnacle Rock below red-roofed hut on skyline will give 125m clearance

Bouilly Port

It is possible to venture further on transit J16 to anchor 400m from the jetty just S of Rocquet beacon. Sound in carefully, avoiding fishermen's moorings and pot markers.

PORTELET BAY
49°10'·13N 02°10'·61W

Historical note

The Janvrins were a leading maritime family in 17th and 18th-century Jersey, owning the largest fleet of merchant ships in the island. Many were built in St Helier for trading and privateering in Canada and Newfoundland. On return to his native isle in 1721, Philippe Janvrin fell victim to the plague and died in quarantine aboard his brigantine *Esther* anchored off Noirmont. He was buried on the islet Ile ès Guerdains, in this bay.

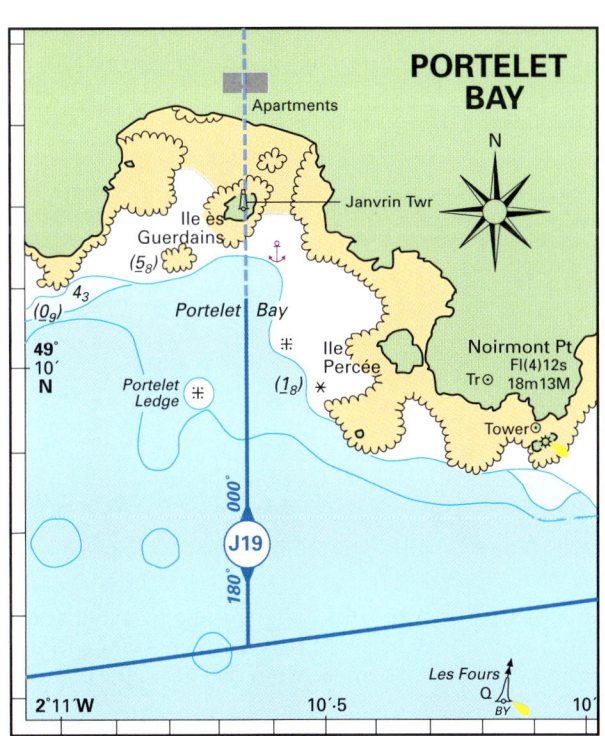

J19 000° Janvrin Tower in line with third block from left

Avoid the drying ledges on the W side of Noirmont Point by approaching with Janvrin Tower bearing due N. When just off the islet alter course to starboard to anchor SE of it. Space is tight and it would be as well to remain on board and maintain an anchor watch. This is a good spot for safe swimming out of the tide and there is an excellent, very popular beach, a short row away. Portelet Bay Café (☎ 728550).

BELCROUTE BAY
49°10'·43N 02°09'·60W

Provides excellent shelter from W and SW winds, but dries at 3·5m and is cluttered with small craft moorings. Anchoring off is recommended and the holding in sand is good. The approach from the S using BA chart 1137 is straightforward noting dangers to the N of the bay, and an isolated drying rock (3·3m) in the S. See *St Aubin Harbour. Approach from the south* above.

1 The Channel Islands

Gorey Harbour

49°11'·80N 02°01'·34W Pier head

CHARTS
British Admiralty
  3655 Jersey and adjacent coast of France
  1136 Jersey – north coast
  1138 Jersey – east coast
Imray
  C33A Channel Islands (North) Plan: Gorey
  2500 The Channel islands and adjacent coast of France Chart Atlas

TIDAL INFORMATION
Tidal levels referred to chart datum
St Catherine's Bay 49°13 N 2°01 W

MHWS	MHWN	MLWN	MLWS
11·1m	8·0m	4·1m	1·4m

TRAVEL INFORMATION
Gorey Pier office ☏ 853616 (hours determined by ferry movements and tides)
VHF Ch 74 during hours
Public telephone boxes on the pier and near bus station at its root.
There is a frequent bus service to St Helier. During the season there are occasional ferry services between Gorey and the French ports of Carteret, Portbail and Granville.

Historical note

'The Village the Oysters Built'. This drying harbour nestling beneath Mont Orgueil Castle (meaning Mount Pride), first appears in 13th-century records as 'Portus Gorryk', a landing place for boats coming from France. Over the years its rough piers came and went but a boom in the oyster fishery business in the early 19th century saw its development into the port of today. Large fleets of oystermen, mostly from the east coast of England, crammed the harbour, and rows of cottages on the pier and in the nearby village were erected for the newcomers. Over-dredging killed the industry but its place was taken by shipbuilding. At its height in the 1860s, large schooners up to 250 tons were being built on the waterfront for trading as far afield as Newfoundland.

Access

The harbour dries completely and is accessible 3 hours either side of HW St Helier.

Shelter

Exposed between S and SE and can be very uncomfortable when gales from this sector combine with large spring tides.

Gorey Harbour from the SW near HW

Approaches to Gorey

From the West (St Helier)

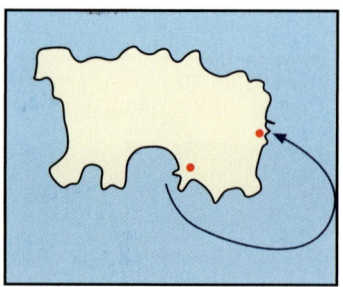

(See plans pages 104–5, 111, 121, 122)

Approach along the S coast to round the SE corner by the Violet Channel ⊕33, the Anquette Channel or the Brett Boat Passage short cut. Aim to be off St Helier no later than half flood and at the SE corner at St Helier HW–0200 when the N-going eddy is building up inshore along the E coast. This will ensure a fair stream all the way, sufficient water and arrival off Gorey just before HW.

If setting out from St Helier, leave by the Red and Green Passage (J11) then the Eastern Passage. Round Demie de Pas light Tower at a distance of 0·2M and when due SSE of the tower, take up a heading of 110°. Transits that will ensure a safe distance off this rocky coastline are shown below (see plan page 111 and views below).

J20 *290° La Corbière LtHo open of La Moye Pt*

In poor visibility an alternative that may be used with caution is as follows:

J21 *292° Noirmont Point Lt Tr well open to the S of Demie de Pas Lt Tr*

When S of Icho Tower (14m) alter course to make good 097° to pass midway between La Conchière (2m) with its S cardinal beacon and Canger Rock W cardinal buoy.

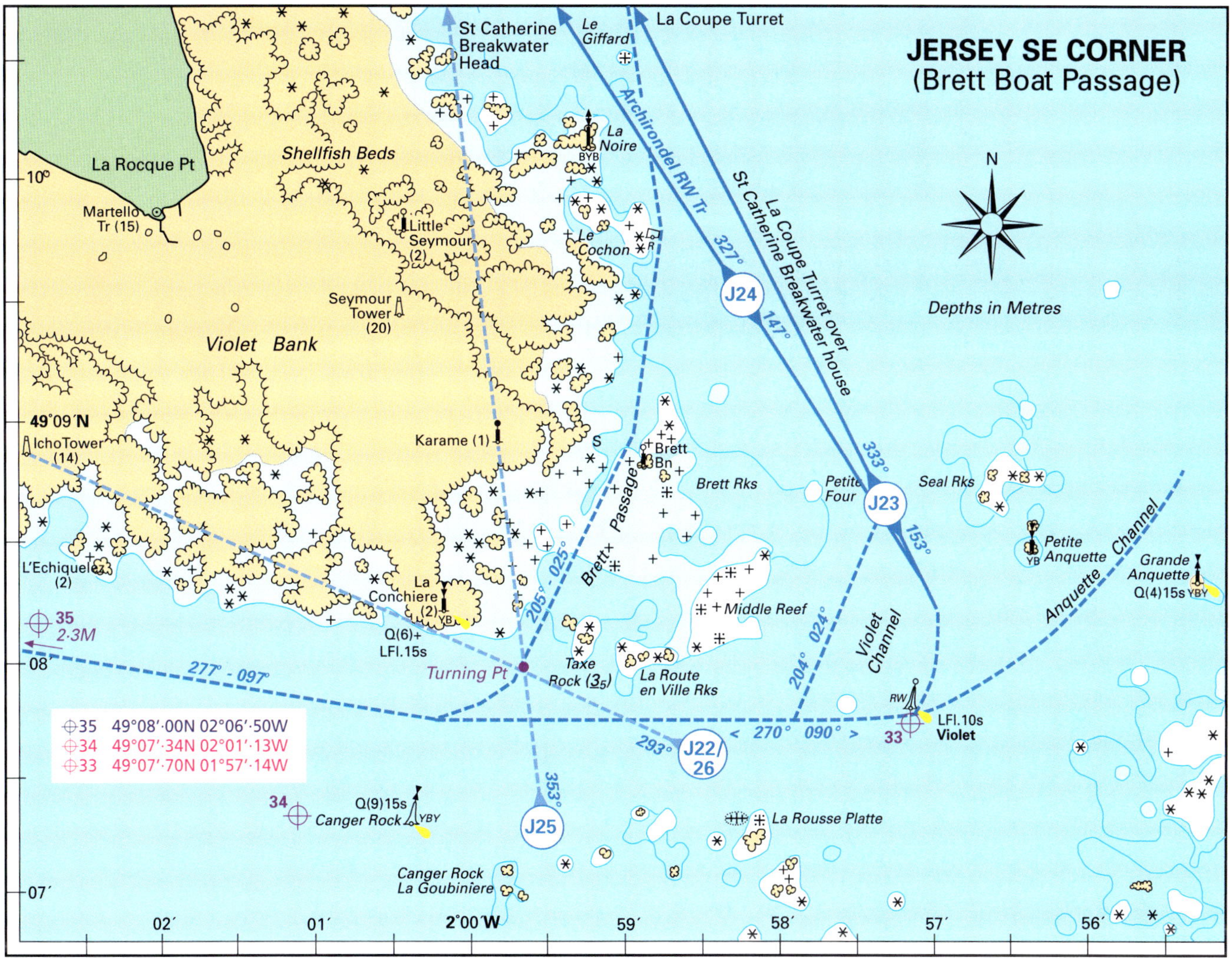

Jersey

JERSEY SE CORNER
(Brett Boat Passage)

Violet Channel (9·0m)

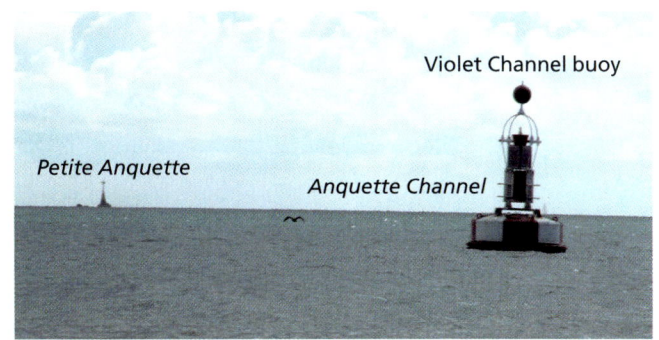

J22 293° Icho Tower open SW of La Conchière Rock (2m) with its lit S cardinal beacon clears SW of Taxe Rock and La Route en Ville Rocks

Identify the Violet Channel RW safe-water buoy ⊕33 a further 2M to the E and proceed towards it with due regard for a strong northerly set which will be experienced here from HW St Helier −0200 to +0300. To assess any set towards Taxe Rock (drying 1·4m) and La Route en Ville Rocks (drying up to 2·0m) Transit J22 is useful as a clearing line:

Pass the Violet Channel buoy either side and take up a northerly heading until the next set of marks (J23) are identified. This transit will be held all the way to Gorey Outer Road.

CHANNEL ISLANDS, CHERBOURG PENINSULA & NORTH BRITTANY

1 The Channel Islands

J23 333° La Coupe turret over St Catherine Breakwater Ho – a prominent white building at the root of the breakwater (Verclut Point). (See plan page 121 and below)

La Coupe turret

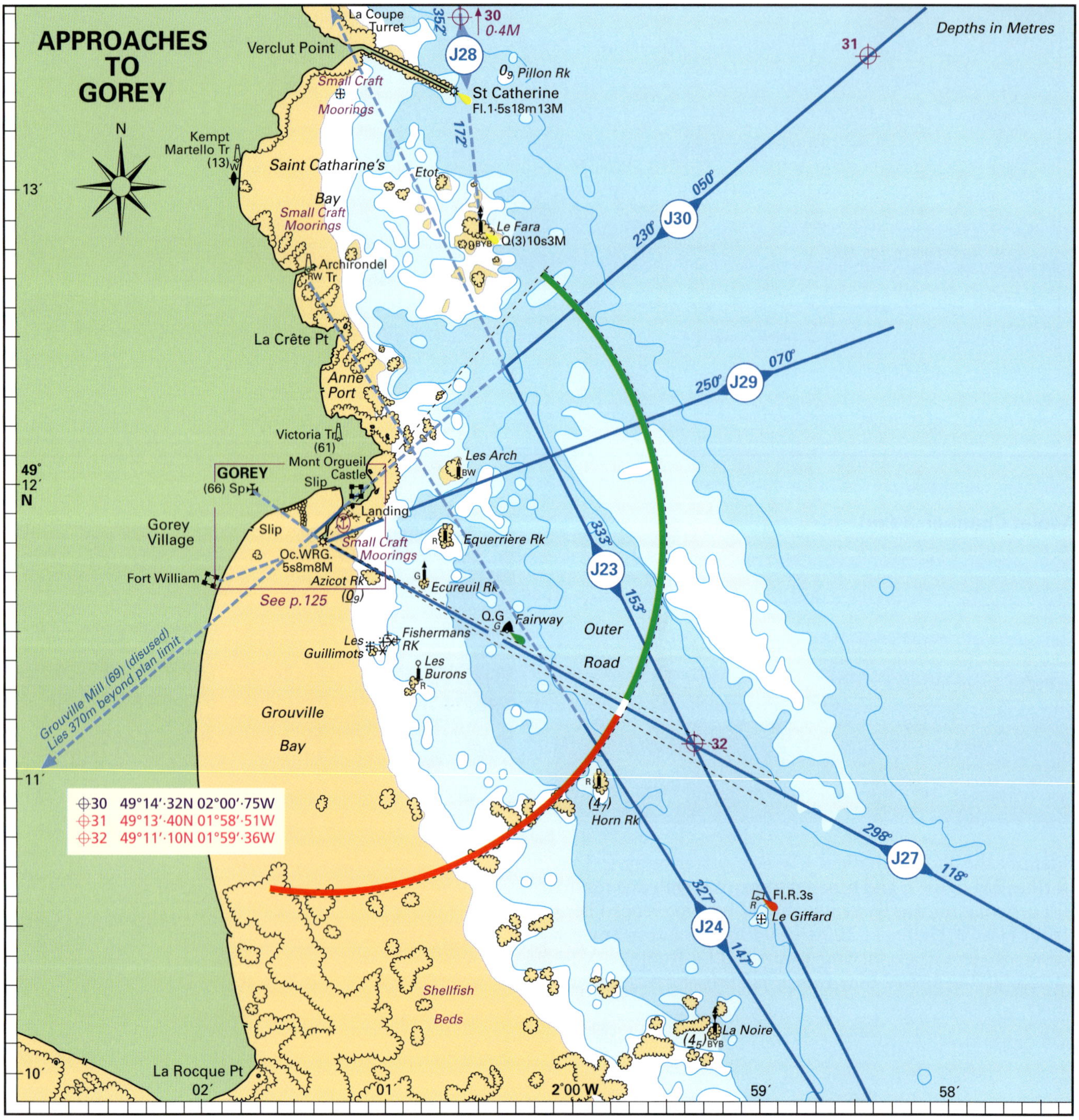

APPROACHES TO GOREY

Depths in Metres

⊕30 49°14′·32N 02°00′·75W
⊕31 49°13′·40N 01°58′·51W
⊕32 49°11′·10N 01°59′·36W

122 CHANNEL ISLANDS, CHERBOURG PENINSULA & NORTH BRITTANY

Jersey

The turret is often difficult to find, even with binoculars, in which case a useful alternative is as follows.

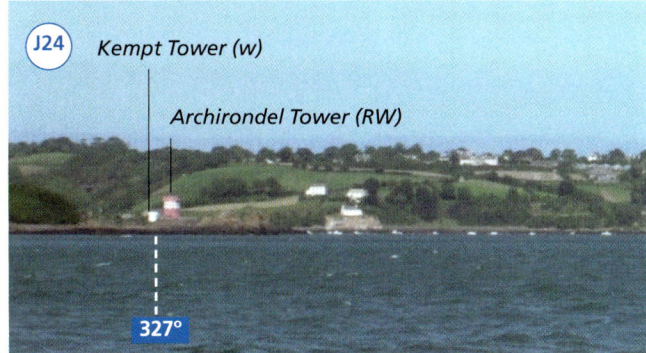

J24 327° Archirondel RW Martello Tower in line with Kempt Tower W behind it or open to the left

Anquette Channel (8·0m)

NE of the Violet Channel buoy is a clean channel 0·75M wide between Grande Anquette and Petite Anquette beacons – a useful alternative to the Violet Channel if proceeding to Carteret or Portbail on the Normandy coast.

BRETT BOAT PASSAGE (1·0m) (S–N)

Chart BA 1138 Jersey – east coast
(See plan page 122)

With sufficient water and good visibility this passage with rocks drying 2m or more on either side provides a useful short cut. Before entering the passage obtain the Brett Passage Turning Point, just under 0·5M SE of La Conchière beacon. This may be fixed by a cross-cut of 2 transits, as follows.

1. J25 353° Karamé beacon in line with St Catherine breakwater end, if visible

2. J26 293° Icho Tower (14m) open SW of La Conchière Rock (2m) with its beacon, at which point turn smartly onto 025°. (For view see J22 above)

Leave Brett beacon 200m to starboard then make good 010° to Le Cochon R and Le Giffard R can buoys, both of which should be left to port. Finally, identify the leading day marks for entry to Gorey J27 298° ⊕32 as described under *Entry to Gorey*.

By night

J27 298°
The only possible approach from the W is by the Violet Channel buoy (LFl.10s) ⊕33 and then onto the leading lights (see *Entry to Gorey* below).

Brett Rocks looking N at an exceptionally low spring tide. The passage is almost dry

Grande Anquette W cardinal lit beacon

Brett beacon. It may be submerged at HW springs

FROM THE SOUTH AND SOUTHEAST

Inbound from Granville, Iles Chausey or St Malo a yacht will be navigating on a falling tide, having departed around HW. The prevailing stream will be NW to W-going, although during the early hours of the ebb there is a more northerly element off the SE corner. Care should be taken to avoid being set towards the reefs that extend some 8M SE from the island to the Normandy coast, forming an almost impenetrable barrier. Two buoys that should be identified en route but given a respectable offing are Frouquier Aubert S cardinal and Canger Rock W cardinal ⊕34. From the latter, take Brett Boat Passage, Violet Channel or Anquette Channel onto the E coast.

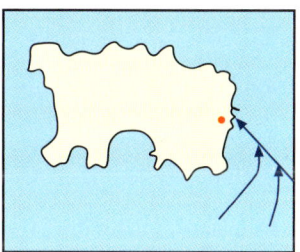

By night

Route via Frouquier Aubert S cardinal buoy, Canger Rock W cardinal buoy ⊕34, Violet Channel buoy (LFl.10s) ⊕33 and the leading lights as described under *Entry to Gorey* below.

FROM THE NORTH

(See plans pages 105, 121, 127)

The approach from the N will normally be with the S-going flood tide, having cleared the Alderney Race around LW St Helier. Route S to pass midway between the Paternosters and Les Dirouilles reefs. Follow the coast to the NE corner, (⊕30) keeping at

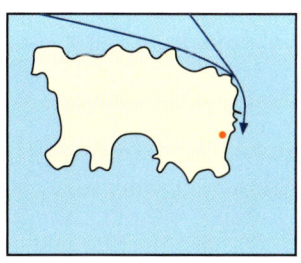

CHANNEL ISLANDS, CHERBOURG PENINSULA & NORTH BRITTANY 123

1 The Channel Islands

least 0·5M off. When St Catherine Breakwater head bears S, take up Transit J28 to clear dangers off the corner. If bound from Guernsey, Herm or Sark, it might be preferable to route via Desormes W cardinal buoy (⊕28) and pass S of the Paternosters. Follow the coast as described above (see *Between Sark and Jersey. Dixcart Bay to Gorey* page 21).

J28 172° ⊕30 *Le Fara E cardinal beacon (lit) open of the end of St Catherine breakwater clears Coupe Rock (2·7m) and Brayes Rocks (dries 1·8m) off La Coupe Point and Pillon Rock (0·9m)*

Leave the breakwater end 100m to starboard and clear Fara E cardinal beacon by at least 0·2M. Note this reef extends some way E of the beacon. Steer due S until Gorey pierhead (whitewashed) bears 250° and with sufficient water enter with:

J29 250° *Fort William house on the distant beach just open to S of Gorey pierhead*

Alternatively, route further S leaving Les Arch BW beacon and Equerrière beacon 400m to starboard and pick up the leading marks in Outer Road (J27).

By night
Approach the N coast by the same route. Stay in the W sector of Sorel Pt (LFl.WR.7·5s) and keep at least 1M off the coast.

FROM THE NORTHEAST
Inbound from Carteret or Les Ecréhous the unmistakable landmark of Mont Orgueil Castle should be kept on a bearing of not less than 230°. Closer in and given good visibility it should be possible to locate Grouville Mill (69m) and transit:

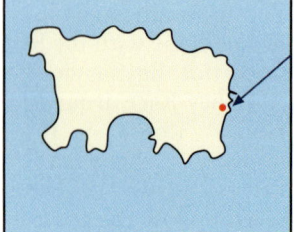

J30 230° ⊕31 *Grouville Mill open to S of Mont Orgueil Castle*

This transit avoids trouble with the reef surrounding Le Fara off St Catherine Bay and enables the navigator to keep any set in check. From half flood to half ebb there is a strong N-going stream inshore.

When 1M mile off, edge S to enter on J29 as above or the leading marks J27 as below.

By night
Until established on the leading light, keep at least 1M off all coastal dangers. Lights for reference are in N–S order:
St Catherine Fl.1·5s
Gorey Road buoy Q.G
Violet Channel buoy LFl.10s
⊕32 is positioned on the entry marks (J27).

Entry to Gorey

J27 298° ⊕32 *E gable end of conspic house to left (W) of church spire positioned above LtHo*

By night
Keep in W sector of DirF.WRG 6m8M (lit 24 hours). Identify Gorey Road Starboard buoy Q.G 0.7M SE of the pierhead. This will be left 80m to starboard. Note that Gorey Castle is floodlit between 2100 and 0000 LT throughout the year.

Caution
Note that the leading line passes close E of Azicot Rock (dries 0·9m), 400m short of the pierhead.

Entry formalities
Gorey is an official port of entry for vessels arriving from outside the Bailiwick of Jersey. A customs and immigration declaration form must be completed on arrival. These may be obtained and delivered at Gorey Pier office.

Jersey

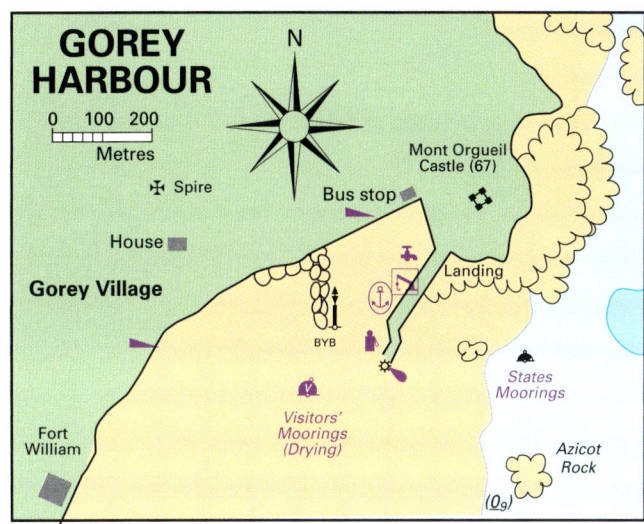

Gorey harbour at half tide

Anchoring and mooring

Outside the harbour
Anchor E of pierhead clear of private moorings. The holding is good in sand. There are 2 deep-water moorings situated about 200m E of pier head. These are orange, flat-topped and marked 'States of Jersey'.

St Catherine Bay to the N offers a further possibility (see below).

Within the harbour
150m W of the pierhead are 12 yellow visitors' buoys. They dry out around LW. Further into the harbour are 5 wall berths alongside where visitors may dry out, and several fore and aft moorings set up on the beach.

Facilities
Fuel Gorey Marine Fuel Supplies ☎ 07797 742384 supply petrol and diesel (duty free) from pumps at pierhead steps. Open 3 hours either side of HW up to 1800 LT, unless the wind is above Force 5. Out of hours by arrangement.
Water At fuelling berth and crane.
Electricity Operated by card obtainable from harbour attendant. There are points at fuelling berth, crane and on each lamppost on the pier.
Crane Max 7 tons.
Shower and toilets Available near fuelling berth.
Scrubbing Either alongside or on the grid near half tide steps. Arrangements should be made with the harbour attendant.
Chandlers None.
Marine and *electrical engineers* On call.
Ashore There is a good selection of bars and restaurants on the pier and in nearby Gorey Village, which has a good shopping centre. Visit the medieval fortress Mont Orgueil for an insight into Jersey history.

CHANNEL ISLANDS, CHERBOURG PENINSULA & NORTH BRITTANY

1 The Channel Islands

Gorey to Grosnez Point (E–W) northabout

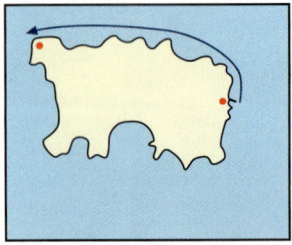

St Catherine Bay
49°13'·33N 02°00'·65W Breakwater head

Historical note
N of Gorey is St Catherine Bay with its breakwater that stretches almost 0·5M out to sea and known as 'The harbour that failed'. This grandiose construction dates from the mid-19th century and was intended to form part of a large fortified harbour in response to the fortification of nearby French harbours of Cherbourg, Granville and St Malo. The stub of the southern breakwater with its red and white tower still remains at Archirondel. The project was doomed from the start, as a harbour peppered with rocks and shallowing waters due to silting is of little use. When the threat from France diminished it was abandoned to remain something of a folly.

Entry
Entry and departure is by the N end of the bay using BA chart 1138 Jersey – East Coast. Note Pillon Rock (0·9m) 0·2M ENE of pierhead, Coupe Rock (2·7m) and Brayes Rocks (dries 1·8m) off La Coupe Point. For marks to clear, see Gorey. From the north, transit J28.

Shelter and anchorage
The bay is sheltered in all but easterlies. Anchor just S of the middle of the breakwater in 3m or more, but do not close it as rocks and debris extend out to 100m along its length and at least 15m off its end (see photo). The holding is good in sand and mud but beware of areas of kelp. Anchoring further into the bay is possible about 0·5M SW of the breakwater clear of private moorings.

A states mooring is situated 200m SE of the slipway. Landing can be made on the slipway at the root of the

breakwater. At the top is a café, telephone box and a stop for the bus to Gorey and St Helier. Nearby is the clubhouse and dinghy park of St Catherine's Sailing Club.

Further S next to the Martello Tower (13m) is St Catherine's RNLI lifeboat station and slip.

North coast harbours and anchorages

JERSEY NORTH COAST
(See plans pages 104–5 and 127)

The contour of Jersey resembles a S-inclined wedge shape. The N coast, in contrast to the S, is generally high, with spectacular stretches of steep cliffs towards its W end, sloping to a more hospitable verdant landscape of wooded valleys and farmland in the E. To be appreciated fully it needs good weather with an absence of onshore winds which can produce swelly conditions, particularly at springs. There are 3 small fishing harbours and a handful of anchorages. There are no dangers more than 0·5M offshore.

Proceeding E–W, pass St Catherine breakwater head with stern Transit J28 to clear rocks immediately N of it (for view see page 124). Before turning NW to follow the coast find transit:

J31 290° Belle Hougue Point is open of conspicuous Tour de Rozel (29m) with its white mark. This will clear dangers off La Coupe Pt

ROZEL
49°14'·23N 02°02'·65W Pier head

A small drying fishing harbour with a cluster of gift shops, a pub (Rozel Bay Hotel), several restaurants and an hotel. The pier was built in the early 19th century to provide shelter for the overflow of oyster boats from Gorey. Today it is the domain of small fishing craft and holidaymakers but is only occasionally visited by small yachts able to take the ground.

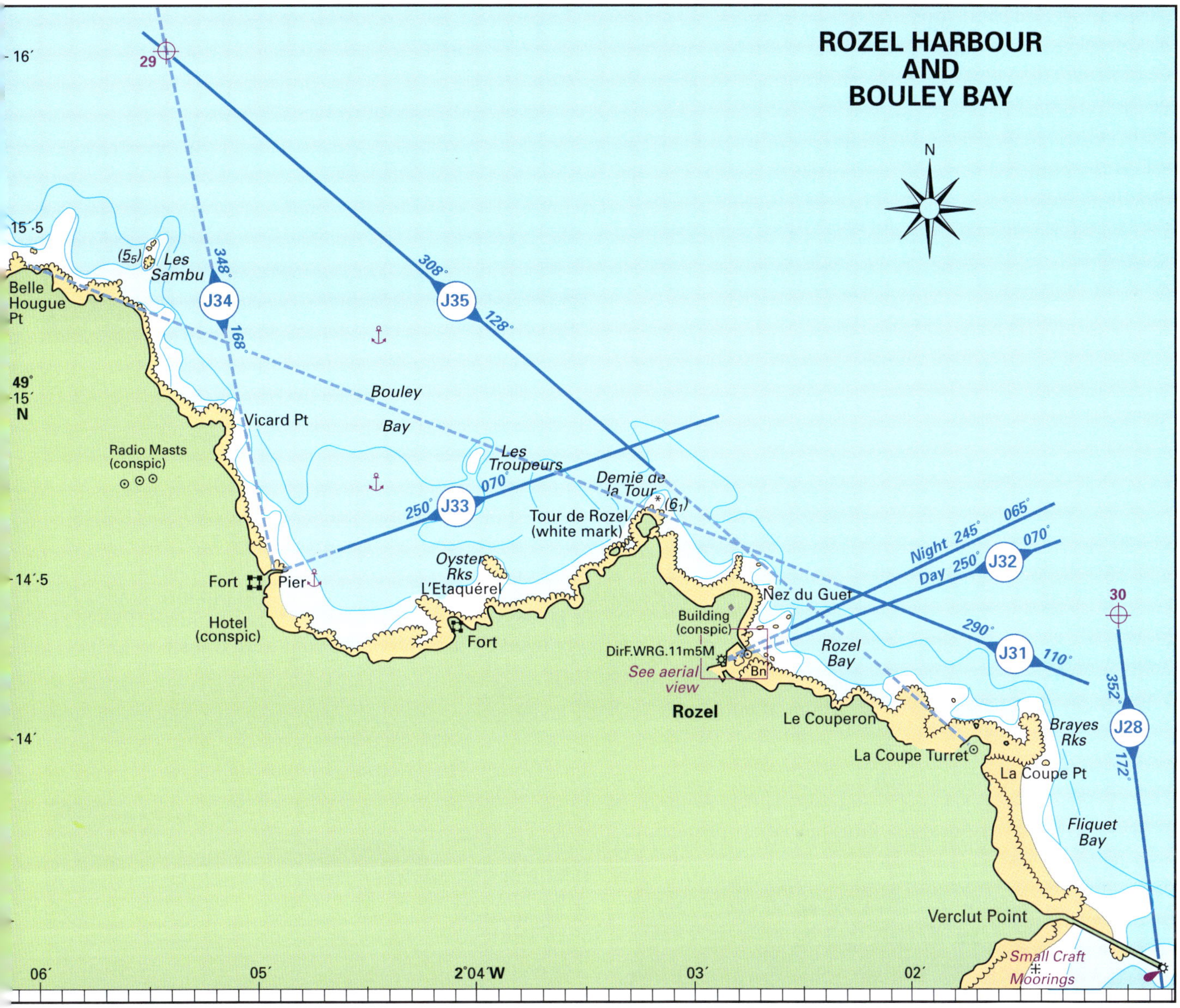

Jersey

ROZEL HARBOUR AND BOULEY BAY

I. THE CHANNEL ISLANDS

Approach

From Transit **J31** identify the white patch on the end of Rozel pier and take the following transit:

J32 250° *A conspicuous buff-coloured gable open of white patch on pierhead*

Note the official rear mark is a slender white light beacon on the slipway on an approach bearing of 245°, but this is seldom visible by day from seaward hence the above alternative. There is a buoyed entry channel (seasonal).

By night

Approach in the white sector of DirF.WRG light.

CHANNEL ISLANDS, CHERBOURG PENINSULA & NORTH BRITTANY

1 The Channel Islands

Anchoring and mooring

Due to the maze of moorings and lines in the harbour, the recommended anchorage lies outside, S of the approach line and clear of moorings. The bottom is mainly sand. Just inside the pierhead are landing steps which may be used briefly by tenders and small craft for off-loading. In suitable conditions and space permitting, a bilge keeler or multihull could safely ground on a sand and shingle beach to the N of the slipway opposite the entrance. Care should be taken not to get 'neaped'.

Shelter

Very good in westerlies and more sheltered than Gorey or St Catherine's Bay in a southerly. Exposed in easterlies when the anchorage and harbour can be untenable with heavy swell.

Supplies and services

Water Standpipe on pier.
Fuel Nil.
Crane Hand operated.
Stores No shops, but there are several snack bars and restaurants in the harbour area.
Transport There is a bus service to St Helier.

Departure

Continuing W leave Rozel on Transit J32 and when Tour de Rozel bears W steer 290° to leave Demie de La Tour (dries 6·1m) off the Tour de Rozel 500m to port.

BOULEY BAY

49°14'·50N 02°04'·70W

A wide bay offering sheltered anchorage in offshore winds. The harbour dries 1·6m and a short pier offers protection to small fishing craft.

Approaches

From east

Steer into the bay between Tour de Rozel and Les Troupeurs (1·8m) with:

J33 250° the right (W) side of Fort Lester over the white patch on the pierhead

From west

A line to clear Les Sambues:

J34 168° ⊕29 The root of Bouley Pier just open of Vicard Point clears Les Sambues (dry 3·4m and 5·5m), the rocky patches extending 0·5M off Belle Hougue Point

If continuing W and not intending to put into Bouley Bay a more comfortable distance off Les Sambues (0·4M) is obtained by using the following stern transit.

J35 128° ⊕29 La Coupe Turret well open of N edge of Tour de Rozel

Anchoring

There is a buoyed channel (seasonal) to the mooring area. Anchor 200m SE of the pierhead clear of moorings. The holding is good in sand. Landing crew alongside is possible in calm conditions and with sufficient water. Use the steps, which have a depth board, or the ladder nearer the pier head. There are few fixing points for lines ashore.

Facilities

There is a hotel, The Black Dog Bar, a pub, and Bouley Bay Dive Centre ☏ 01534 866990. The bus to town takes 30 minutes.

Jersey

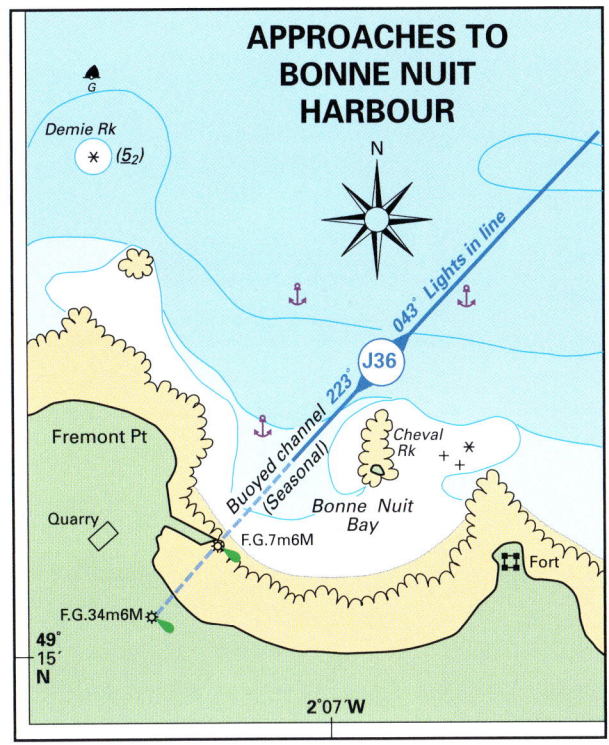

The pierhead at Bonne Nuit

BONNE NUIT HARBOUR

49°15′·09N 02°07′·17W Pier

A small fishing harbour beneath a backdrop of hills over 400ft high. The harbour dries to sand and shingle with rocky patches nearby. It is well traversed with mooring chains and prone to surge in northerlies, so taking the ground is not recommended. As with Rozel, anchoring off and entering by dinghy is the best way to see this quaint harbour with its café. Anchor clear of fishermen's buoys in 2m midway between the pierhead and Cheval Rock.

Historical note

Bonne Nuit takes its name from the priory established here in the 12th century. Not long after the monks returned to France it became a notorious rendezvous for smugglers, which may explain why the atmosphere in certain weathers can be eerie. Since it was a possible landing place for an enemy, La Crete Fort with its barracks was built in the 18th century.

Approach

Identify the above-water Cheval Rock (0·3m) ENE of the pierhead and marked with a pole and radar reflector. Enter with:

J36 223° The leading marks in line. Rear: red mark on hill. Front: pier head

By night

Entry possible with caution with both fixed green leading lights (F.G.6M).

Departure

If proceeding W identify the starboard buoy guarding Demie Rock (dries 5·2m) and leave it to port and keep 0·5M off the coast.

I. THE CHANNEL ISLANDS

CHANNEL ISLANDS, CHERBOURG PENINSULA & NORTH BRITTANY

1 The Channel Islands

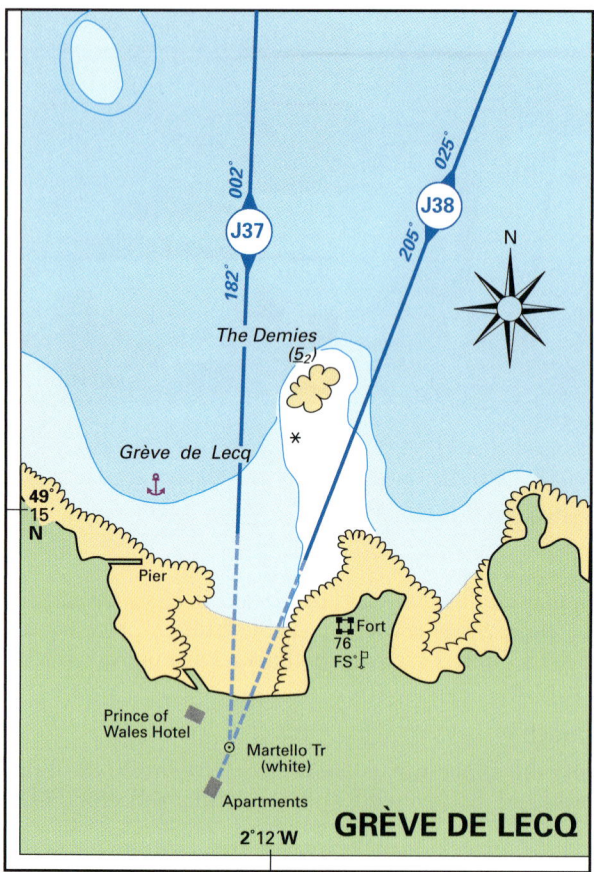

Approach W of the Demies

J37 182° *The tower is open left (E) of left hand edge of Prince of Wales Hotel by its width.*

Approach E of the Demies

J38 205° *The tower is aligned with the middle of the apartments and the road is seen almost on end.*

Both lines will clear The Demies by approximately 160m.

Anchorage

BA chart 1136 shows cables running out from the slipway. An anchorage should be found 180m N of the ruined pier and well clear of these.

GREVE AU LANCON (PLEMONT)
49°15'·60N 02°14'·14W

Although shown as an anchorage on BA charts the bay is seldom visited due to the prevalence of swell. Holding is good in sand but beware of discontinued submarine cables.

Wildlife

The nesting area of Jersey's dwindling puffin colony is among the cliffs between Plemont and Grève de Lecq. Land users and those on the water are asked to steer clear of the nesting sites.

GRÈVE DE LECQ
49°14'·98N 02°12'·12W
(See also plan page 106)

Grève de Lecq has a popular bathing beach with several bars and cafés but the stone pier is destroyed.

The Demies (dry 5·2m) lie 600m north of the E arm of the bay and are the main obstacles in the approach. There is only 0·5m at LWS between the Demies and the beach to the S but from 2m–4m may be found between them and the ruined pier. Approach and anchorage is therefore best made W of the Demies.

Approach from the north

When 0·5M off the shore, note the conspicuous Martello Tr (white) which is the key to clearing the Demies.

Les Ecréhous and Plateau des Minquiers

Local information

TRAVEL INFORMATION
Not applicable

PORTS OF ENTRY
Official Ports of Entry into Bailiwick of Jersey are St Helier and Gorey

CHARTS
British Admiralty
1136 Jersey – North Coast (1:25 000)
3655 Jersey and Adjacent Coast of France (1:50 000)
3656 Plateau des Minquiers and Adjacent Coast of France (1:50 000)

SC 5604 The Channel Islands Leisure Folio:
13 Jersey (1:50 000)
15c Les Ecrehou (1:50 000)
17 Plateau des Minquiers (1:50 000)

Imray
2500 The Channel Islands and adjacent coast of France
Chart Atlas:
9 Jersey & Les Écrehous (1:75 000)
13 Plateau des Minquiers (1:50 000)

SHOM
6937 Jersey - Côte Nord (1:25 000)
7157 De la Pointe d'Agon au Cap de Carteret - Passage de la Déroute (1:48 400)
7160 De Jersey à Guernsey (1:48 300)
7161 Des îles Chausey à Jersey - Plateau des Minquiers (1:48 500)

RADIO
See *Jersey Radio*

NAVIGATIONAL AIDS
None

SUPPLIES AND SERVICES
Les Ecrehous None
Plateau des Minquiers Except for the toilet (the southernmost in the British Isles!), there are no facilities on the island and visitors must bring their own water and supplies with them.

JERSEY COASTAL NATIONAL PARK
All Jersey's offshore reefs are recognised as wetlands of international importance and the main islands are part of Jersey's Coastal National Park Area. Visitors are asked to keep well away from nesting birds and to not interfere with any local wildlife, including plants. A 5 knot speed limit applies within the reefs.

Les Ecréhous looking south

CHANNEL ISLANDS, CHERBOURG PENINSULA & NORTH BRITTANY

1 The Channel Islands

Les Ecréhous

Note: Les Ecréhous has various spellings, including Les Ecrehous and Les Ecrehou.

Historical note

This rocky archipelago between Jersey and Normandy is part of the Parish of St Martin in Jersey and has an interesting history.

Its name, which has varied much over the centuries, is thought to derive from the Scandinavian words *sker-holm* meaning 'rocky islets'. In 1203 they were given to a Norman monastery on condition that the monks maintained a light and said masses for the King. The priory ruins still exist on Maître Ile.

The reef has seen its fair share of wreckings. The first reported was in 1309 when a boat returning from a seaweed-gathering trip was holed at low tide. The captain, thinking the rocks would never be covered, discharged all women passengers on a small rock while the crew swam to safety on La Marmotière. Night fell, the tide rose and at dawn the rock (since known as Pierre des Femmes) was bare. There is a tradition that on stormy nights the shrieks of the drowning can still be heard.

As with Jersey's other offshore possession, Les Minquiers, disputes with the French over sovereignty were not resolved until 1953 when the matter was settled in favour of Jersey. Even so it has since been necessary to defend the flag on occasions. In 1993 invading French fishermen succeeded in hauling down the Union Jack from the flagpole on La Marmotière and replacing it, briefly, with the tricolour and the banner of Normandy.

Three of the rocks have been elevated to the status of island, Maître Ile, La Marmotière and Blanche Ile. All have small buildings known as huts, which just manage to stay above water on the top of spring tides. Their Jersey owners use them as occasional retreats but there have been several notable long-term residents, the most recent being a 14-year stint by the self-styled King of the Ecréhous – Alphonse le Gastelois. He managed quite nicely on a staple diet of wild rabbit, fish and seaweed, supplemented by a bit of help from Jersey friends.

Ashore

There are no restrictions to landing and exploring Marmotière and Maître Ile but visitors should respect the privacy of residents and their properties.

Les Ecréhous is more family friendly than Plateau des Minquiers. Low water springs uncovers large areas of sand leaving natural pools for bathing. This should be undertaken with caution keeping a close eye on the tide.

Wildlife

The reef, which is a protected site, supports a diverse range of wildlife. In addition to breeding colonies of cormorants, shags, oystercatchers and terns, it is a stopover for migrants in the spring and summer. Marine mammals such as bottle-nosed dolphins are common and more recently grey seals have been spotted in the summer months.

> **TIDAL INFORMATION**
> Tidal levels referred to chart datum
> 49°17'·10N 1°55'·50W
>
> | MHWS | MHWN | MLWN | MLWS | MTL |
> |------|------|------|------|-----|
> | 10·9m | 8·4m | 3·8m | 1·3m | 6·1m |
>
> HW +0400 NNW 1·0-2·0 HW+0500 NNW 0·5-1·0
>
> **TIDAL STREAMS (referred to St Helier)**
> In the channel running NNW to Marmotière and round its E side.
> HW–0100 the stream is slack
> HW NNW 1·0-2·0 increasing to 2·5-5·0 or more then decreasing to: HW+0400 NNW 1·0–2·0, HW+0500 NNW 0·5–1·0 (slack), HW+0600 SSE 1·0-2·0 increasing to 2·0-5·0 and even 6·0 E of Marmotière, then decreasing.

Timing a visit

The area should be regarded as open sea at HW springs and can be very rough when accompanied by southerlies. A first visit should be made at neap tides in settled weather, light northwesterlies are best, with good visibility and no risk of fog.

The approach from the SW is best timed on a rising tide to arrive about HW–0200 when the stream is fairly slack. Locals aim to arrive at half ebb having taken a fair stream from the E coast. At that time the sandy ridge joining the two islands is uncovering and rowing ashore becomes easier towards LW.

Caution

Dinghy work and bathing can be dangerous and particular attention should be paid to streams.

Depths

The anchorage and moorings S of Marmotière can be approached at all states of tide with a least depth at the moorings of 1·5m LWS. The Pool (plan page 134) has

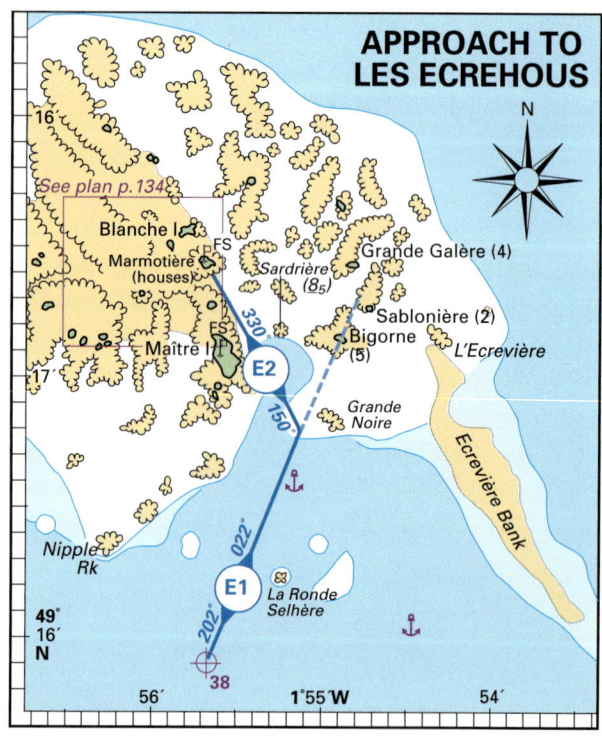

Les Ecréhous & Plateau des Minquiers

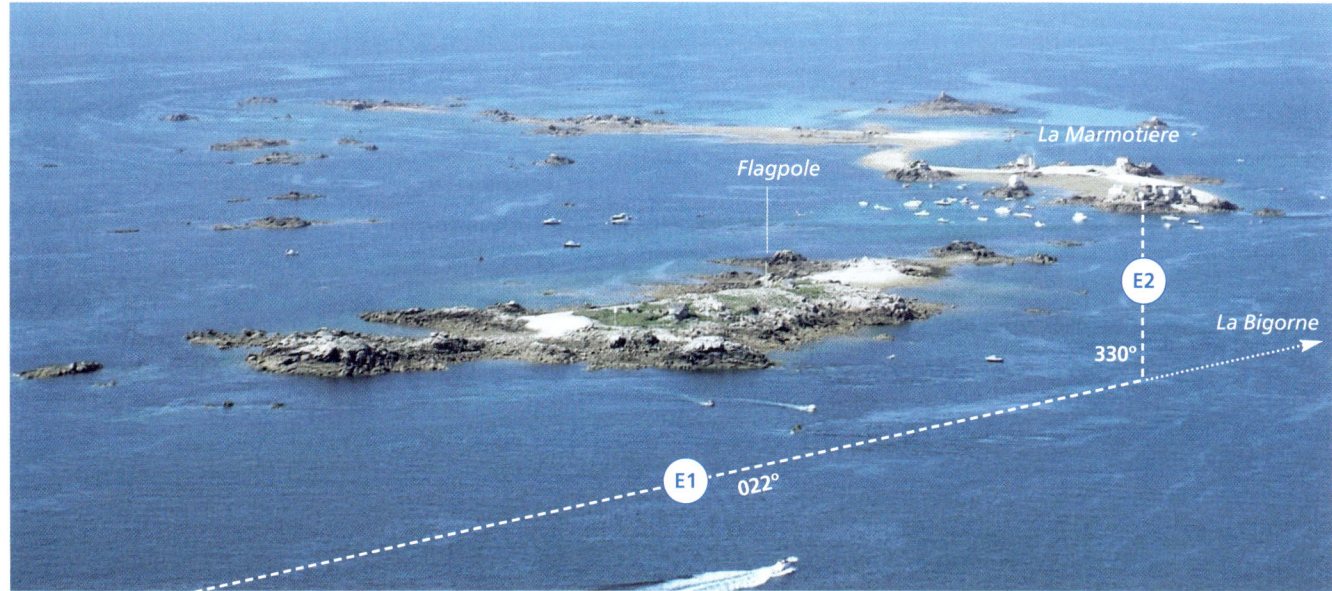

Entry viewed from the south (HW)

Entry viewed from the north (LW)

recently been silting, the sand is ridged, and deep draught vessels that cannot take the ground should enter with caution, if at all. 1m may be found in places to the W at LWS but there is more water at neaps. A reef of *Sargassum muticum* (Japanese seaweed) was reported in the pool in 1995.

Approach (by day only)

Approach from the SW (⊕38) with La Bigorne Rock (5m) on a steady bearing of 022°. This key rock to the E of Maître Ile is identified by its tusk shape – its name derives from a Jersey French word meaning pickaxe. It should be positively identified as early as possible and when on the above bearing take up:

E1 022° ⊕38 *La Bigorne Rock midway between Grande Galère (4m) N and Sablonière (2m) S will clear rocks either side of the approach*

CHANNEL ISLANDS, CHERBOURG PENINSULA & NORTH BRITTANY   133

1 The Channel Islands

When just under 400m short of La Bigorne Rock, look NW to identify the second set of marks:

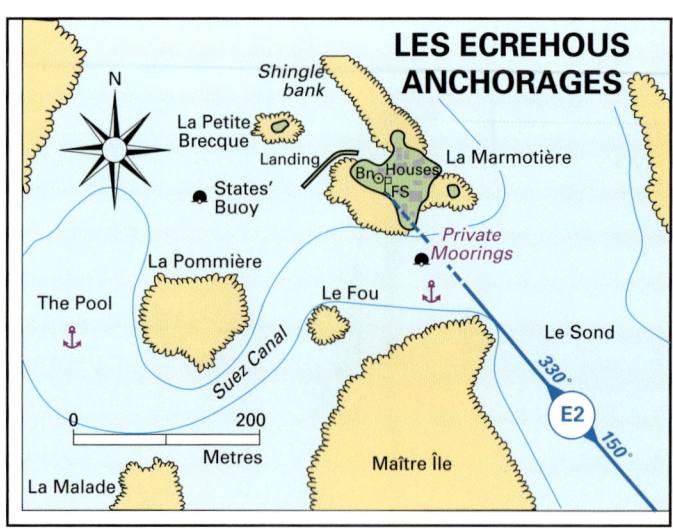

E2 *330° A black board in line with Marmotière flagpole above vertical white stripe*

This transit should be held accurately to clear the drying rock La Sardrière in the centre of Le Sond E of Maître Ile. Approaching the N tip of Maître Ile, a slight deviation to the E may be necessary to avoid drying rocks.

Anchorages

S of La Marmotière

Close S of La Marmotière are several mooring buoys which are private and should not be used without the owner's permission. Alternatively there is good holding, if limited swinging room, for anchoring S of this mooring area. Here the yacht will be just clear of the strong tidal stream in Le Sond.

Drying anchorages and moorings

The aerial view shows several areas in the SW quadrant of La Marmotière where it is possible to dry out on a sandy bottom. There is a States of Jersey maintained mooring buoy (dries) located W of La Marmotière.

The anchorage off La Marmotière can be congested at weekends

134 CHANNEL ISLANDS, CHERBOURG PENINSULA & NORTH BRITTANY

Les Ecréhous & Plateau des Minquiers

The anchorage off La Marmotière

The Pool

This offers the possibility of remaining afloat at LW, if only just at spring tides. Access is about 2hrs either side of HW. Proceed to the States mooring W of La Marmotière, avoiding the S extremity of the islet, then head SW for the private mooring buoys in The Pool. This route will leave La Pommière (dries 3·2m) close to the S. Once familiar with the area entry may also be made via the narrow 'Suez Canal' (also known as 'The Gully') given sufficient water and before Le Fou, Malade and Pommière Rocks are covered. There are no formal marks and a LW reconnaissance is best made beforehand with the dinghy.

The Pool at LWS viewed from the southwest. The yacht is aground, supported by beaching legs

Plateau des Minquiers

48°58'·16N 2°03'·60W (States mooring)

Historical note

This reef, known locally as The Minkies, is Britain's most southerly outpost and at LW springs uncovers a larger area than that of Jersey. Together with Les Ecrehous and the Paternosters, it is a protected RAMSAR site on account of its unique wildlife. For centuries the rare ormer shellfish, considered a local delicacy, has been gathered here at very low 'ormering' tides. Despite the reef's notoriety for treacherous rocks and strong tidal streams, the approach from the N in settled weather with good visibility is straightforward, as is departure to the SE as long as the line is held accurately. The charted S channel should be used for entry or departure with caution.

Maîtresse Ile is large enough to hold a dozen or so small houses, most of which were built by the quarrymen who toiled on the reef in the 18th century. Fort Regent overlooking St Helier is reputed to have been built of granite transported by barge from the Minkies. By the early 19th century local fishermen, fearing there would soon be little left of their valuable fishing grounds, threw the quarrymen's tools into the sea, but they had already had enough and in 1807 emigrated to work for the French on Chausey. Their names can still be seen carved on the rocks.

For centuries French and Jersey fishermen shared the harvest of the Minkies, their harsh lives being immortalised in Victor Hugo's famous novel *The Toilers of the Sea*. In 1953 sovereignty of the reef was confirmed in favour of Britain and the French removed all their buoys. Since then the States of Jersey, with the help of Trinity House, have maintained an excellent system of buoyage and marks around the reef.

TIDAL INFORMATION
Tidal levels referred to chart datum
48°58 N 2°08 W

MHWS	MHWN	MLWN	MLWS	MTL
11·6m	8·9m	4·0m	1·4m	6·5m

Tidal streams referred to HW St Helier
1·0M N of Demie de Vascelin starboard buoy, marking the entrance to the N approach channel to Maîtresse Ile;
HW–0600, W 1·7–0·7 then slack and turning anti-clockwise to:
HW–0500, SE 0·4–0·2 increasing to:
HW–0300, ESE 5·0–2·0 then decreasing to:
HW E 0.4-0·2 slackening and turning anticlockwise to:
HW+0200 WNW 2·3–1·1 with a maximum:
HW+0400 WNW 4·0–1·5

The stream runs SSE and NNW down the channel passing W of Maîtresse Ile with a maximum of 3·5 knots SSE at HW–0400 and 3 knots NNW at HW+0200 (see *Appendix*).

NE of Maîtresse Ile it can attain 7 knots through the Gauliot Passage, occasionally used by locals in small craft.

S of the S Minquiers and SE Minquiers buoys the stream runs E or SE from HW–0500 to HW St Helier with a maximum of 5 knots at springs and W or NW from HW+0100 to HW–0600 with a maximum of 4·7 knots at springs.

CHANNEL ISLANDS, CHERBOURG PENINSULA & NORTH BRITTANY

1 The Channel Islands

Looking NW at LW springs

Looking NE over Maîtresse Ile towards the anchorage north of Grande Gauliot. Les Trois Grunes (drying 9·4m) are visible at the top of this view

View from the N at LWS (see text following page)

Timing a visit and selecting an anchorage

A visit over HW neaps is the best time to make a first acquaintance. Settled weather is essential with at least 3M visibility for identifying marks. Aim to be at the N entrance around half flood so entry is made on a rising tide with decreasing current. Piloting in at an average speed of 4 knots allow about half an hour to reach the Pool (see plan on page 137). At least 3 hours remain to take in some extraordinary scenery before returning on the ebb. From the highest point at the N end of Maîtresse Ile it is possible, on a clear day, to pick out the spire of St Malo Cathedral.

The reef is at its best at LW springs when it becomes the haunt of low water fishermen. The best option is to take the ground, if practicable, in the Pool (dries 1·2m) with its clean sandy bottom and total protection afforded by borders of drying rocks.

Ashore

Caution

Dinghy work can be dangerous and bathing is ill advised. Particular attention should be paid to streams.

There are no restrictions to landing and exploring Maîtresse Ile but visitors should respect the privacy of residents and their properties. In the spring tread carefully to avoid nests and fledglings.

Les Ecréhous & Plateau des Minquiers

Rocher Blanc *Nick Bailhache*

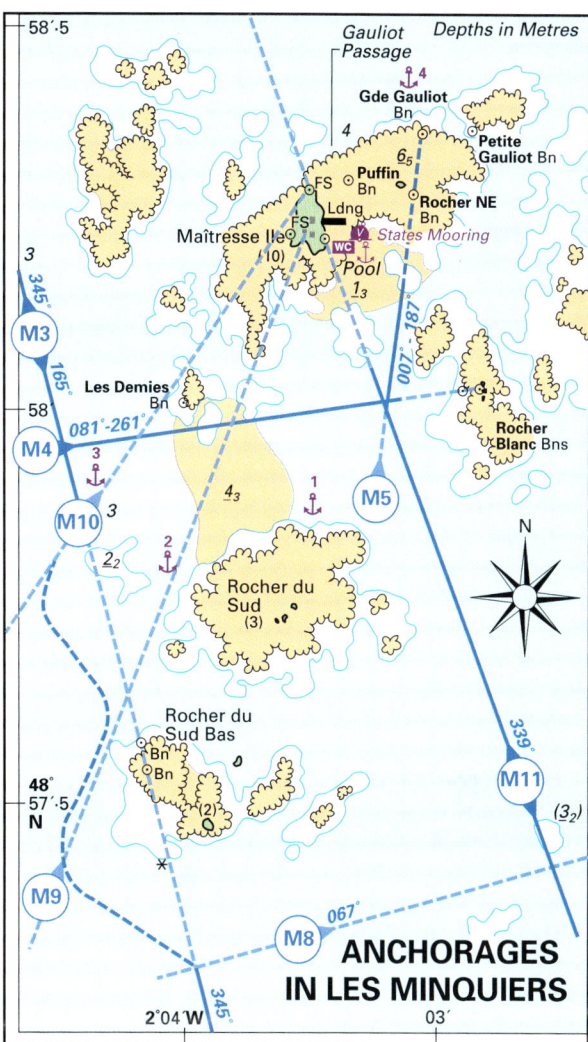

ANCHORAGES IN LES MINQUIERS

There is a Jersey Impôts (Customs) hut on the island which is fitted out with bunks and basic rations for emergency use. The landing pad at the north end of Maîtresse Ile may occasionally be used by Search and Rescue helicopters.

Anchorages

There are a number of alternatives if you wish to remain afloat. The most straightforward of these are as follows (see photos):

1. E of sand bar by Les Demies. This is approximately 400m SE of the beacon
2. S of Les Demies, west of the sand bar. The stream may run hard in a SSE direction after LW
3. SW of Les Demies in the main channel on the Rocher du Sud en Bas marks (M3)
4. NW of Gde Gauliot. To reach this anchorage from the N, round the Jetée des Fontaines de Bas beacon, leaving it to port and steer 151°, with due attention to the tidal stream, on a line between Puffin beacon and Jetée des Fontaines de Bas beacon (astern on the reciprocal 331°). This course leaves the Jetée des Fontaines rocks, drying 7·4m close to port and a rock drying 1·8m close to starboard.

Caution

In view of the dangers in the approach to the anchorage NW of Grande Gauliot, it should not be attempted without local knowledge on board.

Approaches to Maîtresse Ile (The Pool) (by day only)

Caution The Sandbanks

Approaches to The Pool are encumbered by drying sandbanks and arrival is not recommended or may not be possible below half tide St Helier.

The Northern approach (line M3) involves clearing the sandbank around Grune Tar bn. This was drying approximately 3·5m in 2016 having moved E to obstruct the channel.

Final entry to The Pool is limited by depth over the smaller bank around Les Demies (Demics) S of Maîtresse Ile. This dries approximately 3·4m. The cautious limit for crossing this may be extended to 4 hours after HW or even LW at Neaps depending on draught.

Caprice in the Pool off Maîtresse Ile. The fishing boat is on the States mooring

CHANNEL ISLANDS, CHERBOURG PENINSULA & NORTH BRITTANY

1 The Channel Islands

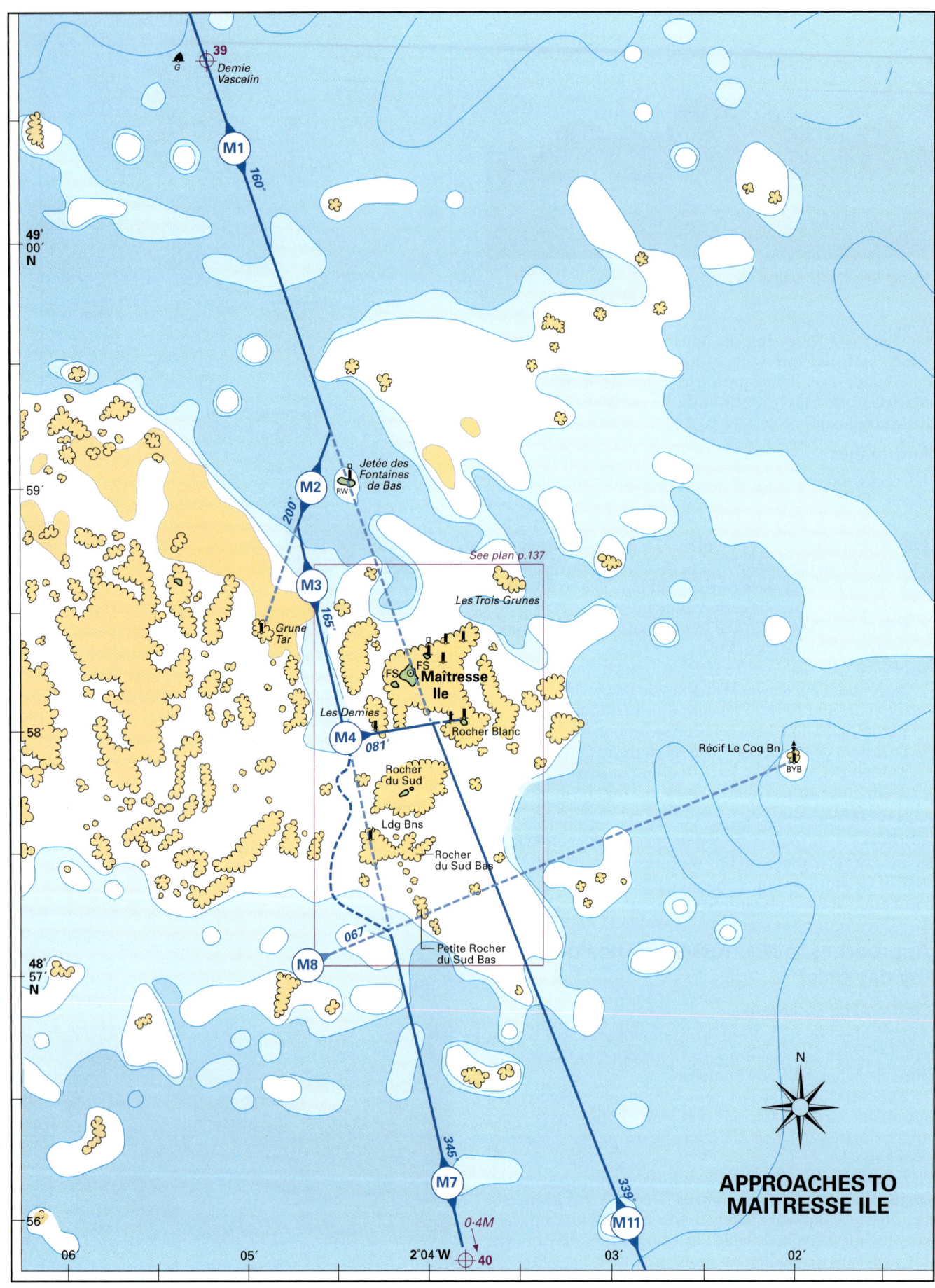

APPROACHES TO MAITRESSE ILE

138 CHANNEL ISLANDS, CHERBOURG PENINSULA & NORTH BRITTANY

Les Ecréhous & Plateau des Minquiers

Northern approach (drying approx. 3·5m)

The following sequence of photographs were taken on a visit under sail. Predicted height of HW St Helier was 8·1m (neaps).

HW–0300 Departure from St Helier marina by S Passage (see *St Helier. From the south* on page 111). Start point is 0·5M W of Demie de Pas LtHo.

HW–0100 At the Demie de Vascelin green buoy Fl.G.3s with radar echo-enhancer (⊕39). This is the key mark for entry and is left close to starboard. Maîtresse Ile is the largest feature to the left (E). The first transit is:

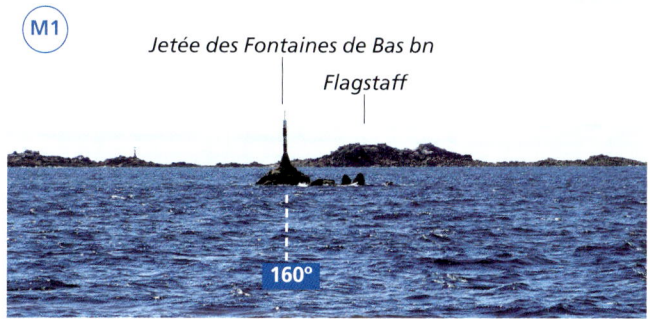

M1 160° ⊕39 Jetée des Fontaines de Bas RW beacon in line with Maîtresse Ile flagstaff (northernmost of two)

At weekends a resident may fly the Union flag making the flagstaff easier to identify. When 200m from the beacon alter to starboard towards a single mark.

M2 200° Grune Tar beacon, a white column with 'T' topmark. Hold on a steady bearing and look for the next distant transit to the S:

M3 165° Rocher du Sud Bas beacons in line

The forward northernmost mark is a pole with two red balls as topmark and the rear S mark is a white concrete column.

Caution

With the sandbank running down the W side of the channel and drying rocks to the E, there is little room to deviate from transit M3. This should be held accurately until Les Demies beacon pole with D topmark is abeam. Look E for the next transit (M4) and make ready to turn to port.

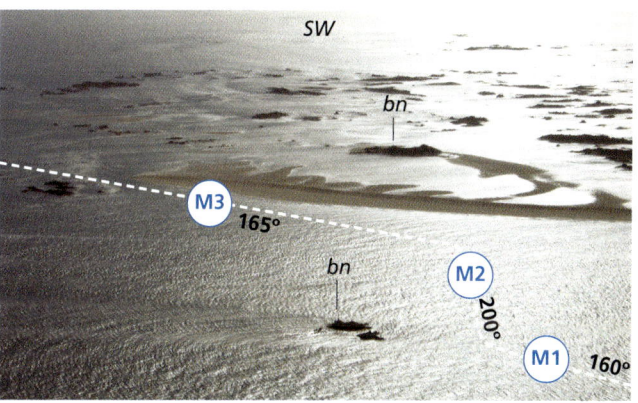

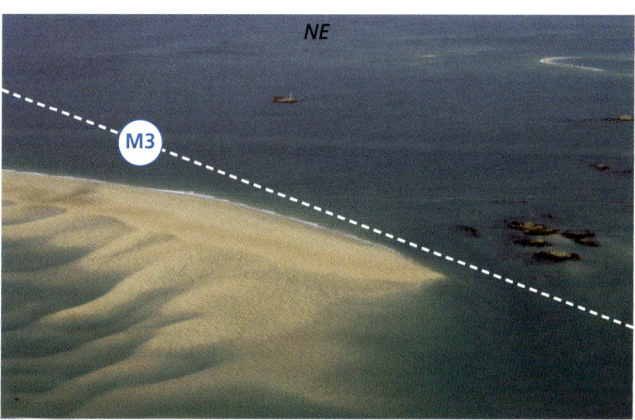

The sandbank northeast of Grune Tar beacon at LWS looking NE

1 The Channel Islands

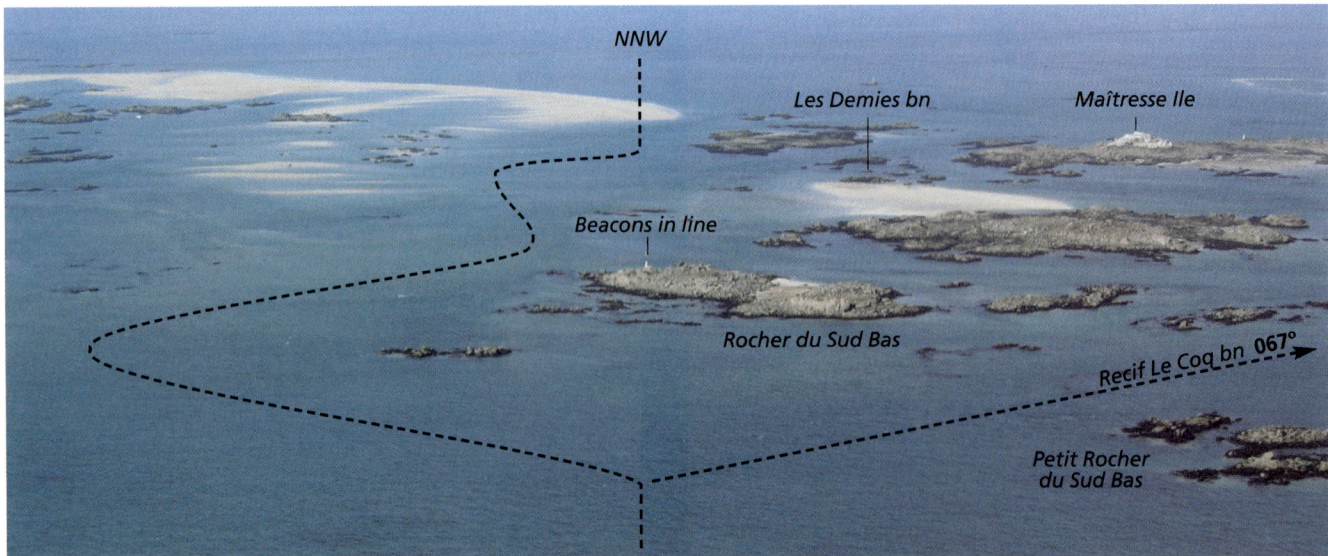

Southern approach on an exceptionally low tide. The sandbank obstructs the channel

M4 081° The Rocher Blanc beacons in transit

The forward mark is a red beacon and the rear E mark is a white painted rock topped with a white pole and + topmark. When just short of Rocher Blanc turn to port onto the final transit.

M5 007° The Rocher NE RW beacon is in line with La Grande Gauliot beacon pole with open diamond topmark

Hold this transit until M6 marks are in transit:

M6 *The most southerly chimney on Maîtresse Ile is in line with the toilet, then head towards the States of Jersey orange mooring buoy in The Pool*

Southern approach (0·3m)

This entry is not easy and should only be attempted after using it for departure, and identifying the dangers at low water.

Entering from the S, leave the SE Minquiers E cardinal buoy 1M to starboard and steer for Maîtresse Ile on 342°. From a distance of not less than 2M, identify the leading beacons on Rocher du Sud Bas.

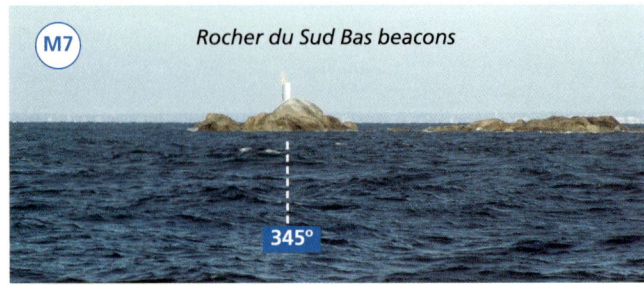

M7 345° ⊕40 *With the beacons in line, make good 345° and identify Récif Le Coq beacon, E cardinal, 2M to starboard*

Les Ecréhous & Plateau des Minquiers

Hold transit of **M7** ⊕*40* until:

Breast mark **M8** *067° Récif Le Coq beacon is just open to the N of the Petit Rocher du Sud Bas rocks (dries 7·3m)*

This transit is the turning point for clearing W of rocks SW of Rocher du Sud Bas (see view on page 15).

Alter to port to make good a WNW course. Hold until:

M9 *NNE The huts on Maîtresse Ile are open to the W of the northernmost Rocher du Sud Bas beacon (pole with two red balls)*

Steer a NNE course, with allowance for stream, leaving the beacons 100–200m to starboard. When abeam, alter course to make good NW until:

M10 The northernmost flagstaff on Maîtresse Ile is just open to the W of Les Demies (Demics) beacon

Regain the transit line **M3** to realign both Rocher du Sud Bas beacons astern on 165°. If proceeding to The Pool turn to starboard with Rocher Blanc beacons in line on 081° (**M4**).

Departure southeast

If there is 4m or more at the States buoy in The Pool, and it is not below half tide, it is possible to leave by this passage on a single transit. The marks are hard to identify from a distance and entry should only be attempted when thoroughly familiar with the area.

There is a toilet on Maîtresse Ile, which is painted on the S side with black/white bands (see view **M11**).

The lower half of the flagstaff is also painted with black/white bands.

The stern transit is the alignment of both these marks.

Britain's southernmost building is a toilet, which doubles as a transit mark

M11 *339° The northernmost flagstaff in line with the toilet*

Hold accurately for at least 2M with due allowance for the tidal stream.

Maîtresse Ile at the top of a large spring tide. There is little to see

II The Cherbourg Peninsula

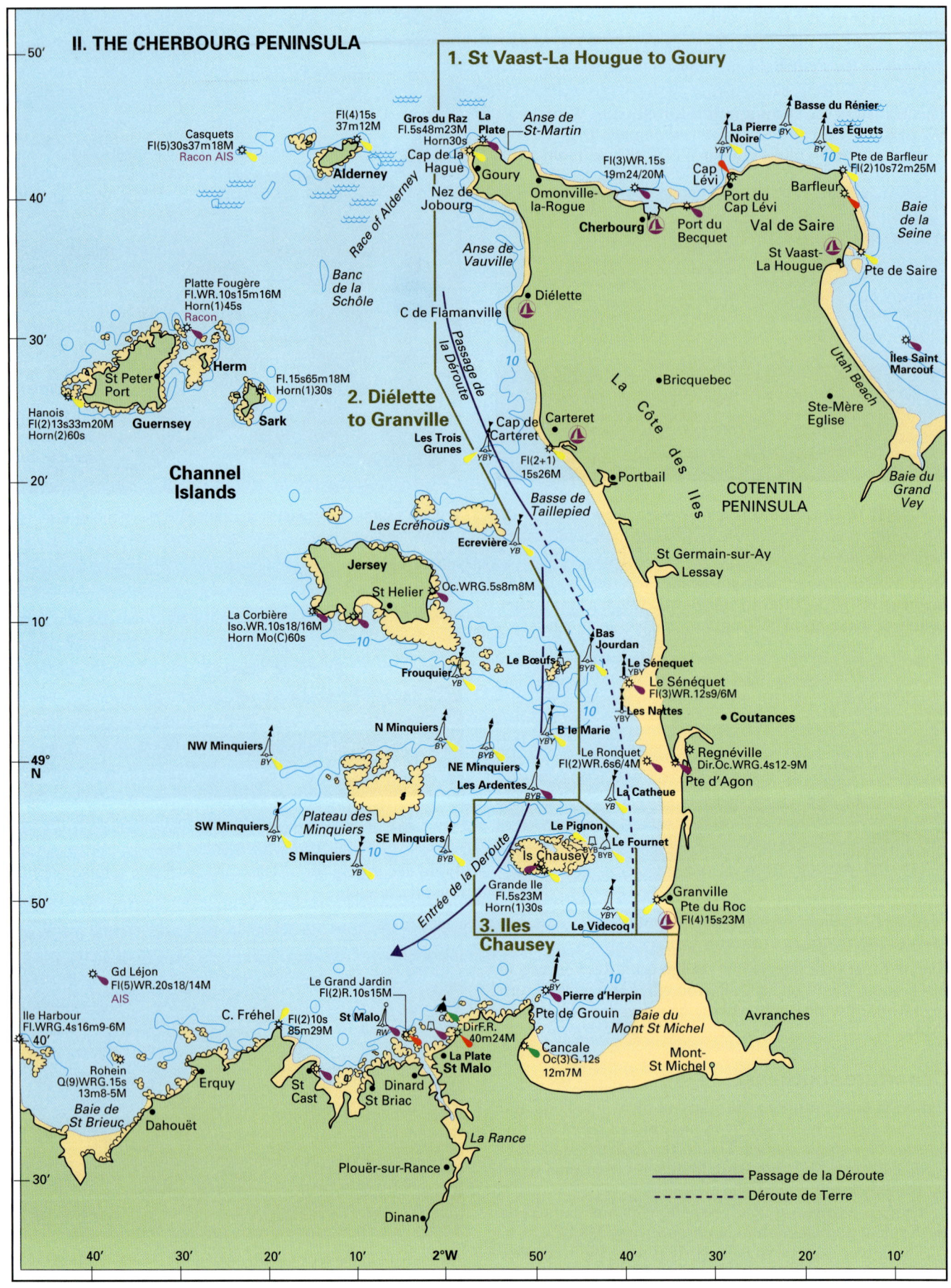

II. The Cherbourg Peninsula
Le Cotentin

Introduction
The Cherbourg Peninsula, known as Le Cotentin after Coutances, its former capital, is within the French department of Manche in the region of Basse Normandie. Normandy shares cultural and historical links with the Channel Islands – Les Iles Anglo-Normandes to the French.

Tides
There is no escape from the strongly tidal waters of the Channel Islands and North Brittany coastal area. The Alderney Race and Le Raz de Barfleur East of Cherbourg call for particular attention. With the exception of Cherbourg all harbours dry although St Vaast-La Hougue, Diélette, Carteret and Granville have marinas that may be accessed over a sill at half tide.

There are no suitable anchorages off any of the harbour entrances on the west coast where one can wait for the tide so arriving on time should be the aim. Iles Chausey may be considered as an alternative in the event of missing the sill at Granville or weather worries.
(See *Caution* page 187.)

Inland
The interior of the Cotentin is as diverse as its coastline and it is worth taking time out to explore its rich countryside and visit some of its many historic sites. Being off tourist routes the roads are generally quiet. Geographically it divides into three areas:

Cap de la Hague
The lonely NW corner is off the beaten track and untouched by tourism. It culminates in the austere headlands of Cap de la Hague, Nez de Jobourg and Flamanville. The latter is dominated by the nuclear reprocessing plant which is open to the public from April to September – a three hour tour.

The old market town of Bricquebec eight miles inland from Carteret has a well preserved 12th century castle.

Val de Saire
The NE corner is promoted as 'an area of verdant landscape that has preserved its bygone charm.' Barfleur, claimed to be 'one of the most beautiful villages of France' has a uniquely peaceful atmosphere and several good seafood restaurants. The oyster port of St Vaast-La Hougue five miles south is a good base from which to visit Utah Beach, the westernmost of the beaches on which American forces landed on D-Day, 6 June 1944. Several wrecks are still visible. Museum: Museé du Débarquement.

The Cotentin Pass is a low plain stretching across the middle of the peninsula between Baie du Grand Vey in the NE to Lessay on the Côte des Iles. Much of this marshland that originally isolated the northern part of the peninsula from the Continent is now a nature park (Parc Natural Régional des Marais du Cotentin et du Bessin). This fascinating area of wetland is home to a variety of wildlife.

Historical
Early times
In prehistoric times sea levels were lower and the landscape looked very different. What is now the Cotentin would have extended into the Atlantic as a low flat plain. As tide

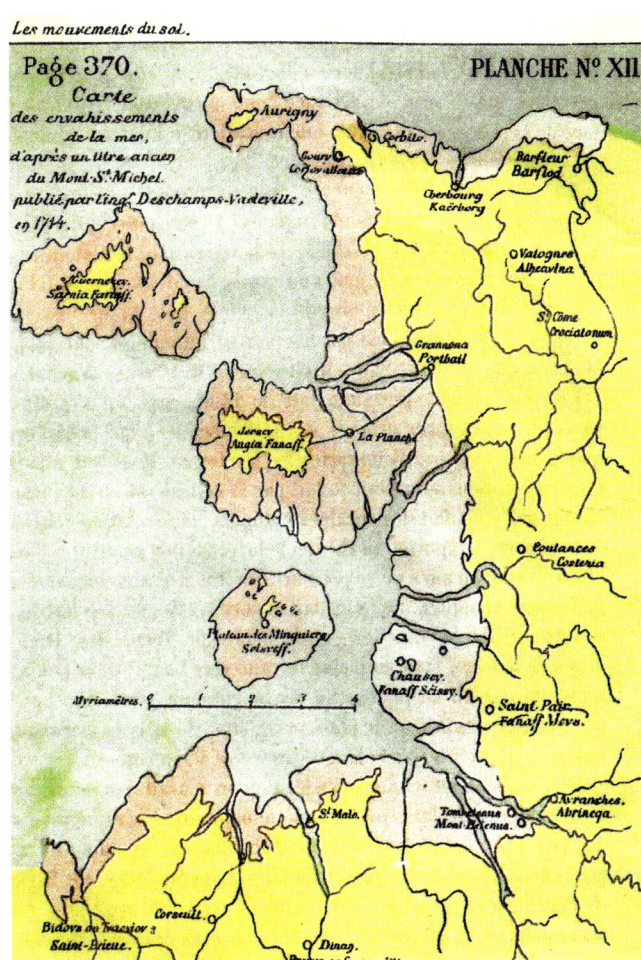

This shows the ancient coastline of Le Cotentin. Jersey, Alderney and Les Iles Chausey are part of the continent and there is no Alderney Race. Guernsey and Sark have always been islands
(Courtesy of La Societé Jersiaise)

II The Cherbourg Peninsula

levels rose around 7000BC areas of higher land became surrounded to form the Channel Islands we know today. There is evidence that Jersey remained linked to the Continent for much longer and it may have been an earthquake and tidal wave in AD709 that caused the final separation. Today it is said that at very low spring tides a man on stilts could, by picking his way, walk from Jersey's southeast corner across to France! See antique plan page 143.

In the first four centuries AD the Romans established settlements in the north and south of The Contentin and also in Alderney (Ridunia), Guernsey (Sarnia) and Jersey (Caesarea). The remains of a Gallo – Roman vessel have been discovered in St Peter Port harbour and a Roman fort may be seen in Alderney.

The Norman Conquest 1066

With the collapse of Rome the Vikings (Norsemen) plundered their way South laying waste the towns of the Cotentin. Their chief, Rollo, became the first Duke of Normandy. His successor, William, invaded and conquered England in 1066 thereby annexing Normandy and its islands to the English crown. When in 1204 England lost Normandy back to the French, Channel Islanders remained loyal to the English crown thereby earning the right to govern themselves.

Though all but the church ceased to be administered from Normandy their laws, language and customs remained largely unchanged. Despite frequent squabbles, brief recapture and periods of war between England and France trade flourished between the Islands and their now foreign neighbours.

In the middle ages piracy and smuggling was rife and the islands exploited their independent status and geographical position as safe havens on merchant shipping routes.

The Battle of Normandy 1944

During the Second World War France and the Channel Islands were occupied by German forces. There are dramatic tales of perilous escapes in frail boats from the Islands across to the Cotentin. On 6 June 1944 (D-Day) British and Allied Forces landed on the beaches east of the Cotentin. The Cotentin campaign is known as 'the war of the hedgerows' as it was fought in the 'Bocage Normand' – an area to the southeast of the peninsula with a landscape of small meadows and orchards enclosed by hedgerows. It took three weeks to liberate the Cotentin peninsula.

Museums and sites (N–S)

Sainte Marie du Mont Musée du Débarquement

Cherbourg Musée Maritime Chantereyne (La Cité de la Mer)

Ste Mère Eglise Airborne Troops Museum

Bayeux Tapestry of The Norman Conquest

Lessay Romanesque Abbey

Coutances Cathedral

Abbaye de la Lucerne (seven miles SE of Granville) Founded in 1143

St Hilaire du Harcourt 13th century fort

Le Mont St Michel World Heritage Site

Détail de la Tapisserie de Bayeux - XIe siécle (detail from Bayeux tapestry, 11th century) *Avec autorisation de la Ville de Bayeux*

1. St Vaast-La Hougue to Goury (40M)

THE COASTLINE

The peninsula's 110M coastline from the Baie du Grand Vey in the Baie de Seine to the border with Brittany at Mont St Michel is diverse. South of Pointe de Barfleur in the Northeast is the short low stretch of the east coast. It has two drying harbours, Barfleur and St Vaast-La Hougue, which have provided havens of peace to generations of sailors seeking shelter from wild westerly weather in the Channel.

The rugged coast and steep cliffs of the North West corner overlooking the Alderney Race and its approaches are reminiscent of the Channel Islands and North Brittany.

Cherbourg in the middle of the north coast is the principal commercial port for the Cotentin. It may be entered at all states of tide and in more or less any weather. At 60 miles from the Solent it is a popular port of call en route to the Channel Islands and Brittany.

West of Cherbourg tidal activity and seas increase towards Cap de la Hague. There are two bays sheltered from westerlies that may be used while awaiting suitable conditions for taking the Alderney Race. Omonville is a small harbour with visitor moorings and further W is Anse de St Martin. With time, calm conditions and some local knowledge aboard you may wish to try the small fisherman's harbour of Goury 0·1M SSW of Cap de la Hague.

LIST OF PORTS

St Vaast-La Hougue *146*

Barfleur *150*

Port du Cap Lévi *157*

Port du Becquet *158*

Cherbourg *159*

Omonville-la-Rogue *164*

Anse St Martin and Port Racine *165*

Goury *166*

Alderney Race in a good mood

Baie de Seine from N

II The Cherbourg Peninsula

St Vaast-La Hougue

49°35'·17N 01°15'·41W light tower head of Long Jetty

TRAVEL
Sea
  Ferries to Cherbourg
  Brittany Ferries ☏ 08 25 82 58 28
  Irish Ferries ☏ 02 33 23 44 44
  Celtic Link Ferries ☏ 02 33 43 23 87
  Manche Iles Express ☏ 08 25 13 30 50
  www.manche-iles.com
  Vedettes 'Jolie France' ☏ 02 33 50 31 81
Air
  Cherbourg (Maupertus) Airport ☏ 02 33 88 57 60
Rail/Bus
  SNCF Cherbourg
  SNCF Valognes
  transports.manche.fr
  Booking and tickets available at Office du Tourisme

CHARTS
  BA 2135 Pointe de Barfleur to Pointe de la Percée (1:48 000)
  Imray C32 Baie de Seine*
  Imray 2110 North France Chart Atlas*
    *both include plan: Saint Vaast-La Hougue (1:20 000)
  SHOM 7090 De la Pointe de Barfleur à Saint Vaast-La Hougue (1:20 000)*
    *includes plan: Port de Saint Vaast-La Hougue (1:7500)
  SHOM 7422 De la Pointe de Barfleur à La Pointe de La Percée – Iles Saint-Marcouf (1:48 000)
  Tidal Stream Atlas: SHOM Baie de Seine

RADIO
  Bureau du Port Ch 9 0900–1200 1400–1700
  Off season: 0900–1200
  Sunday: During gate opening

TIDAL INFORMATION
  Standard port Cherbourg
  Time difference: HW Dover –0240
  HW Cherbourg Springs + 0050 Neaps + 0120

MHWS	MLWS	MHWN	MLWN
6·4	1·1	5·0	2·5

Entry to Marina (max draught 2·3m) is via a gate. Entering vessels have priority.
Times: HW -2h 15–HW +3h 30
During high pressure conditions and at neap tides the above times may be limited by between 30 minutes and 1h 15 minutes.

USEFUL CONTACTS
  Bureau du Port, Quai Ouest ☏ 02 33 23 61 00
    www.saint-vaast.reville.com
    Email porte-st-vaast@saint-vaast-reville.com
  Yacht Club de Saint-Vaast ☏ 06 09 43 71 85
  Club Nautique de la Baie de Saint-Vaast ☏ 02 33 43 44 73
    Email cnbsv@wanadoo.fr
  Office du Tourisme, Quai Ouest ☏ 02 33 23 19 32

SUPPLIES AND SERVICES
Boatyard/Chandlery Le Chantier Naval Bernard
  ☏ 02 33 54 43 47 www.chantier-naval-bernard.com
  Cotentin Nautic ☏ 92 33 88 75 10 www.cotentin-nautic.net
  Email cotentin.nautic@wanadoo.fr
Garage La Longue Rive. Route de St Vaast-Reville
Marine electronics Marelec ☏ 02 33 54 63 82
  Email marelec.electronics@orange.fr
Supermarket 'Super U'
Restaurants La Bisquine, Quai Vauban ☏ 02 33 23 95 82
  Les Fushsias, 20 rue Maréchal Foch ☏ 02 33 43 46 79
Marina Water and electricity on pontoons
Fuel Quai Tourville
Car hire Le Relais du Port ☏ 02 33 88 57 57
  Email relaisduport@orange.fr
Taxi Le Carpentier ☏ 02 33 54 01 84
Market day Saturday

St Vaast-La Hougue and Île de Tatihou looking east

146 CHANNEL ISLANDS, CHERBOURG PENINSULA & NORTH BRITTANY

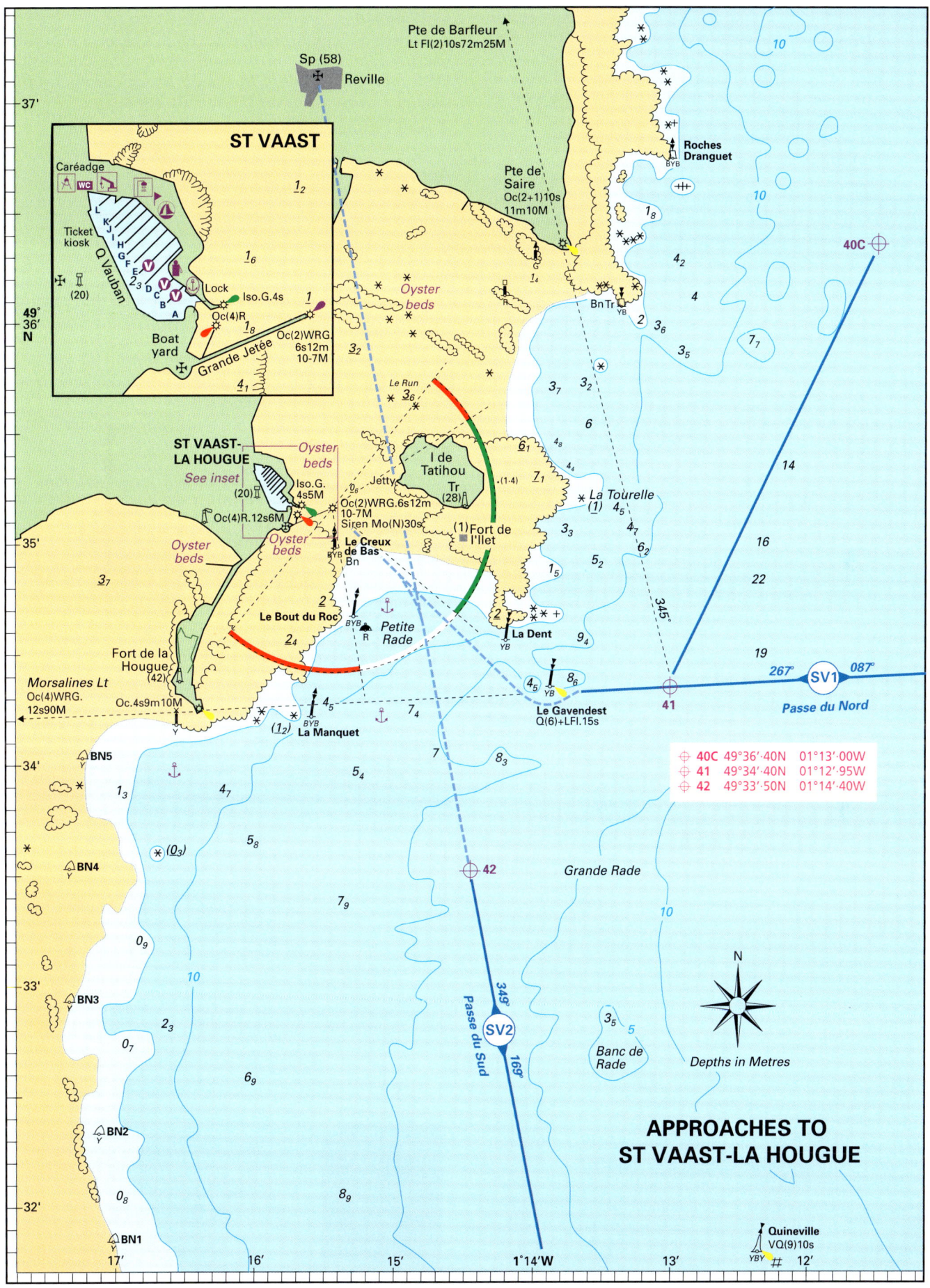

II The Cherbourg Peninsula

Four miles south of Pointe de Barfleur the rocky coastline changes to drying sands which continue south more or less unbroken to the Baie du Grand Vey. Tucked away southwest of Pointe de Saire and totally sheltered from all but easterly winds is the drying Baie de St Vaast with its port and town of St Vaast-La Hougue. Historically this was known as 'La Houge' derived from the Norse word '*haugr*' meaning land surrounded by water.

Thanks to the construction of an inner basin the drying fishing harbour famous for its oyster culture is now also an efficient Port de Plaisance with excellent facilities. This is accessible to craft of up to 2·3m draught via a gate. (See *Tidal Information* page 146.)

While this corner of the Cotentin tends to be seldom visited by Channel Islanders who may be deterred by a long haul up into the Channel and through two tidal races, it is familiar to UK S coast yachtsmen as a quieter and more interesting stop over en route to the Islands and Brittany.

The area is steeped in history and it is worth taking time to visit nearby sites of Ile de Tatihou and Fort La Hougue, both conspicuous by their almost identical forts. (See *Historical* below.)

Historical

The Battle of La Hougue

This clash between French and Anglo-Dutch fleets took place in 1692. It is a cautionary tale that started when the fleet of Louis XIV under Vice Admiral Tourville cast off from Brest bound for La Hougue. Here they were to escort other ships in an invasion of England to help James II recover the English crown. However, the fleet was spotted by a sharp eyed Guernsey Corsair and the element of surprise was lost. They were confronted by English and Dutch fleets off Cherbourg losing several ships. What remained of the fleet including Tourville's vessel attempted to flee to St Malo by what has ever since been known as the *Passage de la Déroute* (described on page 170). Other ships were defeated by the Alderney Race and set north pursued by the English. They sought refuge off Barfleur but it was too late. The order was given to run their ships aground off Ile de Tatihou and the English fire ships moved in. Louis XIV lost 15 of his finest ships of the line.

Following this disaster the military architect Vauban was summoned to fortify La Hougue Bay. This included the towers of La Hougue Fort and Ile de Tatihou. (See *Vauban* page 199).

Visiting Ile de Tatihou

As it is a protected site visitors are controlled. It may be reached on foot at low water when the tidal coefficient is at least 60 ('an average tide'). Alternatively a service is provided by an amphibious vehicle from the harbour. Information and tickets are obtainable from Billetterie de Tatihou, Place Belle Isle on the Quai Vauban. It is not possible to make the crossing in a keel boat.

The Maritime Museum on the island displays several artefacts recovered from the burnt wrecks of Tourville's fleet and is well worth a visit. There is a restaurant within the Vauban tower.

Utah Beach

A modern day conflict took place on this beach a few miles south of St Vaast on 6 June 1944. The Musée de Débarqement at Sainte Marie du Mont chronicles the sequence of events of the Normandy Landings.
☎ 02 33 71 53 35 Email musee@utah-beach.com

Approaches

Approaches are straightforward and there is plenty of sea room.

From the north

An approach from the direction of Cherbourg involves rounding Pointe de Barfleur with its Race that extends three or four miles to the E and NE. For directions see *Barfleur Approaches* page 151.

The coast S to Pointe de Saire should be given a clearance of 1·5M by keeping just outside the 20m depth contour. This might be extended in fresh onshore weather.

PASSE DU NORD

Navigate to a position 1·5M E of Pointe de Saire (⊕40). Continue SSW to join Passe du Nord 0·6M E of La Gavendest S cardinal buoy (⊕41), at which point Barfleur and Pointe de Saire lighthouses will be seen aligned on 345°:

Le Gavendest

Pointe de Saire   Barfleur lighthouse

The transit for Passe du Nord is:

SV1   Fort de la Hougue Tower
Light
Morsalines light tower

SV1 *267°: Fort de la Hougue light beacon Oc.4s9m10M in line with Morsalines light tower Oc(4)WRG.12s90m (inset)*

St Vaast-La Hougue to Goury

Morsalines sectored light is a good mark at night but ineffective by day. An alternative is to align Le Gavendest S cardinal buoy with Fort de la Hougue.

Pass S of Le Gavendest than head NW towards the light tower at the head of the Grande Jetée Oc(2)WRG.6s.

By night: Intercept the transit of lights in line on 267° (SV1). When 0·6M E of Le Gavendest S cardinal lit buoy (⊕41) and with Pointe de Barfleur light Fl(2)10s72M 29M aligned with Pointe de Saire light Oc(2+1)10s11m10M alter course SW until in W sector (310°-350°) of jetty light Oc(2)WRG.6s12m.

Make good 349° to leave Le Gavendest 0·5M to starboard. Enter marina between lights Oc(4)R.12s6M and Iso.G.4s.

From the south

PASSE DU SUD

Approach from ⊕42 with transit:

SV2 *349° Reville church tower in line with end of jetty at W extremity of Ile de Tatihou*

When Le Gavendest buoy is 0·5M abeam to starboard alter course for Grande Jetée light tower.

By night: Approach on 349° in W sector of Grande Jetée light tower. Continue as for Passe du Nord entry as above.

Entry and berthing

The marina is accessible via a gate between HW −2h15 and HW +3 (see *Tidal Information* page 146). Entering vessels have priority. B pontoon is allocated to visitors with a capacity of 100 berths.

Marina southern end

Quai Vauban

Anchorages

If waiting outside for the marina gate to open there are two anchorage areas:

1. 0·25M S of Fort de la Hougue.
2. In Petite Rade E of Le Bout du Roc E cardinal buoy (unlit) or 0·50M to SSE.

Note that the northernmost recommended anchorage in Petite Rade on Passe du Sud transit should be used with caution as it obstructs traffic movements into and out of the harbour.

The quality of the St Vaast oyster is recognised throughout France

II The Cherbourg Peninsula

BARFLEUR (dries)
49°40'30N 01°15'48W (Lighthouse Grande Jetée)

TRAVEL
Gare SNCF Cherbourg
transports.manche.fr
Gare SNCF Valognes
transports.manche.fr

CHARTS
BA 2135 Pointe de Barfleur to Pointe de la Percée (1:48 000)

Imray C32 Baie de Seine*
Imray 2110 North France Chart Atlas*
*both include plan: Barfleur (1:15 000)

SHOM 7090 De la Pointe de Barfleur à Saint Vaast-La Hougue (1:20 000)*
*includes plan: Port de Barfleur (1:7500)
SHOM 7422 De la Pointe de Barfleur à La Pointe de La Percée - Iles Saint-Marcouf (1:48 000)

RADIO
Le Sémaphore de Gatteville (Pointe de Barfleur) Ch 16/10

TIDAL INFORMATION
Standard Port Cherbourg
Difference Cherbourg + 0100 approx

MHWS	MLWS	MHWN	MLWN
6·4	1·1	5·1	2·6

TIDAL STREAMS
Off the entrance to Barfleur the stream sets N from about HW Cherbourg and S from about HW Cherbourg -4 maximum 3 knots. Entry is made between 2 ½ hours either side of HW. Beware of a cross stream in the entrance channel. Off Pointe de Barfleur it is slackest at HW Cherbourg+1. Spring rates inshore are between 1·0 and 3·5 knots.
(See SHOM tidal streams Atlas Baie de Seine)

USEFUL CONTACTS
Bureau du Port, Quai Ouest ☎ 02 33 54 02 48
   www.ville-barfleur.fr
Bureau du Tourisme, Quai Ouest ☎ 02 33 54 08 27
Mechanic. Ets Gúerard, Place du 8 mai ☎ 02 33 54 04 86
Taxi ☎ 02 33 54 11 56
Ecole de Voile de Barfleur www.barfleur_voile.com
La Grande Grève ☎ 02 33 54 79 08

SUPPLIES AND SERVICES
Water and electricity on Quai Henri Chardon
Fuel 2km. Delivery possible
Toilets/showers Off Quai Henri Chardon
Cash Point Credit Agricole Normande, rue Saint Thomas Becket
Restaurant Restaurant du Phare, rue St Thomas Becket
   ☎ 02 33 54 0082
Hotel Le Conquérant. As above

The drying harbour of Barfleur on the NE corner of the Cherbourg Peninsula is a classic grey stone Norman fishing village that has remained remarkably unchanged over the years.

The harbour is mainly dedicated to its fishing fleet, although numerous pleasure craft are moored at its western end. Visitors are accommodated alongside the Quai Plaisance SE of the area below the Church (see Entry page 153).

There are adequate shops for basic victualling and a few restaurants. Bars and cafés overlook the harbour.

Barfleur is perfectly sheltered from Westerlies but exposed to E and NE winds when swell enters the harbour. In such conditions it would be better to look for shelter in the marinas of St Vaast or Cherbourg.

A sheltered port a mile and a half south of Pointe de Barfleur

Barfleur at half-tide

St Vaast-La Hougue to Goury

II. THE CHERBOURG PENINSULA

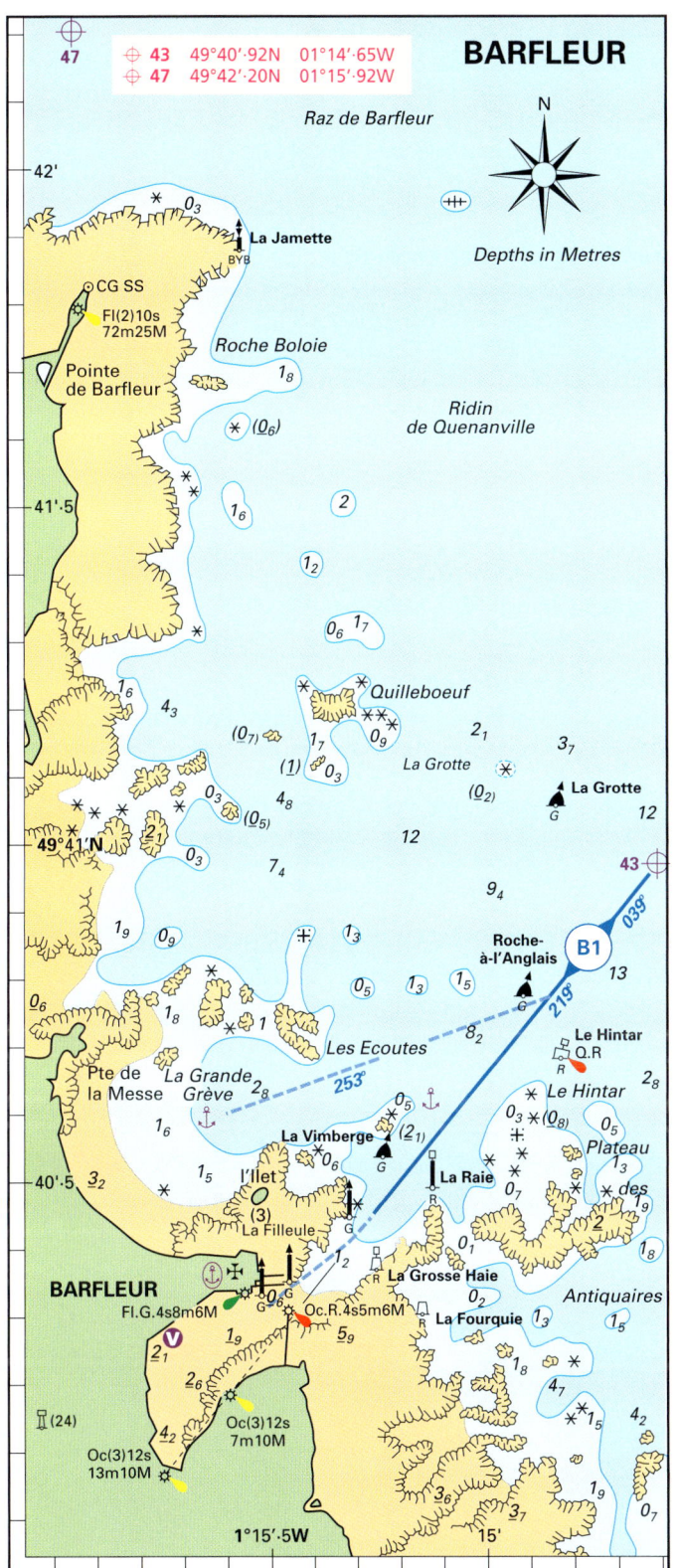

Historical

Barfleur is closely linked to the history of England and was the most important Norman port up to the Middle Ages. Here were built many of the 400 ships, including William Duke of Normandy's flagship the *Mora*, that took part in the invasion of England in 1066.

After the conquest Barfleur was the official port for crossings between Norman England and the Duchy. In 1120 a disaster occurred that was to have dire consequences for the course of English history.

Henry, son of William the Conqueror, was by this time Henry I of England and Duke of Normandy. In November of that year he decided to return to England. Having made arrangements for himself the King entrusted a local captain, the son of William's helmsman in 1066, to carry 300 members of his court including his two sons aboard his ship *La Blanche Nef* (The White Ship). The crossing was delayed by strong northerlies and due, it is said, to the crew having consumed too much wine, the ship was wrecked on a rock (Quillebeuf), between the harbour and Pointe de Barfleur. There was one survivor, a butcher from Rouen, found clinging to the mast.

The tragedy marked the end of Henry I's direct male line and gave rise to problems of inheritance to the English throne. These were not resolved until the reign of Henry II (Plantagenet) in 1154.

Ashore

Barfleur makes few concessions to tourism but there are several options for shore based activity.
- Gatteville Lighthouse
  At 74·85m this is the second highest in France after Ile Vierge in Finisterre. There are 365 steps to the top with panoramic views of the Channel and Val de Saire. It is open every day throughout the year excluding January. Duration of visit 30 minutes.
  Email pharedegatteville@club.fr ✆ 02 33 23 17 97
  www.phare-de-gatteville.fr
- Beach and Ecole de voile: La Grande Grève on N side of the town.
- Gastronomy: Mussels to Barfleur are what oysters are to St Vaast. The local speciality is white mussels which are described as 'Belles, Blondes et Sauvage'.
- Market: Saturday, Tuesday (in season)

Approaches

From the north

Between Pointe de Barfleur and the harbour isolated rocks extend up to 0·8M off the shore. The particular hazard is the Raz de Barfleur.

Pointe and Raz de Barfleur at 2 hours before local LW. Overfalls form as the ebb meets a moderate northwesterly.

CHANNEL ISLANDS, CHERBOURG PENINSULA & NORTH BRITTANY

II The Cherbourg Peninsula

The passage between La Jamette E cardinal and Raz de Barfleur

This extends 3–4 miles E and NE of Pointe de Barfleur and is noted for steep breaking seas even when only a moderate breeze is blowing against the stream. It is therefore advisable to avoid it altogether giving Pointe de Barfleur a clearance of 4M and more in rough weather.

Clearing W of Raz de Barfleur

With local knowledge and in suitable conditions of weather and tide a NW–SE passage is available inshore between Pointe de Barfleur and the Raz. It passes 100m NE of La Jamette E cardinal beacon. The streams in this gap can be intensified. Between La Jamette and the harbour beware of rocks extending up to a mile offshore.

Tidal Streams (southbound)

The SE going flood, which is stronger than the ebb, begins inshore around HW Cherbourg -4. It continues running SE until around HW Cherbourg. During the period the stream off the Pointe is slackest at HW Cherbourg -4 and again at the turn of the stream at HW Cherbourg +1.

Mean spring rates inshore are between 0·9 and 4·0 knots.

0·1m off harbour entrance

There is an inshore reversal when the stream turns before the mainstream offshore.
S going begins HW Cherbourg -4
N going begins HW Cherbourg

From the South and East

These approaches are straightforward. From the south all dangers N of Pointe de Saire will be cleared by keeping outside the 20m depth contour. In offshore winds there is a sheltered anchorage S of Pointe de Landemer marked by Moularde pyramid and E cardinal beacon.

152 CHANNEL ISLANDS, CHERBOURG PENINSULA & NORTH BRITTANY

St Vaast-La Hougue to Goury

Entry
(See plan page 151)

⊕43 is on the leading line 1·0M off entrance. There is a well marked entry channel. The transit is:

B1 *219° Two light towers (W) both Oc(3)12s10M in line*

These may be difficult to see by day and will become obscured behind the Grande Jetée 400m short of the entrance.

Once La Grosse Haie beacon is passed break off to starboard to open up the entrance. This is midway between E jetty light ho (Oc.R.4s) and W jetty light ho (Fl.G.4s). Note the entrance dries 0·6m and the quayside berths dry about 2m.

By night
Lights in line 219°

Mooring
Visitor's mooring is limited to the NW quay beyond the fishing boats. This area dries at about 2m to clean sand and shingle. There are ladders and mooring points alongside.

Note that moorings in the harbour are mainly reserved for local craft.

Anchorages
- La Grande Grève. This bay immediately N of the harbour has an active sailing school and a good beach. To enter, branch off the main channel onto 253° and when abeam La Roche aux Anglais starboard channel buoy.
- Off the main channel N of La Raie port hand channel beacon. The holding in mud, sand and gravel is said to be poor.

Harbour entrance

Le Vimberge in the entry channel

Port de Plaisance

The harbour at HW

II The Cherbourg Peninsula

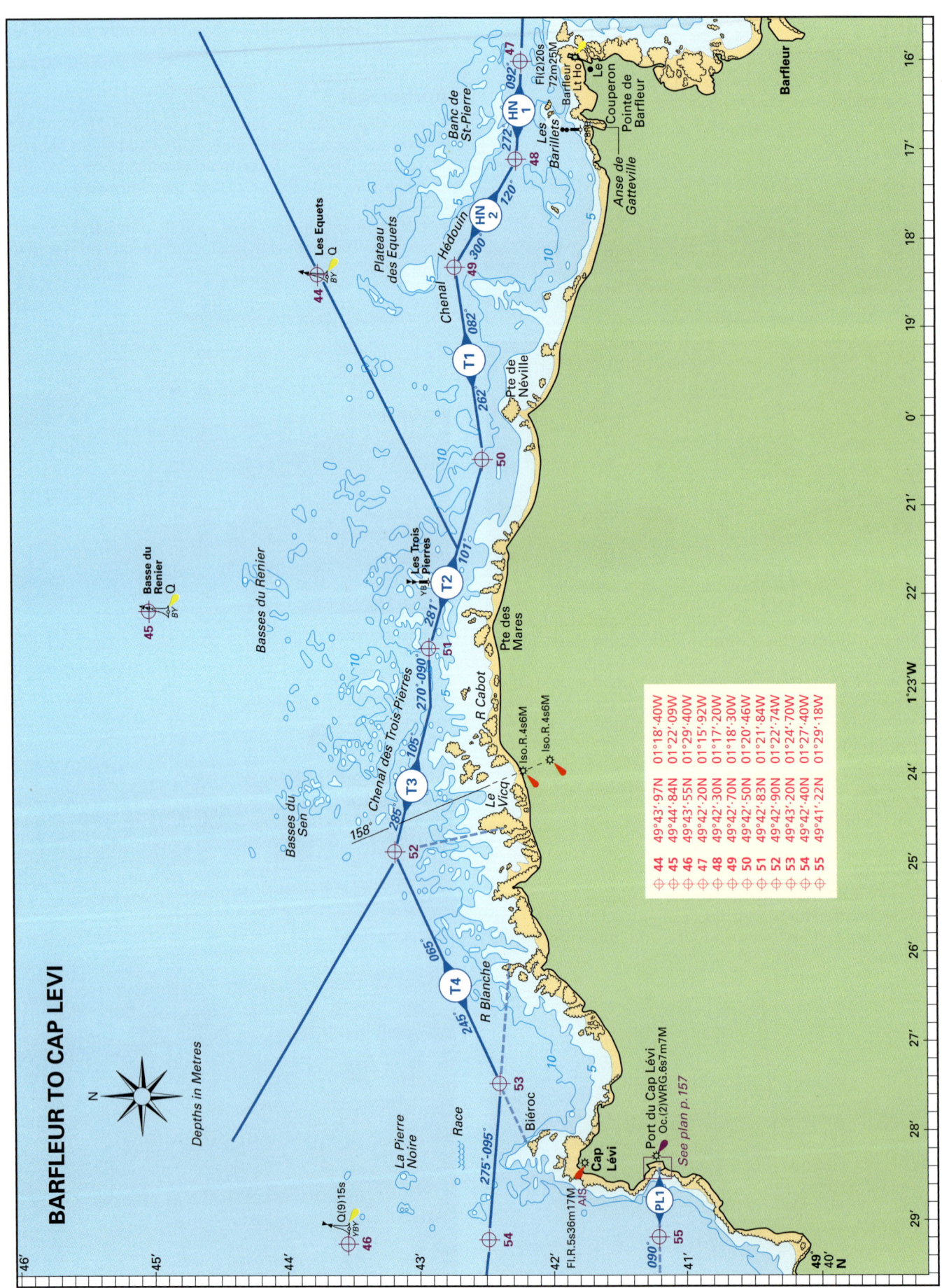

154 CHANNEL ISLANDS, CHERBOURG PENINSULA & NORTH BRITTANY

St Vaast-La Hougue to Goury

MINOR HARBOURS AND ANCHORAGES BETWEEN BARFLEUR AND CHERBOURG

Ports harbours and anchorages
Anse de Gatteville (Havre de Roubaril)
Port du Cap Lévi
Port du Becquet

CHARTS
BA 1114 Approaches to Cherbourg (1:47 800)
SHOM 5609 De la Pointe du Heu à la Pointe de Barfleur (1:20 000)
SHOM 7092 De la Pointe de Nacqueville au Cap Lévi - Rade de Cherbourg (1:20 000)
SHOM 7120 Abords de Cherbourg - Du Cap de La Hague à la Pointe de Barfleur (1:47 800)

TIDAL INFORMATION
As for Cherbourg

Tidal streams
N of Pointe de Barfleur the E going stream slackens off at HW Cherbourg +1 and then runs W for the best part of 6 hours. The turn off Cap Lévi slacks at around HW Cherbourg +5. Streams follow the coast and are weaker inshore. Tidal eddies will be found off Pointe de Barfleur and Cap Lévi where the turn in the stream can preceed that offshore by as much as 2 hours.

The coast between Pointe de Barfleur and Cap Lévi (14M)

This is initially low, flat and featureless – apart from distant church spires. With shoals and reefs extending up to 2·5M off, it has a reputation for uncomfortable seas particularly when wind and tide are opposed. In doubtful weather, including poor visibility, it should be given a clearance of 3·0M, routing via three cardinal buoys positioned on the 20m contour. These are (E–W) Les Equets ($\oplus$44). Basse du Rénier ($\oplus$45) and La Pierre Noire ($\oplus$46).

Inshore route: Chenal Hédouin and Chenal des Trois Pièrres 11M (By day only)

Caution
This route calls for local knowledge. It is best attempted at neap tides, in good visibility and light breezes, preferably offshore.

French Chart *SHOM 5609* Pointe du Heu à la Pointe de Barfleur carries details of these interconnected channels that skirt the shore about a mile off, thus escaping potentially rougher conditions and strong tidal streams offshore. Some of the marks are likely to be elusive even with binoculars so it is recommended to use waypoints positioned at turning points as a back up. From E to W these are listed below with relevant transits.

Note These channels were run when height above chart datum at Cherbourg was 2·1m. There was no noticeable tidal stream.

Pointe de Néville with its conspicuous N cardinal beacon

Chenal Hédouin (5·4M)
$\oplus$47 (49°42'·2N 01°16'·00W)

HN1 *272° Pointe des Mares beacon in line with Pointe de Néville beacon (no view)*
$\oplus$48 (49°42'·22N 01°17'·10W)

(Off transit for identification)

HN2 *300° Stern transit 120° Pointe de Barfleur lighthouse aligned with conspicuous head (if visible) on N side of Les Barillets (dries 3m)*

Les Trois Pierres S cardinal beacon marks the halfway point between Barfleur and Cap Lévi

Chenal des Trois Pierres (1·9M)
$\oplus$49 (49°42'·68N 01°18'·30W)

T1 *262° Cap Lévi lighthouse aligned with house N of des Mares (village) (no view)*
$\oplus$50 (49°42'·50N 01°20'·46W)

View astern from Les Trois Pierres

T2 *281° Stern transit 101° Le Couperon open left (N) of Pointe de Néville N cardinal beacon*

II The Cherbourg Peninsula

⊕51 (49°42'·88N 01°22'·58W) With Pointe des Mares beacon on the quarter bearing 160° take up 270° for 400m. The turning point onto line T3:

Roche Cabot beacon

T3 *(285°) Roche Cabot beacon bearing 194°. Stern transit then is 105°, Houses on Le Couperon open left (N) of Pointe de Néville beacon*

⊕52 (49°43'·46N 01°24'·85W)

T4 *245° Bièroc (5m) bearing 245° open left (S) of Ile Pelée, if visible (no view)*

Take note of Roche Blanche (6m), which does not appear to be white, as this will be needed next.

Biéroc and Cap Lévi lighthouse from NE

⊕53 (49°42'·40N 01°27'·48W)

T5 *275° Stern transit 095° Roche Blanche aligned with Pointe de Barfleur lighthouse (Le Couperon) (no view)*

This line passes midway between Cap Lévi and the Raz du Cap Lévi (see caution under Port du Cap Lévi).

Roche Blanche

⊕54 (49°42'·50N 01°27'·55W)
This marks the end of the channel.

ANSE DE GATTEVILLE (Havre de Roubaril)

49°41'·76N 01°16'·75W (Roche Houmaizel isolated danger beacon)

Air view taken two hours before LWS Barfleur

A narrow drying cove 0·5M W of Pointe de Barfleur and close S of Les Barillets (dry 3m). It is used as a temporary refuge for small craft in settled offshore conditions.

A short mole offers some protection from NW and N. Close N of the entrance is an isolated danger beacon on Roche Houmaizel.

Entry

From Chenal Hédouin transit **MN1** identify Les Barillets (if uncovered) and the isolated danger beacon in front of the cove. The preference is to pass E of the beacon on entry. The E side of the harbour is rocky, elsewhere is firm sand.

Ashore

The nearest village, Gatteville Le Phare, is half a mile inland.

Roubaril at LW with Roche Houmaizel beacon. Gatteville church spire is on the horizon

St Vaast-La Hougue to Goury

PORT DU CAP LÉVI

49°41'·24N 01°28'·34W (light beacon in Port)

STD Code 02 33

TIDAL INFORMATION
Standard Port Cherbourg

SUPPLIES & SERVICES
Fermanville (1·5M) has shops, bar and a restaurant. The following sites are within walking distance of the port and open to the public for guided tours (seasonal):
Fort du Cap Lévi ✆ 02 33 23 68 68
Sémaphore du Cap Lévi ✆ 02 33 54 61 12

Caution: Cap Lévi Race

Wind against tide conditions raise overfalls S of La Pierre Noire buoy N of Cap Lévi.

The advice is to pass outside La Pierre Noire W cardinal buoy to avoid rocks, shoals and the worst of the Race. In light weather it is safe to cut inside at the right state of tide.

The stream runs NE between HW Cherbourg -6 and HW Cherbourg +2h30, after which it runs W until LW. Max rate at springs is 3·3 knots.

This miniscule harbour 5M E of Cherbourg is backed by Normandy countryside and truly out in the sticks. It is almost impossible to find by land but is pinpointed from seaward by the conspicuous Cap Lévi lighthouse 0·5M to the N.

The harbour which dries at between 1·2m and 4m is protected by two small jetties that help to break up the surge and backwash that plagues the harbour in winds between S through W to N. It is well sheltered by the land from the N through E to S.

Small craft moor bows to the quay below the light beacon or fore and aft in the harbour. The bottom is firm flat sand but the S end of the harbour and inner side of the north jetty is rocky.

Historical

Port du Cap Lévi dates from 1786 when a digue and quays were built to enable barges to take on cargoes of granite quarried in nearby Fermanville This was destined for the construction of defences surrounding Cherbourg.

Port du Cap Lévi harbour at HW viewed from S

The harbour at HW from NNW

The port was destroyed by a storm in 1806 and abandoned until 1861 when it was rebuilt in its present form.

Approaches and entry

⊕55 49°41'·22N 01°29'·18W

From the west

This is straightforward. Keep well into the bay to avoid being set into Cap Lévi Race.

From the east

Keep a good 2M off the coast to pass N of La Pièrre Noire N cardinal buoy and avoid rocks, shoals and the Race. Except in light weather, when a short cut may be taken inside at the right state of tide. (See *Inshore channels between Barfleur and Cherbourg* page 155).

Note that an unlit buoy Y is positioned 0·4M W of entrance.

Entry

Is made with:

PL1 *090° white wall with light beacon in between the white marks on each pierhead. Keep close to the end of the southern jetty as the passage between the jetty and the rocks to the N is narrow*

By night

Light inside harbour (Oc(2)WRG.7m17M in white sector (083°–105°).

II The Cherbourg Peninsula

PORT DU BECQUET

49°39'·30N 01°32'·81W Harbour entrance

TIDAL INFORMATION
As for Cherbourg.
The inner side of the N jetty dries 1·4–3m.
The bottom alongside the S quay dries 3–3·4m.

SUPPLIES AND SERVICES
Water and Electricity: W end of harbour at top of slipway.
Restaurant. Le Comptoir du Becquet ① 02 33 22 01 75
Boulangerie and small shops: In Le Becquet

Port du Becquet is a small drying harbour 1M E of Cherbourg used by small fishing and pleasure craft. These are moored bows to at the Quai Sud or fore and aft in the harbour, which is shaped like a lock chamber.

The quay jetty and hard standing are very substantial and all is maintained as an historic showpiece. The harbour is surrounded by classic Norman dwellings which include a restaurant.

Shelter is good except in winds from N to E when a strong send enters the harbour. Seas may break over the jetty in gale conditions.

Historical

The Port was completed in 1783 and has since been rebuilt and strengthened several times to withstand the onslaught of storms. Like Port du Cap Lévi it was used for transporting locally quarried stone for the construction of defences round the port of Cherbourg – and also supplying water to the garrison on Ile Pelée Fort.

Approach and Entrance

Approach is made on transit

PBT1 *186° (⊕56) with marks in line. These are W octagonal towers (front light white; rear light Red). Both Dir Oc(2+1)12s*

Note that there is an unlit buoy (Y) 0·4m NNW of the entrance.

Port du Becquet harbour from W

Transit PBT1 186° White octagonal towers in line

Entry is made between the head of North Jetty and La Tounette beacon tower, a port hand mark at the edge of a rocky ledge (see views).

Berths

Good drying out berths along the inner side of N jetty. The outer end is timber clad with substantial fittings and ladders – a good spot for a yacht to dry out alongside in suitable weather. The bottom is clean and flat but not so good for grounding on the south quay.

By night

Two directional lights, inside harbour, in line.
Fwd: Oc(3)12s8m10M
Rear: Oc(3)R.12s3m7M

Looking into Port du Becquet harbour from east

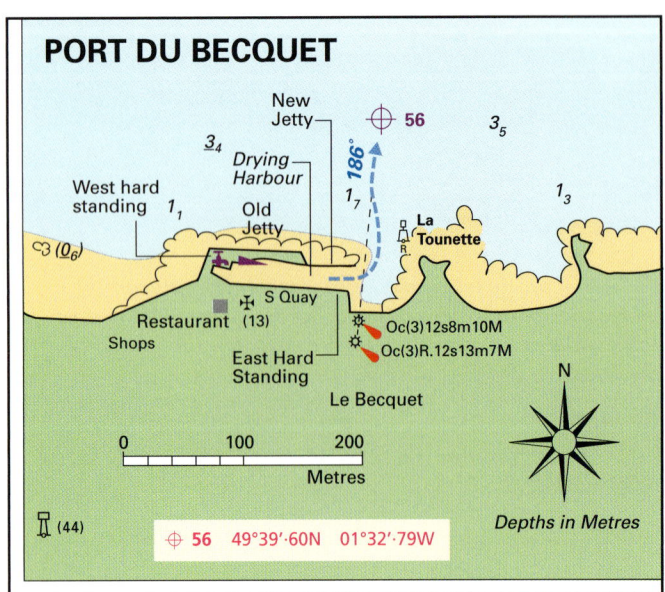

St Vaast-La Hougue to Goury

CHERBOURG
49°40'·46N 01°38'·88W
(Fort de l'Ouest Fl(3)WR.15s)
Pointe de Barfleur lighthouse 12M
Cap de la Hague 15M

TRAVEL
Sea
Brittany Ferries www.brittany-ferries.co.uk ✆ 02 33 88 44 88
   www.brittany-ferries.fr ✆ 0825 828 828
   Cherbourg and Poole, Portsmouth, Rosslare
Manche Iles Express www.manche-iles-express.com
   Channel Islands, Diélette, Carteret, Granville
Condor Ferries www.condorferries.com
   Sailings to Portsmouth

Air
Charter flights only operate from Cherbourg Airport (Maupertus) 5 miles E of the city ✆ 02 33 88 57 60

Rail
The station is 15 minutes walk from the marina. Train connection to Paris. www.sncf com ✆ 02 33 88 66 99

Taxi
Chantereyne Taxis ✆ 02 33 53 36 38

CHARTS
BA 1112 Rade de Cherbourg (1:7500)
BA 1114 Approaches to Cherbourg (1:47 800)

Imray C32 Baie de Seine*
Imray 2110 North France Chart Atlas*
Imray 2500 The Channel Islands and the adjacent coasts of France Chart Atlas*
   *all include plans: Cherbourg (1:40 000), Port de Chantereyne (1:10 000)

SHOM 7086 Rade de Cherbourg (1:7500)
SHOM 7092 De la Pointe de Nacqueville au Cap Lévi - Rade de Cherbourg (1:20 000)
SHOM 7120 Abords de Cherbourg - Du Cap de La Hague à la Pointe de Barfleur (1:47 800)

RADIO
VHF Ch 09/12

USEFUL CONTACTS
Port Chantereyne
Bureau du Port ✆ 02 33 87 65 70
   Email portchantereyne@ville-cherbourg.fr
Hôtel de Ville, Place de la République ✆ 02 33 87 88 89
Office de Tourisme ✆ 02 33 93 52 02
   www.cherbourgtourisme.fr

TIDAL INFORMATION
Cherbourg is a Standard Port

MHWS	MLWS	MHWN	MLWN
6·4	1·1	5·0	2·5

Tidal Streams
-0330 HW Cherbourg E-going starts
+0215 HW Cherbourg W-going starts
3M north of the breakwater the streams start as follows:
HW Cherbourg -0330 E-going
HW Cherbourg +0215 Cherbourg W-going starts
The maximum rates are 3 knots. The rate lessens as the coast is approached and a W-going eddy starts close to the coast and inside the breakwater at about HW -0130. This is particularly useful when proceeding W from Cherbourg as the W –going stream runs for 8 hours inshore.
Care must be taken when approaching from the N to allow for this cross-set, especially at springs, so as not to end up down-tide of the intended entrance.

SUPPLIES AND SERVICES
Berths 1310 + 250 visitors - See *Entry to Port Chantereyne*. (See Anchoring, Berthing and Mooring)

General
Showers and WCs, water and electricity on pontoons
Self-service launderette
Fuel at fuel berth 0800–1145, 1400–1645
30-ton travel-lift and 600kg crane

Yacht clubs
Cherbourg Yacht Club ✆ 02 33 94 28 05

Chandleries and shipyard
Accastillage Diffusion ✆ 02 33 94 15 50
North Sails ✆ 02 33 94 15 51
AMS Marine ✆ 02 33 01 63 63
Cap Loisirs ✆ 02 33 87 58 20
Cherbourg Plaisance ✆ 02 33 53 27 34

Hotels
Hotel Chantereyne, Port de Plaisance ✆ 02 33 93 02 20
Taxi Cherbourg ✆ 02 33 53 36 38

Within walking distance of the marina
Shops and banks: 200m off marina entrance
Supermarket: S of Avant Port
Markets: Several throughout the week. Town Centre. Tues, Thurs and Sat.

Restaurants
Port de Plaisance (2). A wide range in town. Try 'La Cale', Place de la République, sea food specialties ✆ 02 33 93 11 93

Cherbourg from E
Patrick Roach

CHANNEL ISLANDS, CHERBOURG PENINSULA & NORTH BRITTANY

II The Cherbourg Peninsula

160 CHANNEL ISLANDS, CHERBOURG PENINSULA & NORTH BRITTANY

St Vaast-La Hougue to Goury

Fort de L'Ouest

Ile Pelée Fort

Cherbourg is a major commercial port, a ferry terminal, and a Naval base. Its sprawl takes up a large chunk of the coastline between Cap de la Hague in the west and Pointe de Barfleur in the East. It is claimed to be the largest artificial harbour in Europe.

Strategically positioned 60 miles south of the Solent it is a logical port of entry for yachts based in that area and has the distinction of being accessible at all times and in all weathers.

Its large Port de Plaisance, Port de Chantereyne, is the centrepiece of the harbour. It is safe and totally sheltered, offering all the facilities yachtsmen might require. With regular year-round ferry connections with the UK South Coast and a fast rail service into the rest of France, Cherbourg is a practical place for crew changes or a base.

Historical

Visits from the other side of the Channel have not always been friendly. In 1748 the British raided and occupied the town, exposing its vulnerability to attack. Fortifying the port became an obsession that lasted until 1850, first under Louis XVI and then during the Napoleonic era. A heavily fortified 2½ mile long breakwater was built a mile off the coast, enclosing a large area of sheltered water known as Grande Rade. It is claimed to be the largest artificial harbour in the world. Shorter 'digues' further protect the port behind Petite Rade.

During the Second World War the occupying German forces further fortified the coastline against invasion. Cherbourg was liberated on 25 June 1944 following the D-Day landings on the east of the peninsula. The Battle of Cherbourg was a bitter struggle that left the harbour wrecked. One can still see gun shot marks on buildings around the port.

Museums and sites of interest in Cherbourg:
- La Cité de la Mer (Gare Maritime Transatlantique) www.citedelamer.com. Titanic exhibition and French nuclear submarine La Rédoutable, aquarium and underwater exploration.
- Musée de la Libération (Fort du Roule)
- Parc and museum Emmanuel - Liais

Approaches and Entry

There are two main entry points to Cherbourg Grande Rade. The E entrance (Passe de l'Est) and W entrance, Passe de l'Ouest.

The W entrance is more commonly used being wider with 10m least depth. The E entrance is narrowed by dangers N and NE of Ile Pelée and has 8m least depth.

There is also a narrow entrance from the E. Passe Cabart-Danneville (Passe Colignon) cuts between the S end of Digue de l'Est and the shore. It is 93m wide with least depth of 2m so best taken near HW. Tidal stream reaches 3·4 knots.

Passe Cabart-Danneville viewed from E

Caution

Tidal cross set in approaches to Cherbourg.

From west

After rounding Cap de la Hague, pass N of La Platte beacon tower, Basse Bréfort N cardinal buoy and Raz de Bannes N cardinal beacon tower. Head for Passe de l'Ouest (⊕58) and enter on course made good of 142° with initial transit:

CHB2 *142° White triangle at root of Digue du Homet aligned with (back mark) lattice structure on SE corner of Gare Maritime*

This line will leave:

Fort de l'Ouest and its port buoy 60m to port.

Continue across Grande Rade on an ESE heading towards entry to Petite Rade and Port de Chantereyne (Port de Plaisance) described below.

CHANNEL ISLANDS, CHERBOURG PENINSULA & NORTH BRITTANY

II The Cherbourg Peninsula

By night

W Entrance
From ⊕58 the leading lights are –
Front: Dir.2.Q(Hor)
Back: Dir.Q
This leaves:
- Fort de l'Ouest Fl(3)WR.15s and offlying Fl.R.4s to port. (Fort de l'Ouest changes white to red when bearing 122°).
- The head of Digue de Querqueville Fl(2)G.6s6M will be left well to starboard.

In Grande Rade take up next leading line 124° with –
Front: Head of Digue du Homet Q.G.
Back: Q.Iso.G.4s

This leaves –
- La Ténarde N cardinal buoy (lit) 200m to starboard.
- When this is abeam alter course to 110° to clear head of Digue du Hornet.

With Petite Rade entrance open enter on about 205°. Identify marina entrance ahead. The W side is marked Fl(3)G.12s and the opposite side Fl(3)R.12s.

From east

Between Pointe de Barfleur and Cherbourg's E entrance, banks and shoals extend up to 3M offshore up to Cap Lévi. (See directions for this approach in *Minor harbours between Barfleur and Cherbourg* page 155.)

The conspicuous mark from seaward is Ile Pelée Fort. From a position a mile NNW of this or at ⊕57 make good 189° with transit:

CHB1 *189° – 2 pylons E of Petite Rade entrance in line*
Front: White. Back: White with black stripes. These marks may be inconspicuous against the cluttered background but the entrance is spacious and unambiguous. This line leaves:
- Roches du Nord-Ouest port buoy 400m to port
- Tromet tower 600m to port
- La Trinite port buoy 300m to port
- Fort de l'Est 200m to starboard

With Fort de L'Est abaft the beam take up SW heading across Grande Rade towards entrance to Petite Rade. Leave Jetée des Flamands port buoy to port (do not cut inside it) and the end of Digue du Homet to starboard. Continue SSW for half a mile to the Marina entrance.

Digue du Homet encloses the military port of the western side of Petite Rade. Access restricted (see Anchorages)

Entry to Port de Chantereyne

By night

E Entrance
From ⊕57 the leading lights are:
Front: Q
Back: Iso.G.4S
This leaves:
- Roches du Nord-Ouest port buoy Fl.R.2s to port.
- Le Trinite port buoy Fl(4)R.15s
- Ile Pelée Fort Oc(2)WR.6s – changes red to white when bearing 120°

St Vaast-La Hougue to Goury

Port de Chantereyne and Avant Port looking south   SHOM

Turn on to a SW heading for the entrance to Petite Rade leaving Port buoy Q.R. off head of Jetée des Flambards to port and Q.G. on head of Digue du Homet to starboard.
Note The outer end of Jetée des Flambards covers at HW.

Port de Chantereyne

The 100m wide opening is between the marina W mole marked by a G pylon and the NW corner of the large quay with the Gare Maritime marked by a red-topped light tower.

Follow the E wall until the marina opens up to starboard and berth as directed.

Berthing

Visitors berths are on pontoons, N, P, Q and J. Larger vessels up to 25m are accommodated on the N end of H. Call on Ch 09 before entering. Max. depth is 4·5m. The Avant Port to the S now has no berths or facilities for visiting yachts. If arriving at night the waiting pontoon is often the best option.

Anchorage

Anchoring in either of the Rades is discouraged but may, subject to authorisation (VHF Ch 09), be permitted in the following locations:
Grande Rade E side: S of Ile Pelée
             W side: Baie Ste Anne
Petite Rade SE corner: N of marina N mole

Port de Chantereyne. Fuel pontoon and Bureau du Port above

CHANNEL ISLANDS, CHERBOURG PENINSULA & NORTH BRITTANY

II The Cherbourg Peninsula

OMONVILLE-LA-ROGUE

49°42'·35N 01°49'·80W (L'Etonnard)
10M west of Cherbourg

CHARTS
BA 1114 Approaches to Cherbourg (1:47 800)

Imray C33A Channel Islands*
Imray 2110 North France Chart Atlas*
  *both include plan: Omonville-la-Rogue (1:7000)

SHOM 7120 Abords de Cherbourg - Du Cap de La Hague à la Pointe de Barfleur (1:47 800)
SHOM 7232 Du Nez de Jobourg à la Pointe de Nacqueville (1:20 000)*
  *includes plan: Abords d'Omonville-La-Rogue (1:7500)

TIDAL INFORMATION
HW and LW about 10 minutes before Cherbourg

MHWS	MLWS	MHWN	MLWN
6·3	1·1	4·9	2·5

Tidal Streams
2M N of the port the E-going stream starts at -0215 HW Cherbourg and the W-going at +0120 attaining 4 and 5 knots respectively at springs.

SHELTER
From S through W to NW

DEPTH RESTRICTIONS
From 2–7m in anchorage

NIGHT ENTRY
Possible with one directional light

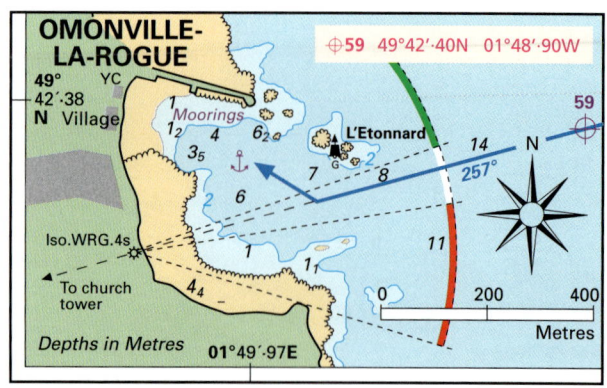

A small harbour protected from the W, but not the E, with few facilities; suitable to wait a favourable stream round Cap de la Hague.

Berthing
There is a clean sandy bottom at the inner end of the breakwater W of the spur halfway along where it dries 1m and where an alongside berth may be found. There are rocks alongside the breakwater to the E of the spur.

Facilities
There are two small cafés/restaurants and a sailing school where there are showers by the harbour, a small shop in the village and more in Beaumont Hague on the main road (5km).

Approaches and entrance

From W and N
The main danger is Les Tatquets rocks (drying 2·6m) which lie 800m N of the breakwater end. Give these a good berth before turning to the SE to pick up the leading line; (⊕59)

OM1 *257° white pylon, red top (Iso.WRG.4s) aligned with church tower*

At night the white sector is 10° wide with green to the N, red to the S. The white sector and the line leads clear S of L'Etonnard rocks and starboard beacon tower.

From E
Leave Raz des Bannes N cardinal beacon tower ½M to the S and from a WNW track pick up the leading line/light as above.

By night
Omonville Iso.WRG4s13m10-7M W sector 252°-262°.

Moorings and anchorage
With L'Etonnard well on the starboard quarter turn into the anchorage. There are four large white visitors' buoys at the E end of the moorings. If occupied, anchor in 5–7m to seaward of them in patchy sand.

Omonville looking SW at half tide

St Vaast-La Hougue to Goury

ANSE DE ST MARTIN (PORT RACINE)

49°42'·41N 01°53'·75W (Port Racine)
2M east of Cap de la Hague

CHARTS
 BA 1114 Approaches to Cherbourg (1:47 800)
 BA 3653 Guernsey to Alderney and Adjacent Coast of France (1:50 000)
 SHOM 7120 Abords de Cherbourg - Du Cap de La Hague à la Pointe de Barfleur (1:47 800)
 SHOM 7158 Du Cap de Carteret au Cap de la Hague - Raz Blanchard (1:48 000)
 SHOM 7232 Du Nez de Jobourg à la Pointe de Nacqueville (1:20 000)

TIDAL INFORMATION
 HW and LW about 20 minutes before Cherbourg with a greater range.

Tidal Streams
 The stream inshore off the Anse sets to the W except for a brief period around HW Cherbourg +0200

SHELTER
 From W through S to ESE

DEPTH RESTRICTIONS
 2·7m in anchorage

NIGHT ENTRY
 Unlit

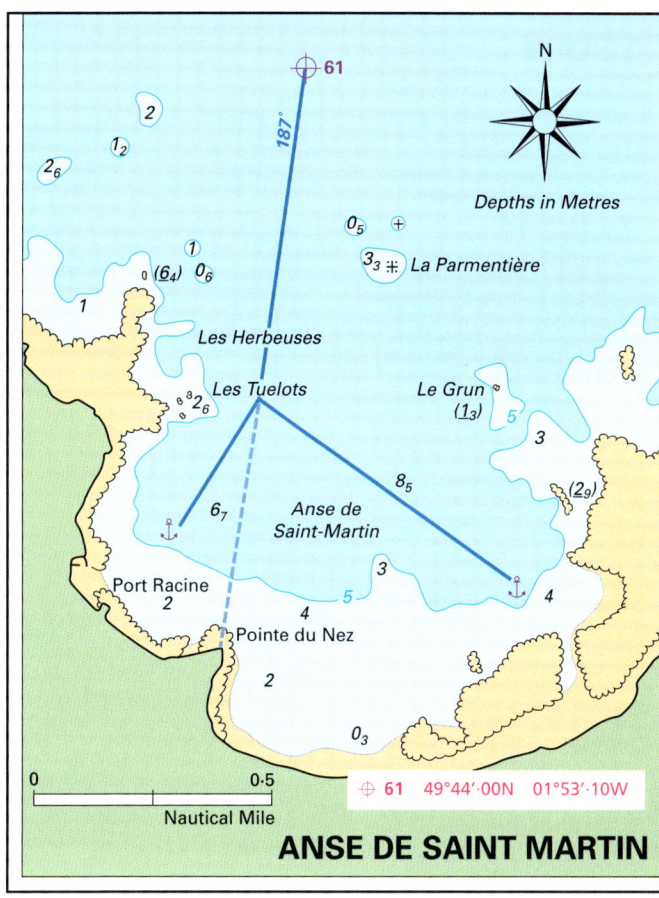

ANSE DE SAINT MARTIN

An open, unlit bay just to the E of Cap de la Hague sheltered from W through S to ESE; safer as a tide-waiting anchorage in easterlies than Omonville.

Berthing
Anchoring only.

Approaches, entrance and anchorage
From a position where La Plate beacon tower bears 285° or at ⊕61 identify Pointe du Nez, a low bluff at the W end of the sandy beach at the head of the bay. Approach this on a track of 187° making allowance for any cross-stream in the offing which can be strong and variable. Pass 300m to the W of Parmentière, a shoal patch drying at CD and 400m to the E of Les Herbeuses rocks (drying 9m but with rocks awash at CD off them). Port Racine, a small drying harbour will soon appear in the SW corner of the bay off which there are a few small boat moorings. Anchor clear of them in 2–3m sand or tuck into the SE corner of the bay in easterly weather.

Facilities
None, except for a small restaurant up the hill from Port Racine. Port Racine claims to be the smallest port in France.

Anse St Martin anchorage beyond minute harbour of Port Racine *Martin Walker*

II The Cherbourg Peninsula

GOURY

49°42'·86N 01°56'·71W (Pierhead Q.R)
0·5M SE of Cap de la Hague Lighthouse (Gros du Raz)

CHARTS
BA 3653 Guernsey to Alderney and adjacent coast of France (1:50 000)
SHOM 7133 Ports de la côte Ouest du Cotentin*
*includes plan: Abords de Goury (1:10 000)
SHOM 7158 Du Cap de Carteret au Cap de la Hague – Raz Blanchard (1:48 000)
SHOM 7232 Du Nez de Jobourg à la Pointe de Nacqueville (1:20 000)

TIDAL INFORMATION
Standard Port: Cherbourg
Differences
HW and LW at Goury is approximately Cherbourg -0100
St Helier +0120
St Malo +0130

MHWS	MLWS	MHWN	MLWN
8·1	1·4	6·6	3·5

Tidal Streams
West of Cap de la Hague the stream is N going from about HW St Malo -2 to HW St Malo +4. Close inshore it is generally half the strength of the main offshore stream. Between HW St Malo +4 and HW -2 it is less than 1·5 knots and variable in direction. The S going stream between HW St Malo +5 and HW -2 is weaker.
The best time to visit Goury is below half tide when the surrounding reefs provide shelter and the stream is slack or nil. (See Passage de la Haize du Raz below)

COMMUNICATIONS
La Hague Signal Station ☏ 02 33 10 03 14
 Daylight hours only
Sémaphore d'Auderville
Lifeboat SNSM Goury ☏ 02 33 93 30 57/02 33 21 20 63
Mairie Auderville VHF Ch 10 ☏ 02 33 52 85 92
 Email marie-auderville@wanadoo.fr

SUPPLIES AND SERVICES
Goury is something of a tourist attraction for its unique scenery. It has a tourist office, restaurant bar and an extraordinary octagonal lifeboat station inside which the boat rests on a turntable that serves two launching slipways. It is open to the public. The nearest shop is ¼ mile at Auderville where there are also several restaurants.

Caution
Goury is not a place to approach in anything less than quiet settled weather and over neaps.

It offers an interesting stopover while waiting for a favourable tide through the Race.

This obscure little harbour with its scattering of buildings is tucked half a mile inside Cap de la Hague lighthouse (Gros du Raz). The wildness of this corner of the peninsula is such that finding Goury can be easier by sea than by land.

Despite its precarious position bordering the Race, the area off the harbour is surprisingly sheltered from the powerful streams offshore and the surrounding land gives protection from N and E winds.

Goury is most vulnerable to westerlies and it is said that strong to gale force winds from this direction combined with spring tides causes heavy swell to enter the harbour.

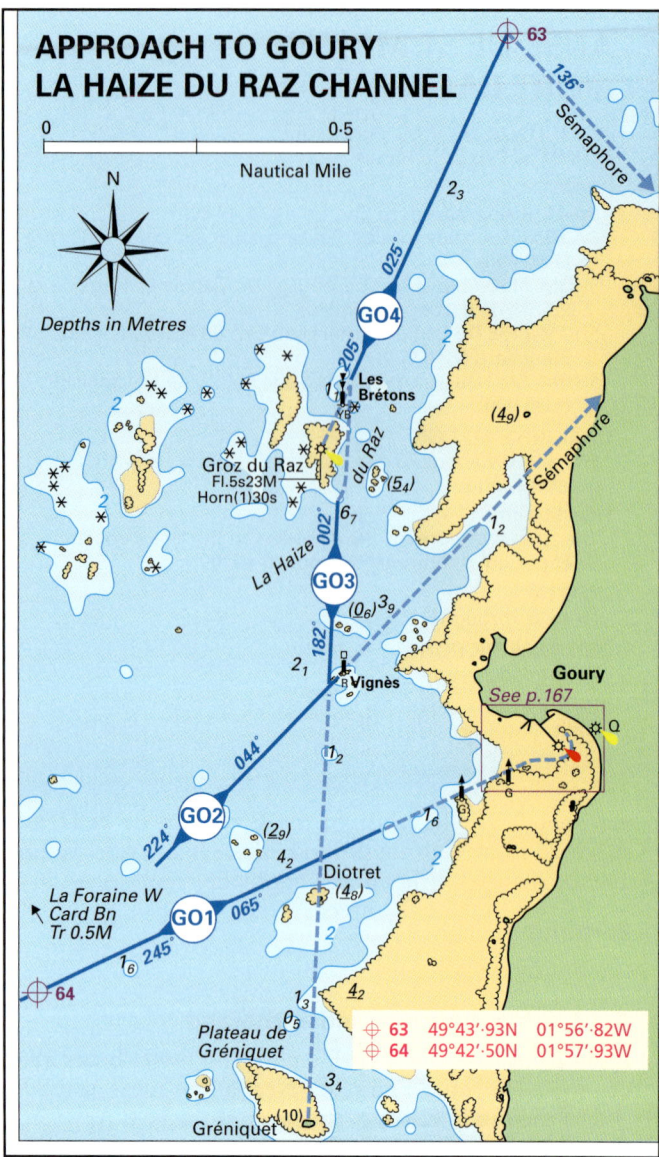

APPROACH TO GOURY
LA HAIZE DU RAZ CHANNEL

⊕ 63	49°43'·93N	01°56'·82W
⊕ 64	49°42'·50N	01°57'·93W

Jet d'Amont

AMARRAGE OBLIGATOIRE DES VISITEURS SUR LES BOUEES JAUNES.

COMPULSORY MOORING FOR ALL VISITORS ON THE YELLOW BUYOS

St Vaast-La Hougue to Goury

Approach and entrance

From SW

From ⊕64 0·5M SE of La Foraine W cardinal beacon tower identify and hold transit:

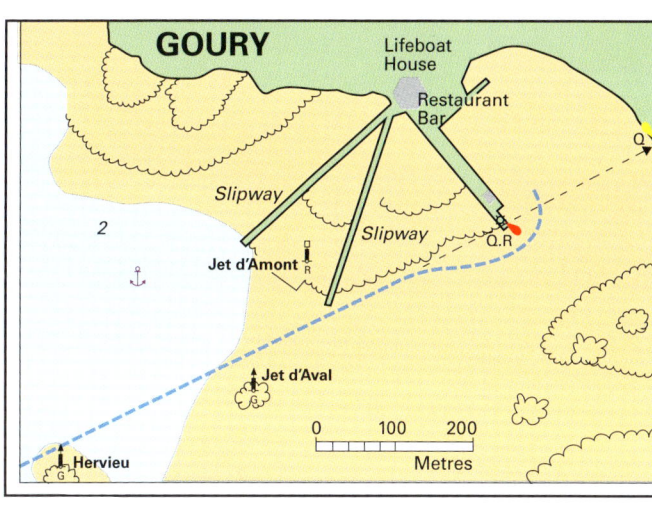

G01 065° Front: Red square within a white square on breakwater end. Back: White pylon to ESE of octagonal lifeboat building

As a secondary mark, alignment of two starboard beacons off the harbour provides a back up:

Front: Hervieu
Back: Jet d'Aval

Both will be left close to starboard followed by Jet d'Amont Port beacon which should be given a clearance of 50m to port to avoid the easternmost lifeboat slipway.

Jet d'Amont and lifeboat station

Goury looking ESE

CHANNEL ISLANDS, CHERBOURG PENINSULA & NORTH BRITTANY

II The Cherbourg Peninsula

Goury from SE

Small craft dried out in the harbour

Anchoring and mooring
At LW neaps in good weather anchoring is possible off the leading line N of Hervieu. Landing may be made on the steps at the foot of Jet d'Amont. Mooring in the harbour is limited to small craft only. It may be possible to dry out alongside the inner face of the 110m long jetty, without obstructing the lifeboat slip. There are patches of firm sand drying 4–5m bordering the beach.

From N
This is by Passage de la Haize du Raz starting from ⊕63 0·7M NNE of Gros du Raz lighthouse.

Gros de Raz lighthouse dominates the scene in Goury

St Vaast-La Hougue to Goury

PASSAGE DE LA HAIZE DU RAZ

In suitable conditions this 3M passage inside Gros du Raz lighthouse provides a short cut round Cap de la Hague taking advantage of inshore tidal eddies (see *SHOM Tide Atlas Golfe Normand–Breton*). There are three straightforward transits which are described here.

From N

Firstly, from ⊕63, a position where Sémaphore d'Auderville bears 136° and Gros du Raz lighthouse bears 205°. Note Les Brétons N cardinal beacon close NNE of it.

Sémaphore d'Auderville

The lighthouse and Les Brétons from SE

Take up transit:

GO4 205° *The left side of the lighthouse aligned with Les Brétons*

Leave Les Brétons 50m to starboard and the lighthouse 80m to starboard. Continue S and when the lighthouse is on the starboard quarter make a small alteration to starboard onto:

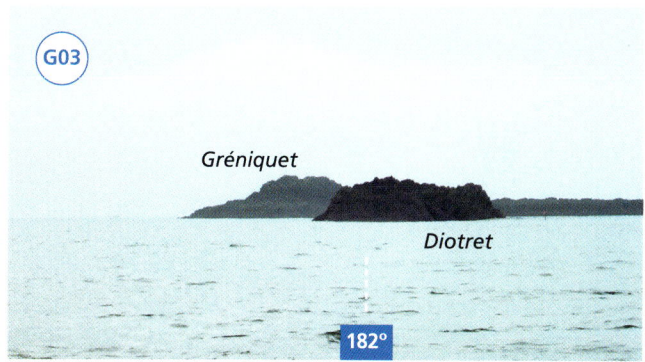

GO3 182° *Diotret (dries 4·8m) aligned as shown with back mark Gréniquet (dries 10m).*

Hold until Vignés port beacon is 100m to port then alter to starboard with stern transit:

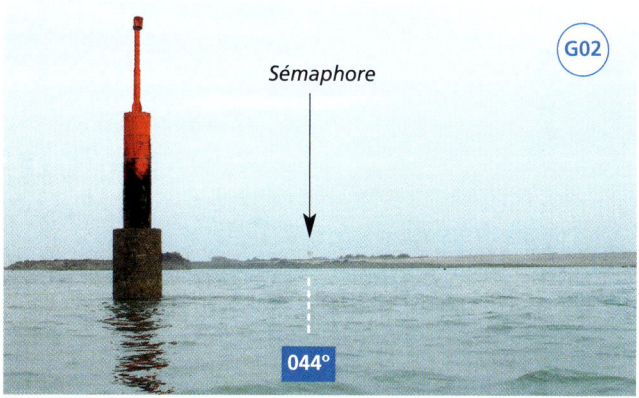

GO2 044° *Vignés port beacon aligned with Sémaphore d'Auderville*

Note If bound for Cherbourg by Passage de la Haize du Raz follow directions for From N in reverse order. Continue NE from ⊕63 – it is possible to take advantage of an inshore eddy that sets E while the mainstream is W going on the ebb.

2. Diélette to Granville (46M)
La Côte des Îles

The west coast 'La Côte des Îles' is, apart from the unsightly development at Cap Flamanville, unspoilt and off the beaten track. It has the longest beaches in Normandy punctuated by minor headlands and sand dunes that shelter the drying harbours of Carteret and Portbail. Further south, rivers and coastal currents have carved wide sandy inlets into the shallow coastal plain such as Havre de Regnéville. These are impenetrable to all but very shallow draughted boats and require local knowledge. Granville is the sole commercial port and main yachting centre on this coast.

LIST OF PORTS

Diélette *172*

Carteret *175*

Portbail *174*

Havre de Regnéville *180*

Granville *184*

Le Mont St Michel and Tomberlaine from the S:
The World Heritage Site of Mont St Michel at the SE extremity of the bay marks the border with Brittany. It is visited by land now that its island status is under threat from encroaching salt marsh. It is hoped that current major hydraulic developments will reverse the process by 2025 when Mont St Michel will become a true island again. (For details on how best to visit Mont St Michel, see St Malo chapter.)

Passage de la Déroute
(See St Vaast-La Hougue, *Historical* page 148)

The 10–15M wide stretch between the Islands and the Normandy coast is known as Passage de la Déroute. It is not detailed on charts and has no specific marks but there is a good scattering of cardinal buoys and beacons marking shoals and reefs. Vigilance, particularly in poor visibility, is a priority at all times. A large scale chart is essential.

La Déroute (See plan page 142)

La Déroute is occasionally used by ferries on the UK to St Malo route. N–S it passes W of Les Trois Grunes W card buoy, between Basse de Taillepied and Les Ecréhous, between Chausée des Boeufs and Plateau de l'Arconie, E of Les Minquiers and Les Ardentes, thence NW of Iles Chausey via Entrée de la Déroute.

The inshore equivalent, *Déroute de Terre*, follows the coast about 5·0M off and carries a least depth of 0·3m. With adequate rise of tide this is not a problem for small craft.

N–S the route passes W of Les Trois Grunes W cardinal buoy, Basses de Portbail landfall buoy, La Basse du Sénéquet W cardinal buoy, Les Nattes W cardinal buoy, Roches d'Agon and E of La Catheue S cardinal buoy and Iles Chausey.

Caution

Between Cap de la Hague and Granville the 60M of west facing coast is at the receiving end of prevailing winds and seas.

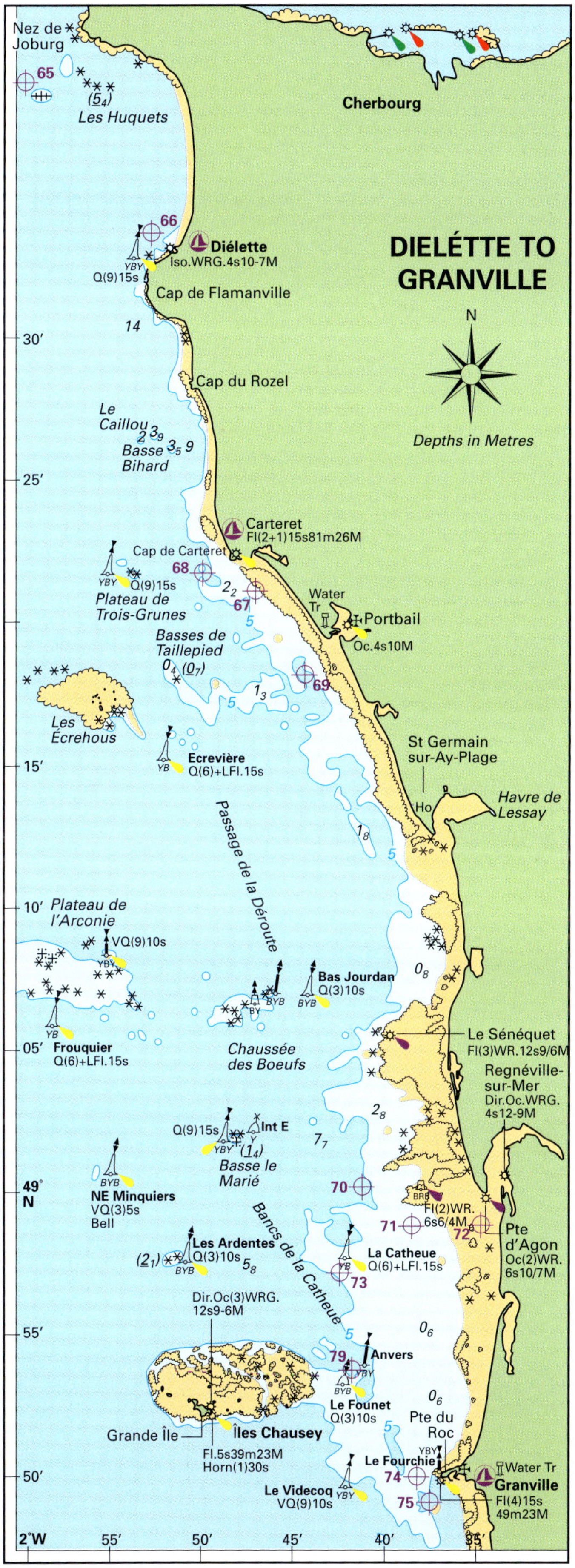

Diélette to Granville

La Côte des Îles at Cap de Carteret

With no islands to shelter behind, no deepwater estuaries and a few harbours with little to offer but drying entrances for much of the time, this shore can become inhospitable to approach in deteriorating onshore weather. In such circumstances St Catherine's Bay on Jersey's East coast and Les Iles Chausey may be the nearest boltholes for shelter.

The Baie du Mont St Michel shallows progressively south of Granville. The tide here is said to run at the speed of a galloping horse on account of an extraordinarily large tidal range – up to 13m. It is therefore not surprising that it is seldom entered by yachts. The border with Brittany is taken to be the Couesnon River at Le Mont St Michel.

Between Pointe du Grouin and St Malo is 10M of rugged northwest facing coast with a few temporary day anchorages and some fine beaches and bays such as Havre de Rothéneuf (see page 205). The coast opens out to the estuary of La Rance with St Malo and St Servan on its eastern bank and Dinard opposite.

⊕ 43	49°40'·92N	01°14'·65W
⊕ 47	49°42'·20N	01°15'·92W
⊕ 65	49°38'·80N	01°59'·00W
⊕ 66	49°33'·36N	01°52'·14W
⊕ 67	49°21'·00N	01°47'·00W
⊕ 68	49°29'·80N	01°49'·51W
⊕ 69	49°18'·35N	01°44'·75W
⊕ 70	49°00'·12N	01°41'·40W
⊕ 71	48°59'·05N	01°38'·00W
⊕ 72	48°58'·95N	01°34'·55W
⊕ 73	48°57'·52N	01°42'·20W
⊕ 74	49°50'·02N	01°37'·60W
⊕ 75	49°49'·30N	01°37'·20W
⊕ 79	48°53'·87N	01°41'·54W

II. THE CHERBOURG PENINSULA

CHANNEL ISLANDS, CHERBOURG PENINSULA & NORTH BRITTANY

II The Cherbourg Peninsula

DIÉLETTE
49°33'·17N 01°51'·82W (W Jetty Lt)
18M SE of Alderney (Braye)
14M N of Carteret
8M SSE of Nez de Jobourg
27M via coast from Cherbourg

TRAVEL
Sea
  Brittany Ferries: Poole/Portsmouth – Cherbourg
  Condor Ferries: Portsmouth – Cherbourg
  Manche Iles Express: Guernsey/Sark/Alderney – Diélette
    (℡ 08 25 13 10 50, www.manche-iles-express.com)
  Vedettes du Cotentin: ℡ 0760 20 20 40
    www.vedettesducotentin.com
Air
  Cherbourg (Maupertus) Airport – 15M
Bus
  MANÉO Line 10 Les Pieux-Cherbourg (30 min)

CHARTS
British Admiralty
  3653 Guernsey to Alderney and adjacent coast
    of France (1:50 000)
Imray
  C33A Channel Islands*
  2500 The Channel Islands and adjacent coast
    of France Chart Pack*
    *both include plan: Diélette (1:15 000)
SHOM
  SHOM 7133 Ports de la côte Ouest du Cotentin*
    *includes plan: Abords de Diélette (1:15 000)
  SHOM 7158 Du Cap de Carteret au Cap de la Hague –
    Raz Blanchard (1:48 000)

RADIO
Cross-Jobourg Ch 16
Port de Diélette (0800-2000 LT) Ch 09

TIDAL INFORMATION
Differences
St Malo: Standard Port +40m
Cherbourg – 1h08m
St Helier +20m

MHWS	MLWS	MHWN	MLWN
9·7	1·2	7·4	3·5

Tidal streams
Off Diélette:
NE going stream starts at HW St Helier-0325
SW going stream starts at HW St Helier +0220
Streams attain max 2kns
During the NE going stream offshore the stream in the harbour runs SE towards the inner jetty (max 1½kns) and an eddy runs W along the inner jetty towards the N part of Jétee Ouest.

Caution
Beware cross stream in the entrance

USEFUL CONTACTS
Bureau du Port ℡ 02 33 53 68 78
  Email portdielette@cc-lespieux.com www.cc-lespieux.com
Office du Tourisme ℡ 02 33 52 81 60
Fuel ℡ 02 33 04 50 37

SUPPLIES AND SERVICES
Marina Water and electricity at pontoons. Two sanitary blocks (E and W). Laundry. WiFi and internet access. Nursery. 40-ton hoist, crane, hard standing for layup.
Fuel 24h
Chandlery, Repairs
  Diélette Plaisance ℡ 02 33 08 30 47
    www.dielette.plaisance@wanadoo.fr
Diver Hague Sud Plongée ℡ 02 33 53 01 13
Sail repairs Voilerie des Iles 06 087 96 35 91
  www.voilerie-des-iles.com
Car hire Information, Bureau du Port
Taxi Durel ℡ 02 33 53 23 24 / 06 08 68 08 67
Shops The nearest shops are in Flamanville village (2M). A more extensive range in the market town of Les Pieux (4M) includes Intermarché in Route du Cherbourg, ℡ 02 33 52 32 06. Local shopkeepers including an excellent fish monger occasionally set themselves up around the marina during the season.
Shuttle bus This free service runs from the Bureau du Port in July and August Monday–Saturday, which stops at Flamanville and Les Pieux. Total journey time including stops is 20 minutes. From Les Pieux there is a public bus to Cherbourg, 40 minutes (See *TRAVEL*).
Restaurants
  L'Escale Bar Brasserie next to Bureau du Port. Speciality: Les Moules (reputed to be the best in the area) ℡ 02 33 52 67 10
  Le Raz Blanchard (on quay) ℡ 02 33 04 14 78
Markets
  Flamanville – Wednesday am
  Le Pieux – Friday am

Diélette to Granville

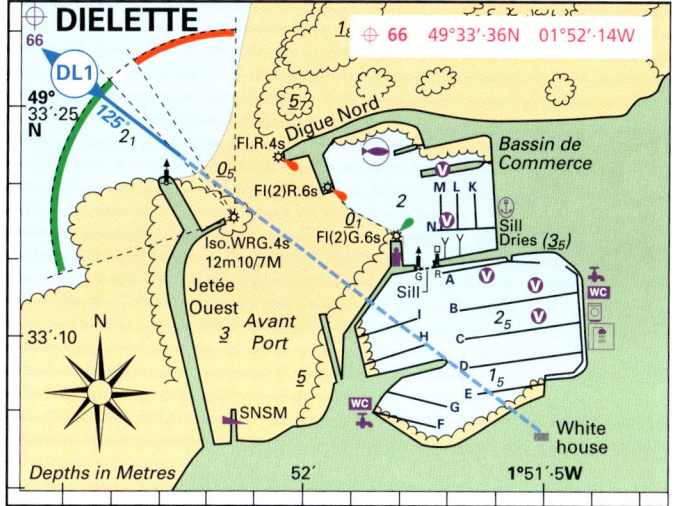

Diélette is promoted as 'the gateway to the Channel Islands' and is proving a popular alternative to Alderney as a staging post for yachts bound south from the north and northeast, or returning home. Being the nearest French port to Guernsey it also attracts weekenders from St Peter Port.

You will not find the noisy high life here but for those that enjoy exploring by bike or on foot there are some exceptional coastal walks from Diélette. The wild countryside of La Hague area is unique to the Cotentin.

Historical
Diélette was once a prosperous iron ore port. The rusting remains of the dolphin and transporter that was used to load bulk carriers are visible a mile SW of the Port.

Approach
The harbour is easily located a mile N of the conspicuous Flamanville Power station with its two enormous towers. Note also, as described above, the remains of two concrete platforms off the coast, 0·25M N of the power station.

Warning
An exclusion zone extends seaward from Flamanville power station with a W cardinal buoy marking its NW extremity. Entry is not permitted under any circumstances.

From the N
S of the Alderney Race are several shoals off Nez de Jobourg (see plan page 171) to be avoided. Pass outside via ⊕65 or with a large scale chart take the mile wide passage between Les Huquets de Jobourg (2M S of Nez du Jobourg) and the shore. If passing outside allow for a cross set towards the reef and inside expect an early turn of the tide.

What was described in the 60s as 'a small artificial harbour used by fishermen as a temporary anchorage in offshore winds' has since been the recipient of large quantities of concrete, transforming it into a substantial harbour complex that provides for ferries, pleasure boaters and fishermen. 'Charm' might not be the first word that springs to mind when describing Diélette but 'functional' is. The Bassin de Plaisance (Marina) lists a wide range of facilities including 420 berths, 70 of which are for visitors, areas of hard standing with crane and hoist, sanitary blocks, laundry, 24 hour surveillance, WiFi and a nursery.

The reality for yachtsmen is that despite a generous window of about seven hours in which to come and go, the harbour is a target for northwesterlies. The wide entrance scoops up waves and swell from the W, making entry potentially dangerous and creating a surge inside. It would be hazardous to approach or leave in strong to gale force onshore winds. (See warning.)

Diélette looking ESE. New pontoons have since been laid in Bassin de Commerce

II. THE CHERBOURG PENINSULA

CHANNEL ISLANDS, CHERBOURG PENINSULA & NORTH BRITTANY

II The Cherbourg Peninsula

From the S
Route to ⊕66 to keep 1·0M off Cap de Flamanville power station. Identify approach transit:

DL1 *125° conspicuous white house (no longer lit) aligned with lighthouse on Jetée Ouest. As an alternative the lighthouse may be aligned with starboard beacon tower NW of it*

Entry
When 0·2M short of Jetée Ouest make a small alternation to port to enter nearer the light house on Digue Nord. The bottom of Jetée Ouest pierhead is rocky. Come to port to enter Bassin de Commerce. Use waiting pontoons ahead or cross the sill into the marina (see *Signals*).

WARNING
The shallow entrance is prone to silting and subject to frequent dredging. Even moderate onshore winds can produce breaking seas off the entrance. It is advisable to make a visual check of conditions before departing the marina. It may be prudent to wait until HW.

Minimum depths
Entrance and Outer Harbour: Dries at 0·1m – 0·2m
Bassin de Commerce: Dredged to 2·0m
Marina: 1·5 to 2·5m depending on position.
(Note that following dredging in 2013 depth in the entrance has increased.)

Limits
With a 1·5m draught it should be possible to enter the harbour at all states of tide except around LW springs.

Diélette. The sill with depth gauge and signals above right
Martin Walker

Entry looking NW from the Avant Port

However it is advised to limit entry and departure to within three hours of HW or if in any doubt to HW when the streams are slack and there is plenty of water.

By Night
Keep in the W sector (135°–145°) of Jetée Ouest light Iso.WRG.4s.
Note advice under *Entry*.

Marina
Pond level is maintained by a gate that dries 5m. The gate drops automatically when there is a rise of 1·5m over the sill which corresponds to approximately 3hr15m before HW depending on the predicted height of tide. It will remain open for a further 3hr15m or so.

Signals
2G + W – two way traffic
3R – Closed

Berthing
On pontoons A B and C. The arrival pontoon is by the bureau du port and the fuel point (24h) is immediately W of the sill.

Drying out
This is possible against the W wall in the Avant Port but it is exposed to NW winds. Dries to 4–5m hard sand. Refer to bureau du port.

The marina looking W

Diélette to Granville

CARTERET

49°22'·08N 01°47'·30W (Light beacon west jetty head)

TRAVEL
Sea
 Ferries: St Helier – Carteret
 Manche Iles Express ☏ (0)2 33 01 10 11 / 01534 80756
  www.manche-iles.com
 Vedettes du Cotentin www.vedettesducotentin.com
Bus
 MANÉO ☏ (0)2 33 05 55 50 www.transports.mnche.fr
 Access to Portbail, Barneville, Bricquebec, Cherbourg, Valognes.
 Monday–Friday 0800–1900. Stop: Old Station

CHARTS
British Admiralty
 3655 Jersey and Adjacent Coast of France (1:50 000)
Imray
 C33A Channel Islands*
 2500 The Channel Islands and adjacent coast of France Chart Atlas*
 *both include plan: Carteret (1:25 000)
SHOM
 7133 Ports de la Côte Ouest du Cotentin*
  *includes plans: Abords de Carteret et Portbail (1:20 000), Carteret (1:10 000)
 7157 De la Pointe d'Agon au Cap de Carteret – Passage de la Déroute (1:48 400)

RADIO
 Cross Jobourg Ch 16
 Carteret Signal Station Ch 10 ☏ (0) 233 04 90 58
 Port de Carteret Ch 09
 Jersey Coastguard Ch 16/82

TIDAL INFORMATION
 Standard Port St Malo or St Helier
 Differences St Malo +0025
 St Helier +0010

MHWS	MLWS	MHWN	MLWN
10·6	1·3	8·1	3·7

The estuary dries out up to one mile offshore. Entry and departure only possible above half tide. The marked channel dries 4m to 4·5m. The Marina sill dries at 5m and may be crossed approximately 2½ hours either side of HW. This window reduces at Neaps.

Tidal streams
 Offshore the flood sets SE from LW up to between one and two hours before HW when a strong NW eddy sets in – first inshore and later offshore. An entry at HW -1 when the stream is slackening is advisable. Getting set N of Carteret is a common mistake. It can be a battle to regain track against a spring ebb – max 4½ knots.

USEFUL CONTACTS
 Bureau du Port ☏ 02 33 04 70 84
  Email contactaport-des-iles.fr
 Yacht Club de Carteret ☏ 02 33 526073
 Office du Tourisme ☏ 02 33 04 94 54 (seasonal)

SUPPLIES AND SERVICES
Chandlery and boatyard Carteret Marine ☏ 02 33 012001
Car hire Yacht Club de Carteret ☏ 02 33 52 60 73 / 02 33 94 32 77 www.francecars.fr
Tabac ☏ 02 33 53 84 93
Market Market day is Saturday in Barneville and Thursday in Carteret.
Taxi Felix ☏ 02 33 52 03 75
 Taxi de la Côtes des Iles ☏ 02 33 04 61 02
Restaurants Le Cap (near ferry terminal) ☏ 02 33 53 85 89
 St Hétier Créperie (in the town) ☏ 02 33 53 81 96

 ⊕ 67 Carteret Lt Ho 49°21'·00N 01°47'·00W
 ⊕ 68 Cap de Carteret 49°29'·80N 01°49'·51W

The entrance near LW springs showing sand banks (2012)

This natural harbour in a drying estuary surrounded by countryside has been a port for centuries. In the days of sail Carteret provided a vital link in the trading routes between the Channel Islands and France. Today the working schooners (*goëlettes*) of that era have been replaced by ferries, pleasure boats and a small fishing fleet. Its Belle Epoque villas recall something of the atmosphere of the fashionable seaside resort that it was in the latter part of the 19th century.

In 1995 a 300 berth marina was developed named 'Le Port des Isles' (spelt the English way as a mark of Carteret's affinity with the Channel Islands). This puts the port on the itinerary as a cruising destination and a pleasant stop over *en route* from the UK south coast to the Islands and Brittany.

Carteret is 23M to the Alderney Race, 14M to Gorey and 20M to St Helier.

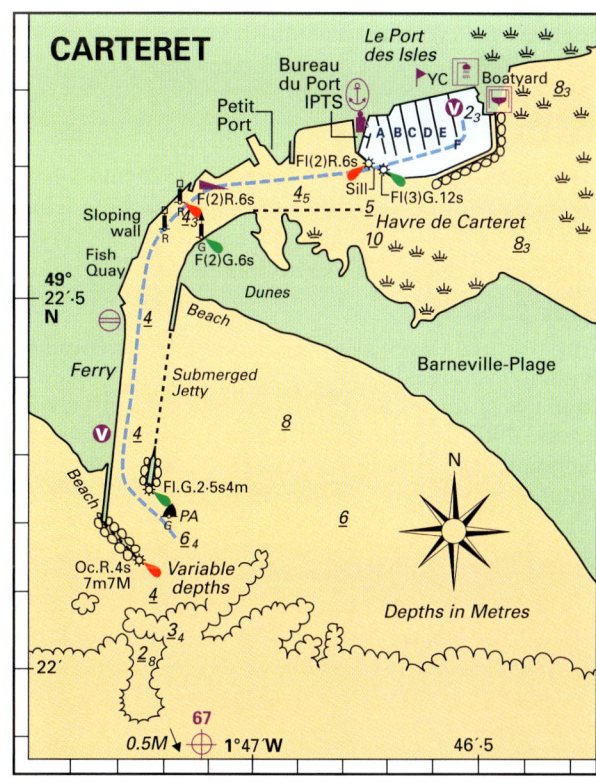

II. THE CHERBOURG PENINSULA

CHANNEL ISLANDS, CHERBOURG PENINSULA & NORTH BRITTANY

II The Cherbourg Peninsula

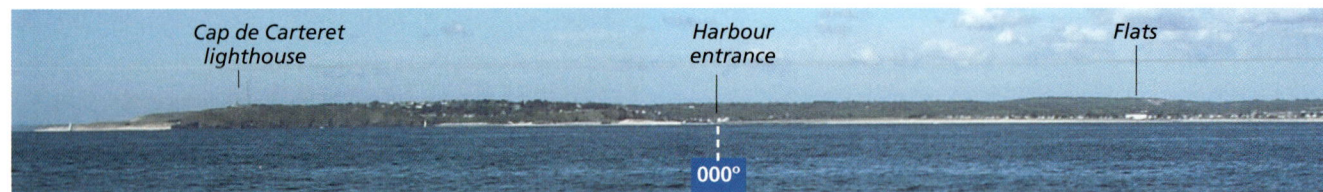

A useful aiming point when closing the coast in the approach is the conspicuous block of flats at Barneville Plage a mile S of Carteret

Ashore

Carteret and its neighbour Barneville merged under one Commune in 1965. In Barneville town (Le Bourg) you will find a wide range of shops. There is also a hypermarket on its outskirts. A walk from the marina via the estuary backwater takes about 30 minutes. Alternatively bikes may be hired from the Tabac. A walk up to Cap de Carteret via the Sentier des Douaniers is rewarded with a spectacular view of the coastline and the protected dunes of Hatainville. There is a good choice of restaurants in the port. The speciality is shellfish.

Le Train Touristique du Cotentin is a string of period carriages drawn by a 1950s diesel locomotive. It runs occasionally between Carteret and Portbail along a stretch of overgrown track – all that remains of the Paris to Carteret line originally laid in the 1890s.

✆ 02 33 04 70 08 / 06 3035 15 71
www.ttcotentin.monsite.orange.fr

Approaches

Caution

In fresh to strong onshore winds the shallow conditions particularly over the *plateau*, *basses* and *bancs*, some of which have drying patches, cause breaking seas. In such conditions entry may be hazardous. In these areas crab and lobster pot floats proliferate and these may not be visible in moderate to rough conditions or after dark. A sharp lookout should be maintained. (See *A local hazard* page 11.)

From the N and W

From Alderney Race it is necessary to keep three miles off the coast, but give Plateau des Trois-Grunes (drying 1·6m) a good clearance. This also applies if approaching from the W.

⊕68 is positioned 1·0M SW of Cap de Carteret.

From the S and SW

Arriving towards the end of the flood involves stemming the N going inshore eddy.

From a position well S (upstream) of the port (⊕67) make good 000° with the entrance seen just open. A useful aiming point when closing the coast in the approach is the conspicuous block of flats at Barneville Plage a mile S of Carteret.

Warning – The Sandbar (See air view page 175)

For centuries mariners have had to contend with this obstacle in the entrance. In May 2012 it was lying against the S side of the outer end of the main W jetty and considered no problem to vessels entering or leaving.

If it moves S and is considered a hazard its position is, during the season, buoyed with a port or starboard mark.

The best water is close to the port beacon

Entry

Enter midway between the starboard beacon at the end of the submersible training wall and the port beacon at the end of the main W jetty. Before the next set of beacons borrow to the N to pass nearer the quay and close to the port beacon thus avoiding the sandbar to the SE. Pass also close to the next isolated port beacon and proceed towards the marina entrance. The channel is dredged to 4·5m W of the marina.

Marina entry

Entry is over a sill (dries 5m) that opens and closes when there is 1·3m over it. This is about 2hr30 either side of HW but less at neap tides.

The Marina sill

By night

There are no leading lights but Cap de Carteret lighthouse Fl(2+1)15s81m26M perched on top of the headland NE of the harbour entrance is unmistakable.

Diélette to Granville

The holding pontoon

Enter between the end of W jetty Oc.R.4s7m and the end of the submersible jetty Fl.G.2·5s4m. Follow the channel that runs NNE parallel to the quay. Pass between, but closer to the port side, the two channel marks Fl(2)R.6s and Fl(2)G.6s.

Here the channel bends to starboard to continue ENE towards the marina sill which is marked with Fl(3)R.12s and Fl(3)G.12s.

Signals
The sill is marked by port and stbd beacons. The port beacon has a depth board and signal lights are positioned S end of marina retaining wall.
3 red = Gate closed
2 Green over white = Gate open

Depth
Retained depth in marina is 2·30m

Berthing
The waiting pontoon is just inside the entrance below Capitainerie du Port. The visitors' pontoon (F) is at the eastern end of the marina.

Facilities
On pontoon: water and electricity.
Yacht Club: showers and toilets.
Fuel: Holding pontoon.
Lift out and lay up with 35-ton travel-lift: NE corner. Operated by Carteret Marine (see *Supplies and services*).

Drying out
This is possible W of the weir S of the marina with authorisation from the Capitainerie.

Yachts wishing to dry out in the East of the Havre must first obtain permission from the Town Hall ☎ 02 33 53 88 29 as this area is outside the jurisdiction of the Harbour Authorities.

The Fish Quay is reserved for fishing vessels only.

The Petit Port may be used for drying out, subject to authorisation by the Bureau du Port

PORTBAIL
49°19'·72N 01°42'·42W Harbour entrance

CHARTS
BA 3655 Jersey and Adjacent Coast of France (1:50 000)
SHOM 7133 Ports de la côte Ouest du Cotentin*
    *includes plans: Abords de Carteret et Portbail (1:20 000), Portbail (1:10 000)
SHOM 7157 De la Pointe d'Agon au Cap de Carteret – Passage de la Déroute (1:48 400)

TIDAL INFORMATION
Standard Port St Malo or St Helier
Differences: St Malo +25
St Helier +10

MHWS	MLWS	MHWN	MLWN
11·4	1·4	8·7	4·0

The approach channel dries 5·2m. Entry and departure possible one hour either side of HW.
When the tidal coefficient is less than 35 (below mean neaps) entry is not possible.

Tidal streams
NE going stream starts at HW St Helier -0325
SW going stream starts at HW St Helier +0220

RADIO
Cross Jobourg VHF Ch 16
Carteret signal station VHF Ch 10 ☎ (0)233 04 90 58
Port / Marina de Portbail VHF Ch 9
Jersey coastguard VHF Ch 16/82

USEFUL CONTACTS
Bureau du Port ☎ 02 33 04 83 48
Office du Tourisme ☎ 02 33 04 02 07
Club Nautique ☎ 02 33 33 10 96

SUPPLIES AND SERVICES
Chandlery, Repairs
    Chandlery, nautical books Portbail Plaisance Place Edmond Laquaine ☎ 02 33 52 98 97
        Email portbailplaisance@wanadoo.fr
Bicycle hire
    Anne Cycles ☎ 02 33 01 28 20
    Eureka ☎ 02 33 04 81 25
Taxi Taxis de la Côte des Iles ☎ 02 33 04 61 02
Supermarket Huit-à-huit: Off Place des Arbres
Market
    Fish market in Place de l'Eglise www.portbail.fr
    General market every Tuesday
Restaurants Restaurant (Le Bourg) Aux Treize Arches, Place Castel ☎ 02 33 04 87 90 www.13arches.com
    Brasserie (Le Port) Le Repère ☎ 02 33 04 35 30 www.lepere-portbail.fr

Four miles SE of Carteret a channel through the low dunes opens out into a large sheltered lagoon of marshland and sand. Within this strange landscape is a small dredged harbour and in the distance at the end of a half mile long causeway (Le Pont de Portbail) is the town. The central feature is L'Eglise Notre Dame which also serves as a navigation mark.

The whole area dries out up to a mile offshore so this is the territory of small bilge keelers and boats with a draught of no more than a metre or so and able to take the ground.

Portbail is a friendly unspoilt place with a captivating atmosphere. If offers adequate facilities for visiting yachts. There is a good range of shops to meet the needs of a small population and several good restaurants.

CHANNEL ISLANDS, CHERBOURG PENINSULA & NORTH BRITTANY

II The Cherbourg Peninsula

Historical

Portbail has been a port since Roman times when it was known as Portus Ballii. The Romanesque Eglise Notre Dame and the nearby site of a unique 6th century hexagonal baptistery are worth visiting. There are guided tours Tuesday to Sunday 1030–1230 (seasonal) which can be arranged with the helpful Office du Tourisme ☎ 02 33 04 02 07.

Approach

WARNING

The coastline is totally exposed to prevailing westerlies between NW through W to S.

There is little to identify the inlet from seaward apart from the RW landfall buoy 1·5M SW of the entrance and a conspicuous water tower (43m) 0·5M inland and 0·75M N of the entrance.

PB1 042° *La Caillourie beacon aligned with spire of Eglise Notre Dame*

Landfall buoy 'PB'   Conspicuous water tower

Entry

The best time to enter is at HW-1 when the stream in the Channel, which can attain 3 or more knots, is slackening.

From a position 400m E of RW landfall buoy 'PB' (⊕69) take up a heading of 042° with transit:

Portbail entrance from the SW

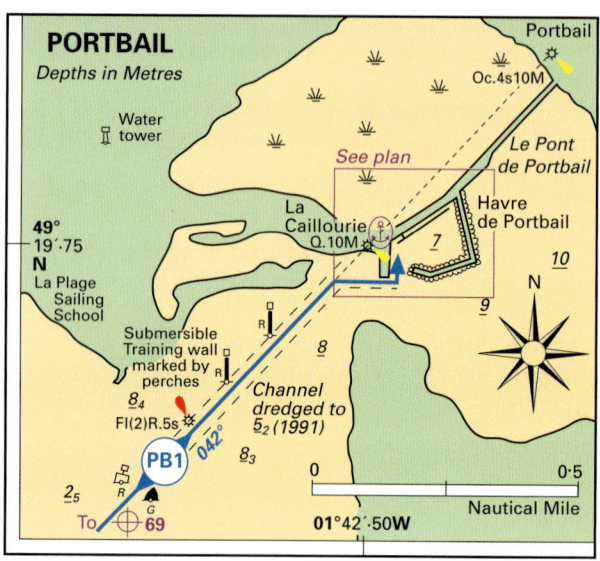

⊕ 69   49°18'·35N   01°44'·75W

178 CHANNEL ISLANDS, CHERBOURG PENINSULA & NORTH BRITTANY

Diélette to Granville

Le Pont de Portbail joins Le Bourg to the Port

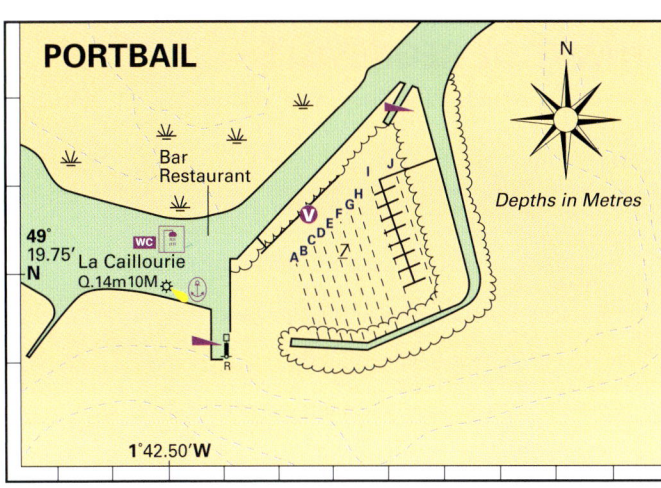

Enter the dredged channel (dries 5·2m) midway between port and starboard buoys. A submersible training wall borders its N edge. There are numerous R posts (eight in 2012) the first being lit (Q(2)R.5s).

The first R post in the channel

The channel at LW with submersible training wall marked by poles. On the right is the base of La Caillourie

A cable short of La Caillourie beacon alter course to starboard to leave the last R pole and jetty end marked by R beacon close to port. Enter mooring area (dries 7m).

Note When training wall is covered there is a least depth of 2·5m in the channel.

The entrance to the mooring area

By night
From landfall buoy 'PB' Fl(2)R.5s5m enter with leading lights Front: La Caillourie Q.14m
Rear: Church spire Oc.4s20m

Mooring
Visitors moor alongside a 150m long drying pontoon NW of the harbour or in the basin on head and stern moorings as directed. Drying out alongside the inner part of the jetty on the slip is usually reserved for fishing vessels but may be used by visitors with prior permission from harbourmaster.

Max length 16m, max draught 2m.

Facilities
Visitors' pontoon – water and electricity.
Toilets and showers, laundry.

View of Portbail harbour from the entrance

CHANNEL ISLANDS, CHERBOURG PENINSULA & NORTH BRITTANY

II The Cherbourg Peninsula

HAVRE DE REGNÉVILLE

49°00'·18N 01°34'·63W (Pointe d'Agon Lighthouse)

TRAVEL
Sea
Ferry between Granville and Jersey March – September incl.
☏ 02 61 08 88 www.manche-iles-com

CHARTS
BA 2669 Channel Islands and adjacent coast of France (1:150 000)
BA 3656 Plateau des Minquiers and adjacent coast of France (1:50 000)
Imray C33B Channel Islands (south) and north coast of France (1:120 000)
SHOM 7133 Ports de la côte ouest du Cotentin (1:20 000)
SHOM 7156 Pointe du Grouin à la Pointe d'Agon (1:48 800)

RADIO
Jersey Coastguard Ch 16/82
Cross Jobourg Ch 16

TIDAL INFORMATION
Standard Port St Malo or St Helier
Time Difference on St Malo +0010
Time Difference on St Helier -007

MHWS	MLWS	MHWN	MLWN
12·5	1·6	10·0	5·0

Duration of flood 5hr
Duration of ebb 7hr

Caution
The mouth of the estuary is narrowed by sand spits which concentrate the tidal streams. This also retards the incoming tide creating a surge in the final 1½ hours before HW which can be alarming. Timing is of the essence for a visit to Regnéville. Slack water is at HW and lasts about an hour. This is the only period in which to arrive, anchor or moor and undertake dinghy work.
On large spring tides banks may be breached and surrounding fields flooded. The mean rate on the flood is 4–5 knots setting NNW but less on the ebb setting S.

USEFUL CONTACTS
Capitainerie/Club Nautique ☏ 02 33 46 36 76
Syndicat d'Initiative 8 Rue du port ☏ 02 33 45 88 71

SUPPLIES AND SERVICES
Adequate shops to meet basic needs.
Water and showers At Campsite near Regnéville landing pontoon.
Boatyard
Chantiers David Smewing 14, Rue du Port 50590 Regnéville-sur-Mer ☏ 02 33 45 75 25
Chantier *Email* smewing@free.fr
Crane, liftout, wintering on terre-plein, restoration, maintenance
Restaurants
La Hostellerie de la Baye ☏ 02 33 07 43 94
Le Jules Gommès ☏ 02 33 45 32 04
Markets
Montmartin-sur-Mer: Wednesday
Château de Regnéville-sur-Mer: Friday (from 1800) July and August
Hauteville-sur-Mer (2½M to the S) Sunday am
Taxi Montmartin-sur-Mer ☏ 02 33 47 62 96

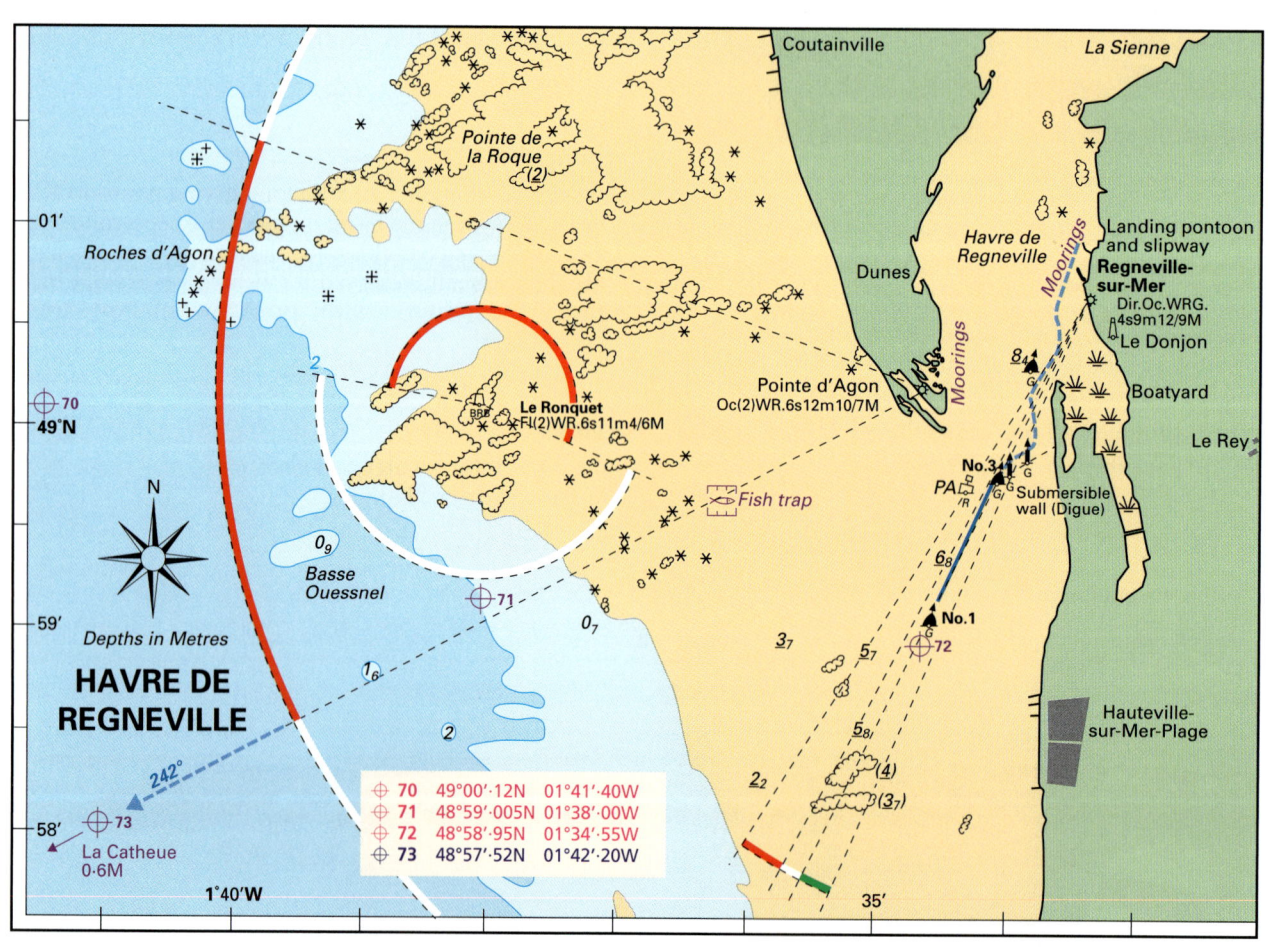

Diélette to Granville

II. THE CHERBOURG PENINSULA

View of estuary with mooring areas off Pointe d'Agon left and Regnéville-sur-Mer, top right

'A magnet for hardy adventurers seeking sand and solitude'
Reeds 2009

Le Havre de Regnéville 10 miles north of Granville is the largest inlet on the 'Côte des Havres'. Here the River Sienne has combined with powerful tides to gouge out this extraordinary estuary. With a reputation for fast flowing streams and its transformation into a desert of sand at low tide, it is a challenging destination for small craft designed to take the ground and equipped with good ground tackle and a reliable tender/outboard motor combination.

Despite the lack of usual yachting facilities it is home to scores of small craft, has two anchorage areas with visitors' moorings and landing pontoons – and there are no rocks.

Historical

As you look over the expansive estuary at low tide it is hard to believe that this was one of the most prosperous ports on the Cotentin peninsula in the Middle Ages. Then it provided a link for trade between Gascony and ports in England. In the 14th century a fortified castle was built to protect the harbour and part of its remains, 'Le Donjon', rises precariously over the village. Its silhouette has been adopted as Regnéville's symbol.

Prosperity returned in the 19th century with the exploitation of limestone, a natural resource in the area. This was quarried in large quantities for the production of quicklime used as a fertilizer and a base for mortar. The enormous kilns (*fouénés*) used in the process may be seen at Rey between Regnéville and Montmartin. Coal for firing the kilns was imported from South Wales in trading schooners. They would come in with the tide, dry out 'Bristol Fashion' on the sands and discharge their cargoes onto horse and carts or barges.

Cotentin fish traps in the outer estuary are stone structures that have been used since the Middle Ages. Fish brought in on the flood tide become trapped on their way out. They are recovered at LW from nets set against the trap gate.

Commercial activity declined by early 20th century due to silting of the estuary but Regnéville continues to be one of the major shell fisheries of the Cotentin. The *pré sale* sheep that graze among the salt marshes are famous for the quality of their meat.

Museums

Fours à chaux du Rey et Musée Maritime.
Château de Regnéville-sur-Mer
Email Musee.regneville@manche.fr.

II The Cherbourg Peninsula

A track through the salt marsh leads to Regnéville village

Landing stage and slipway at Regnéville-sur-Mer are maintained by the Cercle Nautique Regnéville. Drying out alongside is not possible

Ashore

As a protected natural site Regnéville has much to offer in the way of country pursuits, such as walking, cycling and ornithology. It is above all peaceful and off the tourist belt – although there is a Syndicat d'Initiative.

The hamlet of Regnéville-sur-Mer on the east bank is the only habitation in the estuary. Here will be found the usual elements of a small French rural community – *boulangerie*, *boucherie*, *bar tabac*, and a couple of restaurants. There is also a 13th century church and some historical ruins.

For a more substantial shopping centre with a pharmacy, bank and a garage you will need transport to Montmartin-sur-Mer 2M southeast of Regnéville-sur-Mer.

Approaches

The coast is low lying with few conspicuous marks other than the coastal resorts of Agon-Coutainville and Hauteville N and S of the estuary. The key to an approach from any direction is Le Ronquet beacon tower isolated danger mark Fl(2)WR.6s. This is 2·5M W of Pointe d'Agon lighthouse Oc(2)WR.6s.

Le Ronquet tower from the S. It is surrounded by mussel beds

An entry can only be made around HW so the approach will be on a rising tide.

From the north

La Déroute de Terre Passage (see *Introduction* page 170).

Coasting S from the direction of Cap de Carteret aim to keep a distance of 5M off the coast but beware of the dangers that extend a mile out from Le Senequet lighthouse 7M NNW of Regnéville entry channel.

Pass close to Bas Jourdan E cardinal buoy E of the Chaussée des Boeufs and continue S to ⊕70 2·2M W of Le Ronquet tower. Then steer ESE to ⊕71 1·0M S of Ronquet tower. Finally steer E to intercept the entry channel at starboard channel buoy 1 ⊕72.

Note that a yellow buoy numbered 6 1·0M SE of Le Ronquet tower marks the S limit of oyster and mussel beds and should be passed to the S.

From the northwest (St Helier)

This is a good downtide passage with several marks *en route*. After departure S of Demi de Pas beacon tower these are:

Canger rock W cardinal buoy
Le Frouquier Aubert S cardinal buoy
Basse le Marié W cardinal buoy and Internationale E buoy (Y).
Navigate to ⊕71 1·0M S of Le Ronquet beacon tower then ⊕72 at starboard channel buoy No.1.

From the south

Note that the stream turns N off Granville at about HW St Helier -2.

It is a straightforward approach between Iles Chausey and Granville to ⊕71 1M S of Le Ronquet beacon tower. Continue as for Approaches from other directions.

From the southwest

From La Catheue S cardinal buoy (⊕73) make good 075° to starboard channel buoy No.1.

Entry

Caution

The channel buoys are frequently repositioned due to the constantly shifting sandbanks and changes in the direction of the channel.

There are no leading marks for entry but there is a directional light at Regnéville (*see By night*).

From starboard channel buoy No.1 (⊕72) take up a heading of 027° to pass midway between port channel buoy and starboard channel buoy (unnumbered). Leave the two starboard beacons on the digue numbered 5 (outer) and 7 (inner) to starboard after which the channel turns NNW and the final starboard buoy should be left close to port (2012).

From this point the best depths are currently found on the E side of the channel.

182 CHANNEL ISLANDS, CHERBOURG PENINSULA & NORTH BRITTANY

Diélette to Granville

The digue with beacons

The digue at LW

The final mark is a floating sign at which point either continue to the anchorage area close to the shore off Regnéville village or turn towards the anchorage area on the W side of the estuary off Pointe d'Agon lighthouse.

By night
When familiar with entry and departure by day one may with caution and subject to calm, clear conditions attempt a night entry. The only available lights are:

Pointe d'Agon lighthouse Oc(2)WR.6s12m (W sector 063°–110°)

Regnéville-sur-Mer: DirOcWRG.6s12m10M (keep in narrow W sector 027°–029°).

The directional light

All channel marks are unlit so keep a good lookout with the aid of a spotlight for these and craft moored in the estuary.

Depths
The author visited Regnéville on a spring tide with a predicted height of 11·00m at St Helier (coefficient 95).
  Arriving at HW depths were found to be variable which is expected after big spring tides. Soundings taken were as follows:

1M S of Le Ronquet	14m
In channel S of Pointe d'Agon	11m
Off Regnéville village	6–9m

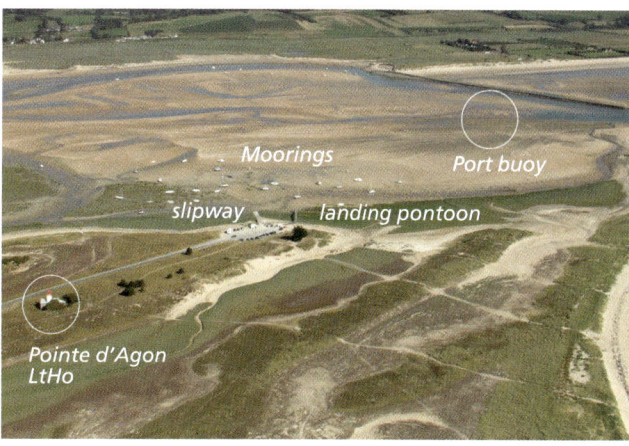
Moorings off Pointe d'Agon

The landing stage at HW

There is less depth off Pointe d'Agon than off Regnéville.
  The bottom is mostly firm sand but there are areas of mud on the foreshore. The estuary dries out at a uniform height of about 10m with some gullies.

Anchoring and mooring
The anchorage area off Pointe d'Agon is bleak but gains some shelter from the sand spit. The Club Nautique (℡ 02 33 46 36 76) advertises a total of 86 anchorage berths and three visitor moorings. Moorings should be considered unreliable. The safer option is to use your own ground tackle (*see Depths*).

Shelter
Regnéville is not a place to be gale bound in westerlies though some shelter is provided by the sand spits, particularly E of Pointe d'Agon. Strong southerlies can create ugly seas in the entrance when wind is against tide.

Regnéville

II The Cherbourg Peninsula

GRANVILLE
48°49'·94N 01°35'·93W (Marina entrance)

TRAVEL
Sea
  Ferries:
  Guernsey/Jersey – Granville
  Manche Iles Express ☎ 015 34 88 07 56 / 02 33 61 08 88
    www.manche-iles.co
  Iles Chausey
  Vedette Jolie-France: www.vedettejoliefrance.com
    ☎ 02 33 50 31 31 / 02 33 50 31 81
Train
  Granville – Paris Montparnasse (3 hours)
  TER (Train Régional) www.ter-sncf.com/basse-normandie

CHARTS
  BA 3656 Plateau des Minquiers and adjacent coast
    of France (1:50 000)
  BA 3659 Cap Fréhel to Iles Chausey (1:50 000)
  Imray C33B Channel Islands and North Coast of France*
    *includes plan: Granville (1:15 000)
  Imray 2500 The Channel Islands and adjacent coast of
    France Chart Pack*
    *includes plan: Granville (1:30 000)
  SHOM 7156 De la Pointe du Grouin à la Pointe d'Agon –
    Baie du Mont-Saint-Michel - Iles Chausey (1:48 800)
  SHOM 7341 Abords de Granville (1:15 000)

RADIO
  Cross Jobourg Ch 16
  Port de Hérel (Marina) Ch 09 HW ±3 hrs
  Port Ch 12 HW ±1½hrs

TIDAL INFORMATION
  Standard Port: St Malo
  Differences: St Malo -10
    St Helier -15

MHWS	MLWS	MHWN	MLWN
12·9	1·2	9·8	4·5

  Tidal Streams off Granville
  N stream starts HW St Malo -2h30
  S stream starts HW St Malo +3h39
  Max 2kns in either direction

Caution
  The Baie de Mont St Michel is renowned for its exceptional tidal range and accelerated streams. Particular caution should be exercised over spring tides when a good percentage should be added to published rates.

USEFUL CONTACTS
  Marina Office ☎ 02 33 50 20 06
  Port ☎ (0)2 33 50 17 75
  Yacht Club Granville ☎ 02 33 50 04 25
  Office du Tourisme ☎ 02 33 91 30 03

SUPPLIES AND SERVICES
  Fuel Pontoon G ☎ 02 33 50 20 06
  Water and electricity On walkways
  General Toilets, showers, internet access, WiFi, weather, bike hire
  Laundry Place Godel
  Chandlery Accastillage Diffusion (Port Hérel)
  Sail repairs Voilerie Granvillaise ☎ 02 33 50 62 28
  Boat Yard 30-ton travel-lift and slip
    Granville Plaisance ☎ 02 33 50 23 82
  Taxi ☎ 02 33 50 50 06 / 02 33 50 01 67

Granville is the largest and most southerly harbour on the Côte des Iles and main port in the Baie de Mont St Michel.

From its origins as a fortified commercial harbour with a large fishing fleet and shipyards, it has developed to accommodate Channel Island ferry traffic and marine tourism. The first marina project, Port Hérel has 200 visitors' berths and excellent dockside facilities. It is accessible over a sill about three hours either side of HW. From seaward the rocky headland of Pointe du Roc with its grey granite barracks may not look particularly inviting but belies the charm of this unpretentious town. Its lower part surrounding the port has a wide range of shops, bars and restaurants and retains the feel of a seaside resort. The upper town and citadel is the cultural and historic heart of Granville, with narrow cobbled lanes, niche restaurants, art galleries and museums. Well worth the climb.

Historical
In the 15th century the English held the town fortifying the promontory as a base from which to attack Mont St Michel then occupied by the French. The town was recaptured in 1442 and gained prosperity through piracy, privateering and cod fishing off Newfoundland. It became a fashionable resort in the 19th century when it was known as 'The Monte Carlo of the North'.

A bizarre incident took place towards the end of the Second World War. German commandos from Jersey, which was not liberated until 9 May 1945, took over the town for an hour and a half long after it had been recaptured by the Allies who were by then well into Germany. Several Americans, British and civilians lost their lives.

Ashore
Shopping: There is a 'Huit-à-Huit' supermarket a short walk from the marina. The nearest hypermarket is out of town and requires a taxi. Market day is Saturday.
Restaurants: There are several around Port Herel and many in the town.
Hotel: Le Herel Hotel and Restaurant (Ibis) overlooking the Marina ☎ 02 33 90 48 08.
Museums: Musée d'Art Moderne
Mont St Michel: For details of escorted treks out to the Mont see St Malo ashore (page 216).

WARNING
While Pointe du Roc and Iles Chausey provide some lee, Granville is exposed to prevailing Westerlies. Strong to gale conditions from this direction combine with shallow waters to make entry dangerous.

Approaches

From the north (Jersey)
The rhumbline from Demi des Pas light tower to a position 0·5M W of Pointe du Roc (⊕74) passes close E of several marks off the E end of Iles Chausey. These should be identified and passed on the correct side.

184 CHANNEL ISLANDS, CHERBOURG PENINSULA & NORTH BRITTANY

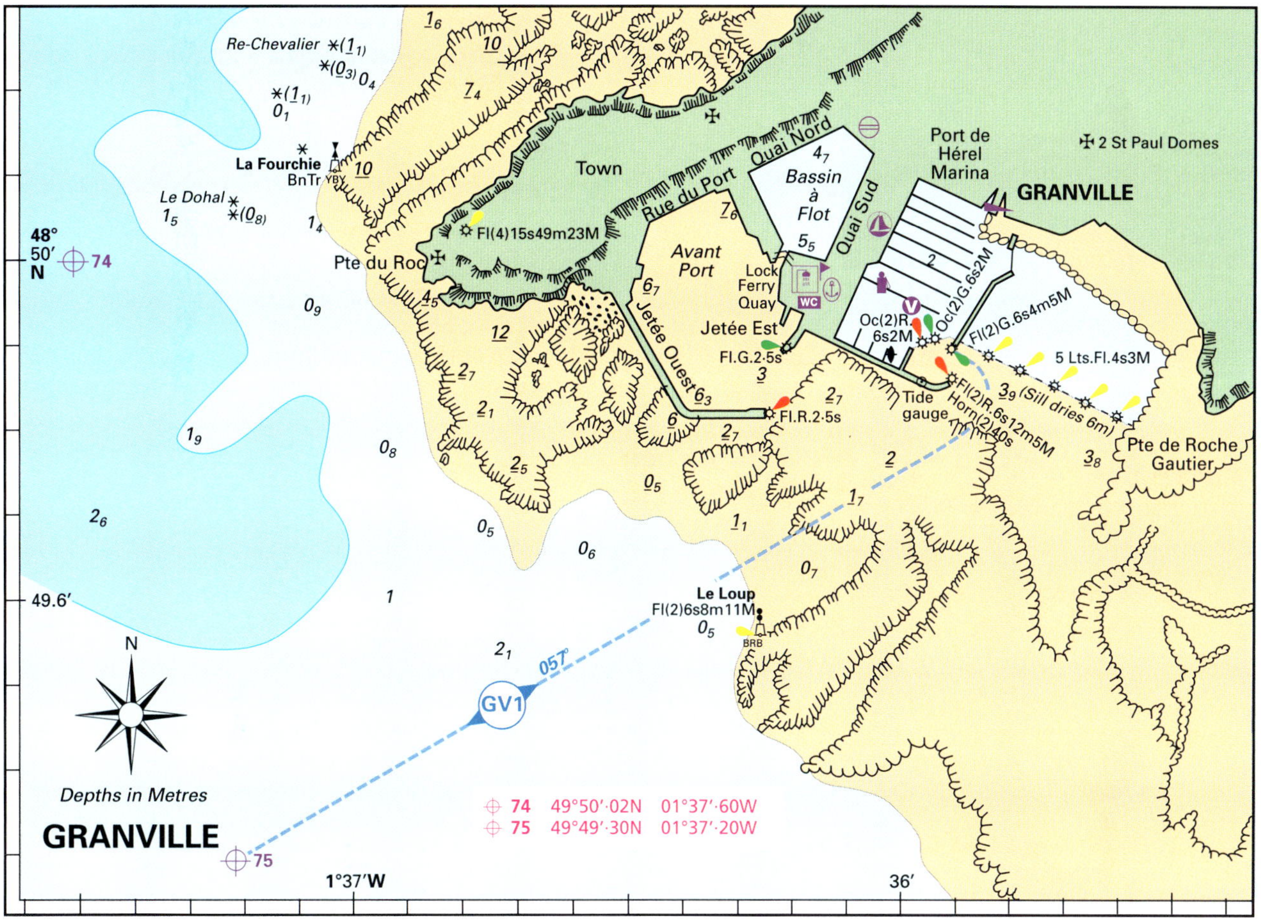

Diélette to Granville

Granville looking NE

CHANNEL ISLANDS, CHERBOURG PENINSULA & NORTH BRITTANY

II The Cherbourg Peninsula

Le Loup Tower

Depth gauge
Entry to Port Hérel

Granville. Enter marina over the sill

From the west (Grande Ile, St Malo)
A straightforward approach with one buoy to identify – Le Videcoq (Lit W cardinal) 4M W of the port.

Entry
WARNING
Keep a sharp lookout for fishpot markers surrounding Pointe du Roc.

From ⊕74 continue SSE to ⊕75 to pass 0·8M S of Pointe du Roc light house (Fl(2)6s).

Aim for a position midway between the Avant Port breakwater end (Fl.R.2·5s) and Le Loup BRB tower (Fl(2)6s), on a heading of 057° towards the marina entrance (Fl(2)R.6s). This is Line **GV1** on the plan.

Depth over the marina sill (dries 5·2m) is indicated on a lit gauge on top of the second breakwater and on the posts either side of the sill. It opens when there is a rise of 1·2m which is about 3hr either side of HW.

Enter between port and starboard posts (both lit).

Visitors' berths: Pontoon G (maximum LOA 15m draught 2·50m) See plan page 185.

Note
The Bassin SE of the marina is solely for the use of dinghy sailors who access it via a sill at the NE corner of the marina or over the submersible wall (dries 6m) marked by poles (lit). Not to be confused with marina sill (dries 5·2m).

By night
Pointe du Roc lighthouse (Fl(4)15s49m22M) is a conspicuous aiming point. An approach from the N passes close to the E end of Chausey off which there are several marks, some unlit (see *Approaches: From the north*.

There are no leading lights but several lit marks which can be obscured against the backdrop of land lights.

Give Pointe du Roc a clearance of at least 0·5M and maintain S until Avant Port breakwater head Fl.R.2·5s and Le Loup tower Fl(2)6s are identified. Enter midway between these lights on 057° towards marina pierhead Fl(2)R.6s. The digital tide gauge next to the light is illuminated. The narrow marina sill is marked Oc(2)R.6s and Oc(2)G.6s.

Anchorage
In suitable conditions this is possible NW of Le Loup tower with reference to the chart. It is advisable to trip the anchor in view of debris on the bottom.

Looking across the Port de Plaisance to the entrance

3. Iles Chausey

48°51'·44N 01°48'·57W
1·2M SE of Crabière de L'Est light beacon

TRAVEL
Granville–Chausey ferry (April to September)
Compagnie Corsaire ℡ 08 25 13 80 50 / 02 33 50 16 36
www.compagniecorsaire.com

Ports of Entry
French mainland port

CHARTS
BA 3656 Plateau des Minquiers and adjacent coast of France (1:50 000)
BA 3659 Cap Fréhel to Iles Chausey (1:50 000)
Imray 2500 The Channel Islands and the adjacent coasts of France Chart Atlas:
15 Îles Chausey (1:25 000)
SHOM 7134 Iles Chausey (1:15 000)*
*includes plan: Sound de Chausey (1:5000)
SHOM 7155 Du Cap Fréhel à la Pointe du Grouin – Approches de Saint-Malo (1:48 800)
SHOM 7156 De la Pointe du Grouin à la Pointe d'Agon – Baie du Mont-Saint-Michel - Iles Chausey (1:48 800)
SHOM 7161 Des îles Chausey à Jersey - Plateau des Minquiers (1:48 500)

RADIO
Jersey Coastguard
Granville Signal Station Chs 16, 80

NAVIGATIONAL AIDS
None

TIDAL INFORMATION
Chausey Sound 48°52'·14N 01°49'·09W

MHWS	MLWS	MHWN	MLWN
13·0	1·9	9·9	4·9

Standard port St Malo
Difference on St Helier –0014

At 11m or more, Chausey's tidal range is one of the largest in Europe. To avoid the mayhem that can occur at HW springs, when, with the exception of Grande Ile and a few pinnacles, the area is open sea, it is better to make an initial visit on a moderate tide. At LW the scene is transformed into a dramatic landscape, leaving a few pools in which to float.

Streams generally conform to the pattern outside, that is easterly on the flood and NW'ly swinging to SW'ly on the ebb. Within the archipelago there are variations.

S of Grand Ile lighthouse
The flood stream sets ENE'ly from HW–0410 to HW+0250 attaining a rate of 2 knots. It turns SW'ly HW+0250.

In The Sound
During the flood and the first hours of the ebb, the stream sets N up The Sound. At half ebb there is a reversal to the S following which there is a brief period of slack before it returns to the N.

Caution
At large spring tides, accelerated rates in The Sound may attain over 5 knots, making dinghy work hazardous. It can also be a wet business when wind and stream are opposed. At such times it is better to wait aboard or ashore for conditions to moderate before crossing The Sound.

CONTACTS
Police ℡ 02 33 52 72 02
CROSS ℡ 02 33 52 72 13

SUPPLIES AND SERVICES
La Boutique general store and bakery (℡ 02 33 50 24 01) for basic provisions including Camping Gaz.
Restaurants and bars Le Bellevue ℡ 02 33 50 80 30. Hotel du Fort ℡ 02 33 50 25 02.
Water There is a standpipe on the main slipway.
Fuel None

This intriguing archipelago of rocks, islets and sandbanks lies 6M NW of Granville on the Normandy coast and 20M SE of St Helier.

Unlike the chaotic sprawl of its neighbouring reef, the Plateau des Minquiers, it is compact with a well defined perimeter and measures a quarter of the size: 6M from E to W and 2·5M from N to S. Dominating the reef is Grande Ile with its conspicuous lighthouse, a fort, two hotels, a small church, a store and a scattering of cottages and gites. It supports Chausey's permanent population of about 10 who live mostly by fishing and catering for the stream of day-trippers from Granville. Among its distinguished residents are the Renault family who converted one of the island's forts into a private holiday château.

The famous maritime painter and ocean traveller M Marin-Marie had his studio here.

The archipelago is penetrated by several narrow well marked channels, most of which converge on Chausey Sound, the main anchorage and landing on the E side of Grande Ile.

Historical

The earliest residents were monks from nearby Mont St Michel but Chausey's history has been far from peaceful. The forts, begun in the 16th century, are evidence of years of rivalry between France and Britain for control of the Baie du Mont St Michel. Their fate was not secured until 1802 when they came under the administration of the Commune of Granville and the British dropped their claim to the archipelago as one of their Anglo-Norman possessions.

A 'threat' of a different kind came from the exploitation of Chausey's much sought-after blue-tinged granite. For nearly 900 years until the early 20th century, armies of quarriers worked on every part of the reef, shipping out vast quantities of stone for the building of quays and ramparts in ports as far afield as London and Bordeaux.

Ashore

A large part of Grande Ile is privately owned but public entry is tolerated. With the main objectives ashore likely to be The Restaurant at L'Hotel du Fort, noted for its seafood, and the general store, much of the island tends

Hotel du Fort   *General store*

The Granville ferry alongside Grande Ile slipway

Iles Chausey

Looking N over the Sound at LW
Nick Bailhache

to be undiscovered by visiting yachtsmen. From the top there are spectacular views over the Sound and some fascinating corners, such as a patch of typical Normandy countryside with minature fields and woodland (bocage) at its centre.

The lighthouse and Le Fort at La Pointe de la Bretagne make an interesting visit. The most convenient beach is at Port Marie.

Nature reserve

The area E of a line from Grande Ile lighthouse and L'Enseigne BW column is a bird sanctuary. No landing in this area is permitted from April to June. This does not apply to L'Ile Aneret (Grande Ancre) 1·1M ENE of Grande Ile lighthouse.

Entry formalities

Chausey is not an official port of entry and there are no permanent customs services. However, *les douanes* launch pays frequent visits and foreign yachts should fly their national and the French courtesy flag and be ready to show passports and registration documents.

Approaches to The Sound

SHOM *chart 7134* shows 12 channels serving the archipelago. Five of the most commonly used are described in this guide. They are aimed on The Sound, the channel of deeper water running up the E side of Ile Grande.

When making the first visit use the straightforward southern entry.

Some key marks:

L'Etat

L'Enseigne BW column

Grande Ile lighthouse

La Chapélle

L'Ancien Sémaphore

Les Epiettes buoy *Tom Vallois*

L'Enseigne

11 The Cherbourg Peninsula

From the southwest
Inbound from the direction of St Malo or from the north, westabout the archipelago, the final approach to Grande Ile will be on an ENE heading. Use Transit C1 (2·3m at Chart Datum):

C1 065° ⊕46 *The gap in Ile Longue in line with Le Tonneau E cardinal beacon will clear S of both La Cancalaise (dries 3·6m) with its beacon and the Roches de Bretagne (dries 5m) (see plan page 193)*

When 200m from this beacon, steer E to leave it 100m to port and join the main entrance from the SSE as described below.

From the southeast
The approach from the direction of Granville is straightforward but if navigating on the first hours of the ebb, guard against being set N towards the edge of the reef.

C2 *Grande Ile lighthouse should be held on a bearing of no less than 280° (see Main entry to The Sound page 193)*

Passage à l'est des Epiettes (reef) (dries 2·3m)
(Plan page 193)
This route passing within 30m of the S end of Ile Longue is used by locals coming in from Granville. It is not recommended below half tide.

The marks are as follows:

C3 292° *The right hand (E) side of the old semaphore in line with Rocher Tourette. This rock is painted white and on top is a stone cross*

From the north

La Grand Entrée (dries 3·5m)
(Plan page 188)
This approach, favoured by Jersey yachtsmen, routes from Demie de Pas lighthouse S of St Helier to La Grande Entrée via both the NE Minquiers and Les Ardentes E cardinal buoys. Departing at or just after LW St Helier ensures that you carry the best hours of the southeasterly stream and arrive well before the stream turns NE at HW St Helier - 0130.

The deadline for crossing the extensive banks down to the Sound is about two hours after local HW. If late, go westabout or, light permitting, take the alternative circuitous route to the Sound by the Chenal Beauchamp, starting from La Petite Entrée.

Conspicuous in the sprawling plateau of rocks is Grande Ile lighthouse. Approach with this on a bearing of 158°. By the time L'Etat W column to the E is bearing 090° you should have aligned the first set of marks:

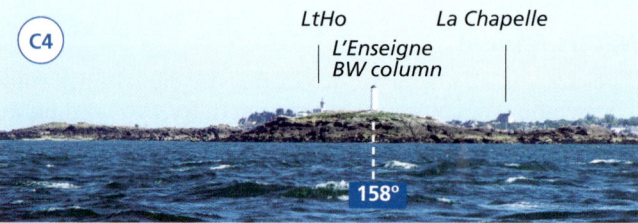

C4 158° ⊕41 *L'Enseigne BW column midway between Grande Ile lighthouse and La Chapelle*

On this line you will pass close E of La Pointue E cardinal beacon and 100m W of Les Longues W cardinal beacon. When the next mark, L'Etardière E cardinal beacon, is almost abeam, be ready to turn SSW onto the next transit which leads over the extensive sandbank:

C5 199° *Le Chapeau and La Massue columns (white) in line*

Iles Chausey

When 50m from Grunes de la Massue E cardinal beacon look SE to identify La Saunière W cardinal beacon and beyond it Le Cochon E cardinal beacon. This transit leads over the shallowest part of the channel, a sandbank drying at up to 4·8m. Then promptly onto:

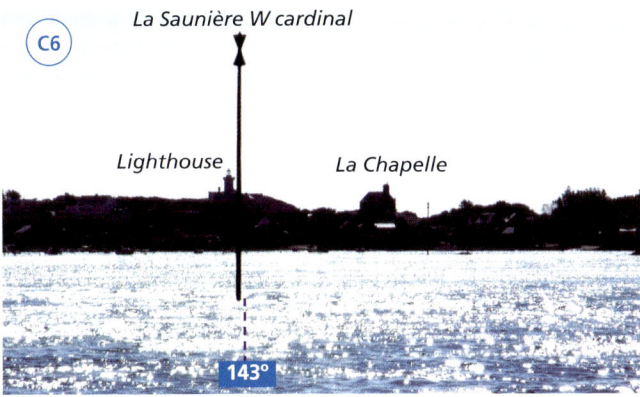

C6 143° La Saunière W cardinal beacon open right of the lighthouse

Hold until 120m short of La Saunière beacon, then course should be altered to starboard to leave it 15m to port. Then take up the final transit:

C7 141° Grande Ile lighthouse in line with Le Cochon E cardinal beacon

Pass between Le Cochon beacon and La Grande Fourche W cardinal beacon. This is the gateway into the Sound anchorage.

La Petite Entrée and Chenal Beauchamp (2·3m)
(Plan page 188)

The deep-water Chenal Beauchamp through the eastern half of the archipelago may be entered from the N at La Petite Entrée W cardinal beacon. This is 0·85M E of La Pointue E cardinal beacon of La Grande Entrée. It terminates at La Tournioure isolated danger beacon SW of Les Huguenans. The Chenal Beauchamp is a succession of cardinal beacons which in the N half are well apart and easily misidentified. Good visibility with the aid of binoculars is essential.

At one point the channel passes through a gap barely 100m wide.

Streams

Throughout the length of Chenal Beauchamp allowance should be made for streams of up to 2 knots. These set NW for nine hours starting HW St Malo -0500 then SE for three hours, but be prepared for variations.

The entry transit is as follows:

C8 ⊕42 174° Gde Ile lighthouse in line with the W face of Grand Ramont (14m), identified by its strip of sand

This will leave La Petite Entrée W cardinal beacon 50m to port.

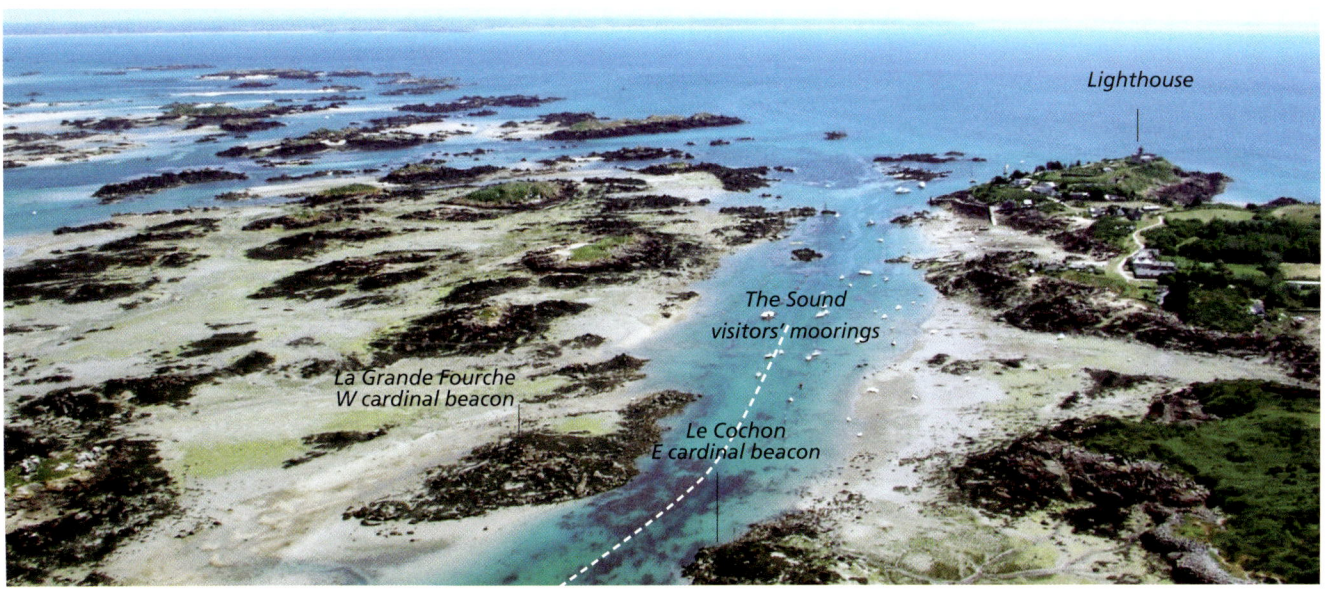

The Sound looking E

II The Cherbourg Peninsula

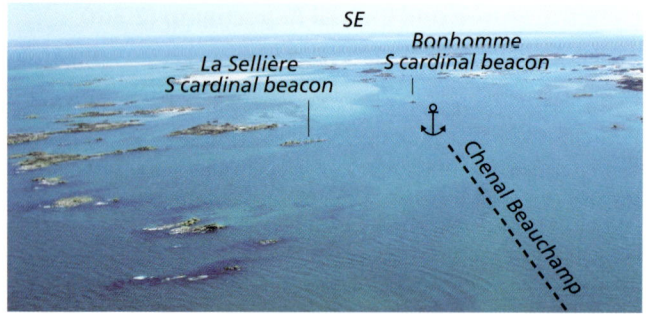

The northern part of the channel is a vast area with few reference points

When 200m SSW of La Petite Entrée beacon identify La Sellière S cardinal beacon to the E and further ahead Le Bonhomme S cardinal beacon. Take up a heading of 115°. The transit is:

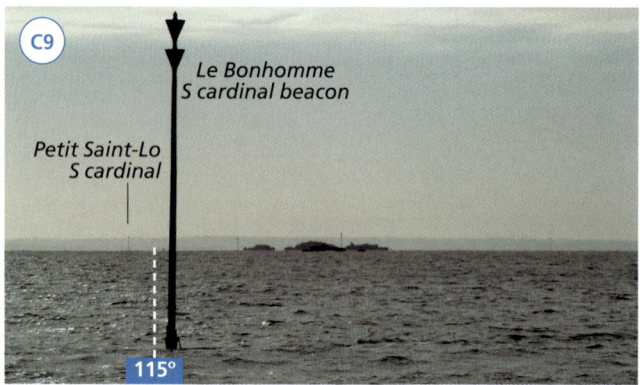

C9 *115° Petit Saint-Lo S cardinal beacon and Le Bonhomme S cardinal beacon in line*

800m along this line, look ENE for a breast mark:

C10 *breast mark 072° La Sellière Rock in line with La Sellière S cardinal beacon*

Now make a slight change of course to starboard onto 121°.

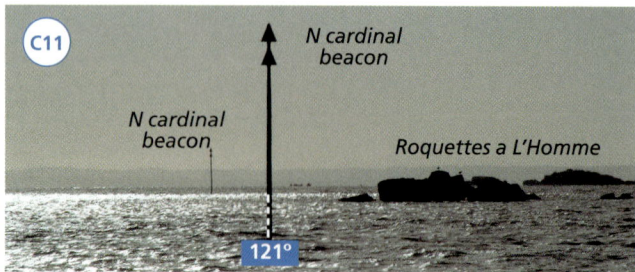

C11 *121° The two N cardinal beacons off Roquettes a L'Homme (dries 10·7m) are aligned (here shown open for clarity)*

This will lead into the narrow gap between Grand St Lo N cardinal beacon and the SE of the two cardinal beacons guarding Roquettes à L'Homme. Once through the gap, alter course SE with stern transit as follows:

C12 *319° La Sellière (9m) in line with the right (E) side of La Petite Mauvaise (9m)*

This line leads into the Beauchamp anchorage described on page 195.

Departing southwards from Beauchamp anchorage

Before clearing out to the S, identify the following three marks:
1. La Culassière (10m), an isolated rock that looks like an inverted yacht hull with its rudder at the W end.
2. L'Etat, the prominent white column on the NE edge of the archipelago (see page 188).
3. Caniard du Sud, if uncovered, is a large clump of rock to the N that dries 12m.

Take up following stern transit:

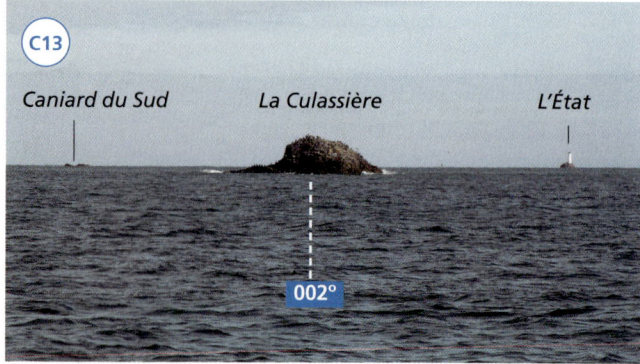

C13 *002° La Culassière midway between Caniard du Sud and L'Etat*

192 CHANNEL ISLANDS, CHERBOURG PENINSULA & NORTH BRITTANY

Iles Chausey

This transit is held all the way S to the exit at La Tournioure isolated danger beacon. This may be passed close (10m) either side but there is more room to the west.

From La Tournioure, the southern entry to The Sound lies 1·7M to the W.

Chenal Beauchamp from the south

This entry, known as La Passe Sud de Beauchamp or Chenal des Roquettes à L'Homme, follows the route described above in reverse. Approach with transit:

Main entry to The Sound (0·3m)

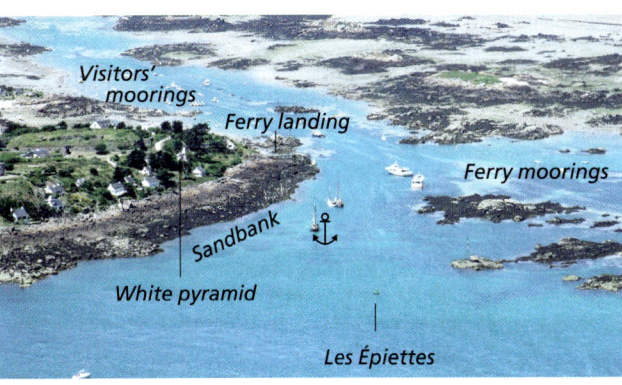

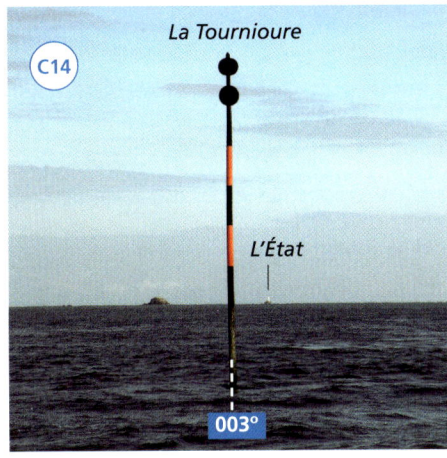

C14 003° L'Etat white column in line with La Tournioure isolated danger beacon

The key is early identification of Les Épiettes starboard buoy which is 300m E of the SE tip of Grande Ile, Pointe de la Tour.

From a position 0·25M SE of the buoy: enter on the marks as follows.

Once past La Tournioure make a minor adjustment to port to pick up:

C13 002° as shown on page 192. (See plan page 188.)

C15 332° ⊕45 L'Enseigne BW column in line with Crabière light beacon. L'Enseigne is only visible with sufficient height of eye

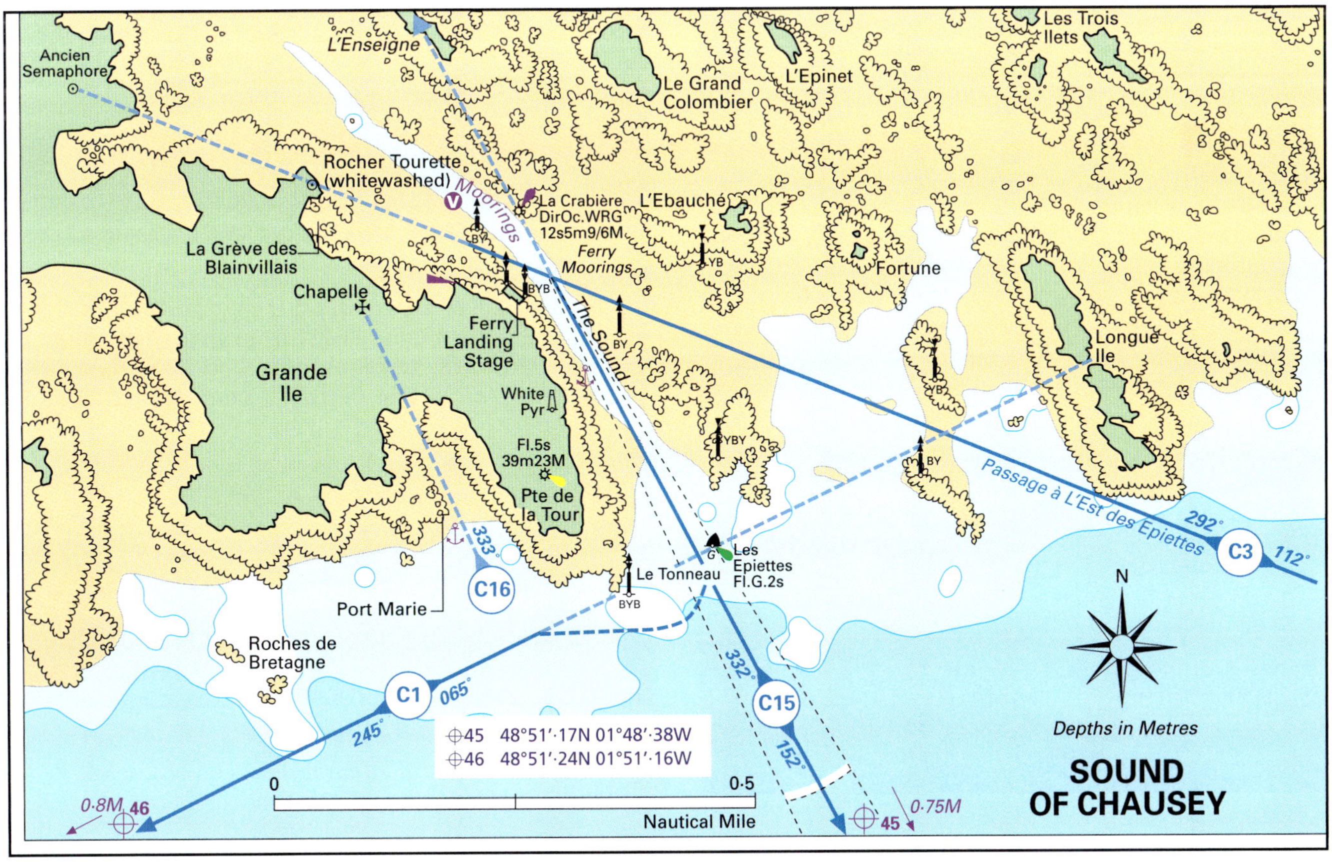

II. THE CHERBOURG PENINSULA

CHANNEL ISLANDS, CHERBOURG PENINSULA & NORTH BRITTANY   193

II The Cherbourg Peninsula

This line leaves Les Epiettes buoy close to starboard and crosses a sandbank NE of the lighthouse over which there is 0·3m at CD. It may be necessary to borrow 25–30m to the E to clear this.

Just short of Crabière light beacon, which should be left 50m to starboard, the entry channel ends and the anchorage begins.

Entry to Chausey by night

The only possible night entry is by the main entry to The Sound from the SE as described on page 193.

At night, approach with Grande Ile light (Fl.5s.39m23M) on a northwesterly bearing. Identify Les Epiettes (Fl.G) and La Crabière Est (Oc.WRG.4s5m9–6M).

Enter in the W sector (329°–333°) of La Crabière Est light. This will leave both Les Epiettes and La Crabière Est 50m to starboard. The anchorage is a sombre place after dark with unlit obstructions, so a good searchlight is a necessity.

Anchoring and mooring

THE SOUND

The Sound from the S at low water

Anchorage

In winds between S and W, this anchorage in the lee of Grande Ile is sheltered but can be swelly over HW in strong to gale force winds from this direction. It is exposed, particularly at HW, in winds between NW and SE.

A short-term anchorage with good holding in sand may be found abeam the white pyramid N of the lighthouse and clear of the leading line (see plan and air view on page 193).

La Grève des Blainvillais

Anchoring further into the Sound is inadvisable due to rocky areas, numerous private moorings and fishing gear. There may also be insufficient room to swing when the stream turns. The safest option is to use the visitors' fore and aft moorings laid by Granville Yacht Club. These are located at the N end of The Sound. At LW springs most will dry out, so attention must be paid to depths. Further S opposite the slipway is a large white conical steel buoy marked Phares et Balises. With a minimum depth here of about 2·6m, this tends to be used by larger deep draughted yachts. In certain conditions it may cause damage to topsides.

The heavy moorings SE of La Crabière light beacon and opposite the ferry landing stage are used by the Granville Ferries. They may be used after the last ferry has left for Granville providing the mooring is vacated before the first ferry arrives the following morning.

Mooring alongside the slipway is prohibited.

Drying out

La Grève des Blainvillais, 300m NW of the slipway, has a beach of flat, firm sand, although there are isolated boulders. Above it are the miniature houses once occupied by stone quarriers.

Port Marie

48°52'·12N 01°49'·46W
(See plan page 193)

This narrow bay on the S coast of Grande Ile below the lighthouse is used by small craft as a fair-weather day anchorage. It offers some shelter from winds between NW and NE. Part of the bay is cordoned off for bathers. It is fringed with rock but the bottom is sand. Approach with:

C16 La Chapelle on a bearing of 333°.

It is possible to remain afloat if the S end of Longue Ile is visible behind Pointe de la Tour, the SE point of Grande Ile.

Iles Chausey

Anchorages in The Channels
(See plan page 188)

There are numerous idyllic anchorages around the archipelago offering total seclusion over the LW period or useful pit stops while waiting for the tide.

In Chenal Beauchamp

From S–N the recommended anchorages are:

W of Les Huguenans
48°52'·29N 01°46'·41W

Anchor in this position or further E around islets of Les Huguenans (see below) with reference to the chart.

Les Huguenans from the NE, a popluar haunt for bilge keelers

The Beauchamp Anchorage
48°53'·30N 01°46'·53W
SE of La Mauvaise (10m)

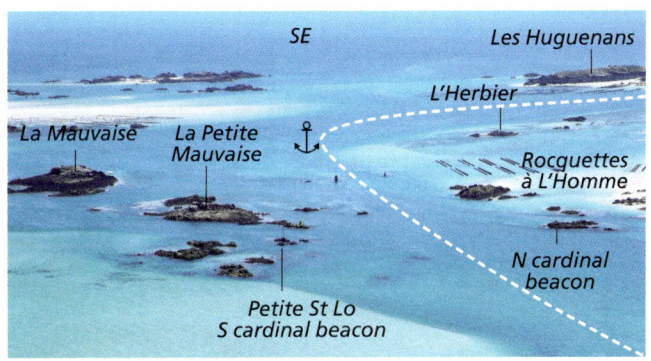

WNW of Le Bonhomme S cardinal beacon
48°53'·98N 01°48'·52W

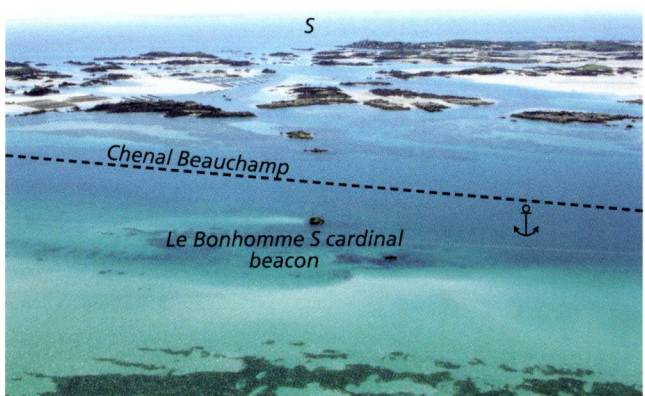

Anchor with reference to SHOM *chart 7134* (see also air view on page 192).

In La Grande Entrée

NNW of L'Enseigne BW column
48°53'·95N 01°50'·54W

This is a useful anchorage just N of the sandbank if waiting for sufficient water to cross the banks further S in the channel.

The antique bisquine *La Cancalaise* is a frequent sight in Chausey waters. She now carries charter parties

III North Brittany

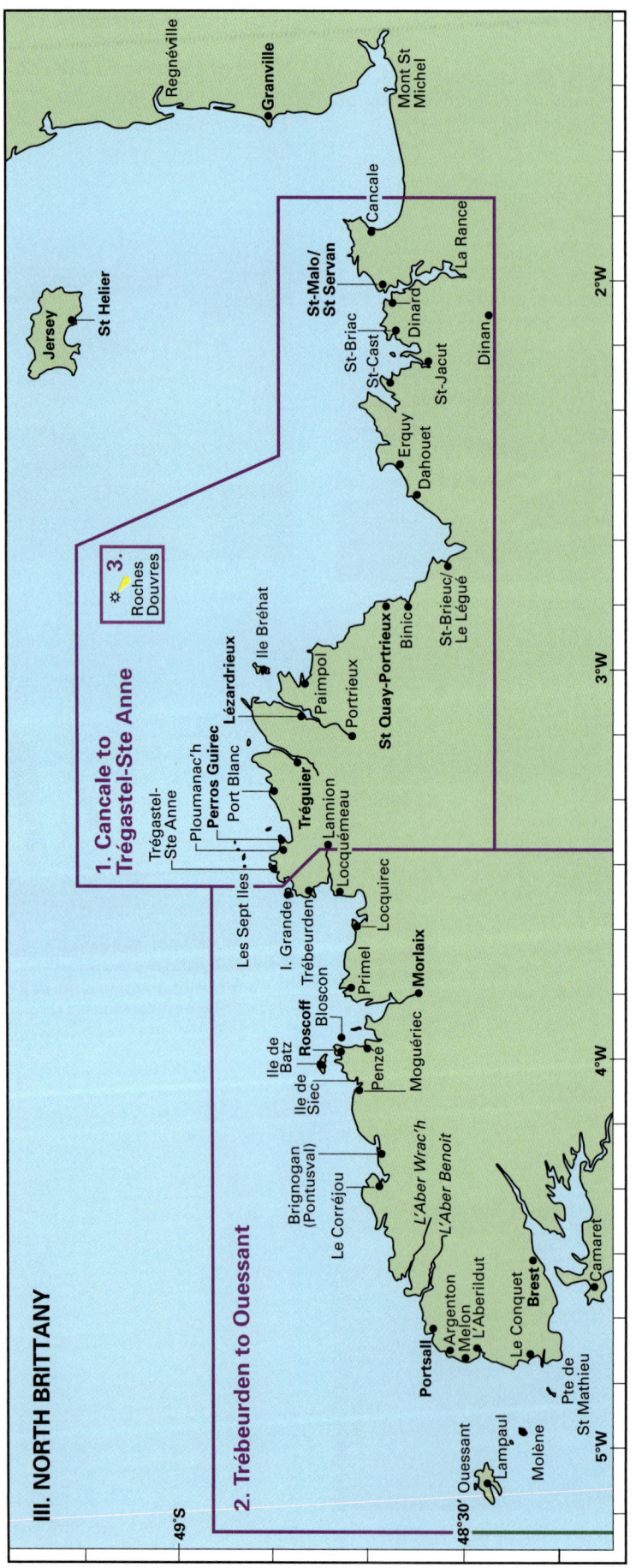

196 CHANNEL ISLANDS, CHERBOURG PENINSULA & NORTH BRITTANY

III North Brittany

Introduction

Brittany is the great maritime region of France often referred to by its ancient name of Armor or Armorica meaning 'Land of the Sea'. Its rugged coastline, its people and their culture have been shaped by it.

As a cruising ground and holiday destination the north coast of Brittany in particular has always held a special appeal for yachtsmen who are drawn by the variety of its scenery and the abundance of harbours, anchorages, deep river estuaries and fine beaches.

With marine tourism as a mainstay of the Breton economy visitors will find excellent facilities and an increasing number of marinas along the 160M length of coast between the Baie du Mont St Michel in the east and Pointe de St Mathieu in the far west. While such developments are convenient they tend to be well patronised during peak season when many may be happier to seek out Brittany's excellent traditional harbours and anchorages. With shallow draught and the ability to take the ground, options are almost unlimited.

Navigation and pilotage

The coast is well endowed with some of France's tallest lighthouses, numerous towers and beacons. It is unusual to be out of sight of land or at least a mark. Navigationally it should be straightforward to a skipper with experience of passage making in strongly tidal waters. However, poor visibility, particularly in the west, is an added challenge for which yacht and crew should be prepared.

Knowing where you are and what the tides are doing at any time is vitally important if unpleasant surprises are to be avoided. An outfit of up to date large scale charts covering planned, and unplanned, entries should be carried as a backup to electronic navigational aids.

Navigation and pilotage here is as complicated as you wish to make it. The advice to those unfamiliar with this coast is to gain experience with main channels and straightforward entrances before moving on to complex situations where there may be little or no room for error.

Tides

Range

The greatest tidal range is in the Baie de St Malo where it can exceed 11m. Further west it is 8m at Ploumanac'h and 6m at Ile d'Ouessant. There are fewer complications cruising North Brittany over neap tides when streams are weaker and anchorages that dry out at springs can be visited. (See *Understanding the Tides*, page 9.)

Rates

Tidal stream rates being influenced by geographical factors become accelerated off headlands, around corners and wherever the stream is constricted through gaps. This effect will be most apparent around half tide when streams are usually at their strongest. Examples of such areas are:

- Round Cap Fréhel
- NE of Ile de Bréhat
- Chenal des Sept Iles
- Chenal de L'Ile de Batz
- Chenal du Four
- Passage du Fromveur (Ile d'Ouessant)

Rates are less inside bays such as:

- Baie de St Brieuc
- Baie de Morlaix

The sheltered rivers of North Brittany are havens for classic boats

Ile Vierge lighthouse at the western extremity of North Brittany

III North Brittany

Direction
The set of the tidal stream tends to follow the coast with variations. It is E going on the flood and W going on the ebb each of about 6hr duration. This means that averaging 7 knots a passage of up to 40M should be possible within 6 hours of ebb or flood.

A W going passage will usually involve departing at HW and arriving at LW so thought should be given to mooring situations at the destination.

For an E going passage the reverse applies. It may involve relocating to deep water on the previous tide in order to be able to get underway at LW.

Cross set
Most approaches along the coast are made across the set of the tide entailing some adjustment of heading. This is where a transit comes in useful. Once marks have been confirmed it is only necessary to hold them in alignment – which can demand concentration.

(See *Understanding the Tides, Standard ports*, page 9 and *Appendix -Tidal Streams* page 364.)

Spires (belfries) proliferate in Brittany. This one at Lézardrieux overlooks Place du Centre

Historical

Armor 'land of the sea'
Brittany's history is one of invasions, feuds and struggle out of which emerged the strongly independent Breton race with close links to Britain. Little is known of the earliest settlers who left the stone structures (megaliths) throughout the region. They date from the Neolithic period, about 5000BC. The standing stones known as Menhirs (long stone in Breton) will be found all over Brittany. Their purpose is believed to focus on pagan rituals but they may also have been of astronomical and navigational significance. The tallest in France, at 10m, is Menhir de Kerloas between Lanildut and Le Conquet. The 'Megalith of Men Marz' near Brignogan shown here was later Christianised by the addition of a stone cross.

The first arrivals in the North West in the 4th Century AD were Celtic tribes from Britain, mainly Cornwall, Wales and Ireland that were threatened by marauding Anglo-Saxons. They brought with them their own culture, religion and a language not dissimilar to modern day Welsh. Breton was still spoken up to 60 years ago in the western half of Brittany (Basse Bretagne) but was later discouraged in favour of French. It might have become extinct had it not been for a modern revival. (See *Appendix – The Breton Language Glossary* page 376)

The Romans who occupied Gaul, modern France, from about 56 BC had named the peninsula Armor (land of the sea). It later became Little Britain shortened to Brittany. They overpowered the Celts and maintained law and order among the tribes until the end of their rule in 400. The barbarian raiders who had driven the Celts from Britain then returned with a vengeance to both sides of the Channel. Tribal feuding and power struggles broke out that were to lead to centuries of anarchy. A new wave of immigrants in 460 included the first Christian missionaries - St Pol from Wales landed first on Ile d'Ouessant and then crossed to L'Aber Wrac'h in North West Brittany. He established a monastery on Ile de Batz and set about routing out paganism. Many towns in Brittany took their names from these early missionaries - St Maclou (Malo), St Servan, St Brieuc, St Pol de Léon, St Lunaire.

In 752 Viking raids and an invasion of Gaul (France) by the Franks (later French) stirred up civil war but by the mid 9th Century the British colonies became unified under a succession of leaders as an independent Duchy of Brittany. This lasted until 1488 when it was defeated and abolished by France. Brittany was finally incorporated into France in 1532.

The megalith of Men Marz near Brignogan

Côte de Granit Rose

198 CHANNEL ISLANDS, CHERBOURG PENINSULA & NORTH BRITTANY

III. Introduction

The 16th and 17th centuries brought an era of economic expansion and prosperity for Brittany. In 1534 the explorer Jacques Cartier from St Malo discovered the St Lawrence estuary and named the new found land 'Canada' for France.

The French Revolution in 1789 was welcomed by the oppressed Bretons although many joined counter-revolutionary movements and uprising continued until 1832. At this time Brittany was divided into five departments which remain today: Côtes-du-Nord, Ile-et-Vilaine (now Côtes d'Armor), Finisterre, Morbihan and Loire Inferieure (now Loire Atlantique).

In the mid-19th Century more than 500,000 Bretons emigrated mostly to Canada where there were already large Breton settlements.

During the first and second World Wars Bretons were recruited in vast numbers and were said to be the backbone of the French Navy.

Château du Taureau, one of the Vauban forts in the approaches to Morlaix

In recent years Breton culture has enjoyed a flowering with renewed interest in its language, traditional music, song and dance. The festivals and *pardons* that are unique to western parts of Brittany provide a rare opportunity to see Breton costume and enjoy local folk music. *Pardons* are religious gatherings held around a particular site on the same date each year.

The Breton Flag *Gwen ha du* (white and black)

The five black stripes represent the five original bishoprics of French speaking Upper Brittany - Rennes, Nantes, Dol, St Malo and St Brieuc. The white bands represent those of lower Brittany - Léon, Cornouaille, Vannes and Tréguier. The ermine is the symbol of the Duchy of Brittany. In the 13th century ermine fur was worn by the Dukes of Brittany as a symbol of authority.

It is customary when in Brittany to fly the Breton courtesy flag below the national flag (*Le Tricoleur*).

Vauban – the military genius who fortified Brittany

A feature of the coast between St Malo and Brest are the numerous forts, towers and defences, many of which serve as navigational marks.

These are, with few exceptions the brainchild of Sebastien le Prestre de Vauban (1633-1707), simply known as Vauban.

This legendary military architect rose to fame during the reign of Louis XIV when France was under constant threat by the Anglo-Dutch coalition. Brittany was particularly vulnerable to attacks and Vauban was tasked with defending strategic sites such as St Malo, Morlaix and Brest. Vauban started his career as a soldier gaining many of his ideas while taking part in sieges. He had enormous capacity for work and is thought to have travelled 180,000 kms in the service of his country. He was given the rank of Marshall but fell from favour through his support of Protestant Huguenots. "A town built by Vauban is safe, a town attacked by Vauban is lost."

Vauban forts to visit:

St Malo (ramparts)
Les Sept Iles (Ile aux Moines fort)
Morlaix (Château du Taureau)
Ile de Ouessant (Phare du Stiff)

La Rance

III North Brittany: 1 Cancale to Trégastel-Ste Anne

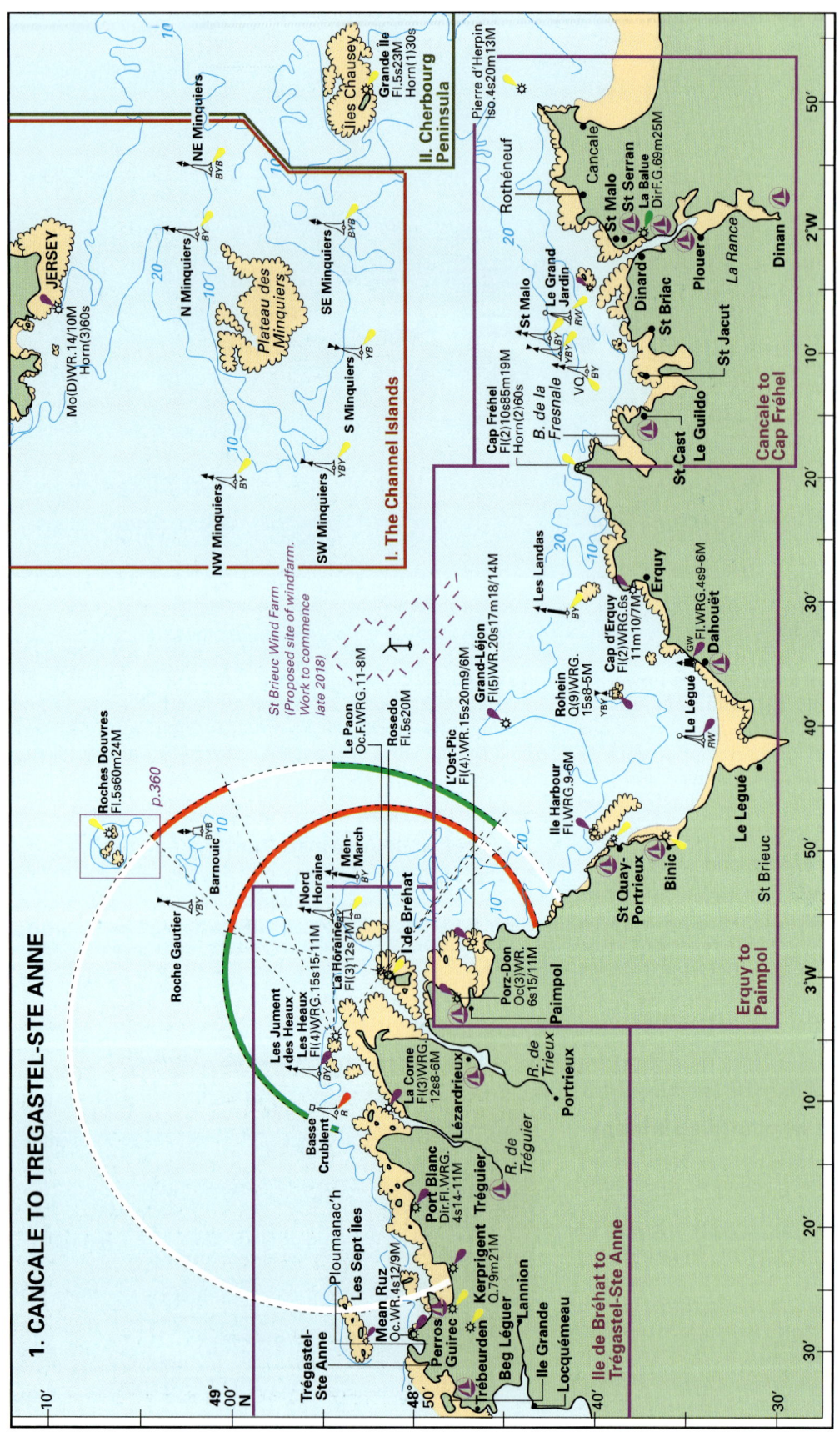

1. Cancale to Trégastel-Ste Anne (80M)

THE COASTLINE

This run of coastline rises from the flat and featureless landscape of the Baie du Mont St Michel where Cancale is the easternmost port of Brittany. It soon becomes rugged, rocky and difficult to access before opening out into the estuary of La Rance. This is the first of Brittany's great rivers and is a cruising area in itself linking both sides of the peninsula via a network of canals.

St Malo and St Servan on the E bank are major yachting centres and ferry terminals. Opposite is the once fashionable resort of Dinard with beaches and wide sandy bays that are havens for small craft able to dry out.

The rocks return with the granite headland of Cap Fréhel before which is the resort and marina of St Cast with 24 hour access.

W of Le Cap is the 24M wide Baie de St Brieuc with reefs in the N and shallows in the S.

On the E side of the bay is the fishing port of Erquy and 5M S, up a small inlet Dahouët is an obscure little port with a modern marina. This coast is shallow and open to Westerlies so is best approached in offshore winds and over neap tides when it may be possible to stay afloat at LW. The W side of the bay has two popular marinas, Binic and St Quay-Portrieux, the latter with 24 hour access. The traditional Breton port of Paimpol lies behind a lock at the W extremity of Anse de Paimpol which almost totally dries to mud at LWS.

The next 25M is dedicated to rocks, islets and river estuaries. This is known as 'Le Côte de Granit Rose' (the Pink Granite Coast) on account of the colour of its strangely weathered rocks. It is the highlight of the North coast of Brittany. At its centre is Ile de Bréhat with some idyllic anchorages and channels that run around the estuaries of the Trieux and Tréguier Rivers. Both have rural marinas upstream.

Continuing W the coastline draws away to the SW with only the small drying bay of Port Blanc as a possible fair weather anchorage. It re-emerges at Perros Guirec – a brash holiday resort with a voluminous marina. N of Perros is the protected site of Les Sept Iles with limited access. To the South is Ploumanac'h, showpiece of La Côte de Granit Rose with a small deep water basin, and the beach resort of Trégastel-Ste-Anne.

St Brieuc wind farm
Work commences on this project during the last quarter of 2018. The site is 17M E of Ile de Bréhat and 10M N of Cap d'Erquay. Sixty-two turbines will be spread over an area of 28 square miles (see plan opposite).

LIST OF PORTS

Cancale and Port de la Houle *200*
Le Havre de Rothéneuf *205*
St Malo *214*
St Servan (Port des Bas-Sablons) *217*
Dinard *219*
La Rance *221*
St Briac-sur-Mer *227*
St Cast *229*
Erquy *233*
Dahouët *235*
St Brieuc – Le Légué *237*
Binic *241*
St Quay-Portrieux *243*
    Port d'Armor Marina *243*
    Vieux Port *246*
Paimpol *247*
Ile de Bréhat *253*
La Rivière du Trieux. Lézardrieux *259*
Pontrieux *263*
Rivière de Tréguier *266*
Port Blanc *271*
Perros Guirec *273*
Les Sept Iles *277*
Ploumanac'h *279*
Trégastel - Ste Anne *281*

III North Brittany: 1 Cancale to Trégastel-Ste Anne

Cancale to Cap Fréhel (23M)
La Côte d'Emeraude

CANCALE AND PORT DE LA HOULE

48°4'·84N 01°51'·10W (Cancale pierhead)
14M SW of Granville 7M ENE of St Malo

CHARTS
BA 3659 Cap Fréhel to Iles Chausey (1:50 000)
SHOM 7131 Du Hâvre de Rothéneuf à Cancale (1:20 000)*
 *includes plan: Port de Cancale (1:7500)
SHOM 7155 Du Cap Fréhel à la Pointe du Grouin–
 Approches de Saint-Malo (1:48 800)
SHOM 7156 De la Pointe du Grouin à la Pointe d'Agon –
 Baie du Mont-Saint-Michel – Iles Chausey (1:48 800)

TIDAL INFORMATION
As for St Malo (Standard port)
Difference St Helier -20

MHWS	MLWS	MHWN	MLWN
12·2	1·5	9·3	4·2

Caution
Exceptional Tidal range

Tidal Streams

Off Herpin Lt Ho:
NW going starts HW St Malo +30
SE going starts HW St Malo -4hr30
Max spring rate: 3·5kns

Off Cancale:
NE going starts HW St Malo –30
SW going starts HW St Malo –4hr
Max spring rate: 1·0kn

USEFUL CONTACTS
Cercle Nautique de Cancale ☎ (0)2 99 89 90 22
Chef du Port. Plage de Port Mer ☎ (0) 2 9989 74 33 /
 06 7562 86 63
Sémaphore de la Pointe du Grouin ☎ 02 99 89 72 29
 Email portdeplaisance@ville-cancale.fr
Comptoir Marine (Chandlers) ☎ (0) 2 99 89 62 25
Tourist Information Rue du Port www.cancale-tourisme.fr

SUPPLIES AND SERVICES
General Water, fuel (in cans), fish markets all on the quay
Supermarket 'Super U' in the own centre
Hardware Mr Bricolage
Transport A free bus service operates between port and town during the season

Cancale is the first and easternmost harbour in Brittany. It is located at the end of the three mile stretch of coast south of Pointe du Grouin which, unusually for Brittany, is totally sheltered from westerlies.

The town of Cancale occupies an elevated position above the coast to the north of its maritime quarter, La Port de la Houle. This is the centre of Cancale's famous oyster culture industry and extensive areas off the harbour are given over to oyster beds (*Parcs à huitres*).

As elsewhere in the Baie de Mont St Michel the sea retreats out of sight at low water springs. Apart from a beach of firm sand and shells where suitable craft can dry out, the harbour is seriously muddy.

Dried out below the fish market *Chris Fairbairn*

Cancale from the SE

Ashore

A lack of facilities for marine tourists is compensated by a wide range of restaurants that line the harbour quay. Eating is big business here and during the season it takes on a Riviera atmosphere as visitors flock into the port to enjoy its seafood specialities.

Most boating activity is centred around the bays north of the harbour – Port Mer, Port Pican and Port Briac (see *Mooring and Anchoring* page 205).

Cancale to Cap Fréhel

La Chapelle de Notre Dame du Verger

Plaques, paintings and photographs cover the walls

Historical

For centuries Cancale has been linked with the sea. In the 18th century its mariners were famous worldwide as *Corsaires*. During the Napoleonic wars it was not unusual for a ship of the French navy to be crewed entirely by men from this port.

In the 18th century and up until the early 20th century three masted brigantines known as Terra-Neuvas, were fitted out in Cancale, St Servan and St Malo for fishing on the Banks off Newfoundland. Their crews were seldom home for more than four months in the winter leaving many communities bereft of their menfolk for most of the year. Cancale was famed for its fishwives, the Cancalaise, who harvested the oysters in their husbands' absence.

Two miles along the coast west of Pointe du Grouin is Anse du Verger and above it the miniscule *chapelle* de Notre-Dame du Verger. There has been a shrine here dedicated to Our Lady, Star of the Sea, since the 10th century. This was venerated by sailors of Cancale who would come here before embarking on a voyage to invoke Our Lady to give a safe return home. Those that did would revisit the chapelle to record their thanks on plaques. These decorate the walls together with several primitive paintings and fine ships' models left by grateful crews.

Approaches

Key marks in the approach are (N to S) – Le Herpin lighthouse (Iso.4s), Roche Herpin, Pointe du Grouin with its semaphore station and close to the E of it Ile des Landes. Cancale church (92m) is conspicuous on the skyline.

From N and W

There are several approaches into Grande Rade de Cancale.

Clear of all dangers northeast of Pointe du Grouin
From a position well east of La Fille N cardinal buoy (unlit) (⊕83) which is northeast of Herpin lighthouse it is a straightforward route south into the Grande Rade de Cancale.

Le Grand Ruet

This ¾ mile wide gap between Herpin lighthouse and Roche de Herpin presents no obstacles though it is better to keep to the SW side to avoid shoals in the middle. (See *Caution* below.)

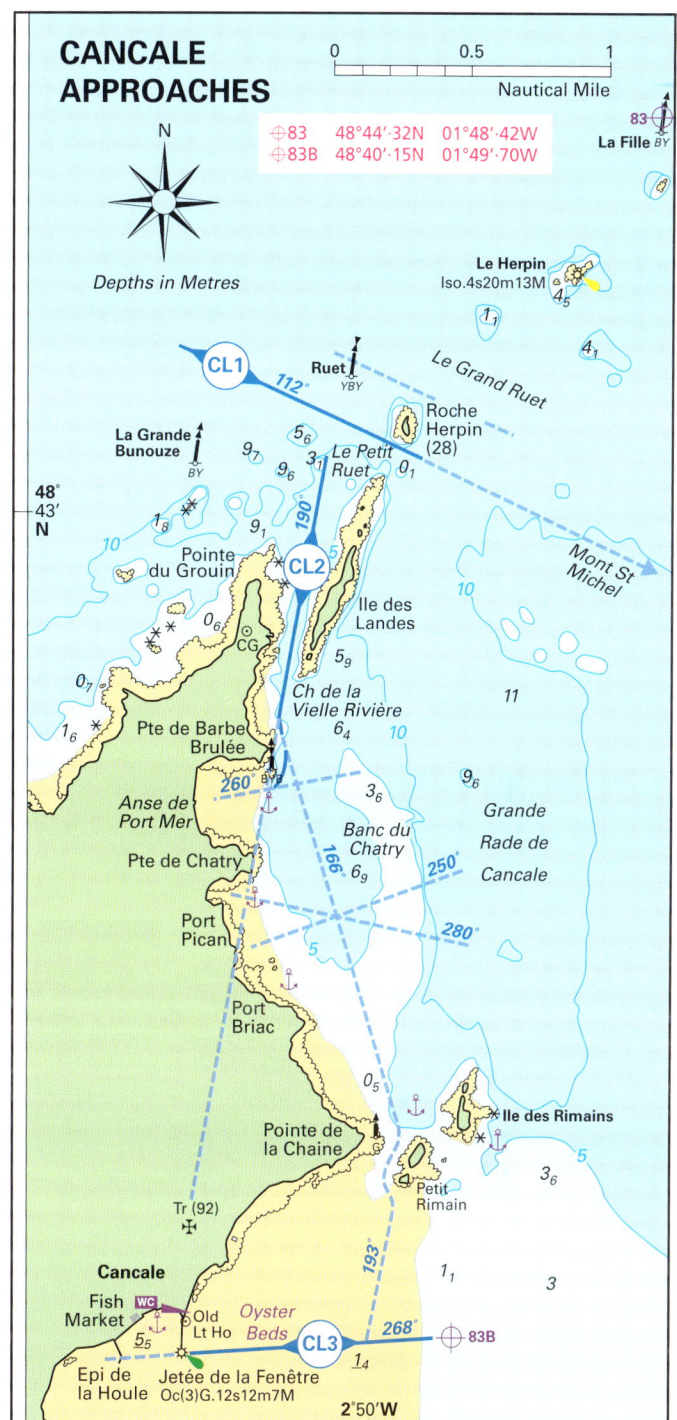

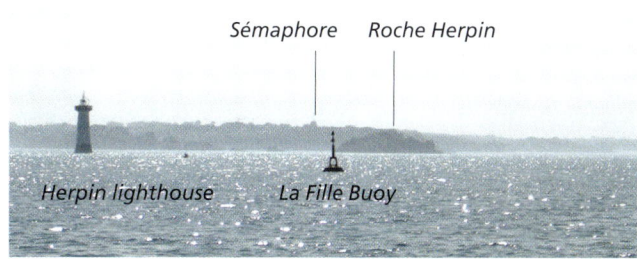

Approaching Pointe de Grouin from the NE

III. NORTH BRITTANY: 1 CANCALE TO TRÉGASTEL-STE ANNE

III North Brittany: 1 Cancale to Trégastel-Ste Anne

Le Petit Ruet (7m)
This shortcut just over 100m wide passes midway between Roche Herpin and N end of Ile des Landes.

First identify Ruet W cardinal buoy and Grande Bunouze N cardinal buoy (both unlit) to the NW and WSW of Roche Herpin.

Steer ESE to pass midway between these buoys with transit:

CL1 *112° Mont St Michel if visible well open right of Roche Herpin (no view)*

This clears Basse des Pignonets (0·1m).

Caution
Accelerated streams occur in these channels particularly at springs when wind against tide conditions may cause overfalls.

Chenal de La Vieille Rivière (6m)
A more interesting option is this narrow (150m) but deep channel between Pointe du Grouin and Ile des Landes.

Approach from the N with transit:

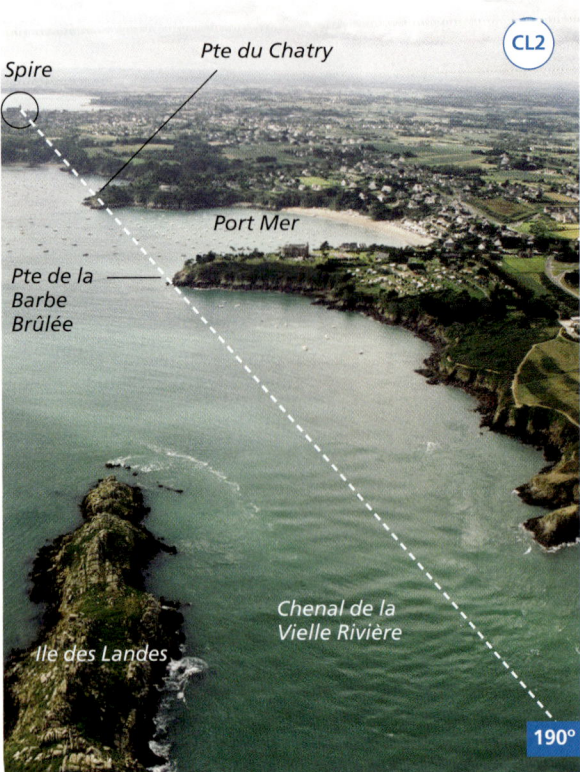

Chenal de la Vieille Rivière CL2 190°

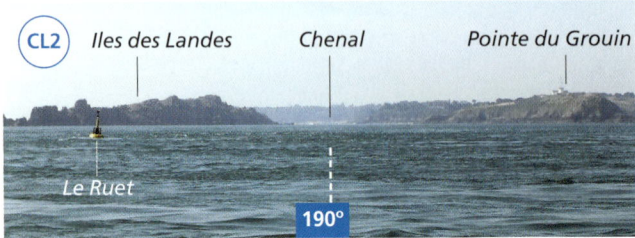

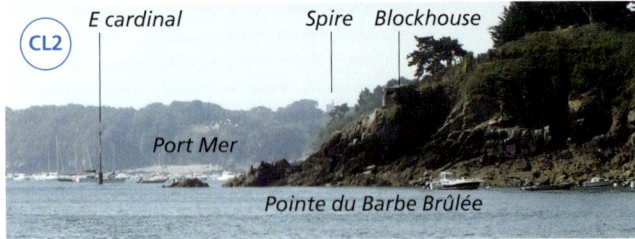

CL2 *190° Cancale church tower open left (E) of Pointe de Barbe Brulée with its E card beacon*

As the channel narrows aim for the middle and when abeam the S end of Ile des Landes come to port to pass Pointe de Barbe Brulée E cardinal beacon 100m to starboard.

The stream described as 'courant violent' on the French chart, runs fast but true through this channel. It sets N reaching 3kns at about HW St Malo but eases to about ½ knot from HW +3 up to HW -1. Patches of overfalls can be expected on large tides.

Cancale may now be reached by passing through the narrow channel (least depth 1·0m) midway between the starboard beacon off Pointe de la Chaine and Petit Rimain, the small island to the SW of Iles des Rimains. Otherwise pass to the E of Ile des Rimains with its fort before turning SW to close Cancale breakwater. (See Entry below.)

From E and NE
There are no dangers in the approaches from this quarter provided Pierre d'Herpin and La Fille its NE outlier and Ile des Rimains and its SW outlier are all left to the W.

Port Mer

Approach Cancale breakwater from (⊕83B) on a track of at least 268° to clear the oyster beds. Transit:

CL3 *268° pierheads in line (no view)*

By night:
Le Herpin Oc(2)6s20m17M.
Cancale jetty head Oc(3)G.12s12m7M.

WARNING Oyster beds *(Parcs à huitres)* cover a large area off Cancale northeast of the port. They are shown on large scale charts which should be studied. On no account anchor in these areas and cross around HW only *Chris Fairbairn*

Cancale to Cap Fréhel

Mooring and anchoring N to S

PORT MER (Firm Sand)
Enter the bay midway between Pointe de Barbe Brulée and Pointe de Chatry on a track of 260°. It is crammed with moorings so anchor well clear. There are several visitor's berths some way offshore but it is recommended to reserve with the *chef du port* before making a visit. (see numbers above).

During the season a water taxi service is available on request (VHF Ch 9).

Above the beach are several bars and restaurants. The Bureau du Port is located at the top of the slipway.

PORT PICAN (Firm sand)
An idyllic smaller bay. The mooring area extends S to Port Briac. Enter on 280°. There is a landing and slipway. No facilities.

Ile des Rimains

Small craft moorings N of La Houle

NE OF PTE DE LA CHAINE (Mud)
Some swell can be expected here, particularly at spring tides.

SE of ILES DES RIMAINS (Sand and mud)
This is nearest the harbour. It is necessary to check depths to find the best position. At neaps it is possible to anchor nearer the harbour but well clear of oyster beds.

PORT DE LA HOULE (Dries between 4·4m and 9·7m)

WARNING
Soft mud up to 3ft deep in places. A depth of 1·7m will be found at the head of Jetée de la Fenêtre at half tide. Entry should be made about 1 hour before HW. On a 30ft tide at St Helier there should be sufficient water to get far enough in to dry out on the beach which is firm sand and shells.

To avoid getting neaped it is recommended to make a visit when the tides are making.

Anchoring in the harbour is inadvisable.

Berthing alongside the inner side of the jetty near the Ancien Phare (old lighthouse) is possible with authorisation. Keep well clear of fishing vessels.

Epi de la Houle - a sheltered corner for drying out

LE HAVRE DE ROTHÉNEUF
48°41'·35N 01°57'·69W (Entry beacon W of Ile Bésnard)

CHARTS
BA 3659 Cap Fréhel to Iles Chausey (1:50 000)
SHOM 7131 Du Hâvre de Rothéneuf à Cancale (1:20 000)
SHOM 7155 Du Cap Fréhel à la Pointe du Grouin - Approches de Saint-Malo (1:48 800)
SHOM 7156 De la Pointe du Grouin à la Pointe d'Agon – Baie du Mont-Saint-Michel – Iles Chausey (1:48 800)

TIDAL INFORMATION
As for St Malo
Difference St Helier –20
The whole bay from the entrance inwards dries at between 2·8m and 8·8m. Entry not possible below half tide.

SUPPLIES AND SERVICES
Water (in cans) obtainable from the Sailing School on the slipway on request.
Shops, restaurants and bars in Rothéneuf village.
Bus connection with St Malo from village square.
Restaurant Le Benetin ✆ 02 99 56 97 www.restaurant-Lebenetin.com
Musée Jacques Cartier ✆ 02 99 40 97 73
SNBSM (Lifeboat) ✆ 02 99 56 16 33

Le Havre de Rothéneuf 4M E of St Malo qualifies as a spacious natural harbour and is the domain of small shallow draught boats able to take the ground. The village of Rothéneuf is a short walk away with a *boulangerie*, *tabac* and a few bars.

This tranquil family beach resort has no organised entertainments and is safe for children and dinghy work. There is an active Cercle Nautique that draws crowds of children to the slipway when the tide is up.

Shelter
The bay is well sheltered from all but Northerlies when a swell can penetrate the entrance. Grounding and refloating can then be an uncomfortable business and it might necessitate a move to the eastern side of the bay (see plan).

Historical
The Rothéneufs
The place takes its name from the Rothéneuf family of privateers and smuggling fishermen that ruled this coast

Rothéneuf *Google Earth*

III North Brittany: 1 Cancale to Trégastel-Ste Anne

in the 16th century. Nearby rocks bear the names of family members – La Bigne, La Haie, Bénétin, Le Grand Chevreuil, Rochefort.

They built ships for trading and set out to rival the famous privateers of St Malo. The Rothéneufs held sway until the mid 18th century when the French Revolution spread family discord, bitter infighting and ultimately their demise.

The family history is immortalised in Les Rochers Sculptés, a weird collection of over 300 sinister figures carved out of the rocks on Pointe de Rothéneuf, the work of a hermit priest, Abbé Fouré, between 1893 and 1909. It is open to the public.

Jacques Cartier Museum Limeölou Manor

A short distance from the village is Le Manoir de Limeölou which was the home of 16th century explorer Jacques Cartier, the greatest of all Malouin seafarers. In 1534 he sailed from St Malo in seach of gold and a western route to the Orient. He discovered new lands including Canada which he claimed for the King of France.

Approach

See plan *St Malo Approaches* (page 208) and chart SHOM 7131 Du Havre de Rothéneuf à Cancale.

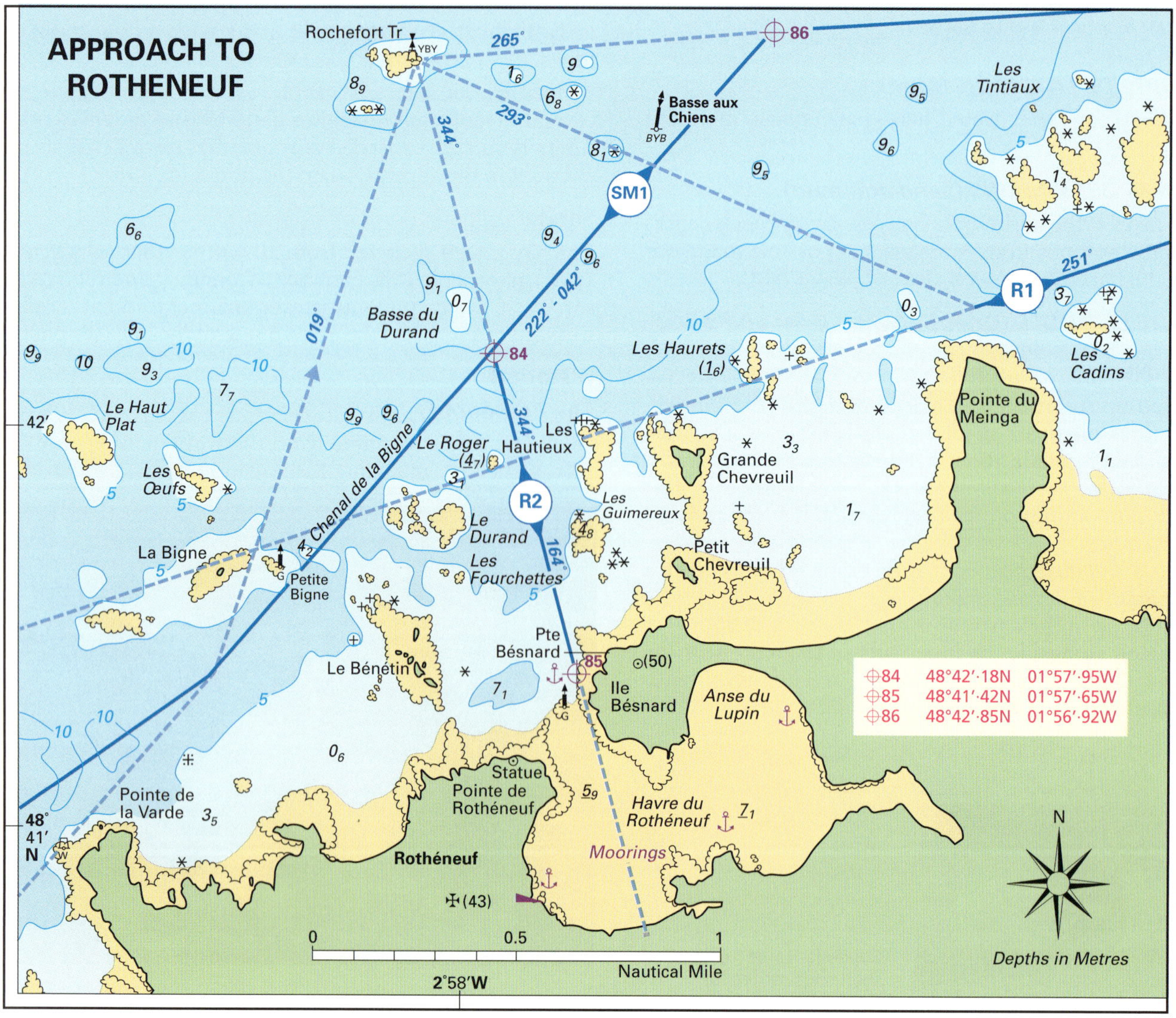

Havre du Rothéneuf from the slipway

Cancale to Cap Fréhel

Caution

Allowance should be made for the tidal stream across the approach line.

Inside Les Tintiaux reef it starts running westward at HW St Malo max 2·7 knots at springs; and starts to the east at LW max 2·5 knots at springs. Off the entrance the west going ebb stream will be weaker, about 1·5 knots.

Final approach is from the eastern end of Chenal de la Bigne (see *Approaches to St Malo* page 209). It should be made on a rising tide when key rocks are visible.

From the east

Rochefort Tower

To enter Chenal de la Bigne involves clearing the extensive reef of Les Tintiaux. The easiest route is to the N.

To clear north. Rochefort tower should be kept on a bearing of no more than 265° and left at least 400m to port.

To clear south of Les Tintiaux use transit:

R1 *251° La Bigne islet midway between Grand Jardin Lighthouse and Ile Cezembre*

The lighthouse is 10M away so fair visibility is needed.

This line passes through a 180m wide gap between Les Tintiaux (dry up to 9·7m) and Les Cadins (dry up to 7·8m). The minimum depth is 3·7m. Hold transit until 200m N of Pointe du Meinga and Rochefort Tower is bearing 293° then alter course NW into clear water to join Chenal de la Bigne transit SM1 222° (see *Approaches to St Malo* page 209).

WARNING

This route should only be attempted with local knowledge aboard, SHOM chart 7131 and in quiet weather.

Entry (dries 2·8m)

This should be made on a rising tide from HW -3. The transit is:

R2 *164° (⊕84 to ⊕85) Large house above beach open of right (W) edge of Pointe Bésnard*

Note that this line leaves Le Roger (dries 4·7m) 180m to starboard and Les Guimereux (dries 4·8m) 200m to port both of which are preferably located before entry. (⊕85 to be used with caution.)

Making allowance for cross set pass midway between Pointe Bésnard and isolated stick beacon with starboard top mark and head towards the mooring area to the S.

Most of the western half of the bay is level hard sand and there are two slipways which make the best landing for the village.

From the west via Chenal de la Bigne

La Bigne and its beacon La Petite Bigne is left to port. Continue until Rochefort tower (W cardinal) bears 344° (⊕84). Break off onto entry transit **R2** *164°*. (See *Entry* above.)

By night

Not possible.

Anchorage

As entry is not possible until half tide it may be necessary to anchor off. Subject to settled weather and offshore winds this is possible 0·25M NNW of starboard bn in entrance, where the bottom is generally firm, flat sand. (Charted depth 1·3m.)

Rothéneuf SE side of the bay looking towards the entrance

III North Brittany: 1 Cancale to Trégastel-Ste Anne

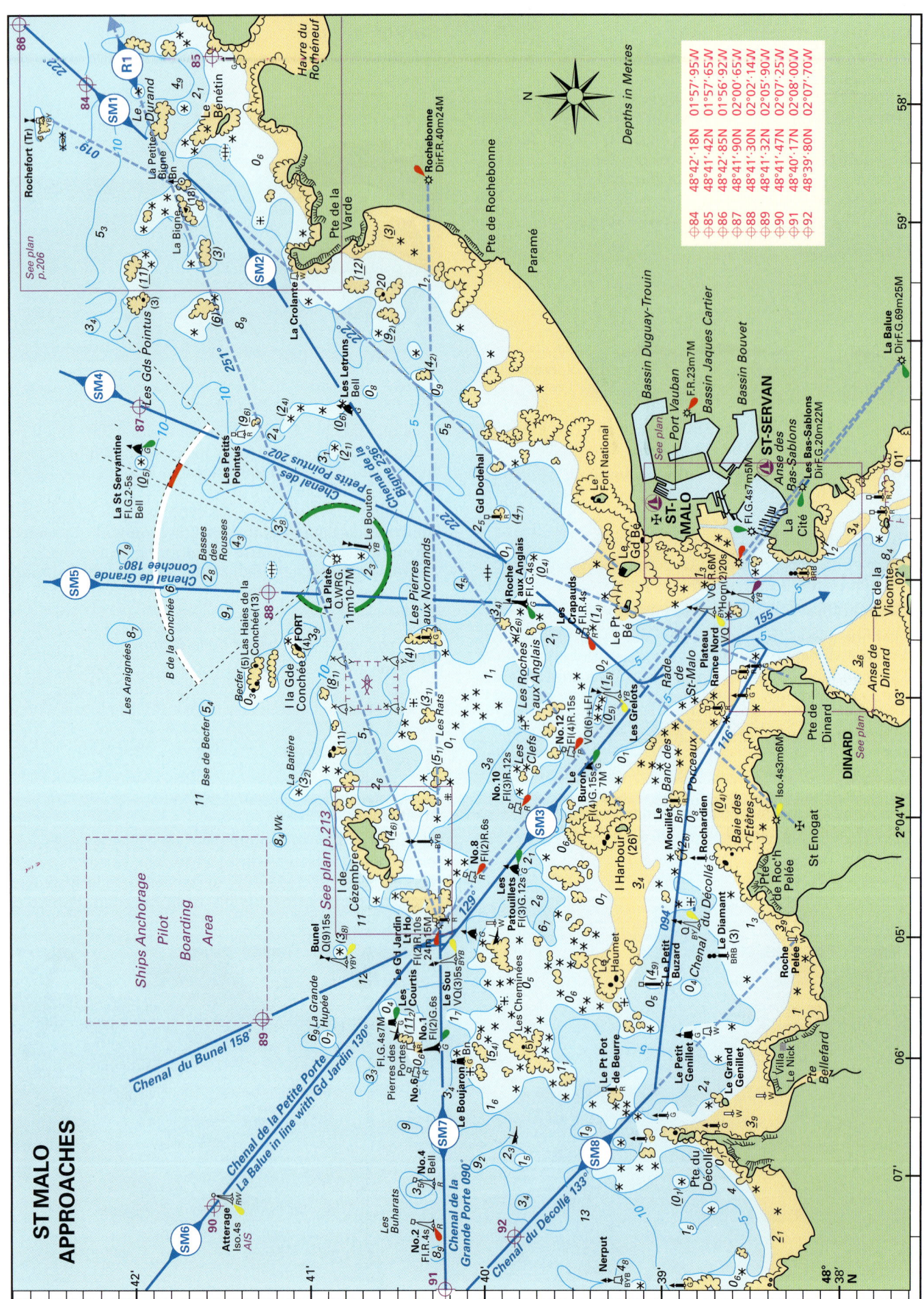

Cancale to Cap Fréhel

Approaches to St Malo, St Servan, Dinard and La Rance

St Malo's approaches are typical of many on the north coast of Brittany. Having arrived at a safe position off your destination you must leave the open sea to pilot your way along a channel between reefs and rocks, and often with a cross stream to contend with. This element of a passage involves good planning, adequate visibility, a large scale chart and knowing exactly where you are in the first place. Key marks to identify off St Malo are from E to W:

- Rochefort Tower (W cardinal) and its reef from S

- La Platte Light tower and La Grande Conchée Fort from ESE

- La Grande Conchée Fort from E
- Ile de Cézembre
- Le Grand Jardin lighthouse Fl(2)10s24m

- St Malo Cathedral from NE

Caution
The channels that converge on Roche aux Anglais buoy (Bigne, Petits Pointus and Grande Concheé) terminate over a shoal area with a minimum depth of 0·3m at chart datum. This may call for a change of plan if arriving at or near LW.

There are seven channels which are described from E to W.

Chenal de la Bigne (0·3m)
By day only

From a position 0·8M E of Rochefort tower W cardinal (⊕86) take up transit:

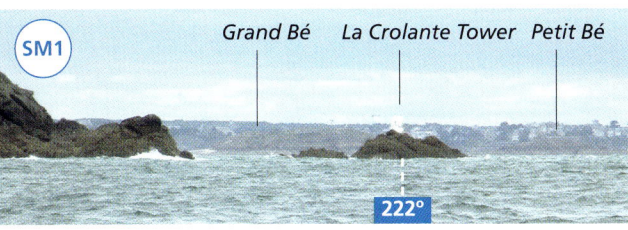

SM1 222° *The right part of Grand Bé aligned with La Crolante Tower*

This will leave Basse aux Chiens E cardinal buoy 100m to starboard and lead through the narrow (300m) gap between La Petite Bigne starboard beacon which is left 75m to starboard and reefs close to port.

0·5M short of La Crolante prepare for an alteration to starboard. The turning point is Rochefort tower bearing 019° (see view opposite). The next transit is:

SM2 236° *Le Buron beacon tower open left (S) of Ile Harbour*

Continue until La Platte tower and La Grande Conchée Fort are aligned on 295° when course should be altered to 222°. There is no reliable transit for the final leg into the deep water of La Rance but there are four marks about 0·35M apart:

- Gd Dodehal port beacon is left 0·25M to port
- Roches aux Anglais starboard buoy Fl.G.4s is left close to starboard
- Les Crapauds port buoy Fl.R.4s is left close to port
- Les Greslots S cardinal lit buoy is left to starboard.

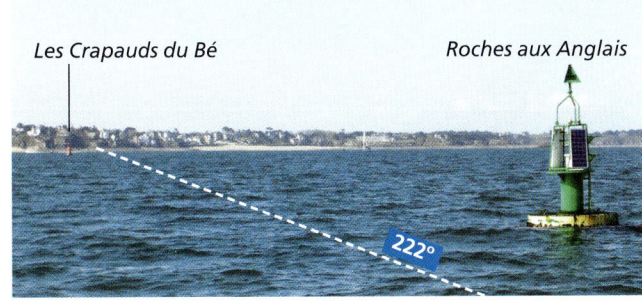

III. NORTH BRITTANY: 1. CANCALE TO TRÉGASTEL-STE ANNE

CHANNEL ISLANDS, CHERBOURG PENINSULA & NORTH BRITTANY

III North Brittany: 1 Cancale to Trégastel-Ste Anne

Entry to St Malo or St Servan
This is made with transit:

SM3 129° *La Balue lighthouse above Les Bas-Sablons lighthouse*

Hold this transit until Plateau Rance Nord N cardinal buoy is abaft the beam then make a small alteration to starboard to give Mole des Noires a clearance of 200m.

By night
Chenal de la Bigne is not possible at night. (See *Chenal de la Petite Porte* page 211.)

La Balue lighthouse

Mole des Noires

Chenal des Petits Pointus (0·3m)

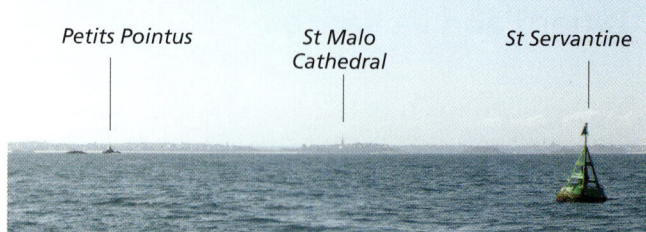

400m E of Saint Servantine starboard buoy (⊕87) take up transit:

SM4 202° *Pointe de Dinard and Dinard spire beyond open to right (W) of Le Petit Bé Fort. (Spire is difficult to identify)*

Leave Les Petits Pointus port beacon (R) 200m to port and Le Bouton S cardinal buoy (S of La Platte light tower) 400M to starboard. The line joins Chenal de La Bigne 0·35M NW of Grand Dodehal port beacon. Continue as for Chenal de La Bigne as described above. (See *Caution* on depths page 209.)

Passing Les Petit Pointus beacon. In the background is La Bigne rock with its beacon La Petite Bigne

By night
With no leading lights and several unlit marks this channel is inadvisable at night until familiarity has been gained by day. Directions are as follows:

First find St Servantine starboard buoy Fl.G.2·5s Bell (⊕87). Leave 400m to starboard and take up a heading of 202°. Keep in W sector of La Platte light tower Q.WRG.11m until well clear of unlit Les Petits Pointus bacon.

Pass 0·35M E of La Plate tower and unlit S cardinal buoy, Le Bouton.

Identify ahead Roches aux Anglais starboard buoy (Fl.G.4s) and leave close to starboard.

Follow directions for Chenal de la Grand Conchée (by night) as described next.

Cancale to Cap Fréhel

Chenal de la Grande Conchée (0·3m)

This is the simplest and most direct approach from the N as used by high speed Channel Island ferries in daylight and subject to sufficient height of tide (see *Caution* page 209).

The published transit has an illusive rear mark so a bearing only may have to suffice:

SM5 *180° distant turreted building on right (W) edge of Le Petit Bé Fort*

The key mark in the approach is La Grande Conchée Fort 1·0M ENE of Ile de Cézembre (see *St Malo approaches* plan page 208).

0·43M NE of the Fort is ⊕88.

The line passes midway between the Fort and La Plate light tower then due S to Roches aux Anglais starboard buoy (Fl.G.4s). *En route* the unlit starboard beacon Les Pierres aux Normandes is left 200m to starboard. Leave Roches aux Anglais starboard buoy close to starboard and alter course to 222°.

Continue as for Chenal de La Bigne described above. (See *Caution* page 209.)

By night

With no leading lights and several unlit marks this channel is inadvisable by night until familiarity has been gained by day. Directions are as follows:

Before closing the coast from the N identify:
La Plate Q.WRG.11m Initially approach on 180° in W sector. Abeam La Grande Conchée Fort (unlit) you enter the G sector. Identify **Roches aux Anglais Buoy** (Fl.G.4s) to the S and hold on a bearing of 180°.
Leave close to starboard and head SW for **Les Crapauds du Bé** buoy Fl.R.4s. Continue SW to intercept Chenal de la Petite Port marks as described below. (See *Caution* page 209.)

Chenal de la Petite Porte (8·6m)

St Malo's main deep water channel is well marked and straightforward by day or night. Be prepared to encounter large commercial vessels.

Entry is made from NW. First identify key marks E–W:
- Ile de Cézembre
- Le Grand Jardin Lighthouse

At Atterage St Malo landfall buoy (Iso.4s) or ⊕90 take up:

SM6 *130° Balue lighthouse (lit 24hr) aligned with Grand Jardin lighthouse*

This line will clear:
- Le Bunel (dries 3·8m) 0·5M WNW of Cézembre and marked by W cardinal buoy (lit)
- Le Grande Hupée (0·7m) reef 0·9M NW of Grand Jardin
- Pierres des Portes (0·4m) reef 200m NE of Les Courtis.

Note that a minor course alteration to starboard is required half a mile before Le Grand Jardin lighthouse (when Les Courtis light tower is abaft the beam) in order to leave it 200m to port. The transit then becomes **SM3** 129°.

Follow the channel till half a mile short of the head of Mole des Noires which should be given a clearance of 200m. Continue towards St Malo Lock or Les Bas Sablons Marina. (See *Entry to St. Malo or St. Servan.*)

By night

Closing the coast from the NW align Le Grand Jardin lighthouse Fl(2)R.10s2m15M with La Balue lighthouse Dir.F.G.68m25M aligned on 130°. This leaves Bunel W cardinal buoy hald a mile to port.

When 0·5M off Le Grand Jardin lighthouse and with Les Courtis light tower (Fl.G.4s14m7M) bearing W come

Atterage St. Malo landfall buoy

III North Brittany: 1 Cancale to Trégastel-Ste Anne

to starboard to align La Balue lighthouse (Dir.F.G 69m) on the skyline above St Servan with Les Bas Sablons (Dir.F.G.20m) in the marina on 128°. This transit is held until 0·4M off Mole des Noires light tower Fl.R.5s11m13M which shold be given a clearance of 200m. Continue towards the dredged channel to the lock (070° with 2F.R. in alignment).

For Bas Sablons Marina see *St Servan entry by night* page 218.

Chenal du Bunel (⊕89 158°)

This minor channel E of Chenal de La Petite Porte has no suitable marks and is unusable by night. It clears W of Le Bunel (dries 3·8m) by 400m and joins Chenal de la Petite Porte 400m WNW of Le Grand Jardin lighthouse.

Chenal de la Grande Porte (5·8m)

This deep water channel offers a direct route into St Malo from the west. It joins Chenal de la Petite Porte 200m W of Le Grand Jardin lighthouse.

The marks are:

SM7 (⊕91) 090° Rochebonne lighthouse aligned with Le Grand Jardin lighthouse.

The backmark is indistinguishable by day without the aid of binoculars.

An alternative backmark by day is the antenna close S of the light (see view).

Enroute marks are:

- Buharats Ouest No.2 port buoy 100m to port
- Buharats Est No.4 port buoy (unlit)
- Basse du Boujaron No.1 starboard buoy close to starboard
- Le Sou E cardinal buoy 100m to starboard.

By night

Lights for joining this Channel are Le Grand Jardin lighthouse Fl(2)R.10s2m15M aligned with Rochebonne lighthouse Dir.F.R.40m24M on 089°. Hold till Le Sou E cardinal is 200m to starboard then come to starboard to join Chenal de la Petite Port as described above.

Chenal du Décolle (dries) – by day only (W to E)

Chart *BA 2700* or *SHOM 7130* is essential for this inshore passage which is a test of pilotage skills. Charted depths may be less than shown in places particularly at the Dinard end, which now dries at about 3·9m and 4·1m due to silting. It should, therefore, be taken around HW and preferably on a rising tide.

From ⊕92 0·7M NNE of Nerput E cardinal bn take up initial transit SM8:

SM8 133° Le Grand Genillet Tower (W) aligned with La Roche Pelée Tower (W)

This line, which should be held accurately, passes midway between Le Petit Pot du Beurre port beacon and La Moulière de Saint-Lunaire starboard beacon and 230m NE of La Pierre aux Bars starboard beacon.

When Le Pierre aux Bars starboard bn (the most easterly of two starboard bns off Pte du Decolle) is bearing W alter course to 094°.

There are then a series of marks to the exit off Pointe de Dinard. These are:

1. Le Petit Genillet starboard beacon tower. Leave 200m to starboard
2. Le Petit Buzard port beacon. Leave 200m to port
3. N cardinal buoy (unnamed). Leave 100m to starboard
4. Rochardien starboard bn. Leave 180m to starboard
5. Le Mouillé port beacon. Leave 200m to port and when it is on the right (E) edge of Île de Harbour fort alter course to 116° for exit 0·75M ahead

6. Les Pierres d'Amourettes port beacon. Leave 0·75m to port

Cancale to Cap Fréhel

Les Pierres d'Amourettes

7. Starboard beacon (unnamed). Leave close to starboard
8. Exit between Les Pourceaux Port beacon to port and Le Moulinet starboard beacon to starboard.

Décolle exit

Drying patch (4·1) close S of Les Pourceaux

By night
Not possible.

Ile de Cézembre
48°40'·50N 2°04'·27W

During the season there will often be a handful of small craft anchored off this islet 2M north of St Malo. The main attraction being its beach which is among the best in the area and a small bar restaurant above it.

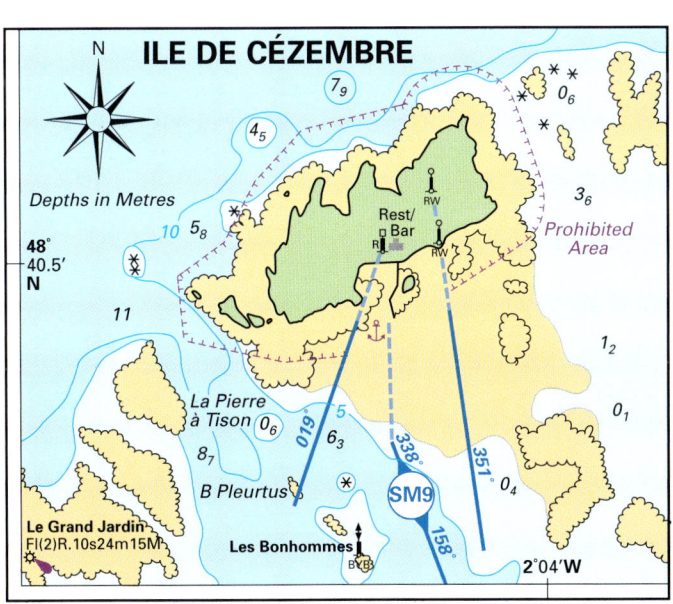

Approach from S
Break off Chenal de la Petite Port at a position 200m SW of Les Clefs d'Aval port buoy (No 10) and track NNW with stern transit:

SM9 *158° Les Burons and Pointe de Dinard*

500m S of the islet is Bonhommes E cardinal beacon which is left 200m to port.

Approach between the clearing lines shown on the plan. (The RW beacons are obscure.)

Anchorage
This should be SSW of the slipway as shown. Beware of the rocky shoreline off the SW end. The bottom is firm sand but as the area dries out extensively, up to 4·6m, it is impractical as a LW anchorage on spring tides.

The anchorage is exposed in any winds with a southerly component.

Historical
Cézembre was fortified by Vauban at the end of the 17th century. It has subsequently been used as a prison, a monastery, a place of quarantine and in the second world war a target for bombing practice. It was heavily shelled in 1944 and a notice on large scale charts warns 'Circulation and anchorage prohibited owing to the existence of explosives'. However anchoring not less than 100m offshore is permitted S of the landing slip (see plan). As of July 2017, the island is accessible thanks to a network of public footpaths.

III North Brittany: 1 Cancale to Trégastel-Ste Anne

ST MALO

48°38'·55N 02°01'·62W
Entry channel to Ecluse du Naye (St Malo lock)

33M S of St Helier 22M SW of Granville

TRAVEL
Sea
Condor Ferries (UK S coast and Channel Islands – St Malo)
① 0045 609 1024 www.condorferries.co.uk
Brittany Ferries (Portsmouth – St Malo)
① 0871 244 1400 / 02 23 18 30 30 www.brittanyferries.com
Vedettes de St Malo (to Dinard, La Rance)
① 02 23 18 02 04 www.vedettes-saint-malo.com

Air
Airlines (Dinard Airport)
Aurigny ① 01481 822886 www.aurigny.com
Ryanair ① 0871 2460000 www.ryanair.com

Train
TGV direct link to Paris from St Malo

CHARTS
BA 2700 Approaches to Saint-Malo (1:15 000)
BA 3659 Cap Fréhel to Iles Chausey (1:50 000)
Imray C33B Channel Islands and North Coast of France*
  *includes plans: St-Malo Approaches (1:55 000),
  St-Malo (1:17 500)
Imray 2500 The Channel Islands and adjacent coast
  of France Chart Atlas:
  14a St-Malo Approaches (1:55 000)
  16 St-Malo & La Rance (1:15 000)
SHOM 7130 Abords de Saint-Malo - De l'île des Hébihens à
  la Pointe de la Varde (1:15 000)
SHOM 7155 Du Cap Fréhel à la Pointe du Grouin -
  Approches de Saint-Malo (1:48 800)

RADIO
Ecluse du Naye Ch 12 (2½hrs either side of HW)
Le Bas Sablons Marina (St Servan) Ch 09

TIDAL INFORMATION
St Malo is a Standard port
Difference on St Helier – 20

MHWS	MLWS	MHWN	MLWN
12·2	1·5	9·2	4·4

Caution
Strong tidal streams. Max rate 4 knots.
The E–W stream generally follows the coastline but inshore directions and rates are modified by headlands and islets. As the stream funnels into La Rance it takes on a SSE direction attaining 4 knots. This is used to advantage by the tidal power station at the Barrage a mile upstream from St Malo. The ebb sets NW and can be equally strong. (see *St Servan Caution – Berthing* page 218)

Cross streams
When following approach channels into St Malo, particularly those orientated N–S, beware of cross set. This is best monitored by observing transits.

CONTACTS
Ecluse du Naye (St Malo lock) ① 02 99 20 25 00, Ch12
Port Vauban Marina ① 02 99 56 51 91
Les Bas Sablons Marina, St Servan ① 02 99 81 81 34
Yacht Club St Malo SNBSM ① 02 23 18 20 30
Tourist Office ① 02 99 56 64 48 www.saint-malo.cci.fr

SUPPLIES AND SERVICES
Fuel Port des Sablons ① (0)2 99 81 71 34
Supermarkets Hypermarkets out of town
  Carrefour: Centre Commercial de la Madeleine
  Intermarché: La Découverte (St Servan)
  Intra Muros – Supermarket Carrefour (Intra Muros)
  Rue St Vincent, (St Servan)
Fish market Tuesday/Friday. Halle au Bleu. Intra Muros
Chandlery and Boatyards In Bassin Duguay-Trouin E of Bassin Vauban are several boatyards offering a range of services such as haul outs, repairs and chandleries.
Enquiries Ville Audrain (by railway station) ① 02 99 564 806 (English spoken)
Restaurants St Malo is reputed to have one of the highest concentrations of restaurants in Europe.
Taxi
St Malo Taxi ① 92 23 181 181
Allo Taxi Malouins ① 02 99 81 30 30

Place Chateaubriand

St Malo is the sort of place every yachtsman should visit at least once in a lifetime. It is the hub of a fascinating sailing area that includes the inland lake of the River Rance stretching as far as Dinan and the Brittany Canals. The historic walled city is a major tourist site.

As a ferry terminal with regular sailings to the Channel Islands and the UK south coast, St Malo is a convenient point for a crew change or longer stay.

Cancale to Cap Fréhel

St Malo looking N

Ashore

The best way to enjoy St Malo is to lock into Port Vauban with its sheltered Marina. This is opposite Porte St Vincent the town's main gate. Inside the walls is a labyrinth of narrow cobbled streets and terraces crammed with restaurants, bars and shops. The cafés in Place Chateaubriand are animated venues where one can sit and watch the world go by or enjoy a bit of impromptu street entertainment in the summer evenings.

A walk round the ramparts, about an hour, provides good coastal views and a chance to check sea conditions. There are good beaches with safe bathing north of the city.

St Malo hosts several yachting events such as The Tall Ships Race, Quebec to St Malo, Cowes to Dinard and La Route du Rhum. At such time berths are in short supply.

Bassin Vauban (above and below)

CHANNEL ISLANDS, CHERBOURG PENINSULA & NORTH BRITTANY

III North Brittany: 1 Cancale to Trégastel-Ste Anne

Dinard ferry (Le Bac de Dinard)
The Bus de Mer leaves the Cale de Dinan outside the SW wall of St Malo every 30 minutes for the 10 minute crossing to Dinard. Tickets obtainable from kiosks at both terminals (see *Dinard* page 220).

Historical
St Malo's origin is a single rock on which a monastery was founded in the 6th century by a monk named Aaron. He was succeeded by St Maclou (St Malo) a Celt of Welsh origin who was Bishop of Aleth, the Gallo-Roman town which became St Servan. As the centuries passed a powerful walled town emerged that successfully resisted four English sieges. Between 1390 and 1594 it was an independent republic owning no allegiance to France or Brittany. 'Ni Français, ni Bretons, Malouins seulement.'

The Malouins were famous seamen, *corsaires* and explorers. Jacques Cartier left St Malo in 1534 to discover Canada. They were also the first colonists of the Falklands – hence the Argentinian name Las Malvinas. (See Rothéneuf on page 205). In the 19th century the docks were developed and the Malouins took up more peaceful pursuits such as fishing where they were one of the main leaders in cod fishery off Newfoundland.

In 1944 most of St Malo was bombed to the ground but subsequently rebuilt through public subscription. Its restoration was finally completed in the 1960s when the elegant spire of the Cathedral St Vincent once again dominated the town.

Museums and sites of interest
The Chateau that makes the NE corner of the city houses the Musée d'Histoire de La Ville. This records the development of St Malo and its seafaring traditions. Well worth a visit.

Fort National de St Malo on Petit Bé is accessible by a causeway at low water.

Mont St Michel
The Abbey is open daily and makes an interesting day trip from St Malo.
By bus: daily during the season departing from Place St Vincent.
By rail: a daily service via Dol and then by bus.
On foot: escorted treks are organised from Le Bec d'Andaine 20km S of Granville.
☎ 02 33 70 83 67 / 0233 89 80 88
www.cheminsdelabaie.com
Further details from the St Malo Tourist Office
☎ 02 99 56 64 48

Entering the lock

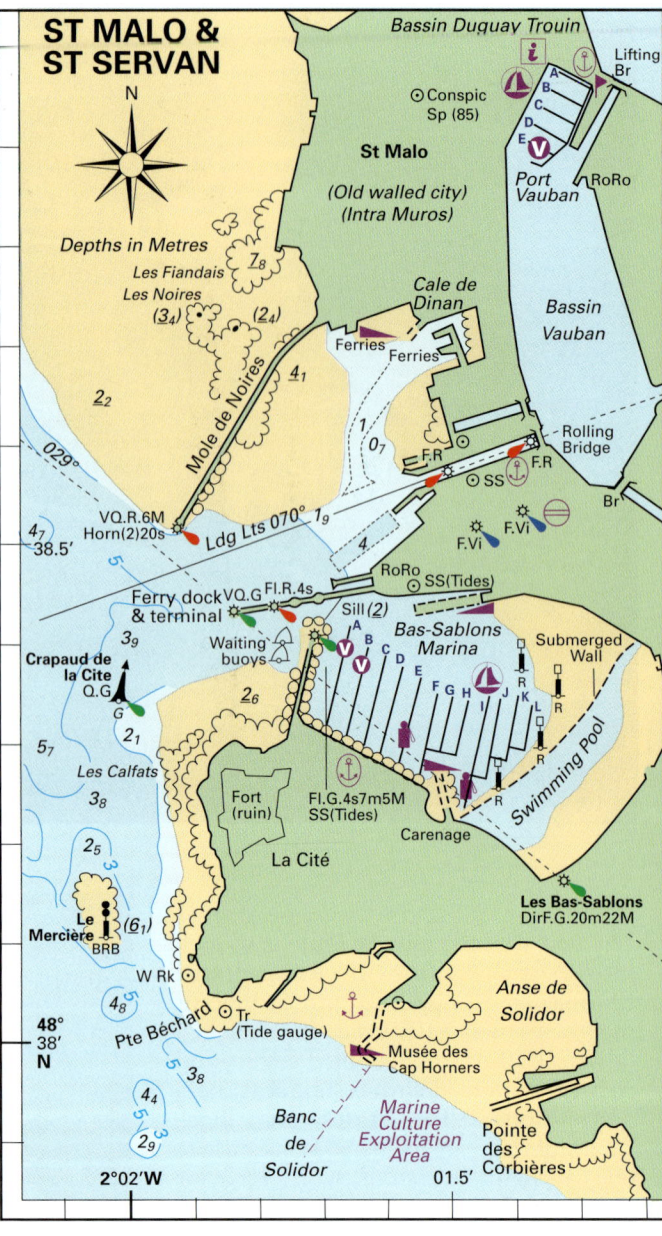

Entry – L'Ecluse du Naye, St Malo Lock

Approach channel
Approach the lock on 070° via the dredged channel 1·5m at chart datum that is in line with the lock.

Times of operation
2½ hours either side of HW with inbound locks normally open at precisely HW -3, HW -2, HW -1, HW, HW +1, HW +2.

Freeflow, when both gates are left open, may occur from HW -1½ to HW is the best but a rare option.

The N side of the chamber normally handles incoming vessels. The lock attendant will advise.

Remember that commercial vessels have priority and it is advisable to brief the crew on heaving lines and tying sheet bends!

By Night
At night the 070° approach is indicated by 2F.R. in alignment.

Cancale to Cap Fréhel

Berthing

Port Vauban Marina (5·5m)
Port Vauban Marina is at the N end of Bassin Vauban. The most southerly of four pontoons (E) is reserved for visitors. Overflow or vessels over 12m use the quay under the city. Getting ashore from here calls for some ingenuity.

Facilities
Comprehensive – but less so alongside quays. Yacht Club (SNBSM) on Quai Bajoyer (E side) welcomes visitors.
Fuel Les Bas Sablons Marina, St Servan.

Bassin Duguay–Trouin (5·5m)
Accessed via a swing bridge in NE corner of Bassin Vauban on request. Used as overflow for vessels over 12m and for special events. Berthing alongside quay only.

Facilities
None.

Anchoring and mooring
Anchoring in or bordering channels and mooring alongside commercial quays is prohibited. There are waiting buoys to the NW of the lock and outside Les Bas Sablons Marina and to the N of the Rance Lock. It is best to avoid such alternatives by planning to arrive between above half tide if intending to lock through.

Dinard on the W bank of La Rance has a limited number of visitors mooring which may be available on prior application. (See *Dinard* page 219.)

ST SERVAN (Port des Bas-Sablons)
48°38'·42N 02°01'·70W Mole des Sablons

Local information
Travel, Charts, Radio, Tidal information (see St Malo)

USEFUL CONTACTS
Bureau du Port  02 99 81 81 34, VHF Ch 12
Email port plaisance@ville-saint-malo.fr

SUPPLIES AND SERVICES
Berths 1,200, including 86 visitors' (pontoons A and B)
Waiting buoys 3 outside marina
Charts, chandlery Voilerie Richard (Marina)
Sail repairs Marc Noel, Technique Voile (Marina)
Fuel (Pontoon 1) Bureau du Port
Haul out 30-ton travel-lift and cranes: Bureau du Port
Slipway (drying out and launching) Bureau du Port
Several boatyards, electricians and marine engineers
Restaurants For the nearest and best selection cross over to Anse de Solidor.
Market day Friday (Place Bouvet)

St Servan merges with St Malo and comes under the same commune but is less tourist orientated. With its shops, cafés, villas and tree lined squares it has the relaxed atmosphere of a traditional French resort.

The town's coastal area is divided by the Aleth peninsula into two contrasting bays. On the north side Anse des Bas-Sablons is taken up by the multi berth marina whereas Anse de Solidor is a natural drying harbour facing the estuary. Its focal point is Le Tour Solidor fort (see *Historical*).

As a yachting destination Port des Bas-Sablons, unlike St Malo, offers a wider period of access over a sill. It has comprehensive facilities on the pontoons and the large hard standing area above.

Ashore
It is a 10 minute walk round the bay to the boulangerie and mini market and a wide range of shops, including

Port des Bas-Sablons looking SE

III North Brittany: 1 Cancale to Trégastel-Ste Anne

supermarket, will be found further uphill on the main street. There are hypermarkets at La Madeleine commercial centre a mile SE of the Marina. 15 minutes by taxi or bus.

Historical

St Servan predates St Malo. Its earliest inhabitants lived in Aleth, a Gallo-Roman town the remains of which can be seen on the peninsula S of the Marina. When Aleth's fortifications finally succumbed to frequent Norman invasions its monastic settlement moved to St Malo with its powerful defences and Aleth declined.

The prominent Tour Solidor in the Anse de Solidor is a 14th century fort built to protect the entrance to The Rance. It is now the Musée des Cap Horners dedicated to Ocean voyagers. Open during working hours except Mondays. Visit highly recommended.

Entry

The Marina is entered S of the ferry berth extension which obscures it from view when approaching from NW. The whole structure is left to port. Note Crapaud de la Cité starboard buoy (G) to starboard which marks the channel to the ferry berth.

The marina breakwater (Mole des Sablons) (Fl.G.4s) and the sill (dries 2m) extending off its end is approached from WSW.

Berthing

There is no escaping the strong tidal streams of the Rance which penetrate over the sill of Les Bas Sablons Marina. Berthing can become a test of boat handling skill, particularly on the vistors' berths near the entrance.

By night

Mole des Noires Fl.R 5s is left 200m to port and W end of ferry berth VQ.G (mounted on top of concrete caisson) is also left to port.

Mole des Sablons (marina entrance) Fl.G.4s is left to starboard.

Caution

If unfamiliar with a night entry into Bas-Sablons the VQ.G marking the W end of the ferry berth can be confusing. It must be left to port (pass W of it).

Three R lights displayed on a mast by the sill prohibit movement in and out of the marina while a ferry is manoeuvring at the adjacent pier (see plan page 216).

Les Bas Sablons Marina

Marina entry. Keep an eye out for traffic

Gauge indicates depth over sill

Access

With a draught of 1·5m there should be sufficient water to cross the sill between approximately HW – 3½ to +4½ at springs and considerably longer at neaps.

Depth over sill is displayed on the breakwater head and on the concrete caisson opposite. A large digital gauge on N side of marina is visible from the entrance by day and night.

Depth

The marina is dredged to 2·5m but less at E end.

Shelter

The marina is sheltered from all directions apart from NW when strong to gale winds can make life uncomfortable at the outer ends of the pontoons nearest the entrance.

Tour Solidor

A useful facility in Les Bas Sablons Marina if you need to dry out. Booking at Bureau du Port

Cancale to Cap Fréhel

DINARD

48°37'·96N 02°03'·03W Dinard slipway *(Cale)*

TRAVEL & CHARTS
See St Malo and St Servan.

TIDAL INFORMATION
Streams in the Anse de Dinard are not as strong as in the Rade de Dinard but are still influenced by activity at the Barrage (Usine Marémotrice). The maximum rate is 3 knots (see also St Malo and St Servan).

USEFUL CONTACTS
Bureau du Port (Capitanerie) ℡ 02 99 46 64 73, VHF Ch 9
  Email port.public@ville_dinard.fr
  Open seven days a week 0700–2100 in the season.
  Tuesday–Sunday 0830–1200 and 1330–1800 out of season.
Yacht Club de Dinard ℡ 02 99 46 14 32
Taxis ℡ 02 99 46 60 74
Dinard Airport (Pleurtuit) ℡ 02 99 46 18 46

SUPPLIES AND SERVICES
Water and electricity on quay and pontoon
Toilets on hard standing near Bureau du Port
Fuel on quay 0800–2000 Monday–Friday subject to a 4m height of tide
Crane 5 ton. Enquire at Bureau du Port
Repairs, maintenance Dinard Marine ℡ 02 99 46 51 56
  www.dinard-marine.com
Mechanic Dinard Nautisme ℡ 02 99 16 47 92

Bureau du Port on Quai de la Perle

Crane and fuelling point accessible at HW

The wet basin is for local boats only

On the west bank of La Rance opposite St Malo the fashionable resort of Dinard has nearly a thousand moorings reserved for small local craft. It is not able to handle visitors except for major events such as the annual Cowes to Dinard Race. However on prior request the Bureau du Port are usually able to assist with short term berthing.

Approaches

If bound for Dinard or La Rance lock break off abeam Les Grelots S cardinal buoy (see plan page 208) and leave Plateau de La Rance with its two cardinal buoys to port. It is worth following a transit up to the lock, particularly at night, to avoid large commercial mooring buoys in the Rade de Dinard (see *La Rance – Access channels to the lock* page 222).

The pontoon serves the lifeboat and can be used temporarily for boarding and dropping off

III North Brittany: 1 Cancale to Trégastel-Ste Anne

The dredged channel into the wet basin is marked by beacons

Anse de Bec de la Vallée

St Malo to Dinard ferry

Mooring and anchoring

Anse de Dinard

A large flat bank drying between 1m and 5m but note that the bottom shelves steeply at the river edge. Within the mooring zone 670 moorings are laid out under the control of the Bureau du Port. These are let out on an annual basis and some are available for short term use by visitors. A water taxi is available in July and August.

The bottom, particularly near the river, is mud and beaching legs are not recommended. Higher up the beach is firm sand drying 3·5m.

WARNING

At spring tides the incoming tide can surge round Pointe de Dinard and into the Bay without warning.

Wet basin off Quai de le Perle

A narrow channel marked by port and starboard beacons and dredged to 1m leads over a sill into a basin with 2m at chart datum. The fore and aft moorings here are private but the area may be entered to access a long pontoon for loading/unloading and, subject to a 4m height of tide, take on fuel and water (see plan page 219).

Anse du Bec de la Vallée

This slipway off La Pointe de Dinard is occasionally used for drying out. The bottom is firm sand. The SE face of the dog leg shaped *cale* may also be used for drying out in suitable conditions.

Ashore

In the late 19th century Dinard developed from the small fishing village of St Enogat into one of the most elegant resorts in France. It was patronised by British and American aristocracy who indulged themselves in the new fashion of sea bathing, gastronomy and gambling. Dinard opened its first casino in 1910 and there were four in operation by 1928. There is now just one.

Dinard retains a fin du siècle atmosphere with its seaside villas, ice cream parlours and English tea rooms.

If based in St Malo and looking for a change of scene you can take the Bus de Mer (Bac de Dinard) that shuttles between Quai de Dinan at St Malo and Dinard every 30 minutes. There are ticket kiosks at either end.

The casino

Cancale to Cap Fréhel

LA RANCE

TRAVEL
Sea
Ferries *(vedettes)*: Have right of way in the Rance and Canal d'Ille et Rance
St Malo – Dinan
www.compagniecorsaire.com ☏ 0825 138 100
Crosières Chateaubriand (Barrage de le Rance)
www.chateaubriand.com ☏ 02 99 46 44 40

Air
Dinard: International airport (Pleurtuit)
Dinan: Airfield

CHARTS
Imray 2500 The Channel Islands and the adjacent coasts of France Chart Atlas:
16 St-Malo & La Rance (1:15 000) - includes continuation to Lyvet (1:25 000)
SHOM 4233 La Rance - De Saint-Malo à l'écluse du Châtelier (1:15 000)

TIDAL INFORMATION
The ebb and flow of the current in the river is controlled by the power stations operation of sluice gates in the Barrage. By manipulation of the level in the basin the flow, either way, through the turbines is maximised. The natural rhythm of the tide is compressed into a four hour period with 'stands' at high and low level when there is no movement at all.

Speed Limits
In La Rance – 10kns
In Canal d'Ille et Rance – 6 kph

Levels
SHOM chart 4233 gives depths at chart datum (CD) which this French chart describes as 'the approximate level of the lowest (natural) tides'. To this level must be added the depth at which the level of being held. The lowest level is considered to be about 4m above CD so there is seldom any problem with depths up to St Suliac. The rate of rise and fall is variable but does not normally exceed 4m per hour. In exceptional circumstances it may fall at a rate of 1m in 15 minutes. It is therefore difficult to calculate the depth needed when anchoring and a good margin for safety should be added.

Currents
These are strongest either side of the turbine sluices in the Barrage, hence the establishment of the 'Zone Interdite' (see warning below). With distance from this area the effect diminishes but it can still be a force to be reckoned with particularly when manoeuvring either side of the lock.

Further information
- A pamphlet published annually by Usine Marémotrice de la Rance contains information on times, levels, signals and regulations. An update on probable changes is published weekly. Both obtainable from St Malo and St Servan Marina Offices.
- www.bretagneinfonautisme.fr
  www.rance-fremur.com
- Telephone and VHF Radio: (see *Radio* and *Useful contacts* below)

Lock working
WARNING
A 'Zone Interdite' (prohibited zone) where navigation, swimming (including dinghy work) is prohibited is established either side of the barrage.

RADIO
Barrage de la Rance Ch 13
St Suliac Ch 9
Plouër-sur-Rance Marina (when office open) Ch 9
CROSS CORSEN keep 24h watch on Ch 16.

USEFUL CONTACTS (see also St Malo)
Barrage de le Rance
Automatic Information Service ☏ 02 99 16 37 33
Lock-keeper ☏ 02 99 16 37 37
St Suliac (Bureau du Port) ☏ 02 99 58 48 80
Plouër-sur-Rance Marina ☏ 02 96 86 83 15
  Email plouer.portplaisance@wanadoo.fr
L'Ecluse du Châtelier ☏ 02 96 39 55 66
Port du Lyvet Marina ☏ 02 96 83 35 57
Dinan (Capitainerie) ☏ 02 96 39 56 44

SUPPLIES AND SERVICES
W bank
Pointe de Jouvante
Restaurant 'Jersey Lilly.'
Private pontoon for patrons only ☏ 02 99 886 592

La Richardais
Dinard St Malo Nautisme ☏ 02 99 16 47 92

La Landriais
Chantier Naval de la Landriais
Le Minihic sur Rance ☏ 02 99 88 56 01

Plouër-sur-Rance
Estuaire Marine Services ☏ 02 96 86 89 39
Saint Samson Plaisance ☏ 02 96 86 95 80

Looking north down La Rance towards St Malo *Patrick Roach*

CHANNEL ISLANDS, CHERBOURG PENINSULA & NORTH BRITTANY

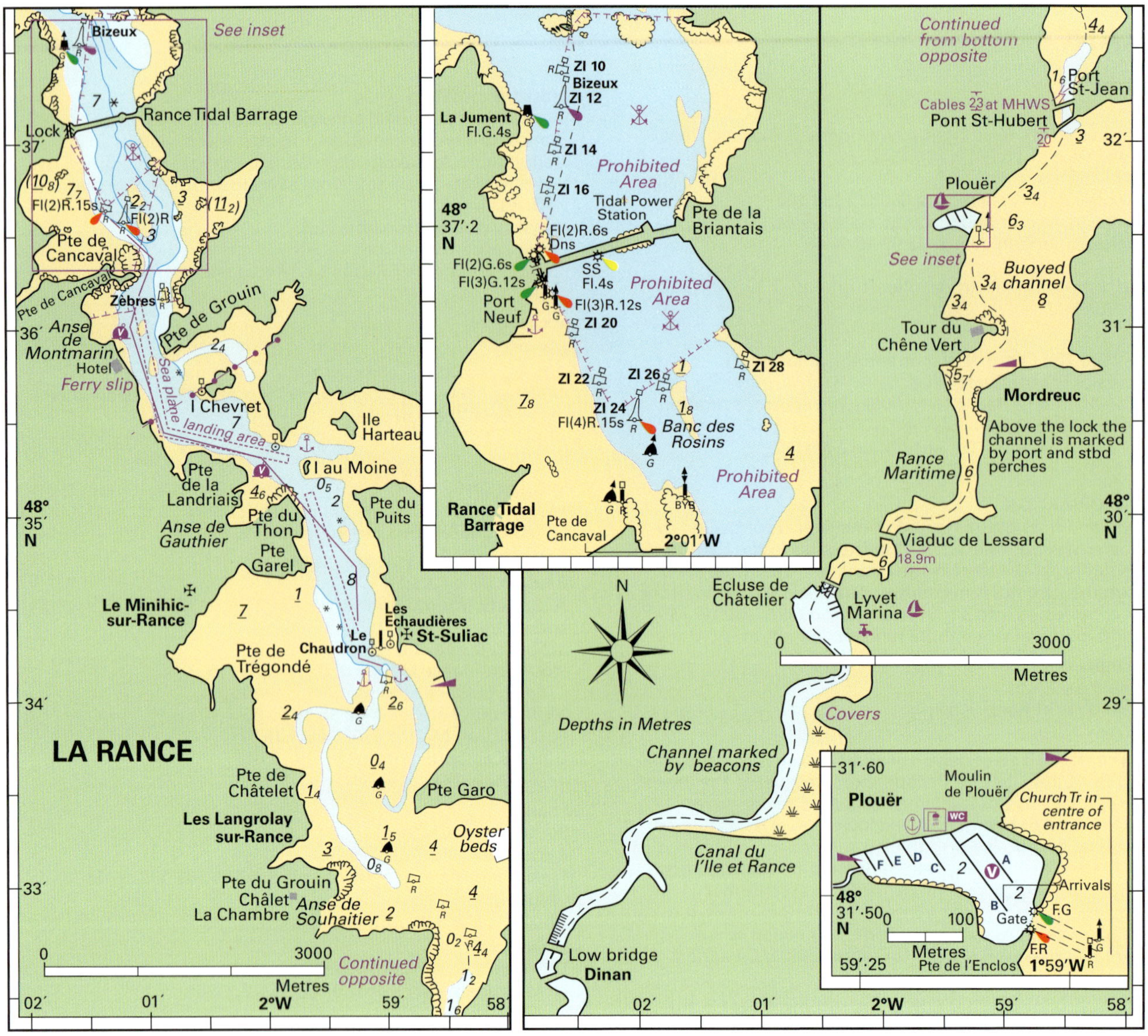

III North Brittany: 1 Cancale to Trégastel-Ste Anne

A visit to St Malo without sampling La Rance is to miss one of Brittany's great river experiences. It offers an escape from the bustle of St Malo or the open sea when the weather is uninviting.

Since the construction of a tidal barrage across the river in the 1960s as part of a hydroelectric scheme, a world first, the river has become a vast sheltered lake entered via a lock. It is possible to sail 12 miles inland as far as the medieval town of Dinan, from where the river becomes the Canal d'Ille et Rance and ultimately the River Vilaine. This provides a useful cross country route via 48 locks to the Bay of Biscay for small mastless vessels drawing no more than 1·3m (see *Inland Waterways of France*, Imray).

Allow at least a couple of days for La Rance. Between the barrage and Dinan is some attractive scenery to be enjoyed, several anchorages, some with public moorings, and marinas at Plouër-sur-Rance and Port de Lyvet behind Le Châtelier lock. Both are described below.

Access channels to the lock

From the N

Route towards the W end of the Barrage via the Rade de Dinard. Pass midway between Pointe de la Vicomte and Bizeux Islet with its statue. Continue up the increasingly narrow channel between the *Zone Interdite* and the shore leaving La Jument starboard beacon 100m to starboard.

The Rade de Dinard looking S towards the Barrage

222 CHANNEL ISLANDS, CHERBOURG PENINSULA & NORTH BRITTANY

Cancale to Cap Fréhel

Approach to the Rance Lock from S

From the S
Having cleared the reef off Pointe de Cancaval head for the W end of the barrage leaving the line of port hand buoys marking the edge of the prohibited zone to starboard.

Waiting buoys
There are four (white) on the seaward side and several on the river side. Both located close to the W barrier of the prohibited zone and marked 'Visitors'. The barrier is a safety net suspended beneath a line of buoys either side of the lock.

Lock entry
The locks work between 0430 and 2030 and when the depth of water outside exceeds 4m. The gates open for incomers on the hour and for outgoers 20 minutes before the hour. Be prepared to pass your draught and mast height to the lockkeeper on demand.

Fishing boats and *vedettes* take precendence over yachts at the locks.

Yachts with masts coming from seaward should precede those without; those with masts going seaward should let those without enter first. This is because the lifting bridge at the N end of the lock clears mastless boats and can then be lowered sooner.

Note The bridge does not now lift for masted vessels between 1200 and 1400 during July and August and at other times. It is recommended to call the Barrage (Ch 13) to check opening time before approaching the lock. The lock operates as normal for non masted vessels subject to their air height. Ropes hang down from the sides of the lock and it is not necessary to make fast securely as there is little turbulence.

Lock entry from N

Caution
When exiting the lock on the river side be prepared for a strong localised W going current setting across the channel.

This emanates from the sluices when they are opening into the river and will be most noticeable on the first inward locking after natural LW.

Lock signals

Signals at the lock:
3 G – Vessels may pass
3 R – No entrance
2 G and 1 W – No movement

Signals on the Barrage:
2 cones point up, white above black –
 Sluices open inwards
2 cones point down, black above white –
 Sluices open seawards.

Timing
While it will always be possible to find at least 4m of depth as far as St Suliac, the advice if proceeding beyond to Le Châtelier Lock is to lock from seaward between three and two hours before HW. Non-stop this should allow time to reach Le Châtelier before the level starts to fall. If unsure first call the lock-keeper to establish deadlines for lock entry. (See *L'Ecluse du Châtelier* page 225.)

From the Barrage to St Suliac (3·5M)
Once clear of the prohibited zone the channel follows a mid river course. The only obstacle to be overcome is the reef close N of Pointe de Concavel. The position of its E cardinal beacon is misleading.

Anchorage is prohibited N of Les Zèbres port beacon tower except for a small area indicated on *4233* and there is a prohibited area on either side of a pipeline which crosses by Ile Chevret, and is marked by beacons. There are also three seaplane landing areas in which anchoring is prohibited.

Anchorages and moorings
With the prohibitions above in mind, it is possible to anchor almost anywhere outside the channel where depth allows. However it is advisable to get as close to shore as possible and to avoid the headlands where the currents are

Typical River Rance scenery. Yachts in Anse de St Hélier a mile S of the Barrage

III North Brittany: 1 Cancale to Trégastel-Ste Anne

strong. The bays are often filled with local boats at moorings but there are sometimes white mooring buoys with no names or numbers on them that are available for visitors. The following are possible anchorages:

1. Anse de Montmarin at the S end of the bay in 4m or closer in. Good landing slip near the hotel reserved for patrons.
2. In the pool N of Ile Chevret in 2m+.
3. In the bay of the S of Ile Harteau.
4. In the bay between Pointe de Langrognais and Pointe du Thon. There are many moorings here and it is difficult to get out of the strong current. Slip and yacht yard. Restaurant at Minihic up the hill.
5. Off St Suliac in 1m+. There are visitors' moorings in 2m off the slip and anchoring is good in mud (see below).

The two bridges viewed from S, pylons are just visible beyond

the river is crossed by power cables and two bridges. The minimum clearance under the most southerly bridge is charted as '20m vertical clearance above high water.'

ST SULIAC

SUPPLIES AND SERVICES
 Bureau du Port ☏ 02 99 58 48 80 (La Mairie)
 Moorings 105 deep water moorings; 2-4 visitors' moorings (Yellow/Orange); 110 drying moorings;
 Water and electricity Ashore S of slip
 WCs at campsite
 Shops Basic shops in the village
 Restaurants La Boucanière (☏ 02 33 15 06 35)
  Guenyuette beach restaurant (S of slipway)
 SNSM lifeboat covering La Rance is based at St Suliac

St Suliac is a charming riverside village with a scattering of basic shops, a restaurant and créperie. There is a good dinghy landing slip but at low levels it dries to soft mud off its end.

From St Suliac to Le Châtelier Lock (6M)

From St Suliac the chart will be needed as the winding channel becomes buoyed and needs to be followed carefully as depths decrease.

2M up on the west side is a pool of deeper water around Port St Hubert. Here it is possible to anchor if necessary and remain afloat but the current runs hard. At this point

PLOUËR-SUR-RANCE
Port de Plaisance

Located one mile S of Port St Hubert and on the W bank (48°31'·5N 01°1'·5W) (See insert on plan page 222)

COMMUNICATIONS
 Bureau du Port: ☏ 02 96 86 83 15 (when office open)
  Manageress: Liliane
  Email plouer.portplaisance@wanadoo.fr
 VHF Ch 9

SUPPLIES AND SERVICES
 Showers, WCs, laundry Next to marina office
 Water and electricity On pontoons
 Drying out Two spaces for drying out alongside the slipway are available for maintenance. Subject to prior arrangement with marina office
 Boatyards
  Estuaire Marine Services, Le Port ☏ 02 96 86 89 39
  Saint Samson Plaisance, Le Port ☏ 02 96 86 95 90
 Restaurants Café Restaurant La Cale de Mordreuc (on slipway) ☏ 02 96 83 20 43
  www.lacaledemordreuc.fr *Email* lacale22@orange.fr
  In village opposite church: Les Causettes ☏ 02 96 86 89 86
  La Gargotte ☏ 02 96 86 99 87
 Shops in Plouër-sur-Rance village (30 minutes' walk) or taxi. The marina office will take orders the evening before for supplying bread and pastries in the morning
 Bike hire Marina office
 Taxi Taxi Direct ☏ 02 96 27 15 87

St Suliac has visitors' moorings, a handful of shops, restaurants and a sailing club

This development of the pond in one of the Rance's old tide mills offers mooring for 240 yachts in a peaceful rural setting. 10 places are reserved for visitors and maximum boat size is 12m length and 1·6m comfortable draught. Minimum depth maintained is 2·0m.

Approach and entry

Identify conspicuous Plouër church spire and align with entrance on 284°.

The channel lies between port and starboard stick beacons. Entry is over a narrow hinged gate which drops when the level has reached 8·2m. Then there will be 1·5m over the gate. Lights and a depth gauge are displayed by the gate.

Cancale to Cap Fréhel

Plouër-sur-Rance. Port de Plaisance looking SE

Marina entrance

Signals
R   Gate closed
RR   Gate out of service
RG   Gate maneuvering
G   Gate open

Waiting buoys (White)
V1 and V2 are located outside the entrance.
Arrival Point
End of Pontoon B.

Continuing in the channel along the west bank you come to Pointe du Chêne Vert with its splendid tower off which is a starboard pole beacon. On the opposite bank is the hamlet of Mordreuc with a slipway. Small craft dry out alongside or on moorings in the river. There is a restaurant, La Cale de Mordreuc, at the top of the slipway with a reputation for excellent home cooking. The nearest shops are in Pleudihen (1·5M).

Pointe and Tour du Chêne Vert

Mordreuc. It is possible to dry out alongside the substantial cale or on the shore either side

The last leg between Mordreuc and the lock at Le Châtelier is narrow and twists and turns between mud banks. There is one bridge, the Lessard viaduct (clearance 18·9m) half a mile before the lock.

The Lessard Viaduct

L'ECLUSE DU CHÂTELIER

Arriving early lie alongside the wall outside the gate (E side). The sill is 6·43m above datum and the lock operates when there is 8·5m rise on the river side (10m at St Suliac). The chamber is 39m long and 7·9m wide. Lines are provided. Expect some turbulence. The road bridge over the lock swings open to accommodate masts.

Operating hours (during season) 0700–2100
☎ 02 96 39 55 66

L'Ecluse de Châtelier from the canal (right)

III North Brittany: 1 Cancale to Trégastel-Ste Anne

La Rance. Le Lyvet looking ESE. The swing bridge is opening to let the yacht in the lock through

Approaching the Port de Dinan. Mooring is on the W bank alongside a walkway and finger pontoons

Canal d'Ille-et-Rance: Port de Lyvet to Dinan (3M)

PORT DE LYVET MARINA

DEPTHS
  Marina quay 1·8m, Bassin 2m
  Canal d'Ille-et-Rance 1·3m to 1·6m (seasonal)
  Dinan (visitors' berths) 1·6m
USEFUL CONTACTS
  L'Ecluse du Châtelier ① 02 96 39 55 66
  Bureau du Port ① 02 96 83 35 57,
  Email portdelyvet@orange.fr
  Open 1000–1200, 1500–1700 during season
SUPPLIES & SERVICES
Berths 254 including 35 visitors (max length 15m)
Water and electricity on pontoons
Showers, WCs ashore
Restaurant Le Livet Gourmand (on quay) ① 02 96 41 45 48

Le Lyvet is a peaceful canalside marina which is popular as a winter base. There are no shops but these will be found in La Vicomté-sur-Rance 1·5M. Its position is on E bank 100m S of Le Châtelier lock.

Before embarking on the 3M stretch of canal to Dinan, it is recommended to obtain updated information on depths from the lock-keeper and Commandant du Port. In April 2013 the author found depths of 1·3m in places and dredging was taking place.

The channel is marked by port and starboard beacons and buoys. Black and white horizontal striped buoys indicate the borders of shallow areas. On departure from Le Lyvet these are left to starboard but sound carefully.

Port de Lyvet

PORT DE DINAN

USEFUL CONTACTS
  Capitainerie ① 02 96 39 56 44
  0800–1900 during season
  0900–1200, 1400–1800 out of season

Berths
100 including 30 for visitors. At Dinan there are quays and a pontoon with short (6m) fingers on the W bank. All are crowded in the summer and there is a steady stream of vedettes when the lock is open.

Facilities
Water and electricity on the pontoons, water taps on the quays; showers, heads and launderette at the Bureau du Port; crane for masts up to 400kg; restaurants and shops, some on the quay otherwise it is a steep climb up the hill through cobbled streets and medieval houses to the main town where there is an abundance.

Travel
Buses and railway to Rennes. Airports Rennes and Dinard.

History
Dinan has a far longer and more important history than its almost-namesake Dinard. The centre of the town has many ancient houses and the ramparts date back to the 13th century. The church of St Sauveur is well worth a visit for its Gothic extravagance and there are many other medieval gems to be seen. The ubiquitous Duchesse Anne, twice Queen of France to different kings, had connections with the town.

La Rance to Biscay via inland waterways

This 140M route across Brittany follows Canal d'Ille-et-Rance and R. Vilaine. It consists of 60 locks and minimum depths of 1·2m with headroom beyond Dinan of about 2·5m. See *Inland Waterways of France* David Edwards-May (Imray).

Steep cobbled lanes lead up from the port to the old town

Cancale to Cap Fréhel

ST BRIAC-SUR-MER
Ile des Hébihens, St Jacut

48°37'·08N 02°08'·23W (Light pillar Dir.Iso.WRG.4s10m)
7M W of St Malo. See plan page 228

TRAVEL
Sea
  Ferry: St Malo
Air
  Dinard Pleurtuit Airport
Road
  30 minutes from St Malo via Barrage de la Rance

CHARTS
  BA 2700 Approaches to Saint-Malo (1:15 000)
  BA 3659 Cap Fréhel to Iles Chausey (1:50 000)
  SHOM 7129 Du Cap Fréhel à Saint-Briac-sur-Mer (1:20 000)
  SHOM 7130 Abords de Saint-Malo - De l'île des Hébihens à la Pointe de la Varde (1:15 000)
  SHOM 7155 Du Cap Fréhel à la Pointe du Grouin – Approches de Saint-Malo (1:48 800)

RADIO
  VHF Ch 09 or 16 (occasional)

TIDAL INFORMATION
  Standard port: St Malo
  Difference: Within 5 minutes and 0·2m

MHWS	MLWS	MHWN	MLWN
12·0	1·4	9·1	4·1

USEFUL CONTACTS
  Harbourmaster (Bureau du Port) ☎ 02 99 88 01 75 (Monday–Saturday 0830–1000)
  Office de Tourisme ☎ 02 99 88 32 47
  Email info@tourisme-saint-briac.fr
  Ecole de Voile ☎ 02 99 88 92 66

SUPPLIES AND SERVICES
Visitors berths Few. Contact Bureau du Port.
Water, toilets and showers W side of Anse de St Briac beach (Le Bechet)
A good selection of shops and restaurants in the town

St Briac is a traditional seaside resort popular with the family holiday maker. It is not a yachting destination but the drying sandy bay is crammed with small craft during the season. A yacht may find fine weather anchorage in 1m or more at neaps at the entrance to the bay. It is open to the NW when better shelter would be found on the W side of the Baie de Lancieux at St Jacut or E of Ile des Hébihens (see plan page 228).

Approach and entrance

This needs a large scale chart of the area *SHOM 7129* is the best.

The approach from ⊕93 is on the leading line of 125° – the white sector of the light pillar at the top of the bay by the bridge (Dir.Iso.WRG.4s10m). It passes between Ile Agot in the NE and Ile des Hébihens in the SW and is well marked with port and starboard beacons.

Le Bechet at low tide

St Briac looking NW

III North Brittany: 1 Cancale to Trégastel-Ste Anne

The anchorage off Ile des Hébihens
Tom Vallois

228 CHANNEL ISLANDS, CHERBOURG PENINSULA & NORTH BRITTANY

Cancale to Cap Fréhel

Anchorages

Between St Briac-sur-Mer and Cap Fréhel to the west are three wide shallow bays – Baie de Lancieux, Baie de L'Arguenon and Baie de la Fresnaie. Their southern halves dry out to expansive areas of flat sand with few landing places. There are also restricted areas due to mussel beds.

Nearer the coast are several drying anchorages worth exploring with large scale chart *SHOM 7129* (Cap Fréhel to St Briac-sur-Mer).

ILE DES HÉBIHENS

48°37'·44N 02°11'·35W

This islet 2M W of St Briac has an attractive anchorage off its SE corner given sufficient water. It is sheltered from N–NW winds. The island is privately owned and landing is restricted. Anchoring is limited to E of a line between La Charbotière E cardinal beacon in the S and Les Jumeliaux in the N (see plan).

PORT DU CHÂTELET, ST JACUT-DE-LA-MER

48°35'·90N 02°10'·92W

This popular holiday resort on St Jacut peninsula is about 2M S of Ile des Hébihens. On its E side are two miniscule drying harbours with extensive mooring areas outside. It is well sheltered from westerlies.

Port du Châtelet is opposite the town but a good walk up to shopping areas. Cale de la Houle Causseul to the N is now silted up and may only be regarded as a landing place.

Port du Châtelet

La Houle Causseul

ST CAST

48°38'·4N 02°14'·5W 4M SE of Cap Fréhel

TRAVEL
Sea
  St Malo (Condor Ferries, Brittany Ferries) – 10M
Air
  Dinard Airport (Aurigny Air Services, Ryanair) – 8M
Bus
  Tibus www.tibus.fr

CHARTS
  BA 3659 Cap Fréhel to Iles Chausey (1:50 000)
  Imray C33B Channel Islands and North Coast of France*
  Imray 2510 North Brittany Chart Atlas*
    *both include plan: Saint-Cast-Le-Guildo (1:20 000)
  SHOM 7129 Du Cap Fréhel à Saint-Briac-sur-Mer (1:20 000)
  SHOM 7155 Du Cap Fréhel à la Pointe du Grouin -
    Approches de Saint-Malo (1:48 800)

RADIO
  VHF Ch 09 (0900–1200, 1400–1800; in season 0800–2100)

USEFUL CONTACTS
  Bureau du Port ☎ 02 96 81 04 43
    Email stcast.plaisance@cotesdarmor.cci.fr
  St Cast Signal Station ☎ 02 96 41 85 30
  Office de Tourisme ☎ 02 96 41 81 52

TIDAL INFORMATION
MHWS	MLWS	MHWN	MLWN
12·0	1·4	9·1	4·1

Minimum depth: 2m

SUPPLIES AND SERVICES
Marina
Pontoon berths 800
Visitors 40 on pontoons
Visitors' moorings Pontoon D marked V
Carénage (drying out) Pontoon F inner end
Hard standing 20-ton boat hoist
Fuel Inner end of fishing pontoon G 24h
WiFi access
Sanitary block Bureau du Port
Centre Nautique Sailing activity on the beach
Restaurant Le P'tit Mousse Restaurant
Le Café Face ☎ 02 96 41 65 62
Town
Chandleries
  Cooperative Maritime ☎ 02 99 82 81 93
  Comptoir de la Mer Le Port ☎ 02 96 41 88 24
Restaurants
  Les Halles ☎ 02 96 41 65 01, La Marinière ☎ 02 96 41
Shops numerous in St Cast-Guildo
Taxis ☎ 02 96 41 86 16 / 02 96 41 72 72

An ambitious project to transform a small drying harbour into a state of the art marina complex is ongoing at St Cast, 10M west of St Malo.

It is well sheltered and straightforward to access at any time without tidal limitations. This is an ideal stop for the sailing family wanting a few days ashore with some beach activity or any yacht planning to visit this area that is looking for a secure base with flexible entry and exit times.

Approach and Entry

Approach from the north

Make for a position one mile east of Cap Fréhel, then shape a course down the eastern side of the peninsula keeping at least one mile off. This will pass Pointe et Fort de la Latte (conspic) and Pointe de St Cast. The only coastal hazards to be avoided are Banc de l'Etendrée, east of Cap Fréhel, the two Basses north of Pointe de la Latte and Les

III North Brittany: 1 Cancale to Trégastel-Ste Anne

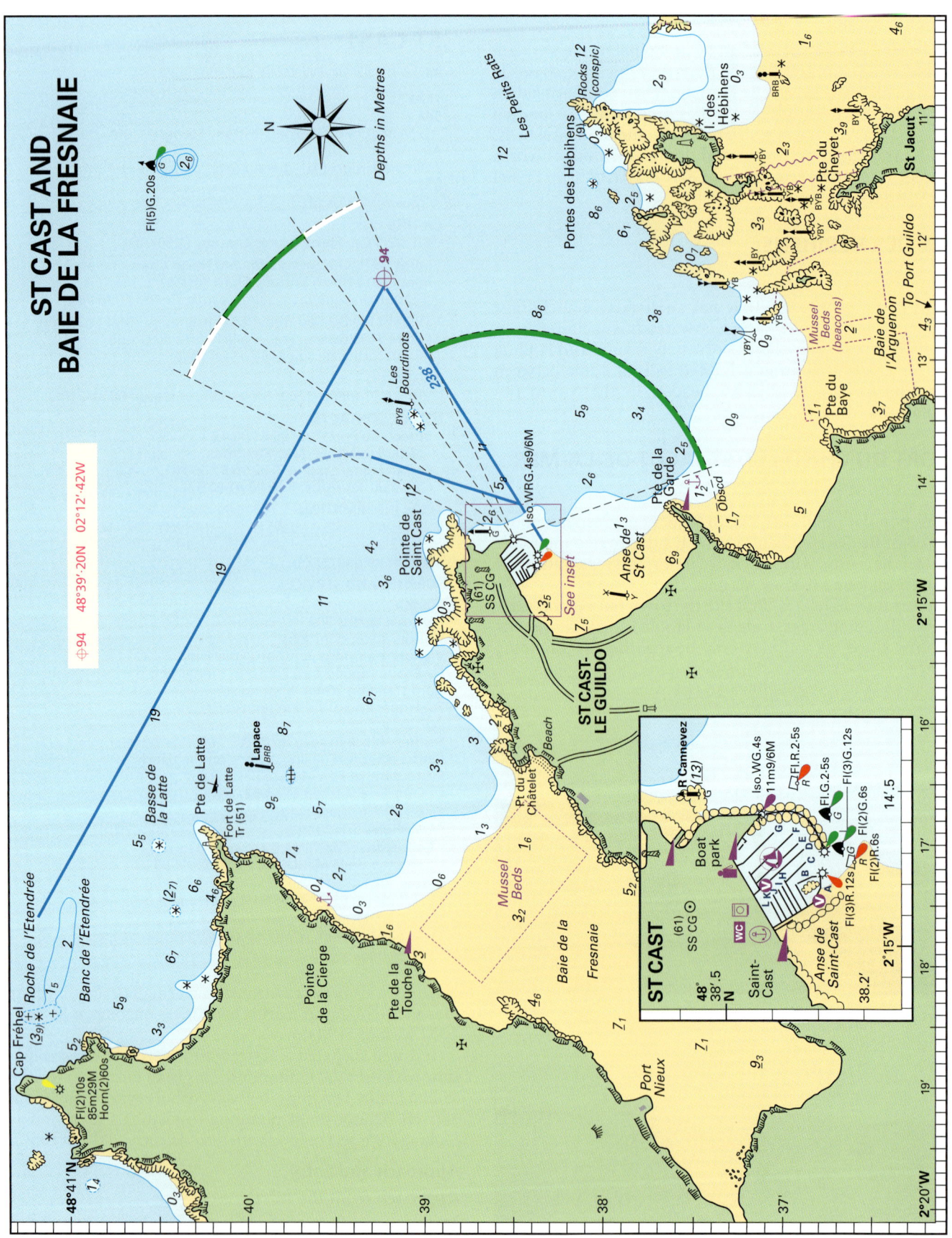

Cancale to Cap Fréhel

Les Bourdinots E cardinal is a key mark in the approach. In the background is Pointe de la Latte

Entry is straightforward

Bourdinots (drying 2m) NE of Pointe de St Cast. This is marked with an E cardinal buoy ⊕94 from where the mole will be seen on a bearing of 238° distant 1·5M.

Approach from the east

Coming from the direction of St Malo via Chenal de la Grande Porte or Passage du Décolle make for a position E of Les Bourdinots E cardinal buoy ⊕94. Then proceed as described above.

Entry

Before entering the buoyed channel visitors should call Port de St Cast on VHF Ch 9 giving length and draught. A marine attendant will escort you to a berth.

By night

End of Mole: Iso.WG.4s11m11/8M, Head of Bec Rond: Fl(3)G.12s, Head of Feuillande: Fl(3)R.12s.

Enter in either of the white sectors. The channel buoys and Les Bourdinots E cardinal buoy are unlit.

The visitors' pontoon

Anchorages

0·5M S of Pointe de Latte

An anchorage well sheltered from westerlies and with good holding in sand. Slipway. Anchorage also possible 200m S of the medieval fort which is worth the climb up from the sea. The tower contains a cannonball factory. Guided tours available.

St Cast Marina from the SE (2009)

III North Brittany: 1 Cancale to Trégastel-Ste Anne

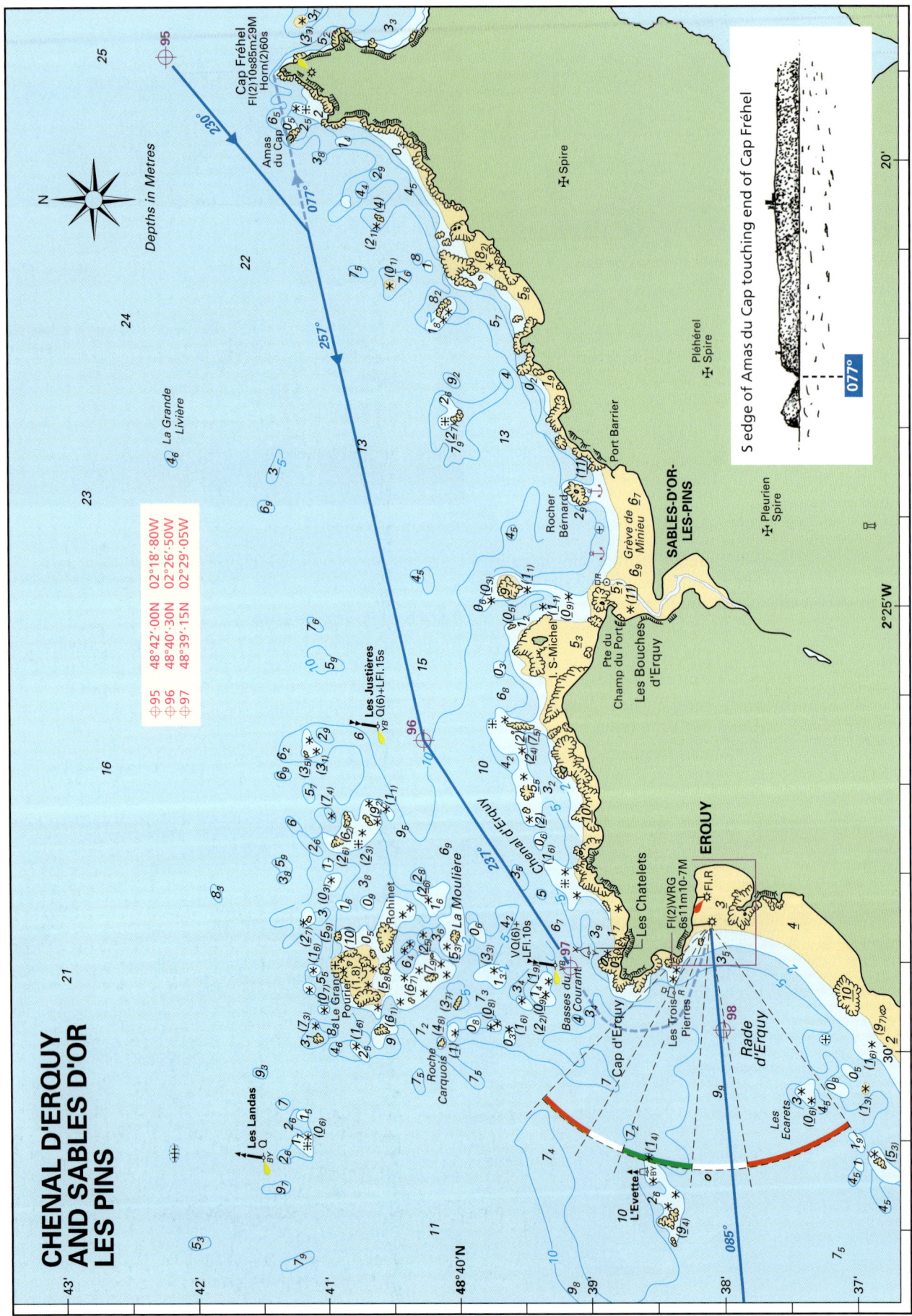

232 CHANNEL ISLANDS, CHERBOURG PENINSULA & NORTH BRITTANY

Erquy to Paimpol (25M)

ERQUY

⊕48°38'·002N 02°28'·76W Vieux Port Pierhead
8M W of Cap Fréhel 5M NE of Dahouët

TRAVEL CONNECTIONS
On land Erquy is most practically reached by road from St Brieuc (14M) which has a stop on the Paris-Brest TGV line.

CHARTS
BA 2029 Ile de Bréhat to Cap Fréhel (1:48 800)
Imray C33B Channel Islands and North Coast of France*
  *includes plan: Erquy (1:20 000)
Imray 2510 North Brittany Chart Atlas*
  *includes plans: Chenal d'Erquy (1:50 000), Erquy (1:20 000)
SHOM 7154 De l'île de Bréhat au Cap Fréhel – Baie de Saint-Brieuc (1:48 800)
SHOM 7310 Baie de Saint-Brieuc (partie Est) – De Dahouët au Cap Fréhel (1:25 000)*
  *includes plan: Port d'Erquy (1:7500)

RADIO
Ch 09 0900–1200 and 1400–1800 in season

TIDAL INFORMATION
Standard port: St Malo
Difference: HW St Malo –0010 LW St Malo –0020

MHWS	MLWS	MHWN	MLWN
11·4	1·5	8·8	4·2

Tidal Streams
HW St Helier –0540 ENE-going
HW St Helier –0045 WSW-going

CONTACTS
Capitainerie ☏ 02 96 72 19 32 / 06 89 75 52
www.ville-erquy.com/fr/port-plaisance.php
Office de Tourisme ☏ 02 96 72 30 12
www.erquy-tourisme.com

SUPPLIES AND SERVICES
Water, Showers, WC Next to Capitainerie Vieux harbour
Fuel Diesel (in cans) from supermarket in town (2·5km)
Restaurants There are four on the quay and more in the town (see Les Ports d'Erquy below)
Chandlery Comptoir de la Mer on the quay
www.comptoirdelamer.com
Regina Plaisance (www.reginaplaisance.com) – in the town
Erquy Guide du Port is online:
www.guide-du-port.com/port-erquy

Les Ports d'Erquy

Since the construction of the Avant Port mole Erquy has become two harbours. The W half of the new port and alongside the E side of the old jetty is reserved exclusively for the fishing fleet. *Plaisanciers* are accommodated in the Vieux Port. Some visitors' moorings are also available on the more exposed E side of the new port. Erquy is a vibrant seaside resort and a major shell fishing port but the reality for the visiting yachtsman is not so good. The port dries at LWS and unless you can take the ground, which is uniformly flat hard sand, the best option might be a short lunchtime stop when weather and tides are right.

It is a snug place in easterlies but should be regarded as totally exposed and prone to swell in winds between W and SSW. The Jetée Ouest provides minimal shelter particularly at HWS.

Finding the shops involves a half mile hike into the town as facilities on the quay are minimal apart from a string of restaurants. Here one can enjoy some of the best seafood Brittany has to offer and keep an eye on your boat at the same time. Le Vivier is reputed to be the best (www.le-vivier-erquy.com). Try also L'Abri des Flots (www.abri-des-flots.fr).

Approach

From E or NW via Chenal d'Erquy

This involves rounding Cap Fréhel and a large rock, Amas du Cap close to the W of it. The coast is then followed down to Cap d'Erquy via Chenal d'Erquy which clears between the reefs extending up to 2·0M off Cap d'Erquy.

Caution

Off Cap Fréhel wind against tide conditions may raise overfalls.

Cap Fréhel is best given a clearance of 1M hence the positioning of ⊕95. *Take up 230° parallel to the coast until the S edge of Amas du Cap is just touching the end of Cap Fréhel and on a bearing 077° (see plan page 232).*

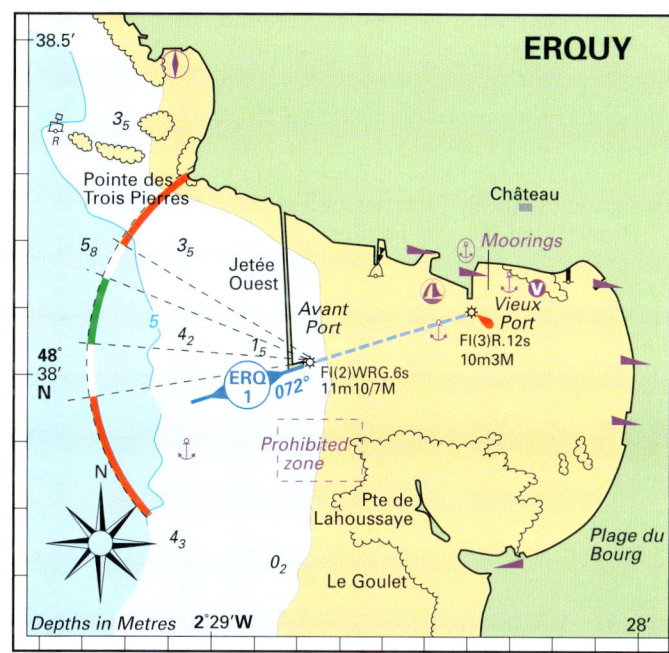

Vieux Port

Hold a course of 257° to ⊕96 S of Les Justières S cardinal buoy at which point alter course to 237° for ⊕97 midway between Cap d'Erquy and Basse du Courant S cardinal buoy.

III North Brittany: 1 Cancale to Trégastel-Ste Anne

Erquy from the W

Keep a good 600m off the Cap. Note the port hand buoy positioned off Pointe des Trois Pierres 0·5M NW of the Avant Port mole.

When the Avant Port (Jetée Ouest) lighthouse bears 120° you are in its northern W sector (see By night) and clear to alter course to the entrance.

From the W (S of Rohein)

Pass 1·5M S of Rohein light tower (YBY) and make good 085°. At night this puts you in the southern W sector of Erquy Avant Port Lt (white tower, red top). (See By night.)

⊕98 is positioned on the rhumbline 0·8M from the light tower on Avant Port (Jetée Ouest) mole.

Note that this approach passes 6·5M S of Plateau des Portes d'Erquy, 1·5W of Cap d'Erquy. It is marked by unlit N cardinal tower l'Evette. Guard being set towards it if navigating with the N setting ebb stream.

If preferred, pass N of this reef or route further S to make entry as from Chenal d'Erquy.

From NW

This part of the bay is less encumbered than the S though the reefs between Rohein and Plateau des Portes d'Erquy still have to be reckoned with – preferably left well to the S.

Entry

Enter harbour with *ERQ1 072° lighthouses in line. This will avoid the prohibited zone to the S*

By night

The best approach is from the west using southern W sector of Jetée Ouest (Avant Port) Fl(2)WRG.6s. Jetée Interieure (Vieux Port) is Fl(3)R.12s.

Anchorage

Yachts must not anchor in the white sector of Jetée Ouest light by day or night. At night an anchor light must be shown.

The recommended anchorage is with the Jetée Ouest light bearing less than 080° and Cap d'Erquy bearing 350°. The bottom is gently shelving and flat so that one can get further inshore with safety at neaps. The part of the harbour inside the inner breakwater mostly dries 3m and is covered with mooring chains.

It would be possible to anchor off the Vieux Port jetty end as shown on plan (but buoy the anchor) and go ashore over HW. The bottom is generally flat firm sand.

Visitors moorings (drying)

There are six buoys (red) situated in the inner harbour (see plan) and additionally several on the extreme E side of the Avant Port which are more exposed and prone to swell. Ground here with caution.

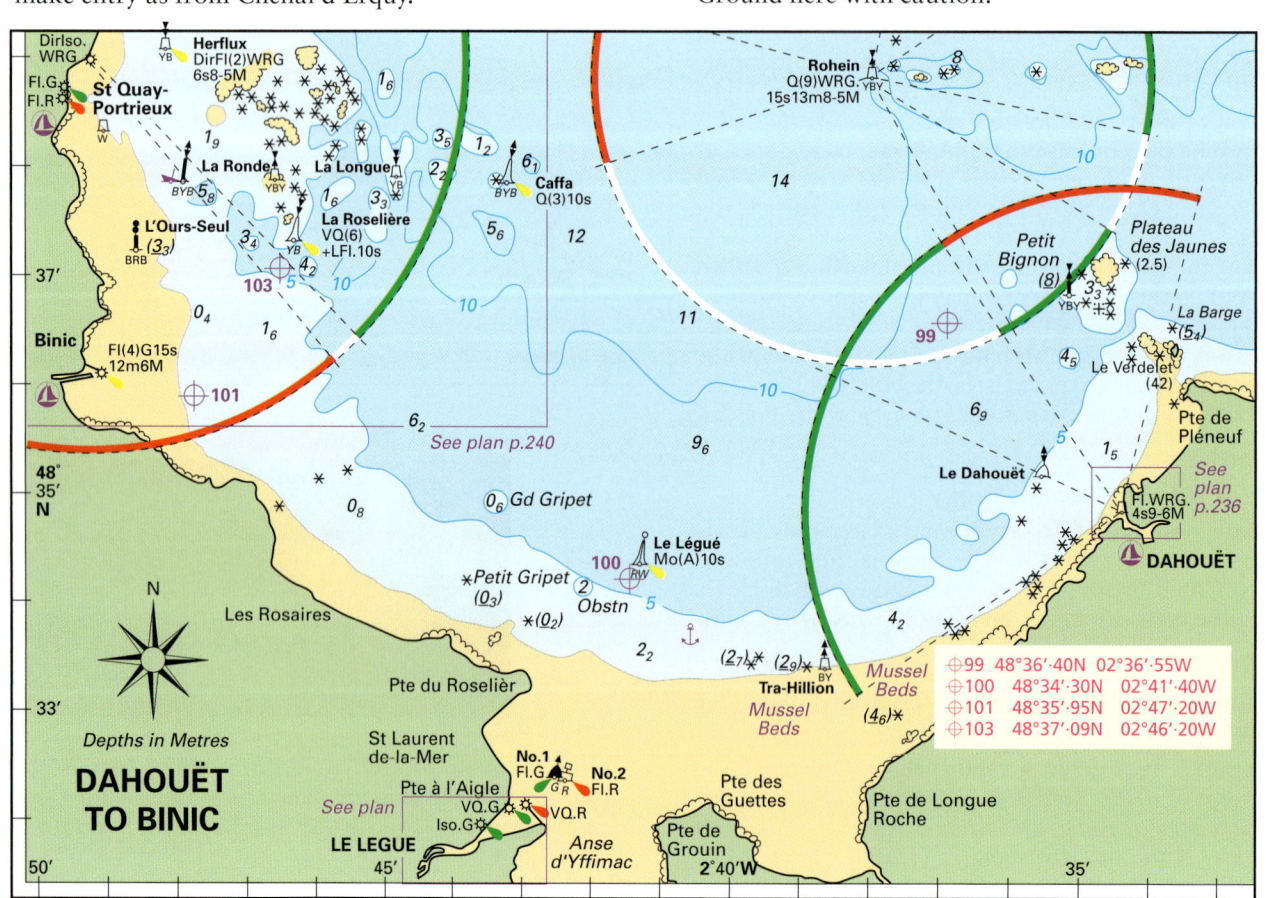

Erquy to Paimpol

DAHOUËT
48°35'·74N 02°34'·17W (Pagoda)
5M SW of Erquy
10M E of Binic

TRAVEL
- Sea
  Ferry: St Malo Condor Ferries
- Air
  St Brieuc airport (35km)
- Train
  Lamballe or St Brieuc – access to TGV
- Road
  Free shuttle between Dahouët-Val-Pleneuf Val Andre – Departs Bureau du Port (seasonal)

See Erquy

CHARTS
BA 2029 Ile de Bréhat to Cap Fréhel (1:48 800)
Imray C33B Channel Islands and North Coast of France*
Imray C34 Cap d'Erquy to Ile de Batz*
Imray 2510 North Brittany Chart Atlas*
  *all include plan: Dahouët (1:10 000)
SHOM 7154 De l'île de Bréhat au Cap Fréhel – Baie de Saint-Brieuc (1:48 800)
SHOM 7310 Baie de Saint-Brieuc (partie Est) – De Dahouët au Cap Fréhel (1:25 000)*
  *includes plan: Port de Dahouët (1:7500)

RADIO
VHF Ch 16/09 over HW during season (range on 09 limited)

TIDAL INFORMATION
Difference on St Malo Standard port
HW St Malo –0010
LW St Malo –0025
HW St Helier –0030

MHWS	MLWS	MHWN	MLWN
11·3	1·3	8·6	4·0

Tidal Streams
HW St Helier – ESE going starts
HW St Helier – W going starts

USEFUL CONTACTS
Bureau du Port ☏ 02 96 72 82 85 / 06 80 07 53 92
  Email portdahouet@pleneuf-val-andre.fr
  www.pleneuf-val-andre.fr
  The Bureau du Port is open around HW
Taxi ☏ 02 96 72 25 04

SUPPLIES AND SERVICES
Marina Water, electricity, showers, hard standing, 10-ton crane.
Fuel (cans) Val Andre 1M
Boatyard Chantier Naval de Port de Dahouët: Quai de Terre-Neuvas
Repairs, mechanic Val Plaisance, Quay du Murier (S Side)
Chandlery Côté Pontons, Marina
Restaurants A few on the Quai Terre Neuvas on the N side of the port

Tucked up an inconspicuous creek at the southern extremity of the east coast of the Baie de St Brieuc is this unusual drying harbour. It might almost be missed were it not for a single N cardinal buoy a mile off the entrance.

There was a time when yachts were deterred from visiting Dahouët due to its lack of facilities and exposure to strong W to NW winds. There was seldom enough space to dry out on the quay and finding supplies involved a walk up the coast to the resort of Pleneuf-Val-André.

Now Dahouët has taken on a new lease of life thanks to the creation of a *bassin à flot* in a sheltered corner at the top of the inlet. Bars, restaurants and a few shops have sprung up on the Quai Terre-Neuvas and providing you do not exceed 12m or draw more than 2·5m you can enjoy the unique atmosphere of this friendly place while your yacht is moored safely alongside a pontoon in the marina.

Historical
In the early 19th century Dahouët was one of the first ports in North Brittany to send three masted barquentines, *terra-neuvas*, to Greenland and the Grand Banks off Newfoundland to fish for cod.

Approaches
WARNING
In strong W-NW winds seas break over the shallow entrance making entry hazardous and causing surge in the harbour. The best time to enter is 2h30m either side of HW assuming a draught of 1·50m.

From the N
Coming from the direction of Cap Fréhel follow directions for Chenal d'Erquy. The conspicuous triangular shaped islet of Le Verdelet off Pointe de Pleneuf will be recognised. This is 1·5M N of Dahouët entrance.

Dahouët looking SE at half-tide

III. NORTH BRITTANY: 1 CANCALE TO TRÉGASTEL-STE ANNE

III North Brittany: 1 Cancale to Trégastel-Ste Anne

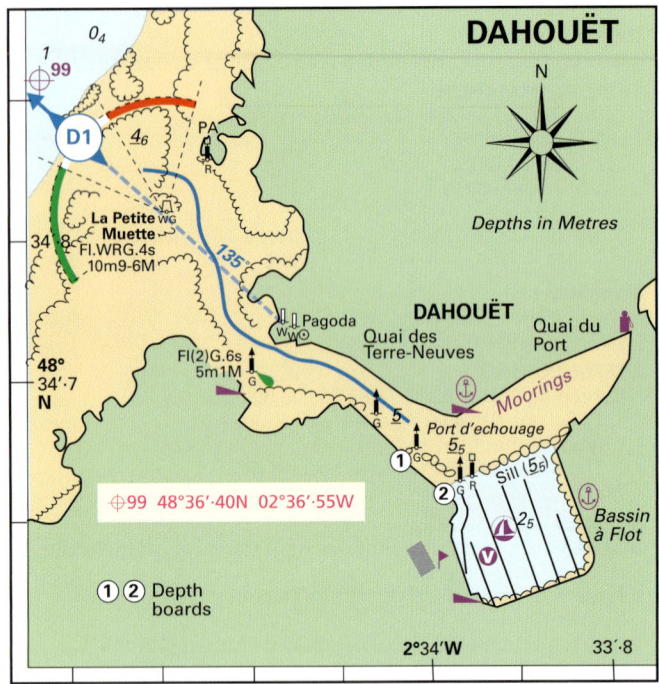

The usual entry is made with transit:

D1 *135°* ⊕*99 La Petite Muette Light Tower (W top G band) aligned with pagoda*

When 50m from the light come to port to commence a turn round N side of the light, returning briefly to original heading towards pagoda. Then head into the entrance leaving:

Two white poles marking edge of slipway close to port.

By night

Entry is made as per day in the W sector of La Petite Muette (Fl.WRG.4s10m9–6M). Beware of unlit N cardinal buoy Le Dahouët at S edge of the W sector.

Leave La Petite Muette 50m to starboard and continue slowly round to 185° on the Fl(2)G.6s which is left to starboard. There are no further lights apart from street and house lights to see the channel.

The channel up the estuary lies midway between N and S quays. Pass midway between the W poles and starboard Lt beacon. There are a further two starboard beacons before the sill. This is crossed between port and starboard beacons, the latter having a depth gauge.

Berthing and moorings

The visitors reception berth is on the western-most pontoon (see plan). There are 20 visitors' berths, max length 12m, max draught 2·5m.

Drying berths

There are several moorings (white buoys) close N of the sill. Use of these is subject to authorisation by the Bureau du Port. Berthing along Quai des Terre-Neuvas is strictly reserved for the fishing fleet.

The entrance looking NW with La Petite Muette

To clear outside Le Verdelet and the Plateau des Jaunes involves a detour. Steer a course to leave Plateau des Portes d'Erquy to the N and Plateau des Jaunes to the S. Entry is made from the NW starting at Le Dahouët N cardinal buoy (⊕99) just under 1·0M off the entrance.

Streams

Note that streams are accelerated to 3 knots off Pointe de Pléneuf and Plateau des Jaunes. The flood is ENE to ESE going and the ebb is reversed.

From the W

From Binic on the W side of the bay the route is comparatively clear. Coming from St Quay-Portrieux the Rochers de St Quay have to be reckoned with. The most southerly danger is La Roselière (dries 3·7m) that is guarded by its S cardinal buoy.

Entry

Depths and guidelines

- The entrance dries at between 4·5m close NW of La Petite Muette to 5·2m just short of the marina sill
- The sill dries at 5·5m retaining a minimum depth in the bassin of 2·5m
- Access over the sill is 2h30mins either side of HW for a draught of 1·5m

Dahouët marina entrance   *Peter Taylor*

ST BRIEUC - LE LÉGUÉ

49°32'·12N 02°42'·88W (NE Jetty Lt)
6M WSW of Dahouët
6M SE of Binic

TRAVEL
Air
  St Brieuc Airport – approximately 3·0M
Train
  St Brieuc Station – on the main TGV line, approximately 2·0M
Road
  Close to motorway
  Bus: Le Légué – St Brieuc
  Taxi: 06 07 57 82 46 / 06 80 48 85 23
  Office du Tourisme: 02 96 33 32 50
  www.baiedestbrieuc.com

CHARTS
  BA 2029 Ile de Bréhat to Cap Fréhel (1:48 800)*
    *includes plan: Port Saint-Brieuc Le Légué (1:10 000)
  Imray C34 Cap d'Erquy to Ile de Batz*
  Imray 2510 North Brittany Chart Atlas*
    *both include plan: Port du Légué (1:20 000)
  SHOM 7154 De l'île de Bréhat au Cap Fréhel –
    Baie de Saint-Brieuc (1:48 800)*
    *includes plan: Port de Saint-Brieuc Le Légué (1:10 000)

RADIO
  VHF Ch 12, 16 ±1h 30mins HW

TIDAL INFORMATION
  Differences:
  St Malo: Standard port
  HW St Malo –0010
  LW St Malo –0020
  St Helier –0030

MHWS	MLWS	MHWN	MLWN
11·4	1·4	8·8	4·0

Tidal Streams
  HW St Helier –0430 S going stream starts
  LW St Helier –0000 N going stream starts

USEFUL CONTACTS
  Harbourmaster, Port du Légué ☏ 02 96 33 35 41
  Port de Plaisance ☏ 02 96 77 49 84 / 06 75 91 67 86
  Lock (opening hours) ☏ 02 96 61 70 86

SUPPLIES AND SERVICES
Bassin à flot No.2
  20 visitors berths, max length 18m, max draught 3m.
Water and electricity occasional points on quay, showers
  Chandlery, boatyard, engineers, electricians, divers.
Fuel on quay N side
Internet access/WiFi available
Restaurants, bars Several bars and a few modest restaurants on
  N & S quays.
Market (St Brieuc) Wednesday

This extensive harbour with its wide quays and boatyards is foremost the commercial port for the nearby regional capital of St Brieuc.

Despite efforts by the local Chamber of Commerce to promote Le Légué as a yachting destination it is primarily a commercial port and should not be compared with the marinas further up the coast.

It does however offer a comprehensive range of professional services nearby that may be of interest to yacht owners. These include refits, restorations, repairs and fabrications. It it also a secure base for long term stays and lay ups.

St Brieuc is an interesting city with good connections by air and rail (TGV) a mile from the port.

Entrance to Le Légué

III North Brittany: 1 Cancale to Trégastel-Ste Anne

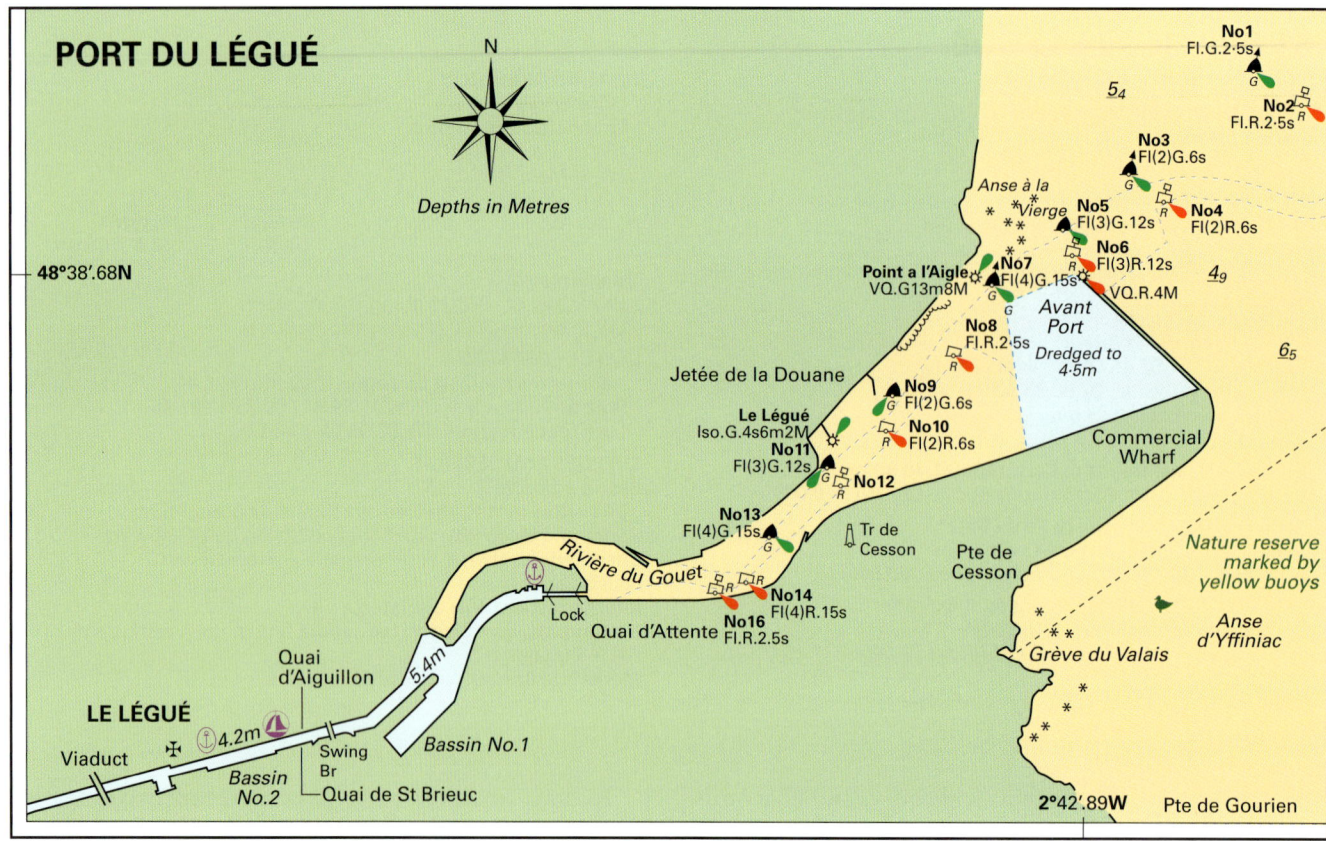

Historical

The inundation of the Baie de St Brieuc by the sea has only occurred in the last 2,000 years. In Roman times forests and cultivated land existed where there is now only drying sand out in the bay.

Le Tour de Cesson, on the hill above the entrance at its narrowest part, was built originally in 1395 but has been blown up, knocked down and rebuilt over the centuries.

St Brieuc is an old cathedral town named after the Celtic monk who arrived with his disciples in the 5th century and converted the district to Christianity. Much of the cathedral is 13th and 14th century.

Le Légué was formerly the base for a fleet of *goëlettes*, the fine two-masted topsail schooners that fished off Greenland and Iceland until the last century.

Approach (see plan page 234)

WARNING

During strong northerlies seas break across the head of the bay and entry should not be attempted.

The entrance to Le Légué, the River Gouët, is at the southernmost limit of navigation. At LWS the bay dries out up to 2·0M off the coast so an approach should only be made on a rising tide to coincide with lock opening. Anchorage in offshore winds is shown on plan page 234.

Lock opens relative to height of tide at St Malo (at local HW)

Up to 9·4m	±1h00
9·4m to 10·3m	±1h15
10·3m to 10·8m	±1h30
Above 10·8m	−2h to +1h30m

From ⊕100 or Le Légué landfall buoy (RW pillar, Mo(A)12s) make 202° with sufficient rise of tide and proceed down the buoyed channel. No.1 starboard buoy (Fl.G.2.5s), No.2 port buoys (Fl.R.2.5s), Pointe d'Aigle jetty head (White tower, green top VQ.G) and Custom House jetty (White column, green top Iso.G.4s) will assist. Proceed up the channel, crossing to the S shortly after passing Tour de Cesson, to the lock gates. The sill dries 5·1m and the locks work HW ±1–2 hours. Vessels may secure to the S wall immediately outside to wait.

Bassin 2 looking E. Quai d'Aiguillon left, Quai de St Brieuc right

Erquy to Paimpol

Passerelle (mobile footbridge) opens to provide access to the W end of the harbour

Locking out

Restaurants on Quai d'Aiguillon

Entry and berthing

The lock is 85m long and 14m wide. The tide gauge on the N side of the entrance indicates depth over the sill, the one on the S side depth above CD.

Turbulence in the lock is noticeable when the gates open so a delay in entering is advisable.

Bassin No.1 on the port hand after leaving the lock is commercial. Bassin No.2 is formed by the canalised part of Rivière de Gouet and is entered through a low swing bridge (*pont tournant*) which opens around lock opening. Proceed through it and towards the viaduct to find a berth alongside the wall preferably on the N side where the shops and cafés are situated (see photograph).

By night

As not all the buoys are lit, a first-off night entry would be unwise until familiar with daylight entry

III North Brittany: 1 Cancale to Trégastel-Ste Anne

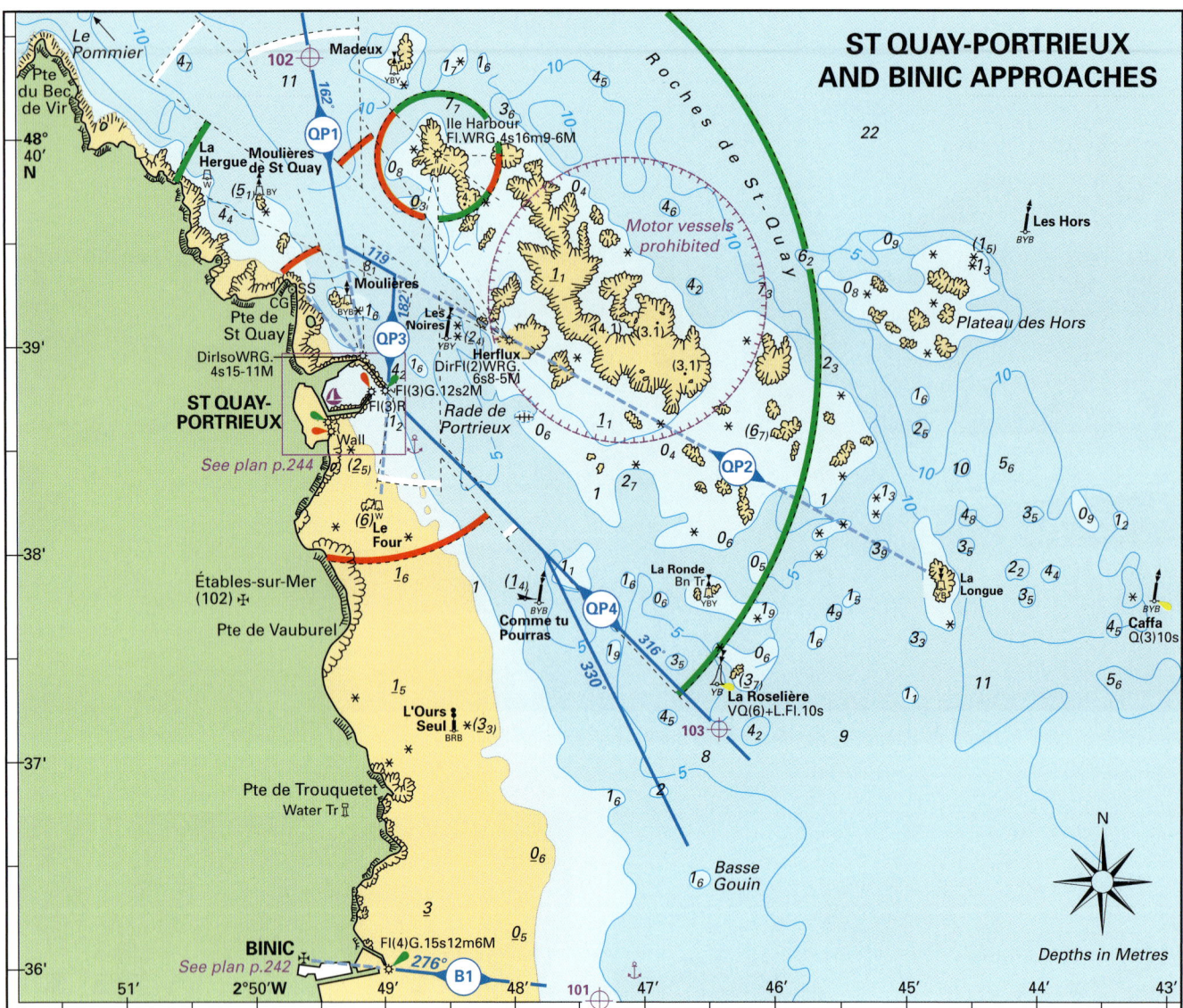

⊕ 101	48°35'·95N	02°47'·20W
⊕ 102	48°40'·51N	02°49'·83W
⊕ 103	48°37'·09N	02°46'·20W

Erquy to Paimpol

BINIC

48°36'·068N 02°48'·92W (Mole de Penthièvre porthand light)
6M NW of Le Légué
3M S of St Quay-Portrieux

TRAVEL
As for St Quay-Portrieux.
Bus to St Brieuc
Taxi
Videment 02 96 71 93 22

CHARTS
BA 2029 Ile de Bréhat to Cap Fréhel (1:48 800)
Imray C33B Channel Islands and North Coast of France*
Imray C34 Cap d'Erquy to Ile de Batz*
Imray 2510 North Brittany Chart Atlas*
*all include plan: Binic (1:12 500)

SHOM 7128 Baie de Saint-Brieuc (Partie Ouest) – De la Pointe de la Tour à l'Anse d'Yffiniac (1:25 000)*
*includes plan: Port de Binic (1:7500)

SHOM 7154 De l'île de Bréhat au Cap Fréhel – Baie de Saint-Brieuc (1:48 800)

RADIO
VHF Ch 09 (working hours)

TIDAL INFORMATION
Differences:
HW St Malo – 0008
LW St Malo – 0025
HW St Helier – 0030

MHWS	MLWS	MHWN	MLWN
11·4	1·3	8·6	4·0

USEFUL CONTACTS
Bureau du Port ☏ 02 96 73 61 86
Email port@ville-binic.fr www.ville-binic.fr
Office de Tourisme Ave Général de Gaulle ☏ 02 96 73 60 12
Doctor ☏ 02 96 69 20 20

SUPPLIES AND SERVICES
Marina 60 visitors' berths. Max length 25m, Draught 2m. Laundry. WiFi. 10-ton crane.
Water and electricity at pontoons
Fuel visitors pontoon E end (see plan)
Showers next to Bureau du Port
Chandlery Marin Ocean, Ave Foch
Restaurants a good range to suit all pockets, including Le Bistro du Port, L'Avant Port
Market Thursday
Shops Boulangérie Jacob, Place de l'Eglise

This harbour is situated in a shallow indentation on the W side of the Baie de St Brieuc enjoying shelter from all but easterly winds. Surprisingly Binic has retained a peaceful unhuried atmosphere over the years challenged only by *La Morue en Fête* – a week long annual event in early summer that celebrates the town's historic links with the cod fishing industry of the 19th and early 20th century.

The marina is conveniently close to the town with bars and cafés alongside and traditional village shopping in the narrow streets behind. Immediately south, over the wall, is an excellent bathing beach – Plage de la Blanche.

History

Binic used to be a considerable port and was the first to break the Basque monopoly of the Newfoundland cod fishery. Hundreds of *terres-neuvas* made the round trip of several months each year to the fishery and then to the south of France to sell their catches.

Approach

The tide retreats up to a mile at LWS exposing flat sands. There are no obstacles apart from Basse Gouin rock (1·6m at datum) and oyster beds in the same area. With sufficient rise of tide approach with transit:

B1 *276° ⊕101 Church spire and Pier head in line*

Binic

III North Brittany: 1 Cancale to Trégastel-Ste Anne

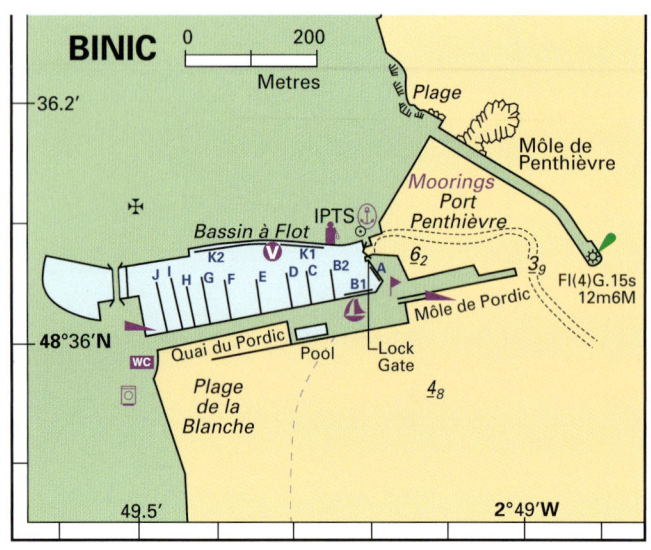

Lock and Bureau du Port

Entry
Round the pierhead close and follow its inner side up to the bend before heading towards the gate. Keep clear of local boats on private moorings in the Avant Port. It is possible to lie alongside the N wall (max length 15m) while waiting for the gate. It dries here at 4·5m and the bottom is sand and thick mud. Plenty of fixing points and several ladders.

By night
Môle de Penthièvre Fl(4)G.15s12m6M.

Marina

Gate
The gate opens when the tide rises to 8·5m and stays open until HW or beyond depending on the height of the tide. On large springs this may be up to HW+2h giving an opening period of 4h.

The gate closes when the level has fallen to 9m. It cannot operate on small tides when the unwary can be 'neaped' in the marina for a day or two.

The table below shows approximate opening periods. These are based on the standard atmospheric pressure (1013 h Pa) and fluctuations of up to 45 minutes can occur. To verify times call port on ☎ 029673 61 86 or VHF Ch 09.

Coefficient
45	<8·7m	No entry, no exit (neaped)
46–56	8·7m–9·5m	HW -45 to HW
55–60	9·5m–10m	HW -1h to HW+1h
60–80	10m–11m	HW -1h30 to HW+1h45
>80	>11	HW -1h45 to HW+2h

Signals
Red and green lights control entry and exit:
Lights off: Port closed
3 reds: Wait
3 greens: Passage authorised
Flashing red: Warning

A timetable of opening is displayed outside the harbour office. There is a sliding bridge by the gate which is opened by the harbourmaster.

View E towards lock

Berthing
There are 60 visitors' berths either side on the first pontoon inside the gate (max 10m) or alongside the long pontoon running along the N wall (max 15m). Depths in the basin vary from 2·5m near the gate to 1·5m further in.

There are no provisions for visitors on the moorings in the Avant Port.

Anchorage
In westerly or settled weather an anchorage may be selected in a suitable depth of water anywhere off the port except in the vicinity of Basse Gouin (1·6m at datum) and *parcs à huitres* (oyster beds)

The long pontoon by the N wall

ST QUAY-PORTRIEUX
Port d'Armor Marina & Vieux Port

48°38'·83N 02°48'·90W (Light tower head of Môle Est)
3M N of Binic
9M S of L'Ost Pic lighthouse

TRAVEL
Air
  St Brieuc Airport 7M
Train
  The nearest station is St Brieuc on the Paris-St Malo-Brest TGV line
Road
  Paimpol 13M

CHARTS
  BA 2029 Ile de Bréhat to Cap Fréhel (1:48 800)
  Imray C33B Channel Islands and North Coast of France*
  Imray C34 Cap d'Erquy to Ile de Batz*
    *both include plan: St-Quay-Portrieux (1:25 000)
  Imray 2510 North Brittany Chart Atlas*
    *includes plans Rade de Portrieux (1:50 000), St-Quay-Portrieux (1:25 000)
  SHOM 7128 Baie de Saint-Brieuc (Partie Ouest) – De la Pointe de la Tour à l'Anse d'Yffiniac (1:25 000)*
    *includes plan: Port de Saint-Quay-Portrieux (1:7500)
  SHOM 7154 De l'île de Bréhat au Cap Fréhel – Baie de Saint-Brieuc (1:48 800)

RADIO
  VHF Ch 09 (24hr) *St Quay-Portrieux*
  VHF Ch 09 (0900-1200, 1330-1730 Mon-Fri) Bureau du Port d'echouage

TIDAL INFORMATION
  Standard port: St Malo
  Differences:
  HW St Malo –0010
  LW St Malo –0035
  HW St Helier –0030

MHWS	MLWS	MHWN	MLWN
11·3	1·4	8·6	4·0

Tidal information
  Streams off St Quay are generally SSE on the flood and NNW on the ebb reaching 3kns.
  HW St Helier -0430 ingoing flood stream starts
  HW St Helier +0115 out going ebb stream starts

USEFUL CONTACTS
  Bureau du Port (Capitainerie) ☏ 02 96 70 81 30
    Night 2000–0700 ☏ 06 63 67 71 77
  Bureau du Port d'echouage ☏ 02 96 70 95 31 / 06 89 105 015
  Doctor Cabinet Médical la Potinière ☏ 02 96 70 54 82

SUPPLIES AND SERVICES
Water and Electricity at pontoons
Shower block Digue Sud (SW corner)
Fuel (diesel, petrol) 24h On reception pontoon below Bureau du Port
Pharmacy Pharmacie de St Quay ☏ 02 96 70 40 27
Bike hire Enquire Bureau du Port
WiFi Accessible within marina
Shops
  Spar supermarket: Quai de la Republique ☏ 02 96 70 40 87
  Boulangerie: Bd du Maréchal Foch ☏ 02 96 70 40 55
Restaurants Bistro La Marine, Quai de la Republique (SE corner of Vieux Port) ☏ 02 96 70 87 38
Market
  Vieux Port: Monday am
  Place de l'Église: Friday am

Port d'Armor Marina

This capacious 1,000 berth deep water marina is accessible at all states of tide, having a minimum depth of between 3m and 4m.

Located half way down the sheltered W side of the Baie de St Brieuc it is well placed for exploring the most popular stretch of the Brittany coast between Paimpol and Ile Bréhat, and the Trieux and Tréguier rivers – all of which are within 25 miles. Three miles S is the attractive little port of Binic with a locked basin in the middle of the town.

St Quay-Portrieux is much used by Channel Islanders for club races and weekend cruising, its main appeal being ease of entry at any time and the assurance of a safe and secure berth on arrival.

St Quay-Portrieux. Port d'Armor Marina

III North Brittany: 1 Cancale to Trégastel-Ste Anne

Alongside the reception and fuel berth. Marina W end

Since opening in 1990 Port Armor has set the standard for a new generation of marinas that are moored out in the depths rather than being a development of existing drying harbours within a town or village setting. Such marinas can be isolated places until the infrastructure has caught up. Prepare for lengthy hikes into the town to find supplies and restaurants.

Approach (see plan page 240)

Approaches are complicated by the extensive Roches de Saint Quay beyond the Rade de Portrieux outside the harbour. There is a good assortment of marks which combined with visibility of at least 3–5 miles and a large scale chart make interesting pilotage exercises.

From the N

From l'Ost Pic lighthouse (see plan page 248) make good 155° towards a position 1M W of Pointe du Bec de Vir ⊕102 (see plan page 240). From here identify the first set of marks:

QP1 162° (⊕102) Moulières de Portrieux E cardinal beacon tower aligned with Lt tower on the bend between Digue Nord and Mole E. At night: Dir.Iso.WRG.4s16m

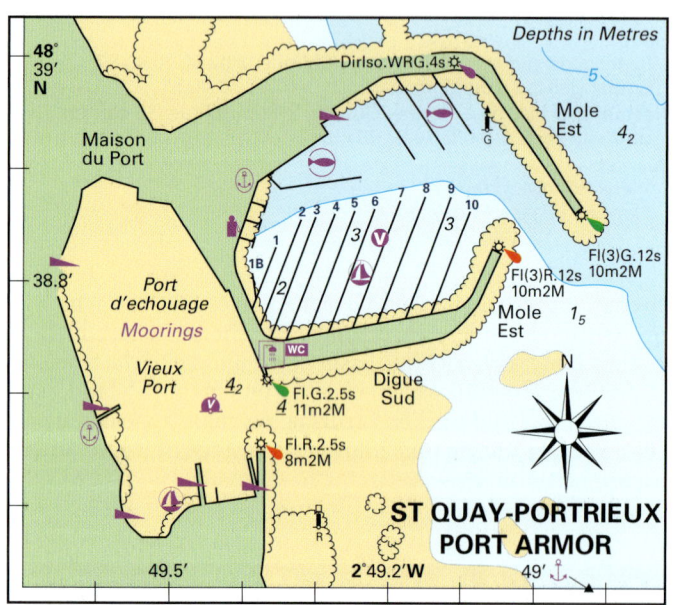

Off St Quay are the Roches de St Quay, with conspicuous Ile Harbour lighthouse Claude Thibault / Alamy Stock Photo

244 CHANNEL ISLANDS, CHERBOURG PENINSULA & NORTH BRITTANY

Erquy to Paimpol

Hold until Pointe de St Quay with its coastguard station is forward of the starboard beam then alter to port onto the next short leg (QP2):

QP2 *119° Herflux Lt tower (W) aligned with La Longue S cardinal beacon tower*

Hold for 0·4M then alter to starboard onto final transit:

QP3 *182° Mole Est Lt tower aligned with Le Four (W)*
Round the head of Môle Est and enter harbour.

From the S

Coming in from the E it is important to identify marks S of Roches du Saint Quay. E–W these are:

- Caffa E cardinal buoy
- Le Longue S cardinal beacon tower
- La Roselière S cardinal buoy – this can be difficult against a low sun.

When 400m abeam (S) of La Roselière, ⊕103, set up approach towards the harbour entrance with transit QP4:

QP4 *316° Breakwater (Mole Est) head Lt tower (G top W base) aligned with CG station*

This line passes:

- La Roselière S cardinal buoy 400m to starboard
- La Ronde W cardinal beacon tower 0·5M to starboard
- Comme tu Pourras E cardinal buoy 300M to port (Note shallow patch 1·1m close E of it).
- Le Four tower (W) 0·25M to port

Entry

During business hours you will normally be met by a marina RIB and led to a berth. Otherwise berth on pontoon 7 or alongside the reception/fuel pontoon below the Bureau du Port for instructions. The N side of the harbour is exclusively the domain of the fishing fleet.

By night

From N by night:

Approach as for 'By day' from ⊕102 (transit QP1) in the white sector of marina elbow light Iso.WRG.4s 162°.

Note that in this red sector you will be too far to starboard, not port. (QP1) Shortly after Herflux light on the port bow (Fl(2)WRG.6s) turns from red to white alter to 119° to bring it ahead and continue until the white sector of Ile Harbour light Oc(2)WRG.6s on the port quarter is entered when turn to 182° (transit QP3) for the breakwater end.

CHANNEL ISLANDS, CHERBOURG PENINSULA & NORTH BRITTANY

III North Brittany: 1 Cancale to Trégastel-Ste Anne

Le Vieux Port

(Fl(3)G.12s to enter the marina. A least depth of 1·3m should be allowed for on this approach.

If continuing S track away SE in the white sector of the breakwater elbow light (Dir.Iso.WRG.4s) making good 138°. This will leave unlit E cardinal buoy Comme tu Pourras 200M to starboard, (Note shallow patch 1·1m at datum close E of it) and La Roselière S cardinal buoy 400m to port.

From S by night
Proceed towards La Roselière buoy to pick up the white sector of the breakwater elbow light Iso.WRG.4s and make good 316°. This passes close to a 1·2m patch; to avoid it, make a small alteration to port into the right hand edge of the red sector until the unlit E cardinal buoy is passed to port when the marina entrance light (Fl(3)R.12s and Fl(3)G.12s can be made for.

If continuing N follow directions for From N by night in reverse sequence.

Le Vieux Port
By contrast, back to back with Port d'Armor is the original Portrieux harbour. With its fine granite piers and period lighthouse it is a reminder of the days when local seamen wintered their *terres-neuvas* bows to the beach at the end of the cod-fishing season off Newfoundland.

It is more favourably located for shops, bars and restaurants. The drying harbour of Portrieux is administered independently of Port d'Armor marina by *La Mairie* (Town Hall).

Access
The harbour dries from 4m at entrance to 5m at N end. The bottom is flat firm sand and mud. On tides of about coefficient 70 (average tide) there is 2m in the entrance 20m after half tide. Access is therefore approximately 3h either side of HW.

Mooring
Eight visitors' buoys, max length 10m.

Chalutiers have first call on drying out alongside walls and this should be considered off limits for *plaisanciers* without authorisation.

Duration of stay: max three days.

Facilities
S of the Vieux Port, La Zone Technique consists of a well equipped boat yard with boat lift, cranes, two slipways and hard standing.

Anchorage
E of old harbour breakwater but clear of entrance the holding is good in sand and mud. Well sheltered from winds between SW and NW and offshore tidal streams.

Café du Port

Erquy to Paimpol

PAIMPOL

48°47'·10N 003°02'·40W
Light ho Head of Jetée de Kernoa
11M NNW of St Quay - Portrieux 4M S of Ile de Bréhat

TRAVEL
Air
   St Brieuc ☎ 02 96 94 95 00
Train
   Regional line connects Paimpol with Pontrieux and Guingamp.
   Le Vapeur du Trieux (Paimpol-Pontrieux) tourist attraction (see Pontrieux) ☎ 08 923 914 27

CHARTS
   BA 2027 Ile Grande to Ile de Bréhat (1:48 700)
   BA 2029 Ile de Bréhat to Cap Fréhel (1:48 800)
   BA 3673 Ile de Bréhat and Anse de Paimpol Entrance to Le Trieux (1:20 000)*
      *includes plan: Port de Paimpol (1:10 000)

   Imray C34 Cap d'Erquy to Ile de Batz*
      *includes plans: Approaches to Rivière de Trieux and Paimpol (1:50 000), Paimpol (1:15 000)
   Imray 2510 North Brittany Chart Atlas:
      5 Approaches to Rivière de Trieux & Paimpol (1:50 000)
      6i Paimpol (1:15 000)

   SHOM 7127 Abords de l'Île de Bréhat – Anse de Paimpol – Entrée du Trieux (1:20 000)*
      *includes plan: Port de Paimpol (1:10 000)
   SHOM 7152 De l'Ile Grande à l'Ile de Bréhat (1:48 700)
   SHOM 7154 De l'île de Bréhat au Cap Fréhel – Baie de Saint-Brieuc (1:48 800)

RADIO
   Ch 09 Capitainerie and Lock – HW ±2h

TIDAL INFORMATION
   Standard port: St Malo or Paimpol
   HW St Malo -0010
   LW St Malo -0035

MHWS	MLWS	MHWN	MLWN
10·8	1·3	8·3	3·8

Tidal Streams based on St. Heller
   A. Between La Jument and Dénou beacon towers:
      HW St Helier -0340 SSE-going starts
      HW St Helier +0405 NNW-going starts
      The maximum rate in each direction is 3½ knots.
   B. At the N end of Chenals Trinité, Lastel and Denou, the S-going stream starts about 15 minutes earlier and the N-going 15 minutes later than the times above.
   C. At the W end of the bay:
      HW St Helier -0515 W-going starts
      HW St Helier +0215 E-going starts
      The maximum rate is 1½ knots

USEFUL CONTACTS
   Bureau du Port ☎ 02 96 20 47 65
   Lock ☎ 02 96 20 90 02
      www.port-paimpol-plaisance.fr
   Taxi Agence Armoricaine ☎ 02 96 20 89 23
   Bureau de Tourisme ☎ 02 96 20 83 16

SUPPLIES AND SERVICES
Boatyard Paimpol Plaisance Quai de Kernoa ☎ 06 32 66 16 69
Chandlery Dauphin Nautic, Quai de Kernoa
Restaurants There is a good selection of eating places around the harbour on both Quai Morand (S) and Quai de Kernoa (E) and in the town
Marina Visitors' berths on pontoons in Bassins 1 and 2 (A)
Water and electricity on quay and at pontoons
Fuel Head of Quai de le Digue (Quai Neuf)
Showers/WC Maison des Plaisanciers next to Capitainerie
There are no accessible beaches.

The port of Paimpol tucked away in the western corner of the Anse de Paimpol four miles in from the open sea offers total shelter behind its lock gates and a chance to enjoy a classic Breton town.

A visit has to fit in with the tides. The whole bay is a sea of mud at LW with only a few fingers of water. To avoid a long wait aim to arrive near high water when there is enough depth in the channel and for the lock.

History

The harbour is surrounded by fine traditional stone buildings and broad quays that echo the prosperous times when Paimpol was known as the 'Cité des Islandais' – the main port in North Brittany for the Icelandic cod and whaling fleets. In its narrow cobbled lanes are numerous bars, bistros and restaurants that were once the haunts of seafarers. There are still traditional boatyards in Paimpol and the town goes into festive mode for an international gathering of classic boats, 'La Fête des Vieux Gréements', held in August every year.

The departure of the fleets every February was the occasion for a famous 'pardon', a religious ceremony lasting for a few days. Until September the town would be bereft of young men whose return was greeted with great celebrations. The ships were either goëlettes (topsail schooners) or dundees (ketches). Hand lines were worked from the ships themselves, hove-to in deep water.

The fishery grew to as many as 50 vessels with 25 crew from this port alone. The last of the *goëlettes*, *La Glycine*, made her final voyage to Iceland in 1935.

Sadly, between 1852 and 1935 up to 2,000 men from ports in this area and 83 ships perished off Iceland.

Approaches

From the S

Chenal de Plouézec (dries 1m)

If approaching from the S the Anse de Paimpol may be entered by the 'back door' passing either side of l'Ost Pic lighthouse. The channel S of the light dries between 1·5m and 2·5m so is not recommended below half tide.

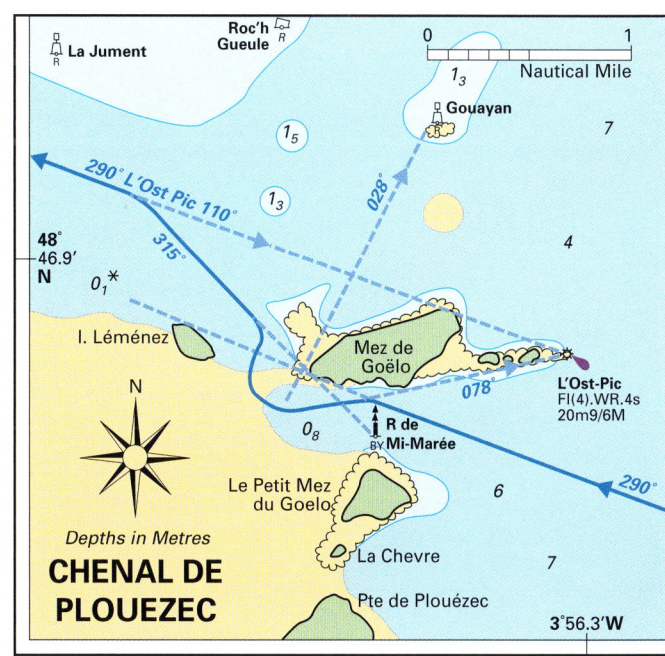

III North Brittany: 1 Cancale to Trégastel-Ste Anne

248 CHANNEL ISLANDS, CHERBOURG PENINSULA & NORTH BRITTANY

Erquy to Paimpol

Approaching l'Ost Pic lighthouse from SE

Roche Mi Marée beacon

Directions are as follows (see plan page 247):

From a position 220m S of L'Ost Pic lighthouse take up transit:

290° the right side of Ile Lemenez lined up with the left side of Mez de Goëlo

This will pass midway between Le Grand Mez de Goëlo and Roche Mi Marée N cardinal beacon.

When L'Ost Pic lighthouse bears 078° alter course to hold this stern bearing until R Gouayan port beacon bears 028°. Make a shallow turn to starboard to pass between Ile Lemenez and the W extremity of Mez de Goëlo. Roll out onto 315° when stern transit:

135° Roche Mi Marée beacon on the right (S) slope of Mez de Goëlo is obtained. Hold this transit until the lighthouse is open left of Grand Mez de Goëlo on 110°. Course may then be altered to join Chenal de la Jument as described below.

From the E
Conspicious marks: N–S
- Ploubazlanec church spire 117m
- La Cormorandière W pyramid
- Les Charpentiers E cardinal beacon tower
- Tour (57m) at Porz-Don
- La Jument port beacon tower
- Paimpol church spire (72m)
- L'Ost Pic lighthouse
- Pointe de Minard

Chenal de la Jument (1·1m)
This is the main channel into which all the minor channels lead. It carries a least depth of 1·1m up to a position 250m N of Roc'h ar Zel beacon. At this point it merges with the leading line up to Paimpol lock (see *Entry*).

From ⊕105 to the NE of l'Ost Pic lighthouse identify transit:

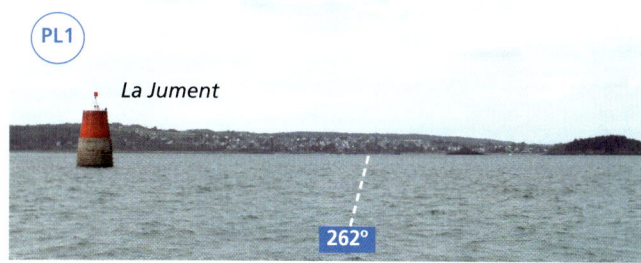

PL1 262° Paimpol church spire aligned with Pointe Brividic 'Sommet' (27m) – a woody hill in front of the town

This line will leave:
- Les Charpentiers E cardinal unlit beacon tower 400m to starboard
- Gouayan port unlit beacon tower 700m to port
- La Gueule port unlit buoy 200m to port
- La Jument port unlit beacon tower 150m to port
- Roc'h ar Zel port unlit beacon 300m to port (see anchorages Anse de Paimpol page 252)

From the N

Chenal du Dénou (3·6m)
This is not an easy channel due to limited marks and exposure to accelerated cross streams of up to 3·5 knots on the spring flood. It is best taken at neap tides when the stream is slack. Visibility of five miles recommended.

PL2 193° Dénou white beacon tower aligned with Plouézec spire

A small alteration to starboard is required to leave Dénou beacon tower 180m to port then come onto a SSW heading to join Chenal de la Jument.

Chenal de Lastel (1·2m)
This is a short channel that links up with Chenal de la Trinité described below. It has more width than Chenal du Dénou but the same comment concerning the streams applies. From a position on transit **BH5** (see Ile de Bréhat below) and with Men Gam E cardinal beacon tower bearing 255° distant 0·5M take up:

PL3 240° Ploubazlanec church spire open right (N) of Ouipoure white beacon tower (Roc'h Grouig Porc'h on SHOM chart 7127)

Once clear of the beacon tower alter course S to join Chenal de la Trinité.

III North Brittany: 1 Cancale to Trégastel-Ste Anne

Chenal de la Trinité (dries 0·3m)

This is the shortest connection between Chenal de Ferlas South of Ile de Bréhat and the leading line into Paimpol. It is interesting from the scenic and pilotage point of view. The stream reaches 5 knots at springs as it funnels past Pointe de la Trinité but sets N or S along the channel which is easier to handle than a cross stream.

There are variations on the initial (or final) stage of this Channel N of La Madeleine W cardinal beacon.

Erquy to Paimpol

East of Les Piliers

Navigate to position 400m to the E of Les Piliers N cardinal beacon tower. From here the transit is:

Quistillic white pyramid to the NE open to the right of Men Bras Logodec (a rock which never covers) on a bearing of 032°. Make good the reciprocal 212° keeping Quistillic open to the right of Logodec to avoid the three Lel-Ouene rocks drying 2·2m if the depth is not enough to clear. Then leave:

- Men Treiz E cardinal beacon 300m to starboard
- Roc'h Château 250m to port
- Roc'h Lème E cardinal beacon 350m to starboard
- La Madeleine W cardinal beacon 200m to port

Looking NE from W of Les Piliers

West of Les Piliers

Navigate to position 800m W of Les Piliers N cardinal beacon tower. From here identify four cardinal beacons to the SE. Chart read your way SE into the gap between the N cardinal beacon Roc'h Ourmelek and the E cardinal beacon Roc'h Lemm. Then steer south to leave Roc'h Lemm 100m to starboard. Continue S to leave La Madeleine W cardinal beacon 200m to port.

To arrive at this point you will have made allowance for crossing a patch with a minimum charted depth of 0·9m and clearing over a rock that dries 0·4m or possibly its close neighbour to the E that dries 0·8m.

Now look to the WNW for turning point.

La Croix lighthouse in line with the coast on the NW side of Pointe de l'Arcouest bearing 300°

Subject to sufficient depth over the area drying 0·3m, alter to 120° to leave Les Fillettes S cardinal beacon 250m to port. When Les Fillettes bears N alter course to starboard to leave;

- Le Taureau starboard beacon 100m to starboard then
- Rollic starboard beacon 100m to starboard
- Men Trieuse port beacon 100m to port
- Roc'h ar Gerroc port beacon 150m to port

When Pointe de la Trinité with its chapel bears 335° make good 155° with Roc'h ar Zel isolated danger beacon almost ahead. This leaves Glividi GRG preferred channel mark 200m to starboard and leads in to the main La Jument channel.

An alternative exit is to branch W at Glividi leaving it to port. This will leave a succession of four starboard beacons to starboard as the channel runs SW. The last beacon should be given a clearance of at least 200m.

Entry

The final 1·5M to the lock is via a buoyed channel that dries between 3·0m and 4·9m. The transit for the leading line is:

264° Alignment of leading marks (see air view):

Front: Kernoa light (red and white hut)
Back: Kerpalud light (white pylon red top)

Marks are difficult to identify against low sun.

By night

Kernoa Q.R 10m
Kerpalud Dir.Q.R 10m

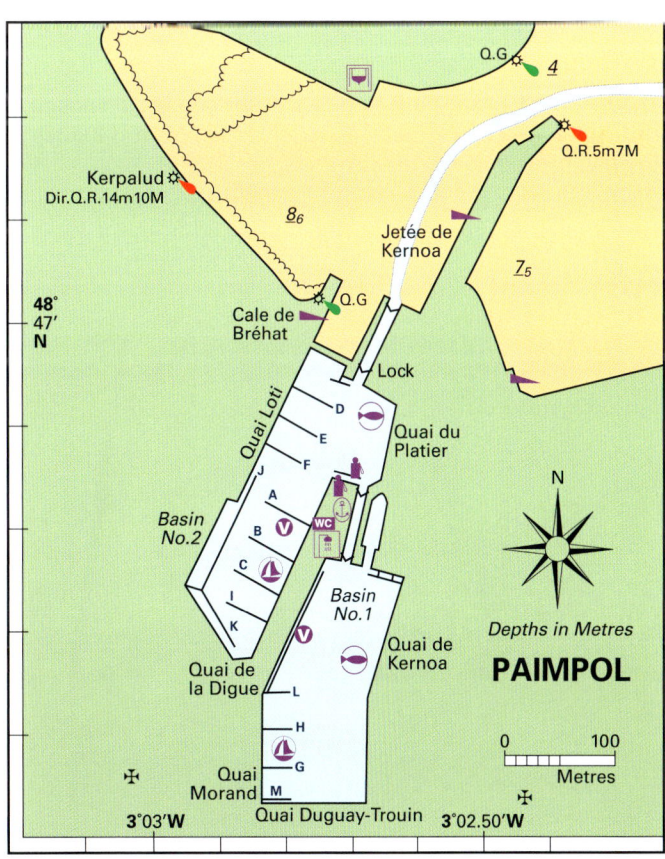

III. NORTH BRITTANY: 1 CANCALE TO TRÉGASTEL-STE ANNE

III North Brittany: 1 Cancale to Trégastel-Ste Anne

Paimpol

The Lock (sill dries 3m)

Turn close round the breakwater end and secure on the E side of the lock if necessary to wait. The lock works for up to 2½ hours either side of HW, is 60m long and 12m wide. With the depth above 8·5m the gates are left open over HW for varying times depending on the height of the tide. In this situation there is often a strong inward flow through the gates before HW.

Berthing

Bassin No. 1 is on the E side of the docks and is reached through another lock that is generally left open. It is mainly for fishing and commercial vessels.

Bassin No. 2 is for yachts and has 20 visitors' berths. The reception pontoon is 'A', the first one ahead from the locks and to the W of the harbour office on the central quay. Maximum length 20m.

Anchorages

In the outer approaches

Anse de Bréhec is 3M S of L'Ost-Pic with a long sandy beach sheltered from S through W to N. It can be approached from Le Taureau beacon tower (isolated danger mark) 1M to the E (landing slip).

In Anse de Paimpol

It is possible to anchor almost anywhere in the Anse clear of the shellfish beds although there are few sheltered areas for yachts. The following are possibilities:

- With La Jument bearing E and Ile St Rion bearing N in a suitable depth. Take care to avoid the 0·6m rock near this position. There is little shelter here and it's a long way from anywhere.
- NNE of Pointe Guilben at the head of the deep approach channel with restricted swinging room.
- An anchor light at night would be a wise precaution as this is on or near the leading line. There is a dinghy landing on the N side of Pointe Guilben above half tide.
- 0·4M NNW of Roc'h ar Zel isolated danger beacon in a finger of deep water
- Off Porz Even in 2·7m with Glividi beacon bearing 190° 200m, to the E of the moorings. This is the most sheltered anchorage from the W but there can be a strong run of tide here and passing traffic. Dinghy landing at Porz Even, a small drying harbour for fishing boats. Inadvisable to leave yacht unattended.

It is recommended to trip the anchor anywhere in the Anse de Paimpol.

Visitors' pontoons

Ile de Bréhat to Trégastel-Ste Anne (26M)
Côte de Granit Rose

ILE DE BRÉHAT

48°50'·10N 03°00'·20W
(Men Joliguet W cardinal lit beacon tower)
4M N of Paimpol, 6M downstream from Lézardrieux

TRAVEL
  Les Vedettes de Bréhat: ☏ 02 96 55 79 50
      www.vedettesdebrehat.com (L'Arcouest terminal)

CHARTS
  BA 2027 Ile Grande to Ile de Bréhat (1:48 700)
  BA 2028 Ile de Bréhat to Plateau Des Roches Douvres (1:48 600)
  BA 2029 Ile de Bréhat to Cap Fréhel (1:48 800)
  BA 3673 Ile de Bréhat and Anse de Paimpol Entrance to Le Trieux (1:20 000)
  Imray C34 Cap d'Erquy to Ile de Batz*
      *includes plans: Approaches to Rivière de Trieux and Paimpol (1:50 000), Port de la Corderie (Ile de Bréhat) (1:15 000), Port Clos (Ile de Bréhat) (1:10 000)
  Imray 2510 North Brittany Chart Atlas:
      5 Approaches to Rivière de Trieux & Paimpol (1:50 000)
      6j Port de la Corderie (Ile de Bréhat) (1:15 000)
      6k Port Clos (Ile de Bréhat) (1:10 000)
  SHOM 7127 Abords de l'Île de Bréhat – Anse de Paimpol – Entrée du Trieux (1:20 000)
  SHOM 7152 De l'Ile Grande à l'Ile de Bréhat (1:48 700)
  SHOM 7153 De l'Île de Bréhat au Plateau des Roches Douvres (1:48 600)
  SHOM 7154 De l'île de Bréhat au Cap Fréhel – Baie de Saint-Brieuc (1:48 800)

TIDAL INFORMATION
  Standard port: St Malo or Paimpol
  HW St Malo -0010
  LW St Malo -0045
  HW St Helier -0025

MHWS	MLWS	MHWN	MLWN
10·3	1·3	7·9	3·8

Tidal Streams
  To NE of Ile de Bréhat
  HW St Helier +0610 SE flood
  HW St Helier +0005 NW ebb

  In Chenal de Ferlas
  HW St Helier +0610 E flood
  HW St Helier +0005 W ebb

  In Kerpont Channel
  HW St Helier +0610 S flood
  HW St Helier +0005 N ebb

USEFUL CONTACTS
  Bréhat Sémaphore Station ☏ 02 96 20 00 12
  VHF Ch 16/10 (day only)

SUPPLIES AND SERVICES
The island's village, Le Bourg, is a 15–20 minute walk along the footpaths from La Chambre or La Corderie anchorages. Around the central square are several small shops including a mini supermarché, boulangerie, cafés, bars, several restaurants and a regular market. Bike hire is also available.

With its colourful rocks and subtropical flora Ile de Bréhat is the showpiece of the Côte de Granit Rose and one of North Brittany's most popular destinations.

It lies within a scattering of islets in the estuary of the River Trieux of which Bréhat is the largest. Being just two miles N to S by one mile E to W and low lying it tends to be inconspicuous from seaward. A network of well marked channels surround the island and once the relevant buoys and towers are identified the way in becomes clear.

Areas of yachting activity are centred around the anchorages of La Chambre and Port Clos in the Rade de Bréhat in the S and Port de la Corderie in the NW. These dry out to a greater or lesser extent so craft that can take the ground have the advantage of being able to edge in further while the rest must anchor out in the tidal stream which can be strong around Bréhat at springs. At night or in the event of deteriorating weather a retreat up the River Trieux to Lézardrieux might be the best move (see *Anchorages* page 257).

From south

III North Brittany: 1 Cancale to Trégastel-Ste Anne

Ile de Bréhat to Trégastel-Ste Anne

Ashore

Bréhat is divided into two halves joined by a single bridge, Pont Vauban. A labyrinth of paths criss-cross the island and it is easy to lose your way. The north half has rolling moorland and rocky outcrops and is best for coastal walks. In the south is Le Bourg and La Chapelle St Michel which at 41m is the second highest point in the island and well worth the climb for extensive views of the estuary.

Despite the deluge of day trippers that are daily ferried into Port Clos during the season Bréhat has managed to retain its peaceful atmosphere and unspoilt scenery. This is at the expense of some *reglementation* and plaisanciers should heed notices on the chart and in the anchorages.

Approaches to Ile de Bréhat from the S

(see plans pages 240 and 248)

Clear of all dangers

N of Roches de Saint Quay the coast is clear up to Basse St Brieuc E cardinal buoy 2M off Pointe de Minard. From here continue NNW to ⊕106 which is positioned on transit **BH5** for Chenal du Ferlas S of Bréhat (see below).

Via Anse de Paimpol

The most direct route across the Anse passes N or S of L'Ost Pic lighthouse and then N to Chenal de la Trinité. For directions see Paimpol approaches which will need to be followed in reverse order for Chenal de la Trinité.

Via Chenal du Ferlas (0·8m)

Approach into Chenal du Ferlas should be made clear S of the shallows E of Ile de Bréhat – Plateau de la Horaine, Plateau du Men Marc'h and Plateau ar C'hign Bras. The streams sweep through this area creating unpleasant conditions particularly over springs and when wind is against tide. (See *Chenal de Bréhat*.)

The published transit for entering Chenal du Ferlas is:

BH5 *(⊕106) 277° La Croix lighthouse aligned with S end of Ile Raguénès. (No view)*

These marks are obscure. An alternative is a single bearing of not less than 280° on Men Joliguet W cardinal lit beacon tower on S end of the Ile de Bréhat – or devise your own transit.

Men Joliguet W cardinal

The narrowing gap between the island and the mainland has frequent marks so reference should be made to the large scale chart. (BA *3673* or SHOM *7127).*

The line should leave:
- Cain ar Monse N cardinal buoy 0·5M to starboard (see plan page 248)
- Lel Ar Serive S cardinal buoy 200M to starboard
- Cadenenou N cardinal buoy 200m to port
- Les Piliers N cardinal beacon tower 400m to port

600m east of Men Joliguet is the opening of La Chambre anchorage (see Anchorages below).

By night via Chenal du Ferlas

From E (see plans pages 248, 254, 255)

There are three directional leading lights which lead through the Ferlas from E to W. Be warned that the sided sectors are inconsistent from one another.

From a position 2M NE of L'Ost Pic lighthouse or at ⊕105 on transit **PL1** pick up the white sector of Men Joliguet (Fl(2)WRG.6s) on a track of 277° (Green to the S, Red to the N), and proceed until between the unlit buoys of Cadenenou and Lel ar Skrev when the red sector of Roch'h Quinonec (Dir.Q.WRG) at the W end of the Chenal will be come visible; continue into the very narrow white sector (257°) and proceed down it exactly until Rompa (unlit) is abeam to starboard (Red to S, Green to N). The white sector of Kermouster (Dir.Fl.WRG.2s) will then be entered on 272° to lead in to Grande Passe de Trieux (Red to S, Green to N) leaving Vielle de Loguivy unlit beacon well to starboard.

From W (see plan page 248)

Only with difficulty as the directional leading lights are aligned to be used from the E.

Approaches to Ile de Bréhat from the N

There are three options for approaching Ile de Bréhat from between NE and NW.

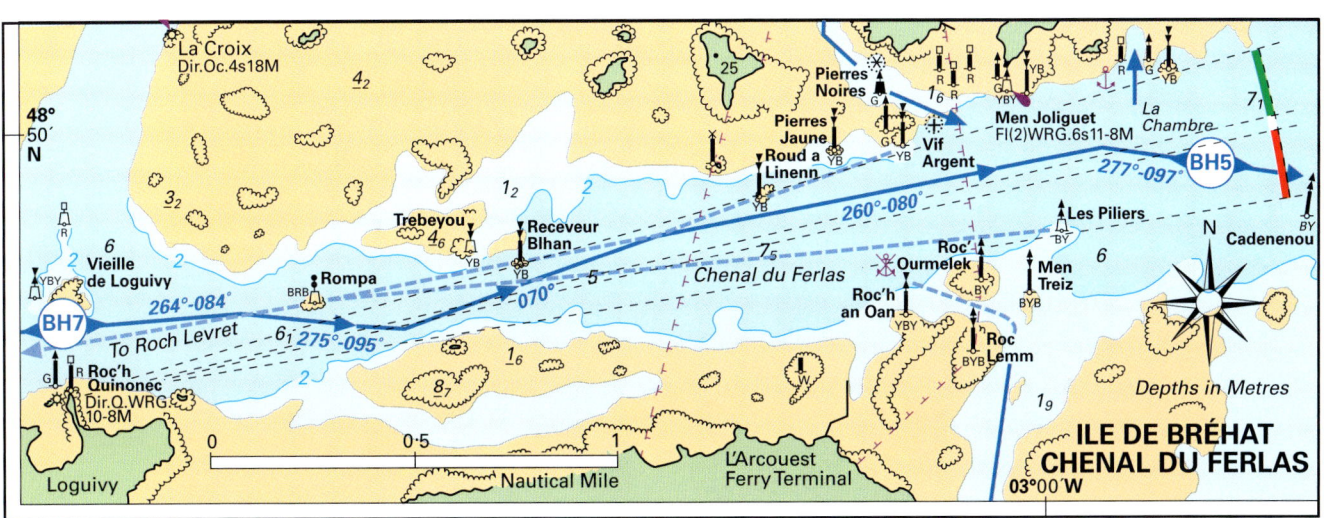

ILE DE BRÉHAT
CHENAL DU FERLAS
03°00'W

III North Brittany: 1 Cancale to Trégastel-Ste Anne

Via Chenal de Bréhat (⊕108) (3·6m)
This deep channel follows a SSE track E of the island to join the Ferlas in the S.

Being fully exposed to the strongest streams that occur on the NE corner of the island it can be rough, particularly so at springs. It cuts through a narrow (200m) gap between Roche Guarine E cardinal buoy, the sole mark, and the shallows of Plateau des Échaudés to the E.

With visibility in excess of 6M it may be possible to identify a mark ahead:

Looking north from junction between the R. de Trieux and Ferlas Channel

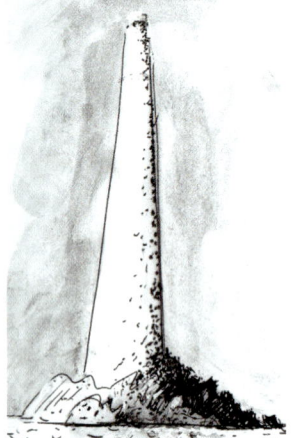

BH6 *167° La Cormorandière W pyramid bearing 167°*

When Cain Ar Monse N cardinal buoy is 400m to port alter course SSW to join transit **BH5** into Chenal du Ferlas (See also *Lézardrieux approaches from S and E*).

BH7 *084° Rompa isolated danger beacon tower aligned with Les Pilliers N cardinal beacon tower*

150m short of Rompa come to starboard to leave it at least 100m to port – there is an outlier drying 3·5m S of it.

Return to a heading of 080° to leave a succession of marks to port:

- Trebeyou S cardinal beacon tower 200m to port
- Receveur Bihan S cardinal beacon 100m to port
- Roud ar Linenn S cardinal beacon 100m to port
- Vif Argent S cardinal beacon 250m to port
- Men Joliguet W cardinal beacon tower (lit) 300m to port
- Les Piliers N cardinal beacon tower 300m to starboard

Via Entrée du R. Trieux (Le Ferlas W–E)
Identify Vielle de Loguivy W cardinal beacon tower at the S end of the Grand Chenal (Entrée du R. du Trieux) (see Lézardrieux from N and W). When the cardinal bears ENE take up 084° to leave it 200m to port. Ferlas Channel is entered with transit:

From the NW
Via Chenal de la Moisie (1·3m) (⊕109)
(see plan page 248)

This provides a direct approach to La Corderie anchorage and Le Kerpont channel on Bréhat's W coast as described below.

For pilotage directions see Lézardrieux approaches from W. Transit **L1** on page 261 (Chenal de la Moisie).

Kerpont Channel from the S

Les Pierres Noires

Ile de Bréhat to Trégastel-Ste Anne

Kerpont Channel from the N

Le Kerpont Channel (dries 2·5m) (see plan page 254)
This narrow N–S cut between the W coast of Ile de Bréhat and Ile de Biniguet (private) is a short but exciting piece of pilotage.

These directions are from the N but it is equally straightforward from the S.

Depths
The length of the channel is charted as drying at 2m but it is safer to assume that at the shallowest point close S of the sole mark, Men ar Gouilh (Men Granouille) starboard beacon, it dries at 2·5m.

It is said that when the slipway at the S end of the Bréhat side is covered the passage is clear for a yacht drawing 1·8m. At any rate it should be taken at or near HW.

Streams
The stream in the Channel can attain 4–5 knots and runs with the direction of the fairway.

Directions
From a position between Men ar Fav port beacon and Ar Morhoc'hed starboard beacon at the S side of the entrance into Port de La Corderie anchorage take up transit:

The slipway is covered

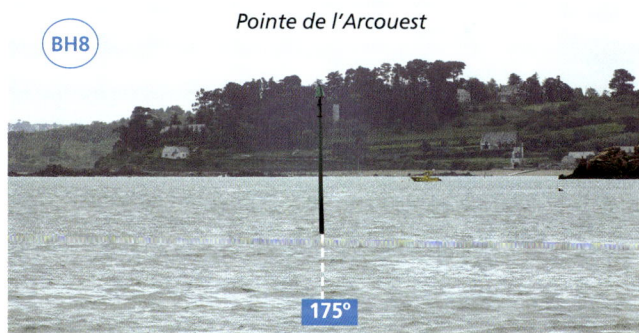

BH8 *175° Men ar Gouilh (Men Granouille) starboard beacon aligned with Tower (white) on Pointe de l'Arcouest*

Leave Men ar Gouilh close to starboard and continue on the line. Pass close but keep clear of the slipway then come to port to leave Les Pierres Noires starboard beacon tower to starboard and out into Rade de Bréhat.

Ile de Bréhat anchorages (clockwise from La Chambre) (see air view)

La Chambre
A small drying inlet on the SE corner. Crowded with moorings and difficult to find anchorage out of the stream even at neaps. Small craft that can take the ground may sneak in further for best shelter and more space.

Men Alann Bay (Port Grève du Guerzido)
Close W of La Chambre. Visitors' moorings are sometimes available outside the buoyed swimming area. Exposed to any wind and swell from the east. Guerzido has the best beach in the island with a bar/restaurant and sailing school.

CHANNEL ISLANDS, CHERBOURG PENINSULA & NORTH BRITTANY

III North Brittany: 1 Cancale to Trégastel-Ste Anne

Port de la Corderie (La Corderie)

Port Clos
A small drying harbour much used by the *vedettes*. Avoid obstructing the slips and jetties. 2m or more can be found at MLWN to the NW of Men Joliguet beacon tower. Craft that can take the ground may use the inner harbour where there is perfect shelter. **Note the prohibited anchorage which covers the W side of the outer harbour.** The *vedette* traffic ceases in the evening. Land at any of the slips.

S end of Le Kerpont
Anchorage is possible in a finger of deep water (2·5m at datum) off the life boat station but keep clear of the channel.

Port de la Corderie
Offers a restricted anchorage to deep draught yachts at the entrance but with more scope at neaps. There are several visitors' moorings in the outer anchorage W of entry beacons. Sound in as close in to the sides as possible to avoid strong tidal streams of the Kerpont Channel.

Bilge keelers and yachts with legs can move further in to dry out on the bottom which, except for a few rocky places, is hard sand with patches of mud. Shelter inside is very good except in a gale from W or NW when one might want to move N or S to avoid wind and swell that may penetrate.

WARNING
Avoid power cable that runs across the harbour marked by beacons.

Landing
There is a slip on north side. Beaches and rocks on the south side are nearer Le Bourg.

Gosrod and La Corderie anchorage

Entry

From the Kerpont Channel
See *Kerpont Channel* page 257.

From Entrée du R. Trieux
From a position in the Entrée where it joins Chenal de la Moisie and Vieille de Tréou starboard beacon tower bears NNW, alter course to 180° to leave Amer de Rosédo W pyramid 300m to port and Men Robin starboard beacon 100m to starboard. When drying rocks to port are cleared pass between port and starboard entry beacons into the anchorage.

Ile de Bréhat to Trégastel-Ste Anne

LA RIVIÈRE DU TRIEUX – LÉZARDRIEUX

48°53'·30N 02°58'·80W
5M upstream from Ile de Bréhat

TRAVEL
Travel in rural Brittany tends to be complicated.
Train
A regional line connects Pontrieux and Paimpol with Guingamp also on the TGV line.
Road
Lézardrieux is about 4M W of Paimpol by road which in turn is about 24M from St Brieuc with its regional airport and a stop on the Paris-Brest TGV line.
Bus: The Guide du Port obtainable from Bureau du Port includes details of a bus line (No.7) between Paimpol and Lannion calling at Lézardreiux Port. www.tibus.fr

CHARTS
British Admiralty
2027 Ile Grande to Ile de Bréhat (1:48 700)
2028 Ile de Bréhat to Plateau Des Roches Douvres (1:48 600)
2029 Ile de Bréhat to Cap Fréhel (1:48 800)
3673 Ile de Bréhat and Anse de Paimpol Entrance to Le Trieux (1:20 000)*
includes plan: Port de Lézardrieux Le Trieux (1:10 000)

Imray
C34 Cap d'Erquy to Ile de Batz*
includes plans: Approaches to Rivière de Trieux and Paimpol (1:50 000), Lézardrieux (1:15 000)
2510 North Brittany Chart Atlas:
5 Approaches to Rivière de Trieux & Paimpol (1:50 000)
6I Lézardrieux (1:15 000)

SHOM
SHOM 7127 Abords de l'Île de Bréhat – Anse de Paimpol – Entrée du Trieux (1:20 000)*
includes plan: Port de Lézardrieux - Le Trieux (1:10 000)
SHOM 7152 De l'Ile Grande à l'Ile de Bréhat (1:48 700)
SHOM 7153 De l'Île de Bréhat au Plateau des Roches Douvres (1:48 600)
SHOM 7154 De l'île de Bréhat au Cap Fréhel – Baie de Saint-Brieuc (1:48 800)

RADIO
Ch 09 *Port de Lézardrieux* 0730–2130 during season

TIDAL INFORMATION
Standard port: St Malo or Paimpol
Differences:
HW St Malo –0020
LW St Malo –0045
HW St Helier –0033
HW Paimpol –0010
LW Paimpol –0020

MHWS	MLWS	MHWN	MLWN
10·5	1·3	5·0	3·7

Tidal Streams
HW St Helier +0610 ingoing flood stream starts
HW St Helier +0055 out going ebb stream starts

USEFUL CONTACTS
Bureau du Port on quay above Pontoon 3 outer marina (N side) ☎ 02 96 20 14 22 / 06 62 74 81 13 VHF Ch 09
Cross Corsen ☎ 02 98 89 31 31
Doctor ☎ 02 96 20 18 30
Pharmacy ☎ 02 96 20 10 05
Semaphore de Bréhat ☎ 02 96 20 00 12
Office du Tourism ☎ 02 96 22 16 45 www.cc-lezardrieux.com
Taxi le Bourdonnec ☎ 02 96 20 15 90

SUPPLIES AND SERVICES
Berths Are spread over inner and outer marinas, moorings and waiting pontoon in the river and drying berths.
Visitors' berths 50 on Pontoon 3 in outer marina. Inner marina berths on request. (See under Anchoring, Berthing and Mooring below).
Fuel (automatic) outer marina Pontoon 3 inner end
Water, electricity At all pontoons
Showers At marina facilities blocks
Yacht club Yacht Club du Trieux on quay between marinas
Chandlery, Boatyard
Trieux Marina ☎ 02 96 20 14 71
Accastillage Diffusion ☎ 02 96 20 14 71
Sailmaker Voilerie Allpurpose ☎ 02 96 20 10 62 www.allpurpose.fr
Restaurants
In the Port Bar du Port overlooking the Marina, sharing premises with Yacht Club. You can eat inside or out in a convivial atmosphere. Extensive menu. Crowded in high season when booking is recommended.
☎ 02 96 20 10 39 *Email* yachtclub22@orange.fr
La Moulin de la Galette ☎ 02 96 20 18 36
In the village Auberge du Trieux 'Gastronomie Créative', Impasse du Four Neuf (off SW corner of Place du Centre) has a reputation for being one of the best on the Trieux. Large parties can be accommodated. Reservation is recommended.
☎ 02 96 20 10 70 www.auberge-du-trieux.com
Market Friday

Lézardrieux yacht harbours looking WNW

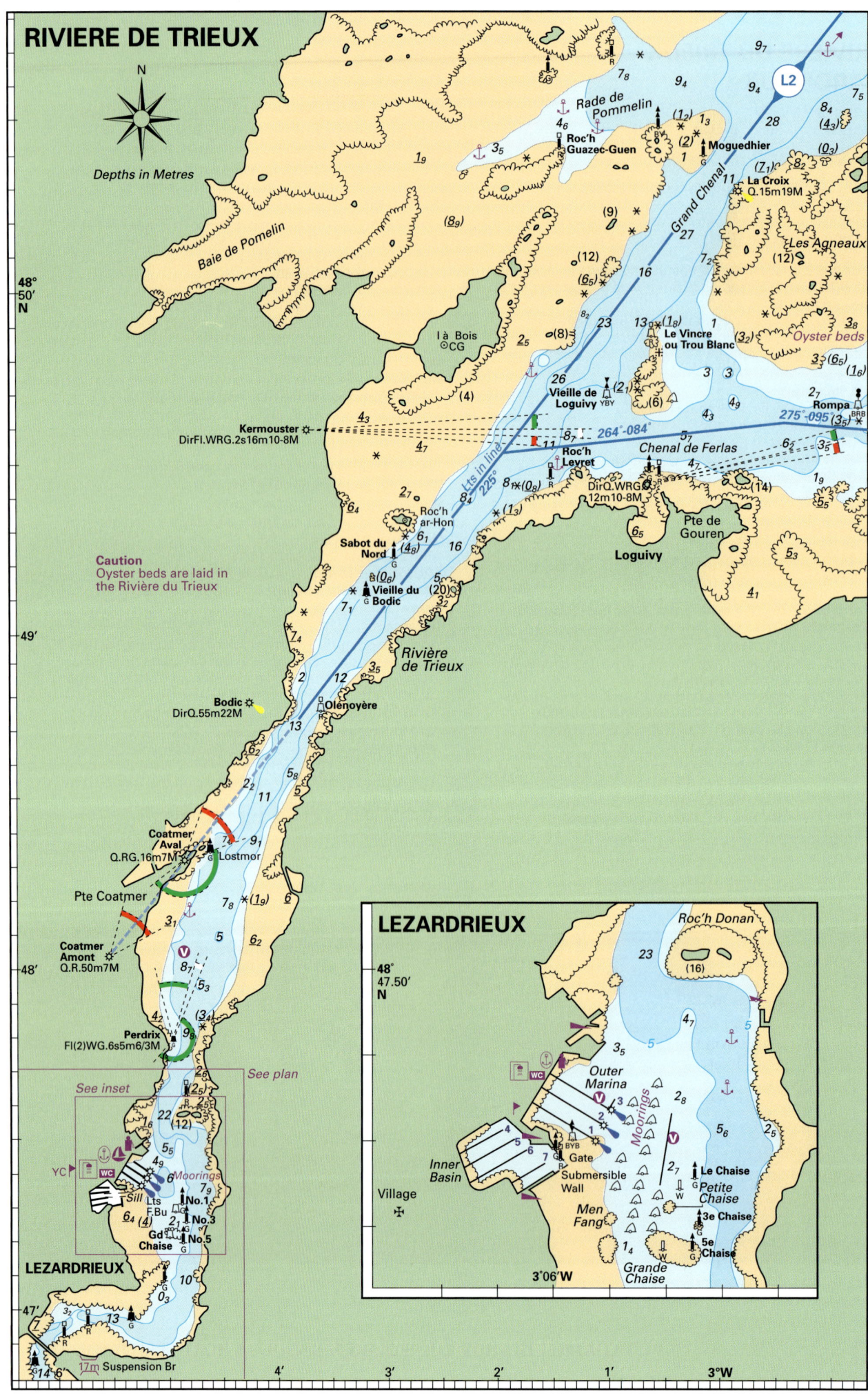

III North Brittany: 1 Cancale to Trégastel-Ste Anne

Ile de Bréhat to Trégastel-Ste Anne

Boats pass La Croix on their way down river

Lézardrieux on the W bank of the Rivière du Trieux is just far enough up the river to be completely sheltered by its wooded banks and the islets in the estuary. It has been a popular haven for generations of yachtsmen especially the British who are drawn to the tranquillity of this deep water estuary. Apart from the development of a new wet basin, and the need for an appeal to patrons 'to make as little noise as possible between 10pm and 7am', *plus ça change*.

During high season marina berths are often in short supply making it necessary to retreat to a buoy or the waiting pontoon in the river. Alternatively and subject to considerations of mast height, draught and the tide you can carry on eight miles up the river to the inland Port of Pontrieux.

Facilities in Lézardrieux are adequate in the port but if shops are required it is a short but steep ascent to the village. Market day in the Place du Centre is on Friday and a colourful occasion.

Approaches (see plans pages 248, 250, 254, 260)

Planning an approach between Les Héaux lighthouse and Anse de Paimpol should take into account the tidal streams that sweep round this corner at up to 4 knots resulting in a cross set that can take some handling at springs.

There are also several shallow banks N and E of Ile de Bréhat, some with drying rocks, which are best avoided in wind against tide conditions at springs when seas may break.

Visibility of at least four miles is required to sight relevant marks.

From the N and W

From Jument des Héaux N cardinal buoy (⊕110) 2·0M WNW of Les Héaux lighthouse make good due E to ⊕109 Chenal de la Moisie or continue further E to the Grand Chenal. (Entrée de la Rivière du Trieux)

Chenal de la Moisie (1·3m) (⊕109)

This is a useful short cut into the Estuary of R. Trieux but is not recommended at LWS or in visibility of less than 5·0M. Positive identification of the marks and **holding the transit accurately is vital** if one is to avoid drying rocks at its N end.

La Moisie

Be prepared for strong tidal cross set.

From ⊕109 (see plan page 248) identify La Moisie E cardinal beacon tower bearing SSE and approach it on a track made good of 160°. Before closing the beacon tower the transit on Ile de Bréhat should be set up:

L1 *160° Chapel St Michel aligned with Amer de Rosédo white pyramid*

The channel is 2·5M long and the tightest point is off An Ogejou Bihan E cardinal beacon. (See plan page 248.)

The line leaves:

- La Moisie E cardinal beacon tower 150m to starboard
- An Ogejou Bihan E cardinal beacon 50m to starboard
- Penn ar Rest W beacon 0·4M to starboard
- Vieille du Tréou starboard beacon tower close to starboard

Entrée de la Rivière du Trieux

Grand Chenal (11m)

A deep, well marked and sheltered channel. ⊕107 is positioned 2·0M on the approach line N of La Horaine beacon tower. Identify key marks. E–W these are:

- La Horaine beacon tower left 1·6M to port
- Les Echaudés port channel buoy left 0·5M to port
- Les Sirlots starboard channel buoy left 400m to starboard
- Petit Pen-Azen port channel buoy and N cardinal beacon tower left 400m and 0·6M to port
- Ile de Bréhat (low lying) E of the channel
- Vieille du Tréou starboard beacon tower left 450m to starboard

The transit is:

L2 *225° Bodic lighthouse aligned with La Croix lighthouse*

III North Brittany: 1 Cancale to Trégastel-Ste Anne

This should be held up to 0·6M short of the lighthouse when a minor alteration to starboard is made to pass between the light and starboard bn Moguedhier. Return to a heading of 218° to follow marks up the river to Lézardrieux (see Approaches from E).

By night
Entrée de la Rivière du Trieux (Grand Chenal)
Leading lights :
Front: La Croix lighthouse Dir.Oc.4s
Back: Bodic lighthouse Dir.Q
Front: Coatmer Aval Q.RG.7M
Back: Coatmer Amont Q.R.50m7M

Chenal de Bréhat (11·5m) (⊕108)
This deep but fair weather channel passes E of Ile de Bréhat to join Le Ferlas channel. It has comparatively long stretches without marks and the transits are distant. Tidal streams may exceed 5kns at springs causing overfalls when wind is against tide. This route is described under *Approaches to Ile de Bréhat from the N* page 255.

From S and E
Navigate to a position 1·5M E of Pointe de Minard (⊕104) then make good 350° up the coast to join the approach line into the Ferlas Channel S of Ile de Bréhat (⊕106). This line leaves:

- Basse de St Brieuc E cardinal buoy close to port
- Les Calemarguiers E cardinal buoy 0·65 to port
- Les Charpentiers E cardinal tower 1·1M to port
- Les Cormorandiers W pyramid 1·25M to port

Chenal du Ferlas (E–W)
Entry into this channel from the East is fully described as far as Men Joliguet W cardinal beacon tower and La Chambre anchorage. (See plans pages 248, 254, 255.)

For the west leg of the Ferlas into the R. Trieux (see page 260) continue on a course of 260° to leave:

- Vif Argent S cardinal beacon 250m to starboard
- Pierre Jaune S cardinal beacon 250m to starboard
- Roud Linenn S cardinal beacon left 100m to starboard
- Identify ahead Rompa isolated danger tower and 400m before the next S cardinal beacon, Receveur Bihan, alter course to leave Rompa at least 100m to starboard – there is an outlier drying 3·5m S of it.
- Maintain heading until 200m S of Vieille de Loguivy W cardinal beacon at which point come to port to enter the Trieux.

By night (see page 255)

Via Anse de Paimpol (Chenal de la Jument (3m) and Chenal de la Trinité (drying 0·3m)
This interesting route starts at L'Ost Pic lighthouse in the SE of Anse de Paimpol and enters Le Ferlas S of Men Joliguet. It has a drying patch of 0·3m. See *Approaches to Paimpol* page 248 and *Approaches to Ile de Bréhat* page 255.

Anchorages, berthing and mooring (N–S)

WARNING
The tidal stream runs strongly past Lézardrieux. Aim to arrive at slack water and moor into the stream whenever possible.

Anchorages on W bank

- 1·3M SW of Min Guen starboard beacon tower 11m. Moderate holding in sand, shells and rocks. Out of the main stream (See pages 248 and 260.)
- Rade de Pommelin: 0·75M NE of Ile à Bois. About 5m. Good holding
- Coatmer anchorage between Lostmor starboard beacon tower and Perdrix starboard light tower. Anchor between northern-most mooring and Lostmor. 5m good holding in mud and shells. (It may be preferable to use mooring buoys to S because of tidal stream and traffic).

Visitors' moorings

- Between Lostmor and Perdrix as above.
- E of marina pontoons and N of La Petite Chaise. Dumbell type waiting buoys, some attached to waiting pontoons.

The marinas
Visitors most commonly use the outer deepwater marina where the northernmost of the three pontoons has visitor berths on both sides and the outer end. Here you can come and go at any time. Some assistance berthing is available during working hours.

Depth: 1·80–2·50m
Max length: 20m
Max draught: 2·50m

The new inner marina is a *bassin à flot* (wet basin) and only accessible about 3 hrs either side of HW. A drying sill and gate retains a pond depth of 2·50m.

Max length: 14m
Max draught: 2·40m

Entry/exit regulated by traffic lights:
2G open
2G + 1W open, two-way traffic
3R closed

Use of this marina is subject to authorisation by the Bureau du Port. For directions call on VHF Ch 9 or ☎ 02 96 20 14 22 / 06 62 74 81 13.

The new inner basin (Bassin à Flot) looking SE

Ile de Bréhat to Trégastel-Ste Anne

PONTRIEUX

⊕48°42'·74N 03°08'·98W
5M upstream from Lézardrieux

TRAVEL
See Le Vapeur de Trieux (page 264) and contacts below

CHARTS
No official chart.

COMMUNICATIONS
Radio – the lock keeper maintains watch on Ch 12 between HW -2 to HW +1
☏ 02 96 95 60 70
Harbourmaster ☏ 02 96 95 34 87
Email Portrieux.plaisance@cotesdarmor.cci.fr
Lock times at www.letrieux.com

TIDAL INFORMATION
As for Lézardrieux (see Upriver to Portrieux 'Timing and Tidal Stream' below).

USEFUL CONTACTS
Office de Tourisme ☏ 02 96 95 14 03 www.portrieux.com
Station, Rue du Port ☏ 02 96 95 60 24
Le Passeur du Trieux (river ferry) ☏ 06 21 07 30 72
Doctor ☏ 02 96 95 18 18
Pharmacy ☏ 02 96 95 60 50
Taxi ☏ 02 96 95 60 43 / 02 96 95 60 69

SUPPLIES AND SERVICES

Port
150 berths including 15 for visitors. Max length: 16m, max draught: 2·2m
Water (domestic use only) on quay
Electricity on quay
Showers Bureau du Port
Laundry Bureau du Port
WiFi Free

Town
800m (10 minute walk) from Bureau du Port in Rue St Yves and town centre – *boulangerie*, pharmacy, *tabac*, petrol/diesel (in cans), *boucherie*, *epicerie* (open every day). Intermarché supermarket on town outskirts ☏ 02 96 95 67 19. Free delivery to boat.
Fuel In cans 24/24
Restaurants Le Schooner Pub 'Restauration Rapide' ☏ 02 96 95 01 57 In town: Numerous
Market On Mondays.

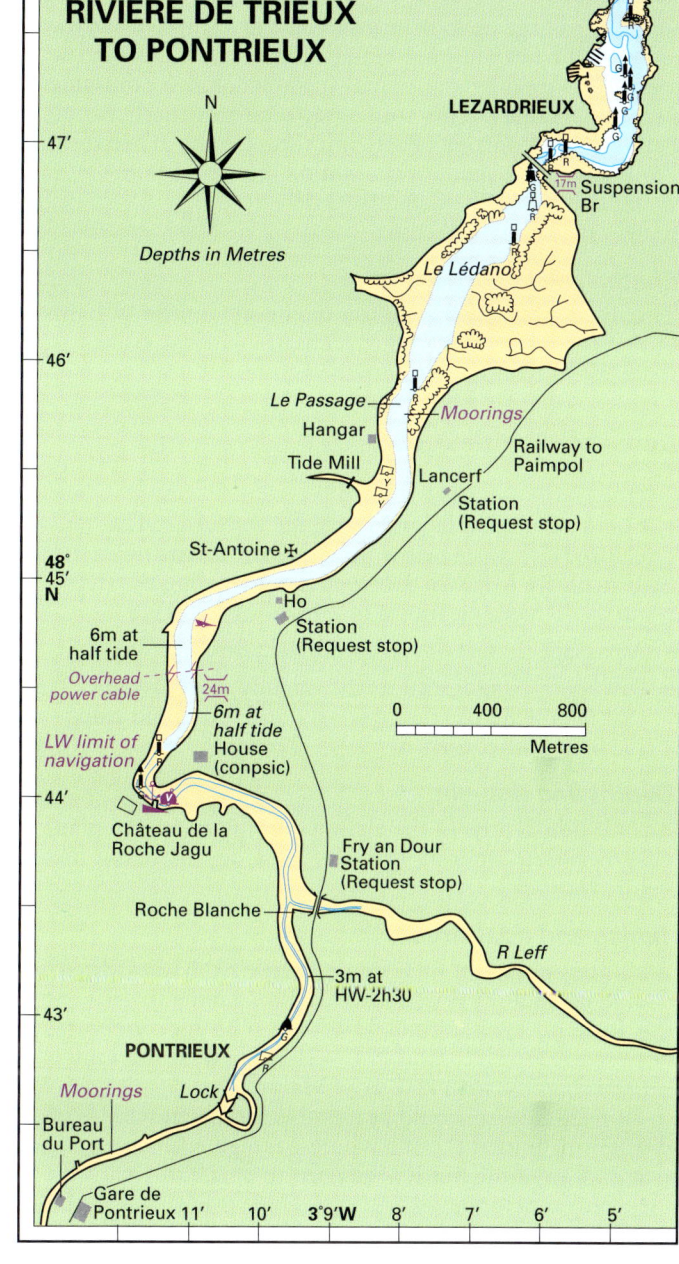

Château de la Roche Jagu

Casting off from Lézardrieux to head inland instead of returning to the open sea may seem like an act of desertion but foraging up rivers is one of the pleasures of cruising this coast. It provides an insight into a different aspect of life in rural Brittany.

Allow an hour with the tide to cover the six miles up to the lock. The narrowing river soon winds through verdant woodland where the only sign of life is likely to be river birds such as herons and egrets.

Once locked into the basin and moored up you are one with a community of river dwellers that enjoy a more peaceful way of life than their coastal counterparts.

Pontrieux is a friendly and unpretentious inland town dating from the 15th century. It grew up at the crossing point of the Trieux before the construction of the bridge at Lézardrieux. It has an attractive centre with cafés, bars and restaurants.

III North Brittany: 1 Cancale to Trégastel-Ste Anne

Le Vapeur de Trieux
On your passage up to Pontrieux you may glimpse a narrow gauge rail track running alongside the river. During the season it is used by an original steam locomotive drawing period carriages. This tourist attraction runs between Paimpol and Pontrieux Port with several halts in between. Bookings can be made at the station in Rue du Port:
☏ 08 92 39 14 27 / 02 96 20 52 06
www.vapeurdutrieux.com.

Chateau de la Roche Jagu
This 16th-century chateau is a major site on the W bank of the Trieux. Its park and gardens are worth a visit.
☏ 02 96 95 62 35   www.larochejagu.fr

Upriver to Pontrieux (5M)

Cautions
- Check your mast height above the waterline. The charted clearance below the bridge at Lézardrieux is 17m above MHWS. A power cable crossing the river further S has a clearance of 24m above MHWS
- A passage in mist or fog could be hazardous
- Beware of commercial traffic, mainly sand dredgers (Sabliers) who use the river around HW. Avoid using the lock at that time

Depths and draught
At half tide depths in the channel up the river (see plan) vary between 2m and 15m the least depths being just before the lock.

Timing and tidal stream
Assuming a draught of 1·5m departure from Lézardrieux should be made at HW (local) -2h30m aiming to arrive at the lock no earlier than HW -1h. The lock operates between HW -2h15 and HW +2h15. HW at the lock is said to coincide with HW at St Malo.

At neap tides it should be possible for a boat with 1·5m draught to undertake the whole passage with sufficient water at any time but it is advised to check this with the lock keeper beforehand.

When it comes to returning downstream lock out 1h30m before HW.

Directions
(Based on a passage made when HW Lézardrieux was 9·65m [Coefficient 104] mean spring). Draught 1·2m.

After departure at local HW -02h30 the river makes a tight double bend before the bridge (clearance 17m). Channel marks should be followed correctly allowing for the accelerated stream. After the bridge the valley opens out into a wide area, Le Lédano. Steer a middle southwesterly course across it.

At the S end of Le Lédano is a port beacon just before a line of private mooring buoys with a landing for the station at Lancerf. At this point, known as Le Passage, the river commences a turn to port – keep well to the outside (E) of the bend. On the W bank are two landmarks – Le Hangar, followed by a tide mail.

Beg An Arvor starboard beacon tower is the first mark upstream of the bridge

Moorings at the S end of Lédano

Le Hangar, once a seaplane base, is a useful landmark on the W bank

Continuing up river you pass a derelict slipway on the east bank with a country house above it. Keeping well to the outside of the next bend note the power cable crossing the river (clearance 24m). A port beacon warns of a sharp 90° bend to port – keep well to the W side. Above the treeline will be seen Château de la Roche Jagu and on the river bend beneath is the Cale de le Roche Jagu, a landing

Château de la Roche Jagu

264   CHANNEL ISLANDS, CHERBOURG PENINSULA & NORTH BRITTANY

Ile de Bréhat to Trégastel-Ste Anne

The Leff – a dead end

place marked by a starboard beacon. From here a pathway leads up to the château. Depths E of the slipway are between 6–8m at half tide and anchorage is possible here providing it is well clear of the channel. Holding is good in mud but one would not want to risk grounding on the steep riverbank. Only on a small neap might it be possible to remain afloat here at LW. An anchor watch should be kept and a light shown after dark.

Depth check

It is said that if the base of the starboard beacon is covered there is sufficient depth for a boat drawing 1·5m to reach the lock.

From the cale transfer smartly to the N bank and follow it closely. At the confluence with R. Leff continue straight on for the lock – do not turn into this dead end.

In the final stretch to the lock there is a starboard buoy, after which the best depth will be found close to the W bank, following by a port buoy and a port beacon. The bottom is uneven and rocky. It is recommended to call the lock keeper on VHF Ch 12 or by phone to give warning of your arrival. While waiting use the 2 waiting buoys - *bouées d'attente* (2) - or the wall by the lock.

Pontrieux basin looking N

The sill dries at 3·5m, the lock is 65m long and 11m wide; the gates will stay open if the tide level exceeds 10m. The high-tension cable over the lock has a clearance of 25m. The basin beyond the lock has between 2m and 4m depth throughout its length.

The Port

It is about 800m from the lock past the industrial quay to the mooring area.

Berthing

There are 160 berths with 40 for visitors, maximum length 25m. There are also moorings in the basin. It is customary to double up at berths and moorings. Tell the harbourmaster if there are elderly or children on board and he will try to get you alongside.

The final bend before the lock

Quai des Sabliers inside the lock

The Maître de Port does his rounds

CHANNEL ISLANDS, CHERBOURG PENINSULA & NORTH BRITTANY

III North Brittany: 1 Cancale to Trégastel-Ste Anne

RIVIÈRE DE TRÉGUIER

48°51'·41N 03°10'·64W (150m W of La Corne lighthouse)
18M W of Lézardrieux
15M E of Port Blanc

TRAVEL
Train
  From Paimpol to Guingamp for TGV Paris-Brest
Road
  Bus: Stop by marina with services to Paimpol and Lannion

CHARTS
  BA 2027 Ile Grande to Ile de Bréhat (1:48 700)
  Imray C34 Cap d'Erquy to Ile de Batz*
    *includes plans: Rivière de Tréguier (1:45 000),
    Tréguier (1:15 000)
  Imray 2510 North Brittany Chart Atlas:
    7 Approaches to Rivière de Tréguier (1:35 000)
    7a Tréguier (1:15 000)
  SHOM 7126 De l'Île Balanec aux Héaux-de-Bréhat –
    Cours du Jaudy (1:20 000)*
    *includes plan: Port de Tréguier (1:7500)
  SHOM 7152 De l'Ile Grande à l'Ile de Bréhat (1:48 700)

RADIO
  Marina Ch 09

TIDAL INFORMATION
  Standard port: St Malo
  Difference
  HW St Malo -0020
  LW St Malo -0050

MHWS	MLWS	MHWN	MLWN
9·9	1·3	7·7	3·6

Tidal Streams
The streams in the river turn at about HW and LW with the ebb at up to 4 knots or more in the river at springs (see Mooring on the marina). Inshore in vicinity of Basse Crublent buoy there is an early turn of the stream. E-going flood starts LW St Malo and W-going ebb starts HW St Malo.

USEFUL CONTACTS
  Harbourmaster Port Plaisance ☎ 02 96 92 42 37 or
    672 707 020
  Office de Tourisme ☎ 02 96 92 22 33
  Taxi MACÉ ☎ 02 96 92 23 95

SUPPLIES AND SERVICES
Water, electricity at the pontoons
Showers on quay next to Bar les Plaisanciers
Diesel Pontoon E available on request when tide is falling at slack water
Boatyard Chantier Naval du Jaudy ☎ 02 96 92 15 15
Chandlery Coper Marine (Pont-Canada) 'La Caverne d'Alibaba le Marin' ☎ 02 96 92 35 72
Shops A wide variety of shops up in the town (15 min walk).
Restaurants close to marina:
  Ty Braise ☎ 02 96 92 15 15
  Hotel de l'Estuaire ☎ 02 96 92 20 77
Market Wednesday morning below cathedral
Bike hire from the harbour office

The Tréguier River, Le Jaudy, has long been considered the best shelter on the north coast of Brittany. With its broad estuary and a long narrowing channel that meanders through the countryside up to Tréguier there can be few better places to end a passage from the UK S coast or the Channel Islands.

It is tempting to make comparisons between this river and its close neighbour to the east, the Trieux or River Pontrieux. Both flow much in the same direction and are of similar length but differ in their destinations.

Unlike the Trieux where there is an option to carry on a further 8M beyond the marina to Pontrieux at Tréguier the Pont Canada above the marina is the limit of navigation for masted vessels.

Tréguier is a fascinating old town with well preserved medieval buildings. It needs at least a day to explore.

Historical

Tréguier takes its name from the 6th century missionary St Tugdual who founded a monastery here. The cathedral of St Tugdual which is one of the finest in Brittany dates from the 9th century. The strange granite spire, a 'honeycomb of irregular openings', was completed in 1787.

St Yves, the 'friend of the poor' lived in Tréguier in the 13th century and is the patron saint of lawyers and advocates. A procession from Tréguier Cathedral to his birthplace at the nearby village of Minihy-Tréguier takes place every third Sunday in May. This is known as the Pardon of the Poor.

Place du Martray in the centre of Tréguier

Cathédral St Tugdual

Ile de Bréhat to Trégastel-Ste Anne

Rivière de Tréguier (Le Jaudy) looking downstream from Tréguier

Approaches

There are three approaches to the estuary for which a large scale chart is essential:

Grande Passe is straightforward by day or night in visibility of 2M of more but transit marks are obscure.

Passe de la Gaine is narrow and dependent on seeing the transit that is 5M or more distant but there is a mark approximately every mile. By day only.

Passe du Nord Est is not so narrow as Passe de la Gaine but 10M visibility is needed to see the distant marks. By day only.

From the W
Grande Passe (4·4m up to La Corne)

This channel is well marked, but the initial transit by day described below is notoriously difficult to locate hence the need to chart read your way.

T1 *137° Port La Chaine lighthouse aligned with Saint-Antoine lighthouse*

First make for a position just under 0·5M due W of Basse Crublent port buoy (⊕111) and take up 137° to leave it 600m to port.

The next marks 1·0M ahead are Le Corbeau port buoy and Pierre à l'Anglais starboard buoy 400m apart. The line passes midway between the two.

The final mark a further 1·0M ahead is Petit Pen ar Guezec starboard buoy which is left 200m to starboard. Make a sharp turn to starboard round the buoy onto 215°:

Basse Crublent port buoy

T2 *215° Roc'h Skeiviec tower (W) against the left hand edge (E) of La Corne lighthouse*

The line passes midway between Le Petit Taureau starboard beacon and Le Trois Pierres N cardinal beacon tower. Come to starboard to leave La Corne 100m to port and Le Taureau starboard buoy close to starboard.

From the N
Passe du Nord Est (0·5m) (By day only)

Caution
This channel lacks en route marks and passes over Basses de Roc'h Hir which has charted depths of at least 0·3m. It is unlikely that Tréguier's spire will be visible from this range.

Approaching the final bend

III North Brittany: 1 Cancale to Trégastel-Ste Anne

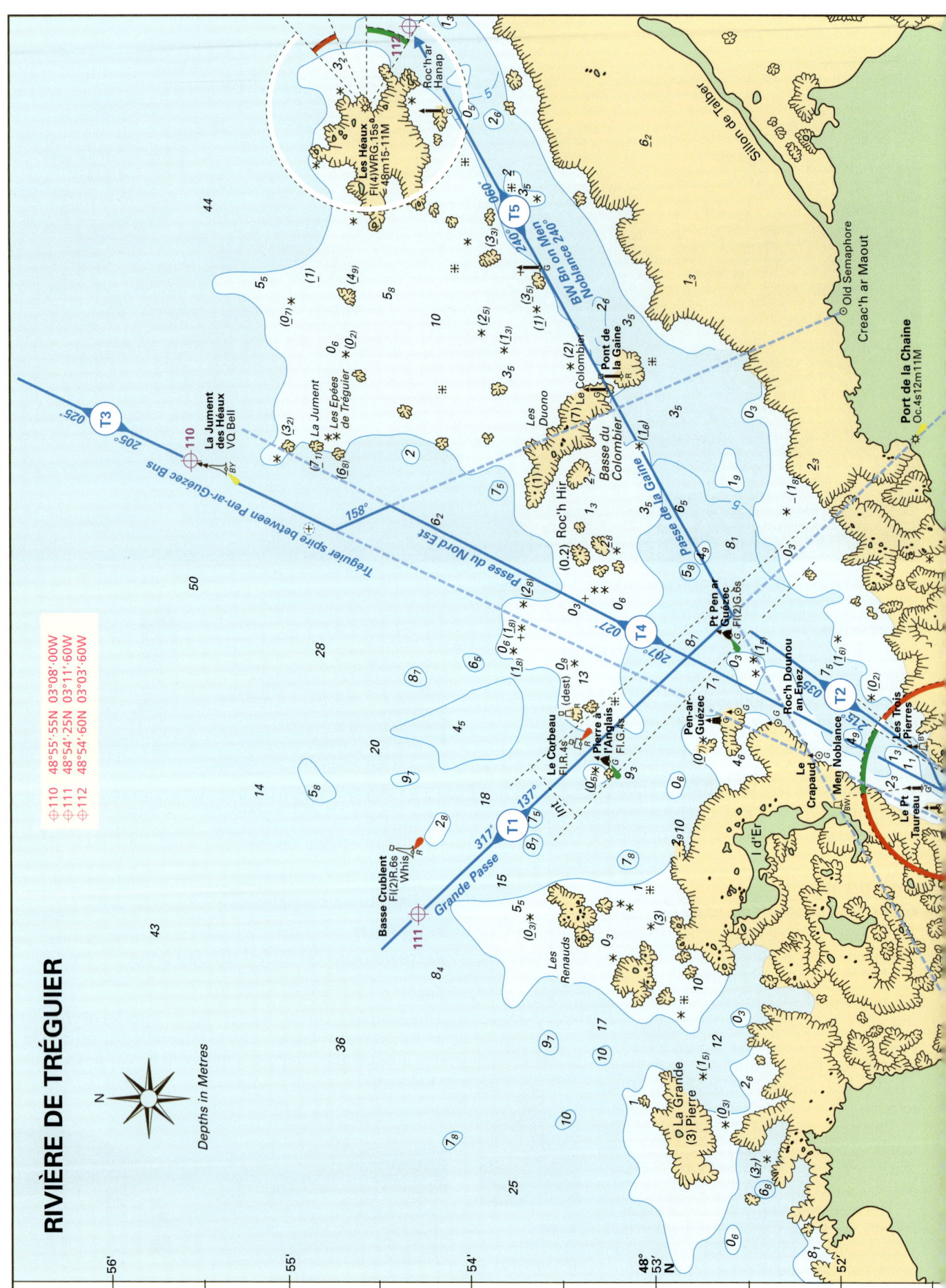

Ile de Bréhat to Trégastel-Ste Anne

III. NORTH BRITTANY: 1 CANCALE TO TRÉGASTEL-STE ANNE

CHANNEL ISLANDS, CHERBOURG PENINSULA & NORTH BRITTANY 269

III North Brittany: 1 Cancale to Trégastel-Ste Anne

From a position 400m N of La Jument des Héaux N cardinal buoy 2·0M WNW of Les Héaux (⊕110) take up 205° with transit:

T3 205° Tréguier Cathedral spire between the two towers of Pen ar Guezec

Hold until 0·4M abeam Les Epées de Tréguier reef. Alter course to SSE and hold for 0·4M to transfer onto:

T4 207° Tréguier Cathedral spire aligned with Roc'h Skeiviec

This leg cuts through the shallow Basses de Roc'h Hir reef between several drying rocks. If uncertain this is the point to stab WSW to Basse Crublent port buoy to join the better marked Grande Passe.

The rest of the channel down to La Corne lighthouse is straightforward.

Pen-ar-Guezec starboard beacon tower and its smaller starboard beacon is left 200m to starboard.

Roc'h Dounou an Enez beacon tower is left 180m to starboard, La Corne lighthouse at least 100m to port and Le Taureau starboard buoy Fl.VQ.G close to starboard.

From the East
Passe de la Gaine (2m up to La Corne) (By day only)

Start from a position 1·8M due E of Les Héaux light house or ⊕109. Note this position is at the N end of Chenal de la Moisie transit L1 (see page 261).

Make good 270° for a further 1M to ⊕112 which is positioned on Passe de la Gaine line. The first transit which is seldom practicable as marks are between 5M and 7M distant is:

T5 240° Amer de Plougrescant (Wall 37m) BW aligned with Men Noblance tower WBW

Note several marks in the first 2M down the line. In NE–SW order these are:

- Conspicious rock Roc'h an Hanaf (Roc'h ar Hanap on BA charts) 600m SE of Les Héaux lighthouse is left 400m to starboard

- Starboard beacon (Basse des Héaux) is left 300m to starboard
- Further starboard beacon is left 100m (only) to starboard
- ¾M ahead is the narrow gap between starboard and port beacons. Pass midway between the two
- 700m SW of the gap and a cat's whisker (about 30m) N of the line is an isolated rock drying 1·6m. This may involve a minor alteration S to avoid.

The most demanding part of the Channel is now behind and the transit T5 should be visible ahead as should the next en route mark Petit Pen ar Guezec starboard buoy. This should be left 120m to starboard. Alter course to 215° with transit T2 as described above (From the W).

Leave La Corne at least 100m to port.

From La Corne inwards (2·0m)

A track of 240° from Banc de Taureau starboard unlit buoy will carry to Guarivinou port hand buoy (Fl.R). From here course may be altered to 195° up the channel.

The channel is well marked and useable at any state of tide but at LWS you would be unlikely to find a metre in places over the last half mile up to the marina. The passage is best made just after LW when the drying banks are uncovered clearly indicating the direction of the channel. It also avoids arriving at the marina when the stream is at its strongest.

There are several blind bends, fish farms and moorings so one needs to stay alert. Tréguier is a commercial port so working vessels can be expected.

By night
Leading lights:
Grande Passe
  Front: Port de la Chaine (Oc.4s11M)
  Rear: St Antoine (Dir.Oc.R.4s15M)
Passe du Nord By day only
Passe de la Gaine By day only

The river is lit.

Anchorages

It is possible to anchor in good holding almost anywhere in the channel but room must be left for the occasional

La Roche Jaune on the Rivière de Treguier

Buoy No 10

Below the château opposite Banc de Ven

coaster, fishing boats and the fish farm craft. A riding light is advisable. Consider:

- Near the Guarivinou buoy in 5m sandy mud. Avoid the rock close to the S of the buoy
- Towards the W of the channel between the starboard Fl.G buoy and Roc'h Don beacon in 5m, mud
- Clear of the moorings and fish farms off Roche Jaune village
- Below the château opposite Banc de Ven below the town in 5m, mud but the banks are steep to and the channel narrow

Anchorage is prohibited between the chateau and the bridge above the marina.

Mooring on the Marina
Caution
Tréguier is sometimes described as 'a nice place to stop… if you can!' referring to the strong run of tide that courses through the marina, particularly on the ebb. This may reach 6 knots at springs causing difficulties manoeuvring.

The answer is to coordinate arrival and departure with slack water – an hour either side of HW or LW – and always moor into the stream.

If waiting for the stream to ease or a vacant berth use the waiting pontoons downstream of the marina.

Visitors are requested to call the Bureau du Port (Ch 09) when in range to give notice of arrival. Berthing directions and assistance on the pontoons will usually be provided during hours of daylight.

The marina looking upstream towards the bridge. E pontoon has been extended to accommodate larger yachts

Ile de Bréhat to Trégastel-Ste Anne

PORT BLANC
⊕48°52'·20N 03°20'·50W (Le Voleur Dir Fl.WRG.4s)
7M W of R de Tréguier entrance
8M E of Perros-Guirec

CHARTS
British Admiralty
 2027 Ile Grande to Ile de Bréhat (1:48 700)
Imray
 C34 Cap d'Erquy to Ile de Batz*
 2510 North Brittany Chart Atlas*
  both include plan: Port Blanc (1:25 000)
SHOM
 7125 Abords de Perros-Guirec – Les Sept Iles – De l'Ile Grande à l'Ile Balanec (1:20 000)
 SHOM 7152 De l'Ile Grande à l'Ile de Bréhat (1:48 700)

TIDAL INFORMATION
HW St Malo –0030
LW St Malo –0050

MHWS	MLWS	MHWN	MLWN
9·6	1·3	7·5	3·6

Tidal Streams
The streams off the coast start as follows:
HW Brest -0450 E-going
HW Brest +0120 W-going

Depths
In the mooring area between Ile St Gildas and Ile des Femmes the chart indicates 7m at datum. It is said that there is seldom less than 4m on all tides except over areas charted as drying.

USEFUL CONTACTS
The Bureau du Port and the sailing school (Cercle Nautic de Port Blanc) share the same area at the E end of the bay. The Harbourmaster will advise on mooring, weather and obtaining supplies. The sailing school is hospitable to visitors who are welcome to use their facilities.
 ℡ 02 96 92 64 96 www.chportblanc.fr
Radio Ch 09 *Port Blanc*
Harbourmaster ℡ 02 96 92 64 96 (0800–1200, 1330–1700)

SUPPLIES AND SERVICES
Visitors' moorings
Water taps at both E and W slipways
WC E and W slipways and also at sailing school
Showers Sailing school
Fuel (in cans) from Garage at Penvénan (2·5km) which is also the nearest source of shops.
Restaurant Grand Hotel Restaurant opposite Bureau du Port.

There are stretches of the Brittany coast where you may never feel totally relaxed unless you are a good distance off, and W of Les Héaux can be one of them. However in quiet settled weather with good visibility and unhurried tides you might consider closing the coast midway between Tréguier and Perros-Guirec to discover the unusual and attractive anchorage of Port Blanc. This just qualifies for the title of 'natural harbour' with seldom less than 4m but the rocks and islets that provide shelter from winds between NE through S to WSW do not extend to the N and it is therefore totally exposed to northwesterlies.

Approach
From E
The key mark is Basse Crublent port buoy at the outer end of Grande Passe onto the R. du Tréguier (⊕111) (see page 268). From here make good 260° for about 6M to ⊕113 on the leading line into Port Blanc described overleaf.

III North Brittany: 1 Cancale to Trégastel-Ste Anne

Caution
This track passes 1M N of Basse Laeres (Barr Laerez) reef (dries 0·6m) which should be identified on the chart.

From W
The key mark is Basse Gauzer port buoy at the outer end of the Le Chenal du Nord-Est into Perros-Guirec. From here maintain the channel (045°) for 0·7M onto the leading line into Port Blanc.

Entry
Identify the key marks on the W side of the deep wide entrance. These are a white painted rock Le Four (2·8) 0·5M W of the line and a white pyramid on Ile du Châteauneuf which is left 200m to starboard on entry. The leading marks are:

PB1 *150° Moulin de la Comptesse (W) aligned with Le Voleur*

Note that Le Voleur while being efficient as a sectored light is partially obscured by trees. An alternative day mark is a W house with grey roof just to the SE of Le Voleur (see view). Similarly the Moulin (back mark) is obscured (2013).

There are several beacons marking the entrance. Opposite the white pyramid on Ile du Châteauneuf are a succession of three port hand beacons and the W extremity of the anchorage is marked by a single starboard beacon, Run Glas.

Looking N across the anchorage

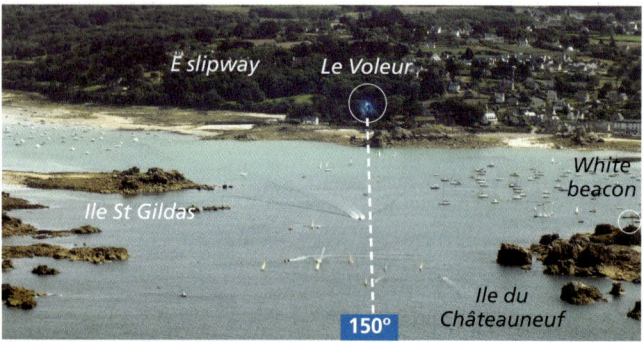

By night
Le Voleur: (Dir.Fl.WRG.4s) W Sector 150°.

Mooring
There are five visitors' moorings. Alternatively anchor clear of them and the channel in 1–4m sand.

Ashore in Port Blanc
There is a slip and jetty drying 1·3m alongside just to the E of Le Voleur – see plan above. This could be used to dry out alongside. The slip or the beach anywhere between Le Voleur and the sailing school can be used to land. There is another slip to the W of the sailing school, a long building 300m W of Le Voleur where the harbourmaster may also be found.

Ile de Bréhat to Trégastel-Ste-Anne

PERROS-GUIREC

48°48'·17N 03°26'·21W (Jetty Head)
7M W of Port Blanc
5·5M E of Ploumanac'h

TRAVEL
Sea
 Ferry: St Malo – Condor Ferries (see St Malo),
 Roscoff – Brittany Ferries (see Roscoff)
Air
 Daily flights Paris Orly - Lannion ☏ 02 96 05 82 22, www.hop.fr
Train
 Station SNCF Lannion (10km), ☏ 02 92 35 35 35. TGV – Brest line

CHARTS
British admiralty
 2027 Ile Grande to Ile de Bréhat (1:48 700)
Imray
 C34 Cap d'Erquy to Ile de Batz*
  *includes plans: Anse de Perros (1:30 000),
  Perros-Guirec (1:15 000)
 2510 North Brittany Chart Atlas*
  *includes plan: Anse de Perros (1:30 000)
SHOM
 7125 Abords de *Perros*-Guirec – Les Sept Iles –
  De l'Ile Grande à l'Ile Balanec (1:20 000)*
  *includes plan: Port de Perros-Guirec (1:10 000)
 7152 De l'Ile Grande à l'Ile de Bréhat (1:48 700)

TIDAL INFORMATION
HW St Malo –0040
Alternatives (approximate):
HW St Helier –0100
HW Paimpol –0030
HW Brest +0130

MHWS	MLWS	MHWN	MLWN
9·3	1·2	7·3	3·8

Tidal Streams
Outside the Bay N of Ile Tomé the SE going flood starts at local HW +0230 reaching 2 knots at springs. The W going ebb also reaches 2 knots at springs.
Inside the Bay at the intersection of Passe de l'Est and Passe de L'Ouest the streams tend to be weak and variable reaching 0·7 knots at springs.
There are accelerated areas where streams may reach in excess of 2 knots at springs. These are where the approach channels pass between Ile Tomé and the coast. Beware also of a SW/NE stream of 2–3 knots in the final approach towards the marina.

RADIO
Radio VHF Ch 09

CONTACTS
Bureau du Port (Capitainerie) ☏ 02 96 49 80 50
 Season 0730–1200, 1330–2000
 Email portplaisance@perrosguirec.com
Port control (marina gate) ☏ 02 96 23 19 03 / 96 49 80 50
Office de Tourisme ☏ 02 96 23 21 15

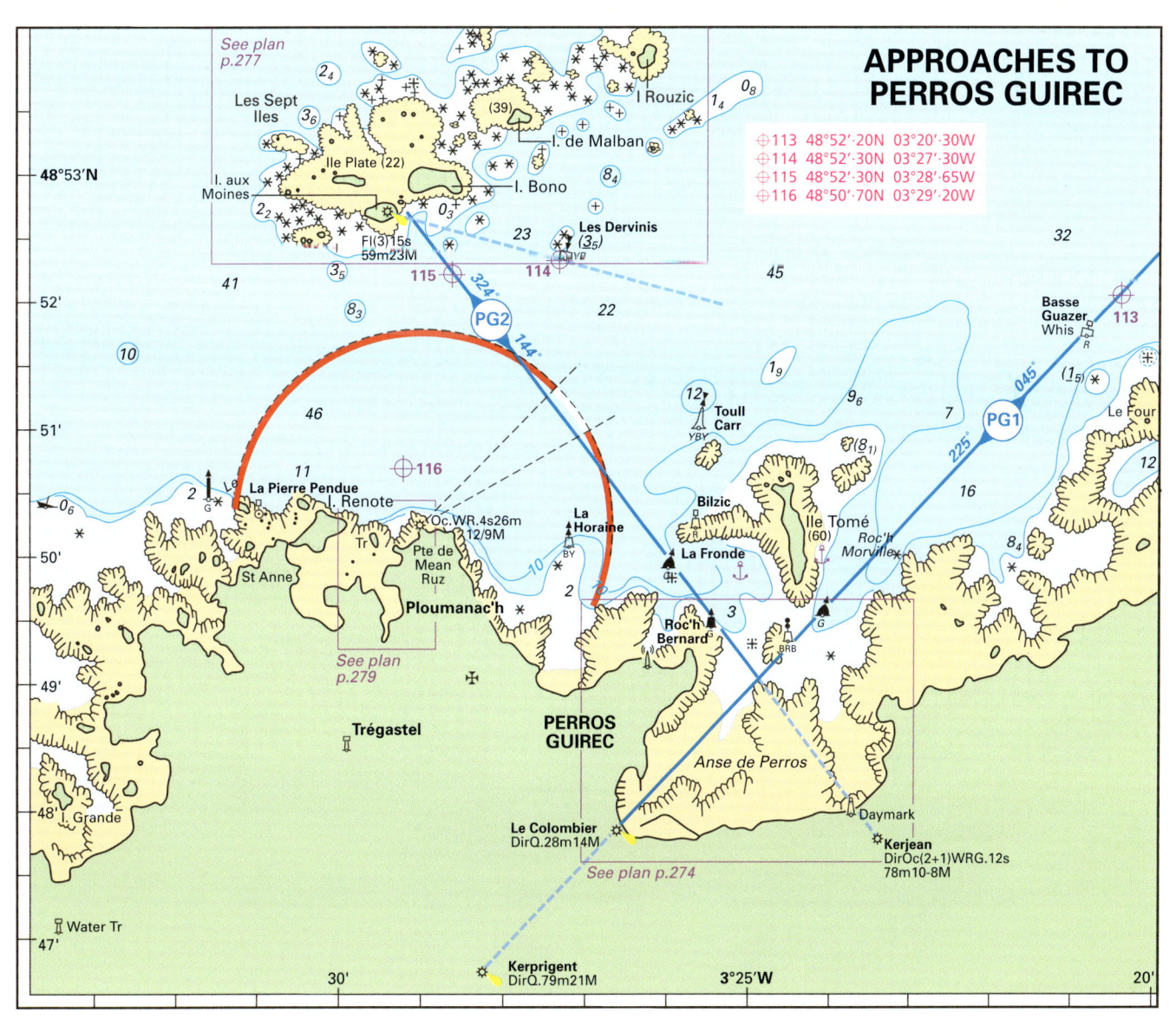

III. NORTH BRITTANY: 1 CANCALE TO TRÉGASTEL-STE ANNE

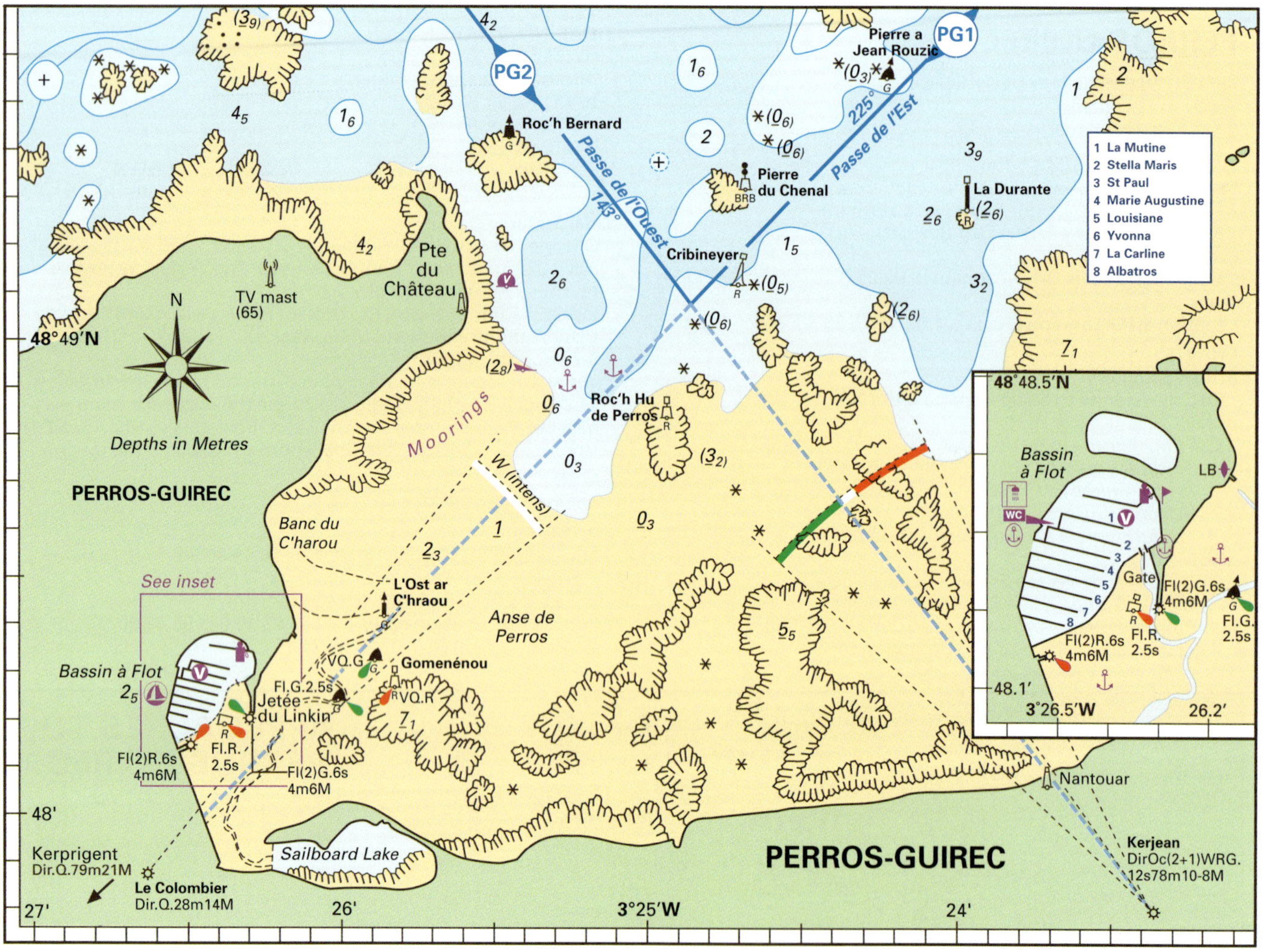

III North Brittany: 1 Cancale to Trégastel-Ste Anne

Perros-Guirec marina from the NE

PERROS-GUIREC (continued)

SUPPLIES AND SERVICES
Marina
Berths 820, visitors': 80, max 20m, draught 2·5m
Water and electricity at pontoons
Fuel 24/7 on isolated pontoon 'La Glycine' adjacent to gate
Showers Bureau du Port (Capitainerie)
Cranes 7 ton, 60 ton on hard standing Jetée du Linkin
WiFi, laundry

In contrast to the historical elegance of Tréguier to the East and the unsophisticated harbours to the W, Perros-Guirec has developed into a sprawling resort that extends along the coast to Ploumanach.

In the season it is 'La France en vacances' attracting holidaymakers from inland cities including Paris with daily flights from Orly to Lannion (6M). It has all the essential amenities – good beaches, highrise hotels, gourmet restaurants, spas and a casino.

To the visiting yachtsman Perros-Guirec's extensive marina in the extreme SW corner of the Anse de Perros offers total shelter and comprehensive facilities but prepare for a long wait in the bay if you arrive at low water. Beamy vessels and multihulls may not get through the main gate which is only 5·8m wide. (See *Anchorages and moorings*.)

Approaches
There are two approaches either side of Ile Tomé which lies to the north of the Anse de Perros. The buoys and beacons at the outer ends of both approaches are sufficient for piloting in good visibility if the leading marks cannot be identified. The final 1M to the gate dries up to 3m at datum.

Approaches are west or east of Ile Tomé viewed here from the north

Looking S out of the narrow entrance *Paul Bryans*

Passe de l'Est (0·4m)
From ⊕113 approach is made with:

Paul Bryans

PG1 *225° Le Colombier lt ho (Q.28m 14M) aligned with Kerprignant Lt Ho (obscured) (Dir.Q.79m21M)*

The channel marks are:

- Basse Guazer port buoy – leave 200m to port
- Pierre à Rouzic starboard buoy – leave 50m to starboard
- La Durante port beacon – leave 600m to port
- Pierre du Chenal isolated danger beacon tower – leave 150m to starboard
- Cribineyer port buoy – leave 150m to port

The line now passes over a 0·4m patch and if avoidance is needed, alter to 270° before reaching Cribineyer and regain the 225° line when Roc'h Hu de Perros port beacon tower bears 180°, or at night well in to the green sector of Kerjean light Dir.Oc(2+1)WRG.12s.

Continue along the line if the tide serves to leave:

Roc'h Hu de Perros port beacon tower 250m to port and L'Ost ar C'hraou starboard beacon 50m to starboard (see plan page 274). The depths now shallow and the head of Jetée du Linkin (Fl(2)G.5s) should be rounded close to starboard. The deeper water from here to the lock gate is close to the W side of the jetée.

Passe de l'Ouest (1·0m)
From ⊕115, 0·5M SSE of Ile aux Moines, navigate to a position about 1M SW of Toull Carr (Les Couillons de Tomé) W cardinal unlit buoy NW of Ile Tomé and identify the leading marks:

PG2 *144° Kerjean Lt Ho (Dir.Oc(2+1) aligned with disused Nantouar Lt Ho (W) on the shore. (see plans)*

As both marks are obscure it will be necessary to chart read to the intersection with Passe de L'Est in Anse de Perros.

III North Brittany: 1 Cancale to Trégastel-Ste Anne

The line will leave:
- Bilzic port beacon tower 200m to port.
- La Fronde starboard buoy 250m to starboard.
- Roc'h Bernard starboard beacon tower 250m to starboard.
- Pierre du Chenal isolated danger beacon tower 400m to port.

As soon as Pierre du Chenal is abeam alter to 190° or more to pick up the Passe de l'Est leading line 225° and avoid the 0·4m patch WSW of Cribineyer. Continue as for Passe de l'Est.

By night
Leading lights:

Passe de L'Est
Front: Le Colombier lighthouse (Dir.Q.14M)
Rear: Kerprignant lighthouse (Dir.Q.W.21M)

Passe de L'Ouest
Kerjean lighthouse (Dir.Oc(2+1)WRG.12s12M)
W sector is 1·6°, red to NE, green to SW.

Moorings
There are five (2013) white visitors' buoys in a minimum of 3m just to the E of Pointe du Château, (also known as Castell Perros) but they can be uncomfortable around HW.

There are three waiting buoys outside the harbour entrance, drying about 3m.

Anchorages
There is generally good holding throughout the Anse de Perros with shelter from the SE through S to NW.
- With Roc'h Hu de Perros tower bearing 120°, 300m. Least depth 2·2m sand and mud.
- At neaps anywhere to the SW of this anchorage as depth allows.
- In westerly weather on the SE side of Ile Tomé about 200m offshore in 3·5m sand and shells. The island is precipitous and uninhabited.
- In easterly weather on the W side of Ile Tomé with the S tip of Tomé bearing 105° 600m. Least depth 5·2m.

As the tide rises and at neaps, anchorage is possible further SW, nearer the port. (See airview on page 274.)

Alongside
Jetée du Linkin
The quay outside the gate is a possible site subject to available space and authorisation of the lockkeeper. It tends to be used by fishing craft. Accessible from about half tide.

Quay des Douanes
Quay des Douanes slipway in the drying zone on the W side of the harbour. This is accessible from about HW – 2h30 but is used exclusively by fishing craft.

A yacht should not be left unattended in either of these locations.

Entry

Signals
Red – No entry/exit
Green – Entry/exit
One way traffic

Marina gate opening
Information ☏ 02 96 23 19 03

Height of Tide	Opening Period
Spring tide, coefficient 70+	HW –1h30 to HW+1h30
Average tide, coefficient 60–70	HW –1h to HW +1h
Between spring and neap tide, coefficient 50–60	HW –1h to HW+0030
Mean neap tide, coefficient 40–50	HW –0030 to HW
Small neap tide, coefficient –40	No opening. 4 days max.

View of Pointe du Château from SE

Jetée du Linkin and the gate at LW

Quai des Douanes

Ile de Bréhat to Trégastel-Ste Anne

LES SEPT ILES

48° 52'·75N 03° 29'·22W (Slipway E end of Ile aux Moines)
6·0M NW of Perros-Guirec
2·7M N of Ploumanac'h

TRAVEL
Sea
Vedettes ply regularly between Les Sept Iles and Perros-Guirec, Ploumanac'h and Trégastel during the season. Routes take you very close in to the gannetry on Ile Rouzic which is fascinating.
  Armor Navigation ☎ 02 96 91 10 00
  www.armor-navigation.com

CHARTS
  BA 2027 Ile Grande to Ile de Bréhat (1:48 700)
  SHOM 7125 Abords de *Perros*-Guirec – Les Sept Iles – De l'Ile Grande à l'Ile Balanec (1:20 000)
  SHOM 7152 De l'Ile Grande à l'Ile de Bréhat (1:48 700)

RADIO
  Nil. Cross Corsen Ch 16

TIDAL INFORMATION
  Standard port: St Malo
  Difference: HW St Malo – 0040
  LW St Malo –0110
  HW Brest +0005

WARNING
Tidal streams run at up to 5 knots in Chenal des Sept Iles between the island and the mainland. Seas can be short and steep with wind over tide.

SUPPLIES AND SERVICES
  Nil. Tourist shop at lighthouse (seasonal)

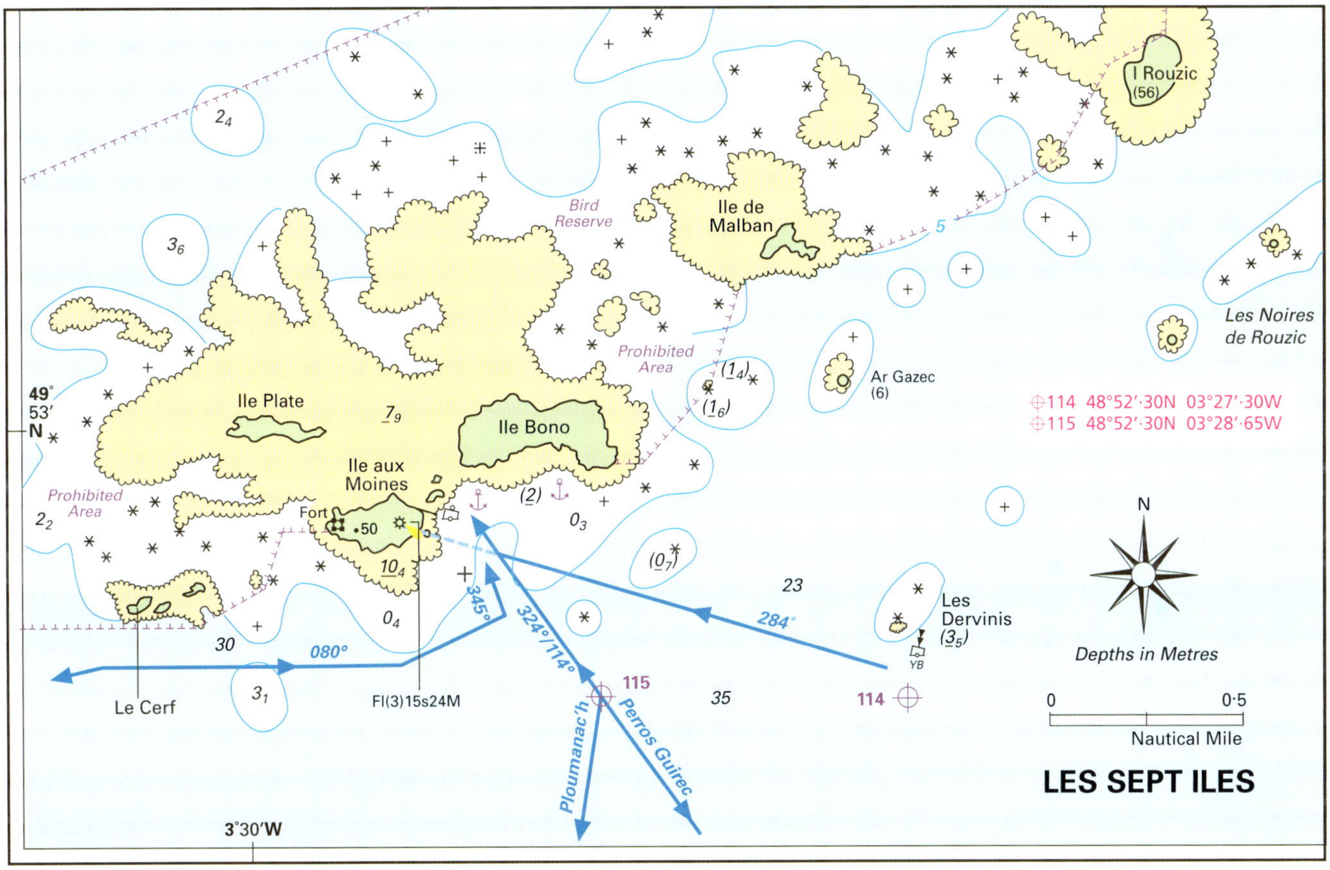

Ile aux Moines (left) and Ile Bono (right) looking NW

CHANNEL ISLANDS, CHERBOURG PENINSULA & NORTH BRITTANY

III North Brittany: 1 Cancale to Trégastel-Ste Anne

Les Sept Iles seen from Mean Ruz lighthouse

The large W mooring is used by ferries

This archipelago lies two miles off the nearest point on the mainland. From E to W it comprises Ile Rouzic, Ile de Malban, Ile Bono, Ile aux Moines (with lighthouse), Ile Plate and three large above water rocks collectively named Le Cerf. The whole area is a bird sanctuary and landing is restricted to Ile aux Moines only where the sole inhabitant, the lighthouse keeper, lives.

It is a good haul from the landing up to the lighthouse where a small shop is maintained in the season. The area N of a line between SE corner of Ile Bono and W side of Ile Rouzic is prohibited.

It was due to the diminishing number of puffins that were almost hunted to extinction that Les Sept Iles became classified as a wildlife reserve in 1976. Other endangered species are the razorbill and guillemot. The most common bird in the islands is the gannet which has taken over the eastern half of Ile Rouzic in vast numbers, giving it the impression of being whitewashed.

Approaches

Approach from the east

From a position 200m S of Les Dervinis S cardinal buoy (⊕114) continue W until right hand (E) edge of Ile aux Moines bears 324° (⊕115) and hold to the slipway (48°52′·75N 03°29′·22W).

Approach from the south

Perros is a popular departure point for Les Sept Iles. Leaving Anse de Perros via Passe de l'Ouest (324°) hold this track for a further 3M after passing La Fronde starboard buoy. This will bring you to ⊕115 where the right hand (E) edge of Ile aux Moines bears 320°. Continue as for Approach for E above.

From the entrance to Ploumanac'h, the nearest point to Ile aux Moines, make good 010° to ⊕115 and continue approach as above. Approaches from S will be crosstide with streams of up to 4 knots at springs.

From W

Keeping outside the 30m line, pass 500m S of the western outliers and make good E until the W end of Ile Bono bears 345°. Hold this track into the anchorage.

Anchorage

The main anchorage lies SE of the gap between Ile aux Moines and Ile Bono with the lighthouse bearing about 270° and the W end of Ile Bono 000°. There is a mooring buoy (W) in the anchorage which is used by vedettes (see photo).

Anchor between the buoy and the pier which has a beacon on the end of it. Do not proceed far N of the buoy towards the strand between the islands as there are two rocks which cover towards HW. The anchorage is protected from the NNE and NE by Ile Bono and from the W by Ile aux Moines. The strand of sand and stones which dries out between the islands, breaks the sea from that direction but otherwise is quite open to southerly winds and should only be used in settled weather. The anchorage is often crowded in daytime especially at weekends.

Another less frequented anchorage lies to the S of the centre of Ile Bono which is less sheltered from the W (see photograph page 277). *SHOM 7125* is really needed to avoid the rocks (drying 0·7m and 0·1m) to the S and a rocky drying area drying 2·2m off the centre of the beach. Landing is now allowed on the beach.

Historical

Ile aux Moines was briefly settled by monks in the 15th century but later by pirates and smugglers. The remains of a Vauban fort dating from 1740 are worth visiting if just for the view. The lighthouse of 1834 was, like that of Les Roches Douvres, bombed in 1944 and subsequently rebuilt.

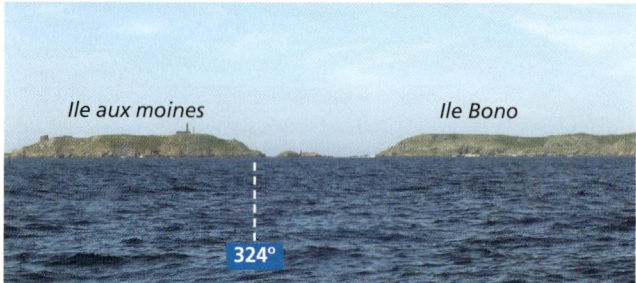

Approach from S

Ile Rouzic gannetry

278   CHANNEL ISLANDS, CHERBOURG PENINSULA & NORTH BRITTANY

PLOUMANAC'H

48°50'·25N 03°29'·00W Mean Ruz Lighthouse
3·5M W of Perros-Guirec
1·5M E of Trégastel

TRAVEL
Bus
 Bus to Perros-Guirec

CHARTS
BA 2027 Ile Grande to Ile de Bréhat (1:48 700)
Imray C34 Cap d'Erquy to Ile de Batz*
Imray 2510 North Brittany Chart Pack*
 *both include plan: Ploumanac'h (1:10 000)
SHOM 7125 Abords de Perros-Guirec – Les Sept Iles –
 De l'Ile Grande à l'Ile Balanec (1:20 000)*
 *includes plan: Port de Ploumanac'h (1:10 000)
SHOM 7152 De l'Ile Grande à l'Ile de Bréhat (1:48 700)

RADIO
Ch 16, 09 Port de Ploumanac'h (seasonal)

TIDAL INFORMATION
Standard port: St Malo
Alternative: Paimpol
HW St Malo -0035
LW St Malo -0110
HW Paimpol -0035
LW Paimpol -0035

MHWS	MLWS	MHWN	MLWN
9·3	1·3	7·3	2·5

Tidal Streams
Tidal streams in Chenal des Sept Iles start at the following times:
HW Brest -0435 SE-going
HW Brest +0130 NW-going
Up to 4 knots spring rate in centre

USEFUL CONTACTS
Bureau du Port (April–September) ☏ 02 96 91 44 31
Ploumanac'h Sémaphore Station ☏ 02 96 91 46 51,
 VHF 16/11

SUPPLIES AND SERVICES
Bureau de Port and facilities at the entrance of the Marina
Wet basin Beyond the narrow drying entrance a sill maintains a wet basin ('Marina') (see Berthing and Anchoring below).
Mooring (on buoys) 20 visitors'. Several drying moorings also available.
Waiting buoys outside (3) marked VPG between No.5 and No.7 channel beacons
Water and electricity at head of both slips
Showers and toilets near Bureau du Port adjacent to sill.
Shops in village (200m)

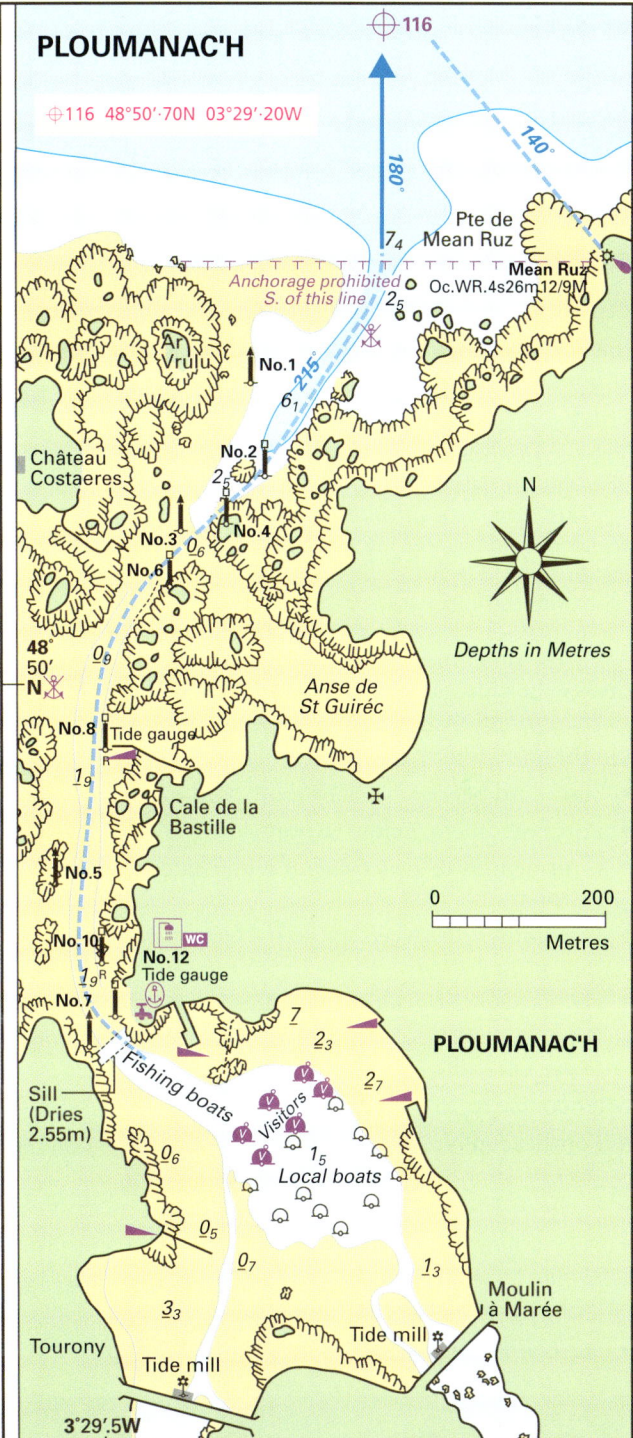

The entrance at LWS

Ploumanac'h is set in a narrow cleft in the coast 2½M due S of Iles aux Moines in the Sept Iles. Surrounded by dramatic rock formations it is the epitome of *La Côte de Granit Rose* (see plan page 273).

An obscure entrance leads through the rocks into a narrow but well-marked channel. As the tide rises it is possible to continue up into a perfectly sheltered bay and remain afloat.

The wet basin is an informal affair where visitors raft up on trot moorings under the direction of a friendly attendant who struggles to find everyone a slot in high season. You will need the tender to get ashore and there are several bars, creperies and restaurants round the harbour.

Due to its limitations Ploumanac'h is not suitable for yachts over 12m long or drawing more than 1·6m.

III North Brittany: 1 Cancale to Trégastel-Ste Anne

Approach (see plan page 273)

The 2M run of coast between Mean Ruz lighthouse off Ploumanac'h and Le Taureau starboard beacon off Tregastel is comparatively clean and may be closed up to half a mile in all but onshore weather. First time visitors may find locating the right opening for Ploumanac'h deceptive. It all hangs on identifying Mean Ruz lt. This sits on the point 200m E of the entrance disguised as another pink rock.

The tidal streams are concentrated through the channel between Les Sept Iles and the coast so an approach from the N will involve keeping a cross stream under control.

Entry

There are no leading marks or a transit other than the home made variety.

Start from a position 0·5M N of the entrance (⊕116) which should be close enough to see the first channel marks inside and Mean Ruz lt ho bearing 140°. Make good 180°. Note that this line passes less than 200m W of drying rocks 250m NW of Mean Ruz.

By the time Mean Ruz is bearing E you must have the line of the channel confirmed and course may be altered to 215° to follow it.

On the entry line you will leave:

- Starboard beacon No.1 180m to starboard
- Port beacon No.2 close to port
- Conspicuous Ile de Costaéres with château to starboard.
- Pass midway between starboard beacon No.3 and port beacon No.4
- Port beacon No.6 close to port
- Port beacon 8 close to port (with tide gauge showing depth over sill)

Alter course to 180° to leave:

- Port beacon No.8B (end of Cale de la Bastille) close to port (with water depth gauge)
- Starboard beacon No.5 close to starboard
- Port beacon No.10 25m to port
- Midway between port beacon No.12 (with tide gauge showing depth over sill) and finally
- Starboard beacon No.7 is the sill (dries 2·55m)

Mean Ruz

Ile de Costaéres with château to starboard on entry

Waiting

If intending to enter the Basin arrival should be timed so there is enough water over the sill to pass straight in. Three waiting buoys in minimum depth 1·5m marked VPG are between No.5 and No.7 channel beacons.

Waiting anchorages outside may be found at Trégastel-St Anne (page 281), Les Sept Iles (page 277) or off Perros-Guirec (page 276).

Berthing and anchoring

There are several rows of dumbbell moorings inside the Basin. There is up to 2m on the middle outer ones but fishing boats tend to occupy them. The water shallows progressively towards the SE corner. There are ostensibly 20 places for visitors up to 12m with a maximum draught of 1·6m.

Anchoring is prohibited as shown on the plan and *SHOM Chart 7125*. For those able to dry out anchorages may be found on generally firm sand either inside the Basin or to the W of the prohibited area.

Bureau du Port

Ploumanac'h looking NW

Ile de Bréhat to Trégastel-Ste Anne

TRÉGASTEL-STE ANNE

48°50'·40N 03°31'·58W (Le Taureau starboard beacon)
2M W of Ploumanac'h. 2M NE of Ile Grande

CHARTS
BA 2027 Ile Grande to Ile de Bréhat (1:48 700)

SHOM 7125 Abords de *Perros*-Guirec – Les Sept Iles –
De l'Ile Grande à l'Ile Balanec (1:20 000)*
includes plan: Mouillages de Trégastel (1:10 000)
SHOM 7152 De l'Ile Grande à l'Ile de Bréhat (1:48 700)

TIDAL INFORMATION
Standard port: Brest
Alternative: Paimpol
HW Brest +0105
LW Brest +0110
HW Paimpol –0035
LW Paimpol –0035

MHWS	MLWS	MHWN	MLWN
9·2	1·4	7·3	3·5

CONTACTS
Capitainerie (July, August) ☎ 02 96 23 49 51 / 02 96 15 92 30
Ploumanac'h Sémaphore Station ☎ 02 96 91 46 51
  VHF 16/11
Office de Tourisme ☎ 02 96 15 38 38
  www.ville-tregastel.fr
Ecole Française de Voile ☎ 02 96 23 45 05

SUPPLIES AND SERVICES
Trégastel has all the facilities of a select family seaside resort with excellent safe beaches and sheltered conditions for water sports and dinghy work.

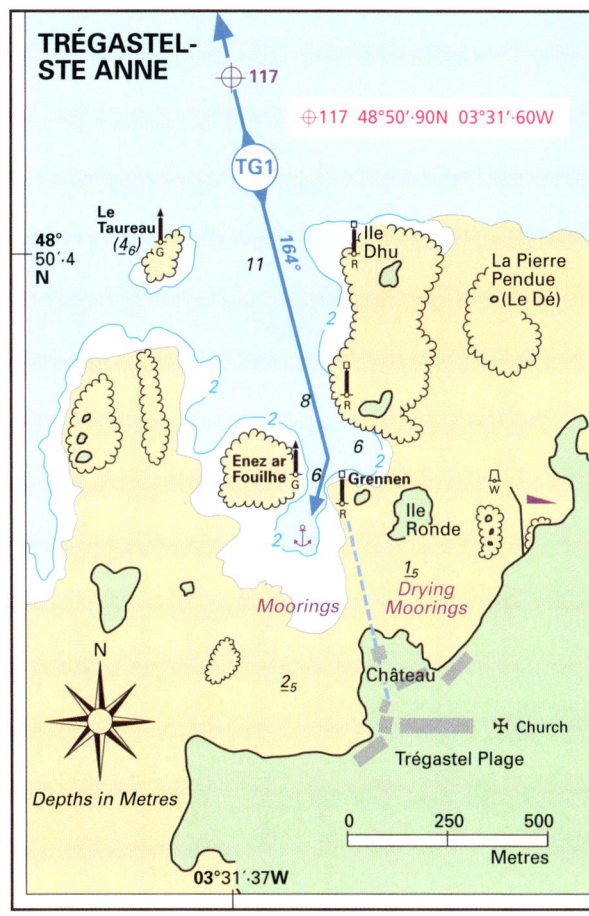

Trégastel and Ploumanac'h back onto each other in this extraordinary landscape but have their differences. Ploumanac'h offers the complete security of its wet basin, whereas Trégastel is an area of anchorages sheltered between ENE through S to WSW by rocks and islets but exposed from N or NW. At LWS the bay is almost completely landlocked with a shallow pool (2m at datum) in which to stay afloat.

Trégastel is the westernmost anchorage on this coast before it takes a dip south-westwards to become temporarily inhospitable. It does not re-emerge until the Trébeurden archipelago 7M to the SW.

Approach
Trégastel's distinctive landmark, Le Dé also known as La Pierre Pendue (the balancing rock) is 500m (¼ mile) E of the leading line. Less conspicuous is Le Taureau starboard beacon 200m W of the line.

La Pierre Pendue

Entry
From ⊕117 on the leading line take up transit:

TG1 164° *Conspicuous château (clocheton) aligned with Grennen port beacon No.6 on W side of Ile Ronde.*

Pass midway between Grennen on Ile Ronde and Enez ar Fouilhe starboard beacon and into the anchorage.

Moorings and anchorage
There are numerous moorings scattered in the bays either side of Ile Ronde. The red ones are for visitors.

Alternatively anchor in suitable depth clear of moorings. The bay SE of Ile Ronde dries 1·5m.

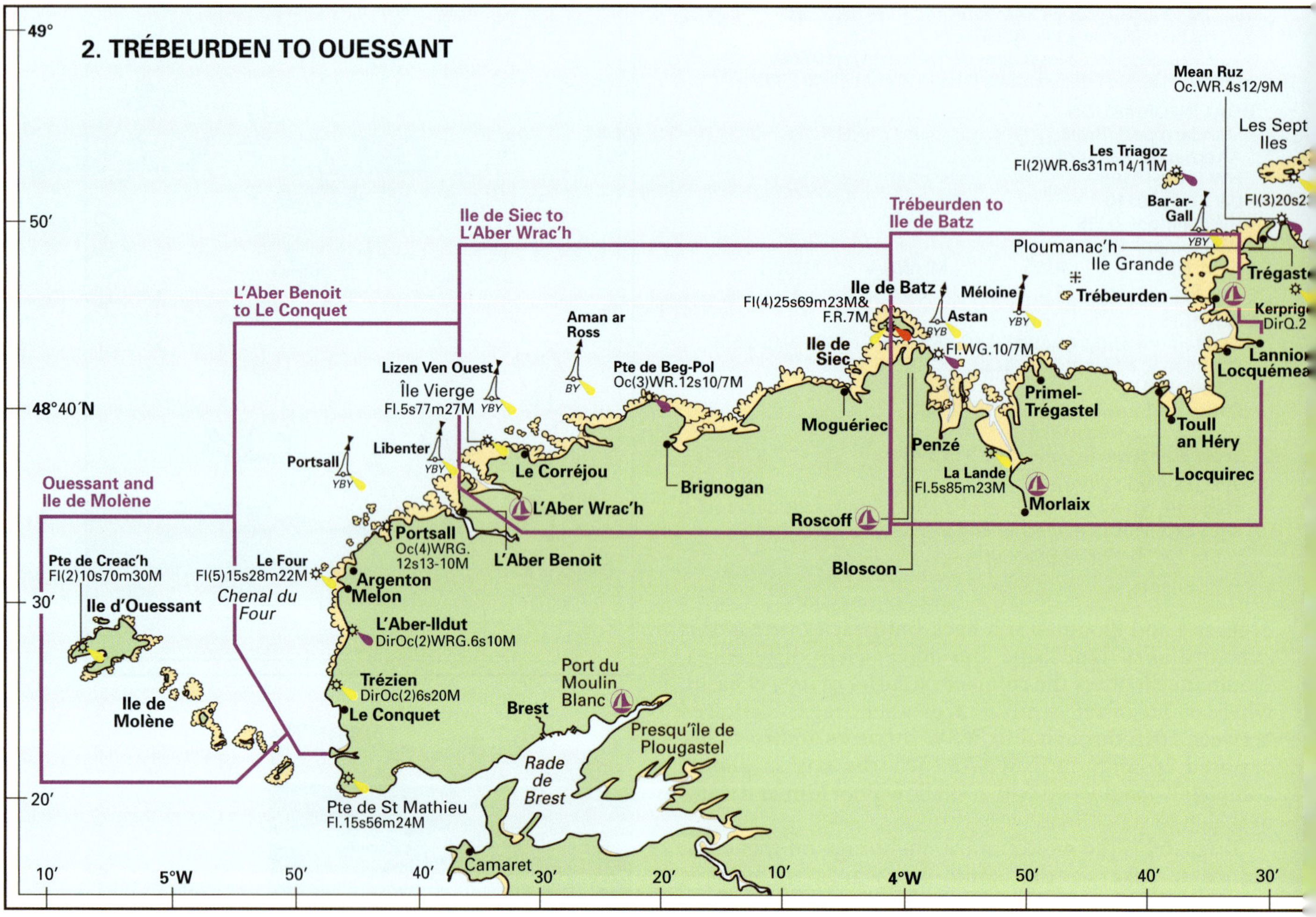

III North Brittany: 2 Trébeurden to Ouessant

Pointe de Primel from W

2. Trébeurden to Ouessant (65M)

THE COASTLINE

The south-southwesterly stretch into the comparatively unspectacular Baie de Lannion is initially broken and inhospitable. It is relieved by a small archipelago comprising of Ile Grande and several smaller islets centered on the marina and resort of Trébeurden.

The southern half of Baie de Lannion is off the beaten track but the estuary of the R. Léguer has a drying anchorage at Le Yaudet suitable for small shallow draught craft and bilge keelers. The drying river itself is hardly worth the diversion as it is no longer possible to navigate up to Lannion. Of two adjacent drying harbours, Locquémeau and Locquirec, the latter is set up for visitors with several drying and some deep water moorings.

Primel Tregastel is a shallow fishing harbour where yachts might feel out of place. The neighbouring Baie de Morlaix has a wealth of small boat anchorages, two rivers – the Morlaix and the Penzé, and at the NW extremity the town and port of Roscoff. It is liberally scattered with reefs, rocks and islets, the largest being the famous Château du Taureau. A good large scale chart is essential for finding your way around.

Roscoff is an historic town with a large secure marina and a cross channel ferry terminal, making it an ideal staging port before taking on the 'corner' of Brittany known as the iron bound coast.

Ile de Batz is separated from Roscoff by Chenal de L'Ile de Batz which is narrow, rocky and prone to accelerated streams. It should be taken at HW by all but shallow draughted yachts. The island is flat and dominated by its lighthouse. An enjoyable place to dry out in shelter and take to a bike.

West of Batz the coast is low-lying and liberally peppered with rocks extending up to 3M offshore. With the exception of Ile Vierge lighthouse (77m) on 'the corner' there are few natural marks and these may be lost in poor visibility and Atlantic swell (*La Houle*).

Whether focussed on escaping the clutches of Channel weather for balmier conditions south of Pointe du Raz, or working northwards, this coast tends to be passed over. However, given time, suitable conditions and shallow draught, there are several openings into wide sandy bays with small drying harbours. Here you will find solitude and a truly Breton atmosphere. Brignogan is an almost natural harbour with a straightforward entrance.

Close south of Ile Vierge is the convenient staging post of L'Aber Wrac'h on La Côte des Abers - a region of sheltered rivers.

Ile d'Ouessant is tall and austere with a rocky coastline and ferocious tidal streams whereas Ile de Molène, between Ouessant and the mainland is low lying surrounded by an archipelago of sandy islets.

Both are protected within the Parc Naturel Marin d'Iroise and straightforward to access from mainland harbours such as L'Aber Wrac'h, L'Aber-Ildut and Le Conquet. Settled weather, good visibility and preferably neap tides are essential for a visit.

It is said that you have no more than a superficial knowledge of Brittany until you have visited Ouessant and Molène.

LIST OF PORTS

Trébeurden Archipelago – Ile Grande 284

Rivière de Lannion (Rivière Léguer) 288

Locquémeau 291

Locquirec 292

Primel-Trégastel 293

Morlaix 295

Rivière de Penzé 305

Roscoff 308

L'Ile de Batz 313

Ile de Siec (or Sieck) 317

Moguériec 318

Brignogan (Pontusval) 320

Le Corréjou 322

L'Aber Wrac'h 325

L'Aber Benoit 328

Portsall 331

Argenton 340

Melon 342

L'Aber-Ildut 344

Le Conquet 346

Ile d'Ouessant and Ile de Molène 349

Toull an Héry, a peaceful bolthole in the estuary of Rivière Douron, a mile south of Locquirec

III North Brittany: 2 Trébeurden to Ouessant

Trébeurden to Ile de Batz (18M)

TRÉBEURDEN ARCHIPELAGO ILE GRANDE

44°46'·40N 03°35'·15W (Breakwater head Fl.G.2·5s)
3M N of Lannion River entrance

TRAVEL
Air
  Lannion airport is 12km ☏ 02 96 05 82 22
Train
  Guingamp station 11km www.sncf.fr
Road
  Bus: Coach link Lannion-Trébeurden
  Ti'bus (transport interurbains) ☏ 0 810 22 22 22
  Cars Verts ☏ 02 96 23 50 32
  CAT ☏ 02 96 46 76 70
  Free shuttle (*navette*) between marina and town (Le Bourg). Seasonal. Information: Capitainerie.

CHARTS
  BA 2026 Anse de Kernic to Ile Grande (1:50 000)
  BA 2027 Ile Grande to Ile de Bréhat (1:48 700)
  Imray C34 Cap d'Erquy to Ile de Batz*
    *includes plan: Trébeurden (1:25 000)
  Imray 2510 North Brittany Chart Atlas*
    *includes plan: Approaches to Trébeurden (1:35 000)
  SHOM 7124 Baie de Lannion – De la Pointe de Primel
    à l'île Grande (1:20 000)*
    *includes plan: Port de Trébeurden (1:7500)
  SHOM 7151 De l'anse de Kernic à l'île Grande (1:48 700)
  SHOM 7152 De l'Ile Grande à l'Ile de Bréhat (1:48 700)

Note: Charts BA 2026 and SHOM 7151 show the whole of Ile Grande but on a small scale and are suitable for approaches only. Large scale SHOM 7124 is indispensable for piloting among the channels and islets N of Trébeurden but unfortunately the N half of Ile Grande is off the top edge of the chart.

RADIO
  Ch 09 (Bureau du Port)

TIDAL INFORMATION
  Standard port: Brest or Roscoff
  Difference
  HW Brest +0105
  LW Brest + 0110
  HW Roscoff +0005
  LW Roscoff +0005

MHWS	MLWS	MHWN	MLWN
9·2	1·4	7·3	3·5

Tidal streams
  Streams off Le Crapaud shoal to the W turn as follows:
  SE/E going HW Brest -0405
  SW/W going HW Brest +0220

Depths
  Much of the area dries to sand and rock. Min depth in channels about 1·9m.

USEFUL CONTACTS
  Capitainerie: ☏ 02 96 23 64 00 / 02 96 23 64 00
    Email portrebeurden@wanadoo.fr
  Office de Tourisme: ☏ 02 96 23 51 64 www.trebeurden.fr
  Capitainerie Communale (Town harbourmaster)
    ☏ 02 96 23 66 93
  Taxi Bernard Le Vot ☏ 02 96 23 55 05 / 06 71 04 56 11

SUPPLIES AND SERVICES
Marina
  Water, electricity at pontoons.
  Showers, launderette next to Capitainerie
  Fuel Pontoon G
  Visitors' buoys (see Moorings & Anchorages)
  Boat hoist/crane
Chandlery Cap Marine, Le Port ☏ 02 96 15 49 49
  Sailing School and Guides: Point Passion Plage,
    Plage de Tresmeur ☏ 02 96 23 51 35 / 06 07 16 47 69
    Email evt@evtrebuerden.com
Boat Yards
  ABC Marine, Chantier du Toëno ☏ 02 96 23 63 55
    www.toeno.fr
  Trébeurden Marine Services ☏ 02 96 15 45 43 /
    06 29 73 17 39
Bike hire Capitainerie
General Spread around the port and along Tresmeur beach to the south are a good range of bars, cafés and restaurants but no down to earth shops. In high season a grocery and boulangerie set up on the quay but for the rest of the time the only option is a long uphill trek into 'Le Bourg'. Here below the church are a number of shops and a bank (with cashpoint). A shuttle between town and port *(navette)* is available in July and August (see Travel).
Restaurants Creperie/Restaurant des Iles.
  Le Port ☏ 02 96 23 51 39
Market Saturday, Place de la Mairie

Trébeurden Marina is sheltered to the W by Ile Milliau

Trébeurden – Ile de Batz

The coast W of Trégastel fragments into reefs, rocks and islets that appear to have been flung into the Baie de Lannion. The message of the two W cardinal buoys that guard this rogue corner is clear – keep out!

At the southern end of the outcrop the coast regains itself opening out into a small archipelago of a dozen low islets, rocky banks and drying sands spread over a three mile length of coast.

Although there are, even at LWS, a few pools of water where shallow draught boats can remain afloat in the lee of islands this is essentially a paradise for boats able to dry out happily on the sands.

Ile Grande in the North shelters the area from that direction. In the S a smaller island, Ile Milliau, barricades the Port of Trébeurden from southwesterlies. The area in between is least sheltered from the W particularly at HW.

The development of a modern marina complex at Trébeurden has raised awareness of this area that hitherto precluded larger yachts. The wet basin is accessible over a sill with a hinged gate for a period of 7 hours around HW and can accommodate yachts of up to 13m length and 2·5m draught.

Ile Grande in the N of the archipelago is, at 1M E to W, the most prominent feature on this coast. It is best approached from the S via the channels from Trébeurden 2M to the S.

Ile Grande is accessible from the mainland by a causeway at its SE corner.

See Ile Grande.

Approaches
With SHOM chart 7124.

From the N
This will be via Le Crapaud (⊕118) and Bar-ar-Gall W cardinal buoys (see plan page 286). From Le Crapaud, the southernmost, take up a southerly course for a mile before coming round to the E and onto the leading line (⊕119).

Alternatively in offshore winds a few miles may be saved on this circuitous route by taking a short cut between Le Crapaud reef and reefs N and S of Ile Losket. Start from a position 1M W of Losket (⊕120). Make good 178° for 2·8M to a position just over a mile WSW of the high NW tip of Ile Milliau (⊕119).

Chenal du Toull Ar Peulven (5·5m)
This secondary approach into the N end of the Trébeurden archipelago is totally exposed to the West so should not be attempted in weather and swell from that direction. It is also initially narrow passing close (100m) to drying rocks.

Port of Trébeurden marina

From a position 1M W of Ile Losket (11) (⊕120) make good 101° with transit:

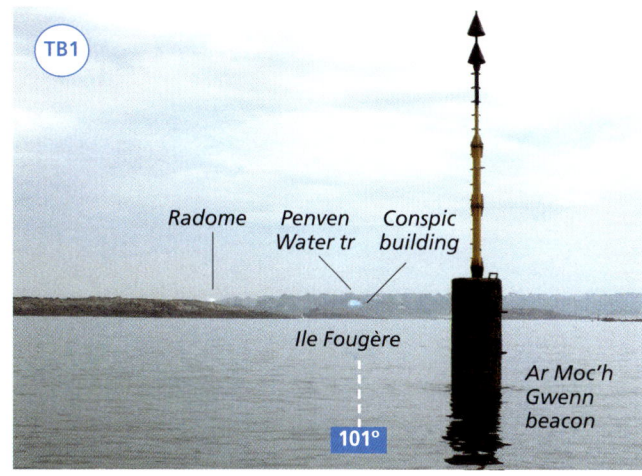

TB1 101° Penven water tower bearing 101° aligned with right (S) edge of Ile Fougère and over the grey roof of a long white building behind the island

An alternative transit involves the more conspicuous Radome (shown on the right edge of SHOM 7151). The transit is then:

095° Radome over the middle of Ile Fougère

(In the view the Radome is opened right for conspicuity.)

The line will clear S of Le Four (dries 3·6m) by just 200m and leave Ar Moc'h Gwenn (Morguen) N cardinal beacon 100m to starboard. With this abeam, there are two alternatives:

Option A
Route to Ile Grande anchorage. Alter course to starboard onto 110° to leave Ar Jalvotenn E cardinal beacon 80m to starboard and clear rocky outcrop S of Ile Fougère. This line will join transit TB2 (below) which leads NE towards Karreg ar Merk anchorage S of Ile Grande. Minimum depth on this line is 1·9m.

TB2 041° Karreg ar Jantil S cardinal beacon aligned with Karreg ar Merk E cardinal beacon tower

This line will leave:
- Karreg ar Jantil close to port
- An Tog Touseg (8) 100m to starboard
- Karreg ar Merk close to port

III North Brittany: 2 Trébeurden to Ouessant

Option B
Route S to Trébeurden
Maintain transit **TB1** *(101°)* until stern transit:

Steer 163° to hold this stern transit. Ar Jalvotenn E cardinal beacon will be left 200m to port. When this line joins transit **TB2** as described above alter course to 221° to hold for 0·25M when an alteration to port onto 178° should be made with stern transit:

TB3 *343° Ar Volenneg (15) the westernmost of two islets off the W end of Ile Aganton aligned with Easternmost point of Ile Losket*

TB4 *358° Les Trois Frères E cardinal beacon aligned with easternmost point of Ile Losket*

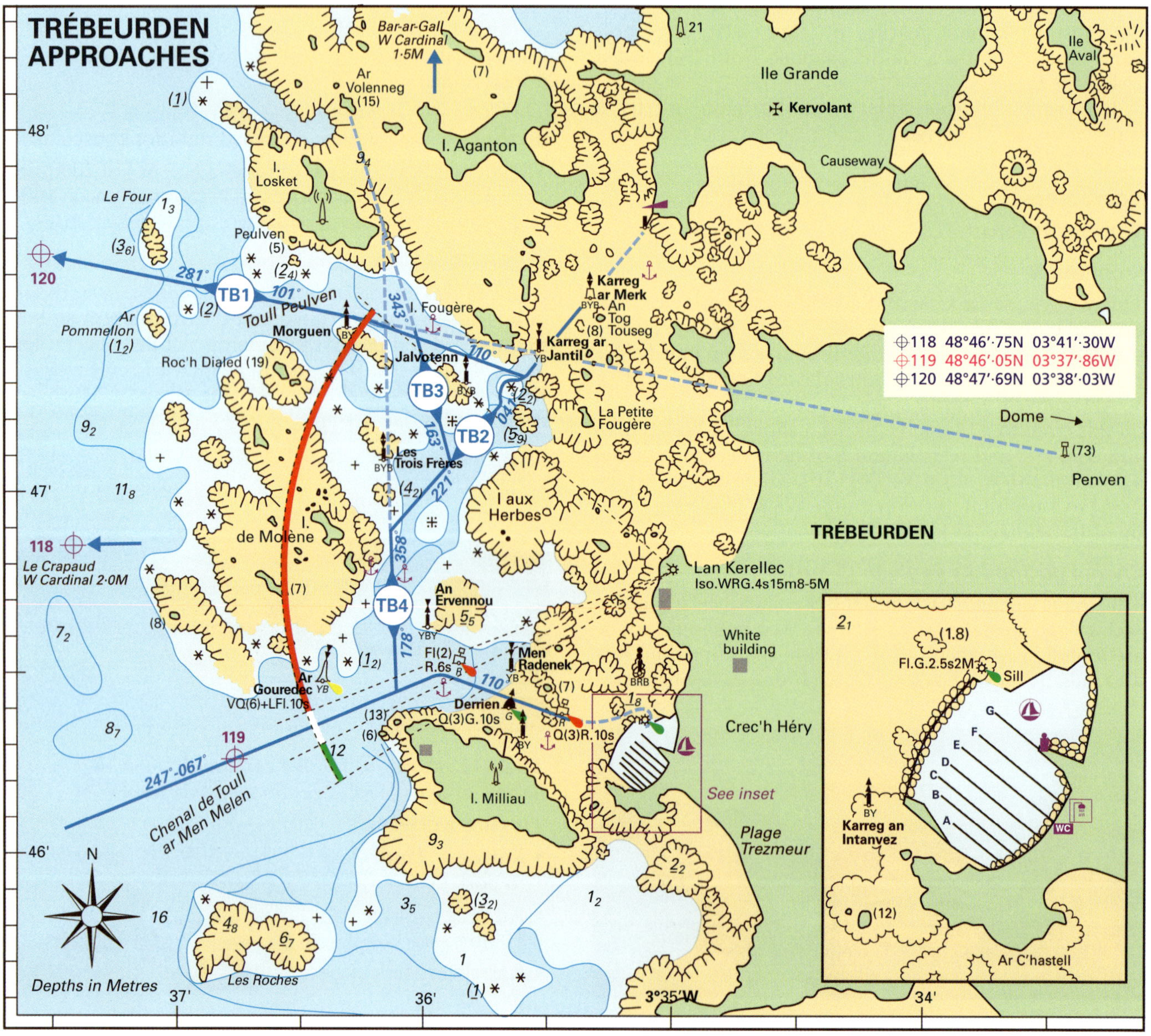

Trébeurden – Ile de Batz

Caution
E of Ile Molene this line crosses an area of rocks that are submerged at datum. A minor deviation to Port (E) at this point might be prudent (see large-scale chart). Chanel de Toull ar Men Melen described below is regained 0·6M SSE of Ile Molène.

From WSW
Navigate to ⊕119 on the leading line giving the whole length of Plateau de la Méloine and Le Crapaud a respectable clearance.

Chanel de Toull ar Men Melen
This is the main entry into Trébeurden. First identify the conspicuous Ile Milliau 0·5M W of the port. Also identify Ar Gouredec (lit) S cardinal buoy.

Position midway between these marks and enter on 067°. To leave Ar Gouredec 200m to port.

Ar Gouredec

Ile Milliau

Fl(2)R.6s   Men Radenek

When just short of the next port buoy (lit) turn to starboard onto about 110° towards marina to leave:
- Port buoy close to port
- Men Radenek S cardinal beacon 200m to port
- Roc'h Derrien starboard buoy (lit) close to starboard

Head then for the end of the breakwater Fl.G.2·5s. Note that there is a rocky patch drying 1·8m 100m WNW of the breakwater end but there will be water to carry over it if the sill can be crossed.

Entrance

Signals

The marina sill viewed from outside

By night
Iso.WRG.4s a Lan Kerellec Pt. Enter 067° in W sector. (See Main Entry from W.)

Marina entry
Call *bureau du port* on Ch 09 to request a berth.

The deeper water is close to the breakwater and round its end which involves a 180° turn to line up with the gate. This should be taken slowly in case boats without masts are leaving. The control lights 100m along the breakwater are:

3R Entry and departure prohibited
2G + 1W Entry and departure allowed (1·5m+ over the sill).

The maintained depths in the marina are from 2·5m near the entrance, to 2m towards the S corner. The water is retained by a wall which dries 3·8m and the height of the sill in the entrance dries 2·1m. The wall on either side of the entrance is marked by port and starboard beacons and there is a depth gauge on either side. The pontoon for visitors is the first one (G) and there appears to be 2·5m depth along its length.

Caution
There is considerable turbulence near the outer end of F and G pontoons for up to 10 minutes after the gate has opened. Yachts here should be well secured and movements through the gate should not be attempted during this time.

Moorings and anchorages off marina entrance
There are a number of moorings to the N of Ile Milliau, 10 of which are for visitors. The yellow ones marked 1–10 are specifically for those waiting to go on to the marina.

An isolated anchorage E of Ile Grande

III North Brittany: 2 Trébeurden to Ouessant

Anchor on sand where there is water to the N of Ile Milliau, between the moorings and the approach channel. At springs this will be exposed to the W and the whole area is open to any NW swell particularly near HW. There is a slip to land on at Ile Milliau on the N side but beware of a rock drying 4·2m just to the N of it marked by a N cardinal beacon.

ILE GRANDE

Position 44°47'·75N 03°35'·10W (Cale SW corner of Ile Grande)

2M N of Trébeurden Marina routing via channels.

This low sandy island is large enough to have its own village, Kervolant, with supermarkets, cafés, bars and restaurants. Round the coast, which measures 4M and may be walked in about 2 hours, are several anchorages. The most popular and nearest the town is on the SW corner. Anchorages on the N and NE side of the island are not so accessible and open to northwesterlies and associated swell.

Approach from Trébeurden

This involves 2 transits and requires visibility of not less than 2M.

Leave the marina as soon as the gate opens and take up Chenal de Toull ar Men Melen. At the port lit buoy briefly follow the Chenal on 247° until:

TB4 *358° Les Trois Frères E cardinal beacon aligned with E'most point of Ile Losket*

For *view* and *Caution* see page 286-7.

When the high point of Ile Molène (pictured below) is abeam look NE for next transit and hold accurately:

TB2 *041° Karreg ar Jantil S cardinal beacon aligned with Karreg ar Merk E cardinal beacon tower*

For view see page 285.

Anchor S of slipway (see plan page 286). The bottom is flat sand and the holding good. Well sheltered. Dries 2m.

Other anchorages

West of Ile Fougère at intersection of Transits TB3 and TB1. Depth at datum 4·9m. Good holding in sand.

SE of Ile Molène

High point of the island bearing 310° distant 370m. Good holding in sand.

Anchorage SE of Ile Molène

RIVIÈRE DE LANNION (R. LÉGUER)

48°43'·92N 03°33'·95W
(Darlasken Vraz starboard beacon tower in estuary)
3M S of Trébeurden
3·5M ENE of Locquémeau

TRAVEL
Lannion is on a branch railway line from Morlaix. Rail and bus connections to St. Brieuc, Morlaix and beyond. There is a small airfield 10km E of the town.

CHARTS
BA 2026 Anse de Kernic to Ile Grande (1:50 000)
BA 2027 Ile Grande to Ile de Bréhat (1:48 700)

Imray C34 Cap d'Erquy to Ile de Batz*
Imray 2510 North Brittany Chart Atlas*
  *both include plan: Le Léguer (1:42 500)

SHOM 7124 Baie de Lannion– De la Pointe de Primel à l'Ile Grande (1:20 000)*
  *includes plans: Le Léguer (Rivière de Lannion) (1:20 000), Port de Lannion (Le Léguer) (1:7500)
SHOM 7151 De l'anse de Kernic à l'île Grande (1:48 700)
SHOM 7152 De l'Ile Grande à l'Ile de Bréhat (1:48 700)

RADIO
Ch 09

TIDAL INFORMATION
Standard port: Brest
Differences
HW Brest +0100
LW Brest +0110
HW St Malo –0025 approximately.

MHWS	MLWS	MHWN	MLWN
9·1	1·4	8·2	3·5

Tidal Streams
Streams in this corner of the bay are generally feeble. The flood sets SE and the ebb NW with modifications inshore. Maximum rate in between 1·5 and 2 knots. At the river entrance the streams begin as follows:

HW Les Héaux – 0600 In going
HW Les Héaux – 0045 Out going (7h)
Most of the estuary and the length of the river above Le Yaudet dries out at springs.
It takes 2hrs for the effect of the incoming tide in the estuary to be felt upstream at Lannion.

USEFUL CONTACTS
Capitanerie Port de Lannion ☏02 96 05 60 70 / 02 96 47 29 64
Affaires Maritimes ☏ 02 96 55 35 00

SUPPLIES AND SERVICES
Le Yaudet The anchorage is on the bend off Le Yaudet. There is a bar, a reputable restaurant and a créperie. It may be possible to obtain basic supplies.
Lannion Shops and restaurants are 20 minutes walk from Pont des Viarmes. Fuel may be obtained in cans. The Bureau de Tourisme is on the N bank 300m beyond the Pont de Viarmes.

The Rivière de Lannion sometimes known as Le Léguer is an opportunity to meander through natural and unspoilt countryside up to the inland town of Lannion. It is however a poor relation of the great rivers elsewhere on Brittany's north coast and is seldom visited. This is due to its location off the beaten track and the fact that apart from a few pools at Le Yaudet in which to anchor both the river and its estuary are totally dry at low water springs. This limits navigation to within 3 hours either side of HW and preferably while the tide is rising.

Trébeurden – Ile de Batz

Lannion. Lannion river entrance looking W

The river is unmarked, shallow and the upper reaches are narrow. A low bridge at the outskirts of the town is the limit of navigation. Here it may be possible to moor alongside a small commercial quay for a brief run ashore before departing downstream while there is still plenty of water. You may even chance drying out alongside to return on the next tide (see the River up to Lannion 3M).

Lannion is a bustling and industrious town with a wide range of shops and restaurants. It is unpretentious and makes few concessions to visitors.

Approach and entrance

From ⊕121 make good a track of 090° on Ben-Léguer light structure (white house amongst trees on a ridge) to leave Kinierbel starboard buoy 400m to starboard. To avoid a rocky patch drying 0·1m, continue until the two green beacon towers on the S side of the estuary are configured as follows:

L1 *140° Westernmost starboard beacon (Darlaskenn Vraz) well open right (S) of Easternmost starboard beacon*

Leave the W one a good 200m to starboard and then the E one 50m to starboard. Keep about 100m off the S bank until the white house among the trees is abaft the beam

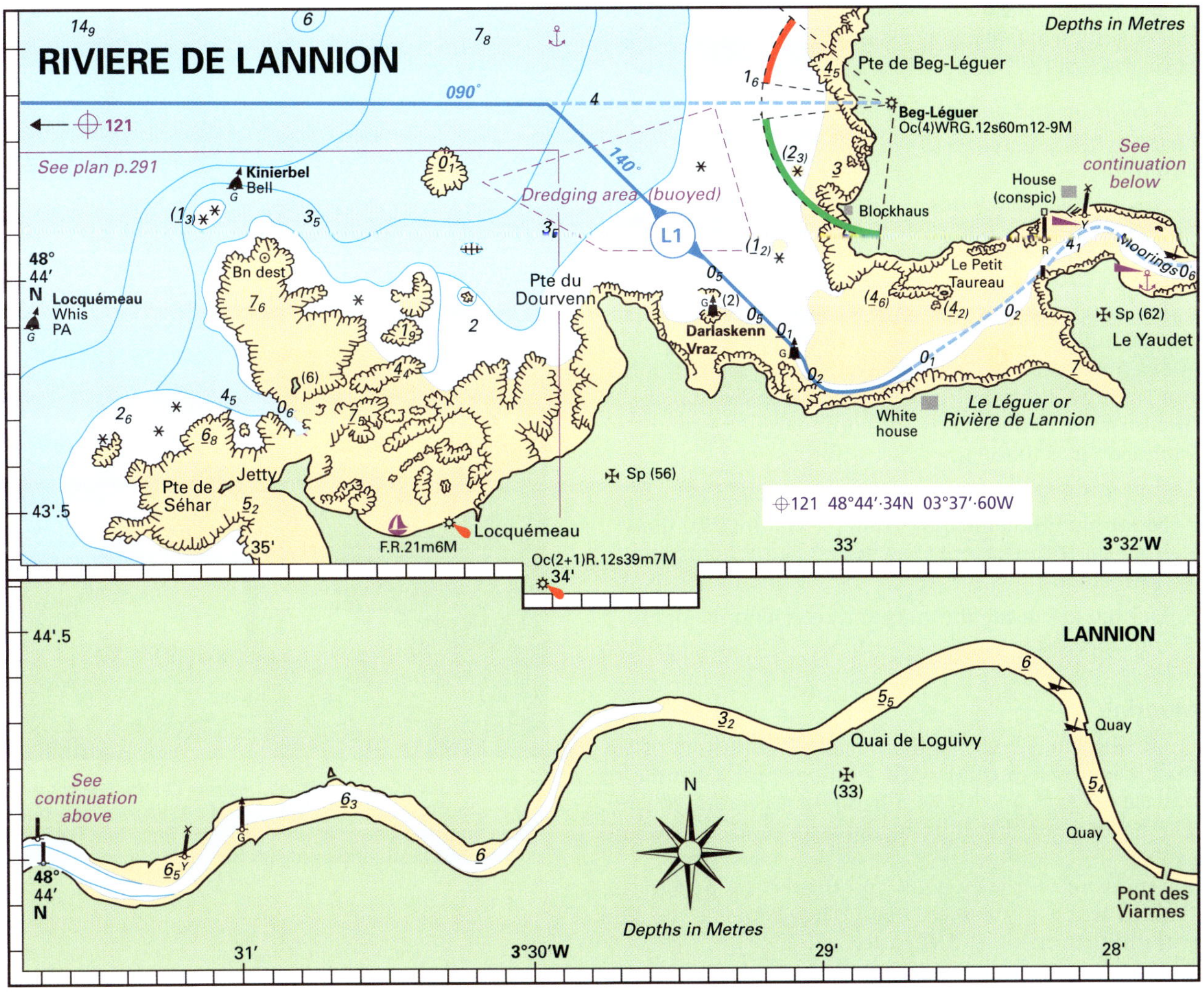

CHANNEL ISLANDS, CHERBOURG PENINSULA & NORTH BRITTANY

III North Brittany: 2 Trébeurden to Ouessant

Quai Maréchal Foch looking downstream from Pont de Viarmes

and slowly turn to head for the slipway and house on the N bank. Leave Le Petit Taureau islet 200m to port and the beacon on the W point close to starboard. The moorings will then show where the channel lies.

Le Yaudet

A small historic village in an elevated position above the S bank. Well worth the walk up from the landing slip. In the bend of the river below are several pools created by sand dredgers. Depths of 1·2m+ at datum may be obtained by sounding.

On the opposite (N) are many small craft moorings and an active sailing school. Anchorage here is complicated by congestion and allowance should be made for swinging at the turn of the tide.

The river up to Lannion 3M

Dries at LWS between 2·6m at Le Yaudet and 5m at Lannion.

The passage should be made within the period HW -3h and HW +3h. The river is narrow, unmarked, and bends continuously. Between steep muddy banks the bottom is uneven and stoney. To avoid the perils of going aground on a falling tide, the passage up and down the river should as far as possible be made on a rising tide.

Navigation ends rather abruptly 300m short of a low road bridge, Pont de Viarmes (clearance 3m) on the W outskirts of Lannion. At this point options might be summed up as follows:

1. Return downstream before HW

2. Moor alongside the only available commercial quay for a short run ashore (3–4 hours) before returning downstream

3. Dry out alongside the quay and return on the next tide. (See *Mooring*.)

Anchorage on the N bank opposite Le Yaudet

Mooring

Quai Maréchal Foch on the S bank 300m short of the bridge is a rough quay with a ladder and a couple of bollards. It is frequently used by sabliers (sand dredgers). The bottom is believed to be flat with mud, stones and rubble.

Opposite on the N bank and nearer the bridge is a cladded area with steps (see view). This should not be used without first making a LW recce.

Pont de Viarmes with Lannion beyond. On the N bank a cladded area with steps is visible. This should not be used without prior inspection. The S bank is Quai Maréchal Foch that is often occupied by local sand dredgers (see view above). No facilities

Trébeurden – Ile de Batz

LOCQUÉMEAU
48°43'·68N 03°34'·88W (1st starboard beacon)
3M S of Trébeurden
3·5M ESE of Locquirec

CHARTS
As for Lannion

TIDAL INFORMATION
HW Brest + 0105
LW Brest + 0110
Harbour dries 5·5m

MHWS	MLWS	MHWN	MLWN
9·1	1·4	8·2	3·5

SUPPLIES AND SERVICES
1M along the shore to village with small shops. *Boulangerie* and *Café du Port* on the quay.
Restaurant Les Filets Bleus is the sole restaurant on the quay with a pleasant view over the port.
☏ 02 96 35 22 26   www.lesfiletsbleus.fr

Locquémeau, S of the Lannion estuary, is a small rather insignificant drying harbour at the W end of a wide rock strewn bay. It is used by small shallow draught boats that can take the ground. It has two quays, an outer at the entrance and an inner S of it. The S side of the inner quay offers the best shelter in the harbour (see *berthing* below).

Approach, entry and berthing

From a position 300m N of Locquémeau starboard whistle buoy identify the leading marks and hold accurately:

LO1 121° Conspicuous white lattice pylon on the beach aligned with W gable shaped lighthouse behind

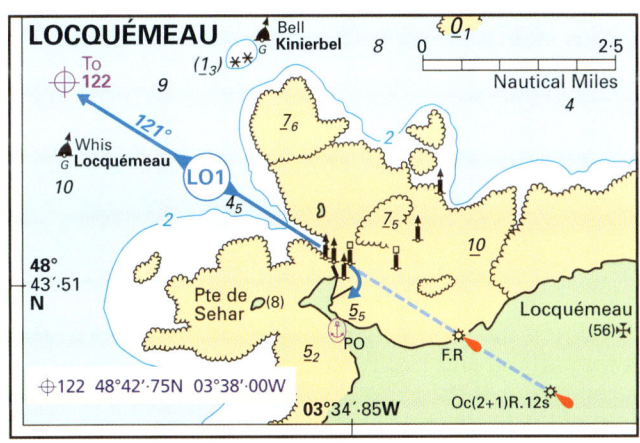
Locquémeau at high tide

The narrow entrance channel off the first starboard beacon

The entrance is narrow but well-marked with three starboard beacons and one port beacon. The first marks the outer end of the slip/breakwater and the next is on the elbow. The leading line must be borrowed to port to leave these two to starboard. When the second is abeam come to starboard to regain the line and pass between the next two beacons. Continue then until the S side of the inner jetty opens up and go alongside on the S side. It has a smooth surface and bollards. The bottom is hard, smooth sand and shingle and dries 5·5m.

Leading marks. White-gabled lighthouse inset

Outer and inner quays

CHANNEL ISLANDS, CHERBOURG PENINSULA & NORTH BRITTANY

III North Brittany: 2 Trébeurden to Ouessant

LOCQUIREC

An attractive backwater in the estuary of the Douron
48°41'·57N 03°38'·68W (Pierhead)
3·5M WSW of Locquémeau
9·5M E of Primel

CHARTS
BA 2026 Anse de Kernic to Ile Grande (1:50 000)
SHOM 7124 Baie de Lannion – De la Pointe de Primel à l'île Grande (1:20 000)
SHOM 7151 De l'anse de Kernic à l'île Grande (1:48 700)

TIDAL INFORMATION
Difference:
HW Brest + 0105
LW Brest + 0110

MHWS	MLWS	MHWN	MLWN
9·1	1·4	8·2	3·5

Tidal streams
Streams in the S of Baie de Lannion are feeble, 1·5kns at the most.

USEFUL CONTACTS
Le Mairie (Town Hall) is the Marine Public Authority (West Wall) ☎ 02 98 67 42 20
Hours: 0830–1200, 1300–1730 and Saturday am
Bureau de Tourisme Place du Port ☎ 02 98 67 40 83
Ecole de Voile, West Wall ☎ 02 98 67 44 57
Taxi ☎ 02 98 67 40 00

SUPPLIES AND SERVICES
Water, electricity A single electrical point and water hydrant on the W wall hardstanding.
WC next to Bureau du Port
Restaurants Several

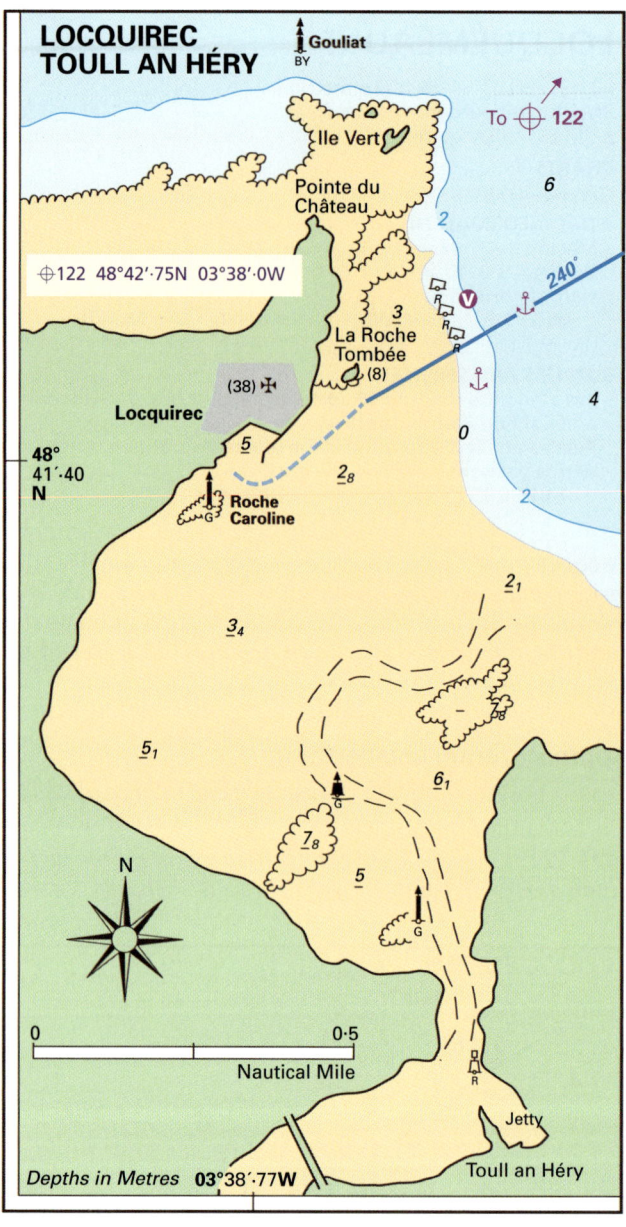

The holiday resort of Locquirec lies in the NW corner of the large sandy estuary of the R. Douron. Its small drying harbour is easy to access 3h either side of HW and is sheltered from N and W. It has a relaxed atmosphere with several restaurants overlooking the harbour.

Approach and entry

From the N
From ⊕122 (off plan) identify the prominent Pointe du Château and the N cardinal buoy, Gouliat, marking its northern outliers. Shape a course to pass about 400m E of Ile Verte and La Roche Tombée (8).

Approach the harbour on a course of 240° leaving La Roche Tombée (8) 200m starboard. Enter between the pierhead and starboard beacon Roche Caroline.

Toull An Héry (see view page 283)
A mile S of Locquirec at the head of the Bay the Douron estuary narrows to form an almost enclosed sandy creek. There is a small roadside settlement Toull An Héry where some supplies might be obtainable. A short jetty offers the possibility of drying alongside but the bottom is very uneven so a good LW recce is essential.

Moorings and anchorages
The harbour has a short jetty with a smooth inner surface (dries 5·5m). Opposite on the W side is a wall with wooden piles, ladders and a slipway. This is also suitable to dry out against. Above it is an area of hardstanding.

Visitors' moorings, drying and deep water are available in the harbour and E of Pointe du Château 0·5M N of the harbour. Use of these is controlled by the Mairie. Anchor ENE of the harbour where the bottom is uniformly sand, ideal for multihulls.

Alongside the quay and hard standing at Locquirec

PRIMEL-TRÉGASTEL

48°43'·20N 03°49'·22W (Pointe de Primel)
9M W of Locquirec   6M E of Roscoff

TRAVEL
Road
Buses run to Morlaix from where there are rail connections onto Roscoff with its ferries. Morlaix has a small airport, as does Lannion 20M to the E.
Taxi ☎ 02 98 72 35 10 / 02 98 67 21 29

CHARTS
BA 2026 Anse de Kernic to Ile Grande (1:50 000)
BA 2745 Baie de Morlaix – Ile de Batz to Pointe de Primel (1:20 000)
Imray C34 Cap d'Erquy to Ile de Batz*
  *includes plan: Primel (1:15 000)
Imray 2510 North Brittany Chart Atlas:
  9 Baie de Morlaix (1:50 000)
  9a Primel (1:15 000)
SHOM 7095 Baie de Morlaix – De l'Ile de Batz à la Pointe de Primel (1:20 000)
SHOM 7124 Baie de Lannion – De la Pointe de Primel à l'Ile Grande (1:20 000)
SHOM 7151 De l'anse de Kernic à l'île Grande (1:48 700)

RADIO
VHF Ch 09 working hours

TIDAL INFORMATION
HW Brest +0105   LW Brest +0115

MHWS	MLWS	MHWN	MLWN
9·0	1·3	7·1	3·4

Tidal streams
The stream turns as follows to the N of Primel:
HW Brest -0430 E-going   HW Brest +0145 W-going

USEFUL CONTACTS
Harbourmaster ☎ 06 22 43 77 58 / 06 09 34 82 37 (office at root of pier)
Tourist office ☎ 02 98 67 31 88

SUPPLIES AND SERVICES
Water, electricity, showers at root of pier.
Fuel (in cans) Le Diben (W side)
Boatyard, chandler at head of bay (L'Abesse)
Shops in Primel-Trégastel (E side) 3M
Restaurant Hotel/restaurant L'Abesse on the W side near the top of the harbour.

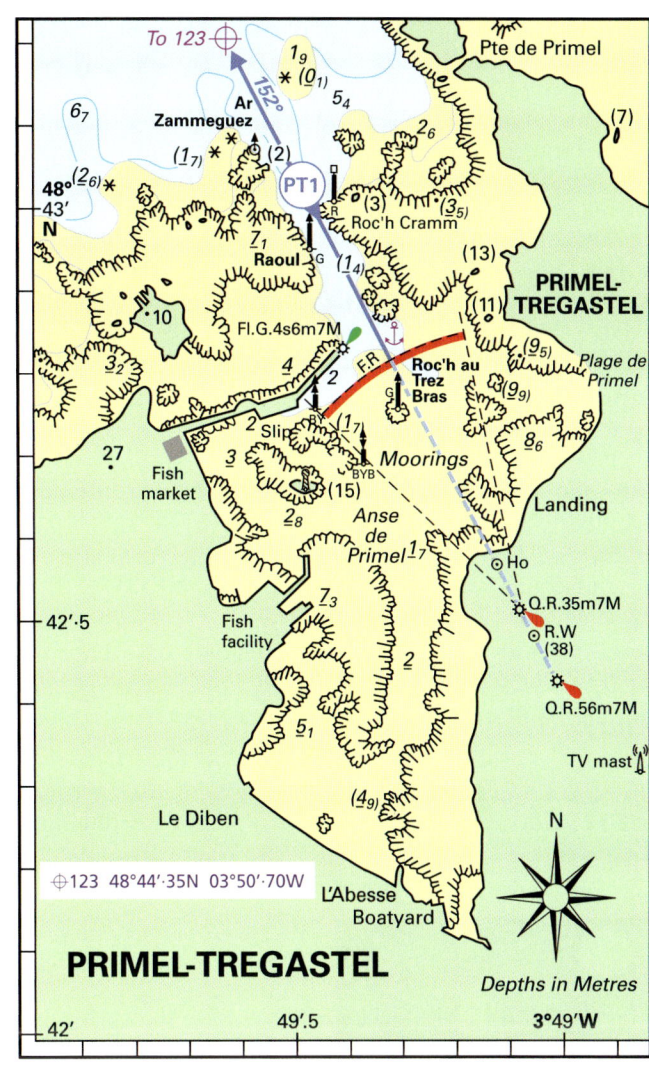

Primel-Trégastel looking S

III North Brittany: 2 Trébeurden to Ouessant

Whether cruising E or W this harbour, with straightforward entrance and at least a narrow tongue of water in which to float, may be worth considering.

It has always been dedicated to the fishing industry, with large *viviers* at Le Diben on the W side. Some concession to plaisanciers, possibly the only one, is the laying of deep water visitors moorings inside the entrance.

The quay, which is the reserve of the fishing fleet, offers a few facilities at its root. The nearest shops are in the resort of Primel-Trégastel about 2–3M E of the harbour. This distance may be reduced by landing the tender when the tide is up the slip below the leading marks (E side).

Approach and Entry

Caution

Any approach into the Baie de Lannion should route clear of offlying dangers:

- Plateau de la Méloine – an area of scattered shoals and drying rocks extending 2M N in a NE–SW direction.
- Les Chaises de Primel – a reef extending 2M ENE from Pointe de Primel.

Entry

The only entry into Primel is 2M W of Les Chaises de Primel. From a position 1·5M NNW of the entrance (⊕123) identify the conspicuous Pointe de Primel and take up:

PT1 *152° Three marks aligned vertically as shown*

The line should be held accurately noting that submerged dangers lie to port, and leave:

- Ar Zammeguez a prominent rock with green and white patch and a starboard beacon 30m to starboard.
- Roch'Cramm a port beacon 30m to port.
- Raoul starboard beacon 20m to starboard.

Ar Zammeguez

Roc'h au Trez Bras

Roc'h au Trez Bras reef is an inconvenience in the middle of the harbour. Keep well clear

- The breakwater end (Fl.G.4s) 50m to starboard looking out for vessels leaving.

Primel is open to the NW and might be dangerous in heavy weather from this direction when the sea is said to break across the entrance.

By night

Align Leading Lights
Lower: Q.R.7M
Upper: Q.R.7M
Breakwater head: Fl.G.4s (will be left to starboard)

Mooring

There are 6–7 visitors' moorings W of Roc'h au Trez Bras in depths that do not dry and these should be used in preference to anchoring.

Anchorages

- Anchor light essential as there can be much fishing boat traffic.
- To the SE of the breakwater as far from it as depths and moorings allow. Two anchors may be needed to restrict swing.
- In the vicinity of Roc'h au Trez Bras where depths and moorings allow.
- If drying out further up the harbour the line of Roc'h au Trez Bras beacon and left hand edge of Pointe de Primel give the line.

Note When the author visited Primel at two hours before local LW neaps the following depths were found:

- At entrance: 9m shelving quickly
- On mooring NW of Roc'h au Trez Bras starboard beacon: 2·7m

Landing and berthing

There are slipways at Le Diben (W side) and below the leading marks (E side) (see plan).

The outer stretch of the breakwater as far as the slip is used by fishing boats but a berth may be found here. Ask at the harbourmaster's office (VHF Ch 9) at the root of the breakwater. This jetty is high and it is recommended to berth alongside one of the ladders.

Trébeurden – Ile de Batz

MORLAIX
48°40′·53N 03°53′·07W (Château du Taureau)
4M SW of Primel
5M SE of Roscoff
For Morlaix city add 6M

TRAVEL
Sea
  Roscoff – Plymouth Ferry: www.brittanyferries.co.uk
Air
  Morlaix Ploujean Airport (2km) ☏ 02 98 62 16 09
  Brit Air ☏ 02 98 63 63 63 www.britair.fr
Train
  Morlaix is on the Paris to Brest TGV line.
      Station ☏ 08 36 35 35 35 www.sncf.fr
Road
  Bus to Roscoff and Lannion

CHARTS
  BA 2026 Anse de Kernic to Ile Grande (1:50 000)
  BA 2745 Baie de Morlaix – Ile de Batz to Pointe de
      Primel (1:20 000)*
      *includes plan: Rivière de Morlaix (1:15 000)
  Imray C35 Baie de Morlaix to L'Aber-Ildut*
      *includes plan: Port de Morlaix (1:15 000)
  Imray 2510 North Brittany Chart Atlas:
      9 Baie de Morlaix (1:50 000)
      9b Port de Morlaix (1:15 000)
  SHOM 7095 Baie de Morlaix – De l'île de Batz à la
      Pointe de Primel (1:20 000)*
      *includes plan: Rivière de Morlaix (1:15 000)
  SHOM 7151 De l'anse de Kernic à l'île Grande (1:48 700)

RADIO
  Ch 09 HW ±2h

TIDAL INFORMATION
  Standard port: Brest
  Difference (Château du Taureau):
  HW Brest +0100 Add 0020 for lock
  LW Brest +0110 Add 0020 for lock
  Difference on HW Roscoff at Lock: +10

MHWS	MLWS	MHWN	MLWN
8·9	1·3	7·1	3·4

  Subtract 0·2m for heights at lock

Tidal streams
  In the vicinity of Château du Taureau the streams start as follows:
  Flood HW Brest –0450
  Ebb HW Brest +0105
  Maximum rate on ebb is 2½ knots which reduces to 1 knot in Rade de Morlaix with no discernible flood in upper reaches.

CONTACTS
  Bureau du Port ☏ 02 98 62 13 14 www.portdemorlaix.fr
  Lock ☏ 06 77 50 15 90
  Office de Tourisme, Place des Otages (close S of viaduct)
      ☏ 02 98 62 14 94 www.morlaixtourisme.fr
  Taxi ☏ 02 98 88 08 32

SUPPLIES AND SERVICES
Yacht Basin 32 Visitors' berths. Max length 12m. Depths 3·5–5·4m alongside quay in N to 1m in S. Larger vessels berth alongside quay.
Electricity and water points at pontoons.
Fuel W side
Facilities block next to Bureau du Port
Bar/café Le Tempo ☏ 02 98 63 29 11 next to Bureau du Port
WiFi Access available
Chandlery Loisirs Nautiques (W bank)
Restaurant Le Viaduc ☏ 02 98 63 24 21
      www.le-viaduc.com (below viaduct)
Market Town centre, Saturday (all day)

The Baie de Morlaix encompasses a wide area bounded by Primel in the east and Roscoff in the west. Apart from a dozen or so islets, the largest being Ile Callot in the W, more than half the bay covers and uncovers with the tide.

Navigationally it is complex but well-marked with a profusion of beacons. These form part of a network of channels that converge on the iconic landmark of Château de Taureau in the estuary of the Rivière de Morlaix. On the West side of the Bay is the secondary estuary of La Penzé River.

The port of Morlaix lies six miles up the river, the last section of which is canalised before the lock which gives access to a large yacht basin in the northern outskirts of the town.

From here it is a 20 minute walk along either bank to find the city centre, and a wide range of shops and restaurants.

Despite the large numbers of yachts that appear to be permanently based here you will not find the flashy dockside facilities of modern coastal marinas such as Trébeurden and Roscoff. At best they may be described as adequate, becoming run down in off season.

Historical
Morlaix is a classic Breton river town, with historical links to the sea. It became prosperous between the 15th and 17th century through the trade and transportation of linen and hemp which included sail cloth for the French Navy. In the 18th century the tobacco trade flourished and survived until recently. Its classic style warehouses line the W bank of the yacht basin (Quai de Léon).

The Molassians have expended much of their energy over the centuries in fracas with the English, notably in July 1522. As a reprisal for recent raids on Bristol by French corsairs a fleet of 60 English ships made a surprise attack on Morlaix. At the time the local nobility were gathered in Guingamp and the merchants were at a fair. Troops entered the town in disguise burning and pillaging houses and churches alike. The townsfolk returned in time to catch the stragglers and took their revenge. A fountain, Fontaine aux Anglais, commemorates this event in Morlaix. It is said that it ran red with English blood.

Following this incident measures were taken to protect the Baie de Morlaix which included the development of the island Château du Taureau into an impregnable fortress (see *Vauban* page 199). From this incident comes the motto of Morlaix: 'If they bite you, bite them back!'

Château du Taureau

III North Brittany: 2 Trébeurden to Ouessant

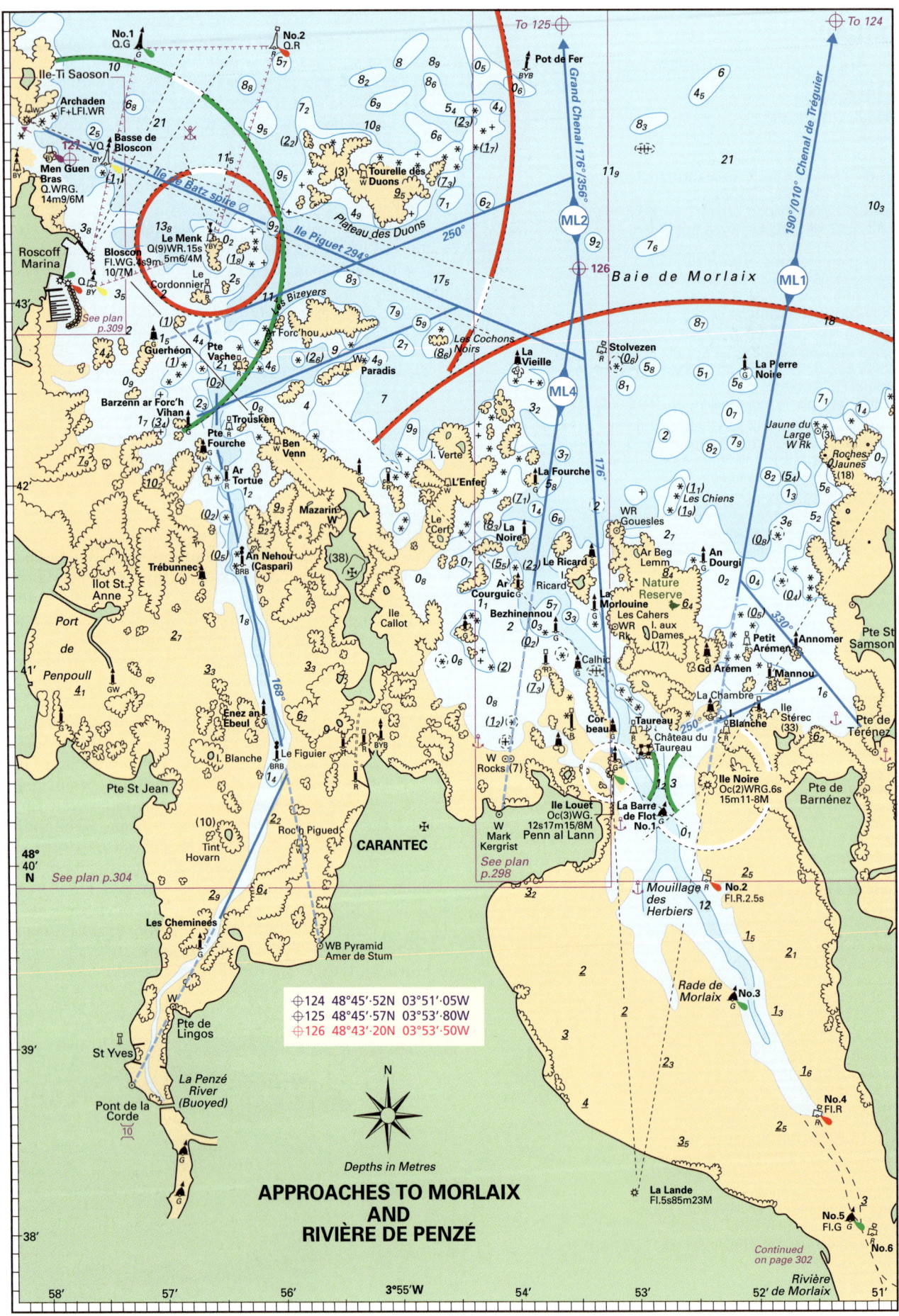

APPROACHES TO MORLAIX AND RIVIÈRE DE PENZÉ

Trébeurden – Ile de Batz

Approaches to Morlaix

Chenal de Tréguier (0·9m)

This is the shallowest approach channel due to a patch of isolated rocks and shoals off its southern end that dry between 0·2m and 0·9m. It should therefore be taken above half tide and on a rising tide. Visibility of not less than 5M is required to see the marks.

The transit is:

ML1 *190° (⊕124) Phare de la Lande aligned with Ile Noire Lighthouse*

This line leaves:
- Méloine W cardinal whistle buoy 400m to port
- La Pierre Noire starboard beacon 400m to starboard
- An Dourgi starboard beacon 400m to starboard
- Pass midway between Grand Aremen starboard beacon tower and Petit Aremen port beacon tower

and La Chambre starboard beacon tower and Blanche port beacon tower.

La Chambre

Note: Drying rocks extend E of La Chambre so make an alteration of course to port (E) to clear before passing between it and Blanche port beacon tower.

Alter course to port on to 207° for about 0·5M to Barre de Flot No.1 buoy.

Ile Noire lighthouse will be left 300m to port.

Grand Chenal (2·0m)

Approach from N with transit:

ML2 *176° (⊕125) La Lande Lighthouse aligned with Ile Louet Lighthouse*

Looking SSE across Baie de Morlaix

III North Brittany: 2 Trébeurden to Ouessant

298 CHANNEL ISLANDS, CHERBOURG PENINSULA & NORTH BRITTANY

Trébeurden – Ile de Batz

The **ML2** transit leaves
- Pot de Fer E cardinal buoy 400m to starboard
- Plateau des Douons tower 1·2M to starboard
- Stolvezen port buoy 200m to port
- Vieille starboard beacon tower 0·4M to starboard
- Ricard starboard beacon tower 100m to starboard
- Ile Ricard 200m to starboard
- La Morlouine starboard beacon tower 100m to starboard
- Roc'h Cahers (4) WR mark 170m to port
- Calhic starboard beacon tower a good 300m to starboard

When Calhic is on the quarter come to port to take up new transit:

ML3 148° The right (W) side of Château du Taureau with its beacon open by two widths

Make a small alteration to starboard to pass clear of Château du Taureau and its beacon. Continue to Barre de Flot No.1 buoy in the river entrance 700m ahead.

By night
Grand Chenal leading lights:
Front: Ile Louet Oc(3)WG.12s12/8m
Rear: La Lande Fl.5s23M

Chenal Ouest de Ricard (5·8m)
This is a deeper alternative to the Grand Chenal.
At a point 600m short of Stolvezen port buoy (⊕126) turn to starboard on to 189° for transit:

ML4 189° (⊕126) The two small W painted rocks of Pierres de Carantec aligned with a W mark on the shore at Kergrist

This line leaves:
- La Vieille starboard beacon tower 400m to starboard
- La Fourche starboard beacon 200m to starboard

When La Noire starboard beacon is on the starboard quarter come to port onto short transit:

ML5 160° Ile Louet Lighthouse aligned with Calhic starboard beacon tower (Here shown open left)

Hold this for 600m then, as Bezhinennou starboard beacon comes abeam make a small alteration to port onto 148°. This should leave Calhic beacon at least 200m to starboard.
   Join **ML3** on 148°.

Chenal Est de L'Ile Callot (Dries 1·1m)
(Curving route on plan page 304.) This channel used by *vedettes* between Roscoff and Château de Taureau is not marked in detail on any charts and calls for local knowledge. Starting from the N no earlier than HW –3, with at least 3M visibility and large scale *SHOM 2095* it does not look difficult. The route N–S follows a generally SE direction and is summarised as follows:

   W of port beacon tower Petite Vache alter course to port to make good 120°. En route marks are then as follows. Leave:
- Ar Vesklik starboard beacon to starboard
- Le Bassin port beacon tower to port
- Les Platines de Callot starboard beacon to starboard

The Chenal E of Ile Louet looking W

III North Brittany: 2 Trébeurden to Ouessant

- Basse Plate beacon to starboard
- Cochon WG starboard beacon tower to starboard
- Petit Cochon starboard beacon to starboard
- Ile Louet to port

Anchorages in Morlaix River Estuary

- **East side of Penn ar Lann**

    Depths: Up to 9m

    Shelter: Good from W but not from other quarters

    Moorings: Occasional visitors' moorings

    Landing: There are several quays and slipways on S side of Penn ar Lann point. Beware small boat moorings.

- **Between Barre de Flot buoy and up-river to Dourduff**

    It is possible to anchor in good holding on either side of the fairway but here is no reasonable landing for dinghies near LW. An anchor light should be exhibited at night. Alternatively leave the main channel to the S of Barre de Flot buoy and anchor in the Mouillage des Herbiers (see plan page 296). Anchoring is prohibited in the channel above Dourduff.

- **Near Pierres de Carantec**

    In settled weather and neap tides only (see plan page 296). Approach on 189° with transit ML4 (189°). (See *Chenal Ouest de Ricard*)

- **Off Pointe de Térénez**

    This is the best anchorage on the E side of the Baie de Morlaix. Situated in the vicinity of Annomer starboard beacon 250m E of Petit Arémen. Good holding in sand.

    Depths: About 2·1m at LWN

    Moorings: Visitors (drying) in the Anse.

TÉRÉNEZ

USEFUL CONTACTS
Capitainerie (Mairie) ☎ 02 98 67 30 06 / 06 22 43 77 58
Sailing School (Le Société des Régates de Térénez)
☎ 02 98 72 33 25
VHF Ch 09

SUPPLIES AND SERVICES
5 visitors' berths, water and electricity at the quay. WC. Slipway.
Restaurants Les Embruns ☎ 02 98 72 39 70
Le Radeau ☎ 02 98 72 44 21

Approaches

From N

Break off Chenal de Tréguier when Annomer starboard beacon and Pointe de Térénez bear 150°. Give the point a clearance of 200m if rounding into the Anse.

Térénez

Térénez has an active sailing school

Anchored off Térénez. Petit Arémen beacon tower in the background

From W

From a point midway between La Chambre starboard beacon tower and I. Blanche port beacon tower at the S end of Chenal de Tréguier take up stern transit:

250° Carantec church aligned with the sentry box at the right hand side (N) of Château de Taureau. This leads midway between Mannou port beacon and Mien Meur port beacon but keep closer to Men Meur (see chart). Steer towards Pointe de Térénez and follow directions from N.

Térénez there is a busy sailing centre with a post office and several restaurants.

The river up to Morlaix

The first 3M from Barre de Flot buoy to the bend at Dourduff is a straight run on 150°/330°. Initially buoys are spaced no more than half a mile apart but become more frequent from Dourduff.

The river shallows from 24m to 0·5m at chart datum by No.4 buoy. It is dry by No.5 buoy. The upper reaches dry at 2·7m.

Buoys give way to beacons and finally posts all of which should be closely kept to if one is to stay in the channel. Note that while buoys are generally positioned on the edge of the channel some of the beacons and posts are set back.

Caution

Navigation above Dourduff at night is not allowed unless a searchlight with an effective beam of at least 200m is carried.

Morlaix yacht basin looking S

Looking downstream from a bend S of Le Dourduff which is seen on the E bank

III North Brittany: 2 Trébeurden to Ouessant

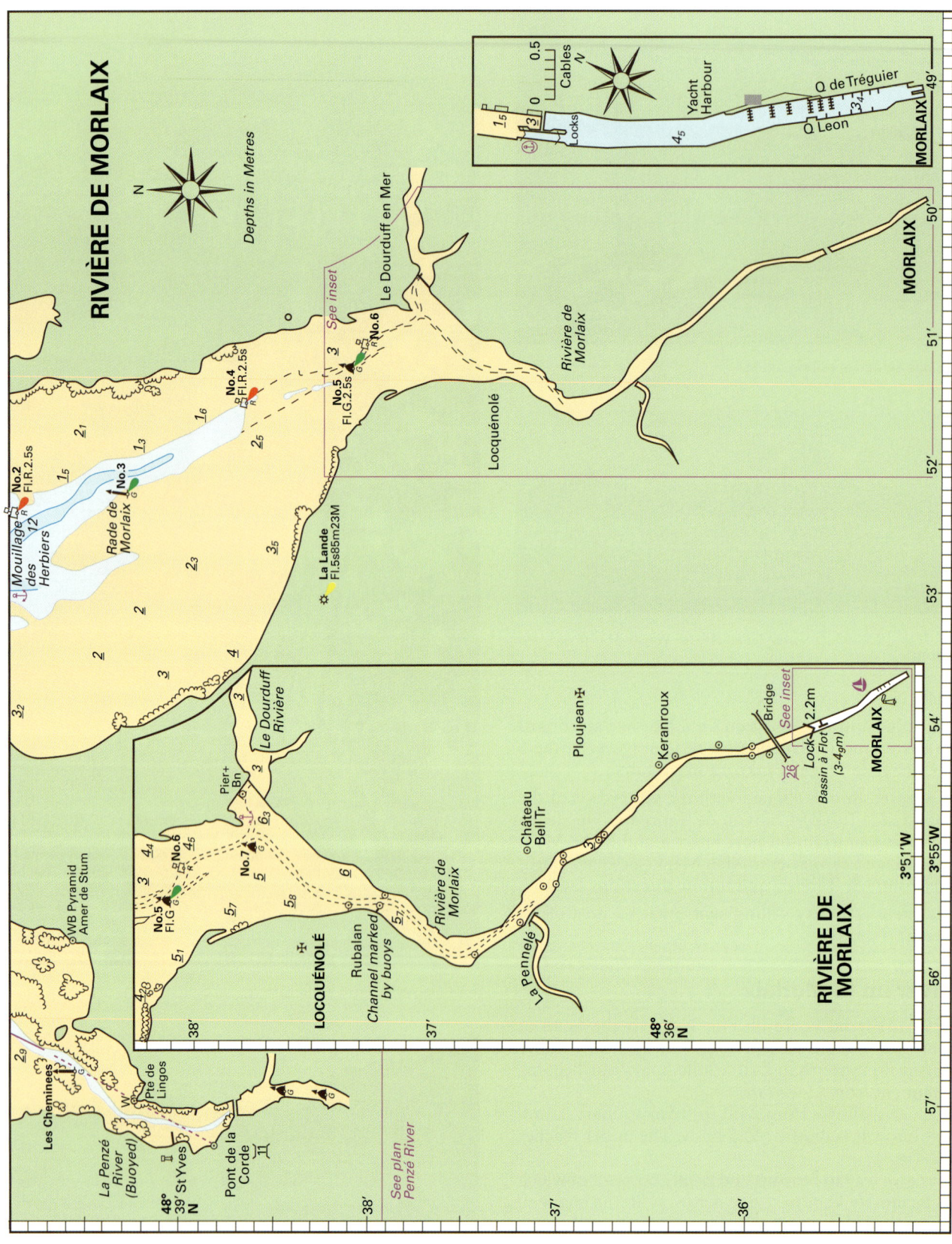

302 CHANNEL ISLANDS, CHERBOURG PENINSULA & NORTH BRITTANY

Trébeurden – Ile de Batz

Morlaix Lock just opening *Peter Taylor*

Lock entrance

The lock is 63m long, 16m wide, the lower sill dries 2·2m and the upper 3·1m. The gate opens three times each HW at HW -1½ hours, HW and HW +1 hour. The tide gauge shows the depth over the lower sill. The bridge below the lock has a clearance of 26m and the power line shown on older charts has been removed. Whilst waiting for the gates to open go alongside the quay on the W side about 150m from the lower gate. Yachts may safely dry out here but not nearer to the lock where there are drying rocks. The aggregate jetty below this quay is a better place to go alongside provided it is not occupied by coasters. The best place to dry out is below the weir alongside the E side of the old entrance where the wall is smooth, has two ladders and a soft mud bottom.

Berthing

Depths in the basin which is over ½M long vary between 1m at extreme S end to 5·4m alongside the quays. At the southern end are the pontoons of the marina. The basin narrows appreciably towards the southern end and large yachts may find some difficulty in turning round if they progress too far in. There is a mobile walkway across the basin halfway down which is pulled aside around lock opening times. There are some 180 pontoon berths and 40 on the quays; maximum length on the pontoons 12m with 30 for visitors, larger yachts go alongside the quays. The arrival berth, where visitors should go to await directions, is alongside the E bank before the harbour office.

Quai de Léon runs along the W side of the Morlaix Yacht Basin

III North Brittany: 2 Trébeurden to Ouessant

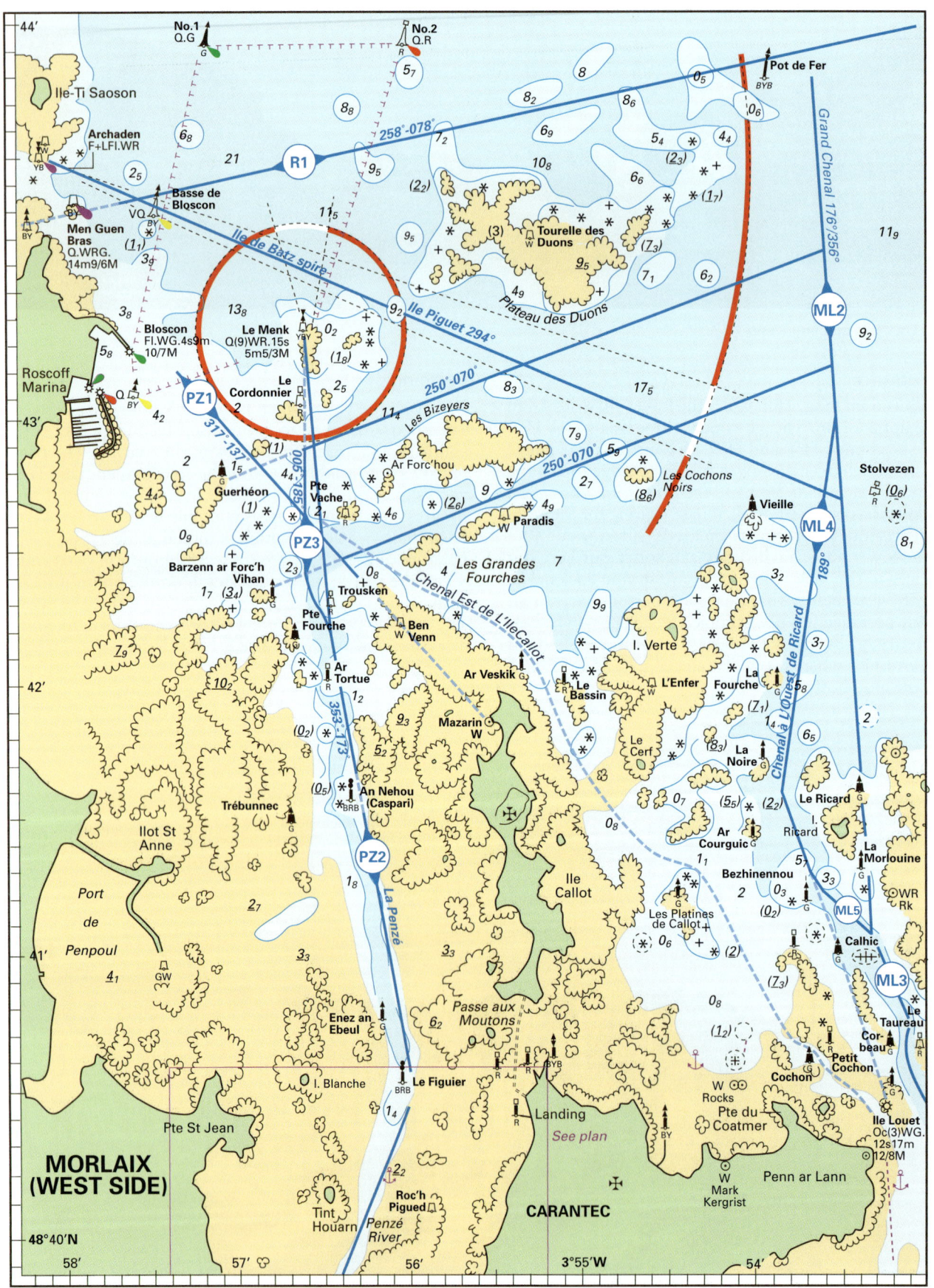

RIVIÈRE DE PENZÉ

Carantec, Ile Callot and Port de Penpoul

48°41'·56N 03°56'·45W (Caspari [An Nehou] isolated danger beacon: Penzé estuary)
2M SSE of Roscoff

TRAVEL
See Roscoff/Morlaix

CHARTS
See Roscoff/Morlaix

RADIO
Nil

TIDAL INFORMATION
Standard port Brest
Alternative: Roscoff
Difference
HW Brest +0010
LW Brest + 0110
HW/LW Roscoff 0000

MHWS	MLWS	MHWN	MLWN
8·9	1·3	7·1	3·4

Streams in river: 2·5–3kns

Depth restrictions
At least 0·9m to Pont de la Corde shallowing to drying 5m at Penzé.

SUPPLIES AND SERVICES
There are a few basic shops, a bar and a restaurant in the village. A water tap is sited near the bridge.

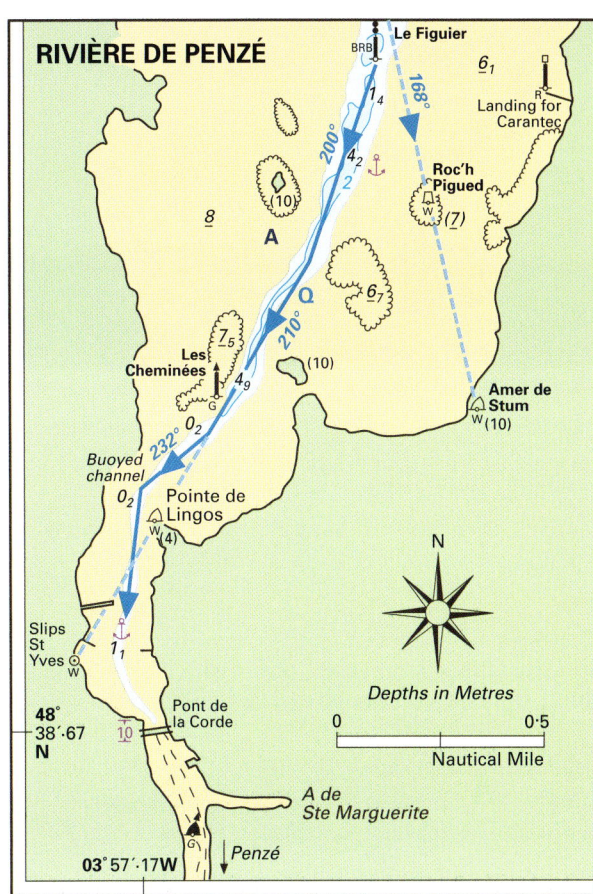

The Penzé River that parallels the Morlaix River 2M to the east is now abandoned by the barges that used to dump sand and building materials on its quays and is seldom visited by yachts. Although something of a backwater compared with its mighty neighbour it possesses rustic charm and that rare commodity, peace. The entry to the river 1½ miles up to Le Figuier isolated danger mark has depths in the channel of between 10m and 27m at datum. Thereafter it peters out to nil at which point the road bridge, Pont de la Corde, crosses the river. Clearance below this and another bridge (rail) further south is said to be 10m. With sufficient water which might involve waiting till half tide one may continue a further 3M up to the village of Penzé where a further low bridge marks the end of navigation. It has a substantial quay and hard standing area.

Historical

On Ile Callot stands the pilgrimage chapel of Notre Dame des Victoires, founded in the 6th century to commemorate a victory over Norse pirates. St Pol de Léon is an ancient cathedral town that has played a leading part in the history of Brittany. Its name is a corruption of St Paul Aurelian, the first missionary who came from Wales in AD540 (see *Historical* on page 198). The cathedral is entirely medieval and its twin spires are one of the most distinctive landmarks of Baie de Morlaix. Close to the S of the cathedral is the thin spire of Kreisker, 250ft high which was built to be the tallest in France, but was subsequently out-built.

St Pol de Léon is a short bus ride from Roscoff.

River approaches

From N (Roscoff)

Starting at Basse de Bloscon N cardinal buoy (⊕127) make good 180° to leave Port de Bloscon breakwater 100m to starboard. The transit then is:

PZ1 *137° Benvenn W pyramid aligned with Mazarin W pyramid (N end of Ile Callot)*

This will leave Guerhéon starboard beacon tower 200m to starboard. When La Petite Vache port beacon tower is abeam at 300m turn to 173° to leave Trousken port beacon tower 180m to port.

Next make a small alteration to port to find stern transit:

PZ2 *353° Trousken port beacon tower aligned with Le Menk W cardinal beacon tower*

Hold a course of 173° to Le Figuier BRB.

If held carefully this will lead close E of both Ar Tourtu port beacon and An Nehou (Caspari) BRB. There are rocks on their W sides.

III North Brittany: 2 Trébeurden to Ouessant

From E
There are two possible approaches. One N and the other S of Les Bizeyers reef (S of Les Duons).

Les Douons Tr

Looking S at LWS

N of Les Bizeyers
- Navigate to a position midway between the tower on Les Duons and Les Bizeyers (8) with its rocks.
- Identify Guerhéon starboard beacon tower to WSW and hold on a steady bearing of 250°.

Caution
Holding a single mark on a steady bearing is demanding particularly with any cross set. The stream here sets SE on the flood and NW on the ebb attaining 2 knots.

- When 0·4M short of Guerhéon look N for transit:

PZ3 005°/185° *Le Menk W cardinal beacon tower aligned with Cordonnier port beacon tower*

- Take up 185° to hold this transit on a back bearing of 005° for 650m when Petite (Pte) Vache port beacon tower is on the beam. A small alteration to port will be required to leave Trousken port beacon tower 180m to port and Petite (Pte) Fourche starboard beacon tower to starboard then look astern for:

PZ2 *353° Trousken aligned with Le Menk. Hold this transit to continue up the river*

S of Les Bizeyer
- From a position where Chenal Ouest de Ricard merges with the Grand Chenal 800m NE of Vielle starboard beacon tower identify to WSW Barzenn ar Forc'h Vihan starboard beacon. Alter course to hold this mark on a steady bearing of 250°. This line will pass:
- Les Cochons Noire (8·6m) 100m to port
- Le Paradis W beacon 100m to port
- Les Grandes Fourches (1m) 100m to port (see *Caution* above)

Pont de la Corde

Anchorage off old ferry on E bank N of Pont de la Corde

Anchoring, mooring and berthing
There is a recommended anchorage with 3·6m at datum in the Channel S of Le Figuier isolated danger mark W of Carantec. The bottom is mud.

Close N of Pont de le Corde is St Yves with quay and slipway. This is the site of the old river ferry. At neaps it may be possible to stay afloat here at LW or alternatively dry out alongside the quay with caution. There is a restaurant nearby.

The quay at Penzé provides a very good surface to lie against and has two ladders (see view). The bottom is level with mud and small stones.

The jetty on the W side at Penzé town looking downstream from the town bridge

Trébeurden – Ile de Batz

Passe aux Moutons between the Morlaix and Penzé rivers. The causeway between Carantec and Ile Callot is clearly visible

CARANTEC

This resort attracts large numbers of holidaymakers in the season. The town of Carantec offers a wide selection of shops and restaurants. It is well sheltered for small boat activities with slipways either side of the headland and moorings. LW uncovers large expanses of flat sand and a causeway drying 5–10m over the Passe aux Moutons to Ile Callot.

At HW this 450m wide gap drying at between 5m and 10m provides a useful short cut between rivers. It is suitable for small craft with no more than 1·5m draught (see *Ile Callot*).

ILE CALLOT

This N-S oriented island, 1½ miles long, separates the Morlaix and Penzé rivers. On the W coast are some fine bays for drying out but anchorage round the island is limited due to surrounding reefs and oyster beds.

The Passe aux Moutons provides a tempting short cut between the rivers. Small local craft drawing no more than 1·5m use this passage between 1 and 2 hours before HW. From the Morlaix River it follows a well-marked northwesterly route passing close SW of Ile Louet. From Petit Cochon starboard beacon it branches WNW to pass N of Pierres de Carantec and two perches marking rocks that dry at 8m and 6·2m. The Passe into the River Penzé is crossed midway between the two islets S of Ile Callot and the beacons off the N tip of the Carantec peninsula.

Caution

This should not be attempted without local knowledge and *SHOM chart 7095* aboard.

PENPOUL (PEMPOUL)

Port de Penpoul is a bite of coastline sheltered by a half mile long breakwater which incorporates an islet, Ilot de Sainte Anne. It shelters an area that dries up to 6m exposing flat featureless sand. It was once the port for St Pol de Léon almost a mile inland but now serves as a major water sports centre that is based at the end of the breakwater. Apart from a landing the shore has nothing of note.

The slip at Carantec

Ile Callot from N

III North Brittany: 2 Trébeurden to Ouessant

ROSCOFF

VIEUX PORT
48°43'·89N 03°58'·26W (0·8M S of Ar Chaden beacon)

PORT DE PLAISANCE (MARINA)
48°32'·22N 03°57'·68W (Bloscon Pierhead)

TRAVEL
Roscoff is well connected:
Sea
  Ferry: Brittany Ferries, Gare Maritime, Port de Bloscon.
    Crossings to Plymouth and Cork
    ℡ 02 98 29 28 13 / 08 71 24 40 744
    www.brittany-ferries.co.uk
Air
  Morlaix Airport ℡ 02 98 62 16 09
Train
  Station in town centre. Morlaix is the nearest TGV station.
    ℡ 02 98 69 70 20 www.ter-sncf.com

CHARTS
BA 2026 Anse de Kernic to Ile Grande (1:50 000)
BA 2745 Baie de Morlaix – Ile de Batz to Pointe
  de Primel (1:20 000)*
  *includes plan: Roscoff (1:10 000)
Imray C35 Baie de Morlaix to L'Aber-Ildut*
  *includes plan: Roscoff (1:20 000)
Imray 2510 North Brittany Chart Atlas:
  9 Baie de Morlaix (1:50 000)
  10f Canal de l'Île de Batz to Roscoff (1:20 000)
SHOM 7095 Baie de Morlaix – De l'Ile de Batz à la
  Pointe de Primel (1:20 000)*
  *includes plan: Ports de Roscoff (1:10 000)
SHOM 7151 De l'anse de Kernic à l'Ile Grande (1:48 700)

TIDAL INFORMATION
Roscoff is a standard port of reference for minor ports between Trébeurden and l'Aber Ildut.
Difference on Brest:
HW + 0100
LW + 0110

MHWS	MLWS	MHWN	MLWN
8·8	1·3	7·0	3·4

DEPTHS
Vieux Port (Vieux Môle S side) dries 3·2m to 5·2m
  Springs 4·5m
  Neaps 1·5m
  Access HW – 2½h to HW + 2½h
Marina 4m
  Access 24/7

SHELTER
Roscoff is particularly exposed to northeasterlies which when strong will create surge in Vieux Port.

CONTACTS
VHF Ch 9 (for marina call *Plaisance Roscoff*)
Taxi Laurent Le Pors ℡ 02 98 67 00 00 www.taxilepors.fr
Vieux Port
  Bureau du Port ℡ 02 98 79 79 49
    Mobile 06 70 50 98 68
  Mairie ℡ 02 98 24 43 00
Roscoff Marina
  Bureau du Port at root of Vieux Môle ℡ 02 98 79 79 49
    Email Plaisance.roscoff@morlaix.cci.fr

SUPPLIES AND SERVICES
Vieux Port
  Water and electricity on quay
  Showers, WCs on quay
  Bureau du Tourism Bassin Sud, next to lighthouse
  Fuel Roscoff Marina, Bloscon
  Epicerie La Ch'tite ℡ 02 98 69 77 82, Rue Gambetta (will deliver to yacht)
  Launderette
  Restaurants numerous. Try: Chez Corinne ℡ 02 98 29 75 42 1, Place de la République or Le Bellevue ℡ 02 98 1 23 38, Rue Jeanne d'Arc, Bd. Sainte-Barbe
Marina
  Berths 671
  Visitors 48 on A, B South and C South
  Max length 25m
  Max draught 3m
  Water, electricity and WCs on walkway
  Showers ashore
  Fuel Pontoons C, B(H24)
  50-ton boatlift on hard standing
  Bus shuttle service between marina and Roscoff (seasonal)

There is a dramatic quality about the way Roscoff's austere granite buildings dominated by a strange medieval church spire appear to rise out of the flat and featureless landscape. It is certainly ancient, its history dating back more than a thousand years, most of which has been closely connected with England. Today cross channel links are maintained by a daily ferry service to and from Plymouth.

Over the years Roscoff has not enjoyed a good reputation with visiting yachtsmen on account of its tidal limitations. The only options have been to dry out alongside a wall in the Vieux Port or moor to a buoy half a mile outside the harbour.

The Chamber of Commerce and Industry of Morlaix have completed a 670 berth deep water marina adjoining the commercial ferry terminal of Bloscon 1M southeast of Roscoff. It will provide a secure base from which to explore the Bay of Morlaix and a convenient staging port for yachts heading for South Brittany or returning up the Channel. It is also good news for those who prefer to dry out in Roscoff harbour as there is now room alongside in the Vieux Port.

Ashore

Roscoff is a friendly place well accustomed to English visitors. Here will be found a wide range of shops and restaurants to suit all pockets. If you want to visit Ile de Batz without a boat in tow there is a regular shuttle between the Gare Maritime on Môle de la Vache and Porz Kernoc'h, the island's harbour (see L'Ile de Batz). Market day is on Wednesdays.

Trébeurden – Ile de Batz

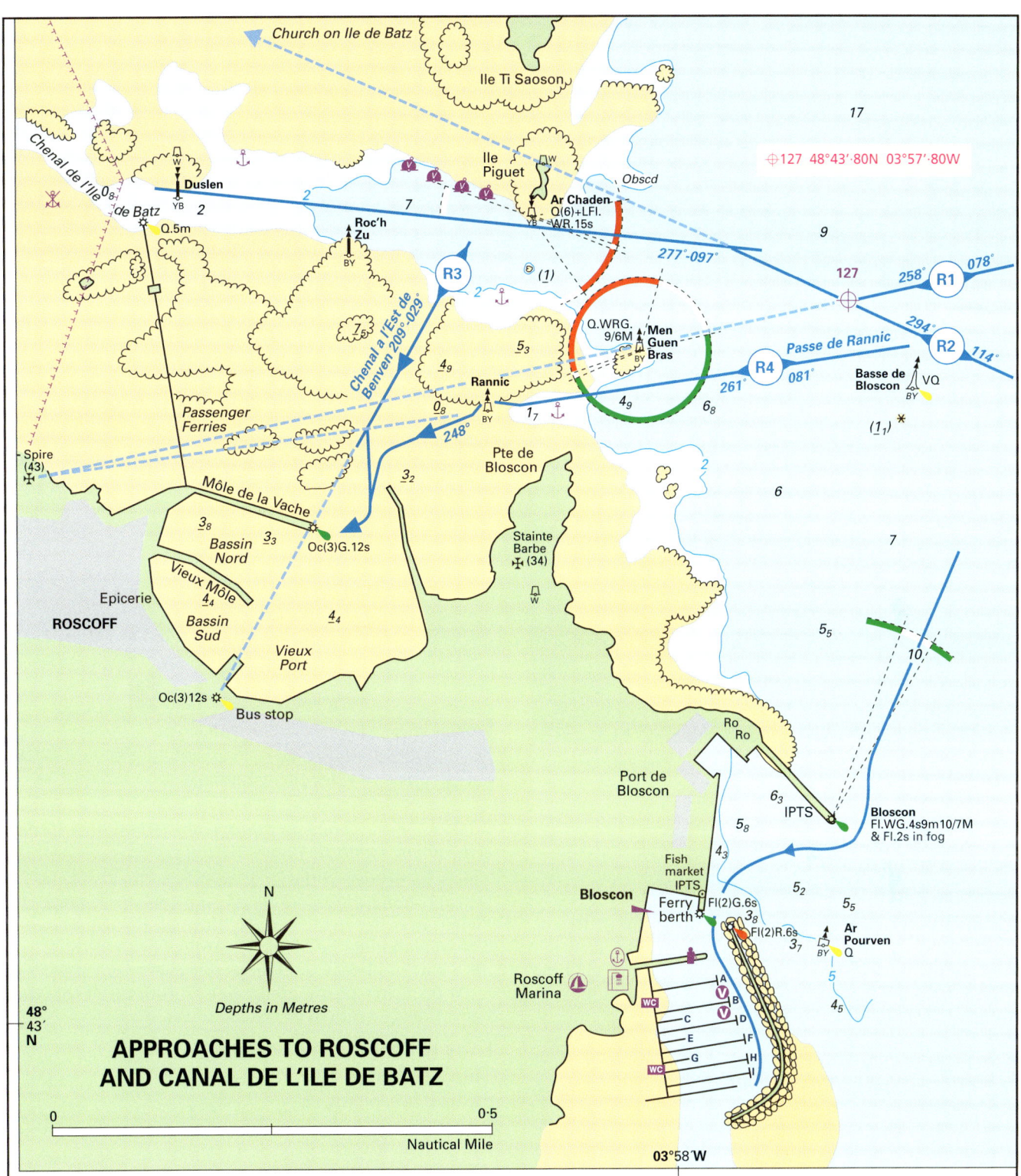

Historical

Roscoff has specialised in onion cultivation since the 17th Century and the Maison des Johnies et L'Oignon Rose folk museum (Rue Brizeux ☏ 02 98 61 25 48) is devoted to the traditional onion sellers known as Johnnies. They would set out for Britain from Roscoff every year and on bicycles laden with onion plaits tout from door to door across the country. Today there are just a few Johnnies left but Roscoff's onions continue to thrive.

III North Brittany: 2 Trébeurden to Ouessant

Roscoff marina with Vieux Port and Ile de Batz in the distance looking NNW

Approaches to Roscoff Marina and Canal de L'Ile de Batz key marks looking NW

Approaches to Roscoff

From the East

Coming down to Roscoff from the direction of Perros Guirec, Ploumanac'h or Trébeuerden involves clearing Plateau de la Méloine and Plateau des Duons. Méloine will usually be passed to the N but the Duons may be passed either side. To clear N the transit is:

R1 258° Align Men Guen Bras tower (300m NE of Pte de Bloscon) with Roscoff spire

To clear S the transit is:

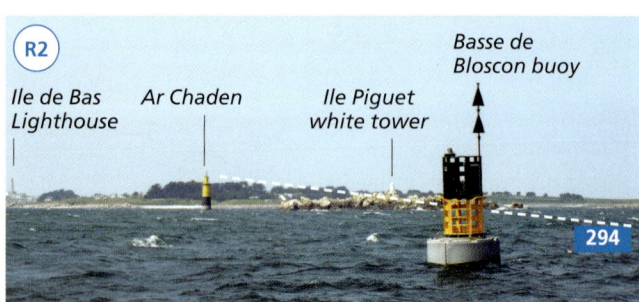

R2 294° Notre-Dame de Bon Secours (Church on Ile de Batz) aligned with Ile Piguet (W tower)

This is ineffective as the back mark is no longer visible. A bearing should therefore be taken on the front mark, Ile Piguet, in order to clear safely through the gap between reefs surrounding Le Menk W cardinal beacon tower and the S part of Plateau des Duons (see chart page 304).

Approaches terminate at ⊕127 400m ENE of Men Guen Bras N cardinal lit beacon tower.

Entry to Canal de l'Ile de Batz

This is made on 277° to pass 50m S of Ar Chaden S cardinal beacon tower.

(Note there are drying rocks close E and SSW of this tower.)

Trébeurden – Ile de Batz

From the West (see plan page 314)
Approach ⊕128 with Ile de Batz lighthouse on a bearing of no less than 070° until Basse Platte N cardinal tower bears 110°. Leave the tower 100m to starboard (see Canal de l'Ile de Batz and Moguériec.

Entry to Roscoff Harbour and Vieux Port
Sufficient water in the entrance should be found at least 2½ hours either side of HW.

Entry is made from the E end of the Canal with transit:

R3 209° Roscoff leading lights (shown open for conspicuity)

Passe du Rannic
This short cut may be used at HW.

From Basse de Bloscon N cardinal buoy take up transit:

R4 261° Roscoff spire aligned with Rannic N cardinal beacon tower

Rannic is left close (30m) to port before altering course to 248° for harbour entrance.

Berthing
The outer harbour has good drying berths along its N and W sides drying from 2·4m to 3m on hard sand but these are reserved for fishing boats and *vedettes* which use the steps. The inner harbour, Vieux Port, dries from 3·2m to 5·2m. The old jetty is rather rough but there are good berths alongside for up to a dozen yachts with six ladders and two steps. The wall is high and the use of warps to hold the yacht in is preferable to masthead lines.

The eastern part of the harbour is not recommended for drying out as it is prone to surge with any swell.

Vieux Port old jetty

The outer harbour has good drying berths along its N and W sides but keep clear of the *vedette* berths

Moorings at W end of Canal de L'Ile de Batz (looking E)

Moorings
The moorings at W end of Chenal de L'Ile de Batz were discontinued 2016. The sole mooring is reserved for Department des Phares et Balises. Getting ashore is only possible three hours either side of HW and it is a long haul.

Anchoring outside
No anchorage outside the port is clear of tidal streams. All are open to the E. Selection will depend on wind direction and whether on springs or neaps.

- Between Ar Chaden and Duslen clear of moorings and as far N as possible. Open to the N and only comfortable for deep draughts at neaps.

III North Brittany: 2 Trébeurden to Ouessant

Marina entrance

- In about 1m just E of the Roscoff leading line with Roc'h Zu N cardinal beacon bearing 285° but note the rock drying 1m close NE of this.

Entry to Roscoff Marina

Approach from N at Basse de Bloscon N cardinal buoy. Round the end of the ferry terminal pier.

Keep a lookout for commercial vessels and avoid access channels (see chart *SHOM 7095 / BA 2745*).

Signals regulate movement into and out of the marina whenever a ferry or merchant vessel is manoeuvring. They can be difficult to see from seaward and before leaving marina berth. The signals are:

```
●      R
●      R    No exit
●      R

●      G
o      W    No entry
●      G
```

Berthing instructions will be passed on VHF Ch 09 on contact before entry. A marina attendant conducts visitors to their allocated berth on A, B or C pontoon.

WARNING

An accelerated stream, most noticeable at springs, runs alongside the E wall of the marina setting S on the flood and N on the ebb. It also runs through the pontoons but less strongly on the W side. It reaches about 1·5kn at half tide. This may cause problems when manoeuvring and the advice is to keep closer to the pontoon side of the channel and be on guard.

Roscoff's new marina looking south

By night

The only night approaches to Roscoff are from the E using W sectors of:

Ar Chaden Q(6)+LFl.WR.15s 8/6M
Men Guen Bras Q.WRG.9/6M

Port de Bloscon is approached from NE in W sector of Bloscon Fl.WG.4s10/7M and in fog Fl.2s.

Entry to Roscoff harbour (Vieux Port) is:
Head of North Môle Oc(3)G.12s aligned with synchronised rear light Oc(3)12s.

Dried out in Portz Kernoc'h. Ile de Batz

Trébeurden – Ile de Batz

L'ILE DE BATZ

48°43'·93N 03°58'·24W Ar Chaden lighthouse

TRAVEL
Regular *vedettes* ply between Roscoff and Ile de Batz. Embarkation is from Nouveau Môle in Roscoff Harbour at HW or the Ferry Pier in the Canal at LW. Roscoff landing in Batz is on the causeway S of Porz Kernoc'h.

CHARTS
British Admiralty
2026 Anse de Kernic to Ile Grande (1:50 000)
2745 Baie de Morlaix – Ile de Batz to Pointe de Primel (1:20 000)
Imray
C35 Baie de Morlaix to L'Aber-Ildut*
*includes plan: Roscoff (1:20 000)
2510 North Brittany Chart Atlas:
9 Baie de Morlaix (1:50 000)
10f Canal de l'Ile de Batz to Roscoff (1:20 000)
SHOM
7095 Baie de Morlaix – De l'Ile de Batz à la Pointe de Primel (1:20 000)
7151 De l'anse de Kernic à l'Ile Grande (1:48 700)

TIDAL INFORMATION
Standard port: Roscoff or Brest
Differences on Brest:
HW Brest +0100
LW Brest –0110

MHWS	MLWS	MHWN	MLWN
8·9	1·3	7·1	3·4

Tidal streams
See Canal de l'Ile de Batz.

USEFUL CONTACTS
Tourist Office On landing quay ✆ 02 98 61 75 70 /
✆ 06 73 55 31 78 iledebatz@orange.fr
Island Tour/Taxi ✆ 06 09 45 23 64 www.taxi-ile-de-batz.fr
Doctor ✆ 02 98 61 79 79

SUPPLIES AND SERVICES
Water, WCs On harbour front
Showers At the Hotel
Boulangerie, alimentation Le Marée Gourmande ✆ 02 98 61 74 33
Restaurants Several around beach and in the town (Le Bourg)
Supermarket Huit à huit ✆ 02 98 61 78 79
Bike hire Les Brissants ✆ 02 98 61 76 34
Le Saout ✆ 06 18 14 72 61
Prigent ✆ 02 98 61 76 91

This peaceful and unspoilt island measuring about two miles long and half a mile at its widest is for the most part low lying and treeless. The lives of its population, about 500, are centred around market gardening, fishing, and tourism in the form of day trippers from Roscoff.

Most activity will be found in Le Bourg that clusters behind the harbour of Porz Kernoc'h. It consists of a handful of shops, bars, creperies and restaurants and a market on Sundays.

The best way to explore the island is to hire a bike or walk round it (distance 7M – allow about 6 hours).

The lighthouse is open to the public during the season and worth a visit. Plodding to the lantern (198 steps) will cost you €2·50 but the view over the island and beyond is outstanding.

Jardin George Delaselle, semi-tropical garden at the east end of the island, is open to the public ✆ 02 98 61 77 76.

Round Island Tour includes both the above sites and others (see *Supplies and Services*).

Mooring, anchoring and drying out
To enter Porz Kernoc'h from Canal l'Ile de Batz leave Ile aux Mouton S cardinal at the outer end of the landing causeway 15m to starboard and head NNW to leave the pyramid (W) of Ile Kernoc'h 50m to port. Select an anchorage clear of moorings and fishing vessels.

The island is most practically visited by boats that can take the ground as the port dries at between 2·6m and 5·4m. At neaps sufficient water may be found in the harbour for anchoring.

For drying out the bottom is firm and mostly sand but beware of some stoney areas. For anchoring off Canal d'Ile de Batz see *Anchoring in the Canal* below.

Porz Kernoc'h from W at LW

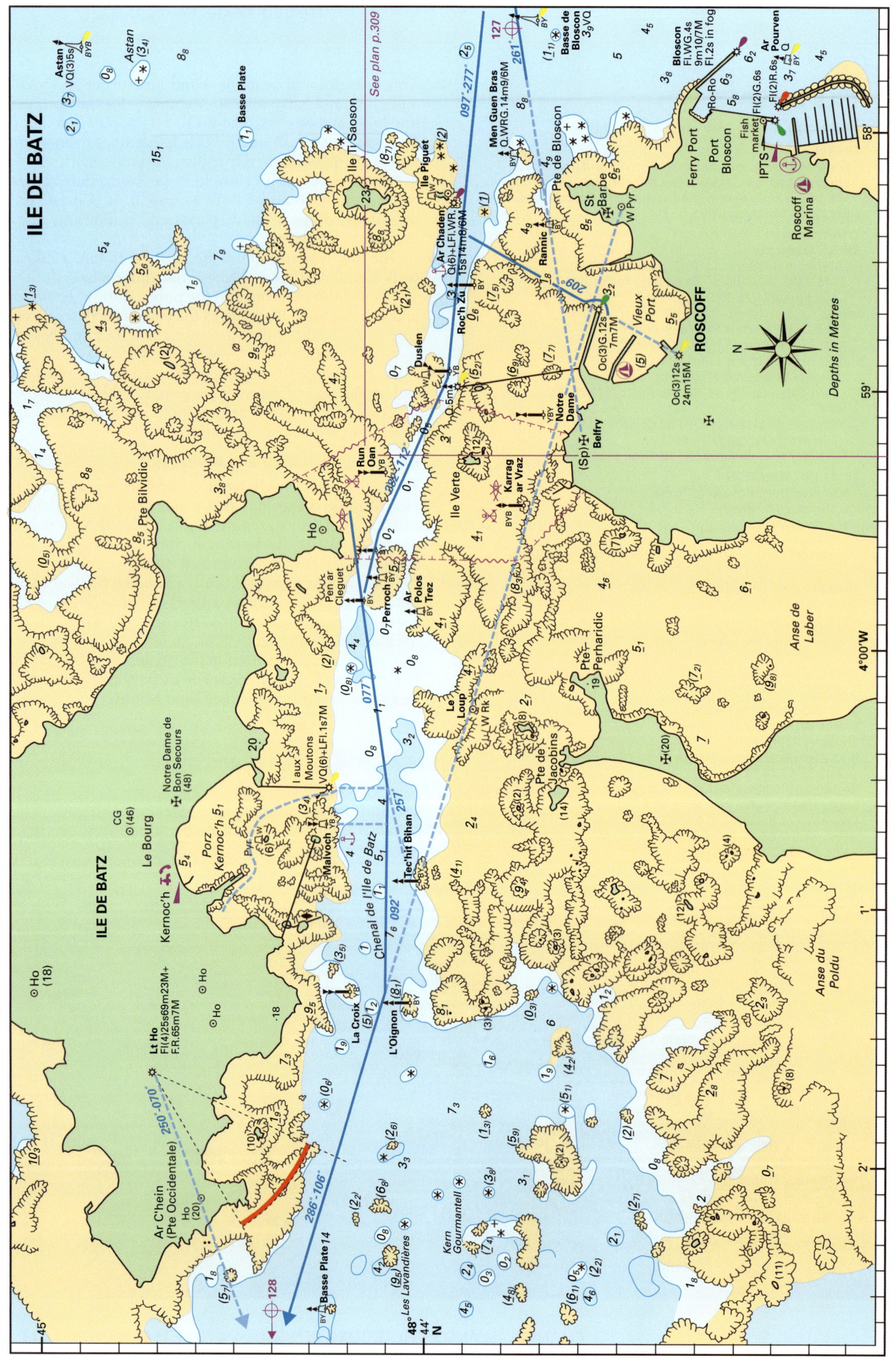

CANAL DE L'ILE DE BATZ

CHARTS
French SHOM chart 7095 (Baie de Morlaix) is the best for transitting the canal and is essential. It is recommended to mark up the succession of dog legs between turning points with courses to be steered.

RADIO
VHF Roscoff Ch 09

TIDAL STREAMS AND DEPTHS
W going stream starts at HW Roscoff +1 (HW Brest +0110).
E-going stream starts at HW Roscoff -5 (HW Brest -0435).
Streams reach 3·5 knots at springs in the narrowest part off Roscoff and follow the direction of the Canal.
At half tide there is a rise of about 5m so the best window for transiting the Canal is between 3 hours before and 3 hours after local HW.

This cut between Ile de Batz and Roscoff is 3·0M long, 100m at its narrowest point and has a least depth of 0·1m. Taken at the right time and in visibility of at least 1·0M it is an interesting exercise in pilotage and preferable to routeing N about the island with its drying rocks up to a mile from the shore and a tidal race. This is mainly eyeball navigation, the essentials being a large scale chart, a hand bearing compass and binoculars.

Pilotage

FROM W

The route through the Canal consists of five dog legs.
Approaching from W a bearing on Ile de Batz lighthouse of no more than 070° will ensure dangers W of the island are cleared.

From ⊕128 which is positioned 0·35M WNW of Basse Plate N cardinal beacon tower take up transit:

1. 106° Pyramid (W) right (S) of Chapelle de Ste Barbe aligned with Le Loup whitewashed rock. This leaves:

2. Basse Plate tower 150m to starboard and leads between La Croix S cardinal beacon and L'Oignon N cardinal beacon. When L'Oignon is 100m to starboard:

L'Oignon

3. Alter course to 092° for half a mile until Tec'hit Bihan N cardinal beacon is on a backbearing of 257° and the S cardinal beacon on the end of the causeway (above) bears N. Come to 077°.

4. Maintain heading towards the southernmost tip of Ile de Batz (Pen ar Cleguet) to clear between two rocks (the northernmost dries 0·8m).

Per Roc'h

5. The next mark ahead is N cardinal buoy marking the NE corner of Per Roc'h reef. This should be left close to starboard. Next:

III North Brittany: 2 Trébeurden to Ouessant

6. Alter to 112° to leave Per Roc'h N cardinal beacon tower 100m to starboard, the N cardinal beacon marking the NE corner of the reef close to starboard and an unmarked S cardinal buoy that replaces Run Oan S cardinal beacon (derelict 2013) 100m to port. Then pass S of Duslen white tower and the S cardinal beacon close S of it. The beacon should be given 50m clearance.

8. Ar Chaden S cardinal beacon tower is left 50m to port. Beware of a 2·0m drying rock 200m ESE of this tower. (See view Roscoff page 310.)

FROM E
Follow **Approaches to Roscoff from E**, then pilotage from W in reverse sequence. Position 50m S of Ar Chaden on an initial track of 274°.

By night
Canal de L'Ile de Batz is unlit.

Anchoring in the Canal
This is prohibited at its E end due to cables (see chart). Elsewhere there are several options but holding may be compromised by tidal stream.

1. Between Ar Chaden and Duslen clear of moorings (see Roscoff) and as far N as depth allows. Exposed in easterlies.
2. SW of Malvoch beacon tower (avoiding Bazenn Malvog 0·1m).
3. S of Ile aux Moutons and E of the causeway clear of Roscoff ferry route.

Mooring
Moorings along the N edge of the channel W of Ar Chaden are available to visitors (see *Roscoff moorings* page 311).

7. Leave Roc'h Zu N cardinal beacon to starboard and finally:

Chenal de l'Ile de Batz looking WNW at LW

Ile de Siec to L'Aber Wrac'h (25M)
Le Pays Pagan

ILE DE SIEC (or SIECK)

48°42'·22N 04°04'·83W (Ile de Siec harbour)
6M SW of Roscoff

CHARTS
As for Moguéric

SUPPLIES AND SERVICES
No resources but the village of Dossen has a bar/crêperie/tabac, Le Fontenoy, by the quay.

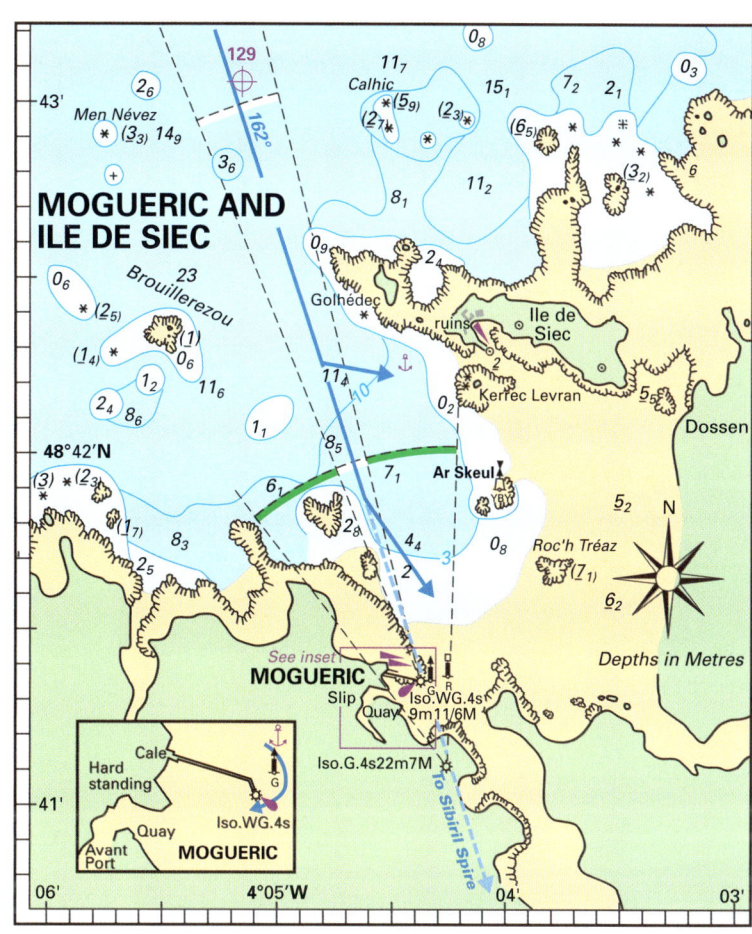

⊕129 48°43'·86N 04°05'·71W

This elusive island 1 mile N of Moguériec and 2·2 miles S of the W extremity of Ile de Batz is barely half a mile long and 24m high. When it is not separated from the mainland by a strip of water it may be reached by foot below half tide over a sandspit (dries 5·5m). The slipway at the village of Dossen is 400m from the SE end of the island. It is privately owned but there is public access to a track around the island. In settled weather small craft use its snug harbour Le Mouillage de Santec which dries at 4m.

History

In 1944, two British airmen were forced to parachute into the sea off the island and, as a reprisal for the help given to them by the inhabitants, all the buildings on Ile de Siec were blown up by the Germans. Another version explaining the reason for the ruins on the island is that arms and explosives were being landed for the Resistance and cached on the island, causing a predictable reaction on discovery. Seventeen of the inhabitants, five from one family, were killed by the enemy and are commemorated by a memorial by the slip at Dossen.

Approach and Anchorage

Ile de Siec shares the same leading line as Moguériec. Follow this line to leave Golhédec (12m) (just to the W of and joined at LW to Ile de Siec) 400m to port, and various drying rocks 600m to starboard. If proceeding to the Siec anchorage turn E after passing Golhédec and sound in with the jetty head bearing 080°. S of the jetty is a pile of rocks, Kerrec Levran which is some 300m E/W.

Berthing

The small harbour is protected by a low breakwater inside of which is a rough jetty. The outer part of this is a slipway running down to the end of the jetty but it is possible to berth at the inner end towards HW. The bottom inside consists of loose boulders and rubble and is not a place to dry out.

Ile de Siec from NW

III North Brittany: 2 Trébeurden to Ouessant

The harbour at HW seen from Plage de Dossen

Kerrec Levran off the harbour. Moguériec on the horizon

Not a place for drying out

MOGUÉRIEC

48°41'·62N 4°04'·3W (Breakwater Head)
6M SW of Roscoff
11M E of Brignogan

CHARTS
BA 2026 Anse de Kernic to Ile Grande (1:50 000)
Imray C35 Baie de Morlaix to L'Aber-Ildut*
Imray 2510 North Brittany Chart Atlas*
  *both include plan: Moguériec (1:32 000)
SHOM 7151 De l'anse de Kernic à l'île Grande (1:48 700)

TIDAL INFORMATION
Differences:
HW Roscoff -0005
HW Brest +0050
LW Brest +0045

MHWS	MLWS	MHWN	MLWN
8·0	1·0	7·0	3·0

SUPPLIES AND SERVICES
Water and WC at the jetty head.
La Marine Hotel, bar, restaurant is the centre of activity in the harbour. It also extends to an occasional *épicerie* for basic stores.
☎ 02 98 29 99 52   www.lamarine-mogueriec.com

This small drying harbour lies on the western side of a sandy river estuary, the Guillec, 3M SSW of Ile de Batz. It should appeal to those that like to explore out of the way harbours and anchorages that are within a short distance of a sheltered port. The surrounding land provides a good lee from easterlies but the whole bay is open to westerlies when the harbour could become precariously swelly in strong conditions.

Moguériec was an ancient Roman port and considered the premier lobster port on the north coast of Finisterre until 1960.

Approach and Entry

(For plan see *Ile de Siec* page 317)
Coming from the Canal de L'Ile de Batz do not turn south too early. At Basse Platte N cardinal tower alter course to 253° with Ile de Batz lighthouse held on a backbearing no less than 070°. This will clear offlying dangers WSW of Ile de Batz. Identify Moguériec leading marks (⊕129) and take up:

MOG 162° *White Tr with green top on breakwater end aligned with near white beacon with green top. On the distant skyline, the spire of Sibiril church is also on the line*

Ile de Siec to L'Aber Wrac'h

The harbour from S

This line passes 0·25M W of Ile de Siec. When 0·5M short of the pierhead and with Ar Skeul W cardinal beacon on the beam alter course to 160° to pass midway between port and starboard beacons off the entrance.

By night
Front: White light tower Iso.WG.4s
Rear: White beacon F.G Keep in the W sector

Depths
The harbour dries at 4–5m. At HW springs a depth of 6m was found in the harbour.

Anchoring and berthing
Anchor 400m NNE off the pierhead or dry out alongside.
   There are three quays, two in the outer harbour and one in the very sheltered Avant Port. The latter is used by the fishing fleet when the tides are high enough. Visitors should keep out of their way. The bottom is generally level and clean.

The focal point of the harbour

Avant Port

III North Brittany: 2 Trébeurden to Ouessant

BRIGNOGAN (Pontusval)

48°40'·66N 04°19'·15W (Ar Neudenn port beacon tower)
4M W of Porsguen
1M E of Pte de Beg Pol Lighthouse
9M E of Le Corréjou
6M W of Morlaix city

CHARTS
BA 2025 Portsall to Anse de Kernic (1:50 000)

Imray C35 Baie de Morlaix to L'Aber-Ildut*
*includes plan: Port du Pontusval (1:15 000)

Imray 2510 North Brittany Chart Pack*
*includes plan: Port du Pontusval (1:25 000)

SHOM 7150 De Portsall à l'Anse de Kernic (1:48 900)

TIDAL INFORMATION
Standard port: BREST
HW Brest +0042
LW Brest +0048

MHWS	MLWS	MHWN	MLWN
8·4	1·2	6·6	3·2

Tidal streams
Tidal streams off the entrance start at the following times:
HW Brest −0440 E-going
HW Brest +0125 W-going

USEFUL CONTACTS
Bureau du Port/Sailing School ☎ 06 26 61 16 55
Mairie ☎ 02 98 83 40 06

SUPPLIES AND SERVICES
Landing slips at Pontusval jetty, extreme SE of bay and W side of the sailing school.
Brignogan village at the distant end of bay is a holiday resort with shops, restaurants and hotels.
Fuel nearest pumps are in Kerlouan (3½M)

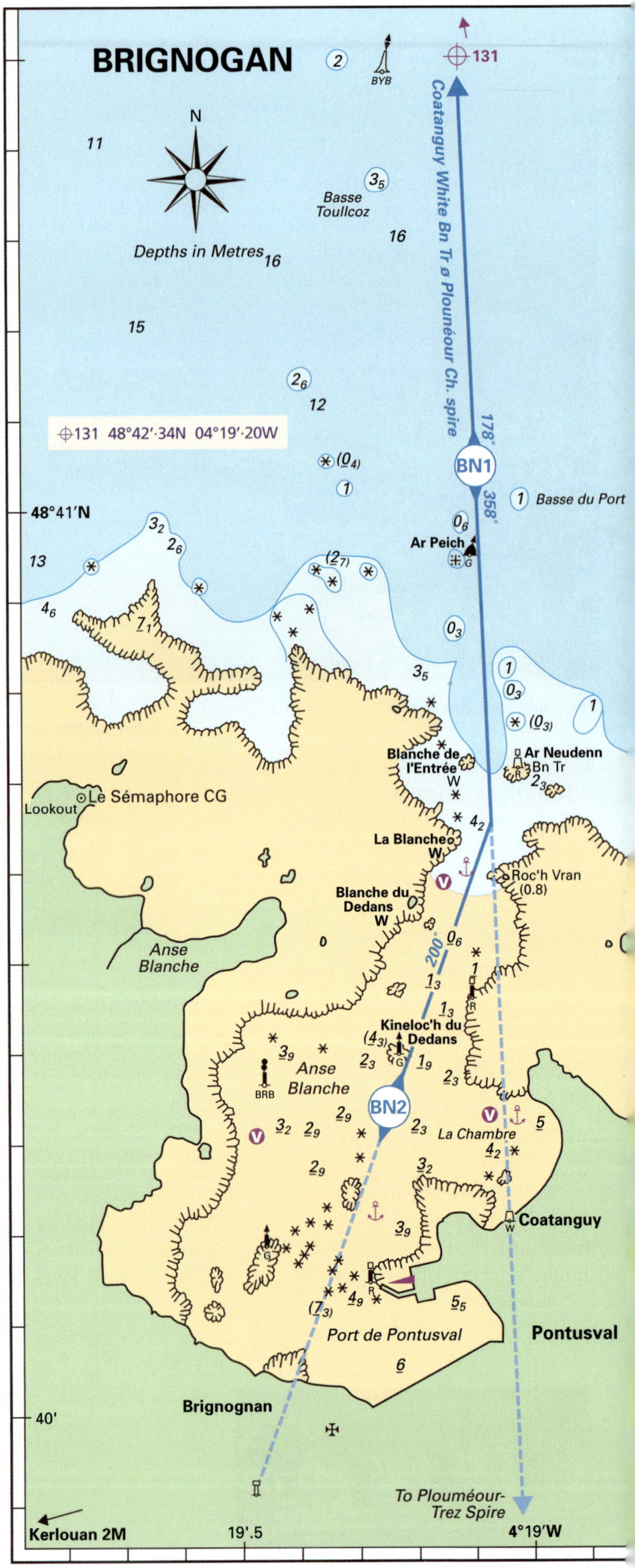

Brignogan Plage is the resort and Pontusval in the extreme SE of the bay is 'Le Port' consisting of a quay and slipway.

This almost landlocked bay is typical of many openings on this stretch of the coast. Tempting in quiet weather and over neap tides but a potential trap if the weather turns nasty with strong onshore winds.

In keeping with most of the harbours between Ile de Batz and L'Aber Wrac'h, Brignogan's entrance involves penetrating the reefs that fringe the coast. Here there are a good selection of marks in the approach which should be made from half tide upwards.

The bay sprawls out into a mass of white sandy beaches with clear shallow water.

Approach
Key marks: E to W

- Vast sandy opening of Grève de Goulven
- Le Sémaphore de Pontusval (or Brignogan)
- Pointe de Beg Pol
- Tall pylon (49m) is 2M inland SSW of Brignogan

Le Sémaphore CG

From ⊕131 make for a position 100m E of Basse Toullcoz E cardinal buoy. Identify the main mark off the entrance Ar Neudenn port beacon tower (48°40'·66N 04°19'·15W) 0·5M E of Le Sémaphore. If possible hold transit of two marks which are likely to be inconspicuous:

Ile de Siec to L'Aber Wrac'h

Brignogan from N (Plouméour Trez spire not visible)

BN1 *178° Back mark Plouméour-Trez church (not to be confused with Brignogan church spire) aligned with white pyramid L'Amer de Coatanguy*

This leaves:

- Ar Peich starboard buoy close to starboard
- Ar Neudenn port tower close to port

If the back mark is obscured, an alternative transit is:

181° L'Amer de Coatanguy aligned with Ar Neudenn. At Ar Peich buoy a small alteration to starboard will be necessary to clear W of dangers 300m N of Ar Neudenn

Continue until La Blanche whitewashed rock in on the starboard beam at which point alter course to SSW with transit:

This leaves:

- Kineloc'h starboard beacon on E end of rock (drying 4·4m) 200m to starboard

Moorings and anchorages

There are (free) visitors' moorings (Y) in the entrance to the bay (see view) and drying moorings at S end of the bay off the beach near the SNSM centre.

Anchorage is best on the E side rather than the W which has rocks and boulders. Anse de la Chambre drying 4·2m is possibly the snuggest (see plan).

Pontusval jetty comprising of a quay and slipway with a rocky headland to the N is the most sheltered part of the bay. The sands here dry at 5m. (See view).

BN2 *200° Water tower well open right (W) of Brignogan church spire*

Anchorage and visitors' moorings in the entrance

III North Brittany: 2 Trébeurden to Ouessant

LE CORRÉJOU

48°38'·25N 04°30'·06 (Barr-Ar-Skoaz port buoy)
8M from L'Aber Wrac'h
10M from Brignogan

CHARTS
BA 1432 Le Four to Ile Vierge (1:25 000)
BA 2025 Portsall to Anse de Kernic (1:50 000)
SHOM 7094 Du Phare du Four à l'île Vierge – Port de l'Aber-Wrac'h (1:25 000)
SHOM 7150 De Portsall à l'Anse de Kernic (1:48 900)

Note: W approach is adequately covered by BA chart 1432 but most of the N approach, which is more complicated, is off the edge of the chart. The smaller scale charts BA 2025 and SHOM 7150 are inadequate for entry.

TIDAL INFORMATION
Standard port: Brest
Difference
HW Brest +0035
LW Brest +0040

MHWS	MLWS	MHWN	MLWN
8·0	1·4	6·4	3·0

Tidal streams
Streams start off the entrance at about the following times:
HW Brest −0400 E-going
HW Brest +0200 W-going

SUPPLIES AND SERVICES
Maison de le Mer at the end of the quay combines Bureau du Port, lifeboat station, Club Nautique de Plouguerneau and bar.
Showers available at the sailing school.
Water on the jetty
Restaurant Le Carré Saint Michel (at W end of harbour)
Shops at Plougeneau 1½M south – a steep hill walk.

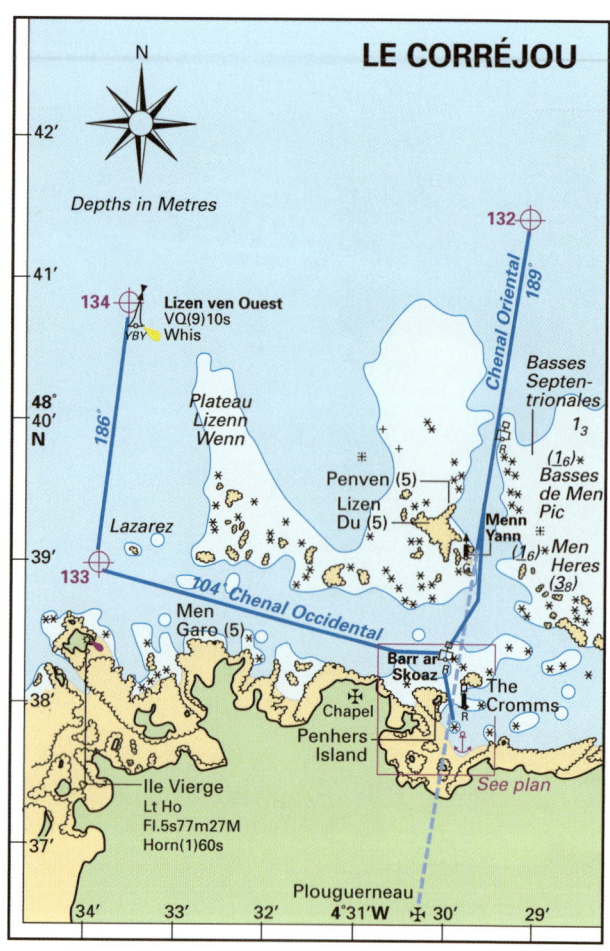

⊕132 48°42'·40N 04°29'·21W
⊕133 48°38'·84N 04°33'·95W
⊕134 48°40'·78N 04°33'·60W

Le Corréjou is an open bay with shelter from the S and W for deep-keeled yachts and more scope for those able to take the ground in the inner bay.

The main industry here is kelp gathering which is carried out by specialist boats with articulated grabs. The kelp is landed at and transported from the jetty.

Approaches

Note The author has not visited Le Corréjou by sea and these directions are based on the work of former author John Lawson.

From N – Chenal Oriental

From ⊕132 identify Plouguerneau belfry which is just to the W of a prominent water tower. With this bearing 189° identify Men Yann, a small rock drying 7·1m with a starboard beacon and align this with the belfry on the bearing. Leave Basses Septentrionales port buoy to port and Penven rock (5) to starboard. Then deviate to port from the transit and leave Men Yann beacon 100m to starboard. Continue on a southerly track of less than 190°

Anchorage and harbour looking SE

Ile de Siec to L'Aber Wrac'h

Le Corréjou looking SW

until 400m S of Men Yann where a starboard buoy must be left to starboard (although this may not be shown on some charts – 2014).

Identify Barr ar Skoaz port can buoy and alter to starboard to leave it close to port. Then turn to port to leave the port beacon 250m E of the N end of Penhers Island close to port on a track of 170°. The channel is very narrow between this port beacon and Penhers but carries a least depth of 3·8m. This entrance is used most frequently by the fishing and kelp boats and it would be prudent to wait if one was leaving rather than meeting it in the narrows by the beacon.

There is a channel used by fishing boats near HW to the W of Penhers Island but it is unmarked and the depths unknown.

From W – Chenal Occidental

This channel is wider than Chenal Oriental and may be preferred. From ⊕134 making good 186° towards Ile Vierge lighthouse until Lazerez port buoy is identified and leave it to port on a track of 104° towards the two pinnacles of Karreg Cromm and Petit Cromm ahead. This track leaves Men Garo (5m) a conspicuous cottage-loaf-shaped rock ¼M to starboard. Chapel St Michel Noblet is hard to pick out in the trees but by then Bar ar Skoaz port hand buoy can be identified and steered for. Leave it close to port on a track of 170° and proceed as for Chenal Oriental.

Anchorages

SE of Penhers Island in from 0·6m and 4m sand.

Anchorage further in to the W may be found but there are several rocky patches to be avoided which are usually visible in clear water. There are a number of small moorings S and E of the slip.

It would be possible to dry out on the end of the jetty W of the slip but ask first as fishermen and the kelp boats use it.

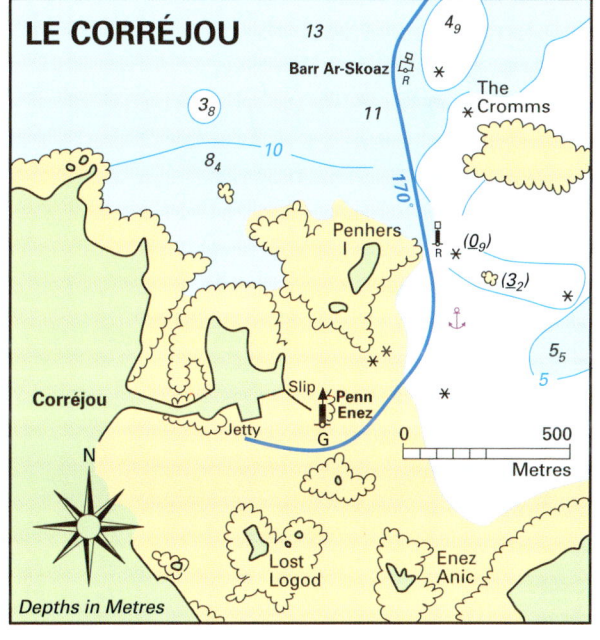

III North Brittany: 2 Trébeurden to Ouessant

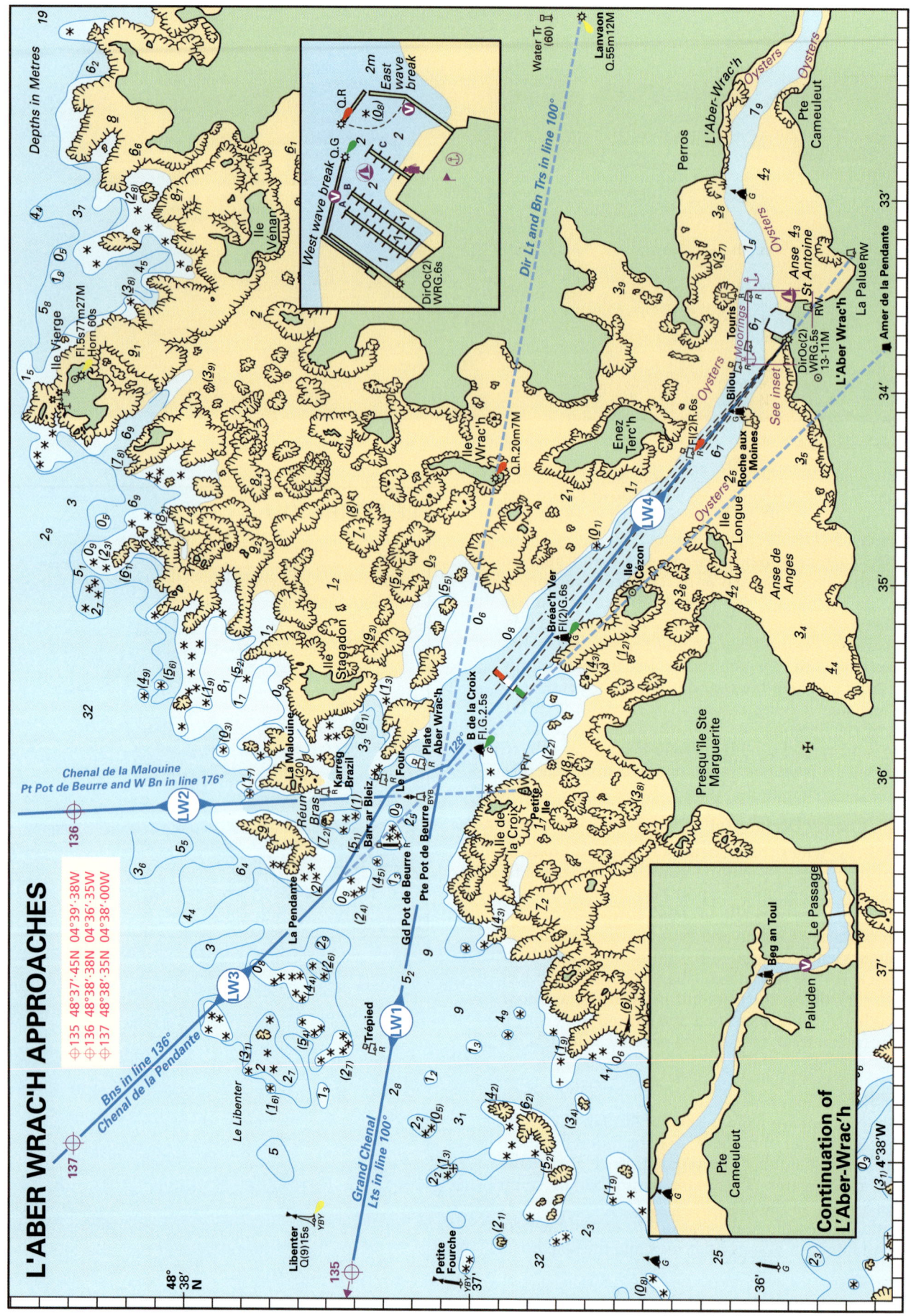

324 CHANNEL ISLANDS, CHERBOURG PENINSULA & NORTH BRITTANY

Ile de Siec to L'Aber Wrac'h

L'ABER WRAC'H

48°35'·90N 04°33'·80W (La Palue lighthouse)
8M from Le Corréjou
6M (by sea) from L'Aber Benoit

TRAVEL
Air
Finist'Air www.finistair.fr
Flights Paris-Brest, Guiparvas Airport (45 mins by road)
Also EasyJet, Air France
Train
www.sncf.com. Paris-Brest 4h30m
Road
Bus: Le Cars des Abers www.carsdesabers.com
Local stop is Landéda Aber-Wrac'h in the port area.
Landéda Bourg 4M. Brest 45M.
Navette shuttle (seasonal): enquire Bureau du Port

CHARTS
BA 1432 Le Four to Ile Vierge (1:25 000)*
 *includes plan: Aber Wrac'h (1:15 000)
BA 2025 Portsall to Anse de Kernic (1:50 000)
Imray C35 Baie de Morlaix to L'Aber-Ildut*
 *includes plan: Approaches to L'Aber Wrac'h &
 L'Aber Benoît (1:30 000)
Imray 2510 North Brittany Chart Atlas:
 12 L'Aber Wrac'h to Argenton (1:40 000)
SHOM 7094 Du Phare du Four à l'île Vierge -
Port de l'Aber-Wrac'h (1:25 000)*
 *includes plan: Aber Wrac'h (1:15 000)
SHOM 7150 De Portsall à l'Anse de Kernic (1:48 900)

RADIO
VHF Ch 09

TIDAL INFORMATION
Standard port: Brest
Difference
HW Brest +0030
LW Brest +0035

MHWS	MLWS	MHWN	MLWN
7·7	1·0	6·1	2·8

Tidal streams
The streams start at the following times off the entrance:
HW Brest -0400 ENE-going
HW Brest +0200 WSW-going
Max 3kns at springs
Max rate in the river 1½kns

USEFUL CONTACTS
Bureau du Port ☎ 02 98 04 91 62
 www.port-aberwrach.com
Office du Tourisme ☎ 02 98 04 05 43
 www.abers-tourisme.com Sub-office at Bureau du Port in season.
Taxis: Abarnou ☎ 02 98 04 84 42 / 06 85 10 52 53

SUPPLIES AND SERVICES
Marina
Water, electricity at the pontoons
Showers facilities block
Fuel Pontoon C inner end
Visitors berths 70 Marina pontoons, 20 buoys in river.
 Max length 50m on pontoons, 18m on buoys
Crane and travel hoist on hard standing
Internet access and WiFi
Up to date weather information display at Bureau du Port
Chandlery Cooperative Maritime
Boatyard, Mechanic
Marine Plaisance ☎ 02 98 04 83 91
Yacht Club des Abers welcomes visitors ☎ 02 98 04 92 60
Victualling No food supplies are available in the port apart from a few basics obtainable over the bar at Café du Port. The nearest supermarket (Utile) is at Landeda (Bourg). This is a long uphill walk of about a mile. Using the local bus or *navette* takes about 4 minutes. (See *Travel*.)
Restaurants
There are barely enough restaurants in the port to accommodate the influx of visitors during the height of the season. Early booking is recommended.
*L'Abri du Canot ☎ 02 29 00 32 11
Markets
The Port: Friday
Landeda (Bourg): Tuesday

This deep-water estuary on the NW extremity of Brittany has long been a popular staging port for yachts bound south towards the Raz de Sein and Biscay or returning up the Channel. At 80 miles from Lizard Point the passage to L'Aber Wrac'h is one of the shortest crossings of the Western approaches.

While it still retains the outpost atmosphere that pervades this coast the marina has been the subject of a major upgrade recently and ranks as the yachting centre of the Abers region. Facilities are as one would expect of a modern marina although a supermarché within walking distance of the pontoons would go down well.

Approaches

There are three deep-water entrances to the river but only Grand Chenal may be used at night. Expect accelerated streams on this corner of the coast for which compensation will be needed in the approaches.

Grand Chenal (4·7m) (⊕135)

The most straightforward channel by day or night – wide and well-marked.

The transit consists of three marks (here shown out of alignment):

LW1 *100° Ile Vrac'h Lighthouse aligned with Lanvaon light tower – and also Plouguerneau church spire*

The conspicuous mark is Libenter W cardinal buoy which is left 220m to port on entry. The line then leaves:

- Trépied port buoy to port
- La Grande Pot de Beurre port beacon tower to port
- Le Petit Pot de Beurre E cardinal tower to port

When south of Plate Aber W'rac'h port buoy break off this line on to 128° to follow the river up to the Marina.

Libenter buoy

III North Brittany: 2 Trébeurden to Ouessant

L'Aber Wrac'h at LWS

Chenal de la Malouine (3m) (⊕136)

This is the obvious approach from the north and east but should not be attempted in fresh to strong onshore winds or when a heavy swell (La Houle) is breaking across the entrance. In such conditions use Grand Chenal.

From a position close W of Lizen Ven Ouest W cardinal buoy make good a course of SW, with allowance for any cross stream, to close the coast to ⊕136 which is positioned on the leading line 0·75M N of La Malouine Rock with Ile Vierge lighthouse bearing E. With La Malouine positively identified prepare to make the run in through the gap between the W end of La Malouine (which is left 100m to port) and the smaller rock La Pendante to the W of it. The transit is:

LW2 *176° Le Petit Pot de Beurre E cardinal beacon tower aligned with white pyramid on Ile de la Croix*

Note Seas often break over the plateau de la Pendante W of the entrance at all states of tide.

Hold transit to pass Petit Pot de Beurre leaving it close to starboard before turning into the river on 128°.

Chenal de la Pendante (⊕137)

This seldom used channel offers no advantage over the Grand and Malouine channels. It passes very close to drying reefs making it unsuitable below half tide. Good visibility is needed to identify the marks. In the absence of sight of the published back mark – black tower with W stripe and orange conical top – use transit:

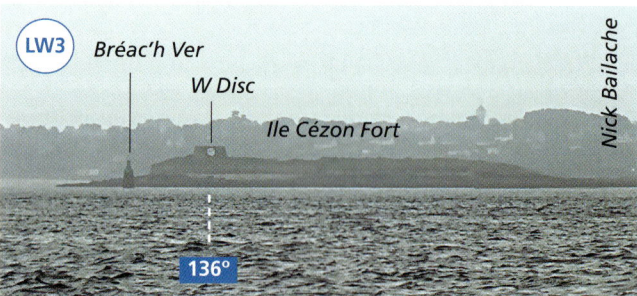

LW3 *136° W disc on Ile Cézon fort just open left (E) of Petit Pot de Beurre E cardinal beacon tower and open right (W) of Bréac'h Ver starboard beacon tower*

Hold this line until La Pendante is 200m to port and when this bears N alter to port to make good 118° for 0·37M to Le Four port buoy. Leave this, and Plate Aber Wrac'h port buoy SSE of it, close to port. When Petit Pot de Beurre is abeam to starboard steer 128° for the final approach up the river towards the marina at La Palue.

The River to La Palue is covered by transit:

LW4 128° La Palue and St Antoine lighthouses in line

This transit is valid by day but for a night approach these marks have been replaced by one single directional light Dir.Oc(2)WRG.6s.

There is also a good sequence of marks to follow up to the marina. Pilotage by the chart is most practicable:
- Plate Aber Wrac'h port buoy to port
- Basse de la Croix starboard buoy to starboard
- Port Bréac'h Ver starboard beacon tower to starboard
- Ile Enez Terc'h port buoy to port
- Roche aux Moines starboard beacon tower to starboard
- Bilou port buoy to port

By night
Grand Chenal only. Leading lights:
Front: Ile Wrac'h Q.R.7M
Rear: Lanvaon DirQ.12M

Entry light:
Dir.Oc(2)WRG.5s13/11M Red sector in N. Green sector in S. Keep to W sector for channel.

WARNING
Approaching from the N the flashing red lights on the many wind turbines can be confusing.

L'Aber Wrac'h Marina

Berthing
A call on VHF Ch 9 to L'Aber Wrac'h marina prior to arrival is recommended for obtaining directions.

Visitors are accommodated inside the W wave break and outside weather permitting. Similarly in the inside of the E wave break but not on the outer N arm which has a rocky area. Additionally several pontoons are available as directed.

There are several visitors' buoys in the river extending as far up as Perros with its quay on N bank.

Shelter
Vulnerable to wind and swell from NW when outer parts of the marina can be uncomfortable.

The marina entrance is between port and starboard pillars
Paul Bryans

Upriver to Paluden
0·5M beyond the marina the river peters out to a narrow stream but still with reasonable depths of 4–5m at LW. On the W bank just before Le Pont du Diable road bridge crosses the river will be found a substantial quay and a scattering of old sheds and dwellings. This is Paluden.

Here drying out is possible alongside the quay where there is about 0·5m at LWS. There are several visitors' moorings, which are subject to dues and anchoring is permitted providing it is clear of moorings.

The quay is well fendered with good fixing points being occasionally used by coasters.

On the opposite side of the river is Le Passage – a quay alongside which it may be possible to dry out.

Facilities
There is a water tap at Paluden but little else. The nearest town is Lannilis a good mile to the S. Water and showers available at Le Passage.

This outsize yacht is dried out alongside the N end of the quay. The official limit is 12m

The anchorage at Paluden. The yacht on the right is anchored clear of the visitors' moorings

L'Aber Benoit to Le Conquet (25M)
Pays d'Iroise

L'ABER BENOIT

45°30'·47N 04°36'·08W (Le Chien isolated danger beacon tower)
6M from L'Aber Wrac'h (by sea)
6M from Portsall (by sea)

TRAVEL
Taxi
  Taxi des Dunes ☏ 06 78 48 66 87

CHARTS
British Admiralty
  1432 Le Four to Ile Vierge (1:25 000)
  2025 Portsall to Anse de Kernic (1:50 000)
Imray
  C35 Baie de Morlaix to L'Aber-Ildut*
    *includes plan: Approaches to L'Aber Wrac'h & L'Aber Benoît (1:30 000)
  2510 North Brittany Chart Atlas:
    12 L'Aber Wrac'h to Argenton (1:40 000)
SHOM
  SHOM 7094 Du Phare du Four à l'Ile Vierge – Port de l'Aber-Wrac'h (1:25 000)
  SHOM 7150 De Portsall à l'Anse de Kernic (1:48 900)

RADIO
VHF Ch 09

TIDAL INFORMATION
Standard port: Brest
Difference:
HW Brest +0025
LW Brest +0030

MHWS	MLWS	MHWN	MLWN
7·8	1·1	6·1	2·9

Tidal streams
Outside the entrance S of Ile Guénioc the streams start as follows:
ENE going flood   HW Brest −0515
WSW going ebb   HW Brest +0010
Rates: 2·5–3 knots
In the river the stream can reach 3 knots at spring tides.

USEFUL CONTACTS
Bureau du Port ☏ 06 19 87 75 39
Movements in the river are managed from a cabin on the N shore inside the entrance and a patrolling attendant in a RIB (VHF Ch 09).

SUPPLIES AND SERVICES
Facilities are limited or non-existent so prepare to rely on own resources.
Water, electricity Available from two sources: on the quay on the N shore marked Port du Village on some plans and on the quay at Stellac'h where there is also a toilet
Boatyard St. Pabu (0·5M)
Restaurants a few options in the scattering of villages inland S of the river. The nearest is at St. Pabu (2M):
Le Charabanc Bar-restaurant ☏ 02 98 89 78 79

This attractive river is off the beaten track and the least visited in the L'Abers region. The main approach from NW involves wending through shallow rock strewn waters and is dependent on sharp visibility to identify marks. It should be made on a rising tide.

On arrival, proceeded by a call on VHF Ch 9, you will be guided up river to a visitors mooring and then left in peace and quiet. To get ashore needs a tender with outboard, the most suitable landing being at Stellac'h quay on the W bank. Drying out alongside here is possible (see views).

From Stellac'h it is a steep walk up from the river to open and rather non-descript countryside interspersed by scattered hamlets.

When planning your next move up or down the coast or perhaps out to Ile d'Ouessant, about 20M, bear in mind that pilotage into or out of L'Aber Benoit is not possible after dark and mist or fog is a hazard on this coast.

Approach

The most common approach is from the NW starting at Petite Fourche W cardinal buoy half a mile SW of Libenter W cardinal buoy. From there to the river entrance, which is taken as Le Chien isolated danger beacon tower, it is three miles of short dog legs, each of about 0·5M between marks. A large scale chart is essential. The order of entry is as follows:

- Petite Fourche W cardinal buoy to port
- Rusven starboard buoy to starboard
- Midway between Basse du Chenal starboard buoy and Basse du Chenal port beacon
- Poul Doun port beacon close to port
- Men Renead starboard buoy to starboard
- La Jument port beacon to port
- Ar Gazel starboard buoy to starboard
- Midway between Le Chien isolated danger beacon tower and Kervigorn starboard buoy

La Jument

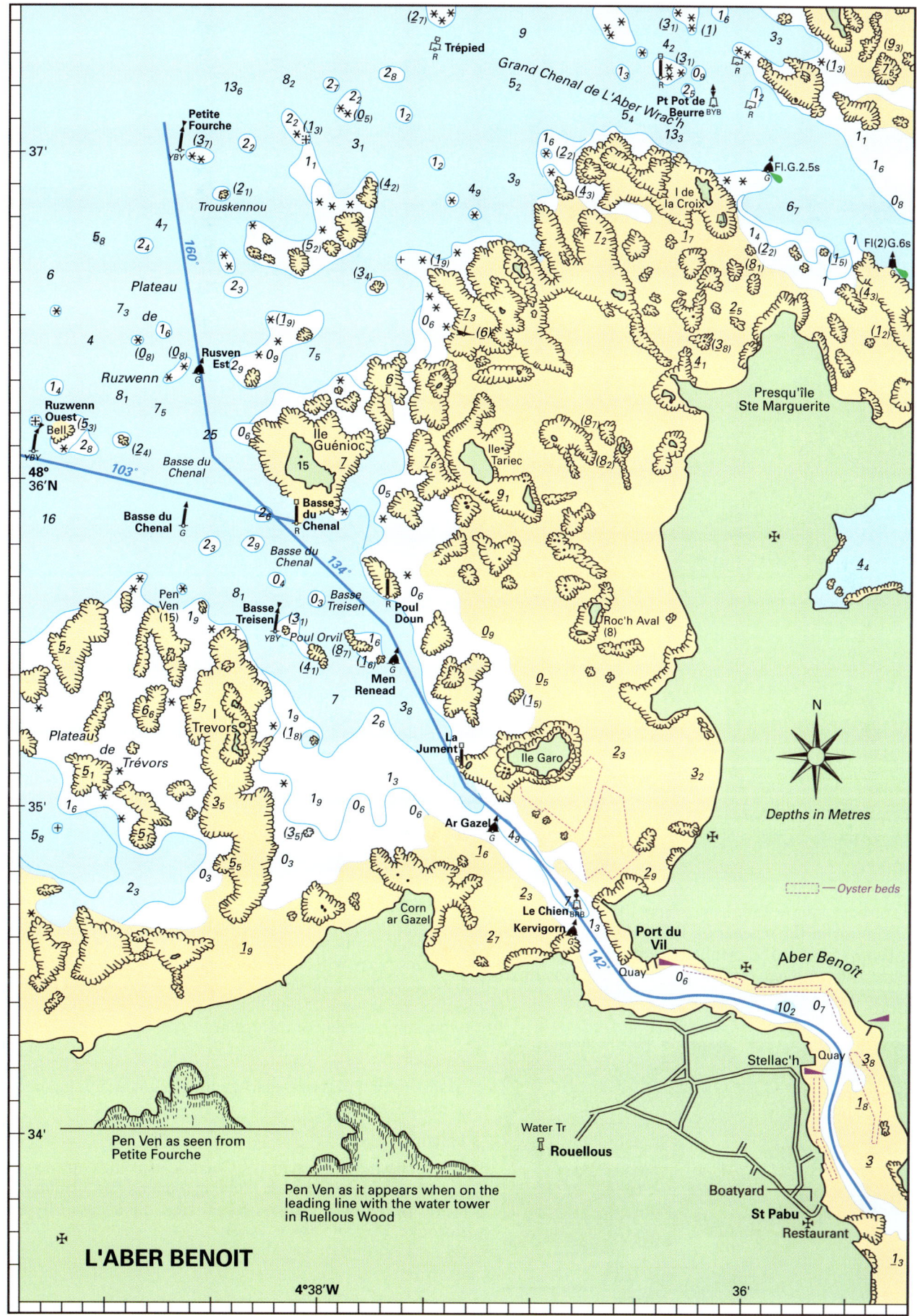

III North Brittany: 2 Trébeurden to Ouessant

Looking downstream from Stellac'h

Le Chien

From the W
This channel may be entered from the W at Basse du Chenal starboard buoy. From a position 400m N of Relec E cardinal buoy in the Chenal du Relec make good 103° to leave Ruzwenn Ouest W cardinal bell buoy close to port and thence 108° to Basse du Chenal starboard buoy then follow *Approach* page 328.

The slipway at Stellac'h

Anchorages and moorings
Anchor as directed or anywhere in the river clear of moorings which now extend above Stellac'h, or pick up a mooring. There is a wide fairway between the lines of moorings in the lower reaches. There are also anchorages to the N or Kervigorn in deep water more suitable in offshore winds. There is a landing at Stellac'h at all stages of the tide.

Berthing
There is a substantial jetty at Stellac'h with a smooth outer side and two ladders; it dries, is used by the occasional fishing boat and a berth may be found here. ½M above this is a slip and a boatyard. There is also a dinghy landing on S bank about half-way along the first reach.

A new jetty with a depth gauge will be found on the N bank just inside the entrance. It is large enough to take a 35 footer alongside, and has a slip close by. There is little ashore on this side of the estuary.

Caution
Manoeuvring in the river when the stream is running hard is best avoided.

Leisure
Good beaches. The island of Guénioc near the entrance to the estuary has prehistoric building remains and a balanced stone that many visitors have tried unsuccessfully to dislodge.

L'Aber Benoit to Le Conquet

PORTSALL (Porsal) and PORTSALL INNER PASSAGE

48°31'·84N 04°41'·28W (Portsall light tower Oc(4) WRG 12s)
8M by sea (Ch. du Rélec) WSW of L'Aber Wrac'h
5M by sea NE of Le Four lighthouse

CHARTS
BA 1432 Le Four to Ile Vierge (1:25 000)
BA 2025 Portsall to Anse de Kernic (1:50 000)
BA 2356 Goulet de Brest to Portsall including
   Ile d'Ouessant (1:50 000)
Imray C35 Baie de Morlaix to L'Aber-Ildut*
   *includes plan: Portsall (1:20 000)
Imray 2510 North Brittany Chart Atlas:
   12 L'Aber Wrac'h to Argenton (1:40 000)
SHOM 7094 Du Phare du Four à l'Ile Vierge – Port de
   l'Aber-Wrac'h (1:25 000)
SHOM 7149 Du Goulet de Brest à Portsall –
   Ile d'Ouessant (1:49 100)
SHOM 7150 De Portsall à l'Anse de Kernic (1:48 900)

RADIO
None

TIDAL INFORMATION
Standard port :Brest
HW Brest +0015
LW Brest +0020

MHWS	MLWS	MHWN	MLWN
7·5	1·0	5·9	2·7

Tidal streams
The streams start at the following times in the channel:
HW Brest –0500 NE-going flood
HW Brest +0130 SW-going edd
Spring rates 3-5 knots in either direction; the rate accelerates in the narrower parts and towards LW.

Marks
The optimum time for the identification of marks is when the tide is 3·6m above CD. The back marks tend to disappear behind the front ones any earlier on the tide.

USEFUL CONTACTS
Bureau du Port ① 02 98 45 19 18 / 06 75 51 89 80
Fuel ① 02 98 48 63 64
Sailing school (Nautisme en Pays d'Iroise) ① 02 98 48 76 23

SUPPLIES AND SERVICES
The Port Visitors' drying (11) in a SE–NW line across the harbour with an additional 3 on beach.
Fuel and water on short mole/slipway (see plan)
Showers Request at sailing school next to Ancre An Or on the quayside.
Shops Barr ar Lann village between Portsall and Kersaint. Hypermarket (Carrefour) Ploudalmèzeau 2M
Restaurant Le Chaumine ① 02 98 48 65 55 (E end of harbour)
Bars, cafés, crêperies Quayside.

Looking WNW over Portsall harbour with Roches de Portsall in the background. The prominent mark at the top right is Corn Carhai lighthouse. The isolated rock at top left is Le Yurc'h

E end of harbour at HW

Portsall (Porsal in Breton) occupies the eastern side of a wide northwest facing bay the southern portion of which is known as Kersaint after the nearby village.

Barricaded behind the formidable sprawl of the Roches de Portsall that extend two miles out from the harbour this is one of mainland Brittany's westernmost outposts.

With difficult approaches, a totally drying harbour and vulnerability to Atlantic wind and swell Portsall is not an

CHANNEL ISLANDS, CHERBOURG PENINSULA & NORTH BRITTANY   331

III North Brittany: 2 Trébeurden to Ouessant

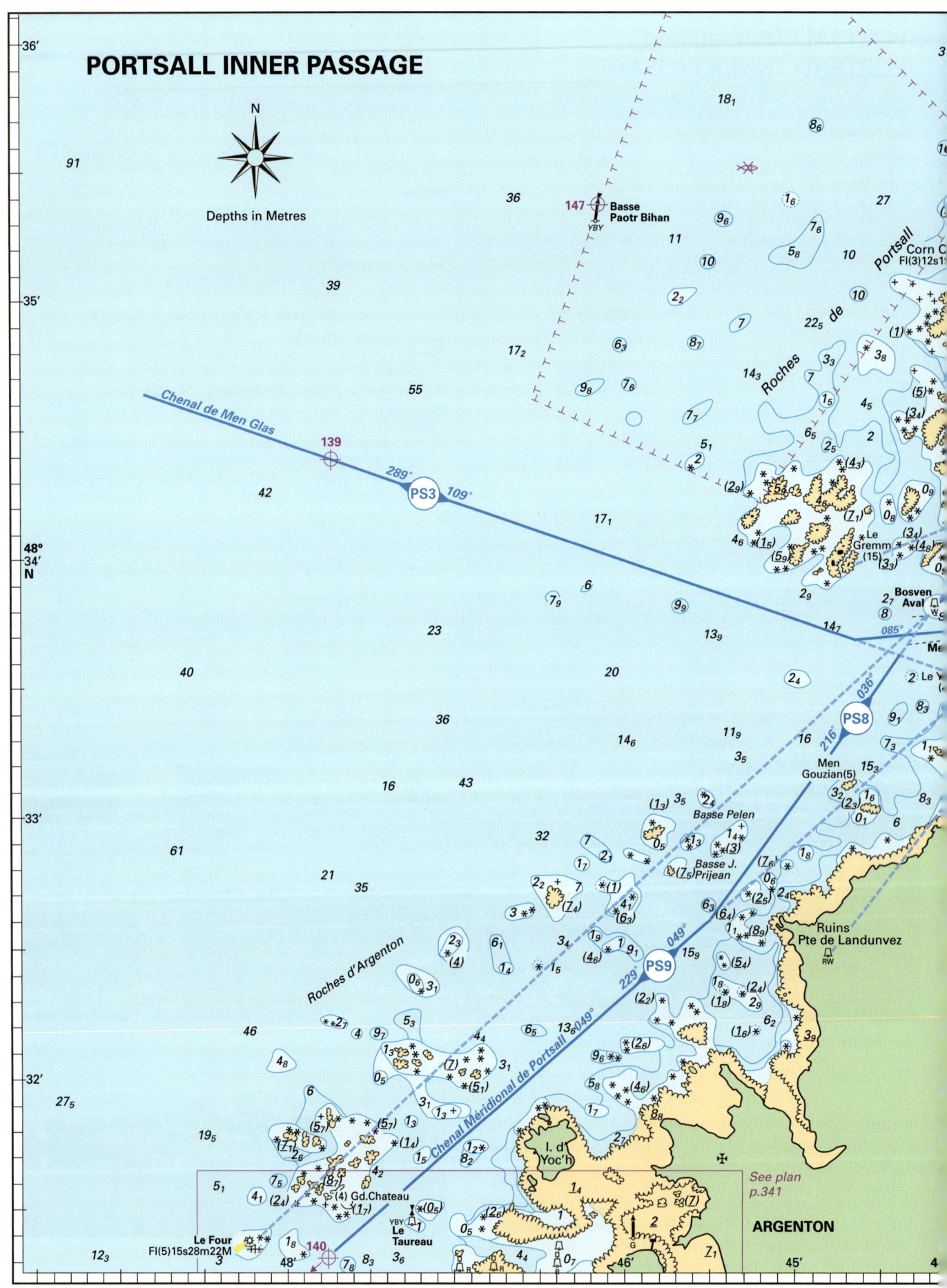

332 CHANNEL ISLANDS, CHERBOURG PENINSULA & NORTH BRITTANY

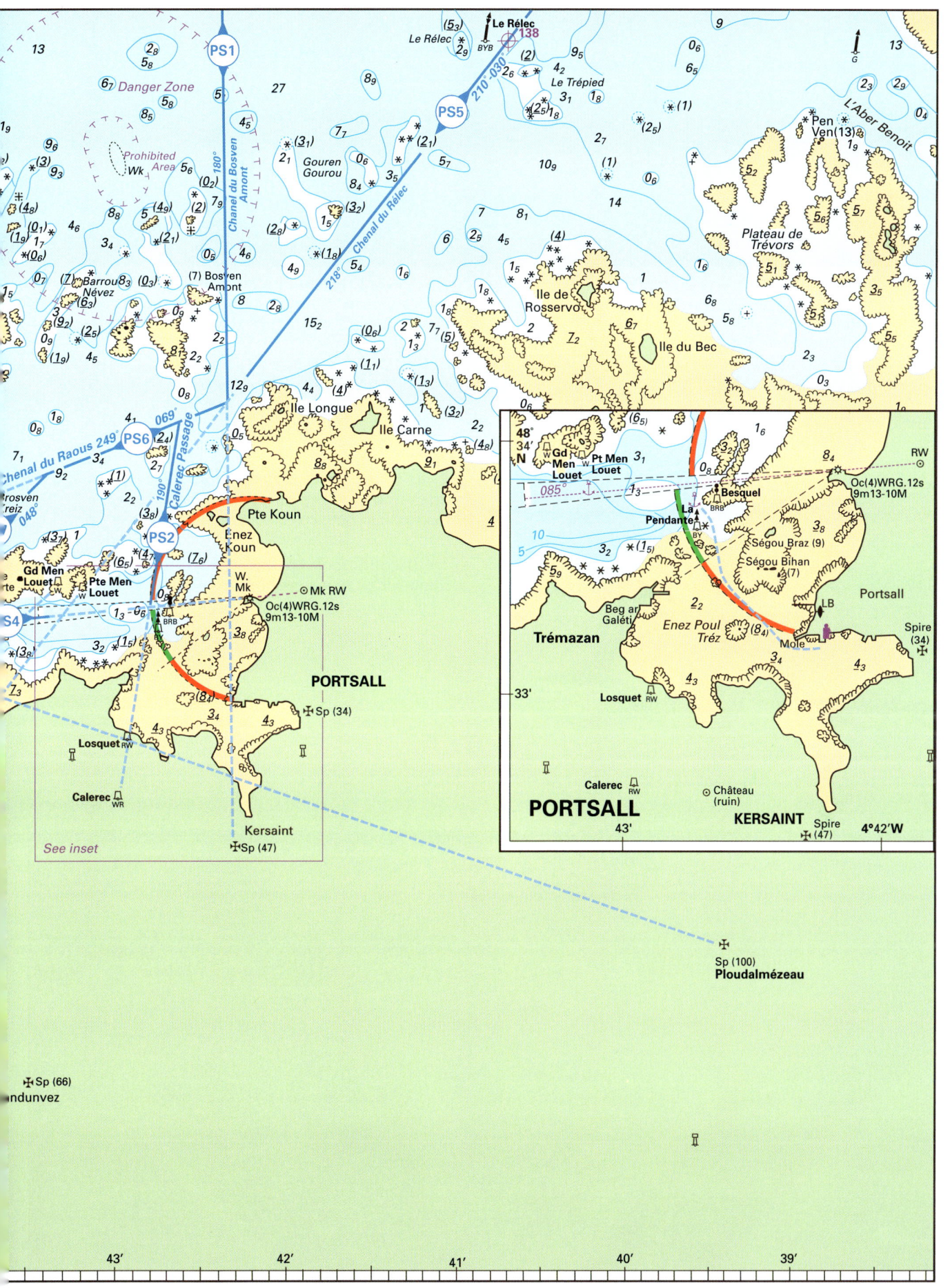

III North Brittany: 2 Trébeurden to Ouessant

attractive proposition for visiting yachts. Even so, local small fishing craft and sailing school dinghies manage to pursue their activities close to the shore when some shelter is derived from the offshore reefs at LW.

On a good day one cannot escape the charm of this peaceful unpretentious harbour. It has an atmosphere reminiscent of the days before much of the Brittany coast became transformed by tourism.

Historical

Portsall entered the history books on 16 March 1978 when the *Amoco Cadiz*, a fully loaded very large crude carrier (VLCC) suffered steering failure off Roches de Portsall. It foundered on Men Goulven rock (dries 4·9m) 1½ miles north of the harbour and broke in two releasing 1·6 million barrels of oil and 4,000 tons of fuel into the sea.

A 12 mile long slick spread east devastating beaches, harbours and marine life as far as Ile de Bréhat. It was the largest oil spill in history at that date.

A museum on the quayside at Portsall, 'Ancre An Or' (anchor in Breton), records this event and the heroic struggle of local communities to restore the environment to its natural state. It has taken several years.

Ancre An Or ☏ 02 98 48 77 49

Approaches

PORTSALL INNER PASSAGE

Chenal du Rélec
Chenal du Raous
Chenal Meridional de Portsall

This passage interconnects with six channels that run within two miles of the shore passing inside Roches de Portsall in the north and Roches d'Argenton in the S. Together they form a short cut between L'Aber Wrac'h and Le Four lighthouse though the only saving is one mile in 10. It should therefore be regarded primarily as an exercise in precision pilotage leaving little room for errors.

The entry channels into Portsall and Kersaint harbour that branch off the main NE–SW channel are covered under 'Entry to Portsall' below.

Caution

The required conditions for attempting these routes are:
- Quiet settled weather
- Visibility of no less than five miles for identification of marks
- Neap tides provide a moderation of the powerful streams that sweep round this corner. They are accelerated between the reefs creating a risk of dangerous overfalls when wind is against tide.

Note If conditions fall below the above minima it is recommended to give the length of this coast a clearance of at least four miles.

The anchor of *Amoco Cadiz* on display outside the Ancre An Or Museum on the quay

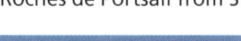

Roches de Portsall from S

Chenal du Rélec (3·5m)

Le Rélec E cardinal buoy, or (⊕138) 200m E of it, should be approached on a track of not less than 210° to avoid the Queyn-an-Treis 1·8m shoal to the N which breaks in any swell below half tide.

Chenal du Rélec leading marks are:

PS5 *218° Petit Men Louet white beacon tower aligned with white beacon with red top on Pointe de Landunvez next to ruins of a semaphore building*

If the visibility is not good enough to identify these marks pass outside Roches de Portsall. This line will leave:

Le Rélec buoy 200m to starboard, Le Trépied shoal (dries 2·5m) close to port and the line of rocks Gouren Gourou close to starboard; there is plenty of water to port of the transit to borrow from at this stage. Leave Ile Longue (6m) 300m to port and when abeam alter to 249° on to the transit for Chenal du Raous.

Chenal du Raous (3·4m)

PS6 *249° Rocks S of Le Gremm aligned with Bosven Kreiz white beacon tower.*

When about 500m from Bosven Kreiz take up transit:

PS7 *228° Le Four Lighthouse just open left (E) of Bosven Aval with its white beacon tower*

The stream will not necessarily be in line with the track in this narrowest part of the passage but the line should be held precisely. Only towards LW will the rocks be uncovered and the channel clearly seen. The immediate dangers are to starboard with Karreg Luth shoal drying 5·2m. To port the shallows to the W of Ile Verte. The extension of Bosven Aval 100m to the E (0·4m) and Seledran rock (dries 0·7m) on the opposite side of the channel (study the chart).

To clear these rocks a minor alteration is required as follows:

When 500m short of Bosven Aval come to port until Bosven Kreiz is bearing 026° and steer the reciprocal (206°). This will leave Bosven Aval 120m to starboard.

At this point you can turn to port onto the Portsall leading line 085° **PS4** as described in *Portsall Entry* on page 336 or continue SW with stern transit **PS8** into Chenal Meridional described below.

Chenal Méridional de Portsall (S bound) (3·3m)

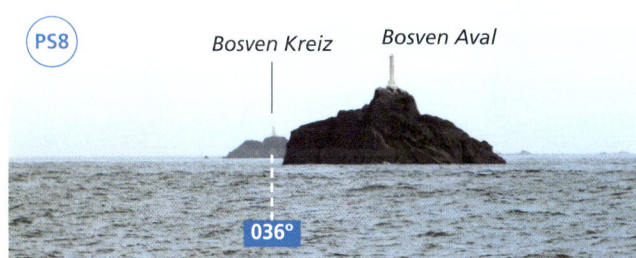

PS8 *036° Stern transit Bosven Aval aligned with Bosven Kleiz*

Steer 216° making adjustment as necessary to hold stern transit.

Abeam Pointe de Landunvez RW beacon tower with ruins

When abeam Pointe de Landunvez RW beacon tower alter course to starboard onto 229° with stern transit:

III North Brittany: 2 Trébeurden to Ouessant

PS9 049° *Grand Men Louet beacon tower and the saddle of Le Yurc'h aligned*

This line leads about 0·3M NW of the prominent Ile d'Yoc'h, about 200m S of Grand Château rock (3m) and leaves Le Taureau W cardinal beacon tower 200m to port. After Le Taureau there is clearer water S of the line. The line then leads into open water about 0·3M S of Le Four lighthouse. Note that there will be extensive overfalls in this area in wind over tide conditions.

Chenal Meridional de Portsall (N bound) (3·3m)

The advantage of a northeastbound passage is that it can be taken on a rising tide and usually with a favourable wind. Also there is a clear passage seaward via Chenal de Men Glas at the half way stage if conditions deteriorate, particularly visibility, and you wish to opt out.

Directions are as for southbound followed in reverse sequence.

Chenal Méridional. Le Four lighthouse and Le Grand Château rock bearing WSW

Entry

From the S

Should be from a position 0·5M SSW of Le Four lighthouse or ⊕140. Steer 049° to join Chenal Méridional de Portsall between Grand Château (6) to port and Le Taureau W cardinal beacon tower to starboard. Initial transit is then:

PS9 049° *Grand Men Louet beacon tower and the saddle of Le Yurc'h aligned (see view at top of page)*

Entry to Portsall from

Chenal de Bosven Amont
Chenal de Calerec
Chenal de Men Glas

From Chenal de Bosven Amont (2·2m) 1M W of Le Rélec E cardinal buoy

Unlike Chenal du Rélec it has no distinguishing enroute mark so the transit marks must be positively identified – if unsure, take the Chenal de Rélec (see *Portsall Inner Passage* page 334-5).

PS1 180° *Kersaint spire visible between Enez Joun islet (16m) and Pointe Koun*

Kersaint spire

This transit leaves Bosven Amont rock (7m) 300m to starboard but there are some outliers a bit closer to the line.

0·4M past Bosven Amont turn to starboard onto Chenal du Raous line - see Portsall Inner Passage transit:

PS6 249° *Rocks S of Le Gremm aligned with Bosven Kreiz white beacon tower*

The harbour may be entered by continuing via Chenal de Calerec (2·0m) as described below:

From S intersection of Chenal du Rélec and Chenal de Bosven Amont

Chenal de Calerec (2·2m decreasing to drying 0·6m)

As a route to the harbour is considered better than Chenal du Raous which involves a detour where seas can be unpleasant. Marks must be positively identified and held exactly. The transit is:

PS2 190° *Pyramide du Calerec (RW) aligned with Pyramide de Losquet (WY)*

The line branches off the early stages of Chenal du Raous (transit **PS6**) at a point 400m into that Chenal.

Initially Chenal de Celerec has a minimum depth of 2·2m but its extension to the harbour entrance crosses a rock drying at 0·6m and passes very close to other drying rocks. It should therefore be used with sufficient rise of tide and caution.

To enter the harbour steer SE to pass midway between Besquel isolated danger beacon tower (without top marks) and La Pendante N cardinal beacon tower, then come to starboard to leave Bihan (9m) 200m to port. Steer to pass close to the end of the mole.

L'Aber Benoit to Le Conquet

From Chenal de Men Glas (10m)

From ⊕139 identify Ploudalmézeau church spire if visible and Le Yurc'h rock (10). The transit:

PS3 *109° Ploudalmézeau church spire (if visible) aligned with Le Yurc'h rock (10)*

Men ar Pic starboard beacon tower will be seen to N of Le Yurc'h. This line leaves the first group of Portsall Rocks with conspicuous Le Gremm (15m) 400m to port.

When Bosven Aval white beacon tower bears 070° turn onto 085° for harbour entrance.

Entry Transit

Entry transit is:

PS4 *085° Two beacons with rectangular columns in line. The light tower is between them*

When 200m short of Besquel isolated danger beacon tower (without top marks) take up a SE heading to pass midway between it and La Pendante N cardinal beacon tower then come to starboard to leave Bihan (9m) 200m to port and enter the harbour as described under Chenal de Calerec.

These low marks may initially be difficult to make out by day. The line leaves:

- Bosven Aval white beacon tower 200m to port
- Men Ar Pic starboard beacon 180m to starboard
- Basse Idi (dries 2·8m) very close to starboard

La Pendante

Mole and slipway

Berthing

Alongside the E side of the jetty where it dries about 4·0m but check at the sailing school as fishing boats use it. The bay is open to the NW and is all hard sand. Grounding and floating off even with the protection of the jetty can be uncomfortable if not dangerous. In these conditions berth around HW and move out before taking the ground.

Anchorage

An anchorage as indicated on the plan will be needed at night, sounding in as far as depth will allow to get out of the stream.

Towards neaps up to 2m can be found to the SE of La Pendante and clear of fishing boat moorings.

The bottom is hard sand. Note that grounding and floating off in NW weather can be very uncomfortable.

III North Brittany: 2 Trébeurden to Ouessant

⊕ 140	48°30'·92N	04°48'·57W
⊕ 141	48°31'·15N	04°48'·20W
⊕ 142	48°31'·40N	04°53'·15W
⊕ 143	48°29'·00N	04°57'·25W
⊕ 145	48°27'·96N	04°48'·48W
⊕ 146	48°21'·65N	04°48'·00W
⊕ 152	48°26'·28N	04°53'·62W
⊕ 153	48°24'·40N	04°50'·50W

L'Aber Benoit to Le Conquet

CHENAL DU FOUR (5·8m)

This wide channel between Ile d'Ouessant and the mainland is well marked by day and night. It is, however, subject to strong tidal streams, particularly at its S end, resulting in moderate to severe overfalls when wind and tide are opposed. As a general rule the worse seas occur in the northern approaches to the channel between L'Aber Wrac'h and Le Four that bear the full brunt of the ocean swell.

WARNING This area is prone to fog and poor visibility. Radar and GPS may alleviate some of the dangers but not remove them so a good look out for the numerous buoys, particularly those that are unlit, should be maintained.
Get the weather and tides right and a fast and enjoyable sail up or down the Chenal du Four can be expected.

CHARTS
BA 2356 Goulet de Brest to Portsall including Ile d'Ouessant (1:50 000)
BA 3345 Chenal du Four (1:25 000)
SHOM 7122 De la Pointe de Saint-Mathieu au phare du Four - Chenal du Four (1:25 000)
SHOM 7149 Du Goulet de Brest à Portsall – Ile d'Ouessant (1:49 100)

TIDAL STREAMS
The timing of the turn of the stream anywhere in the Chenal is much affected by the wind; a S wind will delay the turning of the N-going flood stream and vice-versa.
Between Plâtresses in the N and Pointe de St Mathieu in the S the stream turns roughly as follows:
HW Brest +0600 N-going starts
HW Brest ±0000 S-going starts
The spring rate varies from 0·3 knots at the N end of the Chenal to 5 knots in the acceleration area between Le Conquet and Pte de St Mathieu. The streams obligingly tend to parallel the coast.

MHWS	MLWS	MHWN	MLWN
6·9	1·0	5·4	2·6

Southbound
The best time to arrive off Pointe de St Mathieu going S is at LW slack or HW Brest ±0600. A fair stream will have been carried from the N and will still be fair up Le Goulet to Brest. It will be foul across L'Iroise if going S but by the time Raz de Sein is reached it should be turning fair again. In strong southerly winds or heavy swell this timing, or a little later, will minimise wind/swell conditions off St Mathieu.

Northbound
The choice going N is not so clear-cut. In heavy northerly weather the main consideration will be to minimise the wind over tide conditions N or Kermorvan and it would be prudent to arrive off Kermorvan as the stream turns to the S at HW Brest, and face 5 hours foul stream but easier seas. In good weather and no excessive swell an arrival off St Mathieu at LW slack (HW Brest +0600) will give six hours fair stream and allow L'Aber Wrac'h at least to be reached before HW there.

Tidal streams in La Helle
Streams are generally less intense than those in Le Four only exceeding 3 knots in the NW end of the Channel where it comes under the influence of Passage du Fromveur. Directions and rates in La Helle are between NW and NE going from HW Brest -05h30 to HW Brest (Spring rate 2·5 knots).
Following slack water it becomes S to SW going between HW Brest +00h 30 and HW Brest +05h 30 (Spring rate 3·1 knots).
For best information study SHOM Tidal Stream Atlas Côte Ouest de Bretagne 560 – UJA which graphically sets out the above information.

Chenal du Four, steering S past Les Vieux Moines beacon tower and Pointe de St Mathieu lighthouse

Southbound and on the wind this yacht leaves Le Four close to port *Tom Vallois*

Pilotage (by day or night)

From the N
From a position 3M W of Le Four Lighthouse or ⊕142 take up transit:

CF1 *158° Pte de Kermorvan Lighthouse (Fl.5s) aligned with Pte de St Mathieu Lighthouse (Fl.15s)*

View S on transit CF1 *Bill Harris*

This line will leave:
- Plâtresses N starboard buoy to starboard (Fl.G.2·5s)
- La Valbelle port buoy to port (Fl(2)R.6s)
- Plâtresses SE starboard buoy to starboard (Fl(2)G.6s)
- St Paul port buoy to port (Oc(2)R.6s)
- When Pte de Corsen lighthouse (white hut) (Dir.Q.WRG.33m12-18M) is on the quarter and bears 012° alter to 192° (at night you should be in the W sector of Pointe de Corsen lighthouse)
- Pass midway between Grande Vinotière octagonal port beacon tower (LFl.R.10s) and Rouget starboard buoy (Fl.G.4s)
- When Kermorvan bears 070° alter to 174° and hold until Tournant et Lochrist port buoy is on the beam at which point alter to 145°
- Pass midway between Vieux Moines port beacon tower (Fl.R.4s) and Le Fourmi starboard buoy (unlit). Proceed S or E into Goulet de Brest.

CHANNEL ISLANDS, CHERBOURG PENINSULA & NORTH BRITTANY   339

III North Brittany: 2 Trébeurden to Ouessant

Note: In fine weather these recommended tracks can be safely left, but in heavy weather they should be kept to as the overfalls will be less.

Alternates

If a change of plan is called for due to deteriorating conditions or missing a fair tide there are several options. From N–S:

- L'Aber-Ildut (page 344)
- Anchorage Anse de Pors Moguer 1·0M SE of Pointe de Corsen – see Le Conquet (page 348)
- Anchorage Anse des Blancs Sablons 1·0M N of Le Conquet (page 348)

Chenal de la Helle (9·8m)

A channel that is less used by yachts – unless it offers a better angle on the wind. It is less direct than Chenal du Four if routing N to S or vice versa and also more across the tidal stream.

Despite the name, after the rock La Helle (11m) on the Plateau de la Helle, it is broad and straightforward in clear weather. It is relevant to a passage between the S end of Le Four, Le Conquet for example, and Ile de Molène as the approach via Chenal des Laz branches off La Helle W of Pte de Corsen (see *Ile de Molène approaches*).

From the NW or ⊕143

The transit is **HL1** *138°Kermorvan lighthouse (white square tower Fl.5s) aligned with Lochrist (octagonal W tower + R top (Dir.Oc(3)12s). If marks are obscure Luronne unlit W cardinal buoy and Le Faix N cardinal beacon tower (VQ) will assist*

The transit may be left to join Chenal du Four after passing Le Faix. The turning point is Pointe de Corsen lighthouse (Dir.Q.WRG) bearing E or stern transit:

HL2 *293° Le Faix aligned with Le Stiff Lighthouse on Ile d'Ouessant*

Continue on 113° to join Chenal du Four transit **CF1** *158°* (as described above).

If this option is not taken continue with transit **HL1** *138°* in the W sector of Lochrist to leave:

- Pourceaux N cardinal buoy (Q) to starboard
- St Pierre unlit starboard buoy to port

Rejoin Chenal du Four (as described above).

Argenton entrance looking W from Ile Dolvez at LW

ARGENTON

48°31'·35N 04°45'·76W
4M SW of Portsall
1·7M E of Le Four Lighthouse

CHARTS
BA 1432 Le Four to Ile Vierge (1:25 000)
BA 2025 Portsall to Anse de Kernic (1:50 000)
BA 2356 Goulet de Brest to Portsall including
   Ile d'Ouessant (1:50 000)
BA 3345 Chenal du Four (1:25 000)
Imray C35 Baie de Morlaix to L'Aber-Ildut*
   *includes plan: Argenton (1:20 000)
Imray 2510 North Brittany Chart Atlas:
   12 L'Aber Wrac'h to Argenton (1:40 000)
   12a Argenton (1:25 000)
SHOM 7094 Du Phare du Four à l'Ile Vierge –
   Port de l'Aber-Wrac'h (1:25 000)
SHOM 7122 De la Pointe de Saint-Mathieu au phare
   du Four - Chenal du Four (1:25 000)
SHOM 7149 Du Goulet de Brest à Portsall –
   Ile d'Ouessant (1:49 100)
SHOM 7150 De Portsall à l'Anse de Kernic (1:48 900)

TIDAL INFORMATION
Standard port: Brest
HW Brest +0100
LW Brest +0015

MHWS	MLWS	MHWN	MLWN
7·3	1·0	5·7	2·6

Tidal streams
The streams start at the following times to the W of Le Four light:
HW Brest -0545 ENE-going
HW Brest +0100 WSW-going
The spring rates are 3½ and 2½kns respectively

Depths
Recommended entry is from HW -3. Max draught 2m.

USEFUL CONTACTS
Sailing School: Nautisme en Pays d'Iroise ☎ 02 98 89 54 04
Bureau du Port ☎ 06 06 71 50 29 44

SUPPLIES AND SERVICES
Water from tap on jetty; showers and heads in the sailing school; shops and baker in Argenton; 1M S in Porspoder there is a supermarché, more shops, a garage (with bottled gas), banks and a post office. Restaurants and bars on the S side of the bay. Le Chardon Bleu (☎ 02 98 89 40 34) – speciality seafood. 200m S of the port.

Argenton is a large shallow sandy bay that dries out completely at LWS making it a more suitable harbour at neaps. It might be considered as a waiting room before taking on the Chenal Méridional de Portsall (see page 334).

Although sheltered from the N and S it is open to the W. To be caught here in strong westerlies could be dangerous as heavy swell enters the harbour.

It is a popular dinghy sailing centre and their premises are freely available to visitors – as is advice.

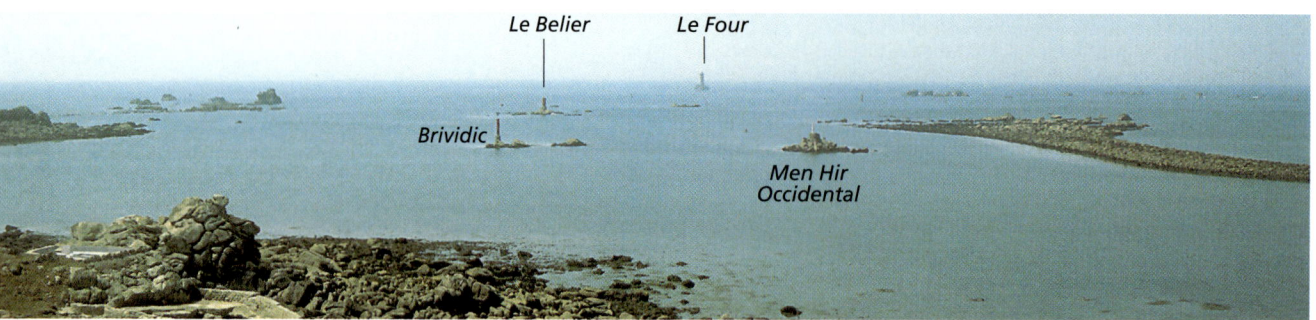

L'Aber Benoit to Le Conquet

Argenton from SE at LWS

Approach and entry

From ⊕141 0·3M S of Le Four identify to the E a succession of three port beacons, Le Belier, Brividic and Les Trois Pierres beyond it. The prominent rock Melgorn Vihan (10) is to the S of Le Belier.

Take up approach transit:

ARG1 *084° Three marks on Ile Dolvez*

Front: stumpy tower on the rocks,
Mid: white tower, Back: white tower with red top
(Note: in 2013 the marks were unpainted).

The line leaves Melgorn Vihan 200m to starboard and Le Belier and Brividic port beacons 250m to port. The channel S of Brividic shoal is only about 100m wide between it and an isolated drying 3m rock to the S so the leading marks need to be identified and kept on by this point.

Leave Les Trois Pierres port beacon tower 200m to port to go to the outer anchorage, or turn to port to go to the inner harbour and drying anchorage leaving Men Hir Occidental white beacon tower well to port.

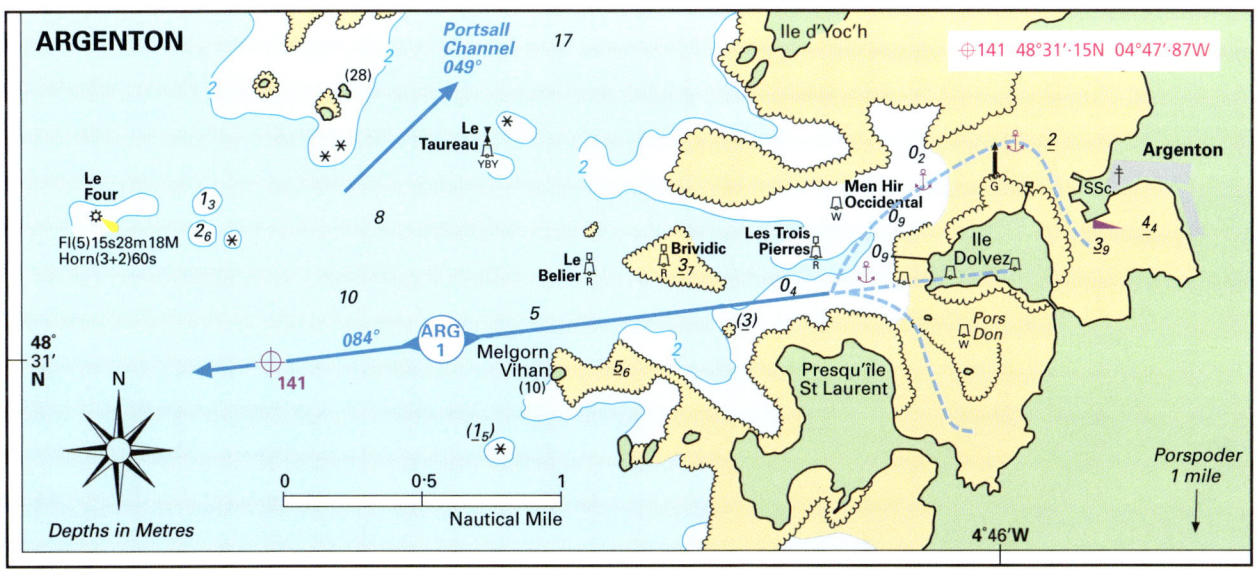

CHANNEL ISLANDS, CHERBOURG PENINSULA & NORTH BRITTANY

III North Brittany: 2 Trébeurden to Ouessant

Anchorages

Outer
Anchor 2·0–0·9m between Les Trois Pierres and Ile Dolvez, mostly sand. The area is more rock-free to the N of the leading line than to the S. 0·9m may be found half way between Men Hir Occidental and the starboard hand beacon to the N of the island. The mooring buoy between Les Trois Pierres and Ile Dolvez is reserved for the lifeboat tender.

Drying out
For yachts that can dry out, the bay to the NE of Ile Dolvez has large areas of weed covered sand mostly drying 2m which would be covered at LW neaps and is sheltered from all directions except the NW.

To go to the inner anchorage pass midway between the old lifeboat house and slip on Ile Dolvez and Men Hir Occidental, leave the starboard hand beacon on the N end of the island to starboard also the rock with a breakwater running out to it.

The rocky promontory above the sailing school, slip and jetty is surmounted by a large Cross of Lorraine.

Harbour
The harbour to the E of Ile Dolvez consists of two slips and a jetty. The slip to the W is weed covered and little used. The large jetty and slip to the E of this is used by a sailing school and the occasional *vedette*. It is possible to berth here (dries 4m) and to dry out but ask at the sailing school. The bay to the SE of this, Pors Don dries 4·4m in its centre.

Pors Don. Small craft moorings S of Ile Dolvez. Exposed to NW'lies

Sheltered drying anchorage in Argenton harbour E of Ile Dolvez

MELON
48°29'·14N 04°46'·35W
2M S of Le Four lighthouse
1M N of L'Aber-Ildut

CHARTS
BA 2356 Goulet de Brest to Portsall including Ile d'Ouessant (1:50 000)
BA 3345 Chenal du Four (1:25 000)
SHOM 7122 De la Pointe de Saint-Mathieu au phare du Four – Chenal du Four (1:25 000)
SHOM 7149 Du Goulet de Brest à Portsall – Ile d'Ouessant (1:49 100)

TIDAL INFORMATION
As for L'Aber-Ildut.

SUPPLIES AND SERVICES
Restaurant on road bordering head of the bay: Le Chenal ☎ 02 98 89 54 36 (www.lechenal.fr)

The harbour looking NW from the slipway

The Anse de Melon is a small drying harbour that is little more than an inlet with a beach. It gains shelter from the land and the low Ile Melon to the W but is exposed at HW and in N–NW winds. There is an outer anchorage on the approach line.

Approaches
The key to the approach is Le Compère rock about 1M NNW of Ile de Melon. This dries 6·6m and will be covered at HW except towards neaps. The approach should be made before 2 hours before HW to be sure of locating it.

First identify the conspicuous tall white radar tower aptly nicknamed 'La Bougie' (the candle) which is shown on *BA 3345* and *SHOM 7122* in a position 0·4M to the SW of Porspoder village. From ⊕144 approach this on transit:

ML1 092° *'La Bougie' in alignment with Le Compère.*

L'Aber Benoit to Le Conquet

Melon looking SE

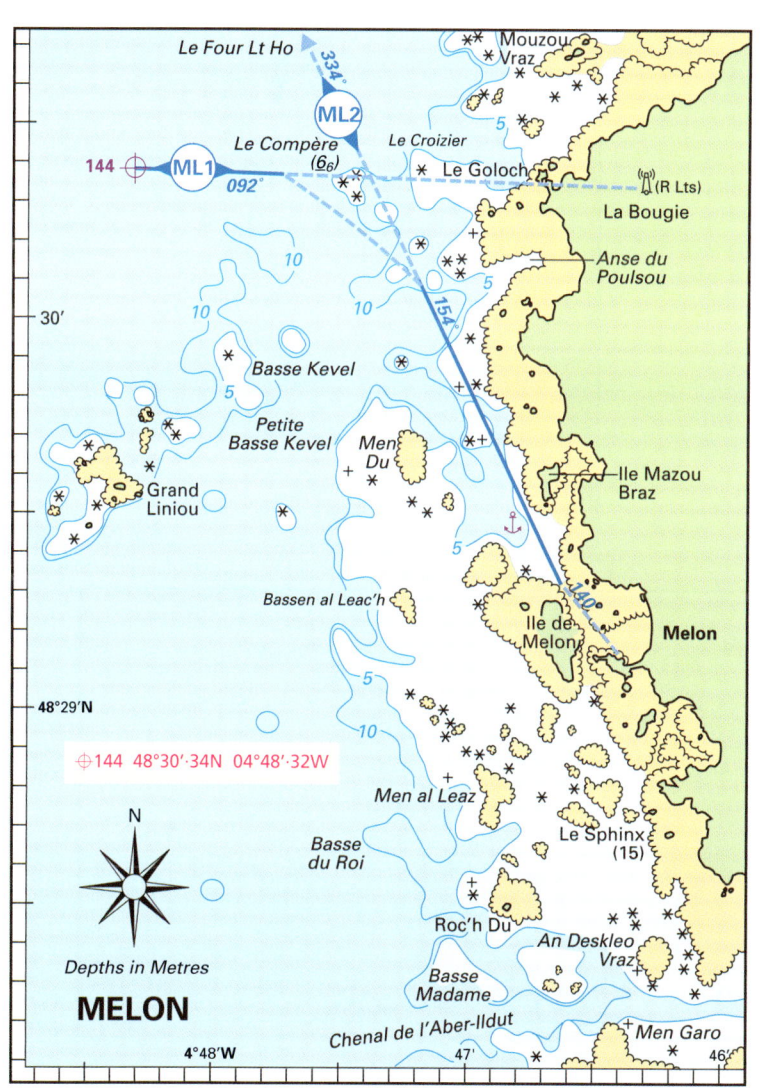

Melon ruined coastguards' hut (Guérite de Melon)

When 200m short of this rock, alter course SE then align it with Le Four on a stern bearing of 334° (Transit **ML2**). Make good 154° on this transit. There is deep water on this approach line but it passes very close to rocks drying 1·2m and it would be prudent to ensure there is sufficient water to clear them. (See *SHOM 7122*.)

The final approach to the anchorage is made with a bearing of 140° on a ruined coastguards' hut. It is said that providing you can see daylight through the door and the window you are on the line!

Anchorage

Anchor in a convenient depth on this line in between 2m and 8m to the N of Ile de Melon.

Enough water and better shelter may be found further in to the narrow channel to the E of Ile de Melon towards neaps but a second anchor may be needed to restrict swing. (See photograph above.)

For those able to dry out some shelter from the N may be found up the channel running E towards the village before the drying moorings start where it dries 5·0m.

III North Brittany: 2 Trébeurden to Ouessant

L'ABER-ILDUT

48°28'·26N 04°45'·56W (Lighthouse)
2·7M SE of Le Four Lighthouse
1M S of Melon
7M N of Le Conquet

TRAVEL
Sea
  Ferries run between L'Aber-Ildut, Ile d'Ouessant and Ile Molène but less frequently than from Le Conquet and are seasonal.
Road
  Bus to Brest (25km)

CHARTS
  BA 2356 Goulet de Brest to Portsall including
      Ile d'Ouessant (1:50 000)
  BA 3345 Chenal du Four (1:25 000)
  Imray C35 Baie de Morlaix to L'Aber-Ildut*
      *includes plan: L'Aber-Ildut (1:20 000)
  Imray 2510 North Brittany Chart Pack*
      *includes plan: L'Aber-Ildut (1:25 000)
  SHOM 7122 De la Pointe de Saint-Mathieu au phare
      du Four - Chenal du Four (1:25 000)
  SHOM 7149 Du Goulet de Brest à Portsall –
      Ile d'Ouessant (1:49 100)

RADIO
  Ch 09 during office hours June–Sept

TIDAL INFORMATION
  Standard port: Brest
  Difference:
  HW Brest +0005
  LW Brest +0015
  Alternative: Roscoff
  HW Roscoff -0050
  LW Roscoff -0048

MHWS	MLWS	MHWN	MLWN
7·3	1·0	5·7	2·8

Tidal streams
  N going stream starts Brest -0600
  S going stream starts Brest +0030
  Max rate about 3M off reaches 3 knots. In the entrance the flood sets E and the ebb NW, max 3 knots.

Depths
  The least depth in the entrance is 3·6m, 3m at deepwater moorings. Max draught 2m.

USEFUL CONTACTS
  Harbourmaster (La Capitainerie) ☎ 02 98 04 36 40 /
      06 12 58 34 85

SUPPLIES AND SERVICES
Water, electricity on waiting pontoons
WC/showers next to Capitainerie
Shops Small old-style épicerie and other outlets including a few restaurants in L'Aber-Ildut. More in Lanildut 0·25M.
Chandlery Accastillage Diffusion, Le Port ☎ 02 98 04 40 72
Boatyard, Engineers on hard standing, Lanildut Marine
  ☎ 02 98 04 33 71.
Fuel Alongside commercial quay
Restaurant Bar L'Abri Côtier, Quai de Cambarell next to capitainerie ☎ 02 98 36 30 18
WiFi Office de Tourisme adjoining the Capitainerie

L'Aber-Ildut the port, not to be confused with Lanildut the village further east (both pronounced with a hard T) is a marvel of Breton organisation. In addition to being Europe's premiere port for the harvesting of seaweed, 30,000 tons a year, it also shelters an active fleet and manages to find up to 300 berths for plaisanciers including 20 for visitors.

As the southernmost of the three Abers (estuaries) it has the shortest usable stretch of river but is the most sheltered from the prevailing westerlies due to the pronounced U-bend inside the entrance. If you are small enough and can take the ground happily mooring further up the river opposite Lanildut village slipway is possible.

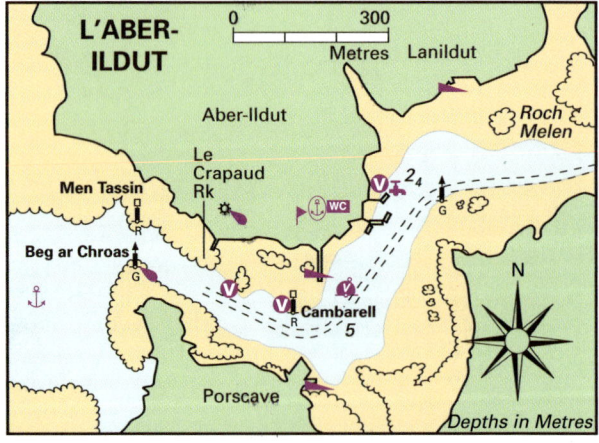

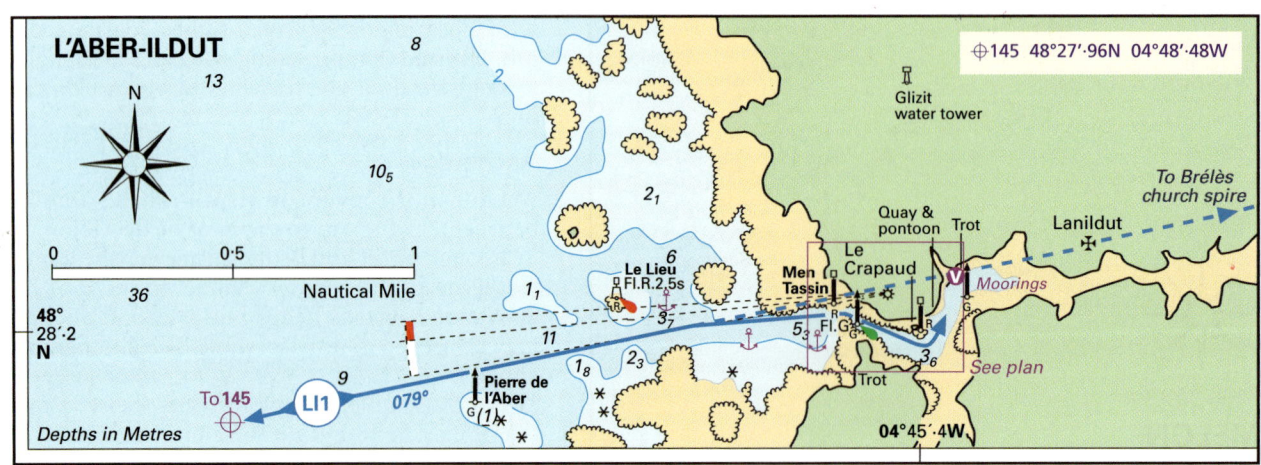

L'Aber Benoit to Le Conquet

Historical
The great disused quarry on the south bank of the river once supplied stone for construction of many of the ocean harbours of France, and for several works in England including the Thames Embankment.

Today it is seaweed that holds sway and you can discover more about this industry at La Maison de l'Algue next to the Office de Tourisme adjoining the Capitainerie.

Approach
The key mark is Le Lieu Port beacon tower just over ½ mile W of the entrance. A prominent water tower to the N also aids location. The recommended approach is with ⊕145 transit:

LI1 *079° Light structure aligned with conspicuous water tower*

On entry this line leaves Pierre de L'Aber starboard beacon 200m to starboard and Le Lieu port beacon tower (Fl.R.2·5s) to port.

By night
Dir.Oc(2)WR.6s12m W: 25M R: 20M.
Le Lieu Fl.R.2·5s
Enter in W sector 081°–085°.

Light structure aligned with conspicuous water tower
Nick Bailhache

Entry (Minimum depth 3·6m)
The narrow channel passes midway between Men Tassin Port beacon and Beg ar Chroas starboard lit beacon (Fl.G.2·5s)

Note: a sandbar (drying 5·3m) has built up close W of these marks where less depth can be expected.

Alter to starboard onto 115° to leave Le Crapaud Rk – a prominent rounded rock close SSE of light structure – close to port. Come to port onto 020° and the river and mooring areas open up.

Caution
Expect streams of up to 3 knots in the river at springs.

L'Aber-Ildut looking W

III North Brittany: 2 Trébeurden to Ouessant

New marina arrangement, L'Aber-Ildut *Nick Bailhache*

Mooring (Max length 12m)

On arrival contact the Capitainerie to obtain instructions.

There are two pontoons with walkways up to the hard standing area. The southernmost is for commercial vessels but may be used subject to space for embarking and disembarking. Max stay 2h.

The second, further N, is reserved for *plaisanciers*. New marina visitors' berths established in the estuary 2017, shown above.

There are three areas where white visitors' moorings marked 'V' will be found:

- SE of Le Crapaud (10m)
- S and SW of the hard standing area (14m)
- Off the landing slip at Lanildut village NE of the port – drying area (4m).

Anchoring

Anchoring within the river is not permitted. In offshore winds and calm conditions anchorage may be found outside clear of the entrance in the following positions:

- Le Lieu beacon tower bearing WNW distant 300m, least depth 3·7m
- Starboard entry beacon bearing ENE distant 300m, least depth 3m in sand

Caution

Beware of commercial movements in and out of the port by day and night. Maintain conspicuity.

LE CONQUET

48°21'·60N 04°47'·00W (port entrance)
7M S of L'Aber-Ildut
2M N of Pointe de Saint Mathieu

TRAVEL
Le Conquet is the hub for Ile d'Ouessant and Ile de Molène ferries. There are also connections with Brest. The main operators are:
Sea
Finist'Mer ☏ 0825 135 235 www.finist-mer.fr

CHARTS
BA 2356 Goulet de Brest to Portsall including Ile d'Ouessant (1:50 000)
BA 3345 Chenal du Four (1:25 000)*
    *includes plan: Port du Conquet (1:10 000)

Imray C36 Ile d'Ouessant to Raz de Sein*
Imray 2510 North Brittany Chart Pack*
    *both include plan: Port du Conquet (1:20 000)

SHOM 7122 De la Pointe de Saint-Mathieu au phare du Four – Chenal du Four (1:25 000)*
    *includes plan: Port du Conquet (1:10 000)
SHOM 7149 Du Goulet de Brest à Portsall – Ile d'Ouessant (1:49 100)

RADIO
Le Conquet Port Ch 08/16

TIDAL INFORMATION
Standard port: Brest
Difference HW Brest +0010
LW Brest +0010

MHWS	MLWS	MHWN	MLWN
7·3	1·0	5·7	2·6

Tidal streams
Streams start at the following times outside the port:
HW Brest -0600 N-going flood
HW Brest ±0000 S-going ebb
Maximum flow 5 knots in main channel

USEFUL CONTACTS
Bureau du Port ☏ 02 98 89 16 98 / 06 30 38 89 56
Bureau du Tourisme ☏ 02 98 89 11 31
Taxi: Gwen Taxi ☏ 02 98 89 07 85 / 06 80 65 42 41

SUPPLIES AND SERVICES
Water Tap on Môle St Christophe Old Harbour
WC at quay
Fuel (in cans)
Shops and restaurants a good range in the town centre.
Les Korrigans Rue Lieut Jourden ☏ 02 98 89 00 45 (service until late)
Le Relais du Vieux Port Hotel/Restaurant, Quai du Drellac'h. Nearby in the Vieux Port and at harbour level. ☏ 02 98 89 15 91 www.lerelaisduvieuxport.com
Market
Chandler Comptoir de la Mer, 3 Rue Lieut Jourden ☏ 02 98 89 01 85

Le Conquet together with L'Aber-Ildut, 7M north, share the distinction of being the westernmost ports of mainland France. They are the only secure harbours off the Chenal du Four but should be approached with caution in any onshore weather.

Located at the S end of Chenal du Four it can be a useful place in which to await a fair tide up the channel. It is sheltered from N through E to almost S but exposed to W although some protection is provided by Ile de Beniguet and Pointe de Kermorvan. Access is straightforward – complicated only by a cross tide in the approach which may exceed 5 knots at springs.

L'Aber Benoit to Le Conquet

Le Conquet looking ESE at LW

The town, a steep climb up from the port, is a lively and attractive place in the season with a good selection of shops and eating places in the narrow streets around the church.

Le Conquet is a logical place from which to visit Ile Molène and Ile d'Ouessant. It is the hub of ferry companies that operate an efficient year round service.

If short of time you can make a comfortable recce of both islands in a day with the high speed ferry. Crossing time is 25 minutes to Molène and 45 minutes to Ouessant.

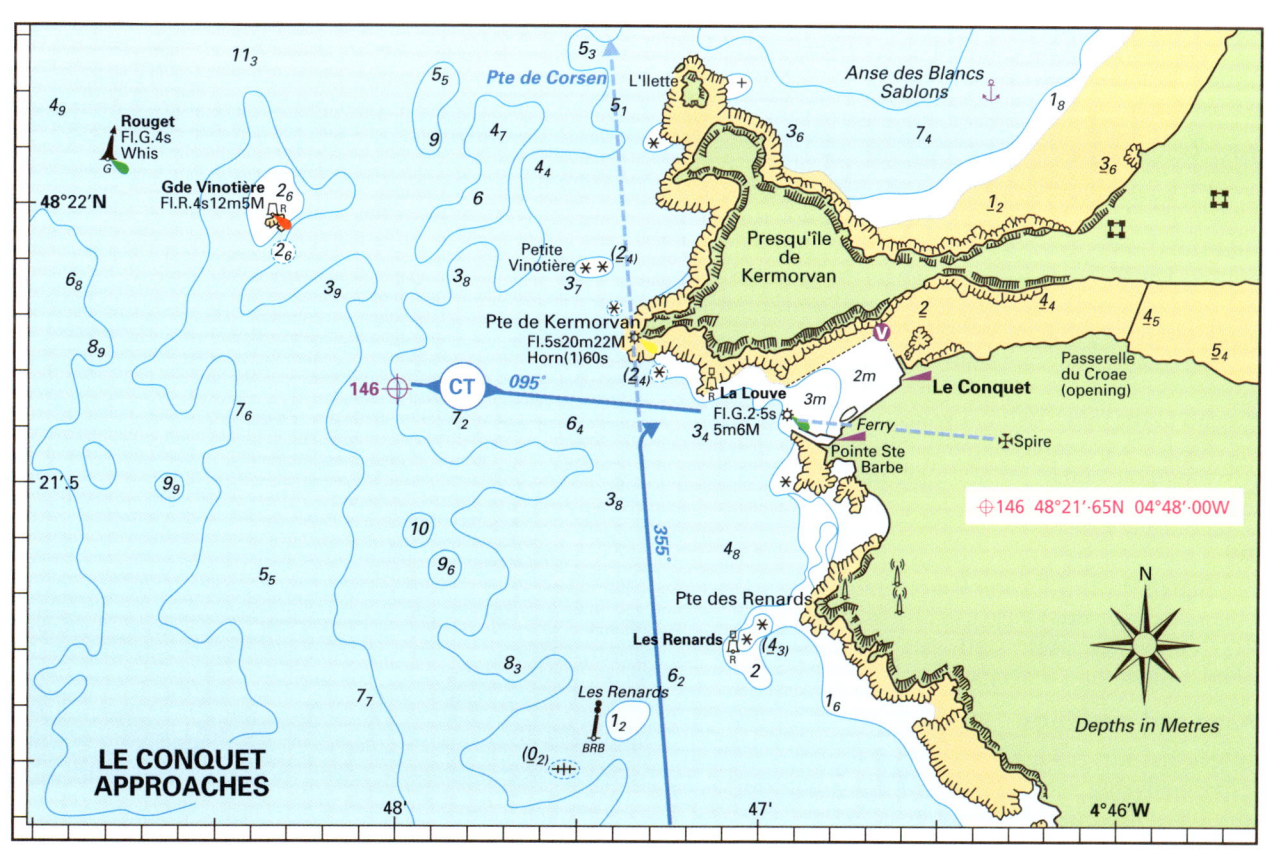

III North Brittany: 2 Trébeurden to Ouessant

Historical
Le Conquet has been the scene of many fights between the French and English who seem to have generally been repulsed. However in 1558 they sacked the town and burnt all the houses except for eight that belonged to English people – surprisingly they still stand today. The church contains the tomb of Père Michel le Nobletz, the seafaring priest who devoted his life to the conversion of pagan inhabitants of Finistère and surrounding islands.

Approach
The key to identifying Le Conquet is the conspicuous white square lighthouse off the point of Presqu'ile de Kermorvan. Other marks are shown below.

From the N
An approach can be made from the Chenal du Four as it passes midway between Grande Vinotière port beacon tower and Rouget starboard buoy. From this point make good 130° for 0·5M to intercept entry transit at ⊕146 making allowance for the stream. The transit below should be held carefully to avoid being set N towards drying rocks off Pte de Kermorvan.

CT 095° (⊕146) Head of Pointe Sainte Barbe môle aligned with church spire

An alternative approach is to break off Chenal du Four at its turning point 0·5M E of St Pierre starboard buoy. From this position make good 174° to ⊕146 and entry transit making allowance for the stream.

From the S
There are two transits, only one usable by night.

By day
Kermorvan lighthouse in line with Pointe de Corsen 355° leads between Les Renards buoy (BRB, two balls) and Les Renards port beacon tower with Le Louvre on starboard bow on this track.

By night
Kermorvan (Fl.5s) in line with Trézien (Dir.Oc(2)6s) 007° leads very close to Les Renards isolated danger buoy (unlit) wreck and shoal, so borrow to the E before reaching it to pass between Les Renards isolated danger buoy and Les Renards beacon (unlit). When the breakwater end (Oc.G.4s) bears 080°, turn towards it.

Entry
Leave the end of the outer W breakwater 50m to starboard watching out for any vessels leaving. There is 4m on the approach, 3m in the outer harbour and 2m up to the inner jetty beyond the slip.

Berthing
The inner side of the breakwater is not suitable for yachts and all the rest of the quays are used by fishing boats and *vedettes*. Quays at far end may be used for loading/unloading but a longer stay unlikely.

Anchorage and moorings
Anchoring is discouraged in the harbour. Keep clear of the *vedette* manoeuvring area and always use a trip line as there are a lot of mooring chains on the bottom. There are three visitors' buoys in the outer harbour on the N side.

Inner harbour (Vieux Port)

Outer harbour with commercial quay and ferry terminal

Alternative anchorages
To await the tide or the fog to clear, Anse des Blancs Sablons over the peninsula N from Le Conquet offers an alternative. There is some shelter from the SW in the southern bight although swell tends to find its way in. In E or N winds Porz Illien clear of the moorings is preferable. All good holding on sand. (See plan page 338.)

Porsmoguer 1·0M S of Pte de Corsen. Anchorage sheltered from N through E to SSE. Simple entrance by chart.

Porz Illien (in foreground) and Anse des Blancs Sablons (Le Conquet) looking SW

Ile d'Ouessant and Ile de Molène

ILE D'OUESSANT (ENEZ EUSSA)

48°28'·5N 05°03'·4W (Le Stiff Lighthouse)
12M WNW of Pte de St Mathieu
12M W of L'Aber-Ildut
Population 850 (2013)

TRAVEL
Sea
Main carrier: Compagnie Penn Ar Bed ☎ 02 98 80 80 80
www.pennarbed.fr
Year round daily sailings from Le Conquet, Brest, Camaret (summer only)
Finist'mer: frequent seasonal sailings from Lanildut, Le Conquet and Camaret ☎ 0825 135 235
Air
Finist'air ☎ 02 98 84 64 87 www.finistair.fr
Daily flights from Brest Guipavas

CHARTS
British Admiralty
2356 Goulet de Brest to Portsall including Ile d'Ouessant (1:50 000)
Imray
C36 Ile d'Ouessant to Raz de Sein*
*includes plan: Baie de Lampaul (Ouessant) (1:30 000)
2510 North Brittany Chart Atlas*
*includes plans: Baie de Lampaul (Ouessant) (1:30 000), Baie du Stiff (Ouessant) (1:30 000)
SHOM
7123 Ile Molène – Ile d'Ouessant – Passage du Fromveur (1:20 000)
7149 Du Goulet de Brest à Portsall – Ile d'Ouessant (1:49 100)

RADIO
Coastguard (Le Stiff) Ch 16
Ouessant Traffic Control Ch 13 (provide navigational assistance and bearings)

TIDAL INFORMATION
WARNING Very strong streams and potentially heavy overfalls around the island.
Standard port Brest
HW Brest +0005
LW Brest ±0005

MHWS	MLWS	MHWN	MLWN
6·9	1·0	5·3	2·5

Tidal streams
Tidal flows are complex especially to the SW of the island where the direction can change in a short distance. The most powerful are at the SE corner followed by the NW corner. In both areas heavy overfalls occur. Generally the rising tide sets to the NE, falling to the SW. Streams start at the following times from HW Brest:

½M NW of Nividic -0550 NE-going. Max 5½kns
+0045 SW-going Max 5½kns
At La Jument +0435 NW-going. Max 4½kns
-0045 S-going. Max 4½ kns

P. du Fromveur -0515 NE-going. Max 9kns
+0045 SW-going. Max 8kns

CONTACTS
Mairie/Harbourmaster ☎ 02 98 48 80 06
Office du Tourisme (Lampaul) ☎ 02 98 48 85 83
Sémaphore (Le Stiff) ☎ 02 98 48 81 50

SUPPLIES AND SERVICES
Water on slipway
Fuel (in cans)
Internet
Bank/ATM
Shops
Bike hire Ouessant Cycles ☎ 02 98 48 83 44 / 06 81 89 11 41
Taxis Ouessant voyages ☎ 06 81 04 31 04
Restaurant Le Roc'h Ar Mor ☎ 02 98 48 80 19
Le Fromveur ☎ 02 98 48 81 30

Ile d'Ouessant – Ushant in English – is the westernmost point of France and more remote and higher than Brittany's other islands. The climate is milder in winter than anywhere else in Brittany. It is prone to fog particularly in the summer months.

Although Ouessant is a major maritime turning point on the world's shipping routes it is not often visited by yachts. The far west of Brittany tends to be regarded as a remote and precarious place with a reputation for powerful tidal streams, overfalls, swell and fog. Nevertheless at neap tides in clear settled weather with light winds an opportunity to visit Ouessant should not be missed. Navigationally it is well within the ability of an experienced costal skipper and a yacht set up for offshore cruising.

The two main anchorages in the island are Lampaul in the West and Le Stiff in the East. The latter is most commonly used by ferries and the supply ship with Lampaul as an alternative should landing in Baie du Stiff be impossible in strong easterlies. There are two temporary anchorages on the south coast – Porz Darland (see plan overleaf and note page 354) and Baie de Penn ar Roch. The north coast, Le Côte Sauvage, is considered to be one

Ouessant Traffic Control Radar Tower and Phare du Stiff

III North Brittany: 2 Trébeurden to Ouessant

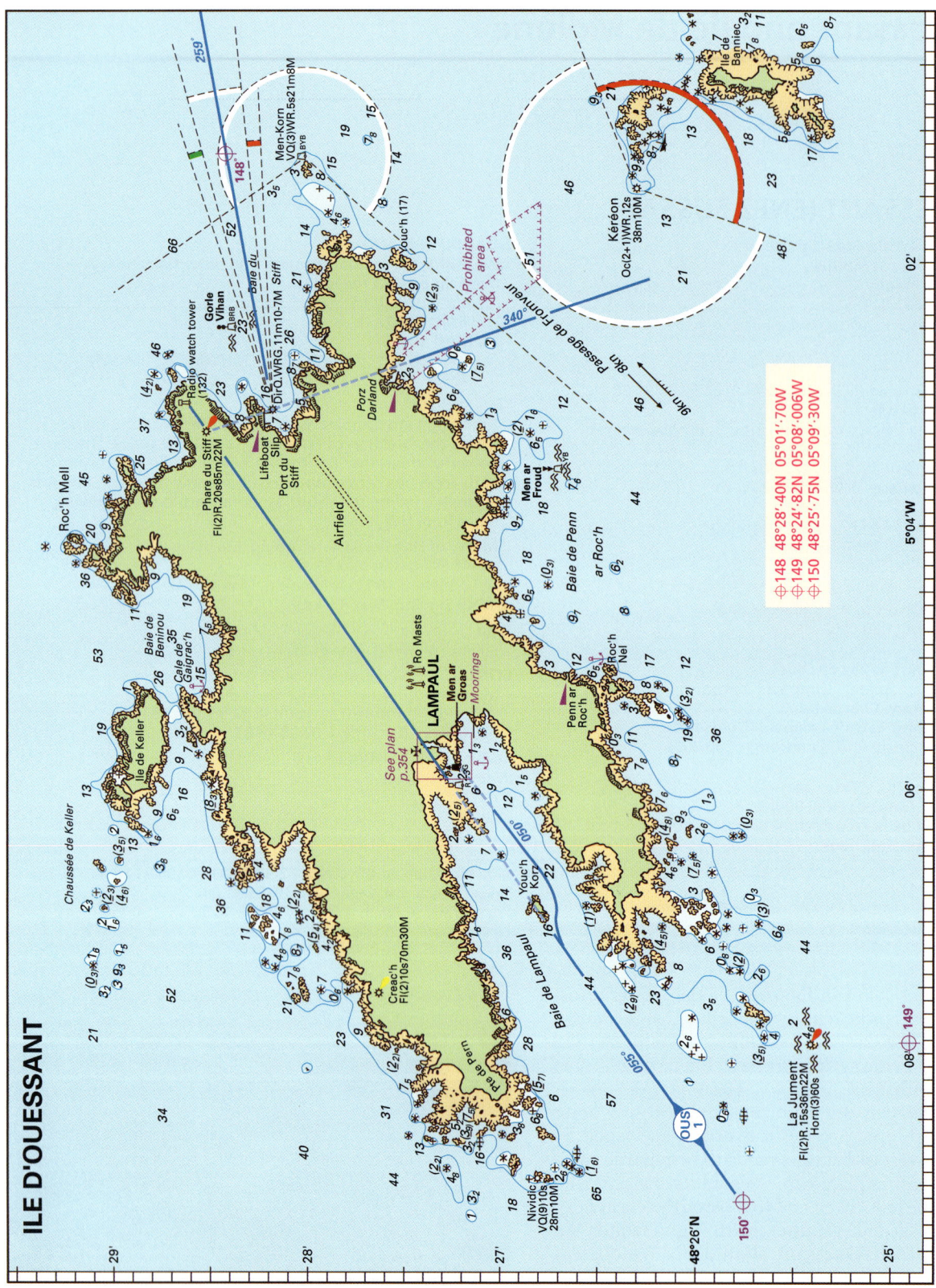

350 CHANNEL ISLANDS, CHERBOURG PENINSULA & NORTH BRITTANY

Ile d'Ouessant and Ile de Molène

Ile d'Ouessant from W

of the most treacherous stretches of coast in France. Being at the receiving end of a 4,000 mile fetch it becomes unpleasant even in moderate onshore winds and is prone to swell that can penetrate round the island. However, one fair weather anchorage on this coast is described below. (See *Cale de Gaigrac'h* page 355.)

Baie de Lampaul in the W is the island's capital and the preferred place to land, conditions permitting, being a short walk into the island's town. The best way to get around in Ouessant is to hire a bike and there are several outlets in Lampaul. Once clear of the town and tourists you cannot fail to be struck by the island's unique atmosphere and awesome silence.

The Museum of Lighthouses and Beacons at Créac'h lighthouse is a half hour peddle from Lampaul and well worth a visit as is Phare du Stiff in the east. This was the first lighthouse to be built in Brittany.

Historical

Enez Eussa (the High Island)

'Qui voit Ouessant, voit son sang' may overstate the island's reputation as a wild place wracked by storms and high seas. Its history is steeped in legends, superstitions and folk-lore that are rooted in a Celtic past. Then it was regarded as the resting place of the souls of the departed and the end of the world.

Ouessant is first mentioned by Pytheas of Marseille in 400BC. In AD512 the Welsh monk St Paul Aurelian landed in the bay that still bears his name – Lan Paul or Porz Pol – and built the first Christian church on the island. It seems that the Ouessantais were reluctant converts reverting to their pagan ways until the end of the 17th century. In the meantime the English had landed in 1388 to massacre the whole population.

The rocks around Ouessant have claimed innumerable wrecks over the centuries. In 1791 the famous Breton writer and politician Châteaubriand was wrecked off Ouessant returning from America. He is buried as requested on Le Grand Bé island off his native St Malo.

Approaches

In planning a passage to Ouessant a study of the tidal atlas for the area should be made. The best is the French *SHOM 560 UJA Côte Ouest De Bretagne* (Goulven to Penmarc'h).

Créac'h lighthouse

The best way to get around in Ouessant is on a bike

III North Brittany: 2 Trébeurden to Ouessant

Port du Stiff

Visitors' moorings outside the harbour

Port du Stiff from the N

L'Aber-Wrac'h is a good point from which to make a passage to the island. It is a straightforward 20M routing via Libenter W cardinal buoy, Portsall W cardinal buoy (⊕147) to ⊕148 0·4M N of Men Korn E cardinal beacon tower(VQ(3)WR.5s) which is 1·3M E of the harbour.

Tidal Streams

The best hours for this passage are between HW Brest +1 and LW Brest. The deadline for arrival is HW Brest -0530 when the stream starts turning NE. The best time to leave L'Aber Wrac'h would therefore be at or just before local HW (HW Brest -0020). The stream will be initially adverse but become SW going by HW Brest +2.

The highly conspicuous landmark of the radar tower (132m) is 0·4M N of the harbour.

Men Korn is left to port on entry

Entry

The entry into Port du Stiff from ⊕148 will be on 259° leaving Men Korn E cardinal beacon tower 0·4M or at least 200m to port and Gorle Vihan isolated danger beacon tower 200m to starboard.

Moorings and anchorages

There is a heavy white mooring buoy for the supply vessel to the S and W of the jetty. Some smaller moorings have been laid inshore of this for visitors, also in the bay S of the jetty.

For anchoring the holding is poor with rocky patches and the area between the ferry mooring and jetty must be kept clear for the ferries to manoeuvre. Otherwise anchor where there is water though it would be unwise to leave a yacht out of view except in very settled weather.

Although apparently sheltered from the S through W to NW, heavy weather from any quarter sends in a large swell which makes the anchorage untenable. There are no facilities nearer than Lampaul apart from a café/bar. The bus journey into Lampaul takes about 20 minutes.

Port du Stiff from the SE

Tidal Streams

The best hours for this passage are between HW Brest +0430 and HW Brest -0530. As this gives just 2 hours of fair tide an earlier departure may be necessary. The deadline for arrival is HW Brest -0530 after which the NE going stream in the Passage du Fromveur starts building up on the SE corner of Ouessant. (See Tidal Streams Atlas.)

From Le Conquet follow directions for the Chenal de la Helle (⊕143) in reverse sequence (on page 340). When in position ¼ mile SSE of Luronne W cardinal buoy and 0·6M NNE of Le Faix N cardinal beacon tower (⊕152) alter course to 270° for ⊕151 1·6M N of Les Trois Pierres. Course may be altered to Le Stiff. Make good 305° to ⊕148.

Entry

See Port du Stiff from the N above.

Lampaul from Port du Stiff (Passage du Fromveur)

This 10M passage follows the S coast from Men Korn E cardinal beacon tower at the SE corner to La Jument lighthouse at the SW corner and then onto the entry transit into the Baie de Lampaul. It would be navigationally straightforward were it not for the strength of the tidal streams in the channel between Ouessant and Ile Bannec 3·0M NW of Molène.

WARNING

This vicious race sets through the 1·3M wide constriction between the SE corner of Ouessant and Le Kéréon lighthouse to the S, its effects extending into the approaches at either end. Rates reach a maximum of 9 knots at springs whereas further W at the SW corner they barely exceed 2 knots in either direction.

Dangerous overfalls form in the Fromveur with SW or NE winds against tide. The passage should therefore be made with light to moderate winds only and a fair tide

Ile d'Ouessant and Ile de Molène

Kéréon lighthouse on the southern border of Passage du Fromveur. It is 2 hours after LWS and the stream is setting strongly NE

running in the same direction. An offshore breeze would be ideal until shelter from the land is lost.

Tidal Streams

Off Kéréon the SSW going stream starts at HW Brest −0030. The NNE going stream starts at HW Brest +0550.

In the middle of the Race the WSW going stream starts at HW Brest +0030. The ENE stream starts at HW Brest −0520.

Leave Le Stiff in time to make Men Korn before the stream turns SW at about Brest +0030. (Note an area of potential overfalls on Basse du Fromveur 700m SE of Men Korn.) After rounding Men Korn take up a SW heading and give the coast a clearance of a good half mile.

Men ar Froud S cardinal beacon tower *Bobby Lawes*

Leave Men ar Froud S cardinal beacon tower a good 400m to starboard. In order to clear dangers on the SW corner keep La Jument lighthouse on a bearing of not less than 255°.

La Jument

Pass 600m SW of La Jument – **do not cut the corner as there is shallow ground 0·5M NW of La Jument** – before taking up a NW heading to join transit:

Bobby Lawes

OUS1 *055° (⊕149) Le Stiff lighthouse or the taller radar tower behind it open to the left of the prominent Youc'h Korz (34m) in the middle of Lampaul Bay*

As Le Stiff will be five miles distant you may well not see it unless visibility is good.

Entrance

Once inside the tidal streams become negligible. Pass Youc'h Korz to the S (an outlier extends 100m to the N of it) and then approach the moorings/anchorage/harbour with Men ar Groas green beacon tower bearing 050° or less to clear the rocks in the N corner of the bay. Mussel beds in the E corner of the bay.

Moorings

There are 24 substantial visitors' moorings in the bay to the S of Men ar Groas beacon tower and a vacant one will nearly always be found. Moorings are free.

III North Brittany: 2 Trébeurden to Ouessant

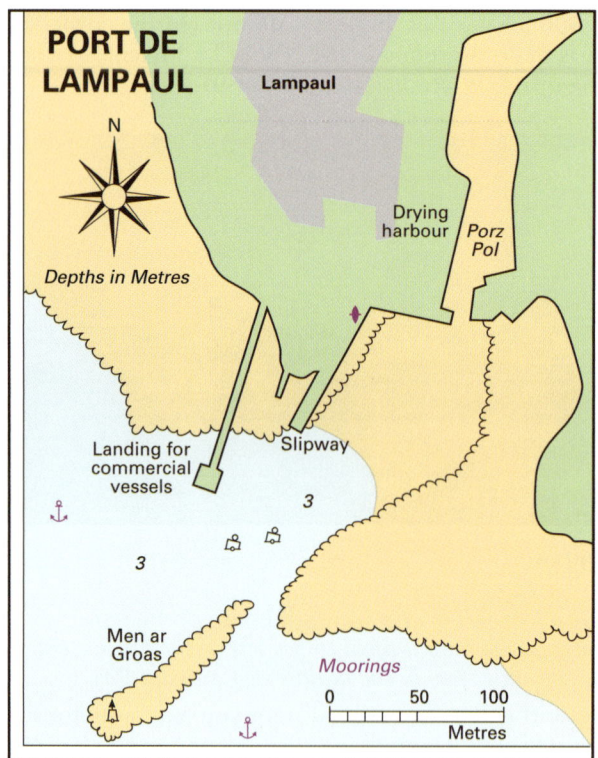

Anchorage

There may be room and water to anchor inside the two beacon towers where some shelter from any sea and swell may be found. There is 2·3m between the beacons shoaling to 0·8m near the jetty but there are many rocky patches.

Outside the beacons water may be found to the E of the moorings in up to 5m sand and mud. Otherwise anchor outside the moorings in generally good holding. The SE side of the bay is much encumbered with fish farms.

Berthing

There is a small inner harbour (Porz Pol) 400m to the ENE inside the beacon towers which dries 3·5m with an entrance less than 8m wide. It is cluttered with local boats and mooring lines. The quays are rough and uneven. Its use by deep draught yachts is not recommended but it might be possible to dry out inside after a prior recce. A number of small boat moorings obstruct the approach.

Porz Pol inner drying harbour at Lampaul

Porz Darland from SE

South coast anchorages

PORZ DARLAND

48°26'·46N 05°02'·98W

A small inlet on the S side of the island with a breakwater and landing slip. A track runs from here to Baie du Stiff to the N. A mooring buoy is sometimes laid in the bay for the supply vessel.

In 2016 a tidal turbine was established 0·9M SE of the breakwater head. At a depth of 30m it presents no hazard to small craft but anchoring, mooring and diving is prohibited within a zone surrounding the turbine and between it and the breakwater. (See plan, page 350.)

Approach and anchorage

Approach with Le Stiff lighthouse bearing 340° but note this disappears when 0·5M off so continue on the same track towards the breakwater. This approach passes 200m E of Men Darland (dries 7·7m). Avoid rocks and patches extending from the NE shore.

In settled weather anchorage may be found close NE of the E boundary of the zone at its N end as shown.

BAIE DE PEN AR ROC'H

48°26'·56N 05°05'·25W

A wide bay on the S side of the island offering little shelter except from the N and NW when it is sometimes used by the supply vessel. There is a landing slip usable at all states of the tide at the W side, and a track to Lampaul. See plan on page 350.

Looking N into Baie de Lampaul. Penn ar Roc'h landing is in the foreground

Ile d'Ouessant and Ile de Molène

Approach and anchorage
Approach with the slip and track bearing 330° and anchor as close in as possible between the slip and Roc'h Nel to the S in 5m. See charts *BA 2694* and *SHOM 7123*.

A north coast anchorage

CALE DE GAIGRAC'H
48°28'·50N 05°05'·30W
500M SSE of Île de Keller

This fair weather anchorage is in the SW corner of Baie de Beninou, a large bight half way along the N coast. It is well sheltered from west-northwesterlies by Ile de Keller and from all southerlies by the land. It is a useful resting point while awaiting a favourable tide. The stream runs strongly along this coast but less so into the bay.

Although the immediate coastline is uninhabited, this corner of the bay has permanent moorings for small local day boats. There is an unpaved track to the moorings from which it is a 20 minute walk to Lampaul. Spectacular scenery.

Cale de Gaigrac'h *Bobby Lawes*

Cale de Gaigrac'h

ILE DE MOLÈNE (ENNEZ MOLENEZ)
48°23'·9N 04°57'·3W
Ancien Môle lighthouse (Dir(3)WRG.12s)
8M WNW of Pointe de St Mathieu
4M SE of Ile d'Ouessant
Population: Less than 200

TRAVEL
Sea
  Ferry – as for Ile d'Ouessant

CHARTS
British Admiralty
  2356 Goulet de Brest to Portsall including Ile d'Ouessant (1:50 000)
  3345 Chenal du Four (1:25 000)
SHOM
  7122 De la Pointe de Saint-Mathieu au phare du Four – Chenal du Four (1:25 000)
  7123 Ile Molène – Ile d'Ouessant – Passage du Fromveur (1:20 000)
  7149 Du Goulet de Brest à Portsall – Ile d'Ouessant (1:49 100)

TIDAL INFORMATION
  Standard port Brest
  HW Brest +0005
  LW Brest +0005

MHWS	MLWS	MHWN	MLWN
6·9	1·0	5·3	2·6

Tidal streams
  In NW channel to N of island the streams start as follows:
  HW Brest -0615 ENE-going
  HW Brest -0015 WSW-going
  Maximum rates 6 knots, up to 9kns in Passage du Fromveur (See Ile d'Ouessant)
  WARNING Very strong streams round the island

USEFUL CONTACTS
  Mairie ☎ 02 98 07 39 05 www.molene.fr
  Gare Maritime ☎ 02 98 07 39 47
  Centre Medico-Social ☎ 02 98 07 39 07
  SNSM (lifeboat) ☎ 02 98 07 39 73
  NB There is no police station or fire service on Molène

SUPPLIES AND SERVICES
  12 (white) visitors' moorings
  Fresh water (scarce) is available at the Mairie
Fuel Saturday afternoon (enquiries: Mairie)
Showers Mairie
Shops Huit à Huit Supérette (supermarket) ☎ 02 98 07 38 81
Tabac ☎ 02 98 07 39 71
Chez Rachel (mobile groceries) ☎ 06 85 29 92 53
Restaurants Chez Rachel Bar Restaurante, Mobile groceries ☎ 06 85 29 92 53
Restaurante L'Archipel ☎ 02 98 07 38 56
Local speciality: Saucisse de Molène (sausage smoked in seaweed)

This miniscule oval shaped island is the largest and only permanently inhabited one within the Molène archipelago which numbers about eight islets. It is ¾ mile N–S and ½ mile E–W rising to 26m. A walk round the island, two miles, takes just over an hour.

The majority of buildings are huddled together around the harbour separated only by narrow alleyways. The dominant features are the church, sémaphore and a tall TV relay mast. The rest of the island is, for the most part, uncultivated heathland crossed by tracks. Molène has four cars but no roads.

III North Brittany: 2 Trébeurden to Ouessant

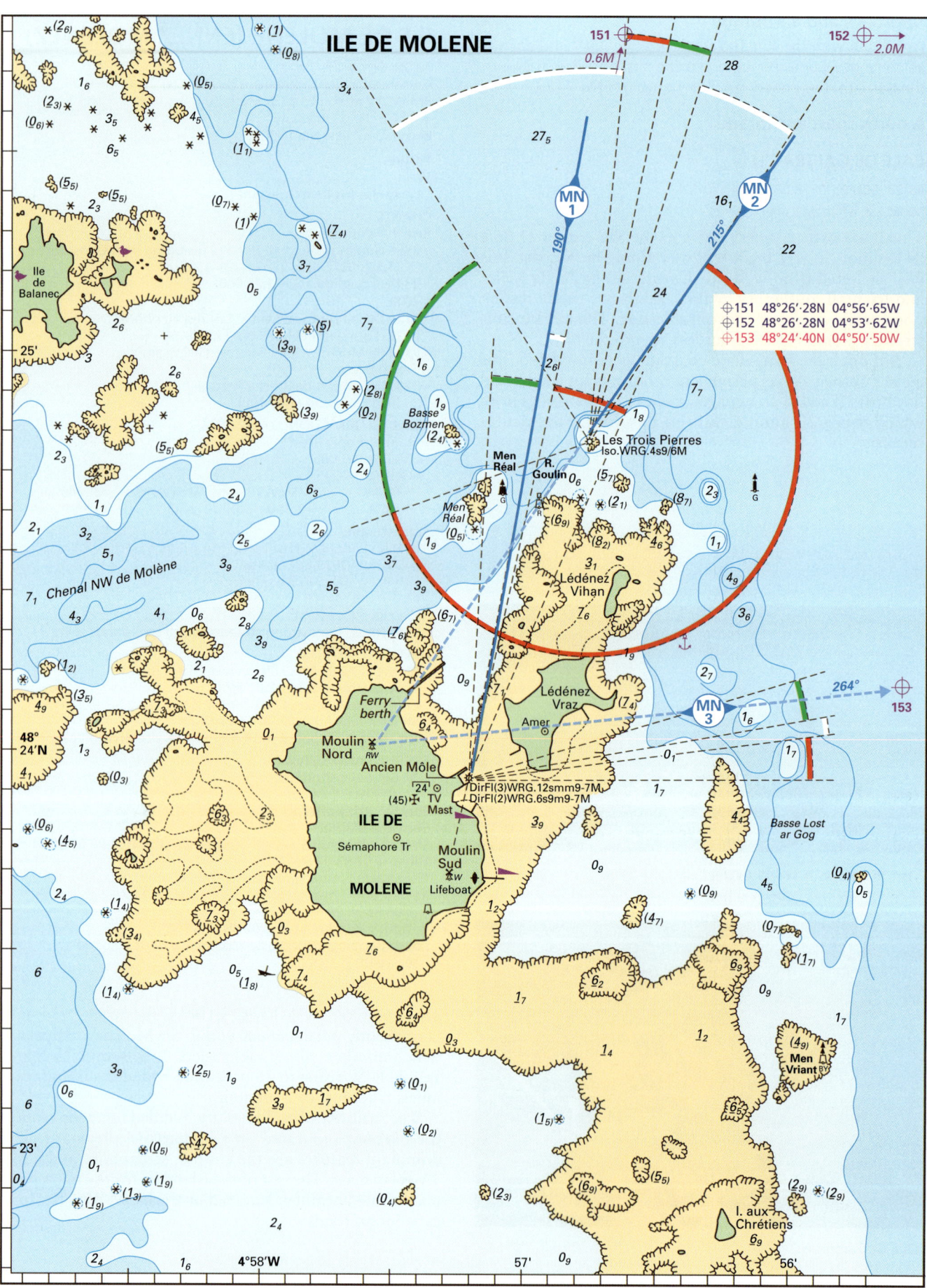

356 CHANNEL ISLANDS, CHERBOURG PENINSULA & NORTH BRITTANY

Ile d'Ouessant and Ile de Molène

Looking N over Molène

Only a handful of local fisherman now work out of Molène and the island has become increasingly dependent on supplies from the mainland to keep its shops stocked up – there is a *supérette* (small supermarket) a short distance from the harbour. Bars, restaurants and a hotel serve the needs of day trippers that are landed from Le Conquet and L'Aber-Ildut during the season.

Winters are hard and there will often be periods when the island is cut off from the world by stormy weather.

Historical

Molène has been inhabited as far back as 5000BC. The Romans called it 'Mediona Insula'. The origin of its present name is thought to derive from the Breton words 'Moal' (bald) and 'Enez' (island), a reference to the absence of trees.

The highest recorded population was 760 in the 1920s after which it started to decline. At that time most of the men were fishermen and helped the women cultivate small areas of land and tend whatever livestock they were able to keep. They were reputed to be the hardiest and most resourceful fisherfolk in Brittany.

Throughout history the Molènais have been the recipients of benefits that enabled them to survive. They became exempt from import duty and property tax in the reign of Louis XIV (1638–1715) as 'they already suffered taxation by the sea, storms and the rocks.'

An event at the end of the 19th century lead to help being given by the British government. On a foggy night in June 1896 the liner *Drummond Castle* returning from South Africa was wrecked on Les Pierres Vertes 3M WSW of Molène. Out of 400 persons on board only three were saved; the bodies of 29 of the passengers are buried in the cemetery and others elsewhere around the island. A cistern for water which the island lacked and a richly jewelled chalice for the church were presented by the English in gratitude for the kindness of the people of Molène. In the *sémaphore* is a small museum about the shipwreck.

La Sémaphore

Les Trois Pierres lighthouse

Approaches

From N

The main deepwater approach and entry (2·4m) is from the N. The key mark is Les Trois Pierres lighthouse (Iso.WRG.4s). Note also conspicuous mast close W of the port.

Make for a position 1·5M N of Les Trois Pierres with it bearing 184 (⊕151). Take up transit:

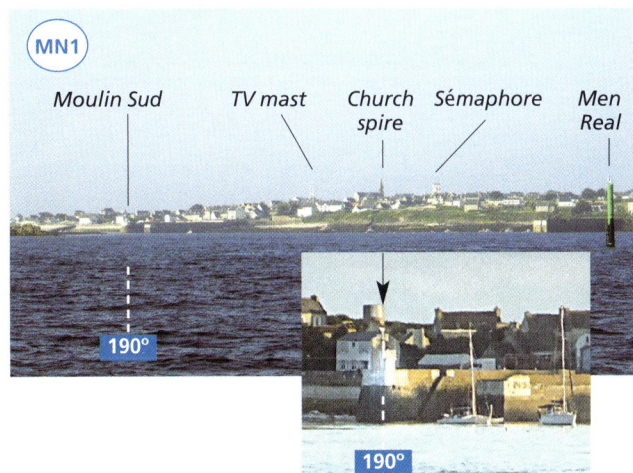

MN1 *190° Moulin Sud aligned with white mark on end of Ancien Môle.*

III North Brittany: 2 Trébeurden to Ouessant

This transit leaves Les Trois Pierres lighthouse (Iso.WRG.4s) 300m to port and:

Passes midway between Basse Men Real starboard beacon tower (Q.G) and Roche Goulin port beacon tower (Q.R). Come to starboard to:

Bring TV mast onto a bearing of 197° and continue into harbour.

Roche Goulin

From NE

Make for a position 0·6M NNE of Le Faix N cardinal beacon tower (⊕152) in the Chenal de La Helle. (See plan page 338.)

Make good 270° for 1·0M and when Les Trois Pierres bears 215° take up transit:

MN2 215° Moulin Nord RW beacon tower aligned with Les Trois Pierres lighthouse

Alter course to leave Les Trois Pierres 200m to port to join **MN1** into anchorage. (Enter as above.)

Moulin Nord is well N of the town

From E – Chenal des Laz

This channel breaks off Chenal de la Helle at position 2·0M WSW of Pte de Corsen (⊕153) (see plan page 338). The transit then is:

MN3 264° Moulin Nord RW beacon tower aligned with white beacon on Ledénez Vraz

This passes between Plateau de la Helle (N) and the extensive reefs surrounding Ile de Quéménès (S). It terminates 1·0M E of Ledénez Vraz when a NNWly heading should be taken up to join transit **MN1** or **MN2** as described above.

At HW springs Chénal des Laz may be extended to cross a bar drying approximately 5m **but local knowledge is needed to find the narrow boat channel into the port.**

WARNING

The indicated stream sets N max 3kns and S max 2kns across this channel.

From W – Chanel NW de Molènes (approx. 2·9m)

This offers a narrow but deep water route to the final N channel approach. It is however indifferently marked and has no formal transit. Using *BA 2694* or *SHOM 7123* it would be an interesting exercise for the skilful navigator well off LW springs, near slack water and in good visibility. (See chart *SHOM 7123*.)

WARNING

Max 4 knot cross stream.

Mooring

The mooring area is SE of the ferry berth on Môle du Bon Retour (N breakwater).

There are 10 white visitors' moorings in between 0·9m and 0·3m SSW of the end of Môle du Bon Retour and to W of lifeboat mooring. Use is regulated by La Mairie ☎ 02 98 07 39 05.

Anchorage

In the pool about 200m SE of the N breakwater head in about 1·9m. Depths decrease to the S of this but it may be possible to creep further in at neaps. The moorings at the S end dry 1·3m.

Berthing

There are drying berths 0·9m and 1·1m alongside the outer end of the môles and there is a slip on the S side of the S arm (Ancien Môle). A drying or alongside berth over HW is a possibility here if not occupied by fishing boats.

Anchorage SE of N breakwater

Anchorage S of Ancien Môle

3. Plateau des Roches Douvres

PLATEAU DES ROCHES DOUVRES

Lighthouse 49°06'·44N 02°48'·82W
Fl.5s60m28M Horn(1)60s

CHARTS
There is no suitable large scale chart covering the area but those listed below provide some information.

BA 2028 Ile de Bréhat to Plateau Des Roches Douvres (1:48 600)

SHOM 7153 De l'Île de Bréhat au Plateau des Roches Douvres (1:48 600)

Pilot books:
Pilote Cotier 6. De Saint-Malo à Brest Alain Cotier

TIDAL INFORMATION
Based on Les Héaux De Bréhat

MHWS	MLWS	MHWN	MLWN
9·15	1·90	7·25	3·85

MTL 5·55
Diff on St Malo   Approx -20 mins
Diff on St Helier   Approx -40 mins

Tidal streams
The area experiences accelerated and unpredictable streams. Maximum rates occur between Plateau des Roches Douvres and Plateau de Barnouic. At half tide Spring rates attain 4·3 knots SE going on the flood and 3·9 knots WNW going on the ebb.

Historical

Positioned between Ushant and the Bays of St Malo and St Brieuc the Plateau des Roches Douvres has long held a reputation as a snare to shipping. In *Toilers of the Sea* published 1886 Victor Hugo refers to the reef as 'a cut throat in ambush in the ocean.'

In the 19th century the idea of erecting a lighthouse on a small islet 20 miles offshore was considered an impossibility. As a compromise it was first constructed in Paris in 1865 of large metal sheets bolted onto an iron

From the south at LW springs

'Those terrible and solitary rocks' *Victor Hugo (1886)*
Those seeking total seclusion and something of a challenge may be interested to venture into this isolated reef lying 28 miles W of St Helier, 25 miles SSW of St Peter Port and 15 miles NNE of Ile de Bréhat. Its conspicuous lighthouse, at 197' the 24th tallest in the world, can hardly be missed on passages between the Islands and NW Brittany. Then it is recommended to pass a comfortable distance off and preferably down tide of the reef. Nevertheless it is possible in suitable conditions and with the right sort of boat to make an entry to land on Roches Douvres islet and savour its extraordinary atmosphere.

framework making it the tallest metal structure in the world at the time. It was then erected as the centrepiece for the Universal Exhibition of 1867, following which it was dismantled and transported to Ile de Bréhat for shipping out to the reef. Workers suffered great hardship living permanently on the rock without shelter and lashed by gales. There were many accidents. Once in place the tower swayed so dangerously that no one would climb to the summit and it proved difficult to find a keeper.

Against all odds the first lighthouse was completed in 1869 and was in service until 1944 when it was bombed by German troops. Its concrete base remains close to the present lighthouse. Work was begun on the new structure in 1950 using granite quarried at Ploumanac'h and Trégastel. It took seven years, several hundred workers and more than 11,000 tonnes of material to complete. From 1971 the light was powered by wind and solar energy but the turbines were later dismantled due to the extreme conditions. The pylons remain. The lighthouse ceased to be manned in October 2000.

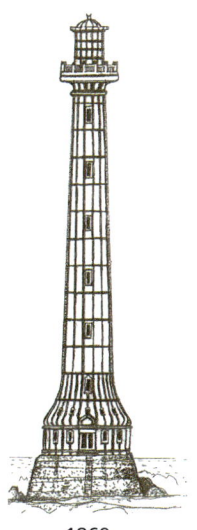
1869

Making a visit

Caution

When planning a visit consider the suitability of your boat to cope with strong and unpredictable tidal streams often accompanied by ocean swell. It should have sufficient turn of speed to get you there and out again within the time limitation. A powerboat or powerful motor sailor might be the best option. Adequate anchor chain is essential.

Prepare also for total isolation. The nearest shelter is around 20 miles away on the Brittany coast and in the event of a problem you may be out of VHF range.

CHANNEL ISLANDS, CHERBOURG PENINSULA & NORTH BRITTANY

III North Brittany: 2 Trébeurden to Ouessant

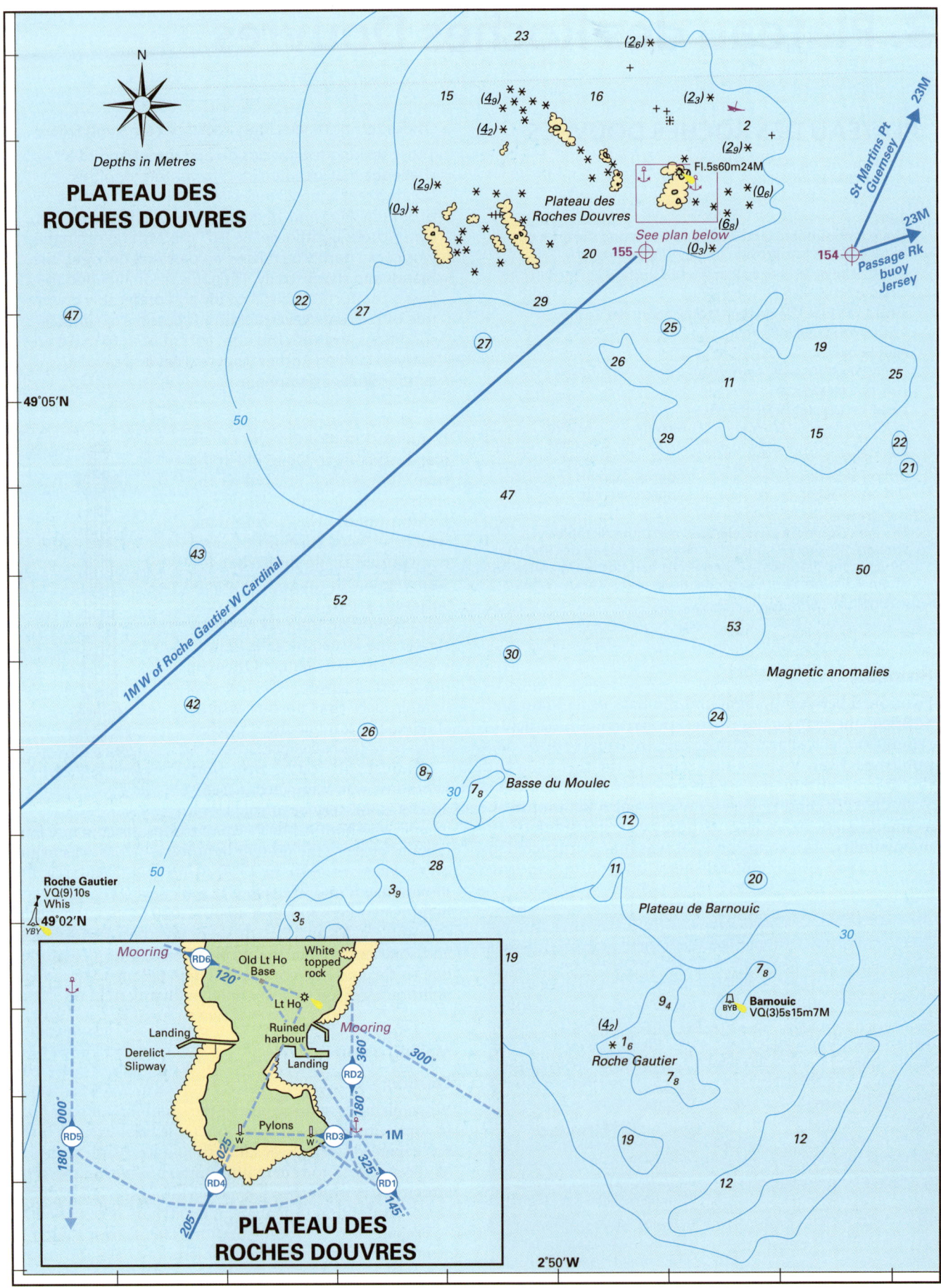

360 CHANNEL ISLANDS, CHERBOURG PENINSULA & NORTH BRITTANY

Plateau des Roches Douvres

Plateau des Roches Douvres is not recommended for an overnight stay as navigation is not possible after dark, or at anytime other than at or near LW as the area gives no protection from wind or swell.

Timing
A visit should be timed to coincide with LW on a moderate spring tide. Slack water will be about 1½ hours either side of local LW (approx St Helier -0040). Quiet settled weather with at least six miles visibility and no swell are prerequisites.

At the top of a spring tide the area is effectively open sea.

All photographs including air views were taken at LW Springs or as stated

East side
50m off the remains of the 'harbour' ESE of the lighthouse.

West side
0·25M WNW of the lighthouse.

Depths throughout the area are considerable and at least 8–10m will be found at LWS in the positions described. The holding is good in sand.

Mooring
As of 2014 Department des Phares et Balises have laid 2 heavy moorings in the vicinity of both landing points described. Each have a large yellow buoy and a long strop.

Approaches

From the east and northeast
To ⊕154 (1M ESE of Roches Douvres lighthouse) is 23M from Jersey (Passage Rock buoy) and the same distance from Guernsey (St Martin's Point lighthouse).

In order to arrive around LW when the stream is slack passages will be taken on most of the ebb. Allowance will need to be made for the WNW–NW-going stream.

E side anchorage and landing

To anchorage (E side)
At ⊕154 the lighthouse which will bear 300°. Identify the concrete base of the earlier lighthouse WNW of the lighthouse. This will be visible but almost closed behind the left hand edge of the lower part of the lighthouse.

Alter course to 270° for approximately 0·7M to obtain transit:

E side at half tide

Anchorages
(See plan.)
There are two preferred anchorages. One SE of the lighthouse and the other W of it. The rock strewn northern half of the reef should not be approached.

RD1 *325° The concrete base on a bearing of 325° and midway between the lighthouse and the easternmost white pylon.*

III North Brittany: 3 Plateau des Roches Douvres

Dries 6·8 m

On this line a conspicuous clump of rock, the highest part of which is charted drying 6·8m is left 200m to starboard. When this is on the beam alter course to port towards the easternmost (right) pylon to clear W (left) of a rock awash at chart datum and very close E of the line. Hold heading until about 50m off the shore which is steep to. Identify transit:

RD2 000° *The easternmost of two white topped rocks N of the lighthouse*

When this rock bears N steer towards it until:

RD3 *Both pylons are in line*

Anchor here or alternatively proceed a little further N to the large yellow mooring buoy. Shelter here is good in westerlies. Close NE of this position a fringe of drying rocks materialises as the tide falls providing shelter from that direction.

Depth found at LW (1·2m at St Helier): 7M.

Landing

This can be made without authorisation but the lighthouse is closed to the public. A French courtesy or Breton flag should be flown. At LW and providing there is no swell the best landing area is south of the ruined quays of the small 'harbour' on the east side. Getting ashore is not easy. Prepare for clambering over kelp covered boulders.

Alternatively, landing can be made west of the lighthouse on the partially ruined slipway that will be found there. A long painter on the tender is required. (See anchorage W side.)

From the south and southwest

Caution

Le Plateau de Barnouic
4M south of Les Roches Douvres is Le Plateau de Barnouic, an extensive reef marked by Barnouic light tower (E cardinal) and Roche Gautier W cardinal lit buoy. (49°02'·013N 002°54'·36W). The rock Roche Gautier 0·7M WSW of Barnouic E cardinal tower dries 4·2m.

The area experiences accelerated streams and can be rough particularly when wind is against tide. It should be given a wide berth.

Similar conditions prevail in the stretch between Barnouic and Roches Douvres. This area also carries a warning of Local Magnetic Anomalies (see chart *BA 2669*).

To ⊕155 about 1·3M SW of lighthouse is 16M from Ile de Bréhat. From a position 1·0M west of Roche Gautier W cardinal buoy make good 050° to ⊕155. Approach with transit:

RD4 025° *The lighthouse on the West white pylon*

362 CHANNEL ISLANDS, CHERBOURG PENINSULA & NORTH BRITTANY

Plateau des Roches Douvres

To anchorage (W side)

From the W

Identify view:

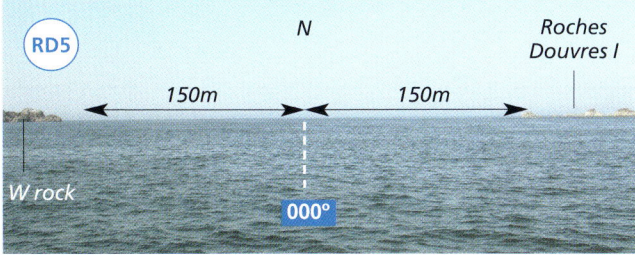

RD5 000° Head N towards the midway point as shown above until looking E you find:

RD6 120° North edge of old lighthouse base against S edge of lighthouse

Anchor in this position or head E to the yellow mooring but do not proceed further north. The bottom is sand and as on the Eastern side LW depths of around 10m will be found. It is sheltered from easterly winds and swell. Drying reefs to the west provide some shelter from that direction. (See also airview above.)

Drying reefs to the W

Landing

This is possible in the area on the crumbling slipway W of the lighthouse some 150m to E. The end is derelict. A long painter on the tender is needed.

Routeing between anchorages

E to W

On departure steer S then follow the shore keeping 75m off. Hold a W heading until well clear of the SW corner. Turn N when View RD5 is identified.

W to E

Head S on line RD5 until W pylon bears E then commence a shallow turn to port to follow the shoreline 75m off.

Ashore

The lighthouse towering above its five-storey keeper's quarters dominates a harsh and desolate scene. Strewn about is the debris of years of struggle – contorted ironwork, crumbling walkways and the remains of tracks set into the surface for transporting truckloads of granite.

Apart from the sight of a seal wallowing in the kelp it is lifeless and strangely silent. No place for loitering.

Old lighthouse base viewed from the lighthouse (above) and from the W mooring as the crew take a lunch break (below)

Appendix

Tidal Streams

Arrows show direction.
Figures show the mean rates of flow in tenths of knots at neaps followed by springs.
06,12 = 0·6 knots neaps, 1·2 knots springs.

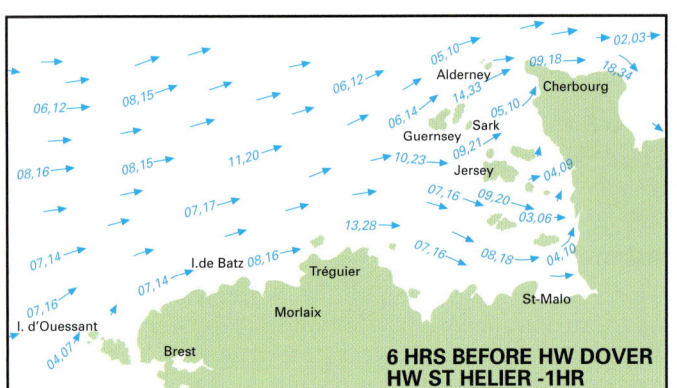

6 HRS BEFORE HW DOVER
HW ST HELIER −1HR

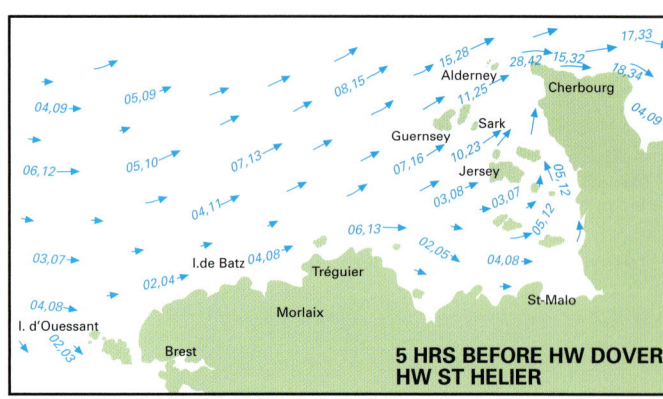

5 HRS BEFORE HW DOVER
HW ST HELIER

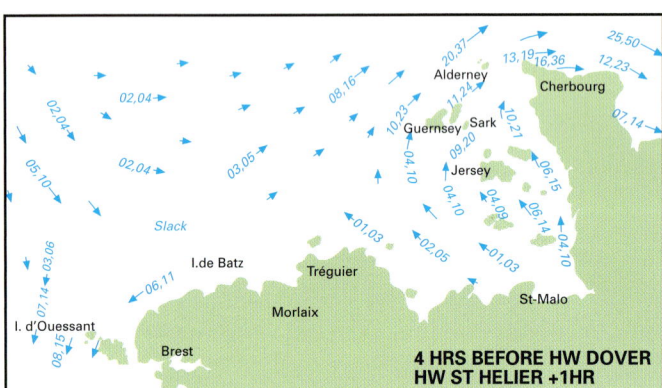

4 HRS BEFORE HW DOVER
HW ST HELIER +1HR

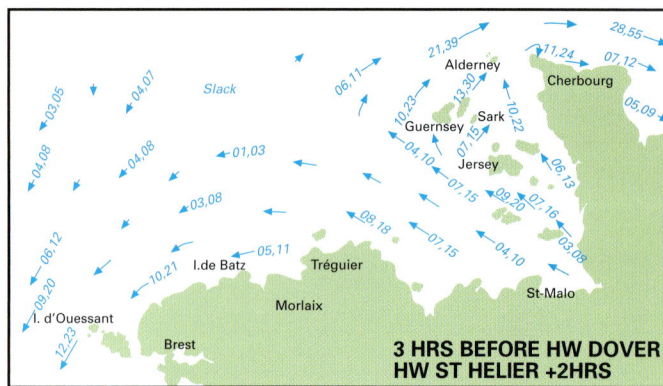

3 HRS BEFORE HW DOVER
HW ST HELIER +2HRS

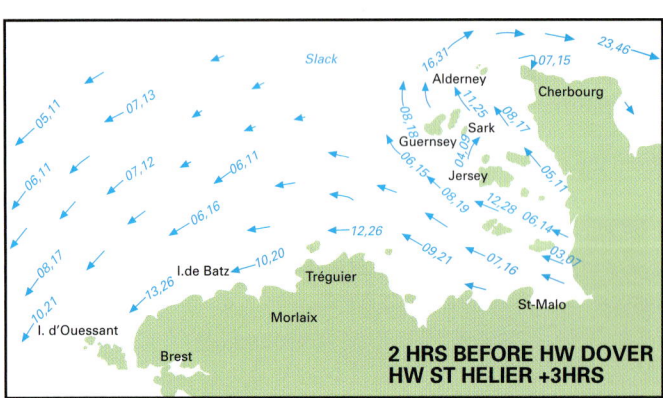

2 HRS BEFORE HW DOVER
HW ST HELIER +3HRS

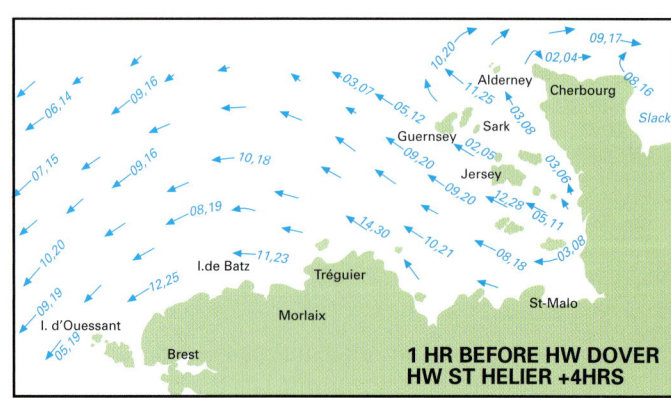

1 HR BEFORE HW DOVER
HW ST HELIER +4HRS

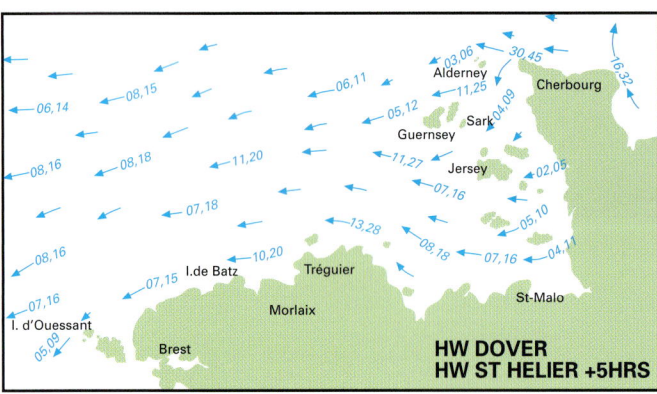

HW DOVER
HW ST HELIER +5HRS

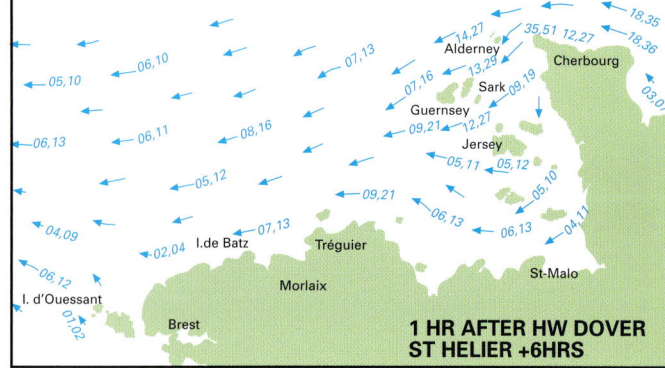

1 HR AFTER HW DOVER
ST HELIER +6HRS

Tidal streams

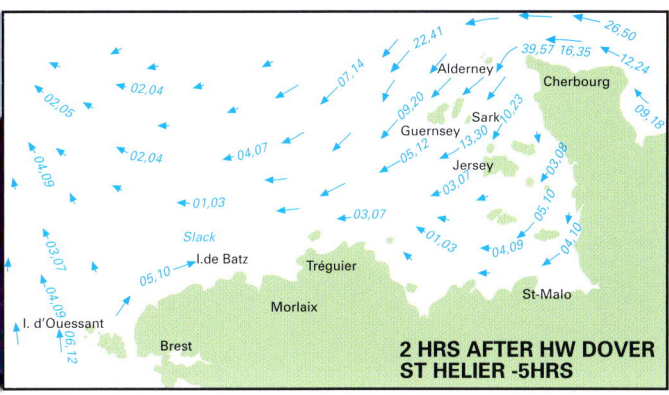
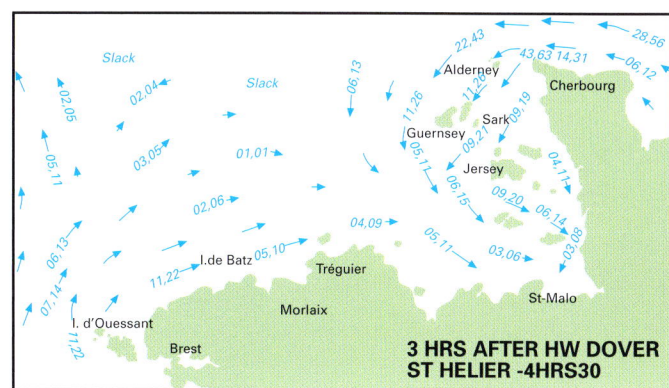
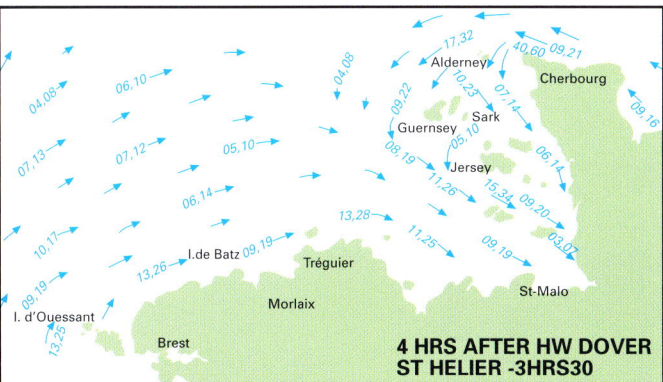
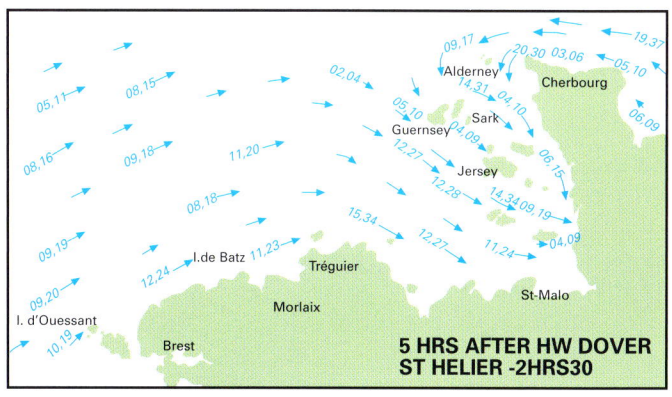
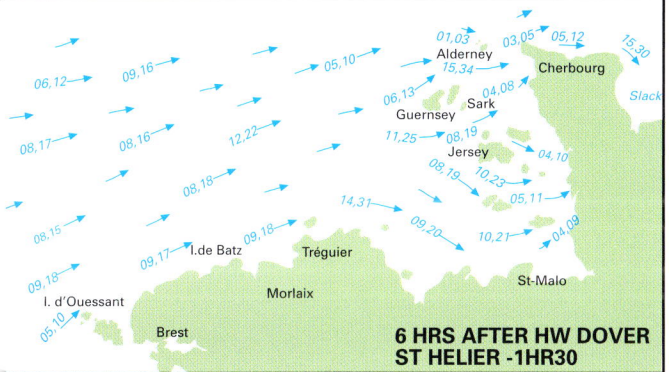

Tidal Streams Alderney and the Swinge

AREAS OF OVERFALLS ～ ALDERNEY RACE AND THE SWINGE

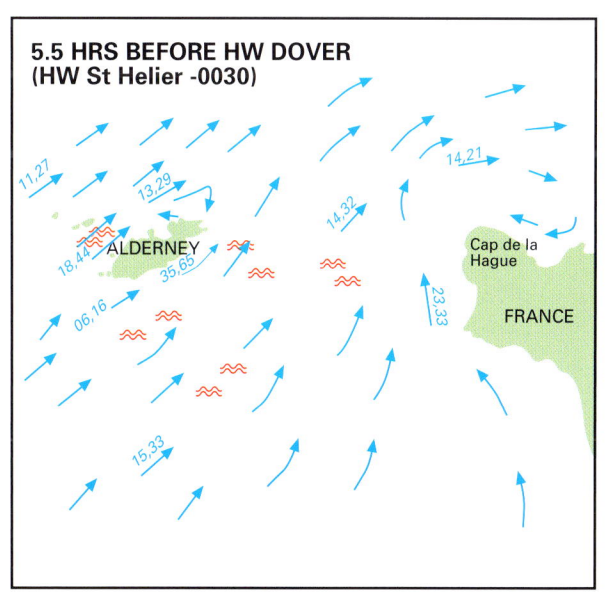

CHANNEL ISLANDS, CHERBOURG PENINSULA & NORTH BRITTANY

Appendix

AREAS OF OVERFALLS ～～ **ALDERNEY RACE AND THE SWINGE**

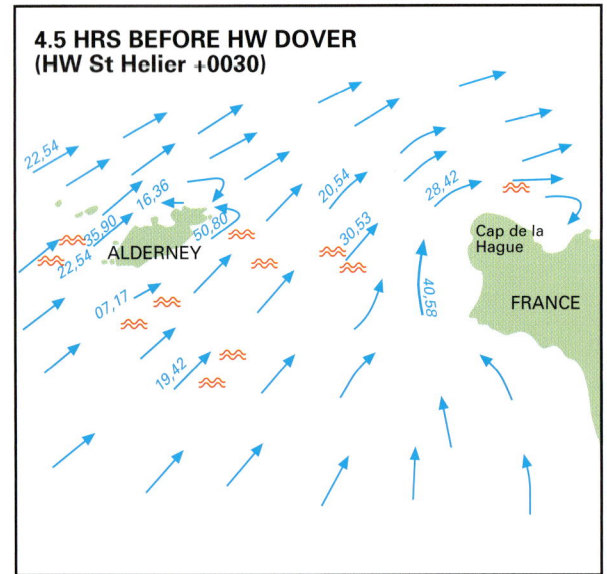

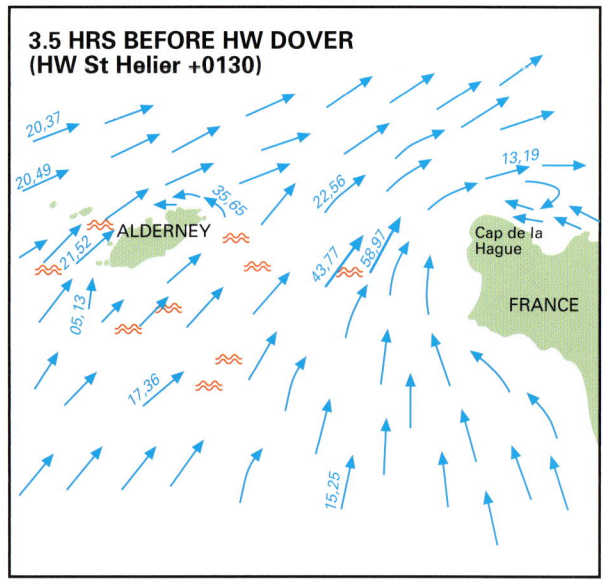

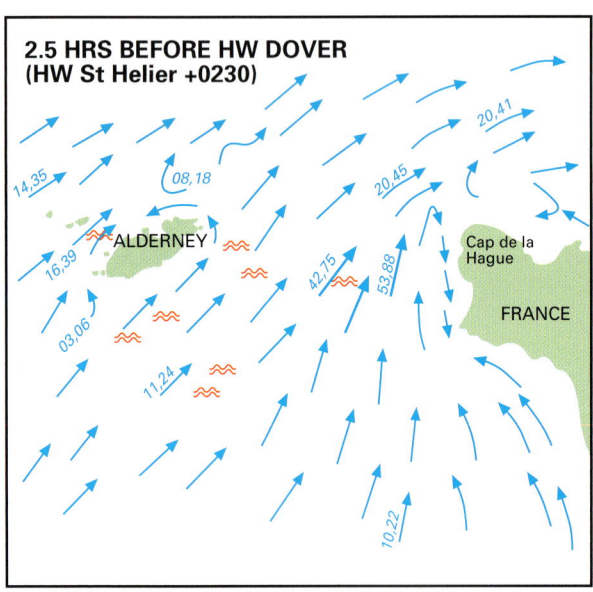

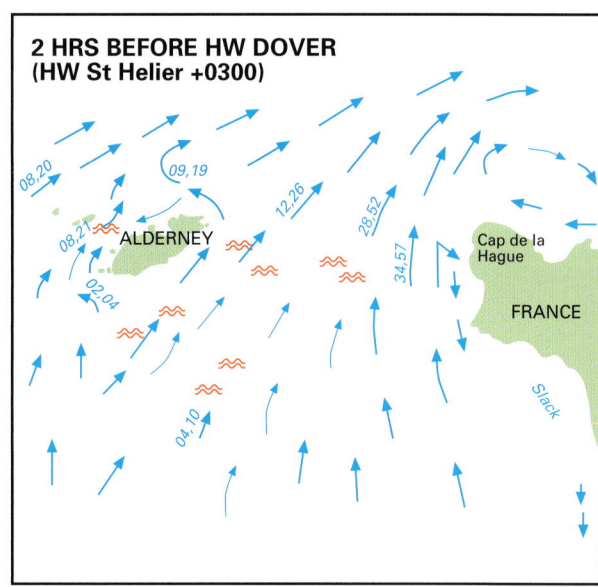

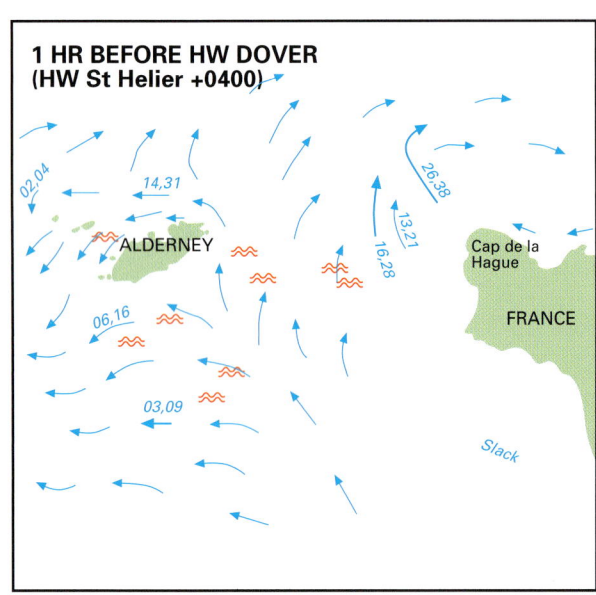

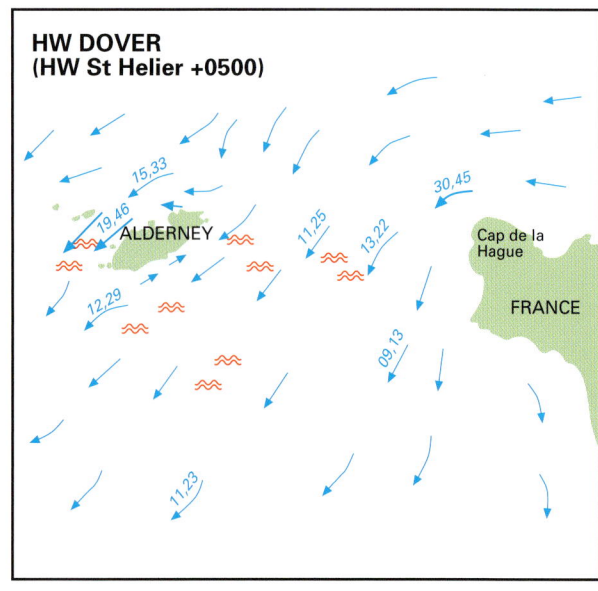

Tidal Streams – Alderney and the Swinge

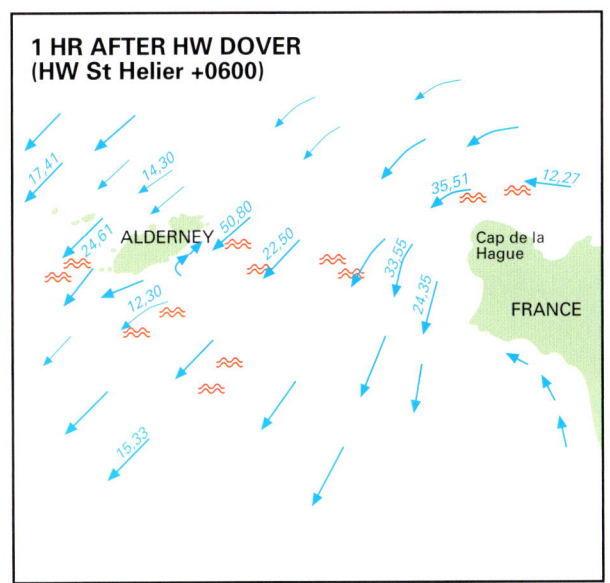

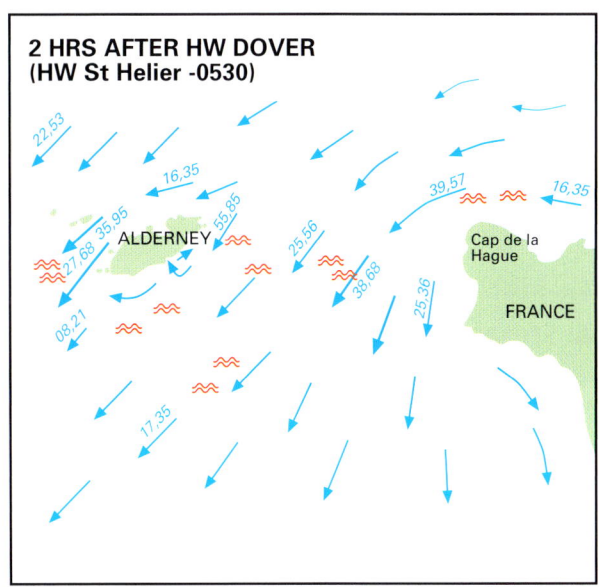

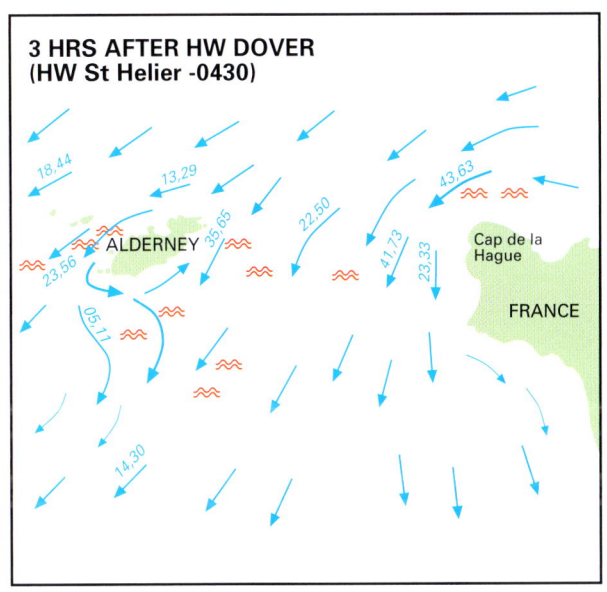

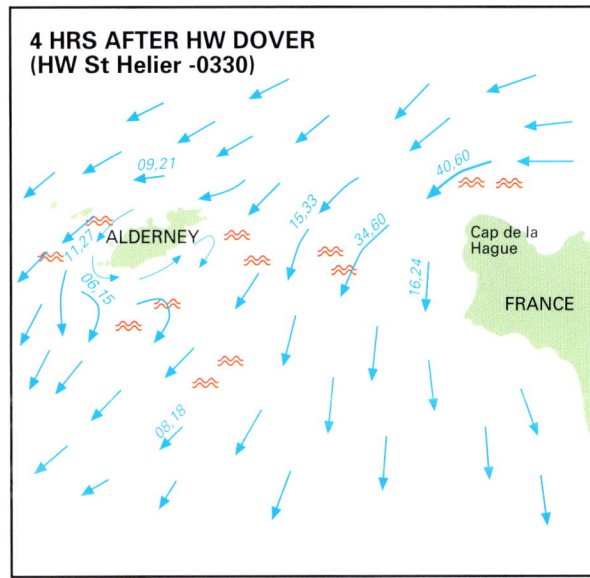

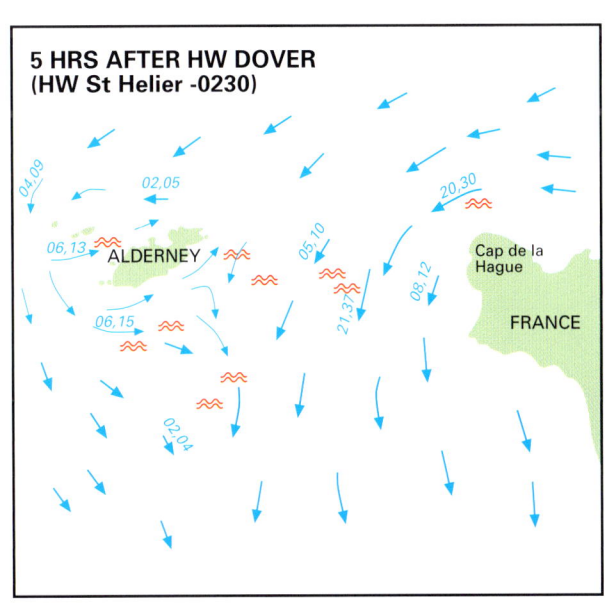

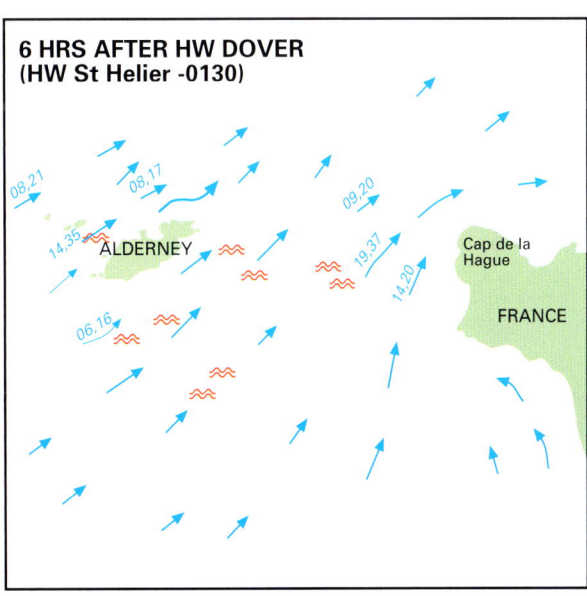

CHANNEL ISLANDS, CHERBOURG PENINSULA & NORTH BRITTANY

Appendix

Tidal Streams Channel Islands

Sources of information:
British Admiralty Tidal Stream Atlas
SHOM Courants de Marée
Local research
R. Adams

Tidal Streams – Alderney

Figures show the mean rates of flow in tenths of knots at neaps followed by springs.
1·4,3·0= 1·4 knots neaps, 3·0 knots springs.

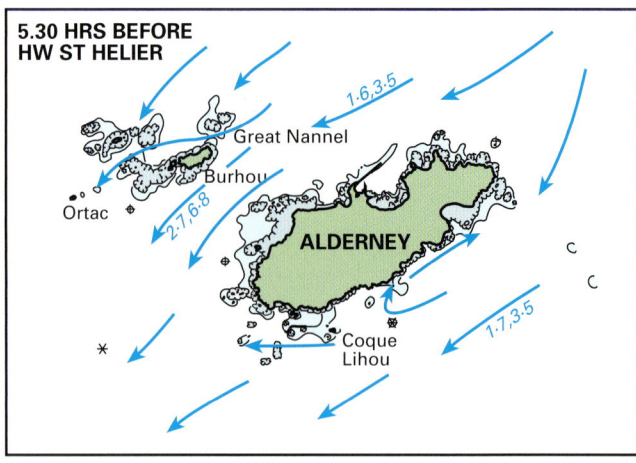

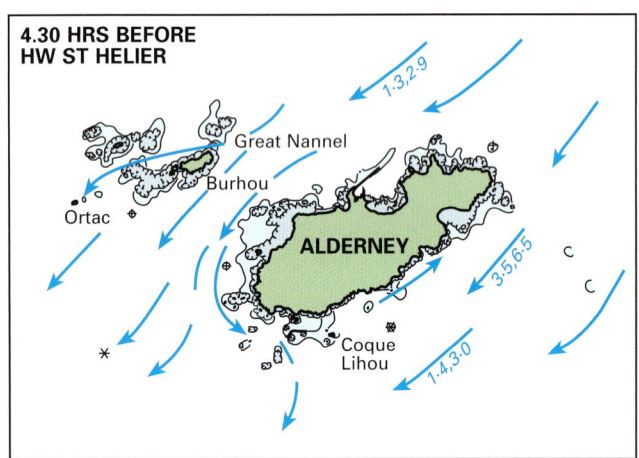

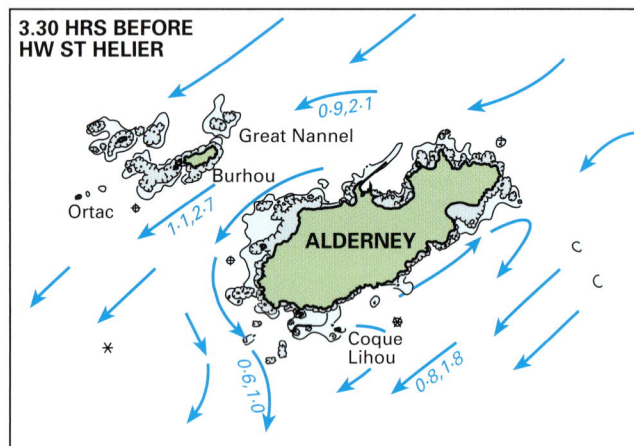

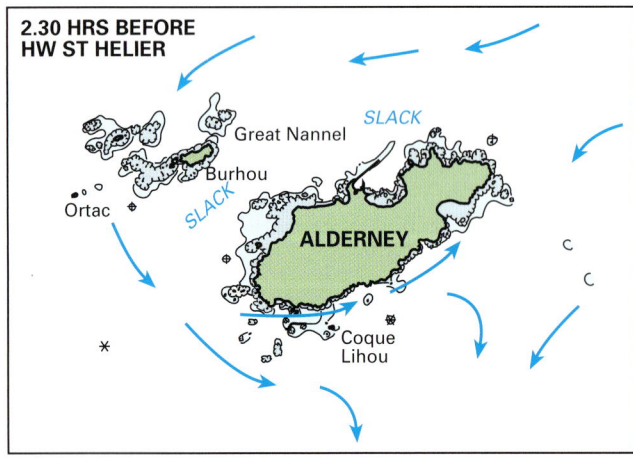

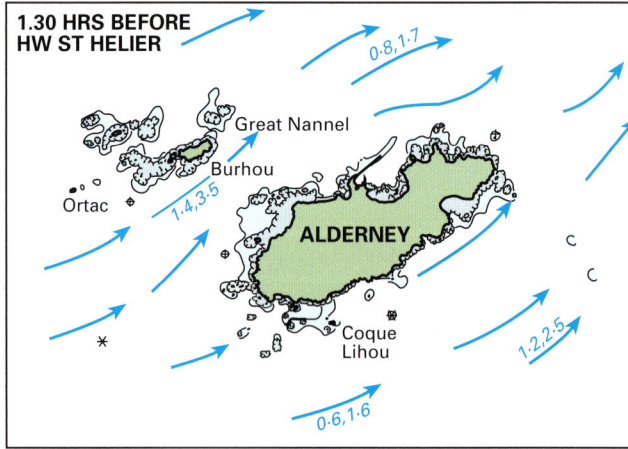

Tidal Streams – Alderney

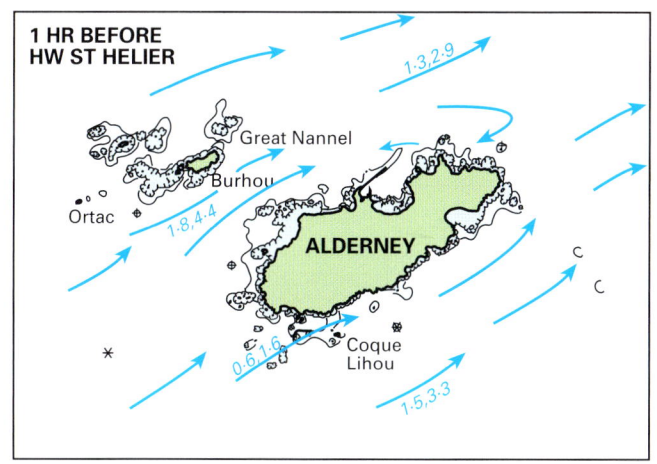
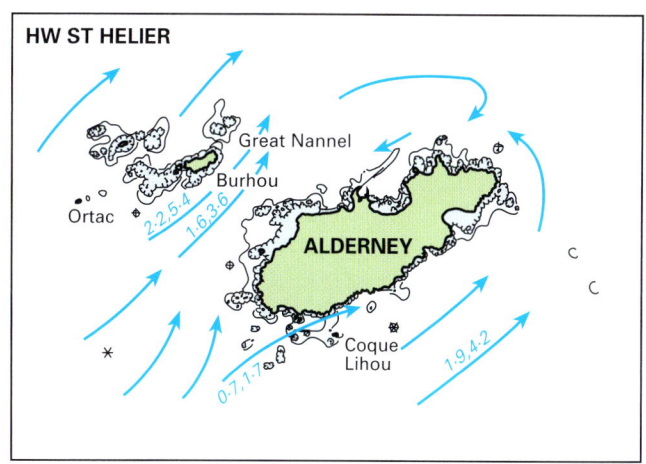
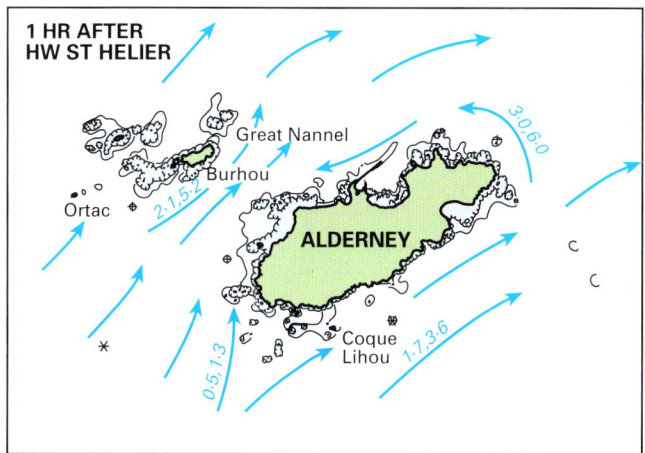
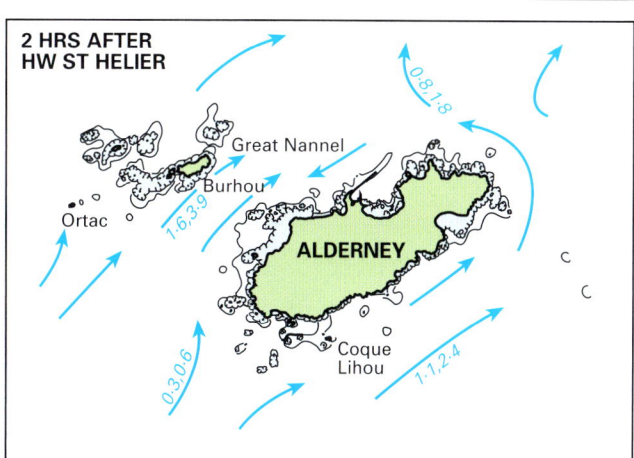
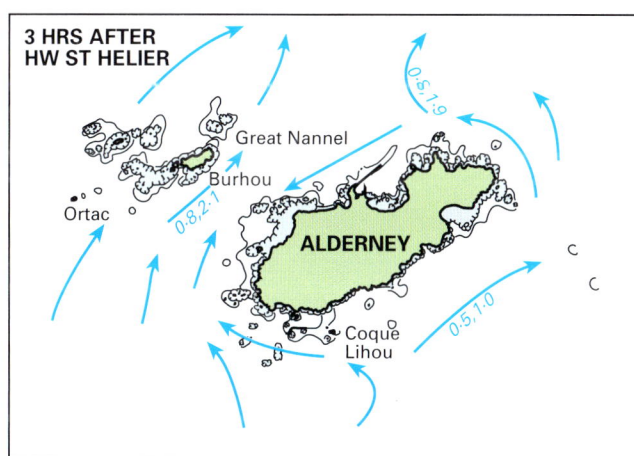
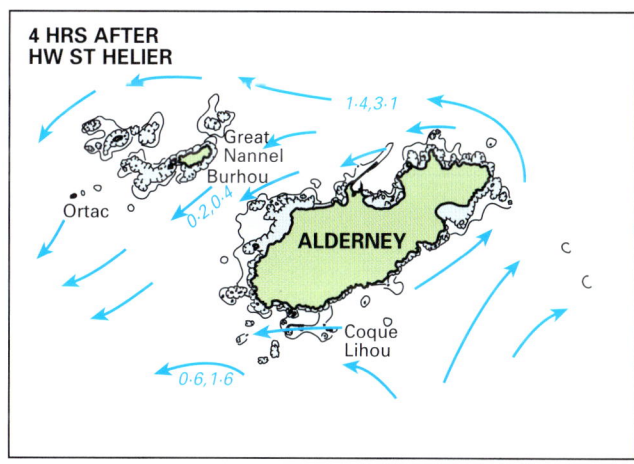
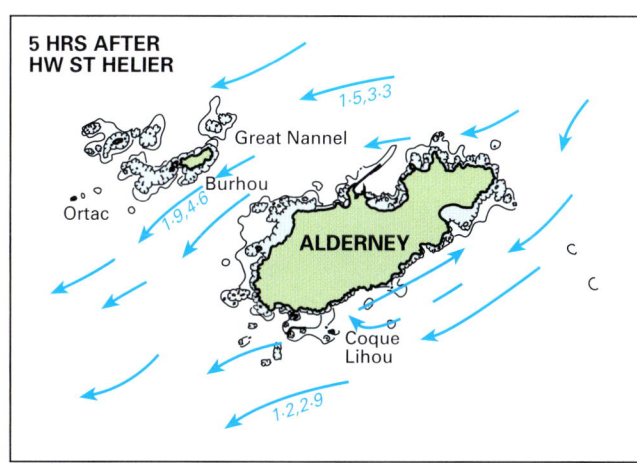
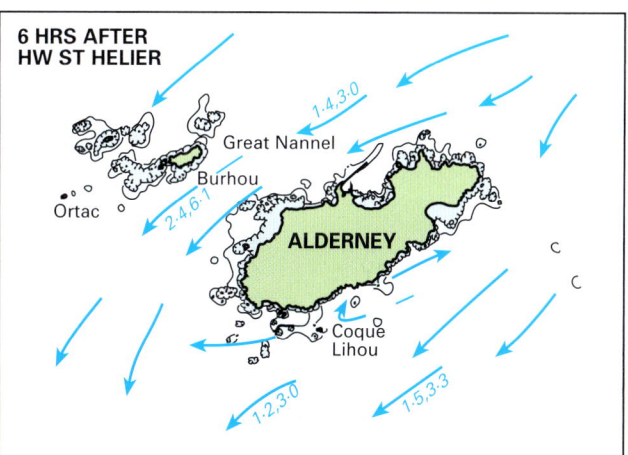

CHANNEL ISLANDS, CHERBOURG PENINSULA & NORTH BRITTANY

Appendix

Tidal Streams – Guernsey

The mean difference of HW St Peter Port based on HW St Helier is +0005 to +0010.

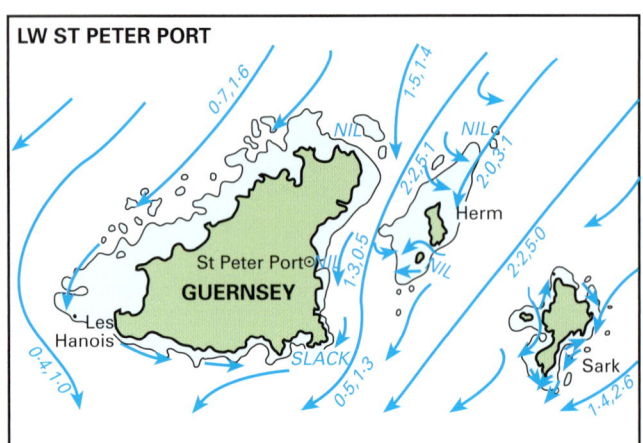
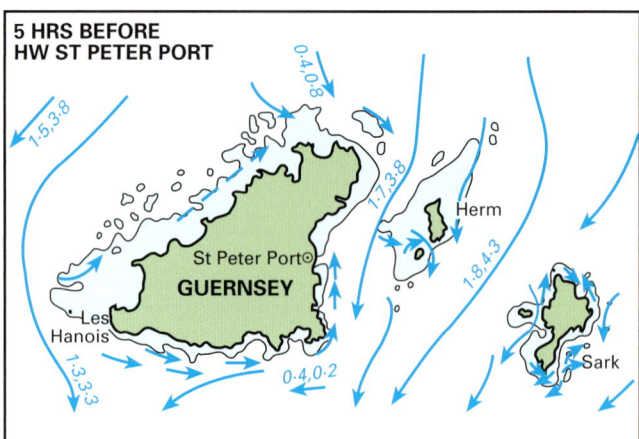
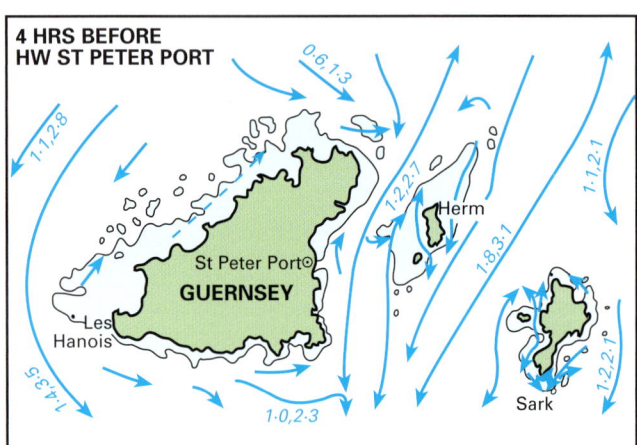
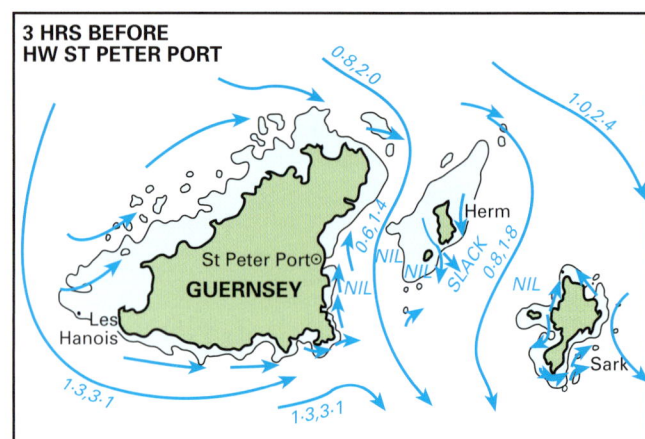
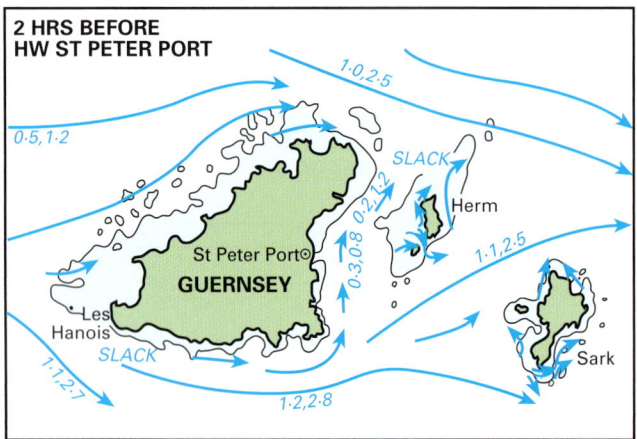
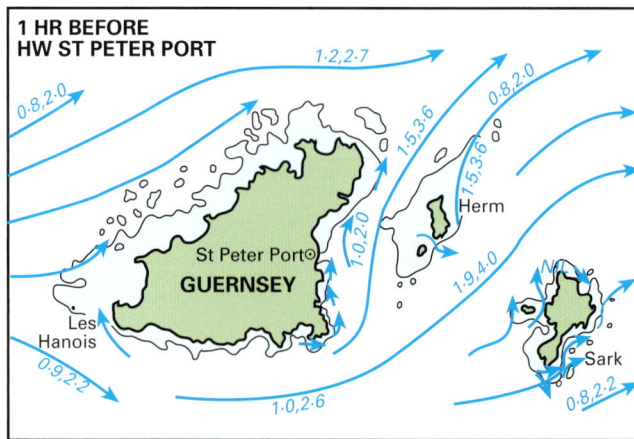

Tidal Streams – Guernsey

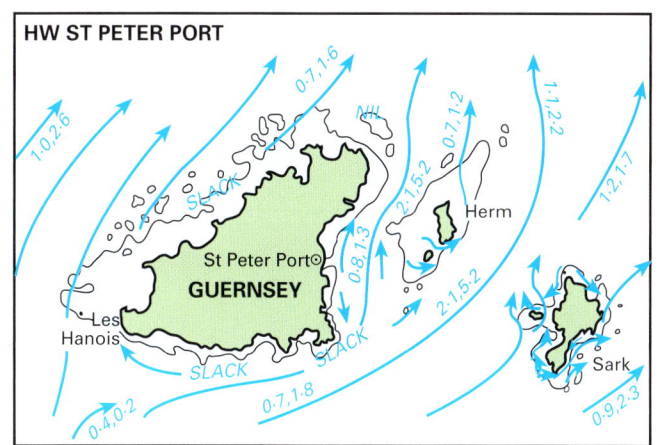
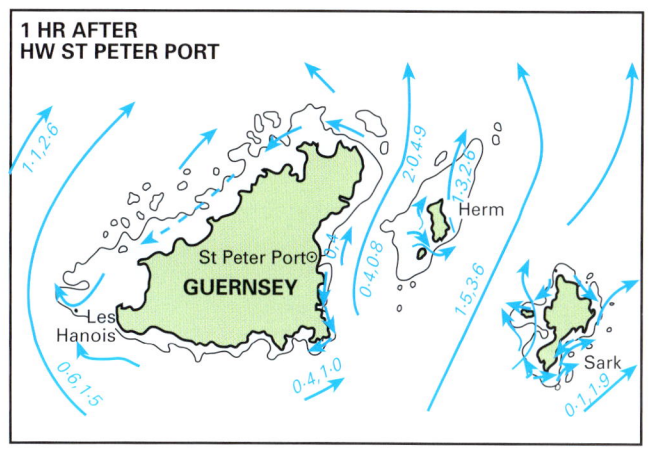
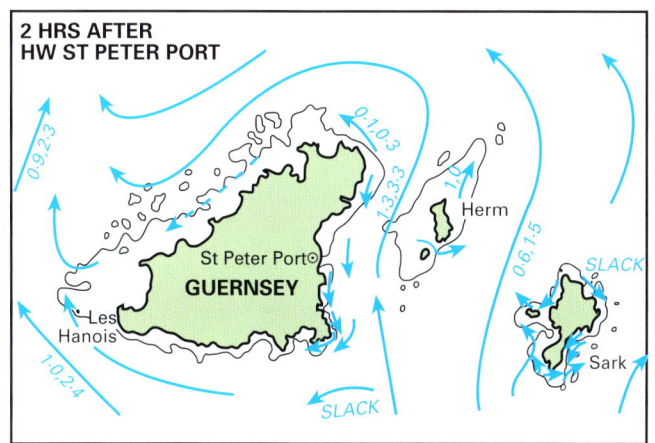
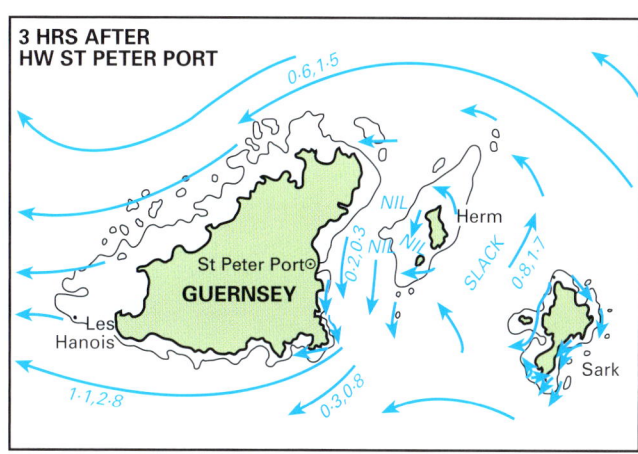
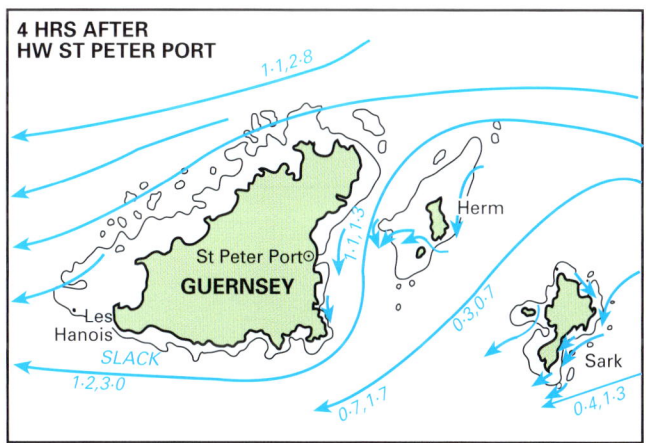
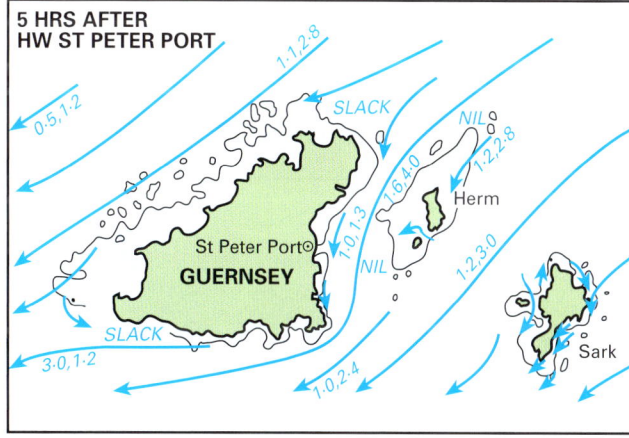

CHANNEL ISLANDS, CHERBOURG PENINSULA & NORTH BRITTANY

Appendix

Tidal Streams – Jersey

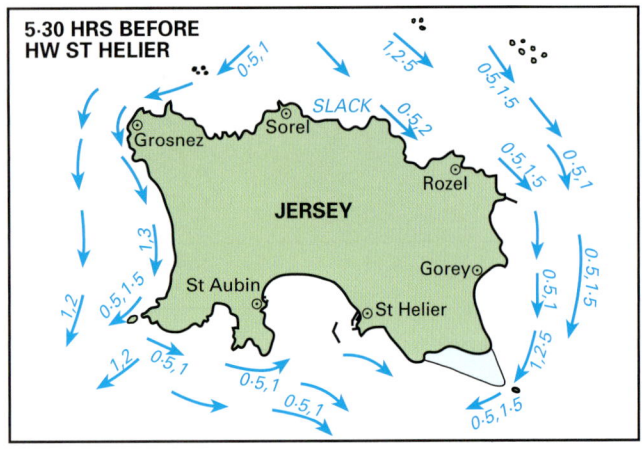
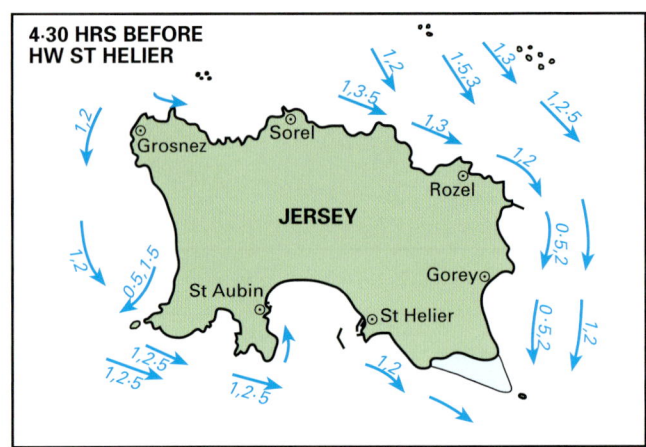
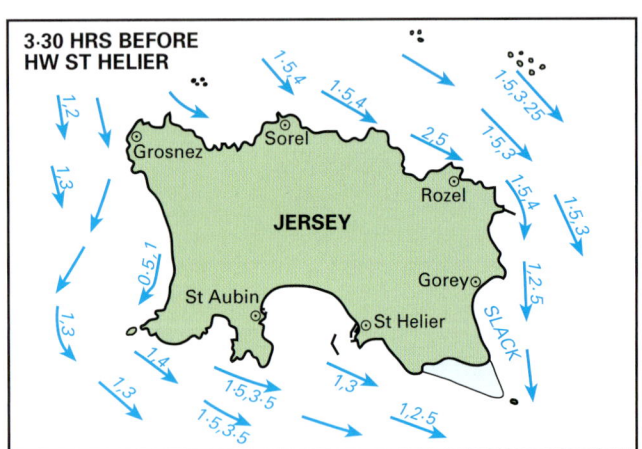
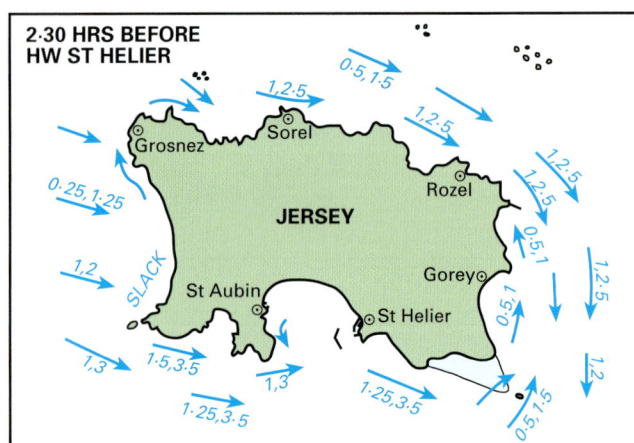
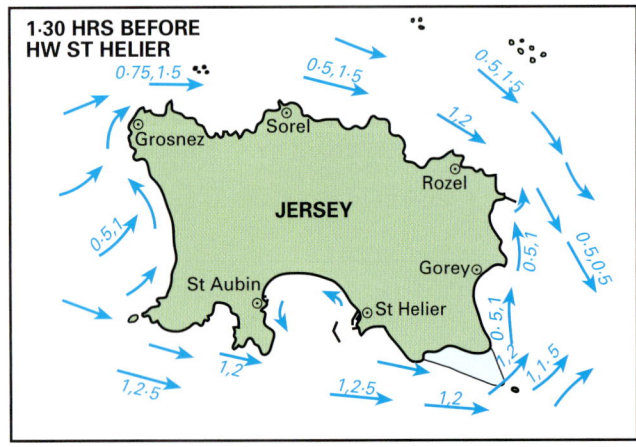
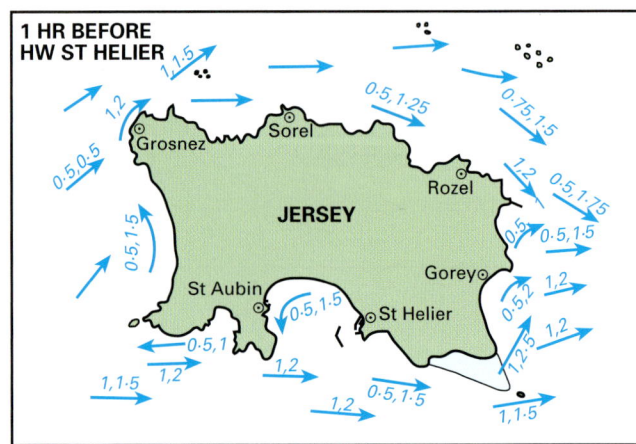

372 CHANNEL ISLANDS, CHERBOURG PENINSULA & NORTH BRITTANY

Tidal Streams – Jersey

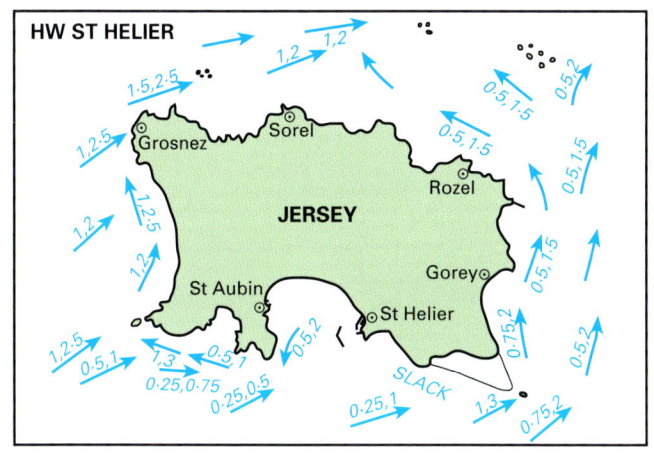
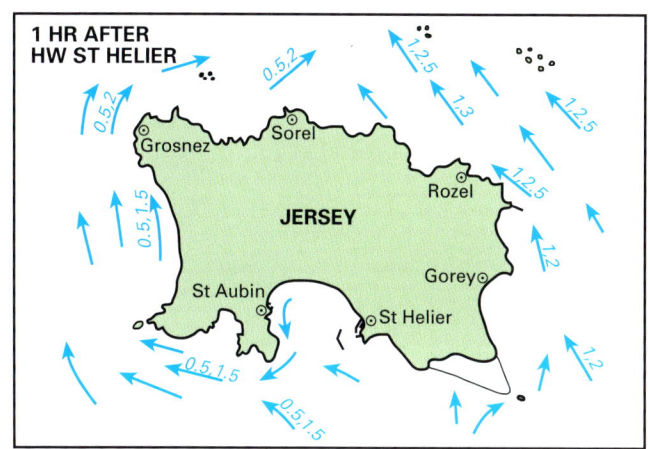
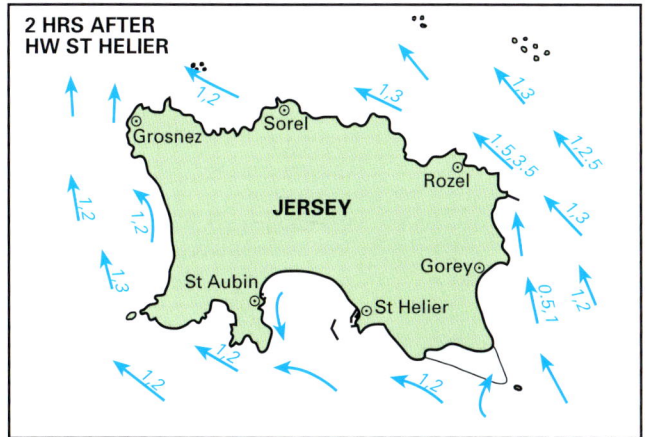
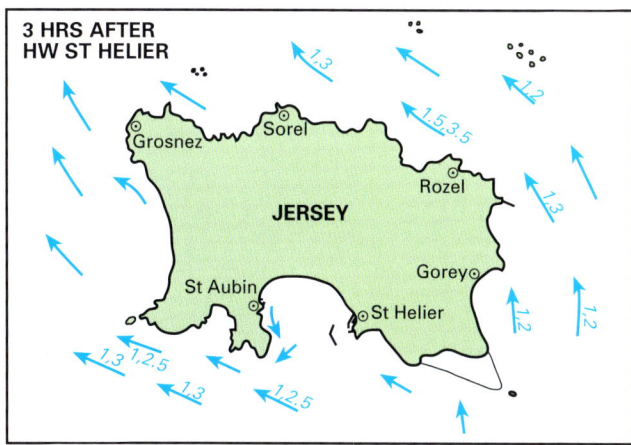
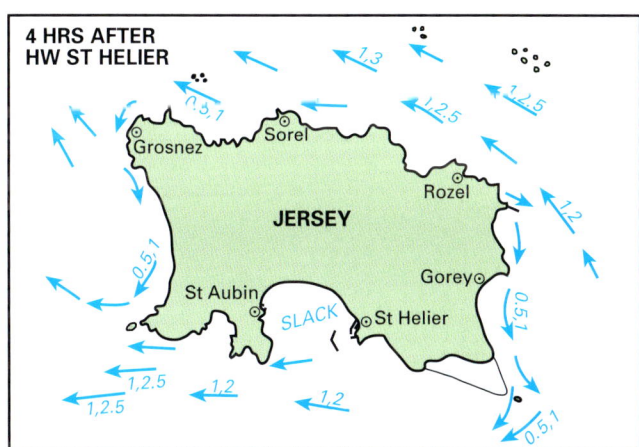
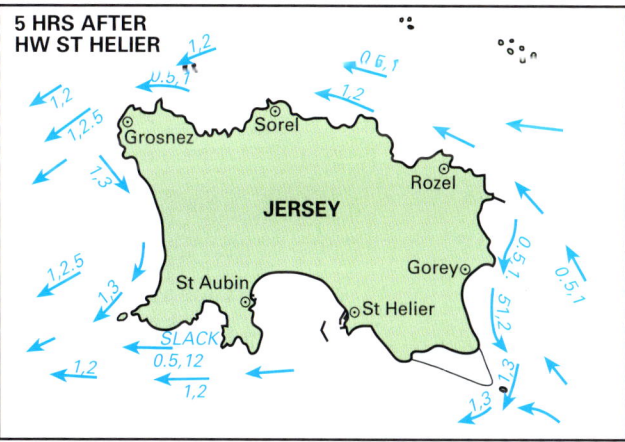

CHANNEL ISLANDS, CHERBOURG PENINSULA & NORTH BRITTANY

Appendix

Channel Island rock names

Rocks and coastal features have long held great significance for Channel Island mariners. Their names are often descriptive of their appearance, their character or just whether they were regarded as a friend or foe to the seafarer. They are mostly of Celtic, Latin and Norse origin.

In recent history the complication of three languages in the islands – French, English and the local patois Jérriais and Guernesiais – has created some confusion for cartographers. It is not uncommon for rocks to be known by a French and an English name.

French	English
Aiguillon	A sharp point or sting
Amont	Upper or upstream
Anquette	Named after Anchetil, a cripple healed by St Helier in 550AD
Ardente	Reddish or 'she who boils'
Aval	Lower or downstream
Baveuse	Foaming rock
Bec	Bill or point of land
Bequet	Point of land
Bigorne	Two pointed heads or pickaxe
Boue	An offshore rock on which waves break
Bouilly, Bouillon	On the boil, excited
Burron	Small hut
Caîne	A chain of rocks
Caramé, Karamay	Grim, rugged
Conchée	Rock covered by bird lime
Conchière	A shell used for signalling, or corner
Conière	Inglenook or corner rock
Coq	Black
Corbière	A place of crows, ravens or cormorants
Coupe	The highest point in a group of rocks
Cracheux	The spitter
Crapaud	Toad
Creux	A crevasse or cave halfway down the cliff
Croute	Croft, small enclosed field
Demie	A rock visible at half tide
Dirouilles	Mischievous dwarfs, seething reefs
Échiquele	Chequered
Écrevière	A place for lobsters or shrimps
Ecureuil	Squirrel
Épé	A sword
Équierrière	A haunt of cormorants
Étacq	Stack
Étoc, Étot	Stump
Fara	A beacon, lighthouse or passage between rocks
Faucheur	The reaper
Ferrière	Iron rock
Four, Fournier	Oven, furnace
Fourdré, Fourché, Frouquie, Fourquie	Forked or jagged-topped rock
Fruquier, Fourchiaux	Forked with twin peaks
Godin	Happy rock
Goubinière	Hands cupped to form a bowl
Gouffre	Abyss, chasm
Goulet or Gouliot	Narrow opening or pass
Grève	A sandy beach, scooped out from a cliff foot, also a shoal, sand bank
Grosnez	Grey cape
Grouin	A cape like a snout
Grunot/Grune	A flat topped rock usually surrounded by deep water and just below surface at low tide
Guet (soft 'G')	Watch (house)
Herbeuse	Grassy
Hocq	Cape, headland, spur of rock
Homet, Hommet, Houmet	A little island; used of smooth rounded islets, rock or boulders of no great height
Hurel	Stony
Jumelles	Twins
Jument	Mare
La Noire	Black
Le Vieux, La Vieille	The old man or woman
Les Cloches	The bells; perhaps rocks once belled (maintained) by the Church or resembling bells
L'Hôpital	A rock where sick seamen were landed
Lit ès chiens	Dog's nest
Longin, Longy	The long one, or one you can coast along
Maurepos	A ground swell, bad anchorage
Moie, Moye, Mouaie	Cape shaped like a heap
Mouille, Mouillière	Soaked or an anchorage, also Mussel rock
Moulet, Mulet, mullet	Mullet
Pêcheresse	Fishing rock
Perelle or Rocquaine	Rocky coast
Pierre	Rock
Pignon	Gable
Pignonet	A small gable end
Pipette	A small pipe
Pont	Bridge, used of a flat rock bridging a gap or channel
Plat	Flat area
Plaquière or Platière	Ledge
Quenon or Quignon	Hunk or lump
Rigdon	Exhilarated dancing
Rochelle, Rochette	Small rocks
Roquet, Rocquaine	
Rond	Round
Ronez	Rock cape
Rougeraie, Rougeret, Rouguet, Rousse	Reddish
Ruaudière	A place of eddies or currents
Sablonnière	Sandpit
Salerie	Fish salting ground
Selle rock	Saddle rock
Sercul	Tail of Sark
Sillette	Rocks on the horizon, reminiscent of a furrow
Silleuse	Rock over which sea breaks
Tête	Head or headland, of a rock above its neighbours
Troupeurs	A line of cavalrymen
Usurie	Doorway, little door
Verclut	The green cleft
Vraiquière, Vachère, Vraquière	Where *vraic* (seaweed) collects or covered with *vraic*

Glossary

The Breton language glossary

Nick Heath

It is of interest, and sometimes actually of value to the navigator, to know the meanings of some of the more common Breton words which appear in place names. Those who have cruised on the Celtic fringes of Britain will recognise some of them; the Irish inish corresponds to the Breton inis, and those who have cruised in West Highland waters will know the meanings of glas and du. I have no pretensions to a knowledge of Breton, but set down here the results of a few investigations.

The pronunciation is, or should be, more like English than French, with the final consonants sounded. The letters c'h represent the final sound of Scottish loch or Irish lough (but not English lock); there is indeed a word loc'h, meaning a lake or pool; ch is pronounced as in shall. The French books and charts do not always distinguish between these, and there may be some errors in this book in consequence. In France, as in England, mobility and the radio/TV are killing regional differences and Raz is now usually pronounced Rah; Penmarc'h, pronounced Penmargh a generation ago, is now often Painmar, and Bénodet has gone from Benodette to Bainoday and collected an accent in the process. The most misleading example of this process is porz, which means an anchorage, possibly quite exposed and/or lacking in all shore facilities, not a port. This gets frenchified into port, and the French word port does mean a port, and not an anchorage, which is anse or rade.

A Breton glossary is hard to use because initial letters are often mutated into others, following complicated rules, depending on the preceding word. I have tried to meet this by suggesting, after the relevant letters, other(s) from which the initial might have come. Suppose that one wants to find the meaning of I. er Gazek (which is quite likely since The Mare seems to be the commonest name given to an islet). There is no word gazek in the glossary, but after G it says 'try K'; kazek means a mare; it mutates into gazek after er. Mutations of final letters also occur, but these do not usually cause difficulty in finding a word.

aber	estuary
anaon	the dead
al, an, ar	the
arvor	seaside
aven	river
B (try P)	
balan, banal	broom
bann, benn	hilltop
barr	summit, top
baz	shoal
beg	point, cape
beniget	cut, slit
benven, bosven	above-water rock
bian, bihan	small
bili, vili	shingle
bir, vir	needle, point
bran	crow
bras, braz	large
bre, brenn	small hill
breiz	Brittany
bri, brienn	cliff
C (try K)	
D (try T)	
daou	two
don, doun	deep
dour	water
du	black
ell	rock, shallow
enez	island
er a, an	the
fank	mud
froud, fred	strong current
freu	river
G (try K)	
garo, garv	rough
gavr	goat
glas	green
goban	shallow
gromell, gromilli	roaring
gwenn	white, pure
hir	long
hoc'h, houc'h	pig
iliz	church
izel	shallow
inis	island
kan(iou), kanal	channel
karn	cairn
kareg	rock
kastel	castle
kazek	mare
kein	shoal
kel(ou)	large rock
ker	house, hamlet
kern	summit, sharp peak
kleuz(iou)	hollow, deep
koad, goad	wood
kornog	shoal
koz	old
kreiz	middle
kriben	crest
lan, lann	monastery
marc'h	horse
melen	yellow
men	rock
mor, vor	sea, seawater
nevez	new
penn	head, point
plou, plo	parish
porz, porzig	anchorage
poul	pool, anchorage
raz	strait, tide race
roc'h	rock
ros	wooded knoll
ruz	red
ster	river, inlet
stiv, stiff	fountain, spring
teven, tevenneg	cliff, dune
toull	hole, deep place
trez, treaz	sand, beach
V (try B, M)	
W (try Gw)	
yoc'h	group of rocks

Road signs can be confusing particularly in Lower (West) Brittany. French charts tend to use Breton place names whereas British Admiralty use English or French

CHANNEL ISLANDS, CHERBOURG PENINSULA & NORTH BRITTANY

Appendix

Waypoints (WGS 84 Datum)

The following lists of waypoints give associated bearings and distances from chart reference points to enable cross-checking of waypoint positions

I. Channel Islands waypoints

ALDERNEY

⊕ number	Lat	Long	Chart reference	Bearing from	Distance from (M)
1	49°43'·75N	02°03'·90W	Quénard Pt lighthouse E	090°	3·8
2	49°44'·65N	02°08'·10W	Quénard Pt lighthouse NE	053°	1·5
3	49°41'·42N	02°15'·22W	Fort Clonque	210°	1·6
4	49°43'·46N	02°14'·90W	Great Nannel	186°	0·8
5	49°44'·76N	02°12'·00W	Braye B'water hd NW	347°	0·97
6	49°44'·56N	02°10'·65W	Braye B'water hd NE	042°	1·0
7	49°42'·38N	02°09'·10W	Essex Castle	126°	1·15

GUERNSEY

⊕ number	Lat	Long	Chart reference	Bearing from	Distance from (M)
8	49°29'·27N	02°28'95W	Roustel beacon Tower	270°	0·1
9	49°31'·30N	02°26'·80W	Tautenay beacon Tower	001°	1·2
10	49°31'·27N	02°27'·78W	Platte Fougère lighthouse	063°	1·0
11	49°25'·64N	02°28°·55W	Lower Hds S Card buoy	180°	0·2
12	49°27'·53N	02°31'·16W	Castle Cornet lighthouse	039°	0·29
13	49°24'·72N	02°31'·40W	St Martins Pt lighthouse	160°	0·7
14	49°24'·37N	02°37'·20W	La Corbière Tower	182°	0·9
15	49°25'·39N	02°41'·28W	Hanois lighthouse SE	140°	0·93
16	49°26'·10N	02°45'·17W	Hanois lighthouse W	270°	2·0

HERM

⊕ number	Lat	Long	Chart reference	Bearing from	Distance from (M)
17	49°30'·56N	02°21'·93W	Grande Amfroque beacon tower	090°	1·75
18	49°28'·21N	02°24'·25W	Noire Pute E	090°	0·5
19	49°27'·25N	02°25'·84W	Noire Pute SW	209°	1·1

SARK

⊕ number	Lat	Long	Chart reference	Bearing from	Distance from (M)
20	49°27'·50N	02°22'·67W	Bec du Nez beacon NW	322°	0·53
21	49°27'·50N	02°21'·60W	Bec du Nez beacon NE	042°	0·56
22	49°26'·95N	02°19'·34W	Pt Robert lighthouse	050°	1·2
23	49°25'·35N	02°16'·65W	Blanchard E cardinal buoy	090°	0·5
24	49°24'·88N	02°20'·20W	Creux Harbour	164°	1·0
25	49°24'·17N	02°20'·68W	L'Etac E	085°	0·9
26	49°23'·63N	02°23'·39W	L'Etac SW	242°	1·0
27	49°25'·25N	02°24'·40W	La Givaude	205°	0·7

JERSEY

⊕ number	Lat	Long	Chart reference	Bearing from	Distance from (M)
28	49°18'·94N	02°18'·13W	Désormes W cardinal buoy	270°	0·1
29	49°15'·91N	02°05'·38W	Belle Hougue Pt	030°	0·7
30	49°14'·32N	02°00'·75W	St Catherine b/water hd N	356°	1·0
31	49°13'·40N	01°58'·51W	St Catherine b/water hd E	087°	1·4
32	49°10'·80N	01°59'·10W	Gorey pierhead	125°	1·8
33	49°07'·70N	01°57'·14W	Violet ch buoy	180°	0·1
34	49°07'·34N	02°01'·13W	Canger Rk W cardinal buoy	270°	0·5
35	49°08'·00N	02°06'·50W	Demie de Pas lighthouse	193°	1·0
36	49°09'·14N	02°16'·00W	La Corbière lighthouse S	202°	1·8
37	49°10'·53N	02°16'·48W	La Corbière lighthouse W	255°	1·0

LES ECREHOUS

⊕ number	Lat	Long	Chart reference	Bearing from	Distance from (M)
38	49°15'·94N	01°55'·65W	La Bigorne Rk	202°	1·3

PLATEAU DES MINQUIERS

⊕ number	Lat	Long	Chart reference	Bearing from	Distance from (M)
39	49°00'·80N	02°05'·00W	Demie de Vascelin buoy	090°	0·1
40	48°55'·40N	02°03'·60W	Maîtresse Ile	175°	2·85

Waypoints (WGS 84 Datum)

The following lists of waypoints give associated bearings and distances from chart reference points to enable cross-checking of waypoint positions

II. Cherbourg Peninsula waypoints

⊕ number	Lat	Long	Chart reference	Bearing from	Distance from (M)
40C	49°36'·40N	01°13'·00W	Pte de Saire	090°	1·5
41	49°34'·40N	01°12'·95W	Fort de la Hougue Tower	097°	2·3
42	49°33'·50N	01°14'·40W	Fort de la Hougue Tower	122°	1·6
43	49°40'·92N	01°14'·65W	Pte de Barfleur lighthouse	134°	1·2
44	49°43'·70N	01°18'·44W	Les Equets buoy	000°	0·1
45	49°44'·84N	01°22'·09W	Basse du Rénier	000°	0·1
46	49°43'·55N	01°29'·40W	La Pierre Noire buoy	000°	0·1
47	49°42'·20N	01°15'·92W	Barfleur lighthouse	000°	0·4
48	49°42'·30N	01°17'·20W	Barfleur lighthouse	120°	0·9
49	49°42'·70N	01°18'·30W	Barfleur lighthouse	120°	1·8
50	49°42'·50N	01°20'·46W	Pte de Néville	000°	0·4
51	49°42'·83N	01°21'·84W	Les Trois Pierres beacon	180°	0·1
52	49°42'·90N	01°22'·74W	Les Trois Pierres beacon	268°	0·6
53	49°43'·20N	01°24'·70W	Les Trois Pierres beacon	275°	1·8
54	49°42'·40N	01°27'·40W	Cap Levi lighthouse	045°	0·9
55	49°41'·20N	01°29'·18W	Port Lévi entrance	270°	0·5
56	49°39'·60N	01°32'·79W	La Tourette beacon tower	006°	0·3
57	49°40'·30N	01°35'·42W	Ile Pelée Fort	348°	1·1
58	49°41'·20N	01°40'·00W	Fort de l'Ouest	315°	1·05
59	49°42'·40N	01°48'·90W	L'Etonnard beacon tower	080°	0·6
60	49°43'·90N	01°51'·15W	Basse Bréfort N cardinal	027°	0·2
61	49°44'·00N	01°53'·10W	Pte Jardiheu Sém	294°	1·5
62	49°44'·00N	01°55'·60W	La Plate tower	009°	0·5
63	49°43'·93N	01°56'·82W	Sém Cap de la Hague	315°	0·48
64	49°42'·50N	01°57'·93W	La Foraine W cardinal	148°	0·48
65	49°38'·80N	01°59'·00W	Nez de Jobourg	227°	2·3
66	49°33'·36N	01°52'·14W	Diélette P'hd	301°	0·64
67	49°21'·00N	01°47'·00W	Carteret lighthouse	147°	1·7
68	49°29'·80N	01°49'·51W	Cap de Carteret	232°	1·0
69	49°18'·35N	01°44'·75W	Fairway Buoy	095°	0·2
70	49°00'·12N	01°41'·40W	Ronquet tower	270°	2·2
71	48°59'·05N	01°38'·00W	Ronquet tower	180°	1·0
72	48°58'·95N	01°34'·55W	Pte d'Agon lighthouse	180°	1·2
73	48°57'·52N	01°42'·20W	La Catheue S cardinal	180°	0·1
74	48°50'·02N	01°37'·60W	Pte du Roc lighthouse	263°	0·5
75	48°49'·30N	01°37'·20W	Pte du Roc lighthouse	200°	0·8

ILES CHAUSEY

76	48°55'·53N	01°51'·46W	L'Enseigne Col NW	339°	2·0
77	48°55'·53N	01°49'·80W	L'Enseigne Col NW	012°	1·9
78	48°55'·67N	01°46'·20W	L'Etat	000°	1·0
79	48°53'·87N	01°41'·54W	Anvers W cardinal buoy	270°	0·3
80	48°51'·17N	01°48'·38W	Grande Ile lighthouse	147°	1·2
81	48°51'·24N	01°51'·16W	Canclais W cardinal beacon	180°	0·7
82	48°53'·67N	01°54'·32W	L'Enseigne Col NW	270°	2·6

Appendix

III. North Brittany waypoints

⊕ number	Lat	Long	Chart reference	Bearing from	Distance from (M)
83	48°44'·32N	01°48'·42W	Le Herpin lighthouse	030°	0·65
83B	48°40'·15N	01°49'·70W	Cancale p'hd	087°	0·95
84	48°42'·18N	01°57'·95W	Rochefort Tower	165°	0·7
85	48°41'·42N	01°57'·65W	Pointe Besnard	237°	0·1
86	48°42'·85N	01°56'·92W	Rochefort Tower	018°	0·85
87	48°41'·90N	02°00'·65W	St Servantine buoy	100°	0·2
88	48°41'·30N	02°02'·14W	Gde Conchée Fort	049°	0·43
89	48°41'·32N	02°05'·90W		324°	0·6
90	48°41'·47N	02°07'·25W	Atterage St Malo buoy	000°	0·1
91	48°40'·17N	02°08'·00W	Buharets W No.2 buoy	262°	0·34
92	48°39'·80N	02°07'·70W	Nerput E cardinal beacon	021°	0·7
93	49°38'·20N	02°10'·60W	Ile Agot	260°	0·64
94	48°39'·20N	02°12'·42W	Les Bourdinots buoy	090°	0·3
95	48°42'·00N	02°18'·80W	Cap Frehel lighthouse	009°	1·0
96	48°40'·30N	02°26'·50W	Les Justières buoy	188°	0·4
97	48°39'·15N	02°29'·05W	Cap d'Erquy	008°	0·4
98	48°37'·95N	02°30'·00W	Erquy Jetée W lighthouse	264°	0·8
99	48°36'·40N	02°36'·55W	Petite Muette lighthouse	135°	2·25
100	48°34'·30N	02°41'·40W	Le Légue landfall buoy	245°	0·25
101	48°35'·95N	02°47'·20W	Binic p'hd	097°	1·15
102	48°40'·51N	02°49'·83W	Pte du Bec de Vir	090°	1
103	48°37'·09N	02°46'·20W	La Roselières S cardinal buoy	170°	0·4
104	48°45'·42N	02°53'·50W	Pte de Minard	083°	1·5
105	48°47'·95N	02°53'·52W	Les Charpentiers	088°	1·6
106	48°49'·58N	02°55'·20W	Les Charpentiers	018°	1·8
107	48°55'·55N	02°54'·92W	La Horaine beacon tower	000°	2
108	48°53'·55N	02°58'·28W	La Horaine beacon tower	270°	2
109	48°54'·52N	03°02'·48W	La Moisie beacon tower	347°	0·7
110	48°55'·55N	03°08'·00W	Jument Les Héaux buoy	000°	0·2
111	48°54'·25N	03°11'·60W	Basse Crublent Port buoy	270°	0·36
112	48°54'·60N	03°03'·60W	Les Héaux lighthouse	084°	1·2
113	48°52'·20N	03°20'·30W	Basse Guazer buoy	035°	0·74
114	48°52'·30N	03°27'·30W	Ile aux Moines lighthouse	114°	1·46
115	48°52'·30N	03°28'·65W	Ile aux Moines lighthouse	130°	0·65
116	48°50'·70N	03°29'·20W	Mean Ruz lighthouse	343°	0·5
117	48°50'·90N	03°31'·60W	Le Taureau	000°	0·5
118	48°46'·75N	03°41'·30W	Le Crapaud W. cardinal	270°	0·5
119	48°46'·05N	03°37'·86W	NW Pt Ile Milieu	253°	1·2
120	48°47'·69N	03°38'·03W	Ile Losket	268°	1
121	48°44'·34N	03°37'·60W	Beg Lége lighthouse	270°	3·15
122	48°42'·75N	03°38'·00W	Pte du Chateau	023°	1
123	48°44'·35N	03°50'·70W	Entrance	332°	1·5
124	48°45'·52N	03°51'·05W	La Meloine W cardinal	270°	0·3
125	48°45'·57N	03°53'·80W	Les Duons Tower	031°	1·65
126	48°43'·20N	03°53'·50W	Ile Ricard	001°	1·7
127	48°43'·80N	03°57'·80W	Men Guen Bras beacon	056°	0·2
128	48°44'·23N	04°03'·25W	Ile de Batz lighthouse	250°	0·98
129	48°43'·86N	04°05'·71W	Ile de Batz lighthouse	250°	2·85
130	48°42'·50N	04°13'·90W	Penven	000°	2·45
131	48°42'·34N	04°19'·20W	Pontsuval CG	015°	1·8
132	48°42'·40N	04°29'·21W	Aman ar Ross N cardinal	253°	1·5
133	48°38'·84N	04°33'·95W	Ile Vierge	007°	0·5
134	48°40'·78N	04°33'·60W	Lizen ven Ouest W cardinal buoy	000°	0·3
135	48°37'·45N	04°39'·38W	Ile Vierge lighthouse	256°	3·64
136	48°38'·38N	04°36'·35W	Ile Vierge lighthouse	272°	1·53
137	48°38'·35N	04°38'·00W	Ile Vierge lighthouse	270°	2·65
138	48°36'·00N	04°47'·75W	Le Rélec E cardinal buoy	270°	0·1
139	48°34'·38N	04°47'·86W	Le Yurc'h (10)	289°	2·7
140	48°30'·92N	04°48'·57W	Le Four lighthouse	197°	0·5
141	48°31'·15N	04°48'·20W	Le Four lighthouse	163°	0·28
142	48°31'·40N	04°53'·15W	Le Four lighthouse	270°	3·2
143	48°29'·00N	04°57'·25W	Le Stiff radar mast	084°	4
144	48°30'·34N	04°48'·32W	Le Four lighthouse	180°	1
145	48°27'·96N	04°48'·48W	Le Four lighthouse	191°	3·65
146	48°21'·65N	04°48'·00W	Pte de Kermovan lighthouse	256°	0·4
147	48°36'·90N	04°46'·15W	Gde Basse Portsall W cardinal buoy	000°	0·2
148	48°28'·40N	05°01'·70W	Men Korn lighthouse	000°	0·4
149	48°24'·82N	05°08'·006W	La Jument lighthouse	180°	0·5
150	48°25'·70N	05°09'·30W	Ousi Youc'h Korz	234°	1·8
151	48°26'·28N	04°56'·65W	Les Trois Pierres lighthouse	004°	1·6
152	48°26'·28N	04°53'·62W	Le Faix Light Tower	020°	0·6
153	48°24'·40N	04°50'·50W	Pourceau N cardinal buoy	052°	0·7
154	49°05'·80N	02°47'·20W	Lighthouse	118°	1·12
155	49°05'·80N	02°49'·20W	Lighthouse	206°	0·55

Further reading

CHANNEL ISLANDS
A People of the Sea Edited by AG Jamieson (Methuen, 1986)

Alderney
The Alderney Story, 1939-1949 Michael St. J. Packe and Maurice Dreyfus (Alderney Society and Museum, 1971)

Guernsey
The Sea was their Fortune Roy McLoughlin (Seaflower Books, 1997)

Herm
Herm: Our Island Home Jenny Wood (Linton, 1986)

Jersey
Balleine's History of Jersey Margurite Syvret and Joan Stevens (Phillimore, 1981)

Les Ecréhous
Les Ecréhous, Jersey. The History and Archaeology of a Channel Islands Archipelago Warwick Rodwell (Société Jersiaise, 1996)

Les Minquiers
Les Minquiers: Jersey's Southern Outpost Jeremy Mallinson (Seaflower Books, 2011)
Les Minquiers. A Natural History Chambers, Binney and Jeffreys (Charonia Media, 2016)

THE CHERBOURG PENINSULA
Pilote Côtier 7 Saint Malo - Iles Anglo-Normande - Dunkerque Alain Rondeau (Praxys, 1999)
Shell Channel Pilot Tom Cunliffe (Imray, 2017)

Iles Chausey
Iles Chausey Abcdaire Gilbert Hurel, Jean-Loup Eve, J-C Tordai

NORTH BRITTANY
Secret Anchorages of Brittany Peter Cumberlidge (Imray, 2016)
Mariners of Brittany Peter Anson (Littlehampton, 1975)
Pilote Côtier 6 Saint Malo - Brest Alain Rondeau (Pen Duick, 1982)
Discovering the History of Brittany Wendy Mewes (Red Dog Books, 2006)
Inland Waterways of France David Edwards-May (Imray, 2010)

Noire Pute

Index

Albert Marina (St Peter Port), 51
Alderney, 23-42
    Channel crossings, 14, 15
    circumnavigation, 34-40
    inter-island passages, 16, 17-18
    tidal streams, 365-9
    waypoints, 376
Alderney Race, 15, 17, 18, 26, 27, 30-31, 145
    tidal streams, 365-7
Alligande Passage, 19, 73, 74, 75
Amas du Cap, 232, 233
Amoco Cadiz, 334
Anquette Channel (Gorey), 120, 123
Anse de Bec de la Vallée (Dinard), 220
Anse de Bréhec, 252
Anse des Bas-Sablons, 217
Anse des Blancs Sablons, 348
Anse de Dinard, 220
Anse de Gatteville, 156
Anse de Melon, 342
Anse de Montmarin, 224
Anse de Paimpol, 247, 252, 255, 262
Anse de St Hélier (Rance), 223
Anse de St Martin, 145, 165
Ar Chaden, 311, 316
Argenton, 340-42

Bac de Dinard (St Malo), 216
Baie de L'Arguenon, 229
Baie de Beninou (Ouessant), 355
Baie de la Fresnaie, 229, 230
Baie de Lampaul (Ouessant), 349, 351, 352-4
Baie de Lancieux, 227, 228, 229
Baie de Lannion, 283-94
Baie de Morlaix, 283, 295-304
Baie de Penn ar Roc'h, 349-51, 354-5
Baie du Stiff (Ouessant), 349, 352-4
Baleine Bay (Sark), 94, 100
Banquette Bay (Sark), 19, 97
Barfleur, 145, 150-53
Barneville, 175
Barnouic, Le Plateau de, 15, 362
Bas Sablons, Port des (St Servan), 208, 209-213, 217-18
Bas-Sablons, Anse de, 217
Bassin Duguay-Trouin (St Malo), 217
Batz, Ile de, 283, 309, 310, 313-17
Bayeux tapestry, 144
Beaucette Marina (Guernsey), 52-4, 78
Beauport (Jersey), 118-19
Bec du Nez (Sark), 19, 97
Bec de la Vallée, Anse de (Dinard), 220
Becquet, Port du (Cherbourg), 158
Les Becquets (Alderney), 37
Bectondu (Channel Islands), 58

Belcroute Bay (Jersey), 117, 119
Belvoir Bay (Herm), 81
Beninou, Baie de (Ouessant), 355
Big Russel, 19, 47, 48, 82
Binic, 240, 241-2
Blanche Ile (Ecréhous), 132
Blancs Sablons, Anse des, 348
Bloscon, 308, 309
Bonit (Boneay) (Alderney), 37
Bonne Nuit Harbour (Jersey), 129
Bono, Ile (Les Sept Iles), 277, 278
books, 379
Bordeaux (Guernsey), 56, 57
Bouilly Port (Jersey), 118, 119
Bouley Bay (Jersey), 128
Braye Harbour (Alderney), 24-5, 26, 28-33, 34
    Channel crossings, 14-15
    inter-island passages, 16, 17-18, 42
Brecquou (Channel Islands), 88, 89, 97
Bréhat, Ile de, 248, 253-8
Bréhec, Anse de, 252
Breton language, 375
Brett Boat Passage (Gorey), 120, 121, 123
Bricquebec, 143
Brignogan, 283, 320-21
Brittany, *Channel crossings*, 14-15, 22
Burhou (Channel Islands), 24, 41-2

Cala de la Houle Causseul, 229
Cale de Gaigrac'h (Ouessant), 355
Callot, Ile, 305, 307
Canal d'Ile de Batz, 283, 309, 310-311, 313-17
Canal d'Ille et Rance, 222, 226
Cancale, 202-5
Cap de Carteret, 171, 176
Cap d'Erquy, 233-4
Cap Fréhel, 229, 232, 233
Cap de la Hague, 27, 143, 145, 166
Cap Lévi & Race, 155, 156, 157
Carantec, 305, 307
Carteret, 175-7
Carteret, Cap de, 171, 176
Casquets (Channel Islands), 24, 26
Casquets TSS, 13, 14, 15
Cézembre, Ile, 213-14
Channel Island Yacht Marina (Beaucette), 52-4
Channel Islands, 4-141
    Channel crossings, 13-15, 22
    inter-island passages, 16-22
    rock names, 374
    tidal streams, 364-73
    waypoints, 376
Chantereyne, Port de, 160, 161, 163

charts & chart datum, 2-3
Chateau de la Roche Jagu, 264
Châtelet, Port du, 229
Chausey, Iles, 187-95, 377
Chausey Sound, 187, 188, 189-94
Chenal Beauchamp (Chausey), 191-3, 195
Chenal de la Bigne (St Malo), 207, 209-210
Chenal de Bosven Amont (Portsall), 336
Chenal de Bréhat, 255-6, 262
Chenal du Bunel (St Malo), 212
Chenal de Calerec (Portsall), 336
Chenal du Décolle (St Malo), 212-13
Chenal du Dénou (Paimpol), 249
Chenal d'Erquy, 232, 233
Chenal Est de L'Ile Callot (Morlaix), 299-300
Chenal du Ferlas (Bréhat), 255, 262
Chenal du Four, 338-48
Chenal de la Grande Conchée (St Malo), 211
Chenal de la Grande Porte (St Malo), 212
Chenal Hédouin, 155
Chenal de la Helle (Chenal du Four), 339, 340, 358
Chenal d'Ile de Batz, 283, 309, 310-311, 313-17
Chenal de la Jument (Paimpol), 249, 262
Chenal de La Vieille Rivière (Cancale), 204
Chenal de Lastel (Paimpol), 249
Chenal des Laz (Molène), 340, 358
Chenal de la Malouine (L'Aber Wrac'h), 326
Chenal de Men Glas (Portsall), 336, 337
Chenal Méridional de Portsall, 335-6
Chenal de la Moisie (Bréhat), 256, 261
Chenal NW de Molènes, 358
Chenal Occidental (Le Corréjou), 323
Chenal Oriental (Le Corréjou), 322-3
Chenal Ouest de Ricard (Morlaix), 299
Chenal de la Pendante (L'Aber Wrac'h), 326-7
Chenal de la Petite Porte (St Malo), 211-12
Chenal des Petits Pointus (St Malo), 210
Chenal de Plouézec (Paimpol), 247-9
Chenal du Raous (Portsall), 335
Chenal du Rélec (Portsall), 334, 335
Chenal des Roquettes à L'Homme (Chausey), 193
Chenal du Toull ar Men Melen (Trébeurden), 287
Chenal du Toull Ar Peulven (Trébeurden), 285-7
Chenal de Tréguier (Morlaix), 297
Chenal de la Trinité (Paimpol), 250-51, 262
Chenal des Trois Pièrres, 155-6
Cherbourg, 14, 15, 27, 145, 159-63
Cherbourg Peninsula (Le Cotentin), 142-95, 377
Chevret, Ile, 223, 224

Index

Cobo Bay (Guernsey), 61, 62
Corbette Passage, 73, 74, 75, 78
La Corbière Boat Passage, 107, 108
Costaéres, Ile de (Ploumanac'h), 280
Côte de Granit Rose, 253-81
La Côte des Iles, 170-86
La Côte Sauvage, 351
Le Cotentin (Cherbourg Peninsula), 142-95
Cotentin Pass, 143
Les Côtes des Havres, 181
Créac'h lighthouse (Ouessant), 351
Creux Harbour (Sark), 90, 91-6
Creux Passage, 73, 74
Crevichon (Channel Islands), 73

Dahouët, 234, 235-6
Danger Rock Passage, 109
Les Demies/Demics Sandbank (Minquiers), 136, 137, 141
depth sounder, 1
depths, 2
Derrible Bay (Sark), 96
Diélette, 172-4
digital charts, 3
Dinan, 222, 226
Dinard, 208, 209-213, 219-20
Dinard, Anse de, 220
Dinard Ferry (Le Bac de Dinard), 216, 220
Dixcart Bay (Sark), 19, 21, 93, 94, 96, 100
Dolvez, Ile (Argenton), 340, 341, 342
Dossen, 317, 318
Dourduff, 300, 301
Douron River, 283, 292
Doyle Passage (Guernsey), 48, 58
Duit Sauvary Passage (Guernsey), 58
Duslen, 311, 316

Eastern Passage (Jersey), 112, 120
Les Ecréhous, 104-5, 131, 132-5, 376
'Electric Passage' (Jersey), 112
electronic charts, 3
Elizabeth Marina (St Helier), 115-16
Ennez Eussa (Ouessant/Ushant), 349-55
Ennez Molenez (Molène), 283, 340, 355-8
equipment, 1-3
Erquy, 233-4
L'Etac (Sark), 93-4
Les Etacs (Alderney), 16, 24, 26, 30, 36, 42

Fermain Bay (Guernsey), 70
Flamanville, 143, 172
Flamanville Power Station, 173
Les Fontaines (Sark), 96
Fontenelle Bay (Guernsey), 59
Fort Doyle (Guernsey), 57-9
Fréhel, Cap, 229, 232, 233
Fresnaie, Baie la, 229, 230

Gaigrac'h, Cale de (Ouessant), 355
Garden Rocks (Alderney), 16, 24, 26, 30, 36, 42
Gatteville, Anse de, 156
glossaries, 374-5
Golhédec, 317
Gorey Harbour (Jersey), 21, 120-25
Goulet Passage, 92
Gouliot Passage, 97, 101
Goury, 145, 166-9
GPS, 1, 3

Grand Chenal (L'Aber Wrac'h), 325
Grand Chenal (Morlaix), 297-9
Grand Chenal (R. Trieux), 261-2
La Grand Entrée (Chausey), 190-91, 195
Grand Fauconnière (Channel Islands), 73, 76, 77
Grand Havre (Guernsey), 60-61
Grande, Ile (Trébeurden), 284-8
Grande Bretagne (Little Sark), 100
La Grande Grève (Barfleur), 151, 153
La Grande Grève (Sark), 97, 98, 99, 101
Grande Ile (Chausey), 187-95
Grande Passe (Tréguier), 267
Granville, 184-6
La Grève de Blainvillais (Chausey), 194
Grève du Guerzido (Bréhat), 257
La Grève de la Ville (Sark), 19, 90, 96
Grève au Lancon (Jersey), 130
Grève de Lecq (Jersey), 130
Gros du Raz, 166, 168, 169
Grosnez Point (Jersey), 107, 108
Guénioc, 330
Guernsey, 43-70
    Channel crossings, 14, 15
    circumnavigation, 44, 57-70
    inter-island passages, 16, 17-18, 19, 20-21
    tidal streams, 370-71
    waypoints, 376
Guerzido, Port/Grève du (Bréhat), 257

Hague, Cap de la, 27, 143, 145, 166
La Haize du Raz Channel (Goury), 166, 168, 169
Hannaine Bay (Alderney), 35-6
Harteau, Ile, 224
Les Hautes Boues (Sark), 98
Havelet Bay (Guernsey), 70
Havre Gosselin (Sark), 97-9, 101
Havre de Regnéville, 180-83
Le Havre de Rothéneuf, 205-7
Havre du Roubaril, 156
Hayes Passage (Le Boursée), 82-4
Hébihens, Ile des, 227, 228, 229
Herm, 19, 45, 71-86
    waypoints, 376
Herm Harbour, 78, 79
history, 5, 143-4, 198-9
    Channel Islands, 5
    Cherbourg Peninsula, 143-4
    North Brittany, 198-9
La Houle, La Port de, 202, 205
La Houle Causseul, Cala de, 229
Les Huguenans (Chausey), 195
The Humps anchorage (Herm), 84-6

Icart Bay (Guernsey), 68
Ile de Batz, 283, 309, 310, 313-17
Ile Bono (Les Sept Iles), 277, 278
Ile de Bréhat, 248, 253-8
Ile Callot, 305, 307
Ile de Cézembre, 213
Ile Chevret, 223, 224
Ile de Costaéres (Ploumanac'h), 280
Ile Dolvez (Argenton), 340, 341, 342
Ile Grande (Trébeurden), 284-8
Ile Harteau, 224
Ile des Hébihens, 227, 228, 229
Ile Louet, 298, 299, 307
Ile de Melon (Argenton), 342, 343

Ile Milliau (Trébeurden), 285, 287-8
Ile aux Moines (Les Sept Iles), 277, 278
Ile de Molène (Ennez Molenez), 283, 340, 355-8
Ile d'Ouessant (Enez Eussa/Ushant), 283, 349-55
Ile Ronde (Trégastel-Ste Anne), 281
Ile de Siec (Sieck), 317-18
Ile de Tatihou, 148
Iles Chausey, 187-95, 377

Jersey, 103-130
    Channel crossings, 14, 15, 22
    inter-island passages, 20-22
    tidal streams, 372-3
    waypoints, 376
Jethou (Channel Islands), 45, 71, 72, 73, 75, 76
Jobourg, Nez de, 143, 173
Jument Rock (Jersey), 108

Kermorvan, 346, 347
Kerrec Levran, 317, 318
Kersaint, 331, 333, 334, 336
Kervigorn, 330

La Baveuse (Sark), 99
La Bette Bay (Guernsey), 68
La Bigorne Rock (Ecréhous), 133
La Chambre (Bréhat), 253, 257
La Collette Yacht Basin (Jersey), 115
La Corbière, 15
La Corbière Boat Passage, 107, 108
La Corderie (Bréhat), 253, 256, 258
La Corne (Tréguier), 270
La Côte des Iles, 170-86
La Côte Sauvage, 351
La Coupée (Sark), 98
La Déroute Passage, 170
La Grand Entrée (Chausey), 190-91, 195
La Grande Grève (Barfleur), 151, 153
La Grande Grève (Sark), 97, 98, 99, 101
La Grève des Blainvillais (Chausey), 194
La Grève de la Ville (Sark), 19, 90, 96
La Haize du Raz Channel (Goury), 166, 168, 169
La Helle, 339, 340
La Houle, La Port de, 202, 205
La Houle Causseul, Cala de, 229
La Jaonnet Bay (Guernsey), 68
La Marmotière (Ecréhous), 131, 132, 133, 134, 135
La Maseline Harbour (Sark), 22, 90-94, 95, 96
La Palue, 327
La Passe Sud de Beauchamp (Chausey), 193
La Penzé River, 283, 295, 296-300, 305-7
La Petite Entrée (Chausey), 191
La Port de La Houle, 202, 205
La Rance, 208, 209-213, 219, 221-6
La Rocque Pendante (Alderney), 37, 39
La Tchué (Alderney), 37
La Vrachière Local Boat Passage (St Helier), 112-14, 117
L'Aber Benoit, 328-30
L'Aber Wrac'h, 283, 324-7
L'Aber-Ildut, 283, 344-5, 346
The Lagoon (Herm), 80
Lampaul, Baie de (Ouessant), 349, 351, 352-4
Lampaul (Ouessant), 349, 351, 352-4

CHANNEL ISLANDS, CHERBOURG PENINSULA & NORTH BRITTANY

Index

Lan Paul (Porz Pol), 351, 354
Lancieux, Baie de, 227, 228, 229
L'Ancresse Bay (Guernsey), 60
Lanildut, 344, 345
Lannion, 283, 288, 289, 290
Lannion, Baie de, 283-94
Lannion, Rivière de, 283, 288-90
L'Arguenon, Baie de, 229
Le Becquet (Cherbourg), 158
Le Boursée (Hayes Passage), 82-4
Le Châtelet, 229
Le Châtelier, L'Ecluse de (Lock), 222, 223, 224, 225, 226
Le Conquet, 283, 346-8
Le Corréjou, 322-3
Le Cotentin (Cherbourg Peninsula), 142-95
Le Gouffre (Guernsey), 68
Le Havre de Rothéneuf, 205-7
Le Kéréon lighthouse (Passage du Fromveur), 352, 353
Le Kerpont Channel (Bréhat), 256, 257, 258
Le Légué, 234, 237-9
Le Lyvet Marina, 222, 226
Le Mouillage de Santec, 317
Le Plateau de Barnouic, 15, 362
Le Portelet (Guernsey), 68
Le Stiff (Ouessant), 349, 352, 353
Le Vapeur de Trieux, 264
Le Yaudet, 283, 290
L'Ecluse de Châtelier (Châtelier Lock), 222, 223, 224, 225, 226
L'Ecluse du Naye (St Malo Lock), 216
Léguer, River (Rivière de Lannion), 283, 288-90
Les Bas Sablons Marina, 217, 218
Les Becquets (Alderney), 37
Les Côtes des Havres, 181
Les Demies/Demics Sandbank (Minquiers), 136, 137, 141
Les Dirouilles (Channel Islands), 123
Les Ecréhous, 104-5, 131, 132-5, 376
Les Etacs (Alderney), 16, 24, 26, 30, 36, 42
Les Fontaines (Sark), 96
Les Hautes Boues (Sark), 98
Les Huguenans (Chausey), 195
Les Minquiers, 15, 131, 135-41
Les Ports d'Erquy, 233-4
Les Sept Iles, 277-8
Les Trois Pièrres (Argenton), 340, 341, 342
Les Trois Pièrres (Molène), 256, 357, 358
L'Etac (Sark), 93-4
Lévi, Cap & Race, 155, 156, 157
Lézardrieux, 248, 259-62
Little Russel, 15, 17, 18, 46-7, 48-9, 58, 82
Little Sark, 93-4, 96, 97-101
Locquémeau, 283, 291
Locquénolé, 302
Locquirec, 283, 292
Longy Bay (Alderney), 35, 37-40
Louet, Ile, 298, 299, 307
Lug of Burhou (Channel Islands), 41, 42
Lyvet Marina, 222, 226

Maître Ile (Ecréhous), 131, 133, 134
Maîtresse Ile (Minquiers), 135, 136, 137, 138-41
marks, 1-2
Mean Ruz (Ploumanac'h), 280
Melon, 342-3

Melon, Ile de (Argenton), 342, 343
Men Alann Bay (Bréhat), 257
Men Hir Occidental, 341, 342
Middle Passage (St Aubin), 116-17
Milliau, Ile (Trébeurden), 285, 287-8
Minkies (Plateau des Minquiers), 15, 131, 135-41
Moguériec, 318-19
Moines, Ile aux (Les Sept Iles), 277, 278
Molène, Ile de (Ennez Molenez), 283, 340, 355-8
Mont Orgueil Castle (Jersey), 124
Mont St Michel, 170, 171, 187, 216
Montmarin, Anse de, 224
Mordreuc, 225
Morlaix, 283, 295-304
Morlaix Lock, 301, 302, 303
Morlaix River, 283, 300-304
Le Mouillage de Santec, 317
Moulin Huet Bay (Guernsey), 68
Musé Passage (Herm), 76, 77

navigation, 1, 9-10, 197
Needles Channel, 15
Nez de Jobourg, 143, 173
Northwest Passage (Jersey), 107, 109
The Nunnery (Alderney), 39

Omonville-La-Rogue, 145, 164
Ortac (Channel Islands), 14, 15, 24, 26
Ouessant, Ile d' (Enez Eussa/Ushant), 283, 349-55

Paimpol, 247-52
Paimpol, Anse de, 247, 252, 255, 262
Paluden, 327
Parfonde Passage, 76, 77
Passage de la Déroute, 170
Passage à l'est des Epiettes (Chausey), 190
Passage du Fromveur (Ouessant), 352-3
passage planning, 1
Passe de l'Est (Perros-Guirec), 275, 276
Passe de la Gaine (Tréguier), 270
Passe aux Moutons (Penzé River), 307
Passe du Nord (St Vaast), 148-9
Passe du Nord Est (Tréguier), 267-70
Passe de l'Ouest (Perros-Guirec), 275-6
Passe du Rannic (Roscoff), 311
Passe du Sud (St Vaast), 149
Paternosters (Channel Islands), 107, 123, 135
Pays d'Iroise, 328-48
Pécheresse (Sark), 91, 92
Pembroke Bay (Guernsey), 60
Pempoul, 305, 307
Penn ar Lann (Morlaix), 300
Penn ar Roc'h, Baie de, 349-51, 354-5
Penpoul, 305, 307
Penzé, 305, 306
La Penzé River, 283, 295, 296-300, 305-7
Percée Passage, 19, 73, 74, 75, 76, 77, 78, 80, 81
Perros-Guirec, 273-6
Petit Bôt Bay (Guernsey), 68
Petit Port (Guernsey), 70
Pierre du Beurre (Burre) Passage (Sark), 99-101
Pierre du Cours (Sark), 93-4, 100
Pierres de Carantec (Morlaix), 300
Plateau de Barnouic, 15, 362

Plateau des Minquiers, 15, 131, 135-41, 376
Plateau des Roches Douvres, 15, 359-63
Pleinmont Ledge (Guernsey), 67
Plemont (Jersey), 130
Plouër-sur-Rance, 222, 224, 225
Ploumanac'h, 279-80, 281
Plymouth, 14
Point Corbière (Jersey), 107, 108, 109
Point la Moye (Jersey), 108
Pointe de Térénez, 300
Pont Vauban, 253
Pontrieux, 261, 263-5
Pontusval, 320-21
The Pool (Ecréhous), 132-3, 135
The Pool (Minquiers), 137, 139-41
The Pool (St Peter Port), 51
Poole, 13-14
Porsal (Portsall), 331-7
Porsmoguer, 348
Port d'Armor Marina, 243-6
Port des Bas Sablons (St Servan), 208, 209-213, 217-18
Port du Becquet (Cherbourg), 158
Port Blanc, 271-2
Port du Cap Lévi, 157
Port de Chantereyne, 160, 161, 163
Port du Châtelet, 229
Port Clos (Bréhat), 253, 255, 258
Port de la Corderie (Bréhat), 253, 256, 258
Port de Dinan, 222, 226
Port Gorey (Little Sark), 100, 101-2
Port du Guerzido (Bréhat), 257
Port à la Jument (Sark), 101
Port de Le Légué, 234, 237-9
Port de Lyvet Marina, 222, 226
Port Marie (Chausey), 189, 194
Port Mer (Cancale), 205
Port de Penpoul, 305, 307
Port Picon (Cancale), 205
Port Racine (Anse de St Martin), 145, 165
Port es Saies (Sark), 98, 99, 101
Port St Hubert, 224
Port du Stiff (Ouessant), 349, 352, 353
Port Vauban Marina (St Malo), 215, 217
Portbail, 177-9
Portelet Bay (Jersey), 119
Le Portelet (Guernsey), 68
Portelet Harbour (Guernsey), 65-7
Portrieux Harbour (Le Vieux Port), 243, 246
Les Ports d'Erquy, 233-4
ports of entry (Channel Islands), 10
Portsall (Porsal), 331-7
Portsall Inner Passage, 331, 332-3, 334-6
Portsmouth, 13-14, 15
Portz Kernoc'h (Porz Kernok), 308, 312, 313
Porz Darland, 349, 354
Porz Illien, 348
Porz Pol, 351, 354
positions, 2
Pot Bay (Little Sark), 96
Primel-Trégastel, 283, 293-4
Putrainez Bay (Herm), 81

Queen Elizabeth II Marina (St Peter Port), 52

Racine, Port (Anse de St Martin), 145, 165
radar, 1
Radome (Jersey), 108
La Rance, 208, 209-213, 219, 221-6

Index

Red & Green Passage (St Helier), 112, 120
Regnéville, 180-83
Rennes, 226
Roche Gautier, 362
Roches Douvres, Plateau des, 15, 359-63
Rocquaine Bay (Guernsey), 63, 64
La Rocque Pendante (Alderney), 37, 39
Ronde, Ile (Trégastel-Ste Anne), 281
Roscoff, 283, 308-312
Rosière Steps (Herm), 73, 74, 78, 79, 80
Rothéneuf, 205-7
Roubaril, 156
Rouge Terrier (Little Sark), 96
Roustel (Channel Islands), 46, 47
Rozel (Jersey), 126-8

Sables d'Or Les Pins, 232
Saignie Bay (Sark), 101
St Aubin (Jersey), 116-17
St Brelade's Bay (Jersey), 118
St Briac-sur-Mer, 227-9
St Brieuc-Le Légué, 234, 237-9
St Cast, 229-31
St Catherine Bay (Jersey), 122, 124, 126
St Helier (Jersey), 104-5, 107-116
    Channel crossings, 14, 15
    inter-island passages, 20-22
St Hélier, Anse de (Rance), 223
St Jacut-de-la-Mer, 227, 228, 229
St Malo, 15, 208, 209-217
St Malo Lock (L'Ecluse du Naye), 216
St Malo-Dinard Ferry, 216, 220
St Martin, Anse de, 145, 165
St Martin's Point (Guernsey), 69, 70
St Peter Port (Guernsey), 49-52, 57
    Channel crossings, 14, 15
    inter-island passages, 16, 17-21, 72, 73-8, 79
St Quay-Portrieux, 240, 243-6
St Sampson (Guernsey), 54-5, 78
St Servan (Port des Bas Sablons), 208, 209-213, 217-18
St Suliac, 224
St Vaast-La Hougue, 145, 146-9
Saints Bay (Guernsey), 68
Santec, Le Mouillage de, 317
Sark, 87-102
    inter-island passages, 19, 21, 22, 78
    waypoints, 376
Sauquet Rock (Alderney), 40
Saye Bay (Alderney), 40
Les Sept Iles, 277-8
Shell Beach (Herm), 81
Shoal Patch (St Helier), 112
Siec (Sieck), Ile de, 317-18
Sillette Passage (St Aubin), 117
Soldiers Bay (Guernsey), 70
Solent, 13-14, 15
South Passage (Jersey), 109-112
Stellac'h, 328, 329, 330
Stiff, Baie du (Ouessant), 349, 352-4
Swashway Channel (Jersey), 107
The Swinge, 17, 18, 27, 29-30, 42
    tidal streams, 365-7

Tatihou, Ile de, 148
technical information, 1-3
Telegraph Bay (Alderney), 36
Térénez, 300-301

tides & tidal streams, 2, 9-10, 13, 143, 197-8, 364-73
Tobars Passage, 73, 76-7
Tomberlaine, 170
Toull An Héry, 292
transit marks, 1-2
Trébeurden Archipelago, 283, 284-8
Trégastel-Ste Anne, 281
Tréguier, 266-71
Tréguier, Rivière (Le Jaudy), 266-71
Trieux, River, 248, 253, 256, 258, 259-65
Les Trois Pièrres (Argenton), 340, 341, 342
Les Trois Pièrres (Molène), 256, 357, 358
Trois Pierres, Chenal des (Barfleur), 155-6

Ushant (Ouessant), 349-55
Usurie Passage, 84-6
Utah Beach, 148

Val de Saire, 143
Le Vapeur de Trieux, 264
Vauban, 199
Vaulto (Alderney), 37
Vermerette (Herm), 74, 75
VHF radio, 1
Victoria Marina (St Peter Port), 51
Vilaine, River, 222
Violet Channel (Gorey), 120, 121-3

waypoints, 2, 376-8
West Corbière Turning Point, 107, 108
Western Passage (Jersey), 107, 109
Weymouth, 14

yacht & equipment, 1-3